Alaska

The complete guide, thoroughly up-to-date

Packed with details that will make your trip

The must-see sights, off and on the beaten path

What to see, what to skip

Mix-and-match vacation itineraries

City strolls, countryside adventures

Smart lodging and dining options

Essential local do's and taboos

Transportation tips, distances and directions

Key contacts, savvy travel tips

When to go, what to pack

Clear, accurate, easy-to-use maps

Books to read, videos to watch, background essays

Fodor's Travel Publications, Inc.
New York • Toronto • London • Sydney • Auckland
www.fodors.com

Fodor's Alaska

EDITOR: Christopher Billy

Editorial Contributors: Mary Engel, Robin Mackey Hill, Sue Kernaghan, Mike Miller, Stanton H. Patty, Don Pitcher, Tom Reale, Melissa Rivers, Heidi Sarna, Helayne Schiff, M. T. Schwartzman (Gold Guide editor), Bill Sherwonit, Kent Sturgis, Eric Troyer, Peggy Wayburn, Howard Weaver

Editorial Production: Nicole Revere

Maps: David Lindroth Inc., *cartographer*; Steven K. Amsterdam, *map editor*

Design: Fabrizio La Rocca, *creative director*; Guido Caroti, *associate art director*; Jolie Novak, *photo editor*

Production/Manufacturing: Mike Costa

Cover Photograph: Fred Hirschmann

Copyright

ISBN 0–679–00157–3

Special Sales

Fodor's Travel Publications are available at special discounts for bulk purchases for sales promotions or premiums. Special editions, including personalized covers, excerpts of existing guides, and corporate imprints, can be created in large quantities for special needs. For more information, contact your local bookseller or write to Special Markets, Fodor's Travel Publications, 201 East 50th Street, New York, NY 10022. Inquiries from Canada should be directed to your local Canadian bookseller or sent to Random House of Canada, Ltd., Marketing Department, 1265 Aerowood Drive, Mississauga, Ontario L4W 1B9. Inquiries from the United Kingdom should be sent to Fodor's Travel Publications, 20 Vauxhall Bridge Road, London SW1V 2SA, England.

PRINTED IN THE UNITED STATES OF AMERICA

10 9 8 7 6 5 4 3 2 1

CONTENTS

On the Road with Fodor's v

About Our Writers *v*
New This Year *v*
Connections *vi*
How to Use This Book *vi*
Don't Forget to Write *vii*

The Gold Guide x

Smart Travel Tips A to Z

1 Destination: Alaska 1

The Many Alaskas *2*
What's Where *5*
Pleasures and Pastimes *6*
New and Noteworthy *9*
Great Itineraries *11*
Fodor's Choice *12*
Festivals and Seasonal Events *15*

2 Cruising in Alaska 17

3 Parks, Wildlife Refuges, and Wilderness Adventures 42

Including Denali National Park and Glacier Bay

4 Southeast Alaska 89

Including Ketchikan, Juneau, Haines, Sitka, and Skagway

5 Anchorage 130

6 South Central Alaska 156

Including Prince William Sound, Homer, and the Kenai Peninsula

7 The Interior 182

Including Fairbanks, the Dalton Highway, and the Yukon

8 The Bush 217

Including Nome, Barrow, Prudhoe Bay, and the Aleutian Islands

9 Vancouver and Victoria 237

10 Portraits of Alaska 255

"Native Alaskans," by Stanton H. Patty *256*
"Alaska: A Geological Story," by Dr. Charles Lane *259*

Maps

Alaska *viii–ix*
Cruise Ships (chart) 28
Parks and Wildlife Refuges
  44–45
Glacier Bay 60
Denali National Park 75
Southeast Alaska 91
Ketchikan 96
Wrangell 101
Petersburg 105
Sitka 108
Juneau 112
Haines 120
Skagway 125

Anchorage 136–137
Anchorage Dining and Lodging
  142–143
South Central Alaska 160
Interior and the Yukon 186
Fairbanks 189
Dawson City 211
The Bush 223
Alaska Peninsula, Aleutians, and
  Pribilofs 225
Gastown and Chinatown 240
Stanley Park 241
Downtown Victoria 247

ON THE ROAD WITH FODOR'S

WHEN I PLAN A VACATION, the first thing I do is cast around among my friends and colleagues to find someone who's just been where I'm going. That's because there's no substitute for a recommendation from a good friend who knows your tastes, your budget, and your circumstances, someone who's just been there. Unfortunately, such friends are few and far between. So it's nice to know that there's *Fodor's Alaska*.

In the first place, this book won't stay home when you hit the road. It will accompany you every step of the way, steering you away from wrong turns and wrong choices and never expecting a thing in return. It includes a wonderful, full-color map from Rand McNally, the world's largest commercial mapmaker. Most important of all, it's written and assiduously updated by the kind of people you *would* hit up for travel tips if you knew them. They're as choosy as your pickiest friend, except they've probably seen a lot more of Alaska. In these pages, they don't send you chasing down every town and sight in Alaska but have instead selected the best ones, the ones that are worthy of your time and money. To make it easy for you to put it all together in the time you have, they've created short, medium, and long itineraries and, in cities, neighborhood walks that you can mix and match in a snap. Just tear out the map at the perforation, and join us on the road in Alaska.

About Our Writers

A Midwesterner who moved to Alaska 15 years ago, **Tom Reale** has traveled extensively throughout the state, writing about it and about wilderness adventures for a variety of publications. He and his wife hunt, fish, camp, backpack, ski, and hike at every opportunity.

Don Pitcher's knowledge of Alaska comes from a dozen seasons spent guiding visitors to brown-bear viewing areas, counting salmon at fish weirs, studying fires in Wrangell-St. Elias National Park, and building trails in rainy Southeast Alaska. He is the author of guidebooks on Alaska, Wyoming, Washington, and Berkeley, California. Today he lives in Anchorage with his wife Karen, and their daughter, Aziza Bali, who was born shortly after Don's deadline for this edition.

New York–based writer and photographer **Connie Saint** updated the Southeast chapter after catching up with relatives in Kodiak and Anchorage. Prior to this trip Connie spent three years writing for **GQ** magazine.

Vancouver-born freelance writer **Sue Kernaghan** is a fourth-generation British Columbian. "The family's been in B.C. so long we've had a swamp named after us," she says. Between Fodor's assignments, Sue writes management books, including the forthcoming *Doing it Different, the Method in Mad Companies*.

M. T. Schwartzman has visited every region of Alaska and has written about the state for several publications. Formerly *Travel Weekly*'s Alaska editor, Schwartzman compiled the Gold Guide, reported the Alaska news in New and Noteworthy, and oversaw this book's cruise chapter.

In his distinguished career at the *Anchorage Times*, **Bill Sherwonit** won more than 10 awards from organizations such as the Associated Press and the Sierra Club. Now a freelance writer who has traveled far and wide in his home state, Sherwonit lent his outdoors expertise to our Parks, Wildlife Refuges, and Wilderness Adventures chapter and diligently updated the Southeast and Bush chapters as well.

New This Year

This year we've expanded the coverage of wilderness activities in Chapter 3. New sections cover the ins and outs of dogsledding, sea kayaking, snowmobiling, horse packing, trail riding, and whale watching. In all cases there's now information on how to prepare for your trip and how to find the best outfitter.

We've also added a new map of Glacier Bay National Park, a stop on many cruises and a favorite destination for flightseeing fanatics, and we've expanded our coverage of lodging in many parts of the state.

Connections

We're pleased that the American Society of Travel Agents continues to endorse Fodor's as its guidebook of choice. ASTA is the world's largest and most influential travel trade association, operating in more than 170 countries, with 27,000 members pledged to adhere to a strict code of ethics reflecting the Society's motto, "Integrity in Travel." ASTA shares Fodor's devotion to providing smart, honest travel information and advice to travelers, and we've long recommended that our readers—even those who have guidebooks and traveling friends—consult ASTA member agents for the experience and professionalism they bring to your vacation planning.

On Fodor's Web site (www.fodors.com), check out the new Resource Center, an online companion to the Gold Guide section of this book, complete with useful hot links to related sites. In our forums, you can also get lively advice from other travelers and more great tips from Fodor's experts worldwide.

How to Use This Book

Organization

Up front is the **Gold Guide,** an easy-to-use section divided alphabetically by topic. Under each listing you'll find tips and information that will help you accomplish what you need to in Alaska. You'll also find addresses and telephone numbers of organizations and companies that offer destination-related services and detailed information and publications.

The first chapter in the guide, Destination: Alaska, helps get you in the mood for your trip. What's Where gets you oriented, Pleasures and Pastimes describes the activities and sights that really make Alaska unique, New and Noteworthy cues you in on trends and happenings, Great Itineraries lays out a selection of complete trips, Fodor's Choice showcases our top picks, and Festivals and Seasonal Events alerts you to special events you'll want to seek out.

Chapters 2 and 3 cover cruising and parks, which are parts of many visitors' experiences. Chapters 4 through 8 discuss the state by region, starting in the southeast part of the state, heading northwest to the Interior, and fanning out to the Bush. Chapter 9 provides succinct information on Vancouver and Victoria. Each regional chapter is divided by geographical area; within each area, towns and other sights of interest are covered in logical geographical order. Throughout, Off the Beaten Path sights appear after the places from which they are most easily accessible. The parks chapter is divided geographically as well, but under geographical headings, parks are alphabetized.

To help you decide what to visit in the time you have, all chapters begin with recommended itineraries; you can mix and match those from several chapters to create a complete vacation. The A to Z section, which ends all chapters, covers getting there, getting around, and helpful contacts and resources.

At the end of the book you'll find Portraits, two essays about the history, peoples, and natural wonders of Alaska. **Stanton Patty** characterizes native Alaskans and **Dr. Charles Lane** describes the state's glaciers, mountains, and other landforms.

Icons and Symbols

★	Our special recommendation
✕	Restaurant
🏨	Lodging establishment
✕🏨	Lodging establishment whose restaurant warrants a special trip
🏕	Campgrounds
🐥	Good for kids (rubber duckie)
☞	Sends you to another section of the guide for more information
✉	Address
☎	Telephone number
☺	Opening and closing times
💲	Admission prices (those we give apply to adults; substantially reduced fees are almost always available for children, students, and senior citizens)

Numbers in white and black circles ③ ❸ that appear on the maps, in the margins, and within the tours correspond to one another.

Dining and Lodging

The restaurants and lodgings we list are the cream of the crop in each price range. Lodging tax in Alaska is 8%–10%. In British Columbia, hotels collect a 10% provincial accommodation tax and a 7% GST.

For restaurants:

CATEGORY	ALASKA*	VANCOUVER AND VICTORIA*
$$$$	over $40	over C$40
$$$	$25–$40	C$30–C$40
$$	$10–$25	C$20–C$30
$	under $10	under C$20

All prices are for a three-course meal, excluding drinks, service, and tip.

For hotels:

CATEGORY	ANCHORAGE*	ELSEWHERE IN ALASKA*
$$$$	over $210	over $120
$$$	$140–$210	$90–$120
$$	$85–$140	$50–$90
$	under $85	under $50

CATEGORY	VANCOUVER AND VICTORIA*
$$$$	over C$200
$$$	C$150–C$200
$$	C$100–C$150
$	under C$100

All prices are for a standard double room in high season, excluding tax and service.

Hotel Facilities

We always list the facilities that are available—but we don't specify whether they cost extra: when pricing accommodations, always ask what's included. In addition, assume that all rooms have private baths unless otherwise noted. Assume that hotels operate on the European Plan (with no meals) unless we note otherwise.

Restaurant Reservations and Dress Codes

Reservations are always a good idea; we note only when they're essential or when they are not accepted. Book as far ahead as you can, and reconfirm when you get to town. Unless otherwise noted, the restaurants listed are open daily for lunch and dinner. We mention dress only when men are required to wear a jacket or a jacket and tie.

Credit Cards

The following abbreviations are used: **AE**, American Express; **D**, Discover; **DC**, Diners Club; **MC**, MasterCard; and **V**, Visa.

Don't Forget to Write

You can use this book in the confidence that all prices and opening times are based on information supplied to us at press time; Fodor's cannot accept responsibility for any errors. Time inevitably brings changes, so always confirm information when it matters—especially if you're making a detour to visit a specific place.

Were the restaurants we recommended as described? Did our hotel picks exceed your expectations? Did you find a museum we recommended a waste of time? Keeping a travel guide fresh and up-to-date is a big job, and we welcome your feedback, positive *and* negative. If you have complaints, we'll look into them and revise our entries when the facts warrant it. If you've discovered a special place that we haven't included, we'll pass the information along to our correspondents and have them check it out. So send us your thoughts via e-mail at editors@fodors.com (specifying the name of the book on the subject line) or on paper in care of the Alaska editor at Fodor's, 201 East 50th Street, New York, New York 10022. In the meantime, have a wonderful trip!

Karen Cure
Editorial Director

Alaska

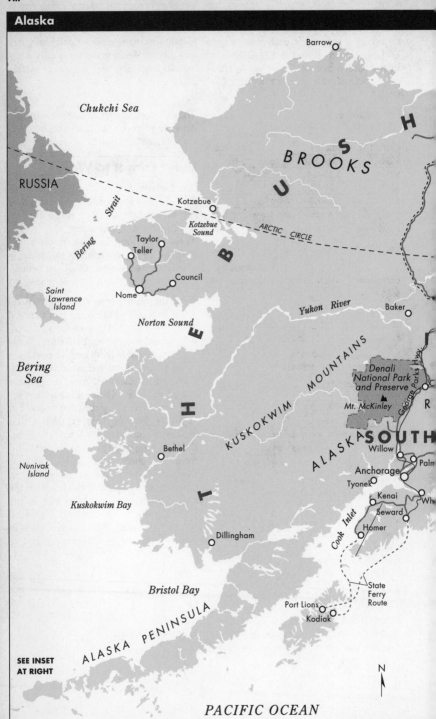

Chukchi Sea

RUSSIA

B R O O K S

S

H

U

Barrow

Kotzebue

ARCTIC CIRCLE

Kotzebue
Sound

Bering Strait

Taylor
Teller

Council

Nome

Norton Sound

Saint
Lawrence
Island

Yukon River

Baker

Bering
Sea

KUSKOKWIM MOUNTAINS

B

E

H

T

Denali
National Park
and Preserve

Mt. McKinley

George Parks Hwy.

R

SOUTH

ALASKA

Willow

Palm

Bethel

Anchorage

Tyonek

Kenai

Wh

Nunivak
Island

Seward

Homer

Kuskokwim Bay

Cook Inlet

Dillingham

Bristol Bay

State
Ferry
Route

Port Lions

Kodiak

ALASKA PENINSULA

SEE INSET
AT RIGHT

N

PACIFIC OCEAN

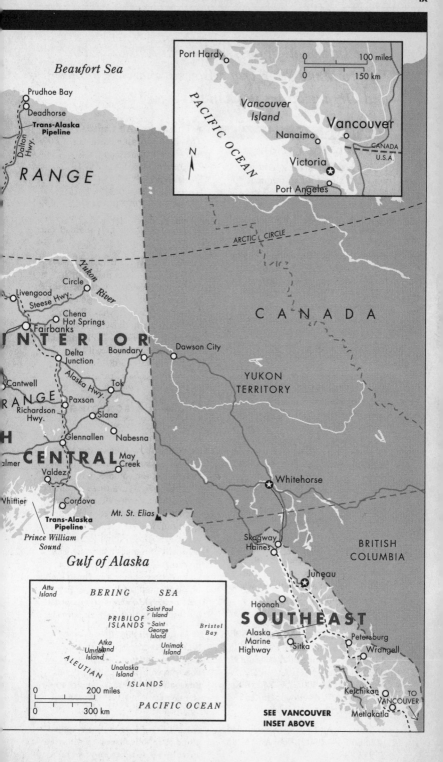

Beaufort Sea

Prudhoe Bay
Deadhorse
Trans-Alaska Pipeline

Dalton Hwy.

R A N G E

Port Hardy

PACIFIC OCEAN

Vancouver Island

Vancouver

Nanaimo

CANADA
U.S.A.

Victoria

Port Angeles

0   100 miles
0   150 km

N

ARCTIC CIRCLE

Yukon River

Circle
Livengood
Steese Hwy.
Chena Hot Springs
Fairbanks

I N T E R I O R

Delta Junction
Boundary
Dawson City

C A N A D A

Cantwell

R A N G E

Richardson Hwy.
Paxson
Slana
Nabesna

Alaska Hwy.
Tok

YUKON TERRITORY

H

C E N T R A L

Palmer

Glennallen
May Creek

Valdez
Whittier
Cordova

Mt. St. Elias

Trans-Alaska Pipeline

Prince William Sound

Whitehorse

Gulf of Alaska

BRITISH COLUMBIA

Skagway
Haines

Juneau

Hoonah

S O U T H E A S T

Attu Island
BERING   SEA

PRIBILOF ISLANDS
Saint Paul Island
Saint George Island

Bristol Bay

Atka Island
Umnak Island
Unimak Island

A L E U T I A N

Unalaska Island

I S L A N D S

0   200 miles
0   300 km

PACIFIC OCEAN

Alaska Marine Highway
Sitka
Petersburg
Wrangell

Ketchikan

TO VANCOUVER

Metlakatla

SEE VANCOUVER INSET ABOVE

SMART TRAVEL TIPS A TO Z

Basic Information on Traveling in Alaska, Savvy Tips to Make Your Trip a Breeze, and Companies and Organizations to Contact

AIR TRAVEL

BOOKING YOUR FLIGHT

Price is just one factor to consider when booking a flight: frequency of service and even a carrier's safety record are often just as important. Major airlines offer the greatest number of departures. Smaller airlines—including regional and no-frills airlines—usually have a limited number of flights daily. On the other hand, so-called low-cost airlines usually are cheaper, and their fares impose fewer restrictions, such as advance-purchase requirements. Safety-wise, low-cost carriers as a group have a good history—about equal to that of major carriers.

When you book, **look for nonstop flights** and **remember that "direct" flights stop at least once.** Try to **avoid connecting flights,** which require a change of plane. Two airlines may jointly operate a connecting flight, so ask if your airline operates every segment—you may find that your preferred carrier flies you only part of the way.

Ask your airline if it offers electronic ticketing, which eliminates all paperwork. There's no ticket to pick up or misplace. You go directly to the gate and give the agent your confirmation number. There's no worry about waiting on line at the airport while precious minutes tick by.

CARRIERS

➤ MAJOR AIRLINES: **Alaska** (☎ 800/426–0333). **America West** (☎ 800/235–9292). **Continental** (☎ 800/525–0280). **Delta** (☎ 800/221–1212). **Northwest** (☎ 800/225–2525). **Reno Air** (☎ 800/736–6247). **United** (☎ 800/241–6522).

➤ SMALLER AIRLINES: **Air North Ltd.** (☎ 800/764–0407).**Yute Air** (☎ 888/359–9883).

➤ TO CANADA: **Air Canada** (☎ 800/776–3000). **Alaska Airlines** (☎ 800/426–0333). **American** (☎ 800/433–7300). **Delta** (☎ 800/221–1212). **Horizon Air** (☎ 800/547–9308). **Northwest** (☎ 800/225–2525). **United** (☎ 800/722–5243. **Kenmore Air** (☎ 206/486–1257 or 800/543–9595) offers direct daily flights from Seattle to Victoria.

➤ FROM THE U.K.: **British Airways** (☎ 0345/222–111) flies from Heathrow to Seattle. **Continental Airlines** (☎ 0800/776–464 or 01293/776–464) from Gatwick, Birmingham, or Manchester via Newark. **Delta** (☎ 0800/414–767) from Gatwick to Cincinnati or Salt Lake City. **United** (☎ 0800/888–555) from Heathrow via San Francisco or Chicago.

CHECK IN & BOARDING

Airlines routinely overbook planes, assuming that not everyone with a ticket will show up, but sometimes everyone does. When that happens, airlines ask for volunteers to give up their seats. In return these volunteers usually get a certificate for a free flight and are rebooked on the next flight out. If there are not enough volunteers, the airline must choose who will be denied boarding. The first to get bumped are passengers who checked in late and those flying on discounted tickets, so **get to the gate and check in as early as possible,** especially during peak periods.

Although the trend on international flights is to drop reconfirmation requirements, many airlines still ask you to reconfirm each leg of your international itinerary. Failure to do so may result in your reservation being canceled.

Always **bring a government-issued photo ID to the airport.** You may be asked to show it before you are allowed to check in.

CONSOLIDATORS

Consolidators buy tickets for scheduled international flights at reduced rates from the airlines, then sell them at prices that beat the best fare available directly from the airlines, usually without restrictions. Sometimes you can even get your money back if you need to return the ticket. Carefully read the fine print detailing penalties for changes and cancellations, and **confirm your consolidator reservation with the airline.**

➤ CONSOLIDATORS: **Cheap Tickets** (☎ 800/377–1000). **Discount Travel Network** (☎ 800/576–1600). **Unitravel** (☎ 800/325–2222). **Up & Away Travel** (☎ 212/889–2345). **World Travel Network** (☎ 800/409–6753).

COURIERS

When you fly as a courier, you trade your checked-luggage space for a ticket deeply subsidized by a courier service. It's all perfectly legitimate, but there are restrictions: You can usually book your flight only a week or two in advance, your length of stay may be set for a certain number of days, and you probably won't be able to book a companion on the same flight.

CUTTING COSTS

The least-expensive airfares to Alaska are priced for round-trip travel and usually must be purchased in advance. It's smart to **call a number of airlines, and when you are quoted a good price, book it on the spot**—the same fare may not be available the next day. Airlines generally allow you to change your return date for a fee. If you don't use your ticket, you can apply the cost toward the purchase of a new ticket, again for a small charge. However, most low-fare tickets are nonrefundable. To get the lowest airfare, **check different routings.** Compare prices of flights to and from different airports if your destination or home city has more than one gateway. Also price off-peak flights—notably the midnight flights out of Anchorage—which may be significantly less expensive.

When flying within the U.S., **plan to stay over a Saturday night** and **travel during the middle of the week** to get the lowest fare. These low fares are usually priced for round-trip travel and are nonrefundable. You can, however, change your return date for a fee ($75 on most major airlines).

Travel agents, especially those who specialize in finding the lowest fares (☞ Discounts & Deals, *below*), can be especially helpful when booking a plane ticket. When you're quoted a price, **ask your agent if the price is likely to get any lower.** Good agents know the seasonal fluctuations of airfares and can usually anticipate a sale or fare war. However, waiting can be risky: The fare could go *up* as seats become scarce, and you may wait so long that your preferred flight sells out. A wait-and-see strategy works best if your plans are flexible. If you must arrive and depart on certain dates, don't delay.

ENJOYING THE FLIGHT

For better service, **fly smaller or regional carriers,** which often have higher passenger-satisfaction ratings. Sometimes you'll find leather seats, more legroom, and better food.

For more legroom, **request an emergency-aisle seat.** Don't sit in the row in front of the emergency aisle or in front of a bulkhead, where seats may not recline.

If you don't like airline food, **ask for special meals when booking.** These can be vegetarian, low-cholesterol, or kosher, for example.

FLYING TIMES

Average travel time from New York to Anchorage is 10 hours; from Chicago, 8 hours; and from Los Angeles, 5½ hours.

HOW TO COMPLAIN

If your baggage goes astray or your flight goes awry, complain right away. Most carriers require that you **file a claim immediately.**

➤ AIRLINE COMPLAINTS: U.S. Department of Transportation **Aviation Consumer Protection Division** (✉ C-75, Room 4107, Washington, DC 20590, ☎ 202/366–2220). **Federal Aviation Administration Consumer Hotline** (☎ 800/322–7873).

WITHIN ALASKA

Commercial air travel to major towns in Alaska is usually by jet or turbo-prop. Scheduled air-taxi and air-charter services provide quick and easy access to smaller towns and remote locales, using propeller-driven bush aircraft that land on wheels, on floats, or on skis. Helicopters are increasingly popular for flightseeing and fast transport (☞ the Getting Around sections of each regional chapter for more specific information).

Most of Alaska's wild places can be reached only by air, but don't consider that a drawback. Small planes have played a legendary part in the state's history: Bush pilots have helped explore Alaska and have been responsible for many dramatic rescue missions. But **be aware that small planes cannot transport more than a limited amount of gear** and cannot fly safely in poor weather. Your drop-off, as well as your pickup flight, is therefore subject to delays, which are sometimes counted in days, not hours. When traveling in remote areas away from any towns or villages, be sure to **carry extra food.**

➤ AIRLINES: **Alaska Airlines** (☞ *above*) for service statewide. **Air North Ltd.** (☎ 403/668–2228; 800/764–0407 in AK) for service from Fairbanks or Juneau to Dawson City and Whitehorse in the Yukon. **Bering Air** (☎ 907/443–5464) for flights from Nome or Kotzebue to smaller communities of the Far North. **ERA Aviation** (☎ 800/866–8394, reservations through Alaska Airlines) for flights to Kenai, Kodiak, Homer, Valdez, Cordova, plus Whitehorse in the Yukon Territory and 17 western Alaska villages. **Frontier Flying Service** (☎ 907/474–0014) for flights out of Fairbanks to points in the Interior. **PenAir** (☎ 907/243–2323, reservations through Alaska Airlines) for flights to Western Alaska including Dillingham, Kodiak, and the Aleutian Chain. **Reeve Aleutian Airways** (☎ 907/243–4700 or 800/544–2248) to Dutch Harbor in the Aleutians. **SouthCentral Air** (☎ 800/478–2550) for flights from Anchorage to Homer and Kenai. **Yute Air** (☎ 888/359–9883) for flights to Aniak,

Bethel, Dillingham, King Salmon, Kotzebue, Nome, and dozens of smaller Bush villages.

AIRPORTS

The major gateway to Alaska is **Anchorage International Airport,** 6 mi from downtown Anchorage. Nonstop service is also available to Fairbanks, Juneau, and Ketchikan. Southeastern Alaska cities are connected through Seattle, while northern locations are reached through Anchorage or Fairbanks. **Vancouver International Airport** is on an island about 14 km (9 mi) south of downtown. There are few nonstop flights to Alaska from the Lower 48 states.

➤ AIRPORT INFORMATION: **Anchorage International Airport** (☎ 907/266–2525). **Vancouver International Airport** (☎ 604/303–3603).

BEARS

If you're lucky—and careful—the sight of one of these magnificent creatures in the wild can be a highlight of your visit. By respecting bears and exercising care in bear country, neither you nor the bear will suffer from the experience. Remember that bears don't like surprises. Make your presence known by talking, singing, rattling a can full of gravel, or tying a bell to your pack, especially when terrain or vegetation obscures views. Travel with a group, which is noisier and easier for bears to detect. If possible, walk with the wind at your back so your scent will warn bears of your presence. And avoid bushy, low-visibility areas whenever possible.

Give bears the right of way—lots of it—especially a sow with cubs. Don't camp on animal trails; they're likely to be used by bears. If you come across a carcass of an animal, or detect its odor, avoid the area entirely; it's likely a bear's food cache.

Don't let bears associate humans with food. Never feed bears. If you're camping, cook away from your tent. Avoid particularly aromatic food like bacon and smoked fish. Store all food and garbage away from your camp-site in airtight or specially designed bear-proof containers. The Park Service supplies these for hikers in Denali and Glacier Bay national parks.

THE GOLD GUIDE / SMART TRAVEL TIPS

If a bear approaches you while you are fishing, stop. If you have a fish on your line, cut your line; don't let bears associate fishermen with fish. If you do encounter a bear at close range, don't panic, and, above all, don't run. You can't outrun a bear, and by fleeing you could trigger a chase response. Keep in mind that most bears just want to be left alone. Help the bear know you're human. Talk in a normal voice. Slowly wave your arms. If traveling with others, stand close together to "increase your size." If the bear charges, it could be a bluff; as terrifying as this may sound, the experts advise standing your ground. If a brown or grizzly bear actually touches you, then drop to the ground and play dead, either flat on your stomach or curled in a ball with your hands behind your neck. If you don't move, a brown bear will typically break off its attack once it feels the threat is gone. But know your bears: If you are attacked by a black bear—typically much smaller but often more aggressive than a brown or grizzly bear—some experts advise that you fight back vigorously.

Finally, don't think bears are the only animal to be treated with caution. Give moose a wide range as well; many a hiker has been charged, and injured, by a moose.

For more information on bears, ask for the brochure "Bear Facts: The Essentials for Traveling in Bear Country" from any of the Alaska Public Lands offices (☞ Parks, Wildlife Refuges, and Wilderness Adventures A to Z *in* Chapter 3).

BIKE TRAVEL

BIKES IN FLIGHT

Most airlines will accommodate bikes as luggage, provided they are dismantled and put into a box. Call to see if your airline sells bike boxes (about $5; bike bags are at least $100) although you can often pick them up free at bike shops. International travelers can sometimes substitute a bike for a piece of checked luggage for free; otherwise, it will cost about $100. Domestic and Canadian airlines charge a $25–$50 fee.

BOAT & FERRY TRAVEL

Travelers looking for a casual alternative to a luxury cruise should **travel as Alaskans do, aboard the ferries of the Alaska Marine Highway system.** When planning your trip, **ask about special onboard programming.** Forest Service naturalists ride the larger ferries in summer and selected winter sailings, providing a running commentary on sights. The Arts-on-Board Program presents educators and entertainers on selected summer sailings. The Alaska Marine Highway ferries travel within Alaska and between Bellingham, Washington, and the towns of the Inside Passage. The Marine Highway links up with British Columbia Ferries in Prince Rupert.

➤ FERRY LINES: **Alaska Marine Highway** (☒ Box 25535, Juneau 99802-5535, ☎ 907/465–3941 or 800/642–0066, ☎ 907/277–4829). **British Columbia Ferries** (☒ 1112 Fort St., Victoria, BC V8V 4V2, ☎ 250/386–3431, ☎ 250/381–5452.

DISCOUNT PASSES

See Bus Travel, *below.*

BUS TRAVEL

Motor coaches, independently or in connection with major tour companies, travel to and throughout Alaska from the United States and Canada.

Island and coastal towns of the Southeast Panhandle are not accessible by bus, except for the two ports at the northern end of the Inside Passage: Haines and Skagway. From here, highways connect with overland routes to South Central and the Interior and with the Alaska Highway.

➤ BUS LINES: **Alaska Direct Bus Lines** (☒ Box 501, Anchorage 99501, ☎ 907/277–6652 or 800/770–6652) operates year-round intercity van service between points in Alaska and the Canadian Yukon on most major highways. **Alaskon Express** (☒ 300 Elliott Ave. W, Seattle, WA 98119, ☎ 206/281–3535 or 800/544–2206), a subsidiary of Gray Line of Alaska, operates intercity service mid-May through mid-September. **Alaska Backpacker Shuttle** (☒ Box 232493,

Anchorage, AK 99523, ☎ 907/344–8775 or 800/266–8625), operates daily vans between Anchorage and Denali National Park. **Greyhound Lines** (☎ 604/662–3222 or 800/661–8747) serves Vancouver. **Quick Shuttle** (☎ 604/244–3744; 800/665–2122 in the U.S.) bus service runs between Vancouver and Seattle.

DISCOUNT PASSES

The **AlaskaPass** allows unlimited travel on bus, ferry, and rail lines in Alaska. Passes are available for 8, 15, 22, or 30 consecutive days of travel ($499, $689, $799, or $939, respectively), as well as for 12 days of travel in a 21-day period ($699) and 21 travel days in a 45-day period ($979).

➤ ALASKAPASS: **AlaskaPass** (✉ Box 351, Vashon, WA 98070-0351, ☎ 206/463–6550 or 800/248–7598 in the U.S., 0800/898285 in the U.K., FAX 206/463–6777 or 800/488–0303).

CAMERAS & COMPUTERS

EQUIPMENT PRECAUTIONS

Always **keep your film, tape, or computer disks out of the sun.** Carry an extra supply of batteries, and **be prepared to turn on your camera, camcorder, or laptop** to prove to security personnel that the device is real. Always **ask for hand inspection of film,** which becomes clouded after successive exposure to airport X-ray machines, and **keep videotapes and computer disks away from metal detectors.**

ONLINE ON THE ROAD

TRAVEL PHOTOGRAPHY

Alaska is one of the premier spots for bird and wildlife photography. Many professional photographers use Kodak's Ektachrome 100, or Fuji's Sensia II or Velvia color slide films under all conditions, though you may want to pack a roll or two of higher-speed film, whether for slides or prints, to catch action shots. Kodak's Ektachrome E200 is an excellent professional-quality slide film for low-light situations. You'll need to take into account the extraordinary qualities of Alaska's slanting light (the sun is never directly overhead, and there are long shadows).

Film—though available in the cities, bush villages, and lodges—tends to be expensive outside of Anchorage, so carry plenty. And be sure to pack extra batteries for your camera. A tripod is useful for almost any Alaskan photography and highly recommended for photographing wildlife.

Keep your camera dry; some people slip their cameras into plastic bags. Long telephoto lenses are useful for many wildlife photos, but wide-angle lenses help show the expansiveness of the Alaskan landscape.

➤ PHOTO HELP: **Kodak Information Center** (☎ 800/242–2424). *Kodak Guide to Shooting Great Travel Pictures,* available in bookstores or from Fodor's Travel Publications (☎ 800/533–6478; $16.50 plus $4 shipping).

CAR RENTAL

Rates in Anchorage begin at $40 a day and $270 a week for an economy car with air-conditioning (not generally needed), an automatic transmission, and unlimited mileage. You're likely to pay at least $50 per day and $300 per week from the major companies; more for four-wheel drives. Reserve well ahead for the summer season, particularly for the popular minivans and sport utility vehicles.

➤ MAJOR AGENCIES: **Alamo** (☎ 800/327–9633, 0800/272–2000 in the U.K.). **Avis** (☎ 800/331–1212, 800/879–2847 in Canada, 008/225–533 in Australia). **Budget** (☎ 800/527–0700, 0800/181181 in the U.K.). **Dollar** (☎ 800/800–4000; 0990/565656 in the U.K., where it is known as Eurodollar). **Hertz** (☎ 800/654–3131, 800/263–0600 in Canada, 0345/555888 in the U.K., 03/9222–2523 in Australia, 03/358–6777 in New Zealand). **National InterRent** (☎ 800/227–7368; 0345/222525 in the U.K., where it is known as Europcar InterRent).

➤ SMALLER AGENCIES: **Payless** (☎ 800/729–5377). **Thrifty** (☎ 907/276–2855 or 800/367–2277).

➤ LOCAL AGENCIES: Local companies are often a good source for low rates, especially on a weekly basis. **Afford-able** (☎ 800/248–3765 in Anchorage or 907/452–7341 in Fairbanks). **Arctic** (☎ 907/561–2990 in Anchorage or 907/479–8044 in Fairbanks). **Denali Car Rental** (☎ 907/276–1230 or 800/757–1230 in Anchorage). **Kodiak Auto Rental** (☎ 907/487–2272 on Kodiak Island). **Rent-A-Wreck** (☎ 907/562–5499 in Anchorage). **U-Save** (☎ 907/272–8728 or 800/254–8728 in Anchorage).

CUTTING COSTS

To get the best deal, **book through a travel agent who is willing to shop around.** When pricing cars, **ask about the location of the rental lot.** Some off-airport locations offer lower rates, and their lots are only minutes from the terminal via complimentary shuttle. You also may want to **price local car-rental companies,** whose rates may be lower still, although their service and maintenance may not be as good as those of a name-brand agency. Remember to ask about required deposits, cancellation penalties, and drop-off charges if you're planning to pick up the car in one city and leave it in another.

Also **ask your travel agent about a company's customer-service record.** How has the company responded to late plane arrivals and vehicle mishaps? Are there often lines at the rental counter?

Be sure to **look into wholesalers,** companies that do not own fleets but rent in bulk from those that do and often offer better rates than traditional car-rental operations. Prices are best during off-peak periods.

➤ RENTAL WHOLESALERS: **Auto Europe** (☎ 207/842–2000 or 800/223–5555, FAX 800–235–6321).

INSURANCE

When driving a rented car you are generally responsible for any damage to or loss of the vehicle. You also are liable for any property damage or personal injury that you may cause while driving. Before you rent, **see what coverage you already have** under the terms of your personal auto-insurance policy and credit cards.

For about $15 to $20 per day, rental companies sell protection, known as a collision- or loss-damage waiver (CDW or LDW), that eliminates your liability for damage to the car; it's always optional and should never be automatically added to your bill.

In most states you don't need a CDW if you have personal auto insurance or other liability insurance. However, **make sure you have enough coverage to pay for the car.** If you do not have auto insurance or an umbrella policy that covers damage to third parties, purchasing liability insurance and a CDW or LDW is highly recommended.

REQUIREMENTS

In Alaska you must be 21 to rent a car, and rates may be higher if you're under 25. You'll pay extra for child seats (about $3 per day), which are compulsory for children under five, and for additional drivers (about $2 per day). Non-U.S. residents will need a reservation voucher, a passport, a driver's license, and a travel policy that covers each driver, in order to pick up a car.

SURCHARGES

Before you pick up a car in one city and leave it in another, **ask about drop-off charges or one-way service fees,** which can be substantial. Note, too, that some rental agencies charge extra if you return the car before the time specified in your contract. To avoid a hefty refueling fee, **fill the tank just before you turn in the car,** but be aware that gas stations near the rental outlet may overcharge.

CAR TRAVEL

Driving to Alaska is a popular alternative to flying or cruising, especially for RVers, but you'll need to **set aside plenty of time.** Though journeying through Canada on the Alaska Highway can be exciting, the trek from the Lower 48 states is a long one. It's a seven-day trip from Seattle to Anchorage or Fairbanks, covering close to 2,500 mi. From Bellingham, Washington, and the Canadian ports of Prince Rupert and Stewart, you can link up with ferry service along the Marine Highway to reach southeastern Alaska.

If you are planning to drive to Alaska, you should **come armed with patience.** Road construction often creates long delays on the Canadian side of the border, so don't plan a tight schedule.

Driving in Alaska is much less rigorous than it used to be, although it still presents some unusual obstacles. Alaskan moose often wander onto roads and highways. If you come across one while driving, it's best to **stop your car and wait for the moose to cross.** The moose will usually move on its own.

Flying gravel is a hazard to watch for along the Alaska and Dalton highways, especially in summer. Rubber matting can help protect your gas tank. A bug screen will help keep gravel and kamikaze insects off the windshield. Use clear, hard plastic guards to cover your headlights. (These are inexpensive and are available from almost any garage or service station along the major access routes.) Don't cover headlights with cardboard or plywood because you'll need your lights often, even in daytime, as dust is thrown up by traffic passing in both directions. (Headlights must be used at all times on the Seward Highway.) State law requires that slow-moving vehicles **pull off the road at the first opportunity if leading more than five cars.** This is particularly true on the highway between Anchorage and Seward, where RV drivers have a bad reputation for not pulling over. Alaskans don't take kindly to being held up en route to their favorite Kenai River fishing spot!

If you get stuck on any kind of road, be careful about pulling off; the shoulder could be soft. In summer it stays light late, and though traffic is also light, one of Alaska's many good samaritans is likely to stop to help and send for aid (which may be many miles away). In winter, pack emergency equipment, a shovel, and tire chains, plus such high-energy food as nuts or chocolate, flasks of hot beverages, and extra-warm clothing and blankets to help you through the wait for aid, should you need it. Do not head out onto unplowed roads unless you are prepared to walk back.

➤ LOCAL RESOURCES: **Alaska Public Lands Information Center** (✉ 250 Cushman St., Suite 1A, Fairbanks 99701, ☎ 907/456–0527, FAX 907/456–0154). *The Alaska Milepost,* available in bookstores or from Alaska Publications (✉ 4220 B St., Suite 210, Anchorage, AK 99503, ☎ 907/561–4772 or 800/726–4707, FAX 907/561–5669), is a mile-by-mile guide to sights and services along Alaska's highways.

CARS

Unless you plan to undertake one of the remote highways (such as the Dalton Highway), you won't need any special equipment. The equipment you do have should be in first-class condition, though, from tires and spare to brakes and engine. Carrying spare fuses, spark plugs, jumper cables, a flashlight with extra batteries, a tool kit, and an extra fan belt is recommended.

GASOLINE

Gas prices in the Anchorage area are comparable to those in the Lower 48, but elsewhere you should expect to pay more. Not surprisingly, prices are highest in the most remote areas, particularly in small villages off the road network where fuel must be flown in. Fuel prices in Canada along the Alaska Highway are also very high.

ROAD CONDITIONS

The Alaska Highway begins at Dawson Creek, British Columbia, and stretches 1,488 mi through Canada's Yukon to Fairbanks; it enters Alaska at Tok. The two-lane highway is hard-surfaced for nearly its entire length and is open year-round. Highway services are available about every 50 mi (frequently at shorter intervals).

The rest of the state's roads are found almost exclusively in the South Central and Interior regions. They lie mainly between Anchorage, Fairbanks, and the Canadian border. Only one highway extends north of Fairbanks, and a couple run south of Anchorage to the Kenai Peninsula. These roads vary from four-lane freeways to nameless two-lane gravel roads and are generally open and maintained year-round. The Glenn

Highway begins at Tok and travels south to Anchorage. The Richardson Highway parallels the Alaska pipeline from Fairbanks south to the port city of Valdez. The Seward Highway heads south from Anchorage through the Kenai Mountains to Seward, with the branch Sterling Highway heading southwest to Kenai and Homer. The George Parks Highway connects Anchorage and Fairbanks, passing Denali National Park en route. The Steese Highway runs northwest of Fairbanks to the Gold Rush town of Circle. The Dalton Highway begins at the end of the Elliott Highway, 73 mi north of Fairbanks, and leads 414 mi to Deadhorse, the supply center for the Prudhoe Bay oil fields. This gravel truck route presents unique challenges; **contact the Alaska Public Lands Information Center if you plan to drive the Dalton Highway.**

RULES OF THE ROAD

Alaska honors valid driver's licenses from any state or country, and the speed limit on most state highways is 55 mi per hour, but much of the Parks Highway between Wasilla and Fairbanks is 65 mi per hour. Unless otherwise posted, you may make a right turn on a red light after coming to a complete stop.

RVS

The secret to a successful RV trip to Alaska is preparation. Expect to do some driving on gravel and on rougher roads than you're accustomed to. Batten down everything; tighten every nut and bolt in and out of sight, and don't leave anything to bounce around inside. Travel light and your tires and suspension system will take less of a beating. Protect your headlights and the grille area in front of the radiator. Make sure you **carry adequate insurance to cover the replacement of your windshield.**

Most of Alaska's roadside campgrounds accommodate trailers, but there are few hookups, except in the private RV parks. Water is available at most stopping points, but it may be limited for trailer use. Think twice before deciding to pull an RV during the spring thaw. The rough, boggy roadbed can be a trial.

CHILDREN & TRAVEL

CHILDREN IN ALASKA

Be sure to plan ahead and **involve your youngsters** as you outline your trip. When packing, include things to keep them busy en route. On sightseeing days try to schedule activities of special interest to your children. If you are renting a car don't forget to **arrange for a car seat** when you reserve. Most hotels in Alaska allow children under a certain age to stay in their parents' room at no extra charge, but others charge them as extra adults; be sure to **ask about the cutoff age for children's discounts.**

FLYING

If your children are two or older, **ask about children's airfares.** As a general rule, infants under two not occupying a seat fly at greatly reduced fares or even for free. In general the adult baggage allowance applies to children paying half or more of the adult fare.

Experts agree that it's a good idea to use safety seats aloft for children weighing less than 40 pounds. Airlines, however, can set their own policies: U.S. carriers allow FAA-approved models but usually require that you buy a ticket, even if your child would otherwise ride free, since the seats must be strapped into regular seats. Airline rules vary, so it's important to **check your airline's policy about using safety seats during takeoff and landing.** Safety seats cannot obstruct the movement of other passengers in the row, so get an appropriate seat assignment as early as possible.

When making your reservation, **request children's meals or a free-standing bassinet** if you need them; the latter are available only to those seated at the bulkhead, where there's enough legroom. Remember, however, that bulkhead seats may not have their own overhead bins, and there's no storage space in front of you—a major inconvenience.

GROUP TRAVEL

When planning to take your kids on a tour, look for companies that specialize in family travel.

THE GOLD GUIDE / SMART TRAVEL TIPS

➤ FAMILY-FRIENDLY TOUR OPERATORS: **Families Welcome!** (✉ 92 N. Main St., Ashland, OR 97520, ☎ 541/482–6121 or 800/326–0724, FAX 541/482–0660). **Grandtravel** (✉ 6900 Wisconsin Ave., Suite 706, Chevy Chase, MD 20815, ☎ 301/986–0790 or 800/247–7651) for people traveling with grandchildren ages 7–17. **Rascals in Paradise** (✉ 650 5th St., Suite 505, San Francisco, CA 94107, ☎ 415/978–9800 or 800/872–7225, FAX 415/442–0289).

CONSUMER PROTECTION

Whenever possible, **pay with a major credit card** so you can cancel payment or get reimbursed if there's a problem, provided that you can provide documentation. This is the best way to pay, whether you're buying travel arrangements before your trip or shopping at your destination.

If you're doing business with a particular company for the first time, **contact your local Better Business Bureau and the attorney general's offices** in your state and the company's home state, as well. Have any complaints been filed?

Finally, if you're buying a package or tour, always **consider travel insurance** that includes default coverage (☞ Insurance, *below*).

➤ LOCAL BBBs: **Council of Better Business Bureaus** (✉ 4200 Wilson Blvd., Suite 800, Arlington, VA 22203, ☎ 703/276–0100, FAX 703/525–8277).

CRUISE TRAVEL

See Chapter 2.

CUSTOMS & DUTIES

When shopping, **keep receipts** for all of your purchases. Upon reentering the country, **be ready to show customs officials what you've bought.** If you feel a duty is incorrect, appeal the assessment. If you object to the way your clearance was handled, get the inspector's badge number. In either case, first ask to see a supervisor, then write to the appropriate authorities, beginning with the port director at your point of entry.

IN AUSTRALIA

Australia residents who are 18 or older may bring back $A400 worth of souvenirs and gifts (including jewelry), 250 cigarettes or 250 grams of tobacco, and 1,125 ml of alcohol (including wine, beer, and spirits). Residents under 18 may bring back $A200 worth of goods.

➤ INFORMATION: **Australian Customs Service** (Regional Director, ✉ Box 8, Sydney, NSW 2001, ☎ 02/9213–2000, FAX 02/9213–4000).

IN CANADA

Canadian residents who have been out of Canada for at least seven days may bring in C$500 worth of goods duty-free. If you've been away less than seven days but more than 48 hours, the duty-free allowance drops to C$200; if your trip lasts 24–48 hours, the allowance is C$50. You may not pool allowances with family members. Goods claimed under the C$500 exemption may follow you by mail; those claimed under the lesser exemptions must accompany you. Alcohol and tobacco products may be included in the seven-day and 48-hour exemptions but not in the 24-hour exemption. If you meet the age requirements of the province or territory through which you reenter Canada, you may bring in, duty-free, 1.14 liters (40 imperial ounces) of wine or liquor *or* 24 12-ounce cans or bottles of beer or ale. If you are 16 or older you may bring in, duty-free, 200 cigarettes and 50 cigars.

You may send an unlimited number of gifts worth up to C$60 each duty-free to Canada. Label the package UNSOLICITED GIFT—VALUE UNDER $60. Alcohol and tobacco are excluded.

➤ INFORMATION: **Revenue Canada** (✉ 2265 St. Laurent Blvd. S, Ottawa, Ontario K1G 4K3, ☎ 613/993–0534, 800/461–9999 in Canada).

IN NEW ZEALAND

Although greeted with a *Haere Mai* (Welcome to New Zealand), homeward-bound residents with goods to declare must present themselves for inspection. If you're 17 or older, you may bring back $700 worth of souvenirs and gifts. Your duty-free allowance also includes

4.5 liters of wine or beer; one 1,125-milliliter bottle of spirits; and either 200 cigarettes, 250 grams of tobacco, 50 cigars, or a combo of all three up to 250 grams.

➤ INFORMATION: **New Zealand Customs** (✉ Custom House, 50 Anzac Ave., Box 29, Auckland, New Zealand, ☎ 09/359–6655, ☎ 09/309–2978).

IN THE U.K.

From countries outside the EU, including the United States, you may import, duty-free, 200 cigarettes or 50 cigars; 1 liter of spirits or 2 liters of fortified or sparkling wine or liqueurs; 2 liters of still table wine; 60 milliliters of perfume; 250 milliliters of toilet water; plus £136 worth of other goods, including gifts and souvenirs.

➤ INFORMATION: **HM Customs and Excise** (✉ Dorset House, Stamford St., London SE1 9NG, ☎ 0171/202–4227).

IN THE U.S.

Non-U.S. residents ages 21 and older may import into the United States 200 cigarettes or 50 cigars or 2 kilograms of tobacco, 1 liter of alcohol, and gifts worth $100. Prohibited items include meat products, seeds, plants, and fruits.

➤ INFORMATION: **U.S. Customs Service** (Inquiries, ✉ Box 7407, Washington, DC 20044, ☎ 202/927–6724; complaints, Office of Regulations and Rulings, ✉ 1301 Constitution Ave. NW, Washington, DC 20229; registration of equipment, Resource Management, ✉ 1301 Constitution Ave. NW, Washington, DC 20229, ☎ 202/927–0540).

DISABILITIES & ACCESSIBILITY

ACCESS IN ALASKA

➤ LOCAL RESOURCES: **Access Alaska** (✉ 3710 Woodland Dr., Suite 900, Anchorage 99517, ☎ 907/248–4777; in AK, 800/770–4488; TTY 907/248–8799; FAX 907/248–0639). **Alaska Snail Trails** (✉ Box 210894, Anchorage 99521, ☎ 907/337–7517 or 800/348–4532) has an eight-passenger minibus designed especially for travelers with disabilities on trips ranging from one to 10 days. **Alaska Welcomes You** (✉ Box 91333, Anchorage, AK 99509, ☎ 907/349–6301 or 800/349–6301, FAX 907/344–3259) has a complete database of accessible accommodations, attractions, and tours. **Challenge Alaska** (✉ 1132 E. 74th Ave., Suite 105, Anchorage 99518, ☎ 907/344–7399 voice and TTY, FAX 907/344–7349).

MAKING RESERVATIONS

When discussing accessibility with an operator or reservations agent, **ask hard questions.** Are there any stairs, inside *or* out? Are there grab bars next to the toilet *and* in the shower/tub? How wide is the doorway to the room? To the bathroom? For the most extensive facilities meeting the latest legal specifications, **opt for newer accommodations,** which are more likely to have been designed with access in mind. Older buildings or ships may have more limited facilities. Be sure to **discuss your needs before booking.**

TRANSPORTATION

➤ BUS TRAVEL: **Alaska Direct Bus Lines** (✉ Box 501, Anchorage 99510, ☎ 907/277–6652 or 800/770–6652) offers a 10% discount to passengers with disabilities for intercity travel. Within Anchorage, **Muni-Lift** (☎ 907/562–8444) provides transportation within the municipal Anchorage area.

➤ CAR RENTAL: **Hertz** (800/654-3131; TTY 800/654–2280) has hand-controlled rental cars in Anchorage.

➤ FERRY TRAVEL: The **Alaska Marine Highway** (☎ 907/465–3941 or 800/642–0066, FAX 907/277–4829) system has elevators on eight of its nine vessels and accessible cabins on its six vessels equipped with staterooms.

➤ FLIGHTSEEING: **ERA Helicopters** (☎ 800/843–1947) has wheelchair lifts at its Juneau and Denali National Park locations.

➤ TAXIS: There are no taxi companies in Anchorage that offer lift-equipped van service. However, they do work directly with the **Muni-Lift service** (☞ Bus Travel, *above*).

➤ TRAIN TRAVEL: The **Alaska Railroad** (☎ 907/265–2494 in Anchorage, 907/456–4155 in Fairbanks, or

800/544–0552, FAX 907/265–2323)
has cars that are accessible for people
who use wheelchairs; cars also have
wheelchair locks and lifts. There are
lifts at the Anchorage, Denali National
Park, and Fairbanks stations, with
one lock-down for service between
these points (there are no lock-downs
between Seward and Anchorage).
The Whittier shuttle train offers free
passage to cars with a plastic DISABLED
PERSON'S PARKING IDENTIFICATION
placard for individuals with tempo-
rary disabilities or with a metal license plate bearing the International
Symbol of Accessibility for travelers
with permanent disabilities (no windshield certificates are accepted).

➤ COMPLAINTS: **Disability Rights
Section** (✉ U.S. Department of Jus-
tice, Civil Rights Division, Box
66738, Washington, DC 20035–
6738, ☎ 202/514–0301 or 800/514–
0301, TTY 202/514–0383 or 800/
514–0383, FAX 202/307–1198) for
general complaints. **Aviation Consumer Protection Division** (☞ Air
Travel, *above*) for airline-related
problems. **Civil Rights Office** (✉ U.S.
Department of Transportation, De-
partmental Office of Civil Rights,
S-30, 400 7th St. SW, Room 10215,
Washington, DC 20590, ☎ 202/366–
4648, FAX 202/366–9371) for problems with surface transportation.

TRAVEL AGENCIES & TOUR OPERATORS

As a whole, the travel industry has
become more aware of the needs of
travelers with disabilities. In the U.S.,
the Americans with Disabilities Act
requires that travel firms serve the
needs of all travelers. Note, though,
that some agencies and operators
specialize in making travel arrangements for individuals and groups with
disabilities.

➤ TRAVELERS WITH MOBILITY PROB-
LEMS: **Access Adventures** (✉ 206
Chestnut Ridge Rd., Rochester, NY
14624, ☎ 716/889–9096), run by a
former physical-rehabilitation coun-
selor. **Accessible Journeys** (✉ 35 W.
Sellers Ave., Ridley Park, PA 19078,
☎ 610/521–0339 or 800/846–4537,
FAX 610/521–6959), for escorted tours
exclusively for travelers with mobility
impairments. **CareVacations** (✉ 5019

49th Ave., Suite 102, Leduc, Alberta
T9E 6T5, ☎ 403/986–6404, 800/
648–1116 in Canada) has group
tours and is especially helpful with
cruise vacations. **Flying Wheels Travel**
(✉ 143 W. Bridge St., Box 382,
Owatonna, MN 55060, ☎ 507/451–
5005 or 800/535–6790, FAX 507/
451–1685), a travel agency specializing in customized tours and itineraries
worldwide. **Hinsdale Travel Service**
(✉ 201 E. Ogden Ave., Suite 100,
Hinsdale, IL 60521, ☎ 630/325–
1335), a travel agency that benefits
from the advice of wheelchair traveler
Janice Perkins.

DISCOUNTS & DEALS

Be a smart shopper and **compare all
your options** before making any
choice. A plane ticket bought with a
promotional coupon may not be
cheaper than the least expensive fare
from a discount ticket agency. For
high-price travel purchases, such as
packages or tours, keep in mind that
what you get is just as important as
what you save. Just because something is cheap doesn't mean it's a
bargain.

CLUBS & COUPONS

Many companies sell discounts in
the form of travel clubs and coupon
books, but these cost money. You
must use participating advertisers to
get a deal, and only after you recoup
the initial membership cost or book
price do you begin to save. If you
plan to use the club or coupons
frequently, you may save considerably. Before signing up, find out what
discounts you get for free.

➤ DISCOUNT CLUBS: **Entertainment
Travel Editions** (✉ 2125 Butterfield
Rd., Troy, MI 48084, ☎ 800/445–
4137; $20–$51, depending on destination). **Great American Traveler**
(✉ Box 27965, Salt Lake City, UT
84127, ☎ 801/974–3033 or 800/
548–2812; $49.95 per year). **Mo-
ment's Notice Discount Travel Club**
(✉ 7301 New Utrecht Ave., Brook-
lyn, NY 11204, ☎ 718/234–6295;
$25 per year, single or family). **Privi-
lege Card International** (✉ 237 E.
Front St., Youngstown, OH 44503,
☎ 330/746–5211 or 800/236–9732;
$74.95 per year). **Sears's Mature
Outlook** (✉ Box 9390, Des Moines,

IA 50306, ☎ 800/336–6330; $19.95 per year). **Travelers Advantage** (✉ CUC Travel Service, 3033 S. Parker Rd., Suite 1000, Aurora, CO 80014, ☎ 800/548–1116 or 800/648–4037; $59.95 per year, single or family). **Worldwide Discount Travel Club** (✉ 1674 Meridian Ave., Miami Beach, FL 33139, ☎ 305/534–2082; $50 per year family, $40 single).

CREDIT-CARD BENEFITS

When you use your credit card to make travel purchases you may get free travel-accident insurance, collision-damage insurance, and medical or legal assistance, depending on the card and the bank that issued it. American Express, MasterCard, and Visa provide one or more of these services, so **get a copy of your credit card's travel-benefits policy.** If you are a member of an auto club, always **ask hotel and car-rental reservations agents about auto-club discounts.** Some clubs offer additional discounts on tours, cruises, and admission to attractions.

DISCOUNT RESERVATIONS

To save money, **look into discount-reservations services** with toll-free numbers, which use their buying power to get a better price on hotels, airline tickets, even car rentals. When booking a room, always **call the hotel's local toll-free number** (if one is available) rather than the central reservations number—you'll often get a better price. Always ask about special packages or corporate rates.

➤ AIRLINE TICKETS: ☎ **800/FLY–4– LESS.** ☎ **800/FLY–ASAP.**

➤ HOTEL ROOMS: **RMC Travel** (☎ 800/245–5738).

PACKAGE DEALS

Packages and guided tours can save you money, but don't confuse the two. When you buy a package, your travel remains independent, just as though you had planned and booked the trip yourself. Fly/drive packages, which combine airfare and car rental, are often a good deal.

ECOTOURISM

Concern for the environment has spawned a worldwide movement called ecotourism, or green tourism. Ecotourists aim to travel responsibly, taking care to conserve the environment and respect indigenous populations. For information about how environmental concerns peculiar to Alaska as well as a list of resources and ecotour operators, *see* Planning a Wilderness Adventure *in* Chapter 3.

GAY & LESBIAN TRAVEL

➤ LOCAL RESOURCES: For information on Gay and Lesbian issues in Alaska, contact **Identity** (✉ 3201 Turnagain St., Anchorage, AK 99517, ☎ 907/ 248–6969.

➤ GAY- AND LESBIAN-FRIENDLY TOUR OPERATORS: **R.S.V.P. Travel Productions** (✉ 2800 University Ave. SE, Minneapolis, MN 55414, ☎ 612/ 379–4697 or 800/328–7787, FAX 612/379–0484), for cruises and resort vacations for gays. **Olivia** (✉ 4400 Market St., Oakland, CA 94608, ☎ 510/655–0364 or 800/ 631–6277, FAX 510/655–4334), for cruises and resort vacations for lesbians.

➤ GAY- AND LESBIAN-FRIENDLY TRAVEL AGENCIES: **Corniche Travel** (✉ 8721 Sunset Blvd., Suite 200, West Holly-wood, CA 90069, ☎ 310/854–6000 or 800/429–8747, FAX 310/659– 7441). **Islanders Kennedy Travel** (✉ 183 W. 10th St., New York, NY 10014, ☎ 212/242–3222 or 800/ 988–1181, FAX 212/929–8530). **Now Voyager** (✉ 4406 18th St., San Fran-cisco, CA 94114, ☎ 415/626–1169 or 800/255–6951, FAX 415/626– 8626). **Yellowbrick Road** (✉ 1500 W. Balmoral Ave., Chicago, IL 60640, ☎ 773/561–1800 or 800/642–2488, FAX 773/561–4497). **Skylink Travel and Tour** (✉ 3577 Moorland Ave., Santa Rosa, CA 95407, ☎ 707/585– 8355 or 800/225–5759, FAX 707/ 584–5637), serving lesbian travelers.

HEALTH

MEDICAL PLANS

No one plans to get sick while travel-ing, but it happens, so **consider sign-ing up with a medical-assistance company.** Members get doctor refer-rals, emergency evacuation or repatri-ation, 24-hour telephone hot lines for medical consultation, cash for emergencies, and other personal and legal assistance. Coverage varies by plan, so **review the benefits of each carefully.**

➤ MEDICAL-ASSISTANCE COMPANIES: **International SOS Assistance** (✉ 8 Neshaminy Interplex, Suite 207, Trevose, PA 19053, ☎ 215/245–4707 or 800/523–6586, FAX 215/244–9617; ✉ 12 Chemin Riantbosson, 1217 Meyrin 1, Geneva, Switzerland, ☎ 4122/785–6464, FAX 4122/785–6424; ✉ 10 Anson Rd., 14-07/08 International Plaza, Singapore 079903, ☎ 65/226–3936, FAX 65/226–3937).

HOLIDAYS

Major national holidays include: New Year's Day (Jan. 1); Martin Luther King, Jr. Day (third Mon. in Jan.); President's Day (third Mon. in Feb.); Memorial Day (last Mon. in May); Independence Day (July 4); Labor Day (first Mon. in Sept.); Thanksgiving Day (fourth Thurs. in Nov.); Christmas Eve and Day (Dec. 24–25); and New Year's Eve (Dec. 31).

INSURANCE

Travel insurance is the best way to **protect yourself against financial loss.** The most useful plan is a comprehensive policy that includes coverage for trip cancellation and interruption, default, trip delay, and medical expenses (with a waiver for preexisting conditions).

Without insurance, you will lose all or most of your money if you cancel your trip, regardless of the reason. Default insurance covers you if your tour operator, airline, or cruise line goes out of business. Trip-delay covers unforeseen expenses that you may incur due to bad weather or mechanical delays. It's important to compare the fine print regarding trip-delay coverage when comparing policies.

For overseas travel, one of the most important components of travel insurance is its medical coverage. Supplemental health insurance will pick up the cost of your medical bills should you get sick or injured while traveling. Residents of the United Kingdom can buy an annual travel-insurance policy valid for most vacations taken during the year in which the coverage is purchased. If you are pregnant or have a preexisting condition, make sure you're covered. British citizens should buy extra medical coverage when traveling overseas, according to the Association of British Insurers. Australian travelers should buy travel insurance, including extra medical coverage, whenever they go abroad, according to the Insurance Council of Australia.

Always **buy travel insurance directly from the insurance company**; if you buy it from a cruise line, airline, or tour operator that goes out of business you probably will not be covered for the agency or operator's default, a major risk. Before you make any purchase, **review your existing health and home-owner's policies** to find out whether they cover expenses incurred while traveling.

➤ TRAVEL INSURERS: In the U.S., **Access America** (✉ 6600 W. Broad St., Richmond, VA 23230, ☎ 804/285–3300 or 800/284–8300). **Travel Guard International** (✉ 1145 Clark St., Stevens Point, WI 54481, ☎ 715/345–0505 or 800/826–1300). In Canada, **Mutual of Omaha** (✉ Travel Division, 500 University Ave., Toronto, Ontario M5G 1V8, ☎ 416/598–4083, 800/268–8825 in Canada).

➤ INSURANCE INFORMATION: In the U.K., **Association of British Insurers** (✉ 51 Gresham St., London EC2V 7HQ, ☎ 0171/600–3333). In Australia, the **Insurance Council of Australia** (☎ 613/9614–1077, FAX 613/9614–7924).

LODGING

APARTMENT & VILLA RENTALS

If you want a home base that's roomy enough for a family and comes with cooking facilities, **consider a furnished rental.** These can save you money, especially if you're traveling with a large group of people. Home-exchange directories list rentals (often second homes owned by prospective house swappers), and some services search for a house or apartment for you (even a castle if that's your fancy) and handle the paperwork. Some send an illustrated catalog; others send photographs only of specific properties, sometimes at a charge. Up-front registration fees may apply.

➤ RENTAL AGENTS: **Europa-Let/Tropical Inn-Let** (☒ 92 N. Main St., Ashland, OR 97520, ☎ 541/482–5806 or 800/462–4486, ℻ 541/482–0660). **Hideaways International** (☒ 767 Islington St., Portsmouth, NH 03801, ☎ 603/430–4433 or 800/843–4433, ℻ 603/430–4444; membership $99) is a club for travelers who arrange rentals among themselves. **Property Rentals International** (☒ 1008 Mansfield Crossing Rd., Richmond, VA 23236, ☎ 804/378–6054 or 800/220–3332, ℻ 804/379–2073).

B&BS

➤ RESERVATION SERVICES: **Alaska Adventures &Accommodations** (☒ 200 W. 34th Ave. No. 342, Anchorage 99503, ☎ 907/344–4676, 888/655–4723, ℻ 907/349–4676). **Alaska Available B&B Reservation Service** (☒ 3800 Delwood Pl., Anchorage 99504, ☎ 907/337–3414, ℻ 800/474–2262). **Alaska Bed & Breakfast Association** (☒ 369 S. Franklin St., Suite 200, Juneau 99801, ☎ 907/586–2959, ℻ 907/463–4453 or 800/493–4453). **Alaska Private Lodgings/Stay With a Friend** (☒ 704 W. 2nd Ave., Anchorage 99501, ☎ 907/258–1717, ℻ 907/258–6613). **Alaska Sourdough Bed &Breakfast Association** (☒ 889 Cardigan Circle, Anchorage 99503, ☎ 907/563–6244). **Mat-Su Chapter, Bed-&-Breakfast Association of Alaska** (☒ Box 873507, Wasilla 99687, ☎ 800/401–7444).

CAMPING

Camping in Alaska needn't be a daunting experience: Think of it as camping elsewhere in the Lower 48, except that the mosquitoes are worse and there's a greater likelihood of a nighttime bear visit. Some newcomers to bear country are uneasy sleeping in a tent, but encounters are rare. The midnight sun can also keep tent campers awake. Whether you're in a tent or an RV, you'll need warm bedding, insect repellent, rain protection, and tight containers in which to **store food inside your vehicle,** where it won't be a temptation for bears.

Public campgrounds in Alaska are operated by the Alaska State Parks Division, the U.S. Fish and Wildlife Service, the Bureau of Land Management, the National Park Service, and the U.S. Forest Service. Car camping in Alaska is limited by lack of roads and access to the many parks that lie off the beaten track. The only national park with car-camping facilities is Denali National Park, and its campgrounds are frequently full. Despite this, car camping remains popular, and attractive campsites fill up fast. For more information on camping and campgrounds, *see* Chapter 3.

➤ INFORMATION: **Alaska Public Lands Information Center** (☒ 605 W. 4th Ave., Suite 105, Anchorage 99501, ☎ 907/271–2737, ℻ 907/277–2744; ☒ 250 Cushman St., Suite 1A, Fairbanks 99701, ☎ 907/456–0527, ℻ 907/456–0154). **U.S. Forest Service Information Center** (☒ Centennial Hall, 101 Egan Dr., Juneau 99801, ☎ 907/586–8751, ℻ 907/586–7928). **Southeast Alaska Visitor Center** (☒ 50 Main St., Ketchikan 99901, ☎ 907/228–6214).

HOME EXCHANGES

If you would like to exchange your home for someone else's, **join a home-exchange organization,** which will send you its updated listings of available exchanges for a year and will include your own listing in at least one of them. It's up to you to make specific arrangements.

➤ EXCHANGE CLUBS: **HomeLink International** (☒ Box 650, Key West, FL 33041, ☎ 305/294–7766 or 800/638–3841, ℻ 305/294–1148; $83 per year).

HOSTELS

No matter what your age, you can **save on lodging costs by staying at hostels.** In some 5,000 locations in more than 70 countries around the world, Hostelling International (HI), the umbrella group for a number of national youth hostel associations, offers single-sex, dorm-style beds and, at many hostels, "couples" rooms and family accommodations. Membership in any HI national hostel association, open to travelers of all ages, allows

THE GOLD GUIDE / SMART TRAVEL TIPS

you to stay in HI-affiliated hostels at member rates (one-year membership is about $25 for adults; hostels run about $10–$25 per night). Members also have priority if the hostel is full; they're eligible for discounts around the world, even on rail and bus travel in some countries.

➤ HOSTEL ORGANIZATIONS: **Hostelling International—American Youth Hostels** (✉ 733 15th St. NW, Suite 840, Washington, DC 20005, ☎ 202/783–6161, FAX 202/783–6171). **Hostelling International—Canada** (✉ 400-205 Catherine St., Ottawa, Ontario K2P 1C3, ☎ 613/237–7884, FAX 613/237–7868). **Youth Hostel Association of England and Wales** (✉ Trevelyan House, 8 St. Stephen's Hill, St. Albans, Hertfordshire AL1 2DY, ☎ 01727/855215 or 01727/845047, FAX 01727/844126); membership in the U.S. $25, in Canada C$26.75, in the U.K. £9.30.

HOTELS & MOTELS

You'll find familiar chains scattered across the state, such as Days Inn, Great Western, Hilton, Holiday Inn, and Sheraton; they will be of similar quality to the individual chain's other U.S. properties. Westmark Hotels is a regional chain, owned by cruise-tour operator Holland America Westours, with 17 locations, including hotels in Anchorage, Fairbanks, Juneau, Kenai, Kodiak, Sitka, and Valdez in Alaska, plus Beaver Creek and Whitehorse in Canada's Yukon Territory. Princess Tours owns a luxury hotel in Fairbanks and lodges outside Denali National Park, near Denali State Park, and on the Kenai Peninsula.

WILDERNESS LODGES

To really get away from it all, **book a remote lodge** with rustic accommodations in the middle of breathtaking Alaskan wilderness. Many are in the river drainages of Bristol Bay, in Southeast Alaska, or in the Susitna drainage near Anchorage. Most of these lodges place a heavy emphasis on fishing; a stay generally includes daily guided fishing trips, as well as all meals. They can be astronomically expensive (daily rates of $250–$600 per person), so if you're not interested in fishing, you won't want to seek these out. Lodges in and near Denali

National Park emphasize the great outdoors. Activities focus on horseback riding, hiking, and natural-history walks. For getting deep into the wilderness, these lodges are an excellent alternative to the hotels and cabins outside the park entrance.

MONEY

CREDIT & DEBIT CARDS

Should you use a credit card or a debit card when traveling? Both have benefits. A credit card allows you to delay payment and gives you certain rights as a consumer (☞ Consumer Protection, *above*). A debit card, also known as a check card, deducts funds directly from your checking account and helps you stay within your budget. When you want to rent a car, though, you may still need an old-fashioned credit card. Although you can always *pay* for your car with a debit card, some agencies will not allow you to *reserve* a car with a debit card.

Otherwise, the two types of plastic are virtually the same. Both will get you cash advances at ATMs worldwide if your card is properly programmed with your personal identification number (PIN).

➤ ATM LOCATIONS: **Cirrus** (☎ 800/424–7787). **Plus** (☎ 800/843–7587) for locations in the U.S. and Canada, or visit your local bank.

EXCHANGING MONEY

For the most favorable rates, **change money through banks.** Although fees charged for ATM transactions may be higher abroad than at home, Cirrus and Plus exchange rates are excellent, because they are based on wholesale rates offered only by major banks. You won't do as well at exchange booths in airports or rail and bus stations, in hotels, in restaurants, or in stores, although you may find their hours more convenient. To avoid lines at airport exchange booths, **get a bit of local currency before you leave home.**

➤ EXCHANGE SERVICES: **Chase *Currency To Go*** (☎ 800/935–9935; 935–9935 in NY, NJ, and CT). **International Currency Express** (☎ 888/842–0880 on the East Coast,

888/278–6628 on the West Coast).
Thomas Cook Currency Services
(☎ 800/287–7362 for telephone
orders and retail locations).

TRAVELER'S CHECKS

Do you need traveler's checks? It
depends on where you're headed. If
you're going to rural areas and small
towns, go with cash; traveler's checks
are best used in cities. Lost or stolen
checks can usually be replaced within
24 hours. To ensure a speedy refund,
buy your own traveler's checks—
don't let someone else pay for them:
irregularities like this can cause delays. The person who bought the
checks should make the call to request a refund.

NATIONAL PARKS

Look into discount passes to **save
money on park entrance fees.** The
Golden Eagle Pass ($50) gets you and
your companions free admission to all
parks for one year. (Camping and
parking are extra). Both the Golden
Age Passport ($10), for those 62 and
older, and the Golden Access Passport
(free), for travelers with disabilities,
entitle holders to free entry to all
national parks, plus 50% off fees for
the use of many park facilities and
services. You must show proof of age
and of U.S. citizenship or permanent
residency (such as a U.S. passport,
driver's license, or birth certificate)
and, if requesting Golden Access,
proof of disability. All three passes
are available at all national park
entrances where entrance fees are
charged. Golden Eagle and Golden
Access passes are also available by
mail.

➤ PASSES BY MAIL: **National Park
Service** (✉ National Capitol Area
Office, 1100 Ohio Dr. SW, Washing-
ton, DC 20242).

OUTDOOR ACTIVITIES
& SPORTS

FISHING

License fees for nonresidents are $10
for a one-day permit, $20 for three
days, $50 for 14 days, and $100 for
an annual license. If you're going to
be fishing for king salmon and keeping what you catch, an additional
stamp is necessary. Stamps cost $10

for one day, $20 for three days, and
$100 annually. Licenses are also
available in-state from sporting-goods
stores, charter-boat operators, and
fishing lodges.

➤ INFORMATION AND LICENSES:
Alaska Department of Fish and Game
(✉ Box 25525, Juneau 99802-5525,
☎ 907/465–4180 for seasons and
regulations, or 907/465–2376 for
licenses).

PACKING

LUGGAGE

How many carry-on bags you can
bring with you is up to the airline.
Most allow two, but the limit is often
reduced to one on certain flights.
Gate agents will take excess baggage—including bags they deem
oversize—from you as you board and
add it to checked luggage. To avoid
this situation, make sure that everything you carry aboard will fit under
your seat. Also, get to the gate early,
and request a seat at the back of the
plane; you'll probably board first,
while the overhead bins are still
empty. Since big, bulky baggage
attracts the attention of gate agents
and flight attendants on a busy flight,
make sure your carry-on is really a
carry-on. Finally, a carry-on that's
long and narrow is more likely to
remain unnoticed than one that's
wide and squarish.

If you are flying internationally, note
that baggage allowances may be
determined not by piece but by
weight—generally 88 pounds (40
kilograms) in first class, 66 pounds
(30 kilograms) in business class, and
44 pounds (20 kilograms) in economy.

Airline liability for baggage is limited
to $1,250 per person on flights within
the United States. On international
flights it amounts to $9.07 per pound
or $20 per kilogram for checked
baggage (roughly $640 per 70-pound
bag) and $400 per passenger for
unchecked baggage. You can buy
additional coverage at check-in for
about $10 per $1,000 of coverage,
but it excludes a rather extensive list
of items, shown on your airline ticket.

Before departure, **itemize your bags'
contents** and their worth, and label

THE GOLD GUIDE / SMART TRAVEL TIPS

the bags with your name, address, and phone number. (If you use your home address, cover it so that potential thieves can't see it readily.) Inside each bag, **pack a copy of your itinerary.** At check-in, **make sure that each bag is correctly tagged** with the destination airport's three-letter code. If your bags arrive damaged or fail to arrive at all, file a written report with the airline before leaving the airport.

PACKING LIST

Wherever you go in Alaska (and especially in the Southeast), **be prepared for rain.** To keep yourself dry, **pack a collapsible umbrella** or **bring a rain slicker.** Not all of Alaska has the fierce winters that are usually associated with the state. Winter in the Southeast and South Central coastal regions is relatively mild—Chicago and Minneapolis experience harsher weather than Juneau. It's a different story in the Interior, where temperatures in the subzero range and biting winds keep most visitors indoors. The best way to keep warm under colder conditions is to **wear layers of clothing, starting with thermal underwear and socks.** The outermost layer should be lightweight, windproof, rainproof, and hooded. Down jackets (and sleeping bags) have the disadvantage of becoming soggy when wet; wool and some of the newer synthetics are the materials of choice. Cold and damp jeans can make you miserable. Footgear needs to be sturdy, and if you're going into the backcountry, be sure it's waterproof. Rubber boots are often a necessity in coastal areas. When wearing snow boots, be certain they are not too tight. Restricting your circulation will only make you colder.

Alaskan summers are mild, though it's a good idea to **bring along rain gear, as sudden storms are common.** An extra sweater or jacket for cool evenings will come in handy.

Befitting the frontier image, dress is mostly casual day and night. Bring along one outfit that is appropriate for "dress up," if you enjoy doing so, though it's not necessary.

UVA/UVB **sunscreen, insect repellent, and sunglasses are necessities.** A pair of binoculars will help you track any wildlife you encounter.

In your carry-on luggage **bring an extra pair of eyeglasses or contact lenses** and **enough of any medication you take** to last the entire trip. You may also want your doctor to write a spare prescription using the drug's generic name, since brand names may vary from country to country. **Never put prescription drugs or valuables in luggage to be checked.** To avoid customs delays, carry medications in their original packaging. And don't forget to copy down and carry addresses of offices that handle refunds of lost traveler's checks.

PASSPORTS & VISAS

When traveling internationally, **carry a passport even if you don't need one** (it's always the best form of I.D.), and make **two photocopies of the data page** (one for someone at home and another for you, carried separately from your passport). If you lose your passport, promptly call the nearest embassy or consulate and the local police.

➤ U.K. CITIZENS: **U.S. Embassy Visa Information Line** (☎ 01891/200–290; calls cost 49p per minute, 39p per minute cheap rate), for U.S. visa information. **U.S. Embassy Visa Branch** (✉ 5 Upper Grosvenor St., London W1A 2JB), for U.S. visa information; send a self-addressed, stamped envelope. Write the **U.S. Consulate General** (✉ Queen's House, Queen St., Belfast BTI 6EO) if you live in Northern Ireland.

➤ AUSTRALIAN CITIZENS: **Australian Passport Office** (☎ 131–232).

➤ NEW ZEALAND CITIZENS: **New Zealand Passport Office** (☎ 04/494–0700 for information on how to apply, 0800/727–776 for information on applications already submitted).

➤ U.K. CITIZENS: **London Passport Office** (☎ 0990/21010), for fees and documentation requirements and to request an emergency passport.

SENIOR-CITIZEN TRAVEL

To qualify for age-related discounts, **mention your senior-citizen status up front** when booking hotel reservations (not when checking out) and before you're seated in restaurants (not when paying the bill). Note that discounts may be limited to certain menus, days, or hours. When renting a car, **ask about promotional car-rental discounts,** which can be cheaper than senior-citizen rates.

The Alaska Railroad offers senior citizens a 50% discount during off-peak months (late September to early May). The Alaska Marine Highway offers discounted fares year-round. Alaska Direct Bus Lines offers a 10% discount for intercity travel.

➤ EDUCATIONAL PROGRAMS: **Elderhostel** (✉ 75 Federal St., 3rd floor, Boston, MA 02110, ☎ 617/426–8056).

SHOPPING

The best buys in Alaska are products of native materials made by Native peoples and other artists and craftspeople living in the state. Before you buy, **make sure local crafts are genuine.** The state has adopted two symbols that guarantee the authenticity of crafts made by Alaskans. A hand symbol indicates the item was made by one of Alaska's Native peoples. A polar bear verifies that the item was made in Alaska. If some items with these tags seem more expensive than you expected, examine them closely and you'll probably find that they are handmade, one-of-a-kind pieces.

Although these symbols are designed to ensure authentic Alaska and Native-made products, **it doesn't mean that items lacking them are not authentic.** This applies in particular to Native artists who may or may not go through the necessary paperwork to obtain the silver hand labels. They often come to town and sell items directly to shop owners for cash. It pays to shop around, ask questions and learn about the different types of Native crafts from around the state.

SIGHTSEEING TOURS

A couple of companies operate sightseeing tours statewide; for local sightseeing outfits in individual cities and towns, *see* Guided Tours *in* the appropriate chapters.

➤ SIGHTSEEING-TOUR COMPANIES: **Alaska Sightseeing/Cruise West** (☎ 206/441–8687 or 800/426–7702). **Gray Line of Alaska** (☎ 907/225–5930 or 800/544–2206, FAX 907/225–9386).

STUDENT TRAVEL

➤ STUDENT I.D.s & SERVICES: **Council on International Educational Exchange** (CIEE, ✉ 205 E. 42nd St., 14th floor, New York, NY 10017, ☎ 212/822–2600 or 888/268–6245, FAX 212/822–2699), for mail orders only, in the United States. **Travel Cuts** (✉ 187 College St., Toronto, Ontario M5T 1P7, ☎ 416/979–2406 or 800/667–2887) in Canada.

TELEPHONES

COUNTRY CODES

The country code for the United States is 1.

LONG-DISTANCE CALLS

Competitive long-distance carriers make calling within the United States relatively convenient and let you avoid hotel surcharges. By dialing an 800 number, you can get connected to the long-distance company of your choice.

➤ LONG-DISTANCE CARRIERS: AT&T (☎ 800/225–5288). MCI (☎ 800/888–8000). Sprint (☎ 800/366–2255).

TOUR OPERATORS

Buying a prepackaged tour or independent vacation can make your trip to Alaska less expensive and more hassle-free. Because everything is prearranged, you'll spend less time planning.

Operators that handle several hundred thousand travelers per year can use their purchasing power to give you a good price. Their high volume may also indicate financial stability. But some small companies provide more personalized service; because they tend to specialize, they may also be more knowledgeable about a given area.

BOOKING WITH AN AGENT

Travel agents are excellent resources. In fact, large operators accept bookings made only through travel agents.

But it's a good idea to **collect brochures from several agencies,** because some agents' suggestions may be influenced by relationships with tour and package firms that reward them for volume sales. If you have a special interest, **find an agent with expertise in that area**; ASTA (☞ Travel Agencies, *below*) has a database of specialists worldwide.

Make sure your travel agent knows the accommodations and other services. Ask about the hotel's location, room size, beds, and whether it has a pool, room service, or programs for children, if you care about these. Has your agent been there in person or sent others you can contact?

Do some homework on your own, too: Local tourism boards can provide information about lesser-known and small-niche operators, some of which may sell only direct.

BUYER BEWARE

Each year consumers are stranded or lose their money when tour operators—even very large ones with excellent reputations—go out of business. So **check out the operator.** Find out how long the company has been in business, and ask several travel agents about its reputation. If the package or tour you are considering is priced lower than in your wildest dreams, **be skeptical.** Try to **book with a company that has a consumer-protection program.** If the operator has such a program, you'll find information about it in the company's brochure. If the operator you are considering does not offer some kind of consumer protection, then ask for references from satisfied customers.

In the U.S., members of the National Tour Association and United States Tour Operators Association are required to set aside funds to cover your payments and travel arrangements in case the company defaults. It's also a good idea to choose a company that participates in the American Society of Travel Agent's Tour Operator Program (TOP). This gives you a forum if there are any disputes between you and your tour operator; ASTA will act as mediator.

➤ TOUR-OPERATOR RECOMMENDATIONS: American Society of Travel Agents (☞ Travel Agencies, *below*). National Tour Association (NTA, ✉ 546 E. Main St., Lexington, KY 40508, ☎ 606/226–4444 or 800/755–8687). United States Tour Operators Association (USTOA, ✉ 342 Madison Ave., Suite 1522, New York, NY 10173, ☎ 212/599–6599 or 800/468–7862, FAX 212/599–6744).

COSTS

The more your package or tour includes, the better you can predict the ultimate cost of your vacation. Make sure you know exactly what is covered, and **beware of hidden costs.** Are taxes, tips, and service charges included? Transfers and baggage handling? Entertainment and excursions? These can add up.

Prices for packages and tours are usually quoted per person, based on two sharing a room. If traveling solo, you may be required to pay the full double-occupancy rate. Some operators eliminate this surcharge if you agree to be matched with a roommate of the same sex, even if one is not found by departure time.

GROUP TOURS

Among companies that sell tours to Alaska, the following are nationally known, have a proven reputation, and offer plenty of options. The classifications used below represent different price categories, and you'll probably encounter these terms when talking to a travel agent or tour operator. The key difference is usually in accommodations, which run from budget to better, and better-yet to best.

➤ SUPER-DELUXE: **Abercrombie & Kent** (✉ 1520 Kensington Rd., Oak Brook, IL 60521-2141, ☎ 630/954–2944 or 800/323–7308, FAX 630/954–3324).

➤ DELUXE: **Maupintour** (✉ 1515 St. Andrews Dr., Lawrence, KS 66047, ☎ 785/843–1211 or 800/255–4266, FAX 785/843–8351). **Tauck Tours** (✉ Box 5027, 276 Post Rd. W, Westport, CT 06881-5027, ☎ 203/226–

6911 or 800/468–2825, FAX 203/
221–6866).

➤ DELUXE/FIRST-CLASS: **Globus** (⊠
5301 S. Federal Circle, Littleton, CO
80123-2980, ☎ 303/797–2800 or
800/221–0090, FAX 303/347–2080).

➤ FIRST-CLASS AND TOURIST-RANGE:
Brendan Tours (⊠ 15137 Califa St.,
Van Nuys, CA 91411, ☎ 818/785–
9696 or 800/421–8446, FAX 818/
902–9876). **Collette Tours** (⊠ 162
Middle St., Pawtucket, RI 02860,
☎ 401/728–3805 or 800/340–5158,
FAX 401/728–4745). **Gadabout Tours**
(⊠ 700 E. Tahquitz Canyon Way,
Palm Springs, CA 92262-6767, ☎
619/325–5556 or 800/952–5068).
Mayflower Tours (⊠ Box 490, 1225
Warren Ave., Downers Grove, IL
60515, ☎ 708/960–3793 or 800/
323–7604, FAX 708/960–3575).
Trafalgar Tours (⊠ 11 E. 26th St.,
New York, NY 10010, ☎ 212/689–
8977 or 800/854–0103, FAX 800/
457–6644).

➤ BUDGET: **Cosmos** (☞ Globus,
above).

PACKAGES

Like group tours, independent vacation packages are available from
major tour operators and airlines.
Packages may include fly/drive
itineraries with bed-and-breakfast
accommodations or ferry-liner tours.
The companies listed below offer
vacation packages in a broad price
range.

➤ INDEPENDENT VACATION PACKAGES:
Alaska Bound (⊠ 310 Howard St.,
Petoskey, MI 49770, ☎ 616/439–
3000 or 888/252–7527, FAX 616/
439–3004). **Knightly Tours** (⊠ Box
16366, Seattle, WA 98116, ☎ 206/
938–8567 or 800/426–2123,
FAX 206/938–8498). **Viking Travel**
(⊠ Box 787, Petersburg, AK 99833,
☎ 907/772–3818 or 800/327–2571,
FAX 907/772–3940).

➤ FROM THE U.K.: **Arctic Experience
Ltd.** (⊠ 29 Nork Way, Banstead,
Surrey SM7 1PB, ☎ 01737/218–
800). **Kuoni Travel** (⊠ Kuoni House,
Dorking, Surrey RH5 4AZ, ☎
01306/742–222). **Vacation Canada**
(⊠ Cambridge House, 8 Cambridge
St., Glasgow G2 3DZ, ☎ 0141/332–
1511 or 0345/090–905).

THEME TRIPS

➤ CENTRAL BOOKING SERVICE: **Alaska
Tours and Lodging** (⊠ Box 35403,
Juneau, AK 99803-5403, ☎ 907/
780–4677, FAX 907/780–4673 or
800/493–4453) publishes *The Alaska
Catalog for Independent Travelers*
and lists dozens of special-interest
operators.

➤ BICYCLING: **Alaska Bicycle Adventures** (⊠ 907 E. Dowling Rd., Ste. 29,
Anchorage, AK 99518, ☎ 907/243–
2329 or 800/770–7242, FAX 907/
243–4985). **Backroads** (⊠ 801 Cedar
St., Berkeley, CA 94710-1800, ☎
510/527–1555 or 800/462–2848, FAX
510/527–1444). **Timberline** (⊠ 7975
E. Harvard, #J, Denver, CO 80231,
☎ 303/759–3804 or 800/417–2453,
FAX 303/368–1651).

➤ BIRD WATCHING: **Wilderness Birding Adventures** (⊠ Box 103747,
Anchorage, AK 99510-3747, ☎ FAX
907/694–7442). **Wings** (⊠ 1643 N.
Alvernon Way, Suite 105, Tucson, AZ
85712, ☎ 520/320–9868, FAX 520/
320–9373).

➤ CAMPING: **American Wilderness
Experience** (⊠ Box 1486, Boulder,
CO 80306, ☎ 303/444–2622 or
800/444–0099, FAX 303/444–3999).
CampAlaska Tours (⊠ Box 872247,
Wasilla, AK 99687, ☎ 907/376–
9438 or 800/376–9438, FAX 907/
376–2353).

➤ CANOEING, KAYAKING, AND RAFT-
ING: **Alaska Discovery** (⊠ 5449
Shaune Dr., Suite 4, Juneau, AK
99801, ☎ 907/780–6226 or 800/
586–1911, FAX 907/780–4220).
American Wilderness Experience
(☞ Camping, *above*). **Alaska Wil-
derness Journeys** (⊠ Box 220204,
Anchorage, AK 99522, ☎ 907/349–
2964 or 800/349–0064, FAX 907/
344–6877). **CampAlaska Tours**
(☞ Camping, *above*). **James Henry
River Tours** (⊠ Box 807, Bolinas, CA
94924, ☎ 415/868–1836 or 800/
786–1830, FAX 415/868–9033).
OARS (⊠ Box 67, Angels Camp, CA
95222, ☎ 209/736–4677 or 800/
346–6277, FAX 209/736–2902). **REI
Adventures** (☎ 800/622–2236).
TrekAmerica (⊠ Box 189, Rockaway,
NJ 07866, ☎ 973/983–1144 or 800/
221–0596, FAX 973/983–8551).

➤ Dog Sledding/Iditarod: **Birch Trails Sled Dog Tours** (✉ 22719 Robinson Rd. Rd., Chugiak, AK 99567, ☎ 907/688–5713, FAX 907/688–5713). **Chugach Express** (✉ Box 261, Girdwood, AK 99587, ☎ 907/783–2266, FAX 907/783–2625). **Far North Tours** (✉ Box 102873, Anchorage, AK 99510, ☎ 907/272–7480 or 800/478–7480, FAX 907/276–6951). **Mush a Dog Team** (✉ 20644 Birchwood Loop Rd., Chugiak, AK 99567, ☎ 907/688–1391, FAX 907/688–7731). **Sky Trekking Alaska** (✉ 485 Pioneer Dr., Wasilla, AK 99654, ☎ 907/373–4966 or 800/770–4966, FAX 907/373–4966). **Sourdough Outfitters** (✉ Box 90, Bettles, AK 99726, ☎ 907/692–5252, FAX 907/692–5612).

➤ Ferry Tours: **Knightly Tours** (☞ Packages, *above*). **Viking Travel** (☞ Packages, *above*).

➤ Hiking: **Alaska Wilderness Journeys** (☞ Canoeing, *above*). **Backroads** (☞ Bicycling, *above*). **Mountain Travel-Sobek** (✉ 6420 Fairmount Ave., El Cerrito, CA 94530, ☎ 510/527–8100 or 800/227–2384, FAX 510/525–7710). **Timberline** (☞ Bicycling, *above*).

➤ Native Tours: **Alaska Airlines Vacations** (✉ Box 69677, Seattle, WA 98168, ☎ 800/468–2248) puts together air/land packages with Native groups in Barrow and Kotzebue. **A.L.E.U.T. Tours** (✉ Unalaska, AK, ☎ 907/581–6001). **Alexander's Overnight River Adventure** (✉ Nenana, AK, ☎ 907/474–3924). **Athabasca Cultural Journeys** (☎ 907/829–2261 or 800/423–0094) arranges for travelers to stay with an Athabascan family in Huslia. **Cape Fox Tours** (✉ Box 6656, Ketchikan, AK 99901, ☎ 907/225–4846). **Dig Afognak** (✉ Afognak Native Corporation, 215 Mission Rd., Ste. 212, Kodiak, AK 99615, ☎ 800/770–6014) invites travelers to join in an archaeological dig near Kodiak. **Gray Line of Alaska** (☎ 907/277–5581 or 800/478–6388) has tours to the Eskimo island of Gambell. **Kiana Lodge** (✉ Box 210269, Anchorage, AK 99521, ☎ 907/333–5866, FAX 907/338–8447). **Northern Alaska Tour Company** (✉ Box 82991, Fairbanks, AK 99708, ☎ 907/474–

8600, FAX 907/474–4767). **Reeve Aleutian Airways** (✉ 4700 W. International Airport Rd., Anchorage, AK 99502, ☎ 907/243–4700 or 800/544–2248, FAX 907/249–2276) has tours to the Aleut community of St. Paul on the Pribilof Islands. **Tour Arctic** (✉ Box 49, Kotzebue, AK 99752, ☎ 907/442–3301, FAX 907/442–2866) has tours of remote northwest Alaskan communities. **Tundra Tours** (✉ Box 189, Barrow, AK 99723, ☎ 907/852–3900 or 800/882–8478) leads tours in the Arctic Circle town of Barrow. For more information on Native tours, contact the Alaska Native Tourism Council (☞ Visitor Information, *below*).

➤ Learning Vacations: **Earthwatch** (✉ Box 9104, 680 Mount Auburn St., Watertown, MA 02272, ☎ 617/926–8200 or 800/776–0188, FAX 617/926–8532) has educational tours where participants assist in the monitoring and breeding of several bird species in Alaska. **National Audubon Society** (✉ 700 Broadway, New York, NY 10003, ☎ 212/979–3066, FAX 212/353–0190). **Natural Habitat Adventures** (✉ 2945 Center Green Ct., Boulder, CO 80301, ☎ 303/449–3711 or 800/543–8917, FAX 303/449–3712). **Nature Expeditions International** (✉ 6400 E. El Dorado Circle, Suite 210, Tucson, AZ 85715, ☎ 520/721–6712 or 800/869–0639, FAX 520/721–6719), in business since 1973, has tours led by scientists that focus on bird-watching, photography, and plant study. **Naturequest** (✉ 934 Acapulco St., Laguna Beach, CA 92651, ☎ 714/499–9561 or 800/369–3033, FAX 714/499–0812). **Oceanic Society Expeditions** (✉ Fort Mason Center, Bldg. E, San Francisco, CA 94123-1394, ☎ 415/441–1106 or 800/326–7491, FAX 415/474–3395) has whale-watching tours. **Questers** (✉ 381 Park Ave. S, New York, NY 10016, ☎ 212/251–0444 or 800/468–8668, FAX 212/251–0890). **Sierra Club** (✉ 730 Polk St., San Francisco, CA 94109, ☎ 415/776–2211, FAX 415/776–0350). **Smithsonian Study Tours and Seminars** (✉ 1100 Jefferson Dr. SW, Room 3045, MRC 702, Washington, DC 20560, ☎ 202/357–4700, FAX 202/633–9250).

➤ NATURAL HISTORY: **Alaska Wildland Adventures** (✉ Box 389, Girdwood, AK 99587, ☎ 907/783–2928 or 800/334–8730, FAX 907/783–2130). **Great Alaska Fish Camp and Safaris** (✉ HC1, Box 218, Sterling, AK 99672, ☎ 907/262–4515 or 800/544–2261, FAX 907/262–8797 in summer). **Victor Emanuel Nature Tours** (✉ Box 33008, Austin, TX 78764, ☎ 512/328–5221 or 800/328–8368, FAX 512/328–2919). **Wilderness Birding Adventures** (☞ Bird Watching, *above*).

➤ PHOTOGRAPHY: **Alaska Up Close** (✉ Box 32666, Juneau, AK 99803, ☎ 907/789–9544, FAX 907/789–3205). **Joseph Van Os Photo Safaris** (☎ 206/463–5383). **Steve Gilroy's Alaska Photo Tours** (✉ Box 141, Talkeetna, AK 99676, ☎ 907/733–3051 or 800/799–3051, FAX 907/733–3052).

➤ RV TOURS: **Alaska Highway Cruises** (✉ 3805 108th Ave. NE, Suite 204, Bellevue, WA 98004, ☎ 206/828–0989 or 800/323–5757, FAX 206/828–3519) combines RV-touring (motorhome provided) with a luxury cruise.

➤ SPORTFISHING: **Alaska Sportfishing Packages** (✉ Box 9170, Seattle, WA 98109, ☎ 206/216–2900 or 800/841–4321, FAX 206/216–2906 or 800/323–2231). **Anglers Travel** (✉ 1280 Terminal Way, #30, Reno, NV 89502, ☎ 702/324–0580 or 800/624–8429, FAX 702/324–0583). **Cutting Loose Expeditions** (✉ Box 447, Winter Park, FL 32790-0447, ☎ 407/629–4700 or 800/533–4746, FAX 407/740–7816). **Fishing International** (✉ Box 2132, Santa Rosa, CA 95405, ☎ 707/539–3366 or 800/950–4242, FAX 707/539–1320). **Great Alaska Fish Camp** (☞ Natural History, *above*). **Rod & Reel Adventures** (✉ 566 Thomson Lane, Copperopolis, CA 95228, ☎ 209/785–0444, FAX 209/785–0447). **Sport Fishing Alaska** (✉ 1401 Shore Dr., Anchorage, AK 99515, ☎ 907/344–8674, FAX 907/349–4330).

➤ WILDERNESS HIGH ADVENTURES: **Alaska-Denali Guiding** (✉ Box 566, Talkeetna, AK 99676, ☎ 907/733–2649, FAX 907/733–1362), in business since 1983, arranges soft and high

adventure in the Talkeetna Mountains and in the Alaska Range. **Brooks Range Aviation** (✉ Box 10, Bettles, AK 99726, ☎ 800/692–5443, FAX 907/692–2185) flies rafters and hikers on demand into the Brooks Range from Bettles and can provide rental canoes. **Ketchum Air Service** (✉ Box 190588, Anchorage, AK 99519, ☎ 907/243–5525 or 800/433–9114, FAX 907/243–8311) can outfit and fly you to remote camps or to a wilderness river for a float fishing trip. **Sourdough Outfitters** (☞ Dog Sledding, *above*) challenges hardy travelers with its backcountry expeditions in the Brooks Range.

TRAIN TRAVEL

The state-owned Alaska Railroad has mainline service connecting Seward, Anchorage, Denali National Park, and Fairbanks. Secondary service links Portage, 50 mi southeast of Anchorage, with Whittier on Prince William Sound. The Portage–Whittier shuttle uses special flatbed railcars designed to carry automobiles; you drive your car onto the train and stay in your vehicle for the half-hour trip. Amtrak serves Seattle and Vancouver; Via Rail Canada serves Vancouver and Prince Rupert, British Columbia.

Travel aboard the Alaska Railroad is leisurely (Anchorage to Fairbanks is an all-day trip), so you can enjoy spectacular scenery along the way. And unlike bus travel, train travel allows you to get up and stretch your legs. Some private tour companies that offer a more glitzy trip between Anchorage and Fairbanks hook their luxury railcars to the train (☞ Tours, *above*). For a less expensive alternative, **ride one of the public dome cars** that are owned and operated by the railroad. Seating in the public cars is unassigned, and passengers take turns under the observation dome. The railroad's public cars are a great place to **meet resident Alaskans.**

Except for the Seward–Anchorage leg, all service operates year-round. Trains run daily in summer; service is reduced from September to May. Dining cars are available on all mainline trains; no food service is available on the Portage–Whittier shuttle.

THE GOLD GUIDE / SMART TRAVEL TIPS

For a scenic and historic trip between Skagway and Fraser, British Columbia, take the White Pass & Yukon Route, which follows the treacherous path taken by prospectors during the Klondike Gold Rush of 1897–98. A bus links the terminal at Fraser with Whitehorse, capital of the Yukon Territory.

➤ RAIL LINES: **Alaska Railroad** (✉ Box 107500, Anchorage 99510, ☎ 907/265–2494 in Anchorage, 907/456–4155 in Fairbanks, or 800/544–0552, FAX 907/265–2323). **Amtrak** (☎ 800/872–7245). **Via Rail Canada** (☎ 800/561–3949). **White Pass & Yukon Route** (✉ Box 435, Skagway 99840, ☎ 907/983–2217 or 800/343–7373; 800/478–7373 in Canada).

DISCOUNT PASSES

See Bus Travel, *above.*

TRAVEL AGENCIES

A good travel agent puts your needs first. Look for an agency that has been in business at least five years, emphasizes customer service, and has someone on staff who specializes in your destination. In addition, **make sure the agency belongs to a professional trade organization,** such as ASTA in the United States. If your travel agency is also acting as your tour operator, *see* Buyer Beware in Tour Operators, *above.*

➤ LOCAL AGENT REFERRALS: **American Society of Travel Agents** (ASTA, ☎ 800/965–2782 24-hr hot line, FAX 703/684–8319). **Association of Canadian Travel Agents** (✉ Suite 201, 1729 Bank St., Ottawa, Ontario K1V 7Z5, ☎ 613/521–0474, FAX 613/521–0805). **Association of British Travel Agents** (✉ 55–57 Newman St., London W1P 4AH, ☎ 0171/637–2444, FAX 0171/637–0713). **Australian Federation of Travel Agents** (☎ 02/9264–3299). **Travel Agents' Association of New Zealand** (☎ 04/499–0104).

TRAVEL GEAR

Travel catalogs specialize in useful items, such as compact alarm clocks and travel irons, that can **save space when packing.**

➤ CATALOGS: **Magellan's** (☎ 800/962–4943, FAX 805/568–5406). **Orvis Travel** (☎ 800/541–3541, FAX 540/343–7053). **TravelSmith** (☎ 800/950–1600, FAX 800/950–1656).

U.S. GOVERNMENT

Government agencies can be an excellent source of inexpensive travel information. When planning your trip, **find out what government materials are available.**

➤ PAMPHLETS: **Consumer Information Center** (✉ Consumer Information Catalogue, Pueblo, CO 81009, ☎ 719/948–3334 or 888/878–3256) for a free catalog that includes travel titles.

VISITOR INFORMATION

The state division of tourism publishes the "Alaska Vacation Planner," a comprehensive information source for statewide travel year-round. Alaska's regional tourism councils distribute vacation planners highlighting their local attractions. The Alaska Native Tourism Council can help you with information on Native American attractions.

➤ STATEWIDE INFORMATION: **Alaska Division of Tourism** (✉ Box 110801, Juneau 99811-0801, ☎ 907/465–2010 or 800/762–5275, FAX 907/465–2287).

➤ REGIONAL INFORMATION: **Alaska's Southwest** (✉ 3300 Arctic Blvd., Suite 203, Anchorage 99503, ☎ 907/562–7380, FAX 907/562–0438). **Inside Passage: Alaska Tours and Lodging** (✉ 369 S. Franklin St., Suite 200, Juneau 99802, ☎ 907/586–4777, FAX 907/463–4961 or 800/493–4453). **Kenai Peninsula** (✉ 150 N. Willow, Kenai 99611, ☎ 907/283–3850 or 800/535–3624 for travel planners only, FAX 907/283–2838). **Prince William Sound** (✉ Box 243044, Anchorage 99524, ☎ 907/344–2867 or 800/216–8377, FAX 907/344–2867). **Southeast Alaska Visitors Information Center** (✉ 50 Main St., Ketchikan 99901, ☎ 907/228–6214).

➤ NATIVE AMERICAN ATTRACTIONS: **Alaska Native Tourism Council** (✉ 1577 C St., Suite 304, Anchorage

99501, ☎ 907/274–5400, FAX 907/263–9971).

➤ BRITISH COLUMBIA AND YUKON: **Supernatural British Columbia** (☎ 800/663–6000). **Tourism Industry Association** (✉ 1109 First Ave., Whitehorse, Yukon Territory Y1A 5G4 Canada, ☎ 403/668–3331, FAX 403/667–7379). **Tourism Yukon** (✉ Box 2703, Whitehorse, Yukon Territory, Canada Y1A 2C6, ☎ 403/667–5340, FAX 403/667–3546). **Tourism Victoria** (✉ 1175 Douglas St., Suite 710, V8W 2E1, ☎ 250/953–2033, FAX 250/361–9733). **Vancouver Tourist InfoCentre** (✉ 200 Burrard St., ☎ 604/683–2000).

➤ IN THE U.K.: **Alaskan Tourist Information Board** (✉ 2 The Billings, Walnut Tree Close, Guildford, Surrey GU1 4YD, ☎ 0891/100–727, FAX 01483/451–361). Calls are charged at 50p per minute at all times.

WHEN TO GO

Because Alaska is so big, each region experiences a different climate, and seasons come and go at different times of the year.

Most visitors choose summer because of the warmer temperatures and long evenings of midnight sun. From June through August, you can expect pleasantly warm, long days—Fairbanks shines under a staggering 22 hours of daylight in late June—and cool, comfortable nights. In summer, the sun does not set for more than 2½ months north of the Arctic Circle (approximately a third of Alaska lies north of this invisible line). Even as far south as Juneau, there is a glow of twilight in the sky at midnight. In winter, of course, the situation is reversed, and the sun does not rise for more than two months in Alaska's northernmost regions. South Central Alaska, including the Anchorage area, gets about 5½–6 hours of daylight in mid-December.

Adapting to this Arctic pattern of light, all life in Alaska crowds everything it can into the long period of sunlight—plants grow profusely (a cabbage can get to be 4 ft wide; a delphinium, 12 ft tall) and bloom furiously. If you're camping during these midsummer months, a sleep shade may be more valuable than a flashlight.

Keep in mind that Alaska is not a land of perpetual ice and snow—97% of the state is snow-free during those long summer days. In fact, in parts of the state, temperatures can reach into the 90s.

Of course, with fair weather comes an onslaught of tourists and generally higher prices for rooms, tours, and transportation. Summer, particularly late June through July, also brings on periodic plagues of mosquitoes, thanks to breakup (when frozen ground thaws), which creates the soggy little bogs these nuisances just love. The peak summer travel months, July and August, are also the rainiest throughout Alaska; rain falls on a typically all-or-nothing Alaskan scale.

The weather can change in dramatic and unpredictable fashion. Storms brewed in the Gulf of Alaska, for instance, can arise in the blink of an eye. The frigid air of the polar regions can mean snowstorms on the 4th of July—and a hot summer day on the 5th! Southwest Alaska and the Aleutian chain are rained and fogged in all too frequently, but just when you've given up on the weather, the clouds will miraculously vanish. Throughout the state, winds are apt to race from the mountains with no warning. These winds are so strong they can wrestle a freestanding tent from your hands and send it tumbling over the tundra.

To avoid the summer crowds and peak season prices, go during spring or fall. May and June are the driest months to cruise. Late August through early September (depending on the latitude) brings special autumn bonuses: Above the brilliant foliage, skies may be unbelievably blue, and the mountains and glaciers are often enhanced by fresh dustings of snow. Daytime temperatures should still be quite pleasant, though evenings get progressively nippier.

Contrary to popular belief, Alaska does not close down for winter. Yes, it gets cold, and the nights grow long, but Alaskans have come up with some rousing means of taking their minds off the weather. Winter is the season for skiing, sledding, ice-skating, ice fishing, and other sports. Major events such as the Iditarod Trail Sled Dog Race, held in March, help both residents and visitors shrug off the cold. The annual Fur Rendezvous, in Anchorage each February, is a raucous, action-packed celebration, highlighted by the traditional Miners' and Trappers' Costume Ball. The long nights are also ideal for viewing the northern lights, particularly in the Fairbanks area.

CLIMATE

What follows are the average daily maximum and minimum temperatures for several Alaskan cities.

➤ FORECASTS: **Weather Channel Connection** (☎ 900/932–8437), 95¢ per minute from a Touch-Tone phone.

ANCHORAGE

Jan.	22F	– 6C	May	55F	13C	Sept.	55F	13C
	7	–14		38	3		40	4
Feb.	25F	4C	June	62F	17C	Oct.	41F	5C
	9	13		47	8		27	– 3
Mar.	31F	– 1C	July	65F	18C	Nov.	27F	– 3C
	14	–10		50	10		14	–10
Apr.	43F	6C	Aug.	63F	17C	Dec.	20F	– 7C
	27	– 3		49	9		6	–14

BARROW

Jan.	– 9F	–23C	May	24F	– 4C	Sept.	34F	1C
	–22	–30		13	–11		27	– 3
Feb.	–12F	–24C	June	39F	4C	Oct.	22F	– 6C
	–25	–32		29	– 2		12	–11
Mar.	– 8F	–22C	July	46F	8C	Nov.	7F	–14C
	–22	–30		33	1		– 5	–21
Apr.	7F	–14C	Aug.	44F	7C	Dec.	– 4F	–20C
	– 8	–22		33	1		–17	–27

FAIRBANKS

Jan.	– 2F	–19C	May	59F	15C	Sept.	54F	12C
	–20	–29		35	2		33	1
Feb.	11F	–12C	June	71F	22C	Oct.	35F	2C
	–10	–23		46	8		18	– 8
Mar.	23F	– 5C	July	72F	22C	Nov.	12F	–11C
	– 4	–20		48	9		– 5	–21
Apr.	42F	6C	Aug.	66F	19C	Dec.	1F	–17C
	17	– 8		44	7		–16	–27

1 Destination: Alaska

THE MANY ALASKAS

ALASKA HOLDS A SPECIAL place in the public imagination. It is a land of otherness, a place where northern lights color the cold winter sky, where the summer sun circles the horizon, where Native people still hunt whale and walrus, where brown bears catch salmon in wide rivers, where mountaineers work their way across glaciers, where bush pilots land floatplanes on remote backcountry lakes, where crab boats toss in the wild stormy waves of the Bering Sea, and where vast stretches of land lie undeveloped and unpeopled. If one word could be applied to Alaska, it would be "wilderness." If you enjoy the outdoors and wild places, you will fall head over heels in love with this vast and extraordinarily beautiful state.

Alaska occupies the westernmost edge of the North American continent; Canada's Yukon Territory lies to the east; Mother Russia is westward just across the Bering Strait. It is a massive place: a map of Alaska superimposed on one of the continental United States would stretch from the Atlantic to the Pacific and from Canada to Mexico. Alaskans enjoy telling how they could cut Alaska in half and still make Texas the third-largest state. Then they brag about having the highest mountain in North America (Mt. McKinley) and the nation's biggest oil field (Prudhoe Bay). Some of its citizens live closer to Japan than to their own state capital, Juneau.

But it is more than scale and geography—and more than a tired list of superlatives—that sets Alaska apart from the rest of the country. For the visitor, Alaska is youth, energy, space, wildness. A traveler to Alaska senses excitement, a feeling of adventure, the moment he or she steps ashore from a cruise ship in a misty port or arrives by jetliner in a northern city where the architecture is a haphazard blend of back-home modern and frontier shabby.

There is something different about Alaska. For many visitors, it is almost like a first trip to a foreign land. Yes, the language is the same. There are Big Macs and JCPenney stores. Summertime temperatures are comfortable, about the same as in Seattle or Vancouver, British Columbia, along the coast; it's even warmer in the interior, where welcome hotel air conditioners hum. Alaska is not the stuff of icy legends in all seasons. But there is also something almost unsettling about Alaska for the first-time visitor. It seems to be a land of many places, many kinds of experiences—too big to comprehend.

That is the key—the many Alaskas.

A grandmother rides a tourist helicopter to walk on a glacier. A few yards from the safe zone selected by the pilot there are deep crevasses that could gulp down a house. "Scary," she says, "but exhilarating." Sea kayakers near Ketchikan paddle past verdant islands, mist rising from the forest after last night's rain. Hundreds of anglers line the banks of the Kenai River on a warm summer weekend, all hoping to pull in a monster king salmon. Far to the west in the village of Kwethluk, a Yup'ik woman prepares for winter, hanging strips of smoked salmon up to dry. A youngster panning for gold in Nome yells out when he finds a shiny flake among the swirling sands, never dreaming that the pan was "salted" by a kindly miner. Late on a June night in Barrow, visitors watch the midnight sun dip almost to the horizon and then bounce upward again like a fiery ball. Boaters on the fabled Yukon River drift with the current, spellbound, watching the high-speed dives of peregrine falcons above rocky cliffs.

Deep in Denali National Park, visitors see grizzly bears bounding across the tundra and moose munching on willows by the road. Near Fairbanks, other visitors reach out to touch a silvery tube—the trans-Alaska oil pipeline, which transports crude from Prudhoe Bay 800 mi across Alaska to Valdez, zigzagging through the wilderness like a giant snake. In Glacier Bay National Park, a small cruise ship is anchored for the night across from the face of a booming glacier. There are volleys of sound, like gunshots, then huge slabs of ice break away and tumble into the bay. Harbor seals ride the ice rafts like stowaways; bald eagles ride the air currents above. In the ship's lounge, passengers are cooling their cocktails with slivers of slow-to-melt glacier ice that is millions of years old.

Near the town of Cordova in Prince William Sound, another realm of glaciers, a lone birder on the delta of the Copper River trains binoculars on a trio of trumpeter swans. Nowhere else in the world can a visitor see such a concentration of trumpeters—as many as 1,000 nest here from late spring into fall. And out in the Pribilof Islands, which seem like dots in the Bering Sea between Alaska and Siberia, the surf crashes on rookeries swarming with thousands of northern fur seals. A cacophony of sound comes from the cliffs above, as millions of seabirds swirl around nest sites.

This is the real Alaska—the many Alaskas—a destination for personal discoveries. But there is more to Alaska for the traveler than spectacular scenery and wilderness experiences. One of Alaska's bests is its warm, welcoming hosts—the people.

That is easy to understand when one realizes that Alaska, in many ways, still is a frontier. Communities are widely scattered, linked mostly by airplanes instead of roads. Residents still depend on one another as in pioneer times. There still are gentle places where doors are never locked and car keys are left in ignitions. Alaska's population of about 607,000 spreads across 586,400 square mi.

BECAUSE THERE ARE SO FEW Alaskans, they band together for common causes—but they also scrap like family. Anchorage and Fairbanks (the two largest cities) thrive on feuding. Hometowners in Fairbanks think Anchorage is too glitzy for Alaska. They joke that "the real Alaska begins about 10 mi outside Anchorage." Partly true: The city does have high-rise hotels, posh restaurants, and Alaska-size Wal-Marts, but it also has world-class cross-country skiing right in town and magnificent Chugach State Park—second largest in America—just a 15-minute drive away. Anchorage residents fire back, calling the much smaller Fairbanks "a hick town, the ice-fog capital of the world." Partly true: Fairbanks does suffer through winters when the thermometer seems perpetually stuck at 20 below zero, but it also experiences delightfully warm summers, and the University of Alaska brings an unexpected level of culture.

The squabbling is all in fun—most of the time.

There have been three ballot measures in the past two decades to move the state capital from Juneau, in Southeast Alaska, to Willow and Wasilla, 70 mi and 40 mi, respectively, north of Anchorage. In 1974 voters approved moving their capital but were deterred eight years later by the cost of constructing a new capitol building.

The scars haven't healed yet from that fray. If Alaska in general has a malady, it would be called regionalism. That's pretty easy to understand, too. Alaska is so big that it has conflicting resource interests. The commercial fishermen of coastal Alaska don't want oil tankers endangering their salmon, halibut, and crab harvests. Business leaders in Anchorage and Fairbanks are unabashed boosters of the petroleum industry that fuels their economies.

Despite kind words for public consumption, there still is residual racism in Alaska. The Native peoples—Eskimo, Indian, and Aleut—continue a long struggle to gain equal footing with Caucasian Alaskans. Old-timers remember not-so-long-ago signs in shop windows that read NO DOGS OR NATIVES ALLOWED. They also remember how Native children were punished in schools for daring to speak their traditional languages. Those days of overt discrimination are over, but tensions still remain just below the surface. Natives complain that their views and cultural traditions are ignored; whites often think all Natives are alcoholics on the government dole.

There is one thing that unites—not divides—Alaskans: their shared memories of being held back as a territory, until statehood in 1959. Those were the days when Alaskans couldn't vote for a U.S. president. In territorial times, their governors were appointed by the president without a vote of the people. When prestatehood Alaskans traveled by air between Alaska and Seattle, they were subjected to customs and immigration inspections. From the time the first statehood bill was introduced in Congress, it took Alaskans 40 years to pin a star to the U.S. flag.

The hard feelings from the statehood fight may help explain some of the headlines outsiders read during the oil-pipeline debate. Environmental leaders and outside editorial writers were about as welcome as influenza when they organized a well-orchestrated (but unsuccessful) battle against construction of the pipeline. Most Alaskans wanted the line, viewing it as a source of revenue for their money-short state—money for schools and social programs. Well, the pipeline was built (completed in 1977), and the Prudhoe Bay oil still flows, supplying America with about one-fourth of its crude.

While the pipeline was under construction, environmentalists were winning a bigger battle: getting more of Alaska set aside by the federal government for national parks, wildlife refuges, wild rivers, and other wilderness areas. Today, Alaska's national parklands stretch from the jade fjords of Southeast Alaska to the tundra of the lonely Arctic—51 million acres covering about 13% of the state. Alaska holds 70% of all parklands in the nation and 90% of all wildlife refuges.

That federal action didn't win enthusiastic support from most Alaskans, who believe Uncle Sam, now controlling 60% of Alaska's land area, still has too much say over the affairs of a sovereign state. For visitors and the tourist industry, however, the parks, refuges, and wild rivers that make up half these federal lands are treasures. They belong to the nation, not just Alaska.

THE ALASKA YOU SEE TODAY is young, high-spirited, and mostly untrampled. There was another kind of Alaska back in the mists of time.

Perhaps 13,000 years ago came the forebears of today's Native peoples. The first travelers to Alaska trekked across land bridges that long ago disappeared under the choppy waters of the Bering Sea, traveling from Asia to the North American continent. They migrated in small waves, following fish and game for food. Some of the nomads continued across the Arctic to Canada and Greenland. Some stayed in what today is Alaska. Others moved on, all the way to the southern tip of South America. You'll find a vibrant culture in the Native villages, where traditions such as ivory and totem carving still are living arts.

The peaceful life of the Native peoples ended in 1741, when the Russians "discovered" Alaska (the Natives, naturally, knew it was there all the time). Alaska became Russian America for 126 years. The Russians, spreading out as far as northern California, came to gather the hides of sea otters and fur seals. At first the Natives fought back—the Tlingits drove them from outposts at Sitka and Yakutat. But it was a battle that the Russians would eventually win.

Russia sold Alaska to the United States in 1867—for $7.2 million, or about 2¢ an acre. (Ironically, $7.2 million was the value of the first shipment of crude oil moved by tanker after the trans-Alaska pipeline was completed.) Alaska's biggest holiday, Alaska Day, on October 18, celebrates this remarkable real estate transaction. Alaska's Russian heritage remains a vivid thread in Alaskan life. You can find it in the family names of the Native peoples who were crushed by their Russian rulers. Left behind, in addition to mixed-blood offspring, were onion-dome Russian Orthodox churches all across Alaska.

Events moved quickly, almost in a blur, soon after Alaska became American territory: gold stampedes through Alaska to the Klondike in Canada's Yukon Territory, followed by gold rushes down the Yukon River and to the beaches of Nome on the Bering Sea and into the hills and valleys around Fairbanks in the heart of Alaska.

During World War II, Japanese planes bombed the U.S. Navy base at Dutch Harbor in the Aleutians in 1942, and a few days later enemy troops occupied two of the Aleutian Islands, Attu and Kiska. A terrible battle was fought at Attu the next year to win back the island. Military records say the percentage of American casualties was second only to the fight for Iwo Jima in the Pacific combat theater.

Some of the GIs stayed in Alaska after the war, rearing families and homesteading. They opened small businesses, put down roots, and joined the pioneers in building a new kind of Alaska. And then came the final momentum that led to statehood in January 1959.

But some folks still aren't convinced that Alaska is in the United States. Not long ago, a Fairbanks man received a letter from an aviation school in Miami, where he had applied for entrance. It said: "We are enclosing proper forms for clearance with the American consulate and for obtaining your visa." And then there was the traveler from California who wrote the Alaska Division of Tourism to ask if American currency could be used in Alaska.

Oh, well. You're going to love Alaska, USA.

You have to applaud a place where the first session of the first territorial legislature (in 1913) approved voting rights for women as one of the first orders of business. It would be another seven years before the amendment granting suffrage to women was added to the U.S. Constitution.

In this colorful land called Alaska, where it sometimes is difficult to distinguish tall tales from true stories, that one is on the record.

WHAT'S WHERE

In a place as big as Alaska, it's no surprise to find incredible variations of geography, topography, and climate. Of the 20 highest mountains in the United States, 17 are in Alaska: the state boasts 19 peaks higher than 14,000 ft. And nearly all of the Southeast lies in a rain forest, the Tongass, while the northernmost part of the state is a desert in terms of precipitation.

Southeast Alaska

The Southeast encompasses the Inside Passage—a century ago the traditional route to the Klondike goldfields and today the centerpiece of Alaska cruises. Here are glacier-filled fjords and the justly famous Glacier Bay National Park. Juneau, the state's capital, is also in the Southeast, as are fishing villages such as Petersburg and Ketchikan, which is known for its totempole carving. An onion-dome cathedral accents Sitka, the onetime capital of Russian America. Each fall, up to 4,000 eagles gather just outside Haines.

Anchorage

Alaska's biggest city (population 240,000) is the state's only true metropolis. You'll find a varied selection of ethnic restaurants and a performing arts center—home to theater groups, an opera company, and an orchestra. The Anchorage Museum of History and Art houses an outstanding collection of historic and contemporary Alaskan art. The brand-new Alaska Native Heritage Center celebrates the rich diversity of the state's original inhabitants. At nearby Lake Hood—the largest and busiest seaplane base in the world—the Alaska Aviation Heritage Museum preserves rare examples of the planes that helped tame the wilderness.

South Central Alaska

Beyond Anchorage, South Central is an outdoor playground for fishing, hiking, wildlife watching, and rafting. The truly adventurous can ski in Valdez; more sedate downhill runs can be found at Mt. Alyeska Ski Resort, 40 mi south of Anchorage. Kodiak, 100 mi offshore in the Gulf of Alaska, is the second-largest island in the United States. Known as the Emerald Island for its green-carpeted mountains, this is the home of the famous Kodiak brown bear, which can weigh up to 1,500 pounds and is the biggest terrestrial carnivore on earth.

The Interior

Bounded by the Brooks Range to the north and the Alaskan Range to the south, the Interior is home to Mt. McKinley, the highest peak in North America, and to Denali National Park. Fairbanks, founded in 1901 by a merchant and a prospector who together struck it rich in their respective endeavors, is today Alaska's second-largest city. Fairbanks is the gateway to the Far North—the towns of the Arctic and the Bering Coast that are connected mainly by air—and to Canada's Yukon Territory, whose Gold Rush history is preserved in towns such as Dawson City and Whitehorse.

The Bush

The Bush, more a spirit than a place, is the last frontier of the Last Frontier. From Nome to Barrow, much of the ground is permanently frozen, and for months at a time the sun never sets—or never rises. In the Arctic are the hardy Eskimo people and the Prudhoe Bay oil fields, near Barrow, America's northernmost community. Prospectors still pan for gold on the beach in Nome, where they are occasionally joined by a wandering polar bear. Only one road leads to the Arctic, the Dalton Highway. Otherwise, the only link between these outposts of civilization is by air or sea—unless you happen to have a sled-dog team, a snowmobile, or a Rollagon (a vehicle specially designed for crossing tundra).

The Alaska Peninsula and Aleutian Islands have steaming volcanoes and fast-changing weather; a highlight is Katmai National Park. The Bering seacoast, a watery wilderness of more than 100,000 square mi, arcs from Bristol Bay to the Arctic Circle.

PLEASURES AND PASTIMES

Bicycling

Biking can be rewarding in accessible parts of the state. The paved-road system is straightforward, and automobile traffic is usually light on most Alaska roads, but the road shoulders can be narrow and people tend to drive fast in rural areas. Unpaved highways are bikeable but are tougher going; expect dust, ruts, and flying gravel.

Anchorage has an excellent bike-trail system—one along the coast and several others inland. Take your bike on the Alaska Railroad to Denali National Park. Although its park road is largely unpaved, it has a good dirt surface and only light traffic. You can also bring your bike on Alaska's ferry system for an extra charge. Use it to explore the Southeast's charming communities and surrounding forests, but come prepared for heavy rain. Companies that rent bicycles in the Southeast seem to cycle in and out of business faster than you can shift gears. Your best bet, if you don't bring your own, is to call local bike shops, parks and recreation departments, or visitor information centers for rental information.

Many Interior residents are avid bikers; mountain biking has become a popular sport here. Fairbanks has miles of scenic bike paths along the Chena River and into the city's outskirts. Most roads have wide shoulders and, of course, offer those incredible Alaska views. Trails used in winter by mushers, snowmobilers, and cross-country skiers are taken over by mountain bikers when the snow leaves.

Boating

With its numerous streams and rivers, Alaska is a natural for waterborne exploration. In the Southeast, the most popular river for running is the Mendenhall; in South Central, it's the Kenai. White-water boaters often spend their weekends playing in the whitecaps of the Nenana River, near Denali National Park in the Interior. Remember that Alaska has some serious white water. Unless you are experienced, do not undertake a boating expedition without a professional guide. Numerous operators run river trips throughout the state (☞ Tour Operators *in* the Gold Guide).

CANOEING➢ Canoes are generally safe and comfortable, and they're suitable for many of Alaska's protected waterways, particularly on the Kenai Peninsula and Southeast's Admiralty Island. It's likely that you'll have one or more portages on a canoe trip, and carrying a canoe over demanding terrain is not easy. Canoes can be transported outside via floatplane, but passengers are not allowed on such trips, requiring a separate (and expensive) flight. You can, however, carry a canoe on a car to your river put-in; excellent Alaskan rivers accessible by car include the Delta, the Gulkana, the Fortymile, and the Beaver Creek.

KAYAKING➢ Sea kayaks are popular among Alaskans; it was the Aleuts who invented the kayak (or *bidarka*) in order to fish and hunt sea mammals. When early explorers encountered the Aleuts, they compared them to sea creatures, so at home do they appear on their small ocean crafts. Kayaks have the great advantage of portability, and some models can be broken down and carried on a ferry or small aircraft. Less practical but perhaps more important advantages are that they give the boater a feel for the water and a view from water level. They are also more stable than canoes. Oceangoing kayakers will find offshore adventures, especially in the Southeast, Prince William Sound, or out of Kenai Fjords National Park or Katmai National Park.

RAFTING➢ Rafts have become increasingly popular in Alaska. They take multiple passengers, are reasonably comfortable, and can be broken down and readily packed for transportation on a human back or via small plane. White water is

Alaska's Top Fish and Their Sources

Species	Common Name	Where Found
Arctic Char (F, S)	Char	SC, SW, NW, I, A
Arctic Grayling (F)	Grayling	SE, SC, SW, NW, I, A
Brook Trout (F)	Brookie	SE
Burbot (F)	Lingcod	SC, SW, NW, I, A
Chinook	King Salmon	SE, SC, SW
Chum Salmon (F, S)	Dog Salmon	SE, SC, SW, NW, I
Coho Salmon (F, S)	Silver Salmon	SE, SC, SW, NW, I
Cutthroat Trout (F, S)	Cutthroat	SE, SC
Dolly Varden (F, S)	Dolly	SE, SC, SW, NW, I, A
Lake Trout (F)	Laker	SC, SW, NW, I, A
Northern Pike (F)	Northern, Hammerhandle	SC, SW, NW, I
Pacific Halibut (S)	Halibut	SE, SC, SW, NW
Pink Salmon (F, S)	Humpie	SE, SC, SW, NW, I
Smelt (F, S)	Smelt	SE, SC, SW, NW, I, A
Rainbow Trout (F)	Rainbow	SE, SC, SW, I
Sheefish (F)	Shee, Inconnu	NW, I
Sockeye Salmon (F, S)	Red Salmon	SE, SC, SW, NW, I
Steelhead (F, S)	Steelie	SE, SC, SW

(F) = *Freshwater*   A = *Arctic*   SC = *South Central*
(S) = *Saltwater*   I = *Interior*   SE = *Southeast*
(F, S) = *Freshwater and Saltwater*   NW = *Northwest*   SW = *Southwest*

almost as thrilling on a raft as in a kayak, although a raft is more cumbersome to handle.

SAILING➤ Recreational sailing is becoming a popular sport in Prince William Sound. This beautiful body of water, with tidewater glaciers and forested islands, has good winds in late summer. Whittier is the usual port of entrance; numerous charter boats are here. Other popular South Central sailing towns are Seward, Valdez, and Cordova. The protected waters of Southeast Alaska have fickle winds, but you'll discover quite a few sailboats in Juneau, Ketchikan, and Sitka.

Dogsledding

Alaskans are crazy for dogs. With more and more mushers offering wintertime tours, visitors can try anything from a half-hour jaunt outside Anchorage to a two-week outing in the Brooks Range or an expedition along the Iditarod Trail. You can participate as much or as little as you like, riding in the basket and being pampered at an overnight lodge or helping harness the dogs and taking a turn on the back of the sled. When choosing a tour, make sure your musher has the experience to han-

dle the unpredictable blizzard, moose encounter, or runaway team. In the summer, some mushers put wheels on their sleds, offering visitors a taste of dogsledding without the snow and cold.

Fishing

With more than 3 million lakes and more coastline than the rest of the United States combined, Alaska has no shortage of fishing spots. People from all over the world come to Alaska for a chance to land a trophy salmon (the record is 97 pounds) or a 200-pound-plus halibut. If you're driving through Alaska, you can fish from the roadside in the Interior. In the Southeast you can sink a line right off the docks. If you're a truly serious fisherman, though, a guided boat charter or a stay at a fly-in fishing lodge is the ultimate Alaska fishing adventure. Many companies offer sportfishing packages that include everything you'll need, from transportation to tackle (☞ Tour Operators *in* the Gold Guide). Bag limits and special provisions vary throughout the state's 12 sportfishing-management areas. For updated sportfishing regulations and hot spots, call the Department of Fish and Game (☞ Parks and Wildlife Refuges A to Z *in* Chapter 3).

Although salmon and halibut are Alaska's most sought-after sport fish, the state counts its species of fish in the hundreds. And although the most popular fishing grounds are in the Southeast and in South Central, less crowded but equally abundant fishing holes can be found in the Interior—particularly the Southwest, where there are many remote lodges and fishing camps.

If you plan to cast your reel, you'll need a fishing license, which you can either buy before you leave home from the Alaska Department of Fish and Game or purchase in sporting-goods stores throughout the state. No fishing license is required in Alaska for kids under 16.

Alaska's sport fish are migratory, and peak runs vary by time and place. Harvests are strictly regulated by the state, and any run may be closed to fishing on any day. Sometimes runs are opened and closed on 24-hour notice. Contact the Department of Fish and Game for announcements.

Flightseeing

The magnitude of Alaska can perhaps best be comprehended from the air. Every major destination from the Southeast to the Arctic has flightseeing services that will show you Alaska from a bird's-eye view. It's an experience not to be missed.

Food

Alaska's primary claim to gastronomic fame is seafood. The rich coastal waters produce prodigious quantities of halibut, salmon, crab, and shrimp, along with such specialties as abalone, sea urchin, herring roe, and sea cucumbers (popular in Japan). If you haven't yet tasted fresh Alaskan salmon, be sure to do so during your trip; there's nothing quite like a barbecued Copper River king salmon! Alaska, unlike Norway, Chile, or British Columbia, does not allow salmon farming, so you can be guaranteed of having wild fish from the ocean. Be sure, however, to ask if the seafood is fresh or frozen, particularly during the off-season. One disappointment is that some Alaskan fishing ports lack a quality seafood restaurant; locals see no need since they can get fish at home any day.

For a distinctive taste of the past, step into a classic Alaskan log roadhouse such as

Gwin's Lodge in Cooper Landing, Chistochina Lodge near Glennallen, or The Forks Roadhouse west of Trapper Creek. The food is basic and hearty, and you're likely to meet the hardscrabble miners, trappers, and other folks who survive in the Bush. Roadhouses are not, however, good places to show up with a "Ban Assault Rifles" bumper sticker.

In general, the quality of Alaskan restaurants is directly proportional to the population. In the smallest villages you may be hard pressed to even find a shop selling greasy burgers and fries. Most larger towns have the requisite McDonald's, Burger Kings, and Subways, along with standard all-American restaurants offering bacon-and-egg breakfasts, iceberg lettuce salads, and fresh-from-the-freezer pizza dough. Fortunately, not everything is this bad. In towns with a significant tourist presence—such as Haines, Homer, Ketchikan, Petersburg, Seward, Sitka, or Skagway—you'll always find a café offering espresso and baked goods, plus at least one restaurant where the food is fresh and delicious. Anchorage, Juneau, and Fairbanks all have a wide range of eateries, with something to please everybody. Not surprisingly, Anchorage—with almost half the state's population—has the best selection, including ethnic food from all corners of the globe, creative seafood restaurants, half a dozen brew pubs, vegetarian cafés, European-style bakeries and delis, and gourmet four-star restaurants.

Alaskan dining is an informal affair: it is virtually impossible to find a restaurant here where formal attire is required. In even the fanciest restaurants, appropriate attire simply means a clean shirt and pants for men, and a pair of pants or a comfortable skirt or dress for women.

Gardens and Giant Vegetables

Alaska has a short growing season, but the days of midnight sun produce some of the biggest blooms you'll ever see. Anchorage beautifies its parks each summer with spectacular plantings, and every August, the Alaska State Fair (☞ Festivals and Seasonal Events, at the end of this chapter), in Palmer, is a showcase for 90-pound cabbages and other oversize vegetables.

National Parks and Forests

Alaska has 15 national parks, preserves, and monuments; two national forests;

and 16 national wildlife refuges. The most visited of all is Denali National Park, site of Mt. McKinley, at 20,320 ft the tallest peak in North America. Wrangell–St. Elias National Park, east of Anchorage, is the largest national park in the United States—six times the size of Yellowstone.

Shopping

Alaska, believe it or not, is a big shopping state. In most respects, shopping in Alaska is not unlike shopping in the contiguous United States. Most of the larger cities have department stores and malls, and they accept the same credit cards you use at home.

NATIVE CRAFTS➤ Among the most prized items sought by souvenir hunters are Native crafts. In particular, look for carvings of walrus ivory, soapstone, jade, and wood, and for items made of fur. You'll find a wide choice of jewelry, mukluks (seal- or reindeer-skin Eskimo boots), masks, totem poles, paintings, and baskets. The state has adopted two symbols that guarantee the authenticity of crafts made by Alaskans: a hand symbol indicates the item was made by one of Alaska's Native peoples; a polar bear marks an item as made in Alaska. Better prices are found in the more remote villages where you buy directly from the artisan, or in craft fairs such as Anchorage's downtown Saturday Market.

Each of the Native groups is noted for particular skills; their wares are sold throughout the state. Eskimo art, native to the Arctic and other areas of the Bush, includes animal carvings of walrus ivory, spirit masks, dance fans, baskets made of baleen (a fibrous material found in the mouths of bowhead whales), and jewelry fashioned from walrus ivory, jade, baleen, or a combination of the three.

The Tlingit of Southeast Alaska are known for their totems and other wood carvings, as well as for baskets and hats woven from spruce root and cedar bark. Tsimshian Indians also work with spruce root and cedar bark, and Haida Indians are noted basket makers and totem and slate carvers.

Athabascans specialize in skin sewing, fur garments, and beadwork. The Aleuts' grass basketry is considered among the best in the world.

OTHER PURCHASES➤ Bringing home smoked and canned salmon allows you to transport a taste of Alaska even if you aren't an angler. In communities with a Russian past, such as Kodiak and Sitka, Russian nesting dolls are easily found in local shops. Books and maps are other popular keepsakes.

Skiing

Although it has no lack of snow or mountains, Alaska is not a big ski destination. There are, however, numerous opportunities for both downhill and cross-country adventures. Visitors can charter a helicopter to go backcountry skiing in the Valdez area, or visit one of the downhill areas near Anchorage, Fairbanks, or Juneau. It's also possible to ski in the summer by chartering a plane to a glacier in Denali National Park. At Juneau, Eaglecrest is across from the city on the slopes of Douglas Island. There is also skiing on the glaciers of the Juneau Ice Field, reached by helicopter. Turnagain Pass, 59 mi from Anchorage on the Seward Highway, is popular with cross-country skiers and snowmobilers. Mt. Alyeska, 40 mi south of Anchorage, is where 1994 Olympic gold-medal champion Tommy Moe perfected his form. Hilltop Ski Area and Alpenglow are small alpine ski areas within 10 mi of downtown Anchorage. Valdez is home to the World Extreme Skiing Championships every April.

NEW AND NOTEWORTHY

Internet Alaska

Dozens of Internet sites now provide Alaskan information and links, but good places to start are the **Alaska Tourism Marketing Council** (www.travelalaska.com), producer of the free Alaska State Vacation Planner, and the **Alaska Visitors Association** (www.visitalaska.org). Get information on federal lands from the **Alaska Public Lands Information Center** (www.nps. gov/aplic). For ferry schedules, contact the Alaska Marine Highway System (www.dot. state.ak.us/external/amhs/home.html).

For Southeast Alaska information, head to the **Southeast Alaska Tourism Council** (www.alaskainfo.org), or to the **Juneau Convention and Visitors Bureau** site (www.juneau.com). Other useful Internet sites include ones for **Anchorage** (www.AlaskaOne.com/acvb), **Fairbanks** (www.fairbanks.polarnet.com), **Kenai Peninsula** (www.AlaskaOne.com/kptmc), and **Southwest Alaska** (www.alaska.net/aswamc).

Native Tourism

Anchorage's $15 million **Alaska Native Heritage Center** (☞ Chapter 5) opens its doors in 1999, providing an introduction to the Native peoples of the state. The center contains re-created villages, craft demonstrations, dance performances, films, and historical displays.

Native groups are becoming increasingly active in hosting visitors, and nowhere is this trend more obvious than in **Juneau,** where Goldbelt Native Corporation holdings now include gift shops, the Mt. Roberts tramway, a Juneau hotel, the Glacier Bay concessionaire, and a cruise tour company. **Alaska Native Tours** (☞ Chapter 4) employs Tlingit and Haida guides who lead tours of Native village sites. Juneau is the embarkation point for two Native-oriented catamaran excursions from **Auk Nu Tours** (☞ Chapter 4).

Elsewhere on the Inside Passage, tours are available in **Ketchikan** from the Ketchikan Indian Corporation (☞ Chapter 4); of course, a visit to Saxman Native Village, just outside town, has long been a staple for anyone interested in Native Alaskan culture.

The **Alaska Native Tourism Council** (✉ 1577 C St., Suite 304, Anchorage 99501, ☎ 907/274–5400) can provide you with a listing of Native tour operators throughout the state, including trips to the North Slope community of **Barrow** and to **St. Lawrence Island** in the Bering Sea.

Alaskan Transportation

In 1998 the **Alaska Marine Highway System** (☎ 907/465–3941 or 800/642–0066) added its newest ferry, the 748-passenger *Kennicott.* Built to serve both the protected waters of Southeast and the open ocean conditions of Southwest Alaska, this is the first new ship added to the fleet in 21 years, and the first large ocean-certified passenger vessel built in the United States since 1952.

In 1998 **Gray Line of Alaska** (☎ 907/586–3773 or 800/544–2206) added the new 120-passenger *Alaskan Dream,* with

daily service between Juneau and Skagway.

Also new in 1998 was the addition of a self-propelled railcar called **The Red Line** (☎ 800/343–7373), with service along the White Pass & Yukon Route connecting Skagway and Whitehorse.

Alaskan Accommodations

Two classic Southeast Alaska lighthouses were recently transformed into lodging places: the **Point Retreat Lighthouse** at the north end of Admiralty Island, and the **Five Finger Lighthouse** between Juneau and Petersburg. Both will open for use in 1999; for details contact the U.S. Coast Guard (☎ 907/463–2267).

Anchorage has seen rapid growth in its lodging options, with the opening of six new hotels in the past two years. Newest of these are the 148-room **Residence Inn** in midtown, the downtown 110-bed **Clarion,** the 50-bed **Ramada Limited** in east Anchorage, and the 102-bed **Fairfield Suites by Marriott** in midtown.

Museum News

Brand-new for 1999 is the beautifully designed **Museum of the Aleutians** (☎ 907/581–5150) in Unalaska. A major focus will be the Aleut peoples and their lives, with many artifacts from an ongoing archaeological dig just a short distance from the museum. Other exhibits cover the Russian period, World War II—when the island was repeatedly bombed by the Japanese—and the fishing industry. (Ironically, much of the fish processed in Unalaska/Dutch Harbor now goes to Japan.)

Funded largely by settlement money from the 1989 Exxon Valdez oil spill, Seward's **Alaska SeaLife Center** (☎ 907/224–3080) opened its doors in 1998. Inside this world-class facility visitors can watch scientists as they study everything from the genetics of herring to Steller sea lion telemetry. Centerpieces are the re-created sea and shore habitats—complete with underwater viewing windows—that house seals, sea lions, marine birds, salmon, and other animals.

Cruise News

For the first time in a long time, the big story in Alaska cruises is smaller ships. Perhaps the biggest surprise is the return of the *Island Princess* (20,000 tons, 640 passengers) to "the Great Land" after a five-year absence. The *Island* will sail on 10- and 11-night cruises. Both include a stop at the picturesque artists' community of Homer. This is the only ship that calls there.

The *Island* is one of just two ships that actually docks in Anchorage. (Most ships call at Seward and transfer passengers by bus.) The other is Crystal Cruises' *Crystal Harmony*, which also sails on 10- and 11-night cruises. Crystal now stands alone at the high end of the cruise market since the withdrawal of Seabourn and Cunard.

Carnival, meanwhile, also has opted for a relatively small ship to replace the *Tropicale*, which is crossing the Pacific to become the flagship of the new Carnival Cruises Asia, a joint venture with Hyundai. Replacing the *Tropicale* will be the *Jubilee* (47,262 tons, 1,486 passengers). Although it's hardly tiny, it's still modest compared with the megaships that have come to Alaska in the past couple of years.

Glacier Bay continues to be the crown jewel in any Alaska itinerary. The National Park Service limits the number of cruise ships that can enter the bay from June 1 to August 30. During this period, the height of the Alaska cruise season, humpback whales feed in the park. Competition for permits to enter is fierce and will probably remain strong. Although the park service granted a 30% increase in permits in 1996, it's still not enough to satisfy demand. A proposal to grant another 42% increase in permits is pending but will probably not be decided until after the year 2000. Carnival Cruise Lines, Celebrity Cruises, Crystal Cruises, Holland America, Norwegian Cruise Line, Princess Cruises, Royal Caribbean, Radisson Seven Seas, and World Explorer Cruises have permits for 1999.

GREAT ITINERARIES

Planning a trip to Alaska requires a careful look at both your interests and finances. The state is far too big and undeveloped for you to be able to see all of it in a short period, so unless you have all summer—and are able to print your own money—you'll need to be very selective. The most popular areas are Southeast and South Central Alaska, but these two lie more than 600 mi apart, so you're not likely to see both in a short visit. Getting into the more remote villages is even more problematic. Although most places have scheduled air service (often in small planes), bad weather may halt flights for days at a time. Don't plan a short trip to such notoriously stormy towns as Kodiak or Unalaska! Your best bet is to look through this book to see what areas appeal to you, and then take into consideration how much time and money you have. Most people on a short trip will be happier seeing just a few places well, rather than spending all their time in trains, planes, and automobiles. After all, you didn't come to Alaska for the airline meals!

If You Have 3 Days

What should you do in a three-day Alaskan visit? Try to get more time off! But if you simply have no other options, fly into Anchorage or Juneau and see sights in the immediate area. In **Anchorage** these would include the Museum of History and Art and the new Alaska Native Heritage Center, a hike in nearby Chugach State Park, a visit to Portage Glacier, and a seafood dinner at Simon and Seafort's or Marx Brothers' Cafe. You might also consider a long day trip to **Whittier** or **Seward** for a glacier cruise, or a flightseeing trip over **Mt. McKinley.**

Travelers to **Juneau** should visit the Alaska State Museum, hike the trails at Mendenhall Glacier, take a half-day boat trip to see the calving glaciers of Tracy Arm, tip a beer at the Red Dog Saloon, ride the tram up Mt. Roberts, and enjoy a meal at the Gold Creek Salmon Bake. For a taste of the wilderness, consider a floatplane flight to Pack Creek on **Admiralty Island,** where you can watch brown bears.

If You Have 5 to 7 Days

A week is sufficient time to get a feel for either South Central or Southeast Alaska. Again, it would be best to choose a hub such as Anchorage or Juneau and head out from there (though other hubs such as Ketchikan or Fairbanks would offer additional options). In South Central Alaska, you could start out in Anchorage with the sites described for the three-day itinerary above, adding **Denali National Park**—a must-see on every visitor's list. Plan on at least three days for this portion of the trip, since the park is 240 mi north of Anchorage; getting out to the most scenic areas requires an all-day bus ride out and back from the entrance. You should also consider spending a night in the **Seward** area, where you could take a boat cruise into Resurrection Bay, visit the new Alaska SeaLife Center, and hike near scenic Exit Glacier. Visitors to Southeast Alaska should start out in Juneau with the sights listed above, adding several days in nearby **Glacier Bay National Park.** Park headquarters in **Gustavus** is a quick jet flight from Juneau, but you'll need to book a cruise up into the bay to see the park's justly famous glaciers and wildlife. If you have the time, ride the state ferry north to the Gold Rush town of **Skagway,** returning to Juneau in a small plane.

If You Have 10 Days

Travelers with 10 days or longer have a multitude of options. It is possible to spend a few days in Southeast Alaska before flying to Anchorage for a taste of South Central, but this trip would leave little time to relax along the way. A better option is to expand upon the itineraries described above.

In South Central Alaska, travelers with more time often choose to explore the **Kenai Peninsula,** fishing for salmon on the Kenai River, and visiting the artist town of Homer. Another popular destination for visitors with more time is the historic copper mining settlement of McCarthy, deep within **Wrangell–St. Elias National Park.** This might be included in a big loop trip that leaves Anchorage for Denali National Park, crosses the Denali Highway to Paxson before heading south to McCarthy, and then continues back to Anchorage (possibly via a ferry trip from Valdez to Whittier). You may also want to consider riding the **Alaska Railroad** north from Denali National Park to **Fairbanks,** where the summer days are long and mild. Sights near Fairbanks include Chena Hot Springs, the University of Alaska Museum, the trans-Alaska pipeline, a Chena River paddlewheel cruise, old-time entertainment at the Malemute Saloon in Ester, and a waterside meal at Pike's Landing. Options for travelers with a limitless credit card would include a two-day bear-watching flight to Brooks Camp in **Katmai National Park,** a guided fly-fishing trip to

a backcountry lodge, or an overnight Eskimo cultural tour of **Barrow** and **Kotzebue.**

A good option for Southeast Alaska travelers with 10 days or more is to ride the state ferry north and return home by jet. (Air service is also available between the towns of Southeast if you want to spend less time aboard the ferries.) You can start your voyage in Bellingham, Washington or Prince Rupert, British Columbia, but this will add a day or two to your travel time on the ferry. A better bet would be to fly to **Ketchikan** and then work your way northward via ferry to Juneau (sights in this area are described above). The fishing and logging town of Ketchikan has magnificent collections of totem poles, plus hiking paths into the lush rain forest just behind town. Scenic **Misty Fjords National Monument**—where you can book a Forest Service cabin—is just a half-hour floatplane ride away. Other places well worth an overnight stop include the Norwegian fishing town of **Petersburg** and the old Russian town of **Sitka.**

FODOR'S CHOICE

No two people will agree on what makes a perfect vacation, but it's fun and helpful to know what others think. We hope you'll have a chance to experience some of Fodor's Choices yourself in Alaska. For detailed information about each entry, refer to the appropriate chapters.

Uniquely Alaska

★ **Alaska Chilkat Bald Eagle Preserve.** Each fall and winter, thousands of bald eagles gather in Southeast Alaska's Chilkat Valley near Haines to feed on chum salmon, making this the largest gathering of eagles anywhere in the world (☞ Chapter 3).

★ **Exit Glacier.** Even longtime Alaskans are wowed by the opportunity to come nearly face to face with this ancient river of ice just outside Seward (☞ Chapters 3 *and* 6).

★ **Halibut Cove.** It's Alaska just as you would imagine it: houses built on stilts huddled against snowy mountains, reachable only by water (☞ Chapter 6).

★ **Kenai Fjords and Resurrection Bay cruise.** A variety of cruises depart Seward daily for scenic tours of the surrounding waters. Spot migrating whales (mid-April), sea lions, sea otters, a multitude of seabirds, and calving glaciers. Half- or full-day and dinner tours are offered from the Seward dock (☞ Chapter 3).

★ **Kennicott Mine and McCarthy.** It's worth the extra time to plan a detour to the historic town of McCarthy and the Kennicott Mine, surrounded by the Wrangell–St. Elias Mountains. There's local color, unforgettable views, and the fascinating history of the once thriving copper mining town that makes this a special place to visit (☞ Chapters 3 *and* 6).

★ **McNeil River bears.** As many as 100 or more brown bears (the coastal cousins of grizzlies) come to this Alaska Peninsula stream each summer to feed on salmon, making this the largest gathering of brown bears in Alaska—and the world (☞ Chapter 3).

★ **Mt. McKinley.** "The High One," when not shrouded in mist, is a sight to behold (☞ Chapters 3 *and* 7).

★ **Sitka National Historic Park.** This park in Alaska's Panhandle region celebrates the transfer of Alaska from Russia to the United States in 1867 and is on the site where the exchange took place (☞ Chapter 4).

★ **Trail of '98.** The actual path of gold prospectors, worn into the coastal mountains a century ago, is visible from period railcars that take excursions to the White Pass Trail outside Skagway (☞ Chapter 4).

Taste Treats

★ **Alaskan Amber.** Brewed in Juneau by the Alaskan Brewing and Bottling Company and served statewide, this beer deserves its widespread praise and numerous awards (☞ Chapter 4).

★ **Blue-ribbon pies.** The pies at the Colony Inn in Palmer are consistent winners at the Alaska State Fair. Try the banana-cream strawberry or one of the fresh fruit pies (☞ Chapter 6).

★ **Buffalo Burgers.** For some genuine frontier fare, stop by Fat Freddie's in Nome for a burger made of buffalo or musk-ox meat (☞ Chapter 8).

★ **Micro Brews.** Brew pubs are the latest trend in Anchorage. There are three new brew pubs in downtown Anchorage: the **Glacier BrewHouse,** the **Railway** **Brewing Company,** and the **Snowgoose Restaurant.** Each offers a brew made on the premises and a menu that ranges from seafood to pizza. (☞ Chapter 5).

★ **Salmon Bake.** The salmon bake, an Alaskan tradition, is perfected at Juneau's Gold Creek Salmon Bake (☞ Chapter 4). There's another salmon bake at Alaskaland in Fairbanks (☞ Chapter 7).

★ **Seafood Garlic Pasta.** The menu at the Double Musky restaurant in Girdwood is full of fabulous dishes, and the combination of fresh seafood, lots of garlic, and a sinful amount of butter is hard to beat (☞ Chapter 5).

Restaurants

★ **Marx Brothers' Cafe.** From the made-at-your-table Caesar salad to the homemade butter pecan ice cream, the food is always memorable at this romantic little Anchorage restaurant. (☞ Chapter 5). $$$$

★ **Glacier Bay Lodge.** If it swims or crawls in the sea hereabouts, you'll probably find it on the menu in the dining room of this lodge, within Glacier Bay National Park. A guest favorite is the halibut *alyeska,* a fillet baked in a rich sauce (☞ Chapter 3). $$$–$$$$

★ **Homestead Restaurant.** Built from logs, this former roadhouse outside Homer specializes in steaks, seasonal seafood, and postcard-perfect views of the mountains and hanging glaciers across Kachemak Bay (☞ Chapter 6). $$$–$$$$

★ **Sacks Café.** Consistently fine and innovative food, a big city feel, and unhurried service make this perhaps the best place in town for lunch or dinner before the theater (☞ Chapter 5). $$$

★ **Seven Glaciers.** This fine-dining spot perched atop Mt. Alyeska in Girdwood offers fabulous views of Turnagain Arm alongside unusual, carefully prepared entrées. The presentation is artful; the service friendly and efficient (☞ Chapter 5). $$$

★ **Ivory Jack's.** The specialty at this small restaurant in the gold-rich hills outside Fairbanks is reindeer in cranberry sauce, but they also serve steaks and seafood. Jack "Ivory" O'Brien used to deal in Alaskan ivory and whale bone here (☞ Chapter 7). $$

★ **The Fiddlehead.** One of Juneau's favorite restaurants, this is a delightful place of light woods, gently patterned wallpaper, stained glass, and historic photos. The food is healthy, generously served, and eclectic (☞ Chapter 4). *$–$$*

After Hours

★ **Midnight sunset.** To have a window seat on a clear summer's eve at Anchorage's Simon and Seafort's is not to be taken for granted. The restaurant's spacious bar is a popular gathering spot for locals and visitors alike (☞ Chapter 5).

★ **Red Dog Saloon.** Juneau's most popular watering hole brings back the raucous days of the Gold Rush—especially when cruise ships are in town (☞ Chapter 4).

★ **Red Onion Saloon.** In this 1898 Skagway landmark, bartenders dressed in period costume serve patrons at the original mahogany bar where "Soapy" Smith might have sat (☞ Chapter 4).

★ **Salty Dawg Saloon.** Near the end of the Homer Spit, this low-hung bar with sawdust floors is a favorite of those who like to carve their names on the tables and shoot pool in the back (☞ Chapter 6).

Places to Stay

★ **Driftwood Inn, Homer.** This clean, unpretentious inn offers a variety of room configurations, a comfortable sitting area with fireplace, and a common eating area with microwave, coffeemaker, and refrigerator. It's great for families (☞ Chapter 6). *$$$$.*

★ **Fairbanks Princess Hotel.** This new luxury hotel, with an expansive deck and manicured lawns in a beautiful setting on the Chena River, is a fine place to relax and watch water-skiers and floatplanes on the river (☞ Chapter 7). *$$$$*

★ **Great Alaska Fish Camp, Sterling.** On Alaska's number-one sportfishing river, this fish camp midway between Seward and Homer combines the personal touches of a family-run lodge with such refinements as an outdoor Jacuzzi, candlelit dinners, and morning coffee delivered to your room (☞ Chapter 6). *$$$$*

★ **Kachemak Bay Wilderness Lodge, Homer.** Located across Kachemak Bay from Homer on the Kenai Peninsula, this lodge offers abundant wildlife, stunning views, and gourmet home-cooked meals in an intimate setting for up to 12 guests, who stay in cabins (☞ Chapter 3). *$$$$*

★ **Kodiak Buskin River Inn.** A restaurant with views of the Buskin River, a honeymoon suite with a heart-shape whirlpool bath, and a full menu of soft-adventure options are amenities at this modern lodge (☞ Chapter 6). *$$$$*

★ **Thayer Lake Lodge, Admiralty Island.** One of Southeast Alaska's pioneer lodges, Thayer Lake is on private land within Admiralty Island National Monument, near Juneau. Visitors here can expect rustic comfort in the midst of the coastal rain forest. (☞ Chapter 3). *$$$$*

★ **Top of the World Hotel, Barrow.** This hotel, on the beach facing the Arctic Ocean, has seafront rooms with views of Arctic pack ice even in the middle of the summer (☞ Chapter 8). *$$$$*

★ **Westin Alyeska Prince Hotel, Girdwood.** Alaska's first all-season resort is a full-service hotel with world-class downhill skiing in winter and hiking in summer (☞ Chapter 5). *$$$$*

★ **Voyager Hotel, Anchorage.** This small, well-appointed hotel is popular with business travelers and those who appreciate fine accommodations at more reasonable prices. It's friendly, with a touch of elegance (☞ Chapter 5). *$$$*

★ **Golden North Hotel, Skagway.** Built in 1898 in the heyday of the Gold Rush, this is Alaska's most historic hotel and has been lovingly restored to reflect the Gold Rush period (☞ Chapter 4). *$$*

★ **June's B&B, Nome.** A genuine gold miner's daughter regales guests with tall tales from Nome's storied past (☞ Chapter 8). *$$*

★ **Across the Bay Tent & Breakfast Adventure Co., Seldovia.** This beachfront hideaway defines camping in comfort. Guests sleep in sturdy, walled tents complete with beds and wood floors. (☞ Chapter 6). *$–$$*

FESTIVALS AND SEASONAL EVENTS

Top seasonal events include the Anchorage Fur Rendezvous in February, the Iditarod Trail Sled Dog Race in March, Juneau's Alaska Folk Festival in April, Sitka's Alaska Day Celebration in October, and Fairbanks's Oktoberfest in the fall. For exact dates, request a copy of the state "Vacation Planner" from the Alaska Division of Tourism (☞ Visitor Information *in the* Gold Guide). More information may also be obtained by calling the phone number listed after each event or contacting the local visitors bureau.

WINTER

➤ JAN.: Bethel's **Kuskokwim 300** is one of the state's premier dogsled races. ☎ 907/543–2911.

➤ MID-JAN.: At Seward's **Polar Bear Jump Off** bare skin meets barely above-freezing water. ☎ 907/224–5230.

➤ MID-JAN.–FEB.: **Sled-Dog Racing** season in Anchorage begins with sprints every weekend. ☎ 907/562–2235.

➤ EARLY FEB.: **Tent City Winter Festival,** in Wrangell, captures the flavor of Alaska's early days. ☎ 907/874–3901.

➤ EARLY FEB.: At the **Cordova Ice Worm Festival,** a 140-ft ice worm parades through city streets. ☎ 907/424–3527 or 907/424–7260.

➤ EARLY FEB.: Participants in the **Yukon Quest International Sled-Dog Race** travel between Whitehorse, Yukon Territory, and Fairbanks. ☎ 907/452–7954.

➤ MID-FEB.: Anchorage's **Fur Rendezvous** delivers more than 150 events— from snowshoe softball to the World Championship Sled-Dog Races. ☎ 907/277–8615.

➤ MID-FEB.: The **International Ice Climbing Festival,** in Valdez, is not for the faint of heart. ☎ 907/835–2984.

SPRING

➤ EARLY MAR.: The **World Ice Art Championships** brings the finest ice artists to downtown Fairbanks. ☎ 907/451–8250.

➤ EARLY TO MID-MAR.: The **Iditarod Trail Sled-Dog Race** stretches 1,049 mi from Anchorage to Nome. More than 70 dog teams compete, and events around the race include a winter carnival. ☎ 907/376–5155.

➤ MID-MAR.: The **Bering Sea Ice Classic Golf Tournament** is played with orange golf balls on the pack ice of the Bering Sea near Nome. ☎ 907/443–5535.

➤ LATE MAR.: The three-day **Camai Dance Festival** in Bethel attracts dance groups from throughout Alaska and also from outside the state. ☎ 907/543–2911.

➤ EARLY APR.: The **World Extreme Skiing Championships** brings the world's best daredevil skiers to Valdez. ☎ 907/835–2108.

➤ EARLY APR.: The **Alaska Folk Festival,** in Juneau, is a mix of music, handmade crafts, and foods. ☎ 907/789–0292.

➤ MID-APR.: The **Alyeska Spring Carnival** holds court at the Alyeska Resort & Ski Area, 40 mi southeast of Anchorage. ☎ 907/754–1111 or 800/880–3880.

➤ LATE APR.–EARLY MAY: During the **Copper River Delta Shorebird Festival** in Cordova, there are tours to beaches to witness the migration of millions of shorebirds. ☎ 907/424–7260.

➤ MID-MAY: The **Little Norway Festival,** in picturesque Petersburg, salutes the town's Scandinavian heritage. ☎ 907/772–3646 or 907/772–4636.

➤ LATE MAY: The **Kodiak Crab Festival** brings good food and a frigid swimming race. ☎ 907/486–5557.

➤ LATE MAY: The **Juneau Jazz Festival** features performances by nationally known musicians. ☎ 907/364–2801.

SUMMER

➤ JUNE: The **Sitka Summer Music Festival** is a monthlong series of chamber music performances. ☎ 907/747–6774.

➤ LATE JUNE: The **Midnight Sun Baseball Game** celebrates the longest day of the year in Fairbanks. The game begins at 10:30 PM without the need for stadium lights. ☎ 907/451–0095.

➤ JULY 4: The **Mt. Marathon Race,** in Seward, is a rugged race up the 3,000-ft mountain. The best vantage is right below the trail's starting point. ☎ 907/224–8051.

➤ MID-JULY: The **World Eskimo–Indian Olympics,** in Fairbanks, tests participants in such skills as ear pulling and the knuckle hop and blanket toss. ☎ 907/452–6646.

➤ LATE AUG.–EARLY SEPT.: The **Alaska State Fair,** in Palmer, displays 90-pound cabbages and other oversize vegetables. ☎ 907/745–4827.

AUTUMN

➤ LATE SEPT.–EARLY OCT.: **Oktoberfest** is celebrated in Fairbanks with German food, polka dancing, and, of course, beer. ☎ 907/456–5774.

➤ MID-OCT.: The **Alaska Day Celebration** brings out the whole town of Sitka to celebrate the day (October 18) the United States acquired Alaska from Russia. The week-long festival includes a period costume ball and a parade. ☎ 907/747–5940.

➤ MID-OCT.: The **Quyana Alaska Native Dance Festival,** in Anchorage, provides a taste of Alaska's Native culture. ☎ 907/274–3611.

➤ MID-NOV.: The **Athabascan Old-Time Fiddling Festival** enlivens Fairbanks with traditional Native music. ☎ 907/456–7491.

➤ LATE NOV.: The **Carrs Great Alaska Shoot-out** takes place at Sullivan Arena, in Anchorage, where some of the best college basketball teams in the country compete. ☎ 907/786–1230.

➤ EARLY DEC.: The offbeat **Bachelor Society Ball/Wilderness Woman Contest,** in Talkeetna, combines competitive athletic events for women with competitive bidding for eligible bachelors. ☎ 907/733–2330.

2 Cruising in Alaska

Alaskan cruises are hot. Many cruise lines are putting their newest and biggest ships here; but those who want to sail with only seven other people instead of 1,700 will find a cruise to suit them, too. Hundreds of thousands of people cruise Alaska's Inside Passage every year, watching in awe as glaciers and snowcapped mountains glide by and sprinting from port to starboard as reports of whale sightings are exchanged. As many ports of call are not accessible by road, cruising in Alaska is an easy, leisurely, and practical way to cover great distances.

By M. T.
Schwartzman

Updated by
Heidi Sarna

ALASKA, IT WOULD SEEM, was made for cruising. The traditional route to the state is by sea, through a 1,000-mi-long protected waterway known as the Inside Passage. From Vancouver in the south to Skagway in the north, it winds around islands large and small, past glacier-carved fjords, and along hemlock-blanketed mountains. This great land is home to breaching whales, nesting eagles, spawning salmon, and calving glaciers. The towns here can be reached only by air or sea. There are no roads; Juneau, in fact, is the only water-locked state capital in the United States. Beyond the Inside Passage, the Gulf of Alaska leads to Prince William Sound—famous for its marine life and more fjords and glaciers—and Anchorage, Alaska's largest city.

An Alaska cruise is no longer the exclusive domain of retirees. Following the latest trend in cruising, more and more families are setting sail for Alaska. The peak season falls during summer school vacation, so kids are now a common sight aboard ship. Cruise lines have responded with programs designed specifically for children and with some discount shore excursions for kids under 12. Shore excursions have become more active, too, often incorporating activities families can enjoy together, such as bicycling, kayaking, and hiking.

For adults, too, the cruise lines now offer more than ever before. Alaska is one of cruising's showcase destinations, so the lines are putting their grandest ships up here. In 1998 Royal Caribbean's new *Vision of the Seas* and Princess Cruises' new *Sea Princess* cruised Alaska for the first time.

Itineraries give passengers more choices than ever before—from Bering Strait cruises, which include a crossing to the Russian Far East, to 10-, 11-, and 14-day loop cruises of the Inside Passage, round-trip from Vancouver. A few smaller boats sail only in Prince William Sound, away from big-ship traffic.

Bingo and bridge tournaments, deck games, contests, demonstrations, and lectures are offered daily. You'll also find trendier pursuits: computer classes, stress-management seminars, and talks on financial planning. Enrichment programs are becoming increasingly popular. Some lines hire celebrity or Native speakers, naturalists, or local personalities.

On the big ocean liners, you can eat practically all day and night. There's often a selection of healthy choices for nutrition-conscious eaters. Some ships coordinate your dining-room meals with your exercise program in the health club.

Nearly every day, your ship will make a port call. Alaska port cities are small and easily explored by foot, but for those who prefer to be shown the sights, ship-organized shore excursions are available. These range from typical city bus tours to flightseeing with a landing on a glacier, charter fishing, river rafting, and visiting Native American communities. The programs change annually as the lines search for just the right mix of leisure and learning (☞ Shore Excursions, *below*).

CHOOSING YOUR CRUISE

Every ship has its own personality, depending on its size, the year it was built, and its intended purpose. Big ships are more stable and offer a huge variety of activities and facilities. Smaller ships feel intimate, like private clubs. For every big-ship fan there is somebody who would never set foot aboard one of these "floating resorts."

The lifestyle and activities available on board, the dining-room dress code, and the quality of the service are all important. Are there one or two seatings in the dining room? If there are more than one, you will not be allowed to arrive and exit as the spirit moves you but instead must show up promptly when service begins—and clear out within a specified time. Equally important are your itinerary, the accommodations, and the cost of the cruise.

Types of Ships

Ocean Liners

All ocean liners have swimming pools, spas, nightclubs, theaters, and casinos, but there are three distinct types. Many **classic liners,** ships constructed between 1950 and 1969 for transatlantic or other ocean crossings, are still sailing in the fleets of many cruise lines. Typically, their cabins are larger than those on vessels built for cruising. Smaller ships may feel cramped because of low ceilings in the lobby and corridors. But on the most opulent vessels, public spaces were designed to inspire and still do. Beginning in the 1960s, ship lines began to create vessels specifically for cruising. Some of these **cruise liners** were brand new; others were converted ferries or freighters. On these ships, outdoor deck space is plentiful; stateroom space is not. Vessels known as **megaships,** the biggest cruise ships ever built, first appeared in the late 1980s and with their immense proportions and passenger capacities, immediately established a new standard of cruise-ship design. These vessels are most easily recognized by their boxy profile: the hull and superstructure rise straight out of the water, as many as 14 stories tall.

Expedition Ships

Vessels of this type are designed to reach into the most remote corners of the world. Shallow drafts allow them to navigate up rivers, close to coastlines, and into shallow coves. Hulls may be hardened for sailing in Antarctic ice. Motorized rubber landing craft, known as Zodiacs, are kept on board, making it possible for passengers to put ashore almost anywhere. However, because the emphasis during cruises aboard expedition ships tends to be on learning and exploring, the ships don't have casinos, shows, multiple bars and lounges, and other typical diversions. Instead, for entertainment they have theaters for lectures, well-stocked libraries, and enrichment programs led by experts.

Coastal Cruisers

Designed more for exploring than entertaining, these are smaller than the expedition ships. They, too, are able to sail to remote waterways and ports, but unlike the expedition ships, they do not have ice-hardened hulls. Some have forward gangways for bow landings or carry a fleet of Zodiac landing craft. Coastal cruisers offer few onboard facilities and public spaces—perhaps just a dining room and a lounge.

The Cruise Experience

Although no two cruises are quite the same, even aboard the same ship, the cruise experience tends to fall into three categories.

Formal

Formal cruises embody the ceremony of cruising. Generally available on ocean liners and cruise yachts sailing for seven days or longer, formal cruises recall the days when traveling by ship was an event in itself. By day, their shipboard lifestyle is generally unstructured. Tea and bouillon may be served to the accompaniment of music from a classical trio in the afternoon. Ashore, passengers may be treated to a champagne beach party. Meals in the dining room are served in a single seating, and passengers are treated to the finest cuisine afloat. Jackets and ties for men are the rule for dinner; tuxedos are not uncommon. Pianists, cabaret acts, and local entertainers provide nighttime diversion. Service is extremely attentive and personalized.

Semiformal

On semiformal cruises, meals are served in two seatings on ocean liners or one seating on small ships; menu choices are plentiful; and the cuisine is on a par with that available in better restaurants. Men wear jackets and ties to dinner most nights. Featured dishes may be prepared table side, and you often are able, with advance notice, to order a special diet, such as low salt or vegetarian. There is a daily program of scheduled events, but there's time for more independent pursuits; passengers with similar interests are often encouraged to meet at appointed times for chess, deck games, and other friendly contests. Production-style shows are staged each evening, but the disco scene may not be too lively.

Casual

Casual cruises are the most popular. Shipboard dress and lifestyle are informal. Meals in the dining room are served in two seatings on ocean liners and one seating on specialty ships; menus are usually not extensive, and the food is good but not extraordinary; your options may be limited if you have special dietetic requirements. Men dress in sport shirts and slacks for dinner most nights, in jackets and ties only two or three evenings of a typical seven-day sailing. Aboard casual ocean liners, activities are more diverse than on formal and semiformal ships, and there is almost always something going on, from bingo to trivia contests. Las Vegas–style variety shows or Broadway revues headline the evening entertainment. Discos rock into the wee hours.

Itineraries

Alaska sailings come chiefly in two varieties: round-trip Inside Passage loops and one-way Inside Passage–Gulf of Alaska cruises. Both itineraries are typically seven days. However, if you want to combine a land tour with your Inside Passage loop, you can only spend three or four days aboard ship. On the other hand, Inside Passage–Gulf of Alaska cruises allow you to spend a full week aboard ship and still take a pre- or post-cruise land tour. A few lines schedule longer one-way or round-trip sailings from Vancouver, San Francisco, or Los Angeles.

Whether you sail through the Inside Passage or along it will depend on the size of your vessel. Smaller ships can navigate narrow channels, straits, and fjords. Larger vessels must sail farther from land, so don't expect to see much wildlife from the deck of a megaship.

Cruise Tours

Most cruise lines give you the option of an independent, hosted, or fully escorted land tour before or after your cruise. Independent tours allow maximum flexibility. You have a preplanned itinerary with confirmed hotel reservations and transportation arrangements, but you're free to follow your interests and whims in each town. A hosted tour is similar, but tour company representatives are available along the route to help out should you need assistance.

On fully escorted tours, you travel with a group, led by a tour director. Activities are preplanned (and typically prepaid), so you have a good idea of how much your trip will cost (not counting incidentals) before you depart.

Modes of tour transportation range from plane to bus, rail to ferry. Most cruise-tour itineraries include a ride aboard the Alaska Railroad in a private, glass-dome railcar. Running between Anchorage, Denali National Park, and Fairbanks, Holland America Westours's *McKinley Explorer* and Princess Tours' *Midnight Sun Express Ultra Dome* offer unobstructed views of the passing land and wildlife.

Of the ocean liner fleet, only the *Vision of the Seas, Rhapsody of the Seas, Universe Explorer, and Norwegian Wind* are not currently offering cruise tour packages with land segments in Alaska; they may, however, have tours in the Canadian Rockies. In addition to full-length cruise tours, many cruise lines have pre- or post-cruise hotel and sightseeing packages in Vancouver or Anchorage lasting one to three days.

Cruise Costs

Per diems (☞ The Cruise Fleet, *below*) are an average daily price for Alaska itineraries during peak season, based on published brochure rates: if you shop around and/or book early you will undoubtedly pay less. In addition to your cruise per diem are extra costs, such as **airfare** to the port city. Only the most expensive Alaska cruises include airfare. Virtually all lines offer air add-ons, which may or may not be less expensive than the latest discounted fare from the airlines. **Shore excursions** can be a substantial expense; the best in Alaska are not cheap. But, skimp too much on your excursion budget, and you'll deprive yourself of an important part of the Alaska experience.

Tipping is another extra. At the end of the cruise, it's customary to tip your room steward, server, and the person who buses your table. Expect to pay an average of $7.50 to $10 per day in tips. Each ship offers guidelines.

Single travelers should be aware that there are few single cabins on most ships; taking a double cabin for yourself can cost as much as twice the advertised per-person rates (which are based on two people sharing a room). Some cruise lines will find roommates of the same sex for singles so that each can travel at the regular per-person, double-occupancy rate.

When to Go

Cruise season runs from mid-May to late September; the most popular sailing dates are from late June through August. Although Alaskan weather never carries any guarantees, sunshine and warm days are apt to be most plentiful from mid-June through August. May and June are the driest months to cruise. For shoppers, bargains can be found both early and late in the season.

Cruising in the low seasons provides plenty of advantages besides discounted fares. Availability of ships and particular cabins is greater in the low and shoulder seasons, and the ports are almost completely free of tourists. In spring, wildflowers are abundant, and you're apt to see more wildlife along the shore, because the animals have not yet gone up to higher elevations. Alaska's early fall brings the splendor of autumn hues and the first snowfalls in the mountains. The animals have returned to low ground, and shorter days bring the possibility of seeing the northern lights. Daytime temperatures along the cruise routes in May, June, and September are in the 50s and 60s. July and August averages are in the 60s and 70s, with occasional days in the 80s.

BOOKING YOUR CRUISE

Using a Travel Agent

Nearly all cruises are sold through travel agents, and having a good agent is often the key to having a pleasant cruise experience. To help ensure you pick an agent who is right for you, first talk to friends, family, and colleagues who have used an agency to book a cruise. The most qualified agents are members of CLIA (Cruise Lines International Association). Agents who are CLIA Accredited Cruise Counsellors or Master Cruise Counsellors have had extensive cruise and ship inspection experience. If you opt for a cruise-only agency (☞ *below*), they should also be a member of NACOA (National Association of Cruise-Oriented Agencies). These agents are also experienced cruisers. Finally, the most reputable agencies, both full-service and cruise-only, are members of ASTA (American Society of Travel Agents). *Remember, though: the best travel agent puts your needs first.*

The size of a travel agency tends to matter less than the experience of its staff. A good cruise agent will ask you many detailed questions about your past vacations, your lifestyle, and even your friends and your hobbies. Only by getting to know you can an agent successfully match you to a ship and a cruise. Never book a cruise with an agent who only asks a few cursory questions before handing you a brochure.

Think of an agent as your travel consultant. Ask the agent any questions you may have about cruising. Most travel agents who book cruises have cruised extensively, and they can help you to decide on a cruise line and a ship. If you have a problem with the cruise line before, during, or after your cruise, they can act as an intermediary.

Of course, you want the best price. It's important, however, not to make price your single greatest concern. Value—what you get for your money—is just as important as the dollar amount you pay. Keep in mind that the advertised prices you see in newspapers are usually for the lowest-grade cabin. A better cabin—one with a window and maybe a private veranda—is likely to cost more. Be wary, however, of agencies that end up quoting prices to you in person that are much higher than the ones advertised: It's a bad sign when an agency advertises drastically lower prices just to get you in the door.

Most agencies have "partnerships" with certain cruise lines, which can work to your advantage. By agreeing to sell a lot of cabins (and therefore, of course, by promoting certain cruise lines) the agency gets a better rate from the cruise line. The agency can then afford to offer a "discounted" price to the public.

When it comes down to it, the very top travel agencies can more or less get you the same price on most cruises, because they'll guarantee that if the cruise line lowers the price in a promotion, you'll get the better deal. Look for an agency that offers this guarantee. Remember, too, that the best agencies are the ones that are willing to go the extra mile for their clients. This means providing free cruise-discount newsletters, cabin upgrades, advice on when and how to get the best deal, and, arguably most important of all, 24-hour service in the event you have a problem.

Spotting Swindlers

Although reputable agencies far outnumber crooks, a handful of marketeers have unfortunately been known to use deceptive and unethical tactics. The best way to avoid being fleeced, if you don't have a well-established relationship with a travel agent, is to pay for your cruise with a credit card, from deposit to full payment. That way, if an agency goes out of business before your cruise departs, you can cancel payment on services not rendered. An agency may be a bad apple if it doesn't accept credit cards. Also be wary of any agency that wants an unusually high deposit (check the brochure). To avoid a disreputable agency, make sure the one you choose has been in business for at least five years. Check its reputation with the local Better Business Bureau or state consumer protection agency *before* you pay any deposits. If a cruise price seems too good to be true, it probably is. It could mean the agency is desperate to bring in money and may close its doors tomorrow. So be wary of agencies that claim they can beat any price.

Agencies to Contact

The agencies listed below specialize in booking cruises, have been in business at least five years, and emphasize customer service as well as price.

CRUISE ONLY

Cruise Fairs of America (✉ 2029 Century Park E, Suite 950, Los Angeles, CA 90067, ☎ 310/556–2925 or 800/456–4386, FAX 310/556–2254), established in 1987, has a fax-back service for information on the latest deals. The agency also publishes a free quarterly newsletter with tips on cruising. Cruise Fairs can make independent hotel and air arrangements for a complete cruise vacation.

Cruise Holidays of Kansas City (✉ 7000 N.W. Prairie View Rd., Kansas City, MO 64151, ☎ 816/741–7417 or 800/869–6806, FAX 816/741–7123), a cruise-only agency with outlets throughout the United States, has been in business since 1988. The agency mails out a free newsletter to clients every other month with listings of cruise bargains—its prices are among the best.

Cruise Line, Inc. (✉ 150 N.W. 168th St., N. Miami Beach, FL 33169, ☎ 305/653–6111 or 800/777–0707, FAX 305/653–6228), established in 1983, publishes *World of Cruising* magazine three times a year and a number of free brochures, including "Guide to First Time Cruising," "Guide to Family Cruises," "Guide to Exotic Cruising," and "Guide to Cruise Ship Weddings and Honeymoons." The agency has a 24-hour hot line with prerecorded cruise deals (updated weekly).

Cruise Pro (✉ 2527 E. Thousand Oaks Blvd., Thousand Oaks, CA 91362, ☎ 805/371–9884 or 800/222–7447; 800/258–7447 in CA; FAX 805/371–9084), established in 1983, has special discounts listed in its monthly mailings to members of its Voyagers' Club ($15 to join).

CruiseMasters (✉ 300 Corporate Pointe, Suite 100, Culver City, CA 90230, ☎ 310/568–2040 or 800/242–9000, FAX 310/568–2044), established in 1987, gives each passenger a personalized, bound guide to their ship's ports of call. The guides provide money-saving tips and advice on whether to opt for a prepackaged port excursion or strike out on your own.

Cruises, Inc. (✉ 5000 Campuswood Dr., E. Syracuse, NY 10357, ☎ 315/463–9695 or 800/854–0500, FAX 315/434–9175) opened its doors in 1981 and now has nearly 200 cruise consultants, including many CLIA Master Cruise Counsellors and Accredited Cruise Counsellors. Its agents are extensively trained and have extensive cruise experience. They sell a lot of cruises, which means the company gets very good prices from the cruise lines. Customer-service extras include complimentary accident insurance for up to $250,000 per cruise, a monthly bargain bulletin ($19 a yr), and a free twice-a-year cruise directory with cruise reviews, tips, and discounts.

Cruises of Distinction (✉ 2750 S. Woodward Ave., Bloomfield Hills, MI 48304, ☎ 248/332–2020 or 800/634–3445, FAX 248/333–9710), established in 1984, publishes a free 80-page cruise catalog four times a year. For no fee you can register to receive notification of unadvertised specials by mail or fax.

Don Ton Cruise Tours (✉ 3151 Airway Ave., E–1, Costa Mesa, CA 92626, ☎ 714/545–3737 or 800/318–1818, FAX 714/545–5275), established in 1972, features a variety of special-interest clubs, including a short-notice club, singles club, family cruise club, and adventure cruise club. Its *CruiseNet* magazine is filled with articles as well as price discounts.

Golden Bear Travel (✉ 16 Digital Dr., Novato, CA 94949, ☎ 415/382–8900; 800/551–1000 outside CA; FAX 415/382–9086) acts as general sales agent for a number of foreign cruise ships and specializes in longer, luxury cruises. Its Cruise Value club sends members free twice-a-month mailings with special prices on "distressed merchandise" cruises that are not selling well. The agency's Mariner Club (for past passengers) offers discounts on sailings and runs escorted cruises for people who would like to travel as part of a group.

Kelly Cruises (✉ 1315 W. 22nd St., Suite 105, Oak Brook, IL 60521, ☎ 630/990–1111 or 800/837–7447, FAX 630/990–1147), established in 1986, publishes a quarterly newsletter highlighting new ships and special rates. Passengers can put their name on a free mailing list for last-minute deals. Kelly is especially good if you're interested in the more expensive cruise lines.

National Discount Cruise Co. (✉ 1409 N. Cedar Crest Blvd., Allentown, PA 18104, ☎ 610/439–4883 or 800/788–8108, FAX 610/439–8086) is a five-year-old cruise division launched by GTA Travel, an American Express representative that has served travelers since 1967. The cruise division specializes in high-end cruises and includes shipboard credits, exclusive to American Express, on most of the sailings it books. A three-times-a-year newsletter highlights the agency's latest discounts.

Ship 'N' Shore Cruises (✉ 1160 S. McCall Rd., Englewood, FL 34223, ☎ 941/475–5414 or 800/925–7447, FAX 800/346–4119), an American Express representative founded in 1987, specializes in affordable cruise-tours around the world. In Alaska, the agency has its own fleet of motor coaches, and its land tours are custom-designed to complement the cruise itineraries of Alaska's major cruise lines.

Vacations at Sea (✉ 4919 Canal St., New Orleans, LA 70119, ☎ 504/482–1572 or 800/749–4950, FAX 504/486–8360), established in 1983, puts together its own pre- and post-cruise land packages and escorted land tours. The agency also publishes a free six-times-a-year newsletter with cruise reviews and discounts.

FULL SERVICE

Ambassador Tours (✉ 717 Market St., San Francisco, CA 94103, ☎ 415/357–9876 or 800/989–9000, FAX 415/357–9667), established in 1955, does 80% of its business in cruises. Three times a year, the agency distributes a free 32-page catalog that lists discounts on cruises and land packages, plus free monthly discount alerts.

Mann Travel and Cruises (✉ 6010 Fairview Rd., Suite 104, Charlotte, NC 28210, ☎ 704/556–8311, FAX 704/556–8303), established in 1975, does 65% of its business in cruises.

Prestige Travel (✉ 6175 Spring Mountain Rd., Las Vegas, NV 89102, ☎ 702/248–1300, FAX 702/253–6316), established in 1981, does 60% of its business in cruises. The agency holds an annual trade show for all its local clients, publishes a quarterly travel catalog, and sends frequent mailings to past customers.

Time to Travel (✉ 582 Market St., San Francisco, CA 94104, ☎ 415/421–3333 or 800/524–3300, FAX 415/421–4857), established in 1935, does 90% of its business in cruises. It mails a free listing of cruise discounts to its clients three to five times a month. Time to Travel specializes in pre- and post-cruise land arrangements and claims its staff of 19 has been nearly everywhere in the world.

White Travel Service (✉ 127 Park Rd., West Hartford, CT 06119, ☎ 860/233–2648 or 800/547–4790; 860/236–6176 prerecorded cruise hot line with discount listings; FAX 860/236–6177), founded in 1972, does most of its business in cruises and publishes a free 40-page brochure listing the latest cruise discounts.

Getting the Best Cruise for Your Dollar

Selecting the right agent greatly increases your chance of finding the best deal. But having a basic knowledge of how and why cruises are discounted can only benefit you in the end. Since your vacation experience can vary greatly depending on the ship and its ports of call, it's best to pick your vessel and itinerary first, and then try to get the best price. Remember, it's only a deal if the cruise you book, no matter what the price, meets your expectations.

Like everything in retail, each cruise has a brochure list price. But like the sticker price on a new car, nobody actually pays this amount. These days, if you asked any 10 cruise passengers on any given ship what they paid, they would give you 10 different answers. Discounts from cruise lines and agencies can range from 5% on a single fare to 50% on the second fare in a cabin, and even two-for-one deals are sometimes offered.

Approach deep discounts with skepticism. Fewer than a dozen cabins may be offered at the discounted price, they may be inside cabins, and the fare may not include air transportation or transfers between the airport and the ship. Finally, do the math. A promotion might sound catchy, but if you divide the price by the number of days you'll be cruising and include the cost of air and accommodations, you might find that the deal of the century is really a dud.

Deals and Discounts

SEASONAL DISCOUNTS

Cruise-brochure prices are typically divided into three categories based on the popularity of sailing dates and weather: high season, shoulder season, and low season. (Some lines divide their Alaska sailings into five seasons.) Before you take advantage of a low-season rate, think about the pros and cons of off-season travel. In Alaska, spring cruises are drier but colder, and fall cruises run the risk of stormy weather as you get into late September and early October.

EARLY-BIRD SPECIALS

More than ever, it's important to book early. This is especially true for the newest ships and for cabins with private verandas—both are selling out quickly. If you wait to book, you'll probably pay more even if you don't get shut out from the ship or cabin of your choice. That's because almost all cruise lines provide a discount for passengers who book and put down a deposit far in advance; an additional discount may be provided if payment is made in full at the time of booking. These discounts, given to passengers who book at least three months before departure, range from 10% to 50% off the brochure rate.

As the sailing date approaches, the price of a cruise tends to go up. Also, the best cabins usually sell out first, and, as the ship fills, you'll be less likely to get the meal seating of your choice.

LAST-MINUTE SAVINGS

In recent years, cruise lines have provided fewer and fewer last-minute deals. However, if a particular cruise is not selling well, a cruise line may pick certain large cruise-only travel agencies to unload unsold cabins. Keep in mind that your choice of cabin and meal seating is limited for such last-minute deals.

Payment

Deposit

Once you have made a reservation for a cabin, you will be asked to put down a deposit. Handing money over to your travel agent constitutes a contract, so before you pay, review the cruise brochure to find out the provisions of the cruise contract. What is the payment schedule and cancellation policy? Will there be any additional charges before you can board your ship, such as transfers, port fees, or local taxes? If your air connection requires you to spend an evening in a hotel near the port before or after the cruise, is there an extra cost?

Most cruises must be reserved with a refundable deposit of $200–$500 per person, depending upon how expensive the cruise is; the balance is due 45–75 days before you sail. If the cruise is less than 60 days away, however, you may have to pay the entire amount immediately.

If possible, pay your deposit and balance with a credit card. This gives you some recourse if you need to cancel, and you can ask the credit-card company to intercede on your behalf in case of problems.

Cancellation

Your entire deposit or payment may be refunded if you cancel your reservation between 45 and 75 days before departure; the grace period varies from line to line. If you cancel later than that, you will forfeit some or all of your deposit (☞ Insurance, *below*). An average cancellation charge is $100 one month before sailing, $100 plus 50% of the ticket price between 15 and 30 days prior to departure, and $100 plus 75% of the ticket price between 14 days and 24 hours ahead of time. If you simply fail to show up when the ship sails, you will lose the entire amount. Many travel agents also assess a small cancellation fee. Check their policy.

Insurance

Travel insurance is the best way to protect yourself against financial loss. The most useful plan is a comprehensive policy that includes coverage for trip cancellation-and-interruption, cruise line default, trip delay (including missed cruise connections), and medical expenses (with a waiver for preexisting conditions).

Without insurance you will lose all or most of your money if you cancel your trip, regardless of the reason. Should your cruise line go out of business, default protection will reimburse you for any payments you've made—or pay to get you home should you find yourself stranded. Another way to protect yourself is to book with a line that belongs to the United States Tour Operators Association (USTOA, ✉ 342 Madison Ave., Suite 1522, New York, NY 10022, ☎ 212/599–6599 or 800/468–7862), which requires members to maintain $1 million each in an account to reimburse clients in case of default. A few cruise lines, such as Holland America Line and Special Expeditions, belong to this organization.

Trip-delay provisions will cover unforeseen expenses that you may incur due to bad weather or sometimes mechanical delays. It's important to compare the fine print regarding trip-delay coverage when comparing policies.

Always buy travel insurance directly from the insurance company; if you buy it from a cruise line that goes out of business, your default coverage will be invalid.

TRAVEL INSURERS

In the U.S., contact **Access America** (⊠ 6600 W. Broad St., Richmond, VA 23230, ☎ 804/285–3300 or 800/284–8300) or **Travel Guard International** (⊠ 1145 Clark St., Stevens Point, WI 54481, ☎ 715/345–0505 or 800/826–1300). In Canada, contact **Mutual of Omaha** (⊠ Travel Division, 500 University Ave., Toronto, Ontario M5G 1V8, ☎ 416/598–4083; 800/268–8825 in Canada).

THE CRUISE FLEET

The Alaska cruise fleet is diverse: of the more than 30 ships deployed in 1999, there are 21 ocean liners, two expedition ships, and 13 coastal cruisers. Passenger capacities range from nearly 2,000 people to fewer than a dozen. Lifestyle aboard these ships also spans the range, from formal to semiformal to casual. Three ships will be making their Alaska debut this year.

Ocean Liners

Classic Liners
CASUAL

Universe Explorer. World Explorer Cruises' strong suit is education, and passengers should not expect the glitz and glamour of some newer ships. The line's vessel (formerly the *Enchanted Seas* of Commodore Cruise Line) was built as a transatlantic liner, but World Explorer has modified it to serve as a floating classroom. Rather than the disco and casino typically found on cruise ships, the *Universe Explorer* has an herbarium and a 15,000-volume library—the largest at sea. Several other public rooms include a forward observation lounge. The *Universe Explorer*'s itinerary incorporates long port stays and an excellent array of shore excursions. On any given sailing, you may travel in the company of four or five experts in history, art, geology, marine life, music, or geography. Cabins are simple and spacious. ⊠ *World Explorer Cruises, 555 Montgomery St., San Francisco, CA 94111, ☎ 415/393–1565 or 800/854–3835. Built: 1958. Size: 23,500 tons. Capacity: 739 passengers. International officers and crew. 4 bars, 5 lounges, fitness center with massage, cinema, card room, library, youth center. Cabin amenities: Color TV. Average per diem: $200–$300.*

Cruise Liners
FORMAL

Crystal Harmony. The *Crystal Harmony* is exceptionally sleek and sophisticated. Spacious and well equipped, the ship has plenty of open deck space for watching the scenery plus a forward observation lounge with oversize windows, set high above the bridge. Unlike most ships in this price category, the *Harmony* serves dinner in the main dining room in two seatings. Passengers may choose to dine in the alternative Asian or Italian restaurants at no extra charge. Cabins are especially spacious; more than half have a private veranda. ⊠ *Crystal Cruises, 2121 Avenue of the Stars, Los Angeles, CA 90067, ☎ 310/785–9300 or 800/446–6620. Built: 1990. Size: 49,400 tons. Capacity: 940 passengers. Norwegian and Japanese officers and an interna-*

28

Cruise Ships

● Port is visited on every cruise
○ Port is only visited on some cruises

IP = Inside Passage
GA = Gulf of Alaska
PWS = Prince William Sound

Type of Ship	Cruise Experience	Cruising Region	Glacier Bay	Haines	Juneau	Ketchikan	Petersburg	Sitka	Skagway	Wrangell	Anchorage	Homer	Seward	Valdez	Victoria	Vancouver
Classic Liner																
Rotterdam	Semiformal	IP/GA	○		●	●		●					●	●		●
Cruise Liners																
Crown Majesty	Semiformal	IP/GA			●	●			○	○	○		●			●
Crystal Symphony	Formal	IP	○		●	●		●	●						●	●
Horizon	Semiformal	IP/GA	○		●	●	●	○	●						○	○ ●
Nieuw Amsterdam	Semiformal	IP	●		●	●		●	●							●
Noordam	Semiformal	IP/GA	○		●	●		●	○				○	●		●
Ryndam	Semiformal	IP/GA	○		●	●		●					●	●		●
Sky Princess	Semiformal	IP			●	●			●						●	●
Song of Norway	Casual	IP		●	●	●		●	●	●					●	●
Statendam	Semiformal	IP	●		●	●			●							●
Tropicale	Casual	IP/GA			●	●		○	●				●	○		●
Universe Explorer	Casual	IP/GA	●		●	●		○	○	●			○	○	○	●
Veendam	Semiformal	IP	●		●	●			●							●
Windward	Casual	IP	○	●	●	●			●							●
Megaships																
Crown Princess, Dawn Princess, Sun Princess	Semiformal	IP/GA	●		●	●			●				●			●
Galaxy	Semiformal	IP	○	○	●	●		○	○						○	●
Legend of the Seas	Casual	IP			●	●	●		●							●
Regal Princess	Semiformal	IP	●		●			●	●							●
Rhapsody of the Seas	Casual	IP			●	●		●	●							●
Star Princess	Semiformal	IP/GA	○		●	●			●				●			●
Cruise Yacht																
Seabourn Legend	Formal	IP/GA		○	○	●	○	○	○		○		○		●	○
Expedition Ships																
Hanseatic	Casual	Bering Sea, GA, and IP	○	○	○	○		○	○	○			○			○
World Discoverer	Casual	Bering Sea, GA, and IP	○					○				○	○			
Coastal Cruisers																
Executive Explorer	Casual	IP	●	●	●	●		●	●	●						○
Sea Bird	Casual	IP	●	○	●	○		●	○							
Sea Lion	Casual	IP	●	○	●	○		●	○							
Spirit of Alaska	Casual	IP	●	●	●	●		●	●	●						
Spirit of Discovery	Casual	PWS												○		
Spirit of Endeavour	Casual	IP	●		●	●	●	●								
Spirit of Glacier Bay	Casual	IP	●		●			●			○		○			
Spirit of '98	Casual	IP			●	●	●	●	●							
Wilderness Explorer	Casual	IP	●		●											
Yorktown Clipper	Casual	IP	○	○	○	○			●	○	○				○	

tional crew. 7 bars, 6 entertainment lounges, fitness center with massage and sauna, casino, cinema, library, video arcade, and smoking room. Cabin amenities: 24-hr room service, refrigerator, robes, TV-VCR. Average per diem: $400–$500.

SEMIFORMAL

Nieuw Amsterdam and Noordam. More traditionally styled than the newest and snazziest ships, these ships both carry aboard a multimillion-dollar collection of 17th- and 18th-century antiques. About the only difference between these identical sisters is the theme of their art: Dutch exploration in the New World aboard the *Nieuw Amsterdam* and in the Old World on the *Noordam*. Unlike their newer sisters, these midsize ships have smaller outside deck areas, tiny gyms, and one-level dining rooms, although outside staterooms are spacious. Tipping is optional, but passengers tend to tip anyway. A resident naturalist sails aboard each Alaska cruise, and the Passport to Fitness Program encourages a healthy diet and exercise. ⊠ *Holland America Line Westours, 300 Elliott Ave. W, Seattle, WA 98119, ☎ 206/281–3535 or 800/ 426–0327. Built: 1983/1984. Size: 33,930 tons. Capacity: 1,214 passengers. Dutch officers and Indonesian and Filipino crew. 7 bars, 3 entertainment lounges, fitness center with massage and sauna, casino, cinema, video-game room, library. Cabin amenities: 24-hr room service, TV. Average per diem: $400–$500.*

Ryndam, Statendam, and Veedam. These ships can best be described as classic-revival, combining the old and new in one neat package. From the outside, they look bigger than their 55,000 tons, thanks to their megaship profile. Inside, they dramatically express Holland America's past in a two-tier dining room, replete with dual grand staircases framing an orchestra balcony—the latter first introduced on the *Nieuw Amsterdam* of 1938. Although the ships are structurally identical, Holland America has given each its own distinct personality in the layout and decor of the public rooms. An abundance of glass, outdoor deck space, and a retractable roof over the main pool make these good ships for Alaska cruising. Great views can be found along the wraparound promenade, from the top-deck observation lounge, and in the glass-lined dining room. All standard outside cabins come with a small sitting area and a real tub; some have private verandas. Tipping is optional, but passengers tend to tip anyway. A resident naturalist sails aboard each Alaska cruise, and the Passport to Fitness Program encourages a healthy diet and exercise. ⊠ *Holland America Line Westours, 300 Elliott Ave. W, Seattle, WA 98119, ☎ 206/281–3535 or 800/ 426–0327. Built: 1994/1993/1993. Size: 55,451 tons. Capacity: 1,266 passengers. Dutch officers and Indonesian and Filipino crew. 5 lounges, 7 bars, fitness center with massage and sauna, casino, cinema. Cabin amenities: 24-hr room service, TV. Average per diem: $400–$500.*

Sky Princess. This ship combines an old-liner atmosphere with the modern touches passengers expect from a cruise ship. The showroom is one of the biggest afloat and public spaces are appointed with a notable collection of contemporary art. Most public rooms command good views of the sea. The Horizon Lounge, for example, offers floor-to-ceiling windows and a view directly over the bow—perfect for sailing in scenic waters. The two dining rooms are of intimate size, are identical in decor, and have windows that provide a reasonably good view of the passing scene. Cabins are spacious. Suites have verandas and bathtubs. ⊠ *Princess Cruises, 10100 Santa Monica Blvd., Los Angeles, CA 90067, ☎ 310/553–1770 or 800/568–3262. Built: 1984. Size: 46,314 tons. Capacity: 1,200 passengers. British officers and European hotel crew. 7 bars, 4 entertainment lounges, fitness center with massage and* *sauna, library, youth and teen centers. Cabin amenities: 24-hr room service, robes, TV. Average per diem: $400–$500.*

Westerdam. As with other Holland America ships, the *Westerdam* carries a multimillion-dollar art collection that evokes the cruise line's storied history. Perhaps most impressive is an antique bronze cannon, cast in Rotterdam, which is strategically positioned in the center of the ship. Also worthy of special note is the dining room. Unlike on many newer ships, where the restaurant occupies a strategic perch with expansive views, on the *Westerdam* it is below decks. But Holland America has turned a negative into a positive; the room is attractively accented with wood, brass, and traditional portholes. Cabins are large, with plenty of storage space; all but the least expensive feature a sitting area with a convertible couch. Tipping is optional, but passengers tend to tip anyway. A resident naturalist sails aboard each Alaska cruise, and the Passport to Fitness Program encourages exercise and a healthy diet. ⊠ *Holland America Line Westours, 300 Elliott Ave. W, Seattle, WA 98119,* ☎ *206/281–3535 or 800/426–0327. Built: 1986. Size: 53,872 tons. Capacity: 1,494 passengers. Dutch officers and Indonesian and Filipino crew. 7 bars, 2 entertainment lounges, fitness center with massage and sauna, casino, cinema, library, video-game room. Cabin amenities: 24-hr room service, TV. Average per diem: $400–$500.*

CASUAL

Jubilee. The *Jubilee* brings Carnival's "Fun Ship" style of cruising to the Last Frontier. The ship offers plenty of open space and has many resortlike qualities, though the Jubilee is not nearly as sharp and state-of-the-art as Carnival's newer vessels. The interior decor is modern and festive, incorporating the entire spectrum of colors. Cabins are of similar size and appearance, comfortable and larger than average; the majority have twin beds that can be made into a king-size bed. Most outside cabins have large square windows rather than portholes. ⊠ *Carnival Cruise Lines, Carnival Pl., 3655 N.W. 87th Ave., Miami, FL 33178,* ☎ *800/327–9501. Built: 1986. Size: 47,262 tons. Capacity: 1,486 passengers. Italian officers and an international crew. 7 bars, 6 entertainment lounges, fitness center with massage and sauna, casino, video-game room, library, playroom. Cabin amenities: 24-hr room service, TV. Average per diem: $200–$300.*

Norwegian Dynasty. Large windows in the public areas, a skylight and three walls of windows in the dining room, a full promenade, and a five-story wall of glass in the atrium all provide good views of Alaska's scenery. There's a substantial amount of open deck space, but the interior does not feel as spacious. Everything feels miniaturized—narrow halls, cramped seating in the dining room, standard cabins (140 square ft) with tight showers, tiny bedside drawers, and inadequate storage. Still, many passengers may prefer this more intimate liner for what it doesn't have: large crowds of people. ⊠ *Norwegian Cruise Line, 7665 Corporate Center Dr., Miami, FL 33126,* ☎ *305/436–0866 or 800/ 327–7030. Built: 1993. Size: 20,000 tons. Capacity: 800 passengers. British officers and an international crew. 4 bars and entertainment lounges, fitness center with massage and sauna, casino, cinema, library, youth and teen centers. Cabin amenities: 24-hr room service, TV. Average per diem: $300–$400.*

Norwegian Wind. It's not the biggest or most extravagant ship afloat, but the *Norwegian Wind* is innovative and intelligently conceived. The most distinctive design features are its extensive terracing and abundant use of picture windows. Instead of one big dining room, three smaller restaurants create a more intimate ambience. Even the biggest, the Terraces, seats only 282 passengers on several levels and has windows on three sides for sea views; the Sun Terrace is similarly attractive. (Your travel agent should specifically request an assignment for you in one of these two dining rooms.) The third dining room, the Four Seasons, is pretty but lacks the terraced layout and picture windows of the other rooms. Extensive use of floor-to-ceiling windows, terraced decks, a wraparound promenade, and picture windows in the cabins make this an ideal ship for taking in the passing scenery. Convertible sofas in the cabins, connecting staterooms, the activity-filled Kids Crew program, a playroom, and a video arcade with games, a jukebox, and a 45-inch color TV make this a good choice for family cruising. ✉ *Norwegian Cruise Line, 7665 Corporate Center Dr., Miami, FL 33126, ☎ 305/435–0866 or 800/327–7030. Built: 1993. Size: 50,760 tons. Capacity: 1,748 passengers. Norwegian officers and an international crew. 13 bars and lounges, fitness center with massage and sauna, basketball court, casino, theater, library, youth center. Cabin amenities: 24-hr room service, TV. Average per diem: $300–$400.*

Megaships
SEMIFORMAL

Crown Princess and Regal Princess. These identical sisters are unmistakable because of the white dome that tops each ship. Underneath is a 13,000-square-ft entertainment and observation area with 270-degree views—perfect for a rainy day in Glacier Bay. A small observation deck below the bridge gives great views, and you're likely to have it all to yourself: it's so well-hidden, it's not even on the deck plan. There's a ⅙-mi high-traction outdoor running track, and the ships carry an impressive contemporary art collection. Cabins are quite spacious, and suites, minisuites, and some standard cabins have private verandas. ✉ *Princess Cruises, 10100 Santa Monica Blvd., Los Angeles, CA 90067, ☎ 310/553–1770 or 800/568–3262. Built: 1990/1991. Size: 70,000 tons. Capacity: 1,590 passengers. Italian officers and an international crew. 9 bars, 5 entertainment lounges, fitness center with massage and sauna, casino, cinema, library. Cabin amenities: 24-hr room service, refrigerator, robes, TV. Average per diem: $400–$500.*

Galaxy and Mercury. With features like video walls and interactive television systems in cabins, both ships are high-tech pioneers, yet at the same time are elegant, warm, and well-appointed. For example, the ships' spas are some of the best at sea. The ships' many large windows (including a dramatic two-story wall of glass in the dining room and wraparound windows in the Stratosphere Lounge, the gym, and beauty salon) and glass sunroofs over their pools bathe the ship in natural light and afford excellent viewing of Alaska's natural beauty. ✉ *Celebrity Cruises, 5200 Blue Lagoon Dr., Miami, FL 33126, ☎ 800/437–3111. Built: 1996/1997. Size: 77,713. Capacity: 1,870 passengers. Greek officers and an international crew. 11 bar-lounges; golf simulator; health club with massage, sauna, and thalassotherapy pool; casino; video-game room; library; playroom. Cabin amenities: 24-hr room service, butler service in suites, minibar, TV. Average per diem: $400–$500.*

Sea Princess, Dawn Princess, and Sun Princess. The brand-new *Sea Princess,* and its sisters, the *Dawn Princess* and *Sun Princess,* offer the greatest number of private balconies (more than 70% of outside cabins have them) of any ships sailing in Alaska. Each has two main show rooms and two main passenger dining rooms; an international food court with a 270-degree view over the bow of the ship; an Italian-style pizzeria; a wine and caviar bar; and a patisserie for coffee and drinks. ✉ *Princess Cruises, 10100 Santa Monica Blvd., Los Angeles, CA 90067, ☎ 310/553–1770 or 800/568–3262. Built: 1995/1997/1998. Size: 77,000 tons. Capacity: 1,950 passengers. Italian and British of-*

ficers and European, American, and Filipino crew. 7 bars, 2 entertainment lounges, fitness center with massage and sauna, basketball court, golf simulator, casino, library, teen and children's center. Cabin amenities: 24-hr room service, refrigerator, robes, TV. Average per diem: $500–$600.

CASUAL

Vision of the Seas and Rhapsody of the Seas. The brand new Vision and the Rhapsody have dramatic balconied dining rooms and tiered showrooms. For great views of the passing scenery, each ship has a "Viking Crown Lounge" on the uppermost deck with wraparound glass. The indoor/outdoor deck area of the Solarium Spas are especially well suited to cruising in often rainy Alaska. The Rhapsody and Vision have relatively large cabins and more balconies than Royal Caribbean's previous megaships. About one quarter of the cabins have private verandas. The ships also have specially designed family suites with separate bedrooms for parents and children. ⊠ Royal Caribbean Cruise Line, 1050 Caribbean Way, Miami, FL 33132, ☎ 800/327–6700 (reservations) or 800/255–4373 (brochures). Built: 1997/1998. Size: 78,491 tons. Capacity: 2,000 passengers. Norwegian officers and an international crew. Fitness center with massage and sauna, 8 bars, 3 lounges, casino, theater, library, youth center. Cabin amenities: TV, 24-hr room service. Average per diem: $300–$400.

Small Ships

Expedition Ships

CASUAL

Hanseatic. The Hanseatic is the world's newest, biggest, and most luxurious expedition ship. Its passenger-to-crew ratio rivals the standards of the world's most expensive ships and, due to its size, there is a varied selection of public rooms. A top-deck observation lounge with 180-degree views offers comfortable, all-weather sightseeing; there's also a glass-enclosed whirlpool. A team of experts, such as naturalists and marine biologists, brief passengers in the Darwin Lounge, a state-of-the-art facility with video and sound systems. (You can also watch the lectures in your cabin.) The experts then accompany passengers ashore. Cabins are unusually spacious, and all have outside views and sitting areas. The ship is popular with Europeans. ⊠ Radisson Seven Seas Cruises, 600 Corporate Dr., Suite 410, Fort Lauderdale, FL 33334, ☎ 800/333–3333. Built: 1993. Size: 9,000 tons. Capacity: 188 passengers. European officers and an international crew. 2 lounge-bars, fitness center, massage, sauna, cinema, library. Cabin amenities: Refrigerator, TV, VCR, tub. Average per diem: $600–$700.

World Discoverer. This true expedition vessel, with a shallow draft and ice-hardened hull, is well equipped for Zodiac landings in intriguing ports of call. Naturalists and other guest lecturers enhance the shore-side experience and give enrichment talks in the theater. Cabins are small, but all are outside. Fares include all shore excursions except flightseeing. ⊠ Society Expeditions, 2001 Western Ave., Suite 300, Seattle, WA 98121, ☎ 800/548–8669. Built: 1974. Size: 3,724 tons. Capacity: 138 passengers. German and Filipino officers, European and Filipino crew, international cruise and lecturer staff. 2 bars, 2 lounges, small gym and sauna, observation lounge, cinema–lecture hall, library. Average per diem: $400–$500.

Coastal Cruisers

CASUAL

Executive Explorer. As the name suggests, the Executive Explorer is a plush ship. Its appointments include rich wood paneling throughout;

deep, padded armchairs in the main lounge; and a gallerylike display of nearly 100 Alaskan prints. The main lounge has forward-facing observation windows; the dining room has color TV monitors. Even the stairwells have picture windows for views of the passing scenery. Outside observation areas include a partially covered sundeck, which gives a lofty perspective four decks above the water—an unusually high perch for such a small ship. Cabins have more artwork, two more big picture windows (unusually large for a ship this size), roomy closets, and other cabin amenities not often found in small-ship cabins. ⊠ *Glacier Bay Tours and Cruises, 520 Pike St., Suite 1400, Seattle, WA 98101, ☎ 800/451–5952 (U.S. and Canada). Built: 1986. Size: 98 tons. Capacity: 49 passengers. American officers and crew. Observation lounge. Cabin amenities: Minibar, refrigerator, color TV, VCR. Average per diem: $400–$500.*

Sea Bird and Sea Lion. These small, shallow-draft ships have the freedom to sail through narrow straits and visit out-of-the-way areas that are inaccessible to big ships. The boats forgo port calls at larger, busier towns and instead spend time making Zodiac raft landings, conducting wildlife searches, and stopping for beachcombing and barbecuing in Tracy Arm. These ships are not for claustrophobics, as the ship's storage capacity, the size of the crew, and the number of public areas have been cut back to carry 70 passengers. All cabins are technically outside staterooms, but Category 1 rooms have only a high port light (a very small porthole). ⊠ *Special Expeditions, 720 5th Ave., New York, NY 10019, ☎ 212/765–7740 or 800/762–0003. Built: 1982/1981. Size: 100 tons. Capacity: 70 passengers. American officers and crew. Bar-lounge, library. Average per diem: $500–$600.*

Spirit of Alaska. Alaska Sightseeing's original overnight vessel is still its coziest. You are never by yourself in the lounge, and meals in the homey dining room resemble a family affair soon after the cruise has begun. Sleek and small, the *Spirit of Alaska* feels like a real yacht. A bow ramp adds to the sense of adventure, allowing passengers to put ashore at tiny islands and beaches few other cruise travelers visit. Toilets and showers are a combined unit (meaning that the toilet is inside the shower). Suites and some outside cabins have TVs, but only for watching videos. ⊠ *Alaska Sightseeing/Cruise West, 4th & Battery Bldg., Suite 700, Seattle, WA 98121, ☎ 206/441–8687 or 800/426–7702. Built: 1980; refurbished: 1991. Size: 97 tons. Capacity: 82 passengers. American/Canadian officers and crew. Bar-lounge, exercise equipment. Average per diem: $400–$500.*

Spirit of Columbia. Although cut from the same mold as Alaska Sightseeing's *Spirit of Alaska,* this ship has one notable feature: a unique bow ramp design that allows passengers to walk directly from the forward lounge onto shore. The interior design was inspired by the national-park lodges of the American West, with a color scheme based on muted shades of evergreen, rust, and sand. All suites and deluxe cabins have a mini-refrigerator, an armchair, and a small desk. The Owner's Suite stretches the width of the vessel; located just under the bridge, its row of forward-facing windows gives a captain's-eye view of the ship's progress. Suites and deluxe cabins have TVs, but only for watching videos. ⊠ *Alaska Sightseeing/Cruise West, 4th & Battery Bldg., Suite 700, Seattle, WA 98121, ☎ 206/441–8687 or 800/426–7702. Built: 1979; refurbished: 1994. Size: 98 tons. Capacity: 81 passengers. American/Canadian officers and crew. Bar-lounge, exercise equipment. Average per diem: $400–$500.*

Spirit of Discovery. Floor-to-ceiling windows in the main lounge provide stunning views of passing scenery for passengers aboard this snazzy cruiser. Blue-suede chairs, a wraparound bench sofa at the bow, and a mirrored ceiling make the chrome-filled lounge look especially swank. From here, passengers have direct access to a large outdoor viewing deck, one of two aboard. This is great for those who don't want to trudge upstairs every time a whale is spotted. Deluxe cabins have mini-refrigerators, and many cabins have extra-large picture windows; two cabins are reserved for single travelers. Toilets and showers are a combined unit (meaning that the toilet is inside the shower). Suites and some outside cabins have TVs, but only for watching videos. ⊠ *Alaska Sightseeing/Cruise West, 4th & Battery Bldg., Suite 700, Seattle, WA 98121,* ☎ *206/441–8687 or 800/426–7702. Built: 1976. Size: 94 tons. Capacity: 84 passengers. American/Canadian officers and crew. Bar-lounge, exercise equipment. Cabin amenities: Refrigerator and TV-VCR in deluxe cabins. Average per diem: $400–$500.*

Spirit of Endeavour. Alaska Sightseeing's newest flagship is also the line's largest. Oak and teak are used throughout the light and airy ship. All cabins are outside with large picture windows for superb views. Some cabins have connecting doors, which make them convenient for families traveling together, and all cabins have TVs and VCRs, but only for watching videos. ⊠ *Alaska Sightseeing/Cruise West, 4th & Battery Bldg., Suite 700, Seattle, WA 98121,* ☎ *206/441–8687 or 800/426–7702. Built: 1984; refurbished: 1996. Size: 99 tons. Capacity: 107 passengers. American/Canadian officers and crew. Bar, lounge, library. Cabin amenities: TV-VCR in all cabins and refrigerator in some. Average per diem: $500–$600.*

Spirit of Glacier Bay. Alaska Sightseeing's smallest overnight cruiser is nearly identical to the line's *Spirit of Alaska*, and its public rooms are even cozier. Wraparound couches and small table-and-chair groupings in the lounge create a living-room feel. Cabins on the lowest deck have no window, just a high port light, but soft, cream-color fabrics help brighten up the ship's tiny accommodations. Toilets and showers are a combined unit (meaning that the toilet is inside the shower). There are no TVs in any cabins. ⊠ *Alaska Sightseeing/Cruise West, 4th & Battery Bldg., Suite 700, Seattle, WA 98121,* ☎ *206/441–8687 or 800/426–7702. Built: 1971. Size: 98 tons. Capacity: 52 passengers. American/Canadian officers and crew. Bar-lounge. Average per diem: $400–$500.*

Spirit of '98. With its rounded stern and wheelhouse, old-fashioned smokestack, and Victorian decor, the *Spirit of '98* evokes the feel of a turn-of-the-century steamer. Inside and out, mahogany adorns this elegant ship. Overstuffed chairs upholstered in crushed velvet complete the Gold Rush–era motif. For private moments, there are plenty of nooks and crannies aboard the ship, along with the cozy Soapy's Parlor at the stern, with a small bar and a few tables and chairs. All cabins are outside with picture windows, and all have TVs, but only for watching videos. ⊠ *Alaska Sightseeing/Cruise West, 4th & Battery Bldg., Suite 700, Seattle, WA 98121,* ☎ *206/441–8687 or 800/426–7702. Built: 1984; refurbished: 1993. Size: 96 tons. Capacity: 101 passengers. American/Canadian officers and crew. 2 bar-lounges, exercise equipment. Average per diem: $400–$500.*

Wilderness Adventurer. This is a friendly ship with the casual comforts of home. The coffee's always on and you'll never need a jacket and tie for dinner. Alaskan art enhances the otherwise simple surroundings, and there's just enough varnished wood to imbue a nautical feel. A library of books and videos has a nice selection of Alaska titles. There are no TVs, but you can watch these tapes—or your own wildlife footage—on the community VCR in the main lounge. The most important asset of this ship are its naturalists, who put their hearts into their work. They lead kayak excursions and shore walks, and get as much of a thrill as the passengers do whenever wildlife is sighted. Cabins, like the rest of the ship, are simple and functional. (The toilet and sink are in the shower.) ⊠ *Glacier Bay Tours and Cruises, 520 Pike St., Suite 1400, Seattle, WA 98101,* ☎ *800/451–5952 (U.S. and Canada). Built: 1983. Size: 89 tons. Capacity: 74 passengers. American officers and crew. Observation lounge. Average per diem: $400–$500.*

Wilderness Discoverer. This latest addition to the Glacier Bay fleet was formerly American Canadian Caribbean Line's *Mayan Prince.* You can expect the same general ambience and genuine enthusiasm from the crew that you would find aboard the *Wilderness Adventurer* (☞ *above*) Glacier Bay Tours and Cruises. ⊠ *520 Pike St., Suite 1400, Seattle, WA 98101,* ☎ *800/451–5952 (U.S. and Canada). Built: 1992. Size: 98 tons. Capacity: 86 passengers. American officers and crew. Observation lounge. Average per diem: $400–$500.*

Wilderness Explorer. The Wilderness Explorer is billed as a "floating base camp" for "active adventure," and that's no exaggeration. Seakayak outings may last more than three hours (a 5-mi paddle). Discovery hikes cross dense thicket and climb rocky creek beds. You'll spend most of your time off the ship—which is a good thing, since you wouldn't want to spend much time on it. Decor-wise, the ship is pleasing enough—mostly late 1960s mod with a dash of old-world leather and even Greek Revival accents. But the public spaces are very limited and the cabins are positively tiny. This ship is not for the typical cruise passenger; it should be considered only by the serious outdoor enthusiast. ⊠ *Glacier Bay Tours and Cruises, 520 Pike St., Suite 1400, Seattle, WA 98101,* ☎ *800/451–5952 (U.S. and Canada). Built: 1969. Size: 98 tons. Capacity: 36 passengers. American officers and crew. Observation lounge. Average per diem: $300–$400.*

Yorktown Clipper. The *Yorktown Clipper* is a stylish coastal cruiser with a casual sophistication. There are only a few public rooms—which are bright and comfortable—and deck space is limited. Onboard naturalists and Zodiac landing craft enhance the emphasis on destination. Floor-to-ceiling windows in the lounge and large windows in the dining room allow sightseeing in all weather. Cabins are all outside, and most have large windows. The crew is young and enthusiastic. ⊠ *Clipper Cruise Lines, 7711 Bonhomme Ave., St. Louis, MO 63105,* ☎ *314/727–2929 or 800/325–0010. Built: 1988. Size: 97 tons. Capacity: 138 passengers. American officers and crew. Bar-lounge. Average per diem: $300–$400.*

Special-Interest Cruises

The **Alaska Marine Highway** (⊠ Box 25535, Juneau, AK 99802, ☎ 800/642–0066, FAX 907/277–4829) has cabins aboard several ferries that serve the communities of southeast and south-central Alaska. Dining is cafeteria-style with good American-style food. Public rooms include an observation lounge, a bar, and a solarium. Many passengers are RV travelers transporting their vehicles (no roads connect the towns within the Inside Passage). Time spent in port is short—often just long enough to load and unload the ship. A weekly departure leaves from Bellingham, Washington, north of Seattle. Service to Alaska is also available from Prince Rupert, British Columbia, where the marine highway system connects with Canada's **BC Ferries.** Cabins on the Alaskan ferries book up as soon they become available, but a number of tour operators sell packages that include accommodations. One of the oldest and largest is **Knightly Tours** (✉ Box 16366, Seattle, WA 98116, ☎ 206/938–8567 or 800/426–2123, FAX 206/938–8498).

Discovery Voyages (✉ Box 1500, Cordova, AK 99574, ☎ 907/472–2558) sails solely within Prince William Sound on the 12-passenger, 65-ft *Discovery*, which was built in the 1950s as a Presbyterian mission boat. To carry guests, the vessel has been completely renovated by owners Dean and Rose Rand, who live aboard the ship year-round. Passenger facilities include six cabins with shared baths and a main lounge/dining room. The ship is also equipped with inflatable skiffs and kayaks for off-ship excursions. Sailings are round-trip from Whittier and Cordova, or one-way between Whittier and Cordova.

Another option for cruising Prince William Sound is the four-passenger *Arctic Tern III,* which is one of the smallest overnight vessels sailing in Alaska. Longtime Sound residents Jim and Nancy Lethcoe operate the boat under the name **Alaska Wilderness Sailing Safaris** (☎ 907/835–5175, FAX 907/835–3765) and charter the 40-ft sloop to small parties of two to four passengers, generally for three days of sailing and kayaking.

A number of interesting and unorthodox cruise vessels travel the Inside Passage, too. One that offers a balance between luxury sailing on an intimate scale (only 12 passengers) and outdoor activities, including up-close-and-personal experiences with wildlife, is **Alaska Yacht Safaris** (✉ 1724 W. Marine View Dr., Everett, WA 98201, ☎ 425/252–6800, FAX 425/252–6038). You can choose from two 120-ft megayachts that weave in and around the inlets, straits, coves, and fjords of the Inside Passage, visiting sites and communities—including Native villages and fishing settlements—that many of the larger vessels cannot reach. The staff of six includes a professional naturalist who provides informal lectures and accompanies passengers on kayaking and fishing expeditions. Most itineraries include flightseeing in Glacier Bay National Park; optional extensions include stays in Denali National Park, the Klondike, or fishing lodges.

For a cruise aboard a former minesweeper, contact the **Boat Company** (✉ 19623 Viking Ave. NW, Poulsbo, WA 98370, ☎ 360/697–5454, FAX 360/697–4213). The 12-passenger *Observer* and 20-passenger *Liseron* were commissioned by the Navy in the 1940s and 1950s, but are now in service to the conservation movement. In the past, organizations such as the Sierra Club have brought groups aboard, and all sailings are designed to raise awareness of environmental issues. The vessels themselves are constructed of wood and finished with accents of brass and bronze, so dismiss any thoughts of boats painted battleship gray.

Similar environmentally oriented programs can be found aboard the 16-passenger *Island Roamer,* a 68-ft sailboat operated by **Bluewater Adventures** (☎ 604/980–3800, FAX 604/980–1800), which has been in business for more than 20 years. The vessel is sometimes chartered by Oceanic Society Expeditions, an affiliate of Friends of the Earth. Bluewater Adventures also has the 12-passenger *Snow Goose,* a 65-ft, steel-hulled motor yacht. Built in 1973, it too has served time as a research vessel. For leisure cruising, the *Snow Goose* has a Zodiac, two kayaks, and a natural-history library.

For something even smaller, **Dolphin Charters** (☎ 510/527–9622, FAX 510/525–0720) uses the *Delphinus* (eight passengers), a 50-ft motor yacht, to explore uncharted coves throughout Southeast Alaska. This vessel is popular with professional photographers, who often hire it for their photographic workshops.

Equally intimate is the eight-passenger *Steller* from **Glacier Bay Adventures** (☎ 907/697–2442). The vessel was built as a research vessel for the Alaska Department of Fish and Game and is staffed by a crew of trained naturalists.

Outside Glacier Bay, another cozy cruise for just six passengers at a time can be booked from **All Aboard Yacht Charters** (☎ 360/898–7300 or 888/801–9004, FAX 360/898–7301). Cruises on the *Sea Play* sail from Seattle to Ketchikan, from Ketchikan to Juneau, and on loops round-trip from Juneau.

Alaska Sea Adventures (☎ 253/927–7147) caters to sportfishing enthusiasts, photography buffs, and amateur naturalists aboard the *Alaska Adventurer*. The ship holds up to 10 passengers and was built in 1980 specifically for cruising the Inside Passage.

SHORE EXCURSIONS

Shore excursions arranged by the cruise line are a very convenient way to see the sights, although you pay extra for this convenience. Before your cruise, you'll receive a booklet describing the shore excursions your cruise line offers. A few lines let you book excursions in advance; all sell them on board during the cruise. If you cancel your excursion, you may incur penalties, the amount varying with the number of days remaining until the tour. Because these trips are specialized, many have limited capacity and are sold on a first-come, first-served basis.

Among the many options available, there are some "musts." At least once during your cruise, try flightseeing—it's the only way you'll grasp the expansiveness and grandeur of the land. Go to an evening salmon feast, where you'll savor freshly caught fish cooked over an open fire in a natural setting. And experience an outdoor adventure—you don't have to be athletically inclined to raft down a river or paddle across a lake.

Because cruise-line shore-excursion booklets present such a great variety of options, we have compiled a selection below of the most worthwhile excursions to help you make your choices. Not all those listed below are offered by all cruise lines. Prices will vary.

Anchorage

Anchorage is a mix of big-city and frontier life. Downtown can be seen on foot, but if you want to see more, it would be best to sign up for a tour.

Cultural

Anchorage City Tour: Highlights of the city include stops at the largest and busiest floatplane base in the world and at the Anchorage Museum of History and Art. ☎ *$30.*

Haines

A small coastal community, Haines was originally settled by the Tlingit Indians. It is known for the work of its local artists, native dancers, and, in the fall, lots of bald eagles.

Adventure

Glacier Bay Flightseeing: If your cruise doesn't include a visit to Glacier Bay, here's a chance to see several of its tidewater glaciers during a low-altitude flight. ☎ *$125.*

Cultural

Chilkat Dancers: A drive through Ft. William Henry Seward includes a dance performance by the Chilkat Dancers, noted for their vivid tribal masks. Some lines combine this tour with a salmon bake. ✉ *$40.*

Dining with a Difference

Chilkat Dancers and Salmon Bake: The narrated tour of Haines and Ft. Seward and a Chilkat Dancers' performance are combined with a dinner of salmon grilled over an open fire. ✉ *$55.*

Scenic

Chilkat River by Jet Boat: A cruise through the Chilkat Bald Eagle Preserve reveals some eagles and—if you're lucky—a moose or a bear. It is a smooth, rather scenic trip, but in summer, you'll see little wildlife. Come October, though, imagine the trees filled with up to 4,000 bald eagles. ✉ *$70–$95.*

Juneau

This is Alaska's capital, where old and new mix in a frontier atmosphere. Juneau's historic center is easy to see on foot. Try to get to the Mendenhall, one of Alaska's "drive-up" glaciers, which is 13 mi outside town.

Adventure

Gold Panning and Gold Mine Tour: Pan for gold with a prospector guide and tour the entrance area of the Alaska-Juneau mine. It's a great tour for kids. ✉ *$40.*

Juneau Ice Cap Adventure: This helicopter or floatplane flight takes you over glaciers to the stark beauty of the Juneau Ice Field—1,500 square mi of solid ice that feeds all the area's glaciers. The longer and more expensive trips include glacier landings. ✉ *$120–$220.*

Mendenhall Glacier Helicopter Ride: One of the best helicopter glacier tours in Alaska includes a landing on an ice field for a walk on the glacier. Boots and rain gear are provided. ✉ *$165.*

Mendenhall River Float Trip: This rafting trip goes down the Mendenhall River, with some stretches of gentle rapids. Professional rafters row; rubber rain boots, protective clothing, and life jackets are provided. Minimum age is six years—and kids love this one. It's an excellent first rafting experience, but you should be in good health. ✉ *$75–$100.*

Dining with a Difference

Floatplane Ride and Taku Glacier Lodge Wilderness Salmon Bake: Fly over the Juneau Ice Field to Taku Glacier Lodge. Dine on outstanding barbecued salmon, then explore the virgin rain forest or enjoy the rustic lodge. There's a large mosquito population here; repellent is available. The tour is expensive, but it consistently gets rave reviews. ✉ *$180–$200.*

Gold Creek Salmon Bake: An all-you-can-eat outdoor meal features Alaska king salmon barbecued over an open alder-wood fire. After dinner, walk in the woods, explore an abandoned mine, or pan for gold. ✉ *$25.*

Scenic

Juneau, Mendenhall Glacier, Gastineau Hatchery Tour: If you don't opt for the helicopter tour, take this bus excursion to see the Mendenhall Glacier and then cross the Gastineau Channel to Douglas for a briefing on commercial fishing and a look at spawning salmon swimming up Alaska's largest fish ladder. ✉ *$30.*

Ketchikan

This is the salmon capital of Alaska, so it's one of the best places to sign on for a fishing charter. Ketchikan is also known for its authentic totem poles and nearby Misty Fjords National Monument, one of Alaska's best flightseeing adventures.

Adventure

Bicycle Tour: Ride along a gently rolling dirt road with spectacular views of the ocean and coastal mountains. Your guides will point out wildlife, talk about local history and geography, and take riders on a tour of a working fish hatchery. ☎ *$75*.

Flightseeing, Misty Fjords: Aerial views of granite cliffs rising 4,000 ft from the sea, waterfalls, rain forests, and wildlife are topped off with a landing on a high wilderness lake. ☎ *$155–$180*.

Mountain Lake Canoe Adventure: You and your guide paddle across a mountain lake in oversize canoes (fast, stable, easy to maneuver) and watch for eagles roosting in the trees. ☎ *$75–$85*.

Sportfishing: Cast your line for Alaska king and silver salmon or halibut along the Inside Passage. All equipment is provided; you buy your license on board. Group size is limited. Fish will be cleaned, and arrangements can be made to have your catch frozen or smoked and shipped home. ☎ *$140–$170*.

Cultural

Saxman Native Village: In a Native village displaying more than 20 totem poles and where the inhabitants still practice traditional arts, you'll learn much about the Tlingit culture. A visit here sometimes includes a tour of downtown Ketchikan. ☎ *$45*.

Scenic

Totem and Town Tour: You'll learn about Ketchikan's native and pioneer history as you travel past Creek Street, boat harbors, working canneries, and a pulp mill. Visit Totem Bight State Park, a salmon hatchery, and the Totem Heritage Center. ☎ *$30*.

Seward

This tiny town, nestled against the mountains on Prince William Sound, is the port for Anchorage. There's not much to see in this one-horse town, but the surrounding wilderness, most of it federal landholdings, is beautiful.

Adventure

McKinley Flightseeing: After a stop at Portage Glacier, continue on past Anchorage for a flight over Denali National Park and view the wildlife on Mt. McKinley's slopes. This trip is often canceled due to weather. ☎ *$275*.

Cultural

Log Cabin/Best of Seward: An orientation tour reveals life in a small Alaskan town. Watch for wildlife while journeying through Resurrection River valley. Visit Exit Glacier (☞ *below*), then spend some time in a log-cabin home listening to the owners spin tales of their interesting lifestyle, and petting their sled dogs. ☎ *$85*.

Scenic

Portage Glacier: The drive along Turnagain Arm to Portage Glacier is one of Alaska's most beautiful. The tour sometimes includes a cruise across the lake on the MV *Ptarmigan* for a close-up view of the glacier. This is a much better choice than the overland tour from Anchorage. ☎ *$80*.

Seward, Exit Glacier, and Sled Dogs: Journey along Resurrection River valley to Exit Glacier, inside Kenai Fjords National Park. A stop at an Alaskan sled-dog training center follows. 🎫 *$50.*

Sitka

Sitka was the capital of Russian Alaska. Good walkers can easily do the town on foot. Otherwise, consider taking the town tour so you don't miss the eagle hospital and the 15 totem poles and towering trees of Sitka National Historical Park. This is also a good port for fishing.

Adventure

Sportfishing: Try for the salmon and halibut that are abundant in these waters. All equipment is provided; you buy your license on board. Your catch can be frozen and shipped. 🎫 *$140–$170.*

Cultural

Sitka Drive: If you'd rather not walk the town, this guided tour includes stops at the Sheldon Jackson Museum, Castle Hill, Sitka National Historic Park, and St. Michael's Cathedral. Sometimes you can see a performance by the New Archangel Dancers, local women who have mastered the intricate timing and athletic feats required for their traditional style of dance. Some excursions include the fascinating Raptor Rehabilitation Center (☞ *below*). 🎫 *$30.*

Nature

Eagle Hospital and City Tour: After a tour of historic Sitka, visit the Alaska Raptor Rehabilitation Center, where injured birds of prey are nursed back to health. 🎫 *$40.*

Skagway

This was the gateway to the Klondike, and the town's wooden sidewalks and false-front buildings stir up memories of Gold Rush fever. The White Pass & Yukon Railroad excursion gives cruise passengers a chance to get high into the mountains. This is also a great place to rent a car for an extraordinarily beautiful drive through Carcross to Whitehorse in the Yukon.

Adventure

Chilkat Bald Eagle Preserve Flightseeing and Float Trip: If your cruise does not call at Haines, this is your chance to see the eagle preserve—although there won't be many birds during the cruise season. The trip begins with a flight over the massive ice field and glaciers of the Chilkat Mountains. After landing in Haines, have a picnic lunch, then board an 18-ft inflatable raft for a gentle float through the Chilkat Bald Eagle Preserve. 🎫 *$150–$240.*

Glacier Bay Flightseeing: If your cruise doesn't include a visit to Glacier Bay, here's a chance to see several of its tidewater glaciers during a low-altitude flight. 🎫 *$110–$135.*

Klondike Bicycle Tour: A van takes you to the top of the Klondike Pass, and you ride 15 mi downhill, enjoying the spectacular views of White Pass and Alaska's scenery along the way. Stops are made to take photographs of the area's glaciers, coastal mountains, and waterfalls. 🎫 *$70.*

White Pass & Yukon Railroad: The 20-mi trip in vintage railroad cars, on narrow-gauge tracks built to serve the Yukon goldfields, runs past the infamous White Pass, skims along the edge of granite cliffs, crosses a 215-ft-high steel cantilever bridge over Dead Horse Gulch, climbs to 2,865 ft at White Pass Summit, and zigzags through dramatic scenery—including the actual Trail of '98, worn into the mountain-side a century ago. It's a must for railroad buffs and great for children. ✆ *$80–$90.*

White Pass Heli-Hiking: This excursion offers the best of Skagway for the fit. Board a helicopter for a flight over the Juneau Ice Field to Glacier Station. From there, it's a 5-mi round-trip guided hike along the Skagway River to an isolated cabin near the base of Laughton Glacier. The hike returns to Glacier Station to board the White Pass & Yukon Railroad for a one-hour ride back to Skagway. ✆ *$210–$265.*

Cultural

Skagway Streetcar: This trip is especially exciting for antique-car buffs, who can ride in the Skagway Streetcar Company's vintage 1930s cars. The tour through town to the Gold Rush Cemetery and Reid Falls is accompanied by a historical narrative. ✆ *$35–$40.*

Scenic

Burro Creek Homestead: Cruise the historic Skagway waterfront to a family-run hatchery set in a modern-day log-cabin homestead. Also view the famed White and Chilkoot passes plus the Gold Rush ghost town of Dyea. ✆ *$60.*

Valdez

Valdez is the terminus for the 800-mi trans-Alaska pipeline. Surrounded by alpine scenery and spectacular waterfalls, Valdez has been called the "Switzerland of Alaska." The town can be walked, but there's not a whole lot to see. This is another good port for flightseeing or a car rental, as a drive through the snowcapped mountains is breathtaking.

Adventure

Columbia Glacier Floatplane Sightseeing: Enjoy aerial views of Valdez and of Shoup Glacier, as well as a section of the pipeline and its terminus. The highlight is touching down in the water for a close-up view of the massive Columbia Glacier. ✆ *$140–$180.*

Keystone River Rafting: This 1½-hour raft trip goes down the Lowe River, through a scenic canyon, and past the spectacular Bridal Veil Falls, which cascade 900 ft down the canyon wall. The bus trip from the ship is narrated. ✆ *$60–$70.*

Cultural

Pipeline Story: Tour the pipeline terminus and hear tales of how the pipeline was built. This is the only way to get into this high-security area. ✆ *$20–$30.*

Wrangell

This small island community is one of the oldest towns in Alaska and the only one to have been governed under three flags—Imperial Russian, British, and American. Its most unusual attractions are the petroglyphs—prehistoric boulder carvings found on a nearby beach.

Cultural

City Tour: Explore Indian history at Shakes Island, the Wrangell Museum, and Petroglyph Beach. ✆ *$20.*

Sawmill: Get a behind-the-scenes view of Alaska's largest and most modern sawmill. ✆ *$30.*

3 Parks, Wildlife Refuges, and Wilderness Adventures

Including Denali National Park and Glacier Bay

Fly over a thundering herd of caribou above the Arctic Circle, watch bears on Kodiak and Admiralty islands, drift past bellowing sea lions on the Kenai Peninsula, wander by volcanoes in Katmai National Park, kayak through icebergs in Glacier Bay, bike up to the Chugach Mountains for a stupendous view of the Cook Inlet and Anchorage, or have a floatplane drop you by a secluded Forest Service cabin and cast your fishing line in complete solitude. Alaska has more than 100 million protected acres to explore.

By Peggy
Wayburn and
Mary Engel

Updated by
Bill Sherwonit

IN THE ALEUT LANGUAGE, the word *Alaska* means "the Great Land"—an appropriate name for the 49th of the United States, the one with more land in parks, wilderness areas, and wildlife refuges than all the other states combined. In fact, about one-third of Alaska's 375 million acres is set aside in protected public lands.

These are lands not only of prodigious scale but of prodigious beauty. Four great mountain ranges—and several smaller ones—sweep through Alaska: one is the highest coastal range in the world; another includes the highest point of the North American continent (Mt. McKinley, 20,320 ft); the third lies north of and roughly defines the Arctic Circle; and the fourth arcs through Alaska's most populous region. In between the mountains there are rugged canyons, treeless valleys, softly rolling hills, flower-filled meadows, limpid lakes, blue-iced glaciers, waterfalls, deep-shadowed rain forests, and spacious tundras. Adding to this wealth are some 47,000 mi of spectacular tidal coastline.

Because of its relative inaccessibility and frequently demanding climate, most of this extraordinary area has remained largely undeveloped since it was acquired by the United States in 1867. (The United States paid Russia all of $7.2 million for this treasure.) First called Indian Country and then made a district, Alaska became a proper territory in 1912. However, except for military and federal reservations and a handful of homesites, the first extensive subdivision of Alaska did not occur until 1959, when the territory achieved statehood.

At that time Congress granted the new state 104 million acres to be selected out of more than 300 million acres of "vacant, unappropriated public land," which up to that time had been administered in Alaska by the Bureau of Land Management (or BLM, the federal agency that is charged with caring for the country's uncommitted public lands). In 1970 another congressional act—the Alaska Native Claims Settlement Act (ANCSA)—gave to Alaska's Native people an additional 44 million acres to be chosen from the remaining unappropriated lands. And in 1980, the Alaska National Interest Lands Conservation Act (ANILCA) established federal protection for about 104 million acres of outstanding Alaska land for the use and enjoyment of all the American people—and indeed of people throughout the world. Gaining passage of this legislation is considered by many to be the most extraordinary environmental achievement in the country's history.

Alaska's protected federal lands now include more than 51 million acres of national parks (administered by the National Park Service), 77 million acres of national wildlife refuges (administered by the United States Fish and Wildlife Service), 26 Wild and Scenic Rivers totaling nearly 2 million acres (administered by federal agencies), and 5.7 million acres of land administered by the United States Forest Service as wilderness areas. (Forest Service "multiple use" lands total more than 23 million acres.) Alaska's remaining vacant and unappropriated public land still administered by the BLM now totals somewhere around 87.7 million acres and will continue to decline as land is allotted. Along with the federally protected lands established in Alaska by the passage of ANILCA in 1980, there are approximately 3.2 million acres of superb lands set aside as state parks.

Because Alaska's public lands are as varied as they are magnificent, recreational opportunities within them are likewise varied. They range from such spectator sports as wildlife viewing to rigorous participatory sports such as mountaineering (there are still many unclimbed peaks

N

Barrow

Chukchi Sea

B R O O K S

RUSSIA

Noatak
National
Preserve

Noatak River

Gates of the Arctic
National Park
and Preserve

ENDICOTT MOU

Cape Krusenstern
National
Monument

IGICHUK
HILLS

Kotzebue

Kiana

Kobuk Valley
National
Park

SCHWATKA MOUNTAINS

Kobuk River

Bettles

Bering
Land Bridge
National
Preserve

*Kotzebue
Sound*

Kobuk

ARCTIC CIRCLE

Bering

Teller

Council

Koyukuk
National
Wildlife
Refuge

Kanuti
National
Wildlife
Refuge

Strait

Nome

*Saint
Lawrence
Island*

Norton Sound

Yukon River

Nowitna National
Wildlife Refuge

I N T E R

*Bering
Sea*

Innoko
National
Wildlife
Refuge

KUSKOKWIM MOUNTAINS

Denali
National Park
and Preserve

Mt. McKinley ▲ Cantwell

Dena
State

*Nunivak
Island*

Yukon Delta
National
Wildlife
Refuge

Bethel

ALASKA

S O U T H

Wasilla

Palme

Anchorage

Tyonek

Kuskokwim Bay

Togiak
National
Wildlife
Refuge

Wood-Tikchik
State Park

Lake Clark
National Park
and Preserve

Kenai

Cook   Inlet

KENAI
PEN.

Whitti

Sewo

Homer

Dillingham

McNeil River
State Game
Sanctuary ■

Kenai National
Wildlife Refuge

Kenai
Fjords
National
Park

*Round
Island*

King
Salmon ■

Katmai
National Park
and Preserve

Shuyak Island
State Park

Kachema
State P

Bristol Bay

Port Lions

Kodiak

Chugach
National
Forest

ALASKA PENINSULA

Aniakchak
National Monument
and Preserve

Kodiak
National
Wildlife
Refuge

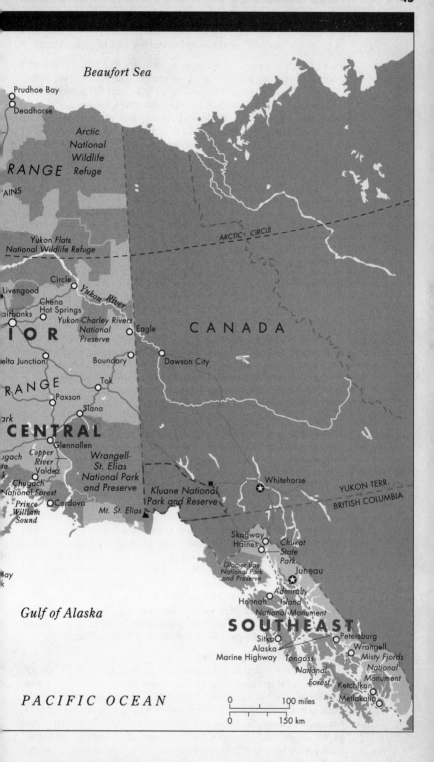

Beaufort Sea

Prudhoe Bay
Deadhorse

Arctic
National
Wildlife
RANGE   Refuge

AINS

Yukon Flats
National Wildlife Refuge

ARCTIC CIRCLE

Circle
Livengood   Yukon River
Chena
Hot Springs
airbanks   Yukon-Charley Rivers
           National   Eagle   CANADA
           Preserve

IOR

elta Junction   Boundary   Dawson City

RANGE   Tok

Paxson
Slana

CENTRAL

Glennallen

ugach   Copper
te   River   Wrangell-
        Valdez   St. Elias
Chugach   National Park   Whitehorse   YUKON TERR.
National Forest   and Preserve   BRITISH COLUMBIA
Prince   Cordova   Kluane National
William   Park and Reserve
Sound   Mt. St. Elias

                                          Skagway
                                          Haines   Chilkat
ay   State
k   Park
                              Glacier Bay   Juneau
                              National Park
                              and Preserve
                                          Admiralty
                              Hoonah   Island
Gulf of Alaska   National Monument

                                       SOUTHEAST
                              Sitka   Petersburg
                              Alaska   Wrangell
                   Marine Highway   Tongass   Misty Fjords
                                    National   National
                                    Forest   Monument
                                          Ketchikan
PACIFIC OCEAN   Metlakatla

                        0   100 miles
                        0   150 km

for intrepid climbers to scale). Many of these lands are only partially accessible: although you can drive to some, you will more often have to go by air—usually air taxi—or boat to the area of your choice.

There are thousands of mountains in this state that not only haven't been climbed, they also haven't been named. The state's most visited parks are Denali National Park and Preserve, Glacier Bay National Park and Preserve, Kenai Fjords National Park, and Chugach State Park, but that doesn't mean a backpacker or kayaker can't have a remote wilderness experience there. Parks closer to roads, and closer to Anchorage and Fairbanks, are likely to have more visitors, but that doesn't necessarily translate into the numbers encountered in parks in the Lower 48. On the other hand, if you're after a truly remote and out-of-the-way experience, you may want to try some of the least-visited places in the state, such as Wood-Tikchik State Park, where one lonely ranger patrols 1.55 million acres, or Aniakchak National Monument and Preserve, south of Katmai, where a ranger can go days or sometimes weeks without seeing a visitor.

Pleasures and Pastimes

Dining

Depending on your mode of travel and destination, dining in Alaska's parks and wilderness areas may turn out to be simple fare prepared on a camp stove. Or, if you happen to be staying at a wilderness lodge, it may equal the finest dining found in Anchorage's best restaurants. In Alaska's coastal areas, you can bet that seafood will be among the menu specialties. And at some lodges your hosts will offer homegrown vegetables and wild game as well. In the more remote parks you're likely to be cooking your own meals. But in several of Alaska's most popular (and, not surprisingly, more accessible) wildlands—for example, Denali, Kenai Fjords, Chugach, and Katmai—it's possible to find restaurants in "gateway" communities just outside the park, refuge, or forest boundaries. For price ranges, *see* the dining chart *in* On the Road with Fodor's.

Fishing

Alaska's parks, refuges, and national forests offer a wide range of sport-fishing opportunities. Depending on your preferred destination, you can fish Arctic rivers for char, grayling, or sheefish; Interior lakes for pike; or coastal streams for rainbow trout and Alaska's five species of salmon. Waters in Southeast, South Central, and Southwest Alaska—for example, those in Tongass National Forest, Lake Clark and Katmai national parks, and Kodiak National Wildlife Refuge—are especially well known around the world for their salmon migrations and healthy populations of native rainbows. The Alaska Department of Fish and Game, National Park Service, U.S. Forest Service, and U.S. Fish and Wildlife Service can provide lists of guides and outfitters. (☞ Visitor Information *in* Parks and Wildlife Refuges A to Z, *below*.)

Hiking and Backpacking

Alaska's parks, refuges, and forests offer some of the world's best opportunities for trekking across wild, pristine landscape. Whether your preference is high alpine, lowland valleys, or coastal forest, there's something here for you. Among the premier wilderness backpacking destinations are Denali, Gates of the Arctic, and Wrangell–St. Elias national parks; the Arctic National Wildlife Refuge; and Chugach and Denali state parks. Nearly all the national and state parks connected to the road system also have maintained trail systems that are appropriate for hikers of all abilities. Those who decide to visit the backcountry should be self-sufficient and educated in backcountry safety as well as low-impact camping and travel. Alaska State Parks, National Park Service, U.S. Forest Service, and U.S. Fish and Wildlife Service can provide additional information on hiking/backpacking opportunities. (☞ Visitor Information *in* Parks and Wildlife Refuges A to Z, *below.*)

Lodging and Camping

Many of Alaska's parklands and refuges have no visitor facilities at all. In fact, it may take you an hour or two by plane to reach the nearest hotel or bed-and-breakfast. Here, backcountry camping experience is necessary to explore the wilderness. Other wildlands have developed campgrounds and/or public-use cabins that may be rented. Most cabins cost $35 or less, a wonderful bargain for those who want shelter and warmth but don't need luxury; they must be reserved in advance. A certain number of parks, refuges, and forests also have wilderness lodges, built on private lands within them or nearby; here you can expect to pay top dollar. Transporting guests and supplies to these remote locations frequently leads to a rate of more than $200 per person per day, including meals. With guided sportfishing, a week at a remote lodge can cost $2,000–$5,000. Some of the road-accessible parklands also have lodging a short drive away; these range from campgrounds and RV parks to bed-and-breakfasts and luxurious hotels and inns. Because available lodging is limited, reservations are a must at most lodges and hotels. For price ranges, *see* the lodging chart *in* On the Road with Fodor's.

Wildlife Viewing

From the brown bears of Admiralty Island and Katmai National Park to the whales, sea otters, and bald eagles of Glacier Bay and Kenai Fjords national parks and the 160,000-member Porcupine Caribou Herd that travels throughout the Arctic National Wildlife Refuge, Alaska's parks, refuges, and forests offer a remarkable variety of wildlife spectacles. Denali National Park is the best known wildlife-watching destination. Tabbed the "Serengeti of the North," Denali is the place in which visitors have the best chance of seeing grizzly bears, Dall sheep, moose, and caribou in a single day—perhaps with a wolf pack sighting added for good measure. But there are numerous other places that annually provide visitors with the wildlife experience of a lifetime. The easiest way for most travelers to see wildlife is to participate in guided tours, though independent travelers can also expect to see plenty of animals if they do their homework before visiting Alaska. (☞ Guided Tours *in* Parks and Wildlife Refuges A to Z, *below.*)

PLANNING A WILDERNESS ADVENTURE

Camping

There are hundreds of campgrounds—both public and private—along Alaska's road system. But those who wish to explore Alaska's vast backcountry will almost certainly have to establish their own campsites (though some park units do have remote tent sites). Before heading into the backcountry, contact the appropriate management agency for any advice or restrictions (☞ Visitor Information *in* Parks and Wildlife Refuges A to Z, *below*). Several variables must be considered whenever camping in the backcountry, including water sources, good drainage (you don't want to end up swamped in heavy rains), protection from high winds, and the presence of any game trails. Campers are also advised to practice "low-impact" camping techniques to minimize damage to the environment. For example: carry out *all* garbage; avoid camping on fragile vegetation, which can be easily trampled; if possible, camp on already established sites; never cut standing trees; wash yourself, your clothes, and your dishes at least 100 ft from water sources; bring a trowel and dig "cat-hole" latrines for human waste at least 100 ft from your camp, water sources, and trails; burn or carry out toilet paper. When traveling in trailless areas (particularly tundra), fan out instead of walking single file, again to avoid trampling vegetation.

Because Alaska's weather is so unpredictable, backpackers should anticipate delays, especially when traveling to and from backcountry areas by plane. It's best to bring more food and fuel than you think you'll need—and be flexible in your travel plans.

Ecotourism

Concern for the environment has spawned a worldwide movement called ecotourism, or green tourism. Ecotourists aim to travel responsibly, taking care to conserve the environment and respect indigenous populations. For a state publication on ecotourism, contact the **Alaska Visitors Association** (⊠ 3201 C St., Suite 403, Anchorage 99503, ☎ 907/561–5733). **REI** (⊠ 1200 W. Northern Lights Blvd., Anchorage 99503, ☎ 907/272–4565) has a helpful brochure titled "Minimum Impact Camping" as well as a useful handout on backpacking equipment needs.

If you want to enjoy the wilderness while limiting your impact on it, the Ecotourism Society, a nonprofit research and advocacy group based in Alexandria, Virginia, gives these tips on choosing a guided-tour operator: look for the use of local guides and well-trained naturalists; predeparture information on local customs and pertinent facts about the ecology of the destination; clear instructions on how to approach wildlife and how to dispose of wastes; and the use of low-impact transportation and limits on group size.

A number of ecotour operators travel to regions covered in this chapter (☞ Guided Tours *in* Parks and Wildlife Refuges A to Z, *below*).

Equipment

Get the best equipment you can afford; it's a must in Alaska.

Backpacking

First decide whether to get a pack with an internal or external frame. If you choose the latter, pick one that balances the pack upright when you set it on the ground; this is a great help in the many areas of Alaska that don't have trees. Internal frames are an advantage when going through brush, which in Alaska is common. A rainproof cover for your pack is a good idea, even if it's just a heavy plastic garbage bag (bring along extras).

Camping

Because winterlike storms can occur at almost any time of year, a four-season tent is highly recommended—one that can withstand strong winds and persistent rainfall. There are few things worse than being stuck in a battered, leaky tent with a storm raging outside. Tie-down ropes and tent flys are essential items, and mosquito netting is another must. For sleeping comfort, bring a sleeping pad to add cushioning and insulation beneath your sleeping bag. You should also carry a lightweight stove; if nothing else, you'll need to boil your water to protect against *Giardia* (an intestinal parasite). Firewood is often a scarce item in Alaska, and what there is may be wet. Also, in keeping with the minimum-impact ethic, the burning of wood in some parklands is now frowned upon or prohibited in order to protect the habitat.

Day Pack

When setting out for a day hike from a base camp, it's wise to carry a pack stocked with a few essentials. These include a knife, preferably a multifunction pocket knife; a first-aid kit, including bandages and moleskin; a cup and spoon, on which you may wish to bang to alert bears (☞ Wildlife Viewing, *below*); a bottle of drinking water; extra candy bars or gorp (nuts and raisins); a warm shirt and windproof rain gear, in case the weather suddenly changes; waterproof matches (you can make these by coating kitchen matches with wax) and other fire starters, such as a candle or heat tab; a flare or flashlight; a topographical map; toilet paper; sunglasses; bug repellent, preferably in nonleaking stick form; duct tape, for all kinds of emergencies; and a compass.

A note about compasses: the farther north you travel, the more the compass needle will be skewed upward and to the east of north by several degrees. U.S. Geological Survey maps show this difference between magnetic and true north—called magnetic declination—at the bottom; with these maps, you can use your compass accordingly—otherwise, allow for this deviation as you do your compass reading.

Terrain

Forests

Forest trails are often wet, especially in coastal lowlands, and they may be soggy or potholed—sometimes they're even blocked with beaver dams. Trails through forested lands are difficult to maintain. The ground stays wet much of the time, and brush grows back quickly after it is cut. Especially nasty is devil's club, a large, attractive plant that is armored thickly with stinging needles. Virtually all hiking country in the Southeast is part of the 17-million-acre Tongass National Forest, administered by the U.S. Forest Service (☞ Visitor Information *in* Parks and Wildlife Refuges A to Z, *below*). Although the service does not consider trail maintenance a top priority, it is a good source for checking the latest condition of backcountry roads and paths.

Rivers

Crossing Alaska's rivers requires care. Many are swift, glacial, silty streams that are harder to read than clear-water streams. Many flow over impermeable bottoms (either rock or permafrost), which means a good rain can raise water levels a matter of feet, not inches, in just a short time. Warm days can also dramatically increase the meltwater from glaciers. Be aware of weather changes that might affect the ease of river crossings. Look for the widest, most shallow place you can find, with many channels. This may entail traveling up- or downstream. A guide who knows the region is invaluable at such times.

A sturdy staff—your own or made from a handy branch—is useful to help you keep your balance and measure the depths of silty water. You may find it easier to uncinch your pack when crossing a swift stream; you can then shed it if you need to. Avoid wearing a long rain poncho; it can catch the water like a sail catches wind and tip you off your feet. For added stability it may help for two or more people to link arms when crossing. Hikers debate the best footwear for crossing Alaskan rivers. Some take along sneakers and wear them through the water; others take off their socks so they will remain dry and can comfort cold feet on the opposite shore. But bear in mind that Alaskan waters are probably frigid, and the bottom's usually rough; bare feet are not advised. One school even advocates wearing your boots—socks and all—and continuing your hike with wet feet.

Tundra

Tundra hiking—especially in higher alpine country—can be a great pleasure. In places, the ground is so springy you feel like you're walking on a trampoline. In the Arctic, however, where the ground is underlaid with permafrost, you will probably find the going as wet as it is in the Southeast, particularly at lower elevations. The summer sun melts the top, often a thin layer above the permafrost, leaving puddles, small lakes, and marshy spots behind. Waterproof footgear is a great comfort. Tundra travel can require the skill of a ballet dancer if the ground is tufted with tussocks (mushroom-shape clumps of grass making slippery, unstable hummocks). This can quickly tire those not used to it.

Wilderness Safety

Alaska's terrain is rugged, demanding care and strength; be sure you're in good shape before venturing into backcountry.

When you're hiking in a national park, national forest, wildlife refuge, state park, or any other kind of protected, administered land, plan to check in and out with a ranger or person staffing the reserve. Be sure to leave plans and an itinerary with at least one trustworthy person before you go. Be as specific as you can about your destination and estimated date of return, and leave the names of people to call in case of an emergency.

Hypothermia—low body temperature—is an ever-present threat in Alaska's wilderness. To help avoid it, be sure to wear warm clothing (in layers) when the weather is cool and/or wet; this includes a good wind- and waterproof parka or shell, warm head- and hand gear, and waterproof boots (☞ Packing *in* the Gold Guide). Be sure to eat regularly and drink enough liquids to stay properly hydrated.

The onset of hypothermia can be recognized by the following symptoms: shivering, accelerated heartbeat, and goose bumps; this may be followed by loss of judgment, clumsiness, loss of control over bodily functions, slurred speech, disorientation, unconsciousness, and in the extreme, death. If you notice any of these symptoms in yourself—whether from overexertion, sweating (which can act as a refrigerating agent), or improper clothing—stop, light a fire, and warm yourself, using your sleeping bag if necessary; a cup of hot tea or another warm drink also helps. If your clothes are wet, change immediately. And be sure to put on a warm hat (most of the body's heat is lost through the head). If the weather is wet and/or windy, it may be necessary to set up a tent to get out of the weather. If you notice these symptoms in a traveling companion, follow the same procedure. The most important thing is to stop heat loss. If there are only two of you, stay together: a person with hypothermia should never be left alone.

Finally, Alaska's waters, even its wild rivers, often carry *Giardia,* which can cause diarrhea and sap your strength. Boil your drinking water in the Bush.

Wildlife Viewing

Alaska is one of the few places in the country where you can easily view wildlife in its natural state. It's unique among the 50 United States for its vast resource of protected wilderness, rich in birds, animals, and fish. Alaska's wild beauty adds a powerful dimension to any wildlife-viewing experience.

Alaska's 375 million acres support nearly 1,000 species of animals—mammals, birds, and fish. The 105 different mammals range from whales to shrews (Alaska's shrews are the smallest of North America's land mammals, weighing ⅒ ounce). The more than 400 species of birds range from hummingbirds to bald eagles, including species found nowhere else in North America. Migrant birds come here annually from every continent and many islands to take advantage of Alaska's rich wetlands, its rivers, its shores, and its tundras. Among the 430 different kinds of fish, there are some weighing more than 300 pounds (halibut) and others that are often less than a pound (Arctic grayling)—both greatly prized by anglers; and there are five different kinds of salmon.

The most prodigious numbers of animals can be seen during periods of migration. The state is strategically located for creatures that migrate vast distances. Some birds, for instance, fly from the southern tip of South America to nest and rear their young on sandbars in Alaska's wild rivers. Others travel from parts of Asia to enjoy an Alaskan summer. Sea mammals congregate in great numbers in the waters of Prince William Sound (some perished in the 1989 oil spill), the Panhandle, the Gulf of Alaska, and the Bering, Beaufort, and Chukchi seas. Tens of thousands of caribou move between Canada and Alaska across the Arctic slope. Anadromous fish by the millions swim up Alaska's rivers, returning unerringly to the place where they were born.

Spotting bear, moose, and other large mammals can be a highlight of a visit to Alaska. Bears live in virtually every part of the state, and though they are often solitary, it is not unusual to see a mother bear with cubs. Several world-class bear-viewing areas attract visitors, from Southeast to Southwest Alaska. Moose abound in the wetter country of the Southeast, as well as in South Central and Interior Alaska. Caribou wander over the tundra country of the Arctic, sub-Arctic, and even South Central, although there are fewer in this part of the state. The coastal mountains of the Southeast and South Central harbor wild goats, while the mountains of the South Central, Interior, and Arctic regions are home to snow-white Dall sheep, which sometimes come down to the streams in the summer. Wolves and lynx, though not so easily seen, live in many parts of the Southeast, South Central, Interior, and Arctic regions, and if you're lucky, a wolf may dash across the road in front of you, or a smaller mammal, such as the Arctic fox, may watch you when you're rafting or even when you're traveling on wheels.

Strategies for Spotting Wildlife
Know what you're looking for. Have some idea of the habitat the wildlife you seek thrives in. Season and time of day are critical. For example, you may want to view during twilight, which during summer in certain parts of Alaska can last all night. Interestingly, winter may be the best time to look for wolves because they stand out against the snow (not true for the Arctic fox, which turns white in winter). You may only have a few hours out of the day during which you can look, and in northern Alaska, there won't be any daylight at all during the winter months.

Be careful. Keep a good distance, especially with animals that can be dangerous (☞ Bears *in* the Gold Guide). Whether you're on foot or in a vehicle, don't get too close. A pair of good binoculars or a scope are well worth the extra weight. The fox you admire may be carrying rabies. Therefore, don't get too close to or touch a fox (if you're traveling with pets, keep them leashed). **Move slowly,** stop often, look, and listen. The exception is when you see a bear; you may want to let the animal know you're there. Avoid startling an animal and risking a dangerous confrontation, especially with a mother bear with cubs or a mother moose with calf. **Keep your hat on** if you are in territory where Arctic terns or pomarine jaegers nest. Both species are highly protective of their nests and young, and they are skillful dive-bombers. Occasionally, they connect with human heads, and the results can be painful.

Be prepared to wait; patience often pays off. And if you're an enthusiastic birder or animal watcher, **be prepared to hike over some rough terrain**—Alaska is full of it—to reach the best viewing vantage. And **respect and protect** both the animal you're watching and its habitat. Don't chase or harass the animals. The willful act of harassing an animal is punishable in Alaska by a $1,000 fine. This includes flushing birds from their nests and purposely frightening animals with loud noises.

Don't disturb or surprise the animals, which also applies to birds' eggs, the young, the nests, and such things as beaver dams. It's best to let the animal discover your presence quietly, if at all, by keeping still or moving slowly (except when viewing bears or moose). If the animal should be disturbed, limit your viewing time and leave as quietly as possible. **Don't use a tape recorder** to call a bird or to attract other animals if you're in bear country, as you might call an angry bear. And **don't feed the animals,** as any creature that comes to depend on humans for food almost always comes to a sorry end.

Best Viewing

Even those traveling by car in Alaska have abundant opportunity to spot wildlife. For those traveling by boat, the **Alaska Marine Highway**— the route plied by Alaska's state ferries—passes through waters rich with fish, sea mammals, and birds. Throughout the Southeast, ferries often provide sightings of whales and virtually always of bald eagles. **Kenai Fjords National Park,** a mecca for those interested in sea mammals and seabirds, provides excellent tour-boat opportunities. Smaller boats and touring vessels are found in such places as **Glacier Bay National Park,** an especially good place to spot humpback whales, puffins, seals, shorebirds, and perhaps a black or brown bear. **Denali National Park and Preserve** is known worldwide for its wildlife; visitors here are likely to see grizzlies, moose, Dall sheep, caribou, foxes, eagles, and perhaps even wolves. And the **Alaska Chilkat Bald Eagle Preserve** hosts the world's largest gathering of bald eagles each fall and winter.

BEARS

To get to **Pack Creek,** on Admiralty Island in the Southeast, fly (air charter) or take a boat from Juneau. Here you'll see brown bears (the coastal equivalents of grizzlies) fishing for spawning salmon—pink, chum, and silver. If you time your visit to coincide with the salmon runs in July and August, you will almost surely see bald eagles and flocks of gulls, too. Permits are required to visit during the peak bear-viewing period; contact **Admiralty Island National Monument** (✉ 8461 Dairy Rd., Juneau 99801, ☎ 907/586–8790).

★ The **McNeil River State Game Sanctuary,** on the Alaska Peninsula in Southwest Alaska, hosts the world's largest gathering of brown bears— as many as 70 have been counted at one time at McNeil Falls—and thus affords unsurpassed photographic opportunities. Peak season, when the local salmon are running, is early June through mid-August. Much-sought-after reservations are available by a lottery conducted in March by the Alaska Department of Fish and Game (✉ 333 Raspberry Rd., Anchorage 99518, ☎ 907/267–2182).

Katmai National Park (✉ Box 7, King Salmon 99613, ☎ 907/246–3305), also on the Alaska Peninsula, has an abundance of bears. In July, when the salmon are running up Brooks River, bears concentrate around Brooks River Falls, resulting in a great view of these animals as they fish, and the spectacle of hundreds of salmon leaping the falls.

You can't be absolutely sure you'll spot a grizzly bear in **Denali National Park** (✉ Box 9, Denali National Park, 99755, ☎ 907/683–2294), but your chances are good. Talk with the staff at the visitor center near the park entrance when you arrive.

Another excellent place to see brown bears is the **Kodiak National Wildlife Refuge,** on Kodiak Island. Contact the refuge headquarters (✉ 1390 Buskin Rd., Kodiak 99615, ☎ 907/487–2600).

BIRDS

If you come on your own, try the following sure and easily accessed bets. In **Anchorage,** walk around **Potters Marsh, Westchester Lagoon,** or along the **Coastal Trail** for shorebirds and waterfowl. The **Anchorage Audubon Society** has a bird-report recording (☎ 907/338–2473). In **Juneau,** visit the **Mendenhall Wetlands State Game Refuge,** next to the airport, for ducks, geese, and swans (there are trails and interpretive signs). In **Fairbanks,** head for the **Creamer's Field Migratory Waterfowl Refuge** on College Road. Here, if you're lucky, you might see sandhill cranes in summer and spectacular shows of ducks and geese in spring.

Great crowds of bald eagles visit the Chilkat River, near **Haines** in Southeast Alaska, each November and December. In the summer, rafting on almost any Alaskan river brings the near certainty of sighting nesting shorebirds, Arctic terns, and merganser mothers trailed by chicks. Approximately 200 species of birds have been sighted on the Pribilofs (☞ Marine Animals, *below*), but you will almost certainly need to be part of a guided tour to get there.

CARIBOU

The migrations of caribou across Alaska's Arctic regions are wonderful to watch, but they are not always easy to time. The U.S. Fish and Wildlife Service and Alaska Department of Fish and Game (☞ Visitor Information *in* Parks and Wildlife Refuges A to Z, *below*) will have the best guess as to where you should be and when. Or you can settle for seeing a few caribou in places such as Denali National Park.

MARINE ANIMALS

At **Round Island,** outside Dillingham in the Southwest, bull walruses by the thousands haul out during the summer, providing a sight unique in the world. Part of the Walrus Islands State Game Sanctuary, Round Island can be visited by permit only. For details, contact the Alaska Department of Fish and Game (✉ Box 1030, Dillingham 99576, ☎ 907/842–1013). Access is by floatplane or, more commonly, by boat. Expect rain, winds, and the possibility of being weathered in. Rubber boots are essential, as are a high-quality four-season tent and plenty of food.

It's easier, but still expensive, to visit the remote **Pribilof Islands**—where about 80% of the world's northern fur seals and 200 species of birds can be seen—but you also may encounter fog and Bering Sea storms. Tours to the Pribilofs leave from Anchorage. Contact the Alaska Maritime National Wildlife Refuge (✉ 2355 Kachemak Bay Dr., Suite 101, Homer 99603-8021, ☎ 907/235–6546 or 907/235–6961) for information.

ADVENTURE VACATIONS

A vacation to Alaska can be a lot more than viewing glaciers—visitors are taking advantage of the increasing number of trips and sports tours that make it possible for ordinary folks to spend a week or two (or three) learning—and performing—feats they've only fantasized about, from horsepacking within sight of Mount McKinley to mushing through some of the state's most challenging landscapes, including Gates of the Arctic National Park. Below you'll find some recommended trips, as well as a checklist of questions to help you choose the right program. When comparing offerings, be sure to ask the following questions:

How much of a deposit is required, and when is the balance due? To reserve a spot, most operators require you to put down a deposit by a particular day and then pay the rest sometime before the starting date.

What is the cancellation policy? In most cases, if you cancel your reservation, you get at least a partial refund, but policies vary widely. Find out how far in advance you must cancel to get a full refund, and ask whether any allowances are made for cancellations due to medical emergencies. If cancellation insurance is available, take it. You'll receive a full refund regardless of why you don't show up as planned.

Are taxes and tips included in the cost? Taxes are generally not included in the quoted price and they can add substantially to the cost of your trip. Depending on the program, you should also ask about gratuities—inquire about which members of the tour personnel customarily get tipped and what the average rate is.

Dogsledding

"Hike!" commands a musher as he releases a brake. They don't call it "mushing" for nothing. The word is from the French _moucher,_ which means "to go fast." And the dogs do. On command, a team of surprisingly small but amazingly strong huskies charge off, howling and yowling excitedly. Of all the wild sporting adventures out there, dogsledding may be the wildest—not only because it's exotic, but because you're literally out in the wilds with pack animals, just like a polar explorer.

Dogsledding is not for everyone. For one thing, you have to like the cold. You also have to like roughing it. Even the nicest accommodations are only a step or two removed from camping, and with camping out comes cooking out. Most importantly, you have to like dogs—a lot. Contrary to the romantic image you may have of sled dogs, they're not all cuddly, clean Siberian huskies. They're often mutts, and often not particularly well-groomed. Here are some questions to ask when choosing your trip:

Will I be driving my own team of dogs? On some mushing trips, participants travel by cross-country skiing or snowshoeing, rather than actually mushing, for at least part of the trip; some introduction to these sports is usually included in your orientation. If you're not interested in skiing or snowshoeing, make sure you'll be given a sled.

How many miles are covered each day? Get a good idea of how strenuous the outfitter's pace is.

What will be my responsibilities on the trip? If you're expecting a relaxing vacation, make sure you don't pick an outfitter who'll have you doing everything from hitching up the dogs to pitching tents.

Outfitters
Far North Tours. Visitors are taken to a musher's kennel for a tour, some background on the history of mushing in Alaska, and instruction on basic techniques. In most cases, participants sit in the sled basket, but they may be given an opportunity to actually drive a sled if they wish and conditions permit. The tours, which include a half-hour sled ride,

last six hours. There is a four-person minimum. ⊠ *Box 102873, Anchorage 99510,* ☎ *907/272–7480 or 800/478–7480,* 𝔽𝔸𝕏 *907/276–6951.*

Redington Sled Dog Rides. Founding father of the Iditarod Trail Sled Dog Race, Joe Redington Sr., and his crew of mushers and dog handlers offer expeditions up the historic Iditarod Trail as well as shorter rides and sled-dog trips into the backcountry. ⊠ *Mile 12.5 Knik Rd., HC30, Box 5440, Wasilla 99654,* ☎ *907/376–5662 or 907/376–6730.*

Sourdough Outfitters. This company offers six- and eight-day sledding trips from January through mid-April through the Gates of the Arctic National Park, one of the last great wilderness areas in the world. They provide all camping gear plus special boots, heavy-hooded parkas, insulated windproof mittens, and snowshoes. ⊠ *Box 90, Bettles 99726,* ☎ *907/692–5252,* 𝔽𝔸𝕏 *907/692–5612.*

Horsepacking

There are no traffic jams and no overcrowded campgrounds on horsepacking vacations. The farther into the wilderness you go, the more untouched and spectacular the landscape usually is. You can also cover a lot more ground with less effort than you can while backpacking. All outfitters who operate on federal lands are required to have a permit. If you strike out on your own, make sure that the outfitter you with does. Here is a list of questions to help you decide which trip is right for you:

How large is the group and how many guides are there? To minimize a horsepacking group's impact on the environment, most are limited to 12 riders. Some go down to just three or four. Most outfits post at least two wranglers for 12 guests, and some bring along another person who serves as cook and/or assistant wrangler.

How much time is spent in the saddle each day and how difficult is the riding? Six hours is a long day in the saddle, and although some outfitters schedule that much, most keep the riding time to about four hours. Most trips move at a walk, and there may be varying opportunities to trot, lope, and even gallop.

What are the meals and accommodations like? On trips into the wilderness, the food is generally straightforward cowboy fare, cooked over a campfire or cookstove. Although a cook goes along on some trips, guides often pull double duty in the kitchen, and often a little help from group members is willingly accepted. If you have any dietary restrictions, make arrangements beforehand. And as far as lodging is concerned, don't allow yourself to be surprised: find out what the rooms are like if you're going to be staying in motels or cabins, and if the trip involves camping, ask about the campsites and about shower and latrine arrangements.

Outfitters

American Wilderness Experience. An orientation dinner kicks off this five-day adventure in the foothills east of Denali National Park, home to Mount McKinley. Riding starts 22 mi south of the park headquarters and, weather permitting, you get breathtaking views of the country's tallest peak on the first and last day of the trip. ⊠ *Box 1486, Boulder, CO 80306,* ☎ *303/444–2622 or 800/444–0099,* 𝔽𝔸𝕏 *303/444–3999.*

Sea Kayaking

One of the country's fastest-growing sports, sea kayaking can be as thrilling or as peaceful as you make it. More stable than a white-water kayak and more comfortable than a canoe, a sea kayak—even one loaded with a week's worth of gear—is maneuverable enough to poke into hidden crevices, explore side bays, and beach on deserted spits of sand.

Anyone who doesn't mind getting a little wet and has an average degree of fitness can be a sea kayaker. The basic stroke is a surprisingly easy push-me pull-you done with a double-bladed paddle; most people pick it up with a minimal amount of instruction. Don't assume, though, that if you've done 10 minutes without tipping over you'll be adequately prepared to circumnavigate Glacier Bay National Park. There's a lot to learn, and until you know your way around tides, currents, and nautical charts, you should go with an experienced guide who also knows what and how to pack and where to pitch a tent. A reputable outfitter can supply such a guide.

In choosing an outfitter, your primary concern should be safety. An outfitter should be equipped with both the proper technical and first-aid gear, and should know what to do with them. Question every outfitter carefully so that you know what you're getting into:

How long have the guides been leading trips and how long have they been leading in the area where I want to go? Generally it is best to have a guide who knows an area very well. A qualified guide's first visit to an area can also be exciting, but *only if* that guide has had extensive experience elsewhere.

What is the weather likely to be? It is important for you to honestly evaluate your own tolerance for cold, dampness, and high winds. Nothing can ruin a trip faster than pervasive discomfort.

What kind of boats are used? Ask whether the outfitter stocks a variety of boats, so you can experiment until you find the kayak that best fits your weight, strength, ability, and paddling style.

Outfitters

Alaska Discovery. One of Alaska's oldest outfitters, this company has been running low-impact, nature-oriented adventure tourism since 1972. Experienced guides know Southeast Alaska intimately, and they emphasize both sea-kayaking skills and safety in their instruction. Destinations include Glacier Bay, Icy Bay, Russell Fjord, and Granite Fjord. ✉ *5449 Shaune Dr., Suite 4, Juneau 99801,* ☎ *907/780–6226 or 800/586–1911,* ℻ *907/780–4220.*

Spirit Walker Expeditions, Inc. This veteran Southeast company offers guided wilderness sea kayaking trips that combine a mix of scenery, wildlife, solitude, and paddling within the Inside Passage. Guides prepare meals, offer instruction, and provide all needed paddling gear. Beginners are welcome. ✉ *Box 240, Gustavus 99826,* ☎ *907/697–2266 or 800/529–2537,* ℻ *907/697–2701.*

Sunny Cove Sea Kayaking Company. Weeklong trips in and around Kenai Fjords National Park in Southcentral Alaska include five nights of camping at Northwestern Fjord, where kayakers can paddle among icebergs, seals, and seabirds as tidewater glaciers calve in the distance. Tours include kayaking equipment and instruction, gourmet camping meals, and lots of chances to see wildlife. ✉ *Box 111283, Anchorage 99511,* ☎ ℻ *907/345–5339.*

Wavetamer Kayaking. Based in Kodiak, in Southwest Alaska, Wavetamer offers guided expeditions around the Kodiak Archipelago and also arranges custom bear-viewing/kayaking tours along the Katmai National Park coast. Both gear and instruction are provided and group sizes are kept small, for minimal environmental impact (typically four to eight people). ✉ *Box 228, Kodiak 99615,* ☎ 📠 *907/486–2604.*

Whale-Watching Cruises

A close encounter with whales in their natural environment can be a thrilling experience. Hearing the resonant whoosh of a cetacean exhaling and witnessing such acrobatics as "spy-hopping" (a whale poking its head straight out of the water for a look around), breaching, and skimming, you can't help but feel their awesome presence.

It's possible to see whales along much of Alaska's coast during the spring and summer months: from the Inside Passage to Prince William Sound, the Kodiak Archipelago, and Kenai Fjords National Park in the South Central region and then north through the Bering, Chukchi, and Beaufort seas, in Arctic waters. A wide variety of whales can be observed, though those most commonly seen on whale-watching trips are killer whales, or orcas, and humpbacks.

Because whales migrate, whale-watching is a seasonal activity. The peak in Alaska waters is June through August—fortunately that's also when most people are visiting the state.

Whale-watching is not the average spectator sport. It's more like a seagoing game of hide-and-seek. Whales are unpredictable, so be prepared to wait and watch patiently, scanning the water for signs. Sometimes it seems that the whales don't want to be watched; other times they might rub up against the boat. Also unpredictable are the weather and sea conditions. You can get wet and chilled, and some people get seasick.

Here are some questions to help determine if a given cruise is right for you:

Which or how many species are likely to be seen? Most cruises travel in or through waters that attract several species, although some focus on a particular type of whale.

What is the best time to take this trip? If you ask, you may find out that the sighting record is better during some months than others.

What kind of boat is used and how many passengers does it carry? You have to weigh the pros and cons of traveling on small vs. large boats. Make sure you know what kind of boat is used for the trip you are considering. A trip with 15 people is certain to be quite different from one with 150.

Tour Companies

Kenai Fjords Tours offers a wide variety of tours into Resurrection Bay and Kenai Fjords National Park in South Central Alaska. They range from three-hour natural history tours to five-hour gray whale–watching tours (April 1 to mid-May only) and full-day cruises to Aialik Bay or Northwestern Fjord. Prime-time whale watching for orcas and humpbacks is June through August. Most of the company's boats are 75 to 95 ft long, with room for 90 to 149 passengers, but it also has a smaller vessel with a 22-passenger limit. ✉ *Box 1889, Seward 99664,* ☎ *907/224–8068 or 800/478–8068.*

Mariah Tours offers the "small-boat alternative" for whale-watching and glacier tours of Kenai Fjords National Park. Their two boats carry no more than 16 passengers each. Mariah runs 8- to 9 ½-hour tours to Aialik Bay and Northwestern Fjord, respectively, from May 1 through September 15. Besides killer and humpback whales, wildlife watchers are likely to see bald eagles, sea otters, sea lions, seals, and thousands of seabirds. ⊠ *Box 1309, Seward 99664,* ☎ *907/224–8623 or 800/270–1238,* ℻ *907/224–8625.*

The **Spirit of Adventure** operates daily trips into Glacier Bay National Park from the dock at Bartlett Cove, near Glacier Bay Lodge. Watching for whales, as well as calving glaciers, is part of the daily routine. Uniformed Park Service naturalists provide local expertise. ⊠ *Bartlett Cove, Box 199, Gustavus 99826, or* ⊠ *520 Pike Tower, Suite 1400, Seattle, WA 98101,* ☎ *907/697–2226 in summer or 800/451-5952,* ℻ *206/623–7809.*

EXPLORING

Choosing where to find adventure in Alaska is as challenging as deciding what to do when you get there. From the Southeast's deep green forests shrouded in curling mists to the golden tundra of the Arctic, from the spruce-lined fjords of the Kenai Peninsula to the joyful streams and meadows of the Interior, many worlds await you. (For more information on the features of each region, *see* Chapters 4–8.)

Southeast

Southeast Alaska (☞ Chapter 4) is a special place of its own, separated from the rest of the state geographically. It's a land not only of high, snowy mountains but also of lush, dark forests and islands at the edge of the sea. This is a place where bald eagles soar overhead, where whales and porpoises glide through the waterways, and where salmon crowd the crystal streams. In the Southeast, you can walk on a glacier and look over one of the continent's last great ice fields. You can explore a muskeg (bog), with its mysterious carnivorous plants, such as the sundew. You can marvel at the slender, silvery waterfalls running down dark, shining cliffs. Alaska "blue days," with their clear, luminous skies, have special meaning here because of their relative infrequency and extraordinary beauty.

In summer the Forest Service sends rangers on the cruise ships and larger state ferries that ply the Marine Highway. The rangers are knowledgeable sources for travelers who want to know more details about the Tongass Forest and the Southeast in general.

Chilkat State Park

Chilkat State Park (⊠ Box 430, Haines 99827, ☎ 907/766–2292) on the Chilkat Inlet in Haines has beautiful and accessible viewing of both the Davidson and Rainbow glaciers. It also has public campgrounds, good if you're traveling the Haines Highway en route to the ferry down the Inside Passage. The Chilkat Valley near Haines is also home to the largest concentration of bald eagles in the world; thousands come to feast on the late run of salmon in the clear, ice-free waters of the Chilkat River, heated by underground warm springs. November and December are the best months for viewing, but a couple hundred eagles reside in the area year-round. The Alaska Division of Parks administers the 49,000-acre **Alaska Chilkat Bald Eagle Preserve,** which protects this unique wildlife resource.

CAMPING

$ ⚠ **Alaska State Parks Campgrounds.** The state maintains four campgrounds (Mosquito Lake, Chilkoot Lake, Portage Cove, and Chilkat) in the Haines area, with a total of 86 camping sites. All four have drinking water, toilets, and fishing opportunities, and all but Mosquito Lake have picnic sites. Length of stay ranges from seven to 15 days.

✉ *Alaska Division of Parks, Haines District Office, Box 430, Haines 99827,* ☎ *907/766–2292. No reservations. No credit cards. Closed in winter.*

GUIDED TOURS

Alaska Cross-Country Guiding and Rafting (☎ FAX 907/767–5522) offers cabin-based fly-in, raft-out trips down the Tsirku River through the Alaska Chilkat Bald Eagle Preserve, plus photo trips to the eagle preserve for small groups only, as well as wilderness backpacking, glacier hiking, and fly-in trips to remote cabins. **Alaska Nature Tours and Backcountry Outfitters** (☎ 907/766–2876, FAX 907/766–2844) conducts bird-watching and natural-history tours through the Alaska Chilkat Bald Eagle Preserve and leads hiking treks in summer and ski tours in winter.

Chilkoot Trail

If you're a strong and experienced backpacker who likes a challenge, you might want to hike the highly scenic, historic Chilkoot Trail, route of the 1897 Gold Rush sourdoughs, from Skagway into Canada. The 41-mi trip can be done in as little as two days, but most hikers will need five to six. Expect steep slopes and muddy, potholed trails, along with exhilarating vistas at the summit over the very different Canadian landscape.

The trail reaches from Dyea to Lake Lindeman and includes a climb up Chilkoot Pass at the United States–Canada border. The National Park Service maintains the American side of the pass as part of the **Klondike Gold Rush National Historical Park.** The trail is good; the forest, mountain, and lake country is both scenic and richly historic, and primitive campsites are strategically located along the way.

The Chilkoot is not, however, an easy walk. There are lots of ups and downs before you cross the pass and reach the Canadian high country, and rain is a distinct possibility. To return to Skagway, hikers must follow a cutoff to **Log Cabin,** on the Klondike Highway. There they can either hitchhike back to town or flag down Gray Line of Alaska's Alaskon Express motor coach (☎ 800/544–2206), fare $22 from Log Cabin, heading south to Skagway from Whitehorse. Or if parties have two cars, they can leave one at Log Cabin for the drive back to Skagway.

For the thousands who complete the hike each year, it is the highlight of a trip to the North Country. For details, maps, and references contact the Klondike Gold Rush National Historical Park visitor center (✉ 2nd Ave. and Broadway, Box 517, Skagway 99840, ☎ 907/983–2921).

Glacier Bay National Park and Preserve

★ **Glacier Bay National Park and Preserve** (✉ 1 Park Rd., Box 140, Gustavus 99826, ☎ 907/697–2230) is one of the jewels of the entire national park system. Visiting Glacier Bay is like discovering the Little Ice Age. It is one of the few places in the world where you can come within inches—depending on your mode of transportation—of 10 tidewater glaciers, which have their base at the water's edge. (Such close proximity is not recommended, however, because of the dangers involved when chunks of the glaciers break off.) They line the 65 mi of narrow fjords at the northern end of the Inside Passage and rise up to 7,000 ft above the bay. With a noise that sounds like cannons firing, bergs the size of 10-story office buildings sometimes come crashing from the "snout" of a glacier. The crash sends tons of water and spray skyward, and it propels mini–tidal waves outward from the point of impact. **Johns Hopkins Glacier** calves so often and with such volume that the large cruise ships can seldom come within 2 mi of its face.

Glacier Bay

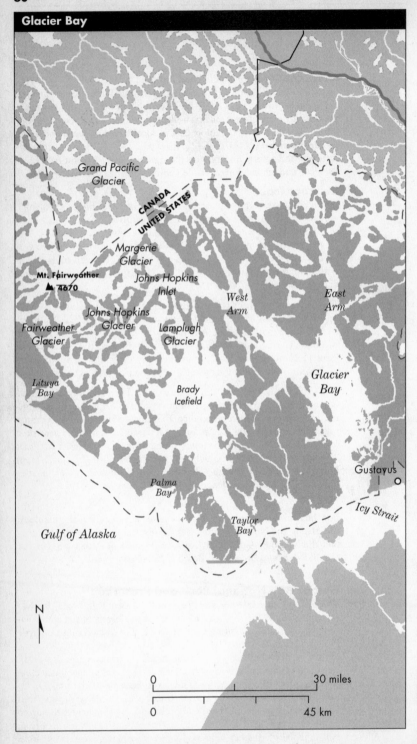

Grand Pacific
Glacier

CANADA
UNITED STATES

Margerie
Glacier

Mt. Fairweather
▲ 4670

Johns Hopkins
Inlet

West
Arm

East
Arm

Johns Hopkins
Glacier

Fairweather
Glacier

Lamplugh
Glacier

Lituya
Bay

Brady
Icefield

Glacier
Bay

Gustavus

Palma
Bay

Icy Strait

Gulf of Alaska

Taylor
Bay

N

0   30 miles

0   45 km

Glacier Bay is a recently formed (and still forming) body of water fed by the runoff of the ice fields, glaciers, and mountains that surround it. Captain James Cook and then Captain George Vancouver sailed by Glacier Bay and didn't even know it. At the time of Vancouver's sailing in 1794, the bay was hidden behind and beneath a vast glacial wall of ice. The glacier face was more than 20 mi across and in places, more than 4,000 ft in depth. It extended more than 100 mi to its origins in the St. Elias Mountain Range. Since then, due to warming weather and other factors not fully understood, the face of the glacial ice has melted and retreated with amazing speed, exposing 65 mi of fjords, islands, and inlets.

It was Vancouver who named the magnificent snow-clad **Mt. Fairweather** that towers over the head of the bay; popular legend says Vancouver named Fairweather on one of the Southeast's most beautiful blue days—and the mountain was not seen again during the following century! An exaggeration, to be sure, but overcast, rainy weather is certainly the norm here.

In 1879, about a century after Vancouver's sail-by, one of the earliest white visitors to what is now Glacier Bay National Park and Preserve came calling. He was naturalist John Muir, both drawn by the flora and fauna that had followed in the wake of glacial withdrawals and fascinated by the vast ice rivers that descended from the mountains to tidewater. Today, the naturalist's namesake glacier, like others in the park, continues to retreat dramatically. Its terminus is now scores of miles farther up the bay from the small cabin he built at its face during his time there.

Glacier Bay is a marvelous laboratory for naturalists of all persuasions. Glaciologists, of course, can have a field day; animal lovers can hope to see the rare glacial "blue" bears of the area (a variation of the black bear, which is here along with the brown bear), whales feasting on krill, mountain goats (in late spring and early summer), and seals on floating icebergs. Birders can look for the more than 200 species that have already been spotted in the park (if you're lucky, you may witness two bald eagles engaging in aerobatics).

A remarkable panorama of plants unfolds from the head of the bay, which is just emerging from the ice, to the mouth, which has been ice free for more than 200 years. In between, the primitive plants—algae, lichens, and mosses—that are the first to take hold of the bare, wet ground give way to more complex species: flowering plants such as the magenta dwarf fireweed and the creamy dryas, which in turn merge with willows, alders, and cottonwood. As the living plants mature and die, they enrich the soil and prepare it for new species to follow. The climax of the plant community is the lush spruce-and-hemlock rain forest, rich in life and blanketing the land around **Bartlett Cove.**

As you sail farther into the great bay, the conifers become noticeably smaller, and they are finally replaced by alders and other leafy species that took root and began growing only a few decades ago. Finally, deep into the bay where the glaciers have withdrawn in very recent years, the shorelines contain only plants and primitive lichens. Given enough time, however, these lands, too, will be covered with the same towering forests that you see at the bay's entrance.

For airborne visitors, **Gustavus,** 50 mi west of Juneau and 75 mi south of Skagway, is the gateway to Glacier Bay National Park. The long, paved jet airport, built as a refueling strip during World War II, is one of the best and longest in Southeast Alaska, all the more impressive because facilities at the field are so limited. Alaska Airlines, which serves

Gustavus daily in the summer, has a large, rustic terminal at the site, and from a free telephone on the front porch of the terminal, you can call any of the local hostelries for a courtesy pickup. Smaller light-aircraft companies that serve the community out of Juneau also have on-site shelters.

Gustavus has no downtown. In fact, Gustavus is not a town at all. The 150 or so year-round residents are most emphatic on this point; they regularly vote down incorporation. Instead, Gustavus is a scattering of homes, farmsteads, arts-and-crafts studios, fishing and guiding charters, and other tiny enterprises peopled by hospitable individualists. It is, in many ways, a contemporary exemplar of the frontier spirit in Alaska.

DINING AND LODGING

$–$$ ✕ **Strawberry Point Cafe.** There's nothing fancy here, just good wholesome cooking that features locally caught seafood, from Dungeness crab to king salmon and shrimp. Alaskan antiques and knickknacks, such as an eclectic bottle collection, enhance this small, homey establishment. Friday night is pizza night. ⊠ *On the dock road,* ☎ *907/697–2227. AE, D, DC, MC, V. Closed in winter.*

$$$$ ✕▦ **Glacier Bay Country Inn.** This picturesque rambling log structure
★ with marvelous cupolas, dormers, gables, and porches was built from local hand-logged timbers yet has modern amenities. Some rooms have antiques and open log-beam ceilings; all have views of the Chilkat Mountains' rain forest and a mountain-modern ambience. Innkeepers Ponch and Sandi Marchbanks will arrange sightseeing and flightseeing tours. They also charter their three boats, each of which sleeps four to six, into Glacier Bay and nearby waters. Theirs is a gourmet kitchen, with foods fresh from the sea and the inn's own garden; reservations are essential, and dinners cost about $24. Among guests' favorites: steamed Dungeness crab, homemade fettuccine, and rhubarb custard pie. Bears and moose might peek in at you from the hay fields. Meals are included in the room rate. ⊠ *Halfway between airport and Bartlett Cove, Box 5, Gustavus 99826,* ☎ *907/697–2288 or 800/628–0912,* ℻ *907/697–2289. 6 rooms with private bath, 4 cabins with private bath. Restaurant, travel services. AE, MC, V. Closed Oct.–Mar..*

$$$$ ✕▦ **Glacier Bay Lodge.** The lodge, the only one within the national park, is constructed of massive timbers and blends well into the thick rain forest surrounding it on three sides. The modern yet rustic rooms (no televisions) are accessible by boardwalks; some have views of Bartlett Cove. If it swims or crawls in the sea hereabouts, you'll find it on the menu in the rustic dining room, which has a water view. A guest favorite is the halibut baked *aleyeska,* a fillet baked in a rich sauce of sour cream, cheese, and onions. Activities include whale-watching, kayaking, and naturalist-led hikes; excursions up the bay leave from the dock out front. ⊠ *Bartlett Cove, Box 199, Gustavus 99826, or* ⊠ *520 Pike Tower, Suite 1400, Seattle, WA 98101,* ☎ *907/697–2226 in summer or 800/451-5952,* ℻ *206/623–7809. 56 rooms. Restaurant, travel services. AE, DC, MC, V. Closed Oct.–Mar.*

$$$$ ▦ **Bear Track Inn.** Built in 1997 of handcrafted spruce logs shipped in from British Columbia (all are from 120 to 150 years old), this family-owned and operated inn sits on a 17-acre property facing majestic Icy Strait. The centerpiece of the inn's soaring 30-ft lobby is the open walk-around fireplace; comfortable overstuffed couches, rustic wooden tables, and moose-antler chandeliers add to the warmth of this space. Forest-green drapes and carpeting complement the pine paneling in the spacious guest rooms, all of which have queen-size beds, a table and chairs, and a large armoire. In addition to offering such local specialties as Dungeness crab, Alaskan spotted prawns, or salmon in parchment, the full-service dining room each night presents guests with a selection of steak, halibut, and salmon fillets. The knowledgable staff will help you design your own customized itinerary of outdoor activities from a long list of options that includes fresh- and salt-water fishing, kayaking, whale-watching, flightseeing and helicopter tours, glacier and wildlife tours, hiking, biking, and golf. The room rate (packages range from one to seven nights) includes air or ferry transportation from Juneau, ground transportation, and meals. ⊠ *255 Rink Creek Rd., Gustavus 99826,* ☎ *907/697–3017 or 888/697–2284,* FAX *907/697–2284. 14 rooms with bath. Restaurant, travel services, airport shuttle. AE, MC, V. Closed Oct.–Apr.*

$$$$ ⊞ **Gustavus Inn.** Built in 1928 and established as an inn in 1965, Gus-
★ tavus Inn continues a tradition of gracious Alaska rural living. In the remodeled original homestead building, rooms are decorated in New England farmhouse–style. Glacier trips, fishing expeditions, bicycle rides around the community, and berry picking in season are offered here. Many guests, however, prefer to do nothing but enjoy the inn's tranquillity and its notable family-style meals. Hosts David and Jo Ann Lesh heap bountiful servings of seafood and fresh vegetables on the plates of overnight guests and others who reserve in advance. The farmhouse-style dining room is down-home cozy; dinnertime is 6:30 sharp. ⊠ *Mile 1, Gustavus Rd., Box 60, Gustavus 99826,* ☎ *907/697–2254 or 800/ 649–5220,* FAX *907/697–2255; in winter,* ☎ *913/649–5220,* FAX *913/ 649–5220. 11 rooms with bath, 2 rooms share bath. Restaurant, travel services, airport shuttle. AE, MC, V. Closed in winter.*

$$–$$$$ ⊞ **Puffin Bed & Breakfast.** These attractive cabins are in a wooded homestead and are decorated with Alaskan crafts. There's also a main lodge with a social area and kitchen for the guests. A full breakfast is included. The owners also operate Puffin Travel for fishing, kayaking, sightseeing charters, and Glacier Bay cruises. There's also a two-bedroom house for rent that's not part of the B&B. ⊠ *¼-mi off of Wilson Rd., Box 3, Gustavus 99826,* ☎ *907/697–2260,* FAX *907/697–2258. 4 cabins, 3 with attached bath. Travel services, airport shuttle. No credit cards. Closed in winter.*

GUIDED TOURS

Glacier Bay is best experienced from the water, whether from the deck of a cruise ship, on a tour boat, or from the level of a kayak. For a list of cruise ships offering trips to Glacier Bay, *see* Chapter 2. During the several hours the ships are in the bay, National Park Service naturalists come aboard to explain the great glaciers, to point out features of the forests, islands, and mountains, and to help spot black bears, brown bears, mountain goats, whales, porpoises, and the countless species of birds that call the area home.

The boat *Spirit of Adventure,* which operates daily from the dock at Bartlett Cove, near Glacier Bay Lodge (☎ 800/451–5952), is smaller than the cruise ships but also has uniformed Park Service naturalists aboard.

Gray Line of Alaska (☎ 907/983–2241 in summer, or 800/544–2206, FAX 907/983–2087) offers Glacier Bay flightseeing tours.

OUTDOOR ACTIVITIES AND SPORTS

The most adventurous way to explore Glacier Bay is by paddling your own kayak through the bay's icy waters and inlets. But unless you really know what you're doing, you're better off signing on with the guided tours. You can book one of **Alaska Discovery**'s (⊠ 5449 Shaune Dr., Suite 4, Juneau 99801, ☎ 907/780–6226 or 800/586–1911) eight-day guided expeditions. Alaska Discovery provides safe, seaworthy kayaks and tents, gear, and food. Its guides are tough, knowledgeable Alaskans, and they've spent enough time in Glacier Bay's wild country to know what's safe and what's not. Kayak rentals for unescorted Glacier Bay exploring and camping can be arranged through **Glacier Bay Sea Kayaks** (✉ Bartlett Cove, Box 26, Gustavus 99826, ☎ 907/697–2257). Twice a day, at 9 AM and 5 PM, its experienced kayakers give orientations on handling the craft plus camping and routing suggestions. The company will also make reservations aboard the regular day boat so that kayakers can be dropped off and picked up in the most scenic country. **Sea Otter Kayak Glacier Bay** (✉ Dock Rd., Box 228, Gustavus 99826, ☎ 907/697–3007) rents kayaks, gives instructions on their use, and supplies essentials like rubber boots, life jackets, maps, and tide tables.

Tongass National Forest

The country's largest national forest, the Tongass (✉ Centennial Hall, 101 Egan Dr., Juneau 99801, ☎ 907/586–8751) stretches the length of Alaska's Panhandle and encompasses nearly 17 million acres, or three-fourths of the Southeast region. Much of the forest is covered by old-growth, temperate rain forest, but it also includes rugged mountains, steep fjords, glaciers, and ice fields within its boundaries. Its lands and waters are home to a wide variety of animals: black and brown bears, bald eagles, Sitka black-tailed deer, mountain goats, wolves, marine mammals and dozens of sea- and shorebird species. Two national monuments within its borders are especially popular with visitors (☞ *below*).

Admiralty Island National Monument (✉ 8461 Old Dairy Rd., Juneau 99801, ☎ 907/586–8790) offers breathtaking vistas when viewed up close in small boats. Admiralty Island is best known as one of North America's richest brown-bear habitats. The island's earliest inhabitants called it Kootznoowoo, meaning "fortress of the bears." Ninety-six miles long, with 678 mi of coastline, Admiralty (the second-largest island in the Southeast) is home to an estimated 1,500 bears, or almost one per square mile. Since 1980 more than 90% of Admiralty's 1 million acres has been preserved as Kootznoowoo Wilderness, within Admiralty Island National Monument. Among its chief attractions is **Pack Creek,** where visitors can watch brown bears feed on salmon. One of Alaska's premier brown-bear viewing sites, Pack Creek is comanaged by the Forest Service and the Alaska Department of Fish and Game. Permits are required during the main viewing season, from June 1 through September 10, and only 24 people per day are allowed to visit Pack Creek from July 5 through August 25. Reservations are available through the monument office beginning March 1.

The monument also has a system of public-use cabins, a popular canoe route, the world's highest density of nesting bald eagles, and some of the region's best sea kayaking and sportfishing.

Misty Fjords National Monument (✉ 3031 Tongass Ave., Ketchikan 99901, ☎ 907/225–2148) is a wilderness of steep-walled fjords, mountains, and islands with an abundance of spectacular coastal scenery, wildlife, and recreational opportunities. Like Admiralty Island, Misty Fjords offers breathtaking vistas when viewed up close in small boats. Travel on these waters can be an almost mystical experience, with the greens of the forest reflected in waters as still as black mirrors. You may find yourself in the company of a whale, see a bear fishing for salmon along the shore, or even pull in your own salmon for an evening meal.

GUIDED TOURS

Alaska Cruises (☎ 907/225–6044 or 800/228–1905 for a free brochure, FAX 907/247–3498) provides cruise or fly-cruise one-day excursions from downtown Ketchikan to Misty Fjords. Boat transport for kayakers is offered to and from Misty Fjords. **Alaska Discovery** (☎ 800/586–1911 or 907/780–6226, FAX 907/780–4220) organizes canoeing, sea kayaking, and wildlife-viewing trips within Tongass National Forest and explores both Admiralty Island and Misty Fjords. **Alaska Sightseeing/ Cruise West** (☎ 206/441–8687 or 800/426–7702) offers boat tours of Misty Fjords.

LODGING AND CAMPING

$$$$ ▣ **Thayer Lake Lodge.** One of Southeast Alaska's pioneer lodges, Thayer Lake is on private land within Admiralty Island National Monument, near Juneau. Bob and Edith Nelson built this small, rustic lodge-and-cabins operation, which houses up to 10 people, after World War II. They did it mostly with their own labor, using local timber for their buildings. Lake fishing is unsurpassed for cutthroat and Dolly Varden trout (though they're not overly large). Canoes and motorboats are available for guests who want to explore the 9-mi-long lake, which laps the sandy beach fronting the lodge. Simple family-style meals are available at the lodge. Rates vary, depending on whether people cook their own meals or eat at the lodge. Travel/lodging packages, including guided trips to Pack Creek, can be arranged. ⊠ *Box 8897 or Box 5416, Ketchikan 99901,* ☎ *907/247–8897 or 907/225–3343,* FAX *907/247–7053. 2 cabins. Dining room, kitchens, hiking, boating, fishing. No credit cards. Closed mid-Sept.–May.*

$ ▣ **U.S. Forest Service Cabins.** Scattered throughout Tongass National Forest, these rustic cabins offer a charming and cheap escape. Most cabins have oil- or wood-burning stoves and bunk beds, but no electricity or running water. Bedside reading in most cabins includes a diary kept by visitors. Add your own adventure. Reservations may be made up to 180 days in advance in person or by mail. ⊠ *U.S. Forest Service Information Center, Centennial Hall, 101 Egan Dr., Juneau 99801,* ☎ *907/586–8751. 150 cabins. No credit cards.*

$ ⛺ **U.S. Forest Service Campgrounds.** Eight Forest Service–maintained campgrounds are scattered through the Tongass Forest; all are accessible from Southeast communities (Juneau, Sitka, Ketchikan, and Petersburg). All have toilets and sites for RVs and tents, but not all provide drinking water. Sites may be reserved in advance at four of the campgrounds (Mendenhall, Starrigaven, Last Chance, and Signal Creek). ⊠ *U.S. Forest Service Information Center, 101 Egan Dr., Juneau 99801,* ☎ *907/586–8751 or 800/280–2267 for reservations. D, MC, V.*

South Central

Anchorage is the gateway to some of Alaska's most spectacular parks and wilderness areas. The city lies near the convergence of two of Alaska's most magnificent mountain systems. To the east of the city and sweeping on to the southwest are the Chugach Mountains, a young, active, and impressively rugged range notable for its high coastal relief. There are near-mile-high valley walls and peaks rising thousands of feet almost directly from the sea. Across Cook Inlet to the southwest march the high volcanic peaks of the Alaska Range, part of the Pacific Ocean's great Ring of Fire, but snowcapped nonetheless. Farther north in the Alaska Range, and visible from Anchorage on clear days, shimmers Mt. McKinley, with Mt. Foraker at its shoulder—the towering granite giants of the North American continent.

Nature lovers can rejoice at the meeting of these two mountain ranges, for it brings together a wide sampling of Alaska's flora and fauna. The Chugach Mountains are a place where both Dall sheep (which roam the Arctic and the Interior but not the Southeast) and mountain goats (found in the Southeast but not in the Interior and the Arctic) dance their way around the heights. Tree species mingle here, too, offering you the chance of seeing the three different varieties of spruce that grow in Alaska—Sitka spruce (from the Southeast, here reaching its northernmost and westernmost limits), black spruce (which does not grow in the Southeast), and white spruce (a tree of the Alaska Peninsula and the Interior). Larch, birch, cottonwood, and aspen here turn golden in the crisp days of late summer and early autumn.

The natural scene in South Central Alaska is not only beautiful, but much of it is easily accessible. From Anchorage, a major hub of Alaska's transportation system, it's possible to travel with relative ease to all parts of the surrounding country. You can go by small plane (Anchorage's Lake Spenard is the busiest floatplane terminal in the United States). You can take the Alaska Railroad north to Denali National Park and Fairbanks or south to Whittier and, during the summer, to Seward and the Kenai Fjords National Park. This train offers one of the greatest rides in the United States: when traveling north on clear days you have unmatched views of Mt. McKinley, and the train may slow down to let a great moose get off the tracks.

Perhaps easiest of all, you can drive from Anchorage to a range of outdoor adventures: canoeing on Swanson Lake or Swanson River in Kenai National Wildlife Refuge or Byers Lake in Denali State Park; sea kayaking in Kachemak Bay or Kenai Fjords National Park; exploring the historic Kennicott copper mine in Wrangell–St. Elias National Park, or traveling on the state ferry to visit Kodiak, with its Russian heritage, or Valdez (en route passing magnificent views of Prince William Sound and the Columbia Glacier). Or if your time is limited, you can drive—or almost walk—to a superlative Alaska park, the Chugach State Park, that lies right outside the city.

Information on all the parks, forests, rivers, and wilderness for which Anchorage is the gateway can be obtained at the Anchorage Alaska Public Lands Information Center (☞ Visitor Information *in* Parks and Wildlife Refuges A to Z, *below*).

Chugach National Forest

Chugach National Forest, adjoining Chugach State Park on its eastern boundary, encompasses nearly 6 million acres to embrace a major part of the Kenai Peninsula as well as parts of Prince William Sound. This national forest has an excellent interpretive center, the **Begich-Boggs Visitor Center** (☎ 907/783–2326), named after two U.S. congressmen who disappeared on a small plane journey out of Anchorage in 1972. There is a splendid view of the photogenic **Portage Glacier**, perhaps Alaska's most visited destination. It is off the Seward Highway, 50 mi southeast of Anchorage. Mountain biking is allowed.

LODGING AND CAMPING

$ ⚏ **U.S. Forest Service Cabins.** Along trails, near wilderness alpine lakes, in coastal forests, and on saltwater beaches, these rustic cabins offer retreats for the solo hiker or a gang of friends. Some cabins are built of logs, some are A-frames. Most have tables, chairs, wood-burning stoves, and bunks, but no electricity, running water, or bedding. Many require a fly-in or boat ride, although some can be reached by car and then foot. Reservations can be made up to 180 days in advance; a $8.65 fee is charged per cabin when making reservations. ⊠ *Chugach National Forest, 3301 C St., Suite 300, Anchorage 99503,* ☎ *907/271–2500, 800/280–2267 reservations.* 🖷 *907/271–2744. 41 cabins. D, MC, V.*

$ ⚠ **U.S. Forest Service Campgrounds.** The Forest Service maintains 18 campgrounds, 14 of them road-accessible, within Chugach National Forest. All of the road-accessible campgrounds have toilet facilities and drinking water. The maximum length of stay is 14 days, except at the Russian River Campground, which has a three-day limit during salmon-fishing season. Most have sites suitable for RVs as well as tents. Reservations (for a fee) are accepted at only a limited number of sites. ⊠ *Chugach National Forest, 3301 C St., Suite 300, Anchorage 99503,* ☎ *907/271–2500 or 800/280–2267 for reservations. D, MC, V accepted for reserved campgrounds. Closed mid-Sept.–late May.*

Chugach State Park

Chugach State Park (⊠ Headquarters, Mile 115, Seward Hwy., HC 52, Box 8999, Indian 99540, ☎ 907/345–5014) is Alaska's most accessible wilderness. Nearly half a million acres in size, the park rises from the coast to more than 8,000 ft, with mountains bearing such colorful names as Williwaw Peak, Temptation Peak, Mt. Magnificent, and Mt. Rumble. The park has nearly 30 trails—from 2 to 30 mi long—totaling more than 150 mi, suitable for shorter hikes, weeklong backpacking, and mountain biking; there are also easy-to-follow cross-country routes. Many of the trails are historic, blazed by early miners who usually sought the easiest passes. There are also some comfortable roadside campgrounds for people traveling by car or bicycle.

The views from high perches in this park are heady. You can look down on the city of Anchorage, observe the great tides in Cook Inlet, gaze north toward McKinley, or delineate the grand procession of snowy peaks across the inlet, marching down the Alaska Peninsula. The most popular alpine perch in Alaska is **Flattop Mountain,** on Chugach Park's western edge, popular with hikers of all abilities. The trailhead is at the Glen Alps parking lot on the hillside above town.

Main trailheads in the park are at the top of O'Malley, Huffman, and DeArmoun roads; south of Anchorage at Potter Valley, McHugh Creek, and Bird Ridge on the Seward Highway; and to the north of town, at Arctic Valley Road (6 mi out) and Eagle River Road (13 mi out).

Eagle River Road leads 12 mi into the mountains from the bedroom community of Eagle River. The **Eagle River Nature Center** (☎ 907/694–2108), at the end of Eagle River Road, has wildlife displays, telescopes for wildlife spotting, and volunteers to answer questions, lead hikes, and host naturalist programs throughout the year. The **Little Rodak Trail** is less than 1 mi long and offers a viewing platform that looks out into the Eagle River valley. The popular **Albert Loop Trail** behind the nature center has natural history displays along its 3-mi route. The nature center is open May–October, Tuesday–Sunday 10–5, and November–April, Friday–Sunday 10–5.

CAMPING

$ ⚠ **Alaska State Park Campgrounds.** Three road-accessible campgrounds are located in Chugach Park, at Eklutna Lake, Bird Creek, and Eagle River. All are within a short drive of Anchorage. The sites have picnic tables, fire pits, water, and latrines and are available on a first-come, first-served basis. The maximum stay ranges from four to 15 nights. ⊠ *Alaska State Parks, HC52, Box 8999, Indian 99540,* ☎ *907/345–5014. 3 campgrounds. No credit cards. Closed in winter.*

Denali State Park

Overshadowed by the larger and more charismatic Denali National Park and Preserve in the Interior, "Little Denali" offers excellent access (it's bisected by the Parks Highway), beautiful views of Mt. McKinley, scenic campgrounds, and prime wilderness hiking and backpacking opportunities within a few miles of the road system. Between the Talkeetna Mountains and the Alaska Range, Denali State Park (⊠ Alaska State Parks, Mat-Su Area Office, HC 32, Box 6706, Wasilla 99687, ☎ 907/745–3975) combines wooded lowlands and forested foothills, topped by alpine tundra. Its chief attraction, other than McKinley views, is the 35-mi-long **Curry-Kesugi Ridge,** which forms a rugged spine through the heart of the park, popular with backpackers. Another destination popular with backcountry travelers is the **Peters Hills,** accessible from Petersville Road in Trapper Creek.

LODGING AND CAMPING

$$$$ 🏨 **Mount McKinley Princess Lodge.** When the sky is clear and Mt. McKinley is visible in the Alaska sky, this new (1997) lodge offers excellent views of North America's highest peak, especially from the lobby with its large stone fireplace. Located on private land inside Denali State Park, this hillside lodge is surrounded by forest and overlooks the Chulitna River. Visitors stay in bungalow-style guest rooms and can go on horseback rides, river-rafting trips, naturalist walks, and alpine hikes. ⊠ *Mile 133.1, Parks Hwy.; reservations: 2815 2nd Ave., Suite 400, Seattle, WA 98121,* ☎ *800/426–0500,* FAX *800/421–1700. 160 rooms, 2 suites. Restaurant, café. AE, DC, MC, V. Closed mid-Sept.–mid-May.*

$ 🏨 **Alaska State Parks Cabins.** Two public-use cabins are in Denali State Park, along the shores of Byers Lake. Both are equipped with bunks, wood-burning stove, table, and benches, but they have no running water or electricity. They must be reserved, up to 180 days in advance. ⊠ *Alaska State Parks Public Information Center, 3601 C St., Suite 200, Box 107001, Anchorage 99510–7001,* ☎ *907/269–8400. 2 cabins. No credit cards. Closed in winter.*

$ ⚠ **Alaska State Parks Campgrounds.** Three roadside campgrounds are within Denali State Park, at Byers Lake, Lower Troublesome Creek, and Denali View North. All are easily accessible from the Parks Highway and have picnic tables, fire pits, drinking water, and latrines. The Byers Lake campground also has a boat launch and nearby hiking trails. Sites are available on a first-come, first-served basis. The maximum stay is 15 days. ⊠ *Alaska State Parks, HC 32 Box 6706, Wasilla 99654,* ☎ *907/745–3975. No credit cards. Closed Oct.–Mar.*

Kachemak Bay State Park and Wilderness Park

Kachemak Bay State Park and Wilderness Park (⊠ Kenai State Parks Office, Box 1247, Soldotna 99669, ☎ 907/262–5581 or 907/235–7024), accessible by boat or plane, protects more than 350,000 acres of coast, mountains, glaciers, forests, and wildlife on the lower Kenai Peninsula. Recreational opportunities include boating, sea kayaking, fishing, hiking, and beachcombing. Facilities are minimal, but there are 20 primitive campsites, five public-use cabins, and a system of trails accessible from Kachemak Bay.

LODGING AND CAMPING

$$$$ 🏨 **Kachemak Bay Wilderness Lodge.** Across Kachemak Bay from
★   Homer, this lodge offers abundant wildlife and stunning views in an intimate setting for up to 12 guests. The main log building has a piano and a big stone fireplace to warm you after a day of hiking, fishing, kayaking, or touring in one of the lodge's five guided boats (some of the guided fly-out trips may cost extra). Scattered throughout the woods, the rustic cabins are decorated with antiques. Dinners spotlight seafood—clams, mussels, crab, and fish—caught in the bay. ⊠ *Box 956, Homer 99603,* ☎ *907/235–8910,* FAX *907/235–8911. 5 cabins. Dining room, hot tub, sauna, hiking, boating, fishing. No credit cards. Closed Oct.–Apr.*

$$ ☷ **Alaska State Parks Cabins.** Three public-use cabins are within Kachemak Bay's Halibut Cove Lagoon area, another is at Tutka Bay Lagoon, and a fifth has been added at China Poot Lake. All but the lakeside cabin are accessible by boat; China Poot must be reached by foot or floatplane. The cabins have wood bunks, table, and chairs, but no running water or electricity. Four of the five sleep up to six people (the other, at Halibut Cove, sleeps eight) and all must be reserved, up to six months in advance. ⊠ *Alaska State Parks Information Center, 3601 C St., Suite 200, Box 107005, Anchorage 99510,* ☎ *907/269-8400. 5 cabins. No credit cards.*

$ ⚠ **Alaska State Parks Campsites.** Twenty primitive, free campsites with pit toilets and fire rings are scattered along the shores of Kachemak Bay across from Homer and are accessible by boat (water taxis operate here daily in summer). The sites are available on a first-come, first-served basis. ⊠ *Alaska State Parks, Kenai Area Office, Box 1247, Soldotna 99669,* ☎ *907/235-7024 or 907/262-5581. 6 campgrounds. No reservations. No credit cards.*

Kenai Fjords National Park

Photogenic Seward is the gateway to the 670,000-acre Kenai Fjords National Park (⊠ Box 1727, Seward 99664, ☎ 907/224-3175). This is spectacular coastal parkland incised with sheer, dark, slate cliffs rising from the sea, ribboned with white waterfalls or tufted with deep-green spruce. Kenai Fjords presents a rare opportunity for an up-close view of blue tidewater glaciers as well as some remarkable ocean wildlife. If you take a day trip on a tour boat out of Seward, you can be pretty sure of seeing sea otters, crowds of Steller's sea lions lazing on the rocky shelves along the shore, a porpoise or two, bald eagles soaring overhead, and tens of thousands of seabirds. Humpback and orca whales are also sighted occasionally. Tours range in length from four to 10 hours. The park's coastal fjords are also a favorite of sea kayakers, who can camp or stay in public-use cabins reserved through headquarters. Backcountry travelers should be aware, however, that much of the park's coastline has been claimed by local Native organizations and is now private property. Be sure to check with park head-★ quarters to avoid trespassing. One of the park's chief attractions is **Exit Glacier,** which can be reached by the one road that passes into Kenai Fjords. There are also trails leading to an overlook of the vast **Harding Icefield.**

GUIDED TOURS

Kenai Fjords Tours (☎ 800/478-8068) has eight charter boats for coastal sightseeing in Resurrection Bay and Kenai Fjords National Park. **Mariah Tours** (☎ 800/270-1238) offers the "small-boat alternative" for wildlife and glacier tours of Kenai Fjords National Park.

Kachemak Air Service (☎ 907/235-8924) is operated by Bill De Creeft, a well-known local pilot with a great knowledge of the area, and his wife, Barbara. He'll fly you to Kenai Fjords or across to Kachemak Bay State Park for sightseeing and can also arrange drop-offs and pick-ups for those who want to explore the parks' backcountry.

LODGING

$$$$ ☷ **Kenai Fjords Wilderness Lodge.** An hour's boat ride from Seward, this wilderness lodge sits within a quiet, forest-lined cove on Fox Island in Resurrection Bay. Visitors stay in cabins tucked inside the spruce forest. Each cabin has expansive views of the bay and surrounding mountains, as well as private baths with shower, two beds, and woodstoves. Meals are served family style in the main lodge building. Hiking trails make it possible to explore the island. Guided kayak trips and coastal wildlife tours can also be arranged. ⊠ *Box 1889, Se-*

ward 99664, ☎ *907/224–8068 or 800/478–8068,* ⊠ *907/224–8934. 8 cabins. Dining area, hiking, travel services. AE, D, MC, V. Closed in winter.*

$$$$ 🏨 **Seward Windsong Lodge.** Built in 1997, this lodge sits in a forested setting near the banks of the Resurrection River, a short drive from either the glacier or downtown Seward. The modern guest rooms feature plaid fabrics, pine accents, and views of the mountains or river. A new restaurant, the Resurrection Roadhouse, specializes in Alaskan meals. A wide array of guided tours can be arranged. ⊠ *Mile 0.6, Exit Glacier Rd., Box 221011, Anchorage 99522,* ☎ *907/224–7116 or 800/ 208–0200 for reservations,* ⊠ *907/245–0400. 48 rooms. Restaurant, travel services. AE, D, MC, V. Closed in winter.*

$ 🏨 **National Park Service Cabins.** Four cabins are managed by Kenai Fjords National Park. Three are along the coast and are for summer use only. Accessible by boat or floatplane, they must be reserved in advance. They're especially popular with sea kayakers. The cabins cost $35 per night; two of the three have a three-night limit, while the other can be reserved for up to nine nights. The park's lone winter cabin is at Exit Glacier and is popular with skiers, mushers, and snow machiners. ⊠ *1212 Fourth Ave., Box 1727, Seward 99664,* ☎ *907/224–3175. 4 cabins. No credit cards.*

Kenai National Wildlife Refuge

The U.S. Fish and Wildlife Service administers nearly 2 million acres on the Kenai Peninsula in one of its prime wildlife refuges. The Kenai National Wildlife Refuge takes in a portion of the **Harding Icefield** as well as two large and very scenic lakes, **Skilak** and **Tustumena.** The refuge is not only the finest moose habitat in the region, but its waterways are great for canoeing and kayaking. The Fish and Wildlife Service maintains a canoe system, campgrounds, and four free cabin shelters, available on a first-come, first-served basis. Two of the cabin shelters are fly-ins; you can hike or canoe to the other two. For information (including canoe rentals), contact the Anchorage Alaska Public Lands Information Center (☞ Visitor Information *in* Parks and Wildlife Refuges A to Z, *below*).

CAMPING

$ ⛺ **Kenai National Wildlife Refuge Campgrounds.** The U.S. Fish and Wildlife Service maintains 14 road-accessible campgrounds in the Kenai refuge, with a total of 130 sites, of which 110 are suitable for RVs, though there are no hookups. All have toilet facilities, and all but three have drinking water. The campgrounds also have picnic tables, fire pits, nearby hiking trails, and fishing. Length of stay ranges from seven to 14 days, except at the Kenai–Russian River Campground, which has a two-day limit due to the immense popularity of the nearby sockeye-salmon fishery. ⊠ *Kenai National Wildlife Refuge, Box 2139, Soldotna 99669-2139,* ☎ *907/262–7021. No reservations. No credit cards.*

Lake Clark National Park and Preserve

When the weather is good, an idyllic choice is the 3.4-million-acre Lake Clark National Park and Preserve (⊠ 4230 University Dr., Suite 311, Anchorage 99508, ☎ 907/271–3751), on the Alaska Peninsula and a short flight from Anchorage. The parklands stretch from the coast to the heights of two grand volcanoes: **Mt. Iliamna** and **Mt. Redoubt,** both topping out above 10,000 ft. The country in between holds glaciers, waterfalls, and turquoise-tint lakes. The 50-mi-long **Lake Clark,** filled by runoff waters from the mountains that surround it, is an important spawning ground to thousands of red, or sockeye, salmon.

The river running is superb in this park; you can make your way through dark forests of spruce and balsam poplars. Or you can hike over the high, easy-to-travel tundra. The animal life here is profuse. Look for bears, moose, Dall sheep, wolves, wolverines, foxes, beavers, and minks on land; seals, sea otters, and white (or beluga) whales offshore. Wildflowers embroider the meadows and tundra in spring, and wild roses bloom in the shadows of the forests. Plan your trip to Lake Clark for the end of June or early July, when the insects may be less plentiful. Or consider late August or early September, when the tundra glows with fall colors.

LODGING

$$$$ ☒ **Farm Lodge.** Near park headquarters in the community of Port Alsworth, the Farm was built as a homestead back in the 1940s and has been a lodge since 1977. As many as 20 guests are housed in two modern duplexes that have carpets and bunk or double beds. Meals are served in the main lodge building, which is surrounded by a large, manicured, and fenced lawn with flower and vegetable gardens. Home-cooked meals feature fresh vegetables from the garden and the greenhouse as well as salmon, wild game, and domestic meats. The lodge also provides flying services (through Lake Clark Air) and guided fishing, backpacking, and river-travel trips. ☒ *Box 1, Port Alsworth 99653,* ☎ *907/781–2211, 907/278–2054 in Anchorage, or 800/662–7661;* FAX *907/781–2215. 5 rooms. Dining room, boating, fishing. D, MC, V.*

Wrangell–St. Elias National Park and Preserve

In a land of many grand and spectacularly beautiful mountains, those in the 9.2-million-acre Wrangell–St. Elias National Park and Preserve (☒ Mile 105.5 Old Richardson Highway, Box 439, Copper Center 99573, ☎ 907/822–5234) have been singled out by many Alaskans as the finest of them all. This is an extraordinarily compact cluster of immense peaks belonging to four different mountain ranges and located toward the southeastern part of the main body of Alaska. Covering an area some 100 mi by 70 mi, the **Wrangells** tower above the 2,500-ft-high Copper River Plateau, and the peaks of Mts. Jarvis, Drum, Blackburn, Sanford, and Wrangell rise 15,000–16,000 ft from sea level. The white-iced spire of **Mt. St. Elias**, in the St. Elias Range, reaches over 18,000 ft; it's the fourth-tallest mountain on the North American continent and the crown of the planet's highest coastal range.

The park's coastal mountains are frequently wreathed in snow-filled clouds, their massive height making a giant wall that contains the great storms brewed in the Gulf of Alaska. As a consequence, they bear some of the continent's largest ice fields, with more than 100 glaciers radiating from them. One of these, the **Malaspina Glacier,** is 1,500 square mi—larger than the state of Rhode Island. This tidewater glacier has an incredible pattern of black-and-white stripes made by the other glaciers that coalesced to form it. Look for it on the coast north of Yakutat if you fly between Juneau and Anchorage.

Rising through many life zones, the Wrangell–St. Elias Park and Preserve is largely undeveloped wilderness parkland on a grand scale. The area is popular with mountain bikers and hikers. The rivers invite rafting for those with expedition experience. The mountains attract climbers from around the world; most of them fly in from Glennallen or Yakutat. The park is largely wilderness, with limited services available in the end-of-the-road town of **McCarthy** and the nearby abandoned **Kennicott Mine,** one of the park's main visitor attractions.

The park is accessible from Alaska's highway system, via one of two gravel roads. The unpaved **Nabesna Road** leaves the Glenn Highway–

Tok Cutoff at the village of Slana and takes visitors 45 mi into the park's northern foothills. The other, better-known route is the **McCarthy Road,** which stretches 60 mi as it follows an old railroad bed from Chitina to the Kennicott River. At the end of the road you must park and cross the river via a footbridge.

Before setting out make sure both you and your car are prepared. The car's jack should be in working order and the spare tire properly inflated, or potholes, old railroad ties, and occasional railroad spikes may leave you stranded.

GUIDED TOURS

St. Elias Alpine Guides (☎ 907/277–6867) offers introductory mountaineering lessons as well as excursions ranging from half-day glacier walks to monthlong backpacking trips. This service, which is owned by experienced mountaineer Bob Jacobs, has been in business more than 20 years. Guided tours of historic Kennicott buildings are also offered.

LODGING AND CAMPING

$$$$ ⊡ **Kennicott Glacier Lodge.** This cozy, modern wooden lodge in the ghost
★ town of Kennicott has fantastic views of the Wrangell and Chugach mountain ranges, as well as the Kennicott Glacier. Rooms are small but clean and nicely furnished. Historical photos of the former copper mine line the walls. Home-cooked meals are served family style; afterward, relax in the spacious living room or on the front porch. Activities include glacier trekking, flightseeing, rafting, alpine hiking, and tours of this former company town that once served the world's richest copper mine. ⊠ *Box 103940, Anchorage 99510,* ☎ *907/258–2350 or 800/582–5128;* 𝔽𝔸𝕏 *907/248–7975. 25 rooms. Dining room, hiking, meeting rooms. AE, D, MC, V. Closed mid-Sept.–mid-May.*

$$$$ ⊡ **Ultima Thule Outfitters.** This remote fly-in-only lodge on the Chitina River in Wrangell–St. Elias National Park and Preserve offers a wonderful opportunity to experience an "air-safari adventure" in America's largest parkland. Besides the breathtaking flightseeing, activities include rafting, climbing, hiking, fishing, mushing, and skiing in the surrounding mountains. The family-style meals feature local foods and homemade bread, pies, and cakes. Oak floors, wallpaper, woodburning stoves, and brass beds offer the comforts of home in these Bavarian-style wilderness cabins. ⊠ *1007 H St., Anchorage 99501,* ☎ *907/258–0636,* 𝔽𝔸𝕏 *907/258–4642. 6 cabins. Dining room, sauna, hiking, boating. No credit cards. Closed Nov.–Feb.*

$ ⚠ **Alaska State Parks Campgrounds.** The state maintains 23 campgrounds in the Matanuska-Susitna–Copper River region. Most can accommodate RVs up to 35 ft long, though electrical hookups are not available. Length of stay varies from four to 15 days. All have toilet facilities, and most have drinking water, picnic sites, fire pits, fishing, and nearby hiking trails. ⊠ *Alaska State Parks, Mat-Su Area Office, HC 32, Box 6706, Wasilla 99654,* ☎ *907/745–3975. No reservations. No credit cards. Closed in winter.*

Interior

The Alaska Range—the "great wall" dividing the Interior from the South Central region—rises more than 20,000 ft. Its grandest member, Mt. McKinley (known among Athabascan-speaking Native people as Denali, or "the high one"), rises 18,000 sky-filling ft from base to peak (one of the highest uplifts in the world); and at 20,320 ft above sea level, it is the highest peak in North America. (Although Mt. Everest reaches more than 29,000 ft above sea level, it rises only 11,000 ft above the Tibetan Plateau.)

This tumultuous landscape was formed by the head-on collision of two tectonic plates. Between them, in the Denali fault system, lies the largest crack in the earth's crust on the North American continent. As high as it is, this barrier between South Central and the Interior Plateau gathers colder weather, and it bears a fine glacial system. These ice-capped mountains give a good idea of the way things were over a large part of the continent during the Ice Age. Flying in a small plane over the black-striped glaciers of the Alaska Range can be a dazzling experience.

Below the high, snowy reaches of the Alaska Range, the lower foothills are often stained with color, evidence of their ancient, restless past. Polychrome Pass in Denali National Park is aptly named: it commands a vista of rose-, orange-, soft brown–, and gray-shaded slopes fingered by swards of green alpine tundra. This high tundra is fine hiking country, but in other areas, the ground is tufted with slippery tussocks, and even the most nimble-footed will be forced into balancing acts.

Below the tundra of the Alaska Range, the trees of the taiga take over: dark spiky spruce, paper birch, aspen, and in the wetter places, cottonwood. The soft green leaves of the deciduous trees shine golden in the autumn. Among and around the trees, fireweed paints the landscape soft magenta. The meadows are blue with lupine in the spring, summer brings succulent berries, and fall touches the berry leaves with crimson. Winter turns this world frigid, white, and crisp with ice.

Stretching farther to the north, the Interior puts the near-vertical terrain of the Alaska Range behind it and assumes a more horizontal character, with low, rounded hills. Tundra and taiga persist, with soft greens spiked by dark spruce trees. There are deep green-gold mossy muskegs, like soggy trampolines underfoot. Lakes gleam like black mirrors. The climate changes: during the summer months, with the sun shining nearly 24 hours a day, heat piles up and lies thick on the land; you may want to go sleeveless at 11 PM. Thunderstorms trailing gauzy streamers of rain move across the landscape. In the winter it gets so cold——50°F or below—that a glass of boiling water flung out a window will explode; parking meters in Fairbanks routinely have electrical outlets for heaters to keep cars from freezing solid. Dry snow glitters in the air. Smog freezes in the Fairbanks bowl.

This part of Alaska has, through many millennia, escaped glaciation and thus formed a refuge for the Ice Age flora and fauna that were crowded out of other areas by ice and intense cold; many species of plants and animals survived only in this refugium, as it is called. Notably, certain species of birds continue to follow age-old patterns of migration and spend summers in the Interior's vast, prodigiously rich wetlands.

Great rivers travel through this landscape: the Tanana, the Nenana, the Kuskokwim, and one of the world's most powerful—the mighty Yukon. (Only four rivers in the Americas have a greater capacity than the Yukon: the Amazon, the St. Lawrence, the Mississippi, and the Missouri.) Twenty miles wide in places, the Yukon travels for 2,300 mi, from Canada to the Bering Sea, and runs through some of the most beautiful country of the Interior Plateau. The Yukon has a firm place in history because it served as a pathway for countless people as they moved through the North American continent (many people still travel the river by boat in the summer and by snowmobile across its frozen surface in the winter).

Fairbanks (☞ Chapter 7) is the principal gateway to the Interior parks, as well as a takeoff point for much of the Arctic wilderness of the bush areas. For more information, contact the Fairbanks branch of the Public Lands Information Center (☞ Visitor Information *in* Parks and Wildlife Refuges A to Z, *below*).

Denali National Park and Preserve

★ The more than 6-million-acre Denali National Park and Preserve (✉ Box 9, Denali National Park, 99755, ☎ 907/683–2294 year-round or 907/683–1266 in summer) is among the most accessible of the large national parks in Alaska; many visitors make the park their primary destination. The visitor center near the park's entrance can fill all your information needs, including the daily schedule for naturalist presentations and sled-dog demonstrations by the park rangers. It's possible to reach the park by car on the George Parks Highway, a well-maintained two-lane road that runs from Fairbanks to Anchorage. The park itself is closed to private vehicles beyond the Savage River Checkpoint (near Mile 14.8, about 14 mi inside the park) to enhance wildlife-viewing opportunities. Shuttle buses travel as far as Wonder Lake, nearly 90 mi from the park entrance; seats can be reserved in advance by calling 800/622–7275 or faxing a request to 907/264–4684. Making the entire trip to Wonder Lake and back will take 10 hours or more, but the shuttle system is such that you can get off along the route and catch another bus in either direction. Adult prices for the shuttles range from $12 to $30 and are in addition to the reservation fee of $4 and the park entrance fee of $5 per person or $10 per family. The buses get early morning (wee hours) starts to take advantage of the best wildlife-viewing hours. As for getting to the park, bus lines run regularly out of both Fairbanks and Anchorage to Denali (the park is 120 mi south of Fairbanks and 240 mi north of Anchorage); another alternative is the Alaska Railroad, which provides a pleasant and interesting way to reach the park from either city.

Denali National Park is one of the world's best and easiest places to see wildlife in their natural environment. Nowhere in the world is there more spectacular background scenery, although Mt. McKinley, alas, is wreathed in clouds about 65% of the time. Nearly every wild creature that walks or flies in South Central and Interior Alaska inhabits the park, and many are readily visible along the 91-mi road that winds from the park entrance to Wonder Lake and Kantishna, an historic mining community in the heart of the park. While providing transportation into the park, bus drivers point out Dall sheep finding their way along the dizzying slopes, grizzlies and caribou frequenting stream bottoms and tundra, moose that prefer the forested areas both near the park entrance and deep in the park, and the occasional wolf that may dart across the road. Keep in mind that, as one park lover put it, "this ain't no zoo." You might hit an off day and have few viewings—enjoy the surroundings anyway. Under any circumstances, don't feed the animals or birds (a mew gull or ground squirrel may try to share your lunch).

Both day hiking and backpacking can be excellent in Denali. Overnight packing into the backcountry is possible with a permit from rangers at the visitor center. This is bear country, and the park service provides backpackers with bear-proof food containers. Use of these containers is mandatory. You can plan your itinerary with park rangers and use the shuttle bus for transportation to and from your starting point. No weapons are permitted in the park. Climbing the great mountain may be every mountaineer's dream, but too many visitors have created a real litter problem on its snowy slopes. If you feel you must attempt the peak, talk to the park-service people about procuring a guide for this Himalaya-class expedition. Climbers are now required to pay a

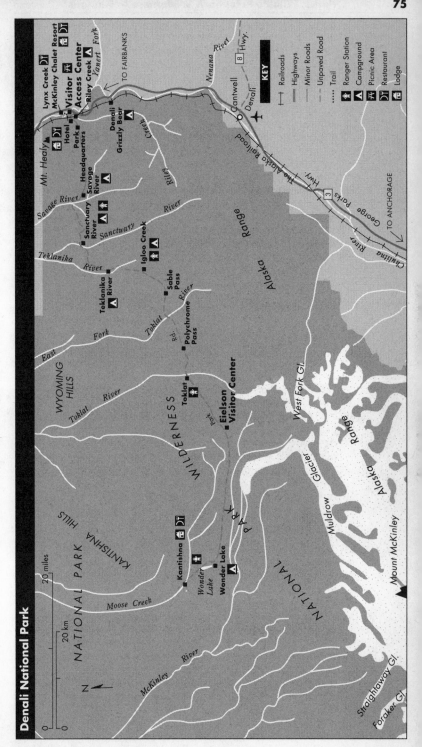

Denali National Park

TO FAIRBANKS

TO ANCHORAGE

KEY
- Railroads
- Highways
- Minor Roads
- Unpaved Road
- Trail
- Ranger Station
- Campground
- Picnic Area
- Restaurant
- Lodge

Lynx Creek
McKinley Chalet Resort
Visitor Access Center
Riley Creek
Mt. Healy
Hotel
Park Headquarters
Denali Grizzly Bear
Savage River
Sanctuary River
Igloo Creek
Teklanika River
Sable Pass
Polychrome Pass
Toklat
Eielson Visitor Center
Kantishna
Wonder Lake

Nenana River
Vanert Fork
Riley Creek
Savage River
Sanctuary
Teklanika River
East Fork
Toklat River
Toklat Rd.
Park Rd.
Moose Creek
Wonder Lake
McKinley River

WYOMING HILLS
KANTISHNA HILLS
WILDERNESS
NATIONAL PARK
NATIONAL PARK

Alaska Range
West Fork Gl.
Muldrow Glacier
Glacier
Alaska Range
Mount McKinley
Straightaway Gl.
Foraker Gl.

The Alaska Railroad
George Parks Hwy.
Chulitna River
Cantwell
Denali
3
8 Hwy.

N

20 miles
20 km

fee whenever visiting McKinley or neighboring Mt. Foraker. Contact the park's mountaineering ranger headquarters in Talkeetna for more information (☎ 907/733–2231). Denali summer weather can vary from hot and sunny to near freezing and drizzly, and those changes can occur within a few hours, so you'll want to bring along appropriate clothing.

DINING, LODGING, AND CAMPING

$–$$$ ✕ **The Perch.** This fine-dining restaurant with a simply furnished interior is located atop a forested hillside, and its bay windows present a 360-degree view of the surrounding Alaska Range foothills. The Perch serves breakfast, lunch, and dinner, offering home-baked breads and desserts along with steak, seafood, and box lunches. ⊠ *Mile 224, Parks Hwy., Denali Park,* ☎ *907/683–2523. AE, MC, V.*

$–$$$ ✕ **Tamarack Inn.** Dine on American cuisine by the light of a fireplace at this inn, which houses one of the best-known restaurants on the road from Anchorage to Fairbanks. It serves lunch and dinner in summer, and dinner only in winter. ⊠ *Mile 298, Parks Hwy., 6 mi south of Nenana,* ☎ *907/832–5455. AE, D, DC, MC, V. Closed Wed. in summer, Mon.–Wed. in winter.*

$–$$ ✕ **Lynx Creek Pizza.** This casual restaurant 1 mi north of the park entrance is a popular hangout for locals and features pizza, sandwiches, salads, ice cream, and some Mexican entrées. Guests order at the front and seat themselves at picnic-table benches. ⊠ *Mile 238.6, Parks Hwy.,* ☎ *907/683–2547. AE, D, DC, MC, V. Closed in winter.*

$–$$ ✕ **McKinley/Denali Salmon Bake.** This rustic building 1 mi north of the park entrance serves breakfast, lunch, and dinner and looks as if it might blow away in a stiff wind. Baked fresh salmon tops the menu; steaks, burgers, and chicken are also available. Shuttle service is provided to area hotels. ⊠ *Mile 238.5, Parks Hwy.,* ☎ *907/683–2733 in summer. AE, MC, V. Closed Oct.–Mar.*

$$$$ ✕🏨 **Denali Princess Lodge.** This hotel overlooking the Nenana River has large rooms decorated in rich forest colors. Complimentary shuttle service is offered to the park and railroad station. The large Summit Dining Room offers an estimable view and fine dining. Burgers and more casual fare are available at the Cruiser's Café, which can also supply picnic lunches. ⊠ *Just off Parks Hwy., 1 mi north of the park entrance, Box 110, Denali 99755,* ☎ *907/683–2282,* 𝖥𝖠𝖷 *907/683–2545; off-season* ☎ *800/426–0500,* 𝖥𝖠𝖷 *206/443–1979. 280 rooms. Restaurant, bar, café, outdoor hot tubs. AE, DC, MC, V. Closed mid-Sept.– mid-May.*

$$$$ 🏨 **Camp Denali and Northface Lodge.** Camp Denali is a group of log
★   cabins in the heart of the park (at the end of the park road), with limited electricity and shared bathrooms. Many consider it the best place to stay in the park because of its rustic charm and delicious home cooking (the dining room is for guests only). The lodge has private baths and other amenities and it's the only one within Denali Park that has a view of Mt. McKinley. The owners also run Northface Lodge, just 1 mi from Camp Denali. Both knowledgeable staffs acquaint you with the surrounding wilderness and lead evening natural-history programs and guided outings. Activities include hiking, mountain biking, flightseeing, and canoeing. ⊠ *Box 67, Denali Park 99755,* ☎ *907/683–2290,* 𝖥𝖠𝖷 *907/683–1568. 17 cabins. Dining room, boating, bicycles. No credit cards. Closed mid-Sept.–early June.*

$$$$ 🏨 **Denali Crow's Nest Log Cabins.** These spartan cantilevered log cabins 1 mi north of the park entrance are on a forested hillside and offer good river and mountain views. Each has its own baths. ⊠ *Mile 238.5, Parks Hwy., Box 70, Denali Park 99755,* ☎ *907/683–2723,* 𝖥𝖠𝖷 *907/ 683–2323. 39 rooms. Restaurant, bar, hot tub.. MC, V. Closed in winter.*

$$$$ 🏨 **Denali National Park Hotel.** This is the only hotel within Denali Park (it's just 1½ mi from the park entrance). Built in 1939, the original McKinley Park Hotel had 200 rooms and was intentionally located a short walk from the railroad depot, to make it more accessible to Denali visitors. It burned down in 1972 and was replaced by the present modular structure that is more functional than luxurious. A staging area for tour-bus trips into the park, the hotel is also a popular gathering spot; it seems there's always a bustling crowd in the lobby. Among its attractions are a restaurant, snack bar, espresso stand, gift shop, and 300-seat auditorium where naturalist programs are presented each afternoon and evening throughout the summer. Denali Park Resorts (⊠ 241 W. Ship Creek Ave., Anchorage 99501) runs this hotel and two others: McKinley Chalet Resort, with 343 rooms, and McKinley Village Lodge, with 50 rooms. ⊠ *Next to the train depot in the park, Box 87, Denali Park 99755,* ☎ *907/276–7234 or 800/276–7234,* FAX *907/ 258–3668. 100 rooms. Restaurant, lounge, snack shop. AE, D, MC, V. Closed mid-Sept.–mid-May.*

$$$$ 🏨 **Denali River Cabins.** This cluster of riverside cabins next to McKinley Village Lodge offers cozy comfort along the Nenana River. The cedar-sided cabins have double beds and are connected by boardwalk to the river. The management operates park excursions and a courtesy shuttle service to and from the train depot. ⊠ *Mile 231, Parks Hwy., Box 25, Denali Park 99755,* ☎ *907/683–2500,* FAX *907/683–2502. 54 units. Hot tub, sauna. MC, V. Closed in winter.*

$$$$ 🏨 **Denali River View Inn.** This newer hotel sits atop a bluff overlooking the Nenana River at Mile 238.4 of the Parks Highway, just north of the park entrance. Rooms are modern with private baths and simply appointed in a blue-and-beige color scheme. Each has a view of the river. And being above the highway rather than along it, they offer a quiet experience. ⊠ *Box 49, Denali Park 99755,* ☎ *907/683–2663,* FAX *907/683–7433. 12 rooms. Courtesy van. D, MC, V. Closed mid-Sept.–mid-May.*

$$$–$$$$ 🏨 **Denali Cabins.** This cabin complex near the highway has hot tubs and barbecue grills; all units have private baths. Complimentary shuttle service to the park visitor center is provided. ⊠ *Mile 229, Parks Hwy., Box 229, Denali Park 99755,* ☎ *907/683–2643,* FAX *907/683– 2595; off-season* ☎ *907/258–0134 or 888/560–2489,* FAX *907/243– 2062. 43 cabins. MC, V. Closed mid-Sept.–mid-May.*

$–$$$ ⛺ **Grizzly Bear Cabins and Campground.** This campground with cabins is just outside the park, along the Nenana River. Both walk-in tent sites and RV sites are available for camping, while cabins range from rustic shelters with minimal facilities to those equipped with kitchens and full baths. ⊠ *Mile 231, Parks Hwy., Box 7, Denali Park 99755,* ☎ *907/683–2696, 907/683–1337 winter only. D, MC, V. Closed in winter.*

$ ⛺ **McKinley RV Park and Campground.** This campground is about 10 mi outside the park. It has a variety of RV sties, from "basic" to those with full electricity, water, and sewer. Two-person tent sites are also available, as are a dump station, public showers, ice, and propane. ⊠ *Mile 248.5, Parks Hwy., Healy 99743,* ☎ *907/683–2379 or 800/ 478–2562.*

$ ⛺ **National Park Service Campgrounds.** There are seven campgrounds inside the park: three are open to private vehicles for tent and RV camping, three are reached by shuttle bus only and are restricted to tent camping, and one is for backpacking only. All have toilet facilities, most have drinking water, and a couple have nearby hiking trails. All are open from late May to September, depending on snow conditions, and cost $6–$12 a night plus a one-time $4 reservation fee; one is open year-round. You can apply for a site at the visitor center, but it's wise to reserve in advance. ⊠ *Denali National Park Headquarters, Box 9, Denali Park 99755,* ☎ *907/683–2294 for information, 907/272–7275 or 800/622–7275 for reservations. AE, D, MC, V. All but Riley Creek (no visitor facilities) closed in winter.*

GUIDED TOURS

Privately operated bus trips with boxed snacks are available through **Denali Park Resorts.** The Tundra Wildlife Tour costs $61, and the shorter Natural History Tour costs $34 (☎ 907/276–7234 or 800/276–7234 for information).

Alaska-Denali Guiding (☎ 907/733–2649) and **Mountain Trip** (907/345–6499) guide climbing expeditions on Mt. McKinley and other Alaska Range peaks (experience required). Alaska-Denali Guiding also leads backpacking trips in both Denali state and national parks.

OUTDOOR ACTIVITIES AND SPORTS

Mountain biking is allowed on the park's dirt road. Visitors with a taste for white-water adventures will find parts of the Nenana River, just north of the Denali Park entrance, to their liking. Several privately owned raft and tour companies operate along the Parks Highway near the entrance to Denali, and they schedule daily rafting, both in the fairly placid areas on the Nenana and through the 10-mi-long Nenana River canyon, which contains some of the roughest white water in North America.

Denali Outdoor Center (☎ 907/683–1925) takes adventuresome people on guided trips down the Nenana River rapids in inflatable kayaks. No river experience is necessary. The kayaks, called Duckies, are easy to get out of, stable, and self-bailing. The company also offers a variety of rafting trips and a white-water kayaking school. All gear is provided.

Denali Raft Adventures (☎ 907/683–2234, FAX 907/683–1281) launches its rafts several times daily on two- or four-hour, all-day, and overnight scenic and white-water floats on the Nenana River. Courtesy pickup at hotels and the train depot is available.

Three companies offer daily white-water and scenic raft trips on the Nenana River: **Alaska Raft Adventures** (☎ 800/276–7234, FAX 907/258–3668). **McKinley Raft Tours** (☎ 907/683–2392, FAX 907/683–2581). **Nenana Raft Adventures** (☎ FAX 907/683–2628).

Steese Mountain National Conservation Area and White Mountain National Recreation Area

The Bureau of Land Management (⊠ BLM Headquarters, 1150 University Ave., Fairbanks 99709, ☎ 907/474–2200) administers the Steese Mountain National Conservation Area and the White Mountain National Recreation Area. Both these preserves are accessible by car. The White Mountain Recreation Area has limited camping facilities from June to November. The BLM also has three campsites on the Taylor Highway between Tok and Eagle at Miles 48.5, 82, and 160.

LODGING AND CAMPING

$ ⛺ **BLM Public-Use Cabins.** The BLM manages 10 public-use cabins in the White Mountain NRA, with 300 mi of interconnecting trails. They are designed primarily for winter use by dog mushers, snow machiners, and cross-country skiers, but a few are also used by backpackers in summer. The cabins have bunk beds, woodstoves, cooking stoves, lanterns, tables, and chairs. ⊠ *BLM Headquarters, 1150 University Ave., Fairbanks 99709,* ☎ *907/474–2200 or 800/437–7021. 10 cabins. Permits are required and available up to 30 days in advance. AE, MC, V.*

$ △ **BLM Campgrounds.** The BLM manages five road-accessible campgrounds in the Steese Highway area and another along the Dalton Highway. They all have picnic tables, fire pits, latrines, and well water. They're available on a first-come, first-served basis. ⊠ *BLM Headquarters, 1150 University Ave., Fairbanks 99709,* ☎ *907/474–2200. No credit cards.*

OUTDOOR ACTIVITIES AND SPORTS

The BLM (☞ *above*) maintains the moderately difficult 20-mi **Summit Trail,** from the Elliott Highway, near Wickersham Dome, north into the White Mountain National Recreation Area. This hiking trail can be done as a day hike or overnight backpacking trip. It quickly rises into alpine country with 360-degree vistas that include lots of wildland, the trans-Alaska pipeline, and a pipeline pump station. You can see many wildflowers in early summer. Look for the parking lot at Mile 28.

Wild and Scenic Rivers

BLM (☞ *above*) is also in charge of three Wild and Scenic Rivers, each of which offers a special wilderness experience. **Beaver Creek** rises in the White Mountain NRA and makes its easy way north; if you have enough time, it's possible to run its entire 268-mi length to the Yukon (if you make a shorter run, you will have to go out by small plane). There's good fishing as well as scenery. Lively clear-water **Birch Creek** is more of a challenge, with several rapids along its 126 mi. Moose, caribou, and birds are easily spotted. Four- to five-day float trips are possible; access is at Mile 94 of the Steese Highway. This stream winds its way north through the historic mining country of the Circle District. The takeout point is at the Steese Highway Bridge, 15 mi from Circle. From there Birch Creek meanders on to the Yukon River well below the town.

The beautiful **Fortymile River** offers everything from a 38-mi run to a lengthy journey to the Yukon and then down to Eagle. Its waters range from easy Class I to serious Class IV (possibly Class V) stretches. Only experienced canoeists should attempt boating on these rivers, and rapids should be scouted beforehand. Canoeing on this river is popular among Alaskans; the Taylor Highway offers several access points.

Yukon–Charley Rivers National Preserve

The 126-mi stretch of the **Yukon River** running between the small towns of Eagle and Circle (former Gold Rush metropolises) has been protected in the 2.5-million-acre Yukon–Charley Rivers National Preserve (⊠ National Park Service, 201 First Ave., Doyon Building, Fairbanks 99701, ☎ 907/456–0281). As its name suggests, this parkland also covers the pristine watershed of the **Charley River,** a crystalline whitewater stream flowing out of the Yukon-Tanana uplands. This waterway provides fine river running. You can put in a raft or a kayak (via small plane) at the headwaters of the Charley and travel 88 mi down this joyful, bouncing river.

In great contrast to the Charley, the Yukon is dark with mud and glacial silt and is an inexorably powerful stream. Only one bridge has been put across it: that built for the trans-Alaska pipeline north of Fairbanks. The river surges deep, and to travel on it in a small boat is a humbling, if magnificent, experience. You can drive from Fairbanks to Eagle (via the Taylor Highway off the Alaska Highway) and to Circle (via the Steese Highway), and from either of these arrange for a ground-transportation shuttle back to your starting city at the end of your Yukon River trip. Weeklong float trips down the river from Eagle to Circle, 150 mi away, are popular. For information, contact the National Park Service in Eagle (☎ 907/547–2233). Those planning a trip here should note that there are no developed campgrounds or other visitor facilities within the preserve itself, though low-impact backcountry camping is permitted.

The Bush

Rimming Alaska as they do, the state's bush areas vary as widely as the terrain they occupy. There is the Arctic, a fragile land inhabited year-round by a variety of wildlife that has adapted to its short summers and long, dark winters. These animals share the other special qualities of the Far North—immense space, extreme winter cold, and deep quiet. There is the Northwest, bounded by the icy waters of the Arctic Ocean and the Chukchi and Bering seas, where whales and thousands of other sea mammals pass by. Here are traces of inhabitants dating back 12,000 years. There is western Alaska, which includes the wet country so important for fish and bird life. Finally the Southwest, where the Alaska Peninsula stretches to meet the Aleutian chain of islands, which also supports immense populations of birds and sea mammals.

Aniakchak National Monument and Preserve

Aniakchak, an extraordinary living volcano, rises to the south of Katmai. It has one of the largest calderas in the world, with a diameter averaging 6 mi across and small **Surprise Lake** within it. Although Aniakchak erupted as recently as 1931, the explosion that formed the enormous crater occurred before history was written. Because the area is not glaciated, geologists place the blowup after the last Ice Age. It was literally a world-shaking event. Marking the volcano's significance, in 1980 Congress established the 138,000-acre Aniakchak National Monument (⊠ National Park Service, Box 7, King Salmon 99613, ☎ 907/246–3305), with an adjacent 376,000-acre national preserve.

This is wild and forbidding country, with a climate that brews mist, clouds, and winds of great force much of the year. Although the **Aniakchak River** (which drains Surprise Lake) is floatable, it has stretches of Class III and IV white water navigable only by expert river runners, and you must travel through open ocean waters to reach the nearest community, Chignik Bay (or get picked up by plane, along the coast); this makes the run something of an expedition. The best way to enjoy Aniakchak is to wait for a clear day and fly to it in a small plane able to land you on the caldera floor or on Surprise Lake. However you choose to see it, it's an unforgettable experience. But be aware that there are no visitor facilities here; you must be prepared to be self-sufficient.

Arctic National Wildlife Refuge

The 18-million-acre Arctic National Wildlife Refuge, lying wholly above the Arctic Circle, is administered by the U.S. Fish and Wildlife Service and contains the only protected Arctic coastal lands in the United States (and some of the very few protected in the world), as well as millions of acres of mountains and alpine tundra, in the easternmost portion of the Brooks Range. This is the home of one of the greatest remaining groups of caribou in the world, the **Porcupine Caribou Herd.** The herd, numbering around 160,000, is unmindful of international boundaries and migrates back and forth across Arctic lands into Canada, flowing like a wide river over the permafrost. Other residents here are grizzly and polar bears, Dall sheep, wolves, musk ox, and dozens of varieties of birds. As in many of Alaska's more remote parks and refuges, there are no roads here, no developed trails, campgrounds, or other visitor facilities. This is a place to experience true wilderness—and to walk with care, for it is fragile here. You can expect snow to sift over the land in almost any season. Many of the refuge rivers are runnable, and lovely lakes are suitable for base camps (a Kaktovik or Fort Yukon air taxi can drop you off and pick you up). The hiking, too, can be invigorating. For refuge information, contact the Fairbanks office of the Public Lands Information Center (☞ Visitor Information *in* Parks and Wildlife Refuges A to Z, *below*).

Bering Land Bridge National Preserve

The frozen ash and lava of the 2.8-million-acre Bering Land Bridge National Preserve (✉ National Park Service, Box 220, Nome 99762, ☎ 907/443–2522) lie between Nome and Kotzebue immediately south of the Arctic Circle. The **Imuruk lava flow** is the northernmost flow of major size in the United States, and the paired maars (clear volcanic lakes) are a geological rarity.

Of equal interest are the paleontological features of this preserve. Sealed into the permafrost are flora and fauna—bits of twigs and leaves, tiny insects, small mammals, even remnants of woolly mammoths—that flourished here when the Bering Land Bridge linked North America to what is now Russia. Early people wandered through this treeless landscape, perhaps following the musk ox, whose descendants still occupy this terrain. There are a remarkable 250 species of flowering plants in this seemingly barren region, and tens of thousands of migrating birds. More than 100 species, including ducks, geese, swans, sandhill cranes, and various shorebirds and songbirds, come here from around the world each spring. You may hear the haunting call of loons on the many clear lakes and lagoons.

The Bering Land Bridge National Monument has no facilities. Access is largely by air taxi, although there is a road north of Nome that passes within walking distance.

Cape Krusenstern National Monument

Only 10 mi northwest of Kotzebue, the 560,000-acre Cape Krusenstern National Monument (✉ National Park Service, Box 1029, Kotzebue 99752, ☎ 907/442–3890) has important cultural and archaeological value. This is a coastal parkland, with an extraordinary series of beach ridges built up by storms over a period of at least 5,000 years. Almost every ridge (there are 114 of them) contains artifacts of different human occupants, representing every known Arctic Eskimo culture in North America. The present Eskimo occupants, whose culture dates back some 1,400 years, use the fish, seals, caribou, and birds of this region for food and raw materials much as their ancestors did. They are also closely involved in the archaeological digs in the park that are unearthing part of their own history.

Cape Krusenstern is a starkly beautiful Arctic land shaped by ice, wind, and sea. Its low, rolling gray-white hills scalloped with light green tundra attract hikers and backpackers. The monument is valuable also for human and historical reasons, and it should be experienced as something like a marvelous living museum. It's possible to camp in the park, but be mindful, as are the Native people when they rig their big white canvas tents for summer fishing, that any tent pitched along the shore is subject to fierce winds.

Check with the National Park Service in Kotzebue (☞ Kobuk Valley National Park, *below*) about hiring a local guide to interpret this unusual scene. The monument, which has no visitor facilities, is accessible by air taxi and by boat from Kotzebue.

Gates of the Arctic National Park and Preserve

The Gates of the Arctic National Park and Preserve includes more than 8.2 million acres north of the Arctic Circle, in the center of the Brooks Range. This is parkland on a scale suitable to the country; it includes the **Endicott Mountains** to the east and the **Schwatka Mountains** to the southwest, with the **Arrigetch Peaks** in between. *Arrigetch* is an Eskimo word meaning "fingers of a hand outstretched," which aptly describes the immensely steep and smooth granite peaks that have attracted many mountaineers. To the north lies a sampling of the Arctic foothills, with their colorful tilted sediments and pale green tundra. Lovely lakes are cupped in the mountains and in the tundra.

The village of Bettles is a dropping-off point for the Gates of the Arctic, which has no developed trails, campgrounds, or other visitor facilities (though there is a wilderness lodge on private land within the park). You can fly in commercially and charter an air taxi into the park. For more information, contact the Fairbanks Alaska Public Lands Information Center (☞ Visitor Information *in* Parks and Wildlife Refuges A to Z, *below*) or the National Park Service (✉ 201 First Ave., Doyon Building, Fairbanks 99701, ☎ 907/456–0281).

LODGING

$$$–$$$$ ⊡ **Peace of Selby Wilderness.** Because of its location along Selby/Narvak Lake within Gates of the Arctic National Park, staying at Peace of Selby allows you to explore one of the world's last great wilderness areas, the Brooks Range. The main lodge includes a dining area, guest rooms, and bathroom facilities; guests wishing to rough it may stay in sleeping bags and cook their own meals in a rustic log cabin or a large canvas "wall" tent. Cabins and wall tents are also available at two remote lake sites and along the Kobuk River. Peace of Selby specializes in custom guided wilderness expeditions that may include hiking, wildlife photography, river floating, and fishing. Late winter and early spring activities include guided dog mushing expeditions and Nordic skiing. ✉ *Box 86, Manley Hot Springs 99756, ☎ FAX 907/672–3206. 3 rooms, 1 cabin, wall tents. Dining room, hiking, boating, fishing. No credit cards. Closed Dec.–Jan.*

OUTDOOR ACTIVITIES AND SPORTS

Contact **Sourdough Outfitters** (✉ Box 90, Bettles 99726, ☎ 907/692–5252, FAX 907/692–5612) for summer river trips (from family float trips to wild-rapid running and fishing expeditions) and winter dogsled and snowmobile trips in the Brooks Range.

Katmai National Park and Preserve

For an extraordinary perspective on the awesome power of volcanoes, visit the 4-million-acre Katmai National Park and Preserve (✉ National Park Service, Box 7, King Salmon 99613, ☎ 907/246–3305). This park is a wild, remote landscape at the northern end of the Alaska Peninsula, bordering Shelikof Strait across from Kodiak Island, 290 mi southwest of Anchorage. Moose and almost 30 other species of mammals, including foxes, lynx, and wolves, share the scene with bears fishing for salmon from stream banks or in the water. At the immensely popular **Brooks Falls and Camp,** you can be sure of seeing brown bears when the salmon are running in July. Unlike Pack Creek and McNeil River State Game Sanctuary, with their strict viewing limits, no special permits are required here, though there is now a $10 day-use fee at Brooks. Ducks are common; so are whistling swans, loons, grebes, gulls, and shorebirds. Bald eagles perch on rocky pinnacles by the sea. More than 40 species of songbirds alone can be seen during the short spring and summer season. Marine life abounds in the coastal area, with Steller's sea lions and hair seals often observed on rock outcroppings.

Compared with roads and facilities at Denali National Park, those at Katmai are quite primitive, but therein lies the park's charm. The first visitors to the Katmai area arrived more than 4,000 years ago. There is some evidence, in fact, that Native Alaskan people inhabited Katmai's eastern edge for at least 6,000 years. On the morning of June 1, 1912, a 2,700-ft mountain called **Novarupta** erupted. The earth shook in violent tremors for five straight days. When the quakes subsided, rivers of white-hot ash poured into the valley. A foot of ash fell on Kodiak, 100 mi away. Winds carried the ash to eastern Canada and as far as Texas. While Novarupta was belching pumice and scorching ash, another explosion occurred 6 mi east. The mountaintop peak of **Mt. Katmai** collapsed, creating a chasm almost 3 mi long and 2 mi wide. The molten andesite that held up Mt. Katmai had rushed through newly created fissures to Novarupta and been spewn out. Sixty hours after the first thunderous blast, more than 7 cubic mi of volcanic material had been ejected, and the green valley lay under 700 ft of ash. Everyone fled from Katmai and other villages; no one was killed.

By 1916 things had cooled off. A National Geographic expedition led by Dr. Robert F. Griggs reached the valley and found it full of steaming fumaroles, creating a moonlike landscape. The report on what Griggs dubbed the **Valley of Ten Thousand Smokes** inspired Congress in 1918 to set it and the surrounding wilderness aside as a national monument. Steam spouted in thousands of fountains from the smothered streams and springs beneath the ash and gave the valley its name. Although the steam has virtually stopped, an eerie sense of earth forces at work remains, and several nearby volcanoes still smolder.

The Native peoples never returned to their traditional village sites, but many now live in other nearby communities. They are joined by sightseers, anglers, hikers, and other outdoor enthusiasts who migrate to the Katmai region each summer. Fish and wildlife are still plentiful, and a few "smokes" still drift through the volcano-sculpted valley.

No roads lead to the national park, at the base of the Alaska Peninsula. Planes wing from Anchorage along Cook Inlet, rimmed by the lofty, snowy peaks of the Alaska Range. They land at King Salmon, near fish-famous Bristol Bay, where passengers transfer to smaller floatplanes for the 20-minute hop to **Naknek Lake** and Brooks Camp. Travel to this area is also possible by private boat. All visitors are required to check into the park ranger station, next to Brooks Lodge, for a mandatory bear talk.

From Brooks Lodge, a daily tour bus with a naturalist aboard makes the 23-mi trip through the park to the **Valley Overlook.** Hikers can walk the 1½-mi trail for a closer look at the pumice-covered valley floor. (Some consider the return climb strenuous.)

The Katmai area is one of Alaska's premier sportfishing regions. It's possible to fish for rainbow trout and salmon at the **Brooks River,** though seasonal closures have been put in place to prevent conflicts with bears, and only fly fishing is permitted. For those who'd like to venture farther into the park, seek out the two other backcountry lodges, Grosvenor and Kulik (☞ Dining and Lodging, *below*), set in prime sportfishing territory, or contact fishing guide services based in King Salmon. A short walk up the Brooks River brings you to Brooks Falls, where salmon can be seen from a viewing platform (on a trail separated from the river to avoid confrontations with bears) as they leap a 6-ft barrier.

GUIDED TOURS

Katmai Air Services (☎ 907/246–3079 in King Salmon; 800/544–0551 in Anchorage) can arrange flightseeing tours of the park. **Katmailand** (⊠ 4550 Aircraft Dr., Suite 2, Anchorage 99502, ☎ 907/243–5448 or 800/544–0551, FAX 907/243–0649) puts together packages to Katmai National Park.

LODGING AND CAMPING

Of the following lodging choices, only Chenik Camp is outside Katmai National Park. Brooks Lodge and Brooks Camp are more central compared to Grosvenor Lodge and Kulik Lodge, which are in remote backcountry.

$$$$ ⊞ **Brooks Lodge.** All the attractions of Katmai National Park are at
★ this lodge's doorstep: world-class fly-fishing for rainbow trout, lake trout, Arctic grayling, and salmon; brown-bear viewing; and tours to the Valley of Ten Thousand Smokes. Accommodations are in detached modern cabins complete with showers, private toilet facilities, heat, and electricity; they accommodate two to four people. The cabins surround the main lodge, which boasts a spectacular view of aquamarine Naknek Lake; it has a semicircular stone fireplace and dining area where buffet-style meals are served three times daily. ⊠ *Katmailand, 4550 Aircraft Dr., Suite 2, Anchorage 99502,* ☎ *907/243–5448 or 800/544– 0551,* FAX *907/243–0649. 16 cabins. Bar, dining room, hiking, fishing. MC, V. Closed mid-Sept.–May.*

$$$$ ⊞ **Chenik Camp.** This rustic camp is along Kamishak Bay, in the heart of Southwest Alaska's bear country, only 2 mi from the world-famous McNeil River State Game Sanctuary. Cabins have room for six to eight visitors, and there's a traditional sod-roof Finnish sauna, a bathhouse with chemical toilet, and a small lodge with dining area, fireplace, library, and picture windows that overlook the ocean. There is no indoor plumbing or electricity. Bear viewing is the number-one activity. ⊠ *Box 956, Homer 99603,* ☎ *907/235–8910,* FAX *907/235– 8911. 3 cabins without bath. Dining room, sauna, hiking, boating, fishing, library. No credit cards. Closed mid-Aug.–early June.*

$$$$ ⊞ **Grosvenor Lodge.** Once you've arrived at this remote Katmai Park lodge, reachable only by floatplane, you have access by motorboat to numerous rivers and streams filled with sport fish. The lodge can accommodate six people in three cabins with heat and electricity and a shared separate bathhouse. The main lodge houses a kitchen, dining room, lounging area, and bar and has an excellent view of Grosvenor Lake. ⊠ *Katmailand, 4550 Aircraft Dr., Suite 2, Anchorage 99502,* ☎ *907/243–5448 or 800/544–0551,* FAX *907/243–0649. 3 cabins without bath. Bar, dining room, fishing. MC, V. Closed Oct.–May.*

$$$$ ⊞ **Kulik Lodge.** Located along the gin-clear Kulik River, between Nonvianuk and Kulik lakes, this remote wilderness lodge also is reachable only by floatplane; it accommodates up to 20 anglers and is popular as a base for fly-out fishing to hot spots in the surrounding Katmai wilderness. Guests stay in two-person cabins with electricity and private baths. In the evening, when fishing's done for the day, guests gather in the spruce lodge, which has a large stone fireplace, dining area, and bar. ⊠ *Katmailand, 4550 Aircraft Dr., Suite 2, Anchorage 99502,* ☎ *907/243–5448 or 800/544–0551,* FAX *907/243–0649. 9 cabins with bath. Bar, dining room, fishing. MC, V. Closed Oct.–May.*

$ ⚠ **Brooks Campground.** This park-service campground is near Brooks Lodge, where campers can pay to eat and shower. There are designated cooking and eating shelters, latrines, well water, and a storage cache to protect food from the ever-present brown bears. Reservations are required. ⊠ *Katmai National Park, Box 7, King Salmon 99613,* ☎ *907/246–3305 or 800/365–2267 for reservations. D, MC, V. Closed mid-Sept.–May.*

Kobuk Valley National Park

Kobuk Valley National Park lies north of the Arctic Circle. Its 1.14 million acres contain remarkable inland deserts, the **Great Kobuk Sand Dunes,** and are home to interesting relict (or remnants of otherwise extinct) flora. In addition to the **Kobuk River,** this park contains two smaller rivers that provide delightful running, the Ambler and the Salmon. These brilliantly clear streams are accessible by wheeled plane, and each offers a good week's worth of pleasure (if the weather cooperates).

Kobuk Valley National Park is, like most other Alaska parks, undeveloped wilderness with no visitor facilities. It's a good place for backpacking and river trips. Nearby is Kotzebue, where the National Park Service has a visitor center. The villages of **Kobuk** and **Kiana** both provide immediate takeoff points and have air service. For information on the park, contact the Fairbanks Alaska Public Lands Information Center (☞ Visitor Information *in* Parks and Wildlife Refuges A to Z, *below*; or the National Park Service, ✉ Box 1029, Kotzebue 99752, ☎ 907/442–3890).

Kodiak National Wildlife Refuge

The 1.6-million-acre Kodiak National Wildlife Refuge (✉ 1390 Buskin Rd., Kodiak 99615, ☎ 907/487–2600) lies partly on Kodiak Island and partly on Afognak Island to the north. Seeing the Kodiak brown bears, weighing a pound at birth but up to 1,200 pounds when full grown, is worth the trip to this rugged country. The bears are spotted easily in July and August, feeding along salmon-spawning streams. Charter flightseeing trips are available to the area, and exaggerated tales of encounters with these impressive beasts are frequently heard.

LODGING

$ ⊡ **Kodiak Refuge Public-use Cabins.** It's possible to rent one of eight recreation cabins (accessible by floatplane or boat) within the refuge for up to seven days (longer in the off-season). Located along the coast and on inland lakes, the cabins include bunks with mattresses, kerosene heaters, tables, and benches. Reservations are awarded through quarterly lotteries, held on the first of January, April, July, and October. ✉ *1390 Buskin Rd., Kodiak 99615, ☎ 907/487–2600). Reservations required. No credit cards. Cabins on inland lakes are usually not accessible in winter.*

Noatak National Preserve

Adjacent to Gates of the Arctic National Park, the 6.5-million-acre Noatak National Preserve (contact the Fairbanks Alaska Public Lands Information Center—☞ Visitor Information *in* Parks and Wildlife Refuges A to Z, *below*; or the National Park Service, ✉ Box 1029, Kotzebue 99752, ☎ 907/442–3890) takes in much of the basin of the Noatak River. This is the largest mountain-ringed river basin in the United States that is still relatively wild (part of it is designated a Wild and Scenic River). The Noatak River offers particular pleasures to river runners, with inviting tundra to camp on and the Poktovik Mountains and the Igichuk Hills nearby for good hiking. Birding can be exceptional: horned grebes, gyrfalcon, golden eagles, parasitic jaegers, owls, terns, and loons are among the species you may see.

Shuyak Island State Park

The 46,000-acre Shuyak Island State Park (✉ Alaska State Parks, Kodiak District Office, HCR 3800, Kodiak 99615, ☎ 907/486–6339) is one of the newest—and most overlooked—units in the state parks system. At the northern end of the Kodiak Archipelago, it's accessible only by plane or boat. Its rugged outer coastline is balanced by a more protected system of interconnected bays, channels, and passages that make the park a favorite with sea kayakers. It also offers excellent wildlife viewing, especially for seabirds and sea mammals, and top-notch sportfishing for salmon.

LODGING AND CAMPING

$$ ⌂ **Alaska State Parks Cabins.** Alaska State Parks maintains four recreational public-use cabins on Shuyak Island. All are accessible by boat or plane only. The cabins may be rented for up to seven days. Each has a woodstove, propane lights, hot plate, four bunks, outside shower and wash area, cooking utensils, and pit toilets. ⊠ *Alaska State Parks, Kodiak District Office, HRC 3800, Kodiak 99615,* ☎ 907/486–6339, FAX *907/486–3320. 4 cabins. Reservations up to 180 days in advance. MC, V.*

$ ⚠ **Alaska State Parks Campgrounds.** The state also has three road-accessible campgrounds (Ft. Abercrombie, Buskin River, and Pasagshak) on Kodiak Island, with a total of 35 tent sites. All have toilets, drinking water, and fishing, and two have nearby hiking trails. Camping at Pasagshak is free; the campgrounds at Ft. Abercrombie and Buskin River charge $10 a night. ⊠ *Alaska State Parks, Kodiak District Office, HRC 3800, Kodiak 99615,* ☎ 907/486–6339, FAX *907/486–3320. No reservations. No credit cards. Closed in winter.*

Wood-Tikchik State Park

The Wood-Tikchik State Park (⊠ Box 3022, Dillingham 99576, ☎ 907/842–2375 from mid-May–Oct. 1; ⊠ 3601 C St., Suite 1200, Anchorage 99503, ☎ 907/269–8698 the rest of the year), 300 air mi southwest of Anchorage, has two separate groups of idyllic, interconnected lakes. These 1.55 million acres make Wood-Tikchik the nation's largest state park and are superb country for canoeing, rafting, kayaking, fishing (the salmon make solid red pools at the mouths of the lakeside streams), wilderness rambling, or simply enjoying the lovely scenery. You can also go from **Dillingham,** the closest city, by boat or by air to view the walruses offshore on **Round Island** within **Walrus Islands State Game Sanctuary** (☞ Wildlife Viewing, *above*).

PARKS AND WILDLIFE REFUGES A TO Z

Getting Around

By Air Taxi

Pilots can land you with precision on a glacier or river gravel bar and pluck you back up a week later. A list of certified air-taxi operations is available from the **Federal Aviation Administration** (⊠ Flight Standards District Office, 4510 West International Airport Rd., Anchorage 99502-1088, ☎ 907/271–2000). Individual parks and Alaska Public Lands Information Centers (☞ *below*) also can supply lists of reputable air-taxi services. Make your reservations in advance, and plan for the unexpected; weather can delay a scheduled pickup for days.

By Car

To reach **Denali National Park and Preserve,** drive south from Fairbanks on the George Parks Highway, or north from Anchorage on the Glenn Highway to the Parks Highway. To reach **Wrangell–St. Elias National Park and Preserve,** go northeast from Anchorage on the Glenn Highway to Glennallen, then south on the Richardson Highway to the visitor center at Copper Center. McCarthy, the park's principal backcountry gateway, is accessible via the McCarthy Road, a 60-mi-long gravel roadway. To reach **Kenai Fjords National Park,** as well as trails in the Kenai Peninsula, take the Seward Highway south out of Anchorage. Several state park units, including Chugach and Denali, are also accessible from the highway system.

By Ferry

The **Alaska Marine Highway System** (☎ 907/465–3941 or 800/642–0066, ℻ 907/277–4829) allows river runners, cyclists, and hikers to reach destinations along the Inside Passage and other coastal areas in South Central and Southwest Alaska. Sea kayakers can take a ferry to Misty Fjords National Monument or Glacier Bay National Park and Preserve in Southeast Alaska.

By Train

Denali National Park and Preserve and Seward, gateway to Kenai Fjords National Park, can be reached on the **Alaska Railroad** (☎ 907/265–2494 or 800/544–0552). Southeast Alaska's only railroad, the **White Pass Yukon Route** (☎ 907/983–2217 or 800/343–7373), operates summer excursions between Skagway and the White Pass Summit.

Contacts and Resources

Guided Tours

The following tour-guide operators offer adventure travel with an environmental bent.

STATEWIDE

Alaska Discovery (✉ 5449 Shaune Dr., Suite 4, Juneau 99801, ☎ 907/780–6226 or 800/586–1911, ℻ 907/780–4220). **Alaska Rainforest Tours** (✉ 416 Harris St., Suite 201, Juneau 99801, ☎ 907/463–3466, ℻ 907/463–4453 or 800/493–4453). **Alaska River Adventures** (✉ Box 725, Cooper Landing 99572, ☎ 907/595–2000 or 888/836–9027, ℻ 907/595–1533). **Alaska Women of the Wilderness Foundation** (✉ Box 773556, Eagle River 99577, ☎ 907/688–2226, ℻ 907/688–2285). **CampAlaska Tours** (✉ Box 872247, Wasilla 99687, ☎ 907/376–9438 or 800/376–9438, ℻ 907/376–2353). **Mountain Travel–Sobek: The Adventure Company** (✉ 6420 Fairmount Ave., El Cerrito, CA 94530–3606, ☎ 510/527–8100 or 800/227–2384, ℻ 510/525–7710). **National Audubon Society** (✉ 700 Broadway, New York, NY 10003, ☎ 212/979–3066, ℻ 212/353–0190). **Sierra Club** (✉ 85 2nd St., San Francisco, CA 94105, ☎ 415/977–5500, ℻ 415/977–5795).

SOUTHEAST

Alaska Cross-Country Guiding and Rafting (✉ Box 124, Haines 99827, ☎ ℻ 907/767–5522). **Baidarka Boats** (✉ Box 6001, Sitka 99835, ☎ 907/747–8996, ℻ 907/747–4801). **Spirit Walker Expeditions, Inc.** (✉ Box 240, Gustavus 99826, ☎ 907/697–2266 or 800/529–2537, ℻ 907/697–2701).

SOUTH CENTRAL

Alaska Wilderness Travel (✉ 715 W. Fireweed La., Suite E, Anchorage 99503, ☎ 907/277–7671 or 800/478–7671 in Alaska; outside AK, 800/544–2236; ℻ 907/277–4197). **Alaska Wildland Adventures** (✉ Box 389, Girdwood 99587, ☎ 907/783–2928 or 800/334–8730, ℻ 907/783–2130). **Coastal Kayaking & Custom Adventures Worldwide** (✉ 414 K St., Anchorage 99501, ☎ ℻ 907/258–3866 or ☎ 800/288–3134). **Stan Stephens Cruises** (✉ Box 1297, Valdez 99686, ☎ 800/992–1297, ℻ 907/835–3765).

INTERIOR

Redington Sled Dog Rides (✉ Mile 12.5 Knik Rd., HC30, Box 5440, Wasilla 99654, ☎ 907/376–5662 or 907/376–6730). **Yukon River Tours** (✉ 214 2nd Ave., Fairbanks 99701–4811, ☎ 907/452–7162, ℻ 907/452–5063).

Sourdough Outfitters (✉ Box 90, Bettles 99726, ☎ 907/692–5252, FAX 907/692–5612). **Wavetamer Kayaking** (✉ Box 228, Kodiak 99615, ☎ FAX 907/486–2604). **Wilderness Alaska** (✉ Box 113063, Anchorage 99511, ☎ 907/345–3567, FAX 907/345–3967).

Visitor Information

Before making a winter trip, discuss the safety of your route and consider taking an avalanche-awareness course at the **Alaska Mountain Safety Center** (✉ 9140 Brewster Dr., Anchorage 99516, ☎ 907/345–3566).

Alaska Department of Fish and Game (✉ Box 25526, Juneau 99802, ☎ 907/465–4100). **Alaska Division of Tourism** (✉ Box 110801, Juneau 99811, ☎ 907/465–2010, FAX 907/465–2287). **Alaska State Parks Information** (✉ 3601 C St., Suite 200, Anchorage 99503, ☎ 907/269–8400, FAX 907/269–8401). **Anchorage Alaska Public Lands Information Center** (✉ 605 W. 4th Ave., Suite 105, Anchorage 99501, ☎ 907/271–2737, FAX 907/265–2323). **Fairbanks Alaska Public Lands Information Center** (✉ 250 Cushman St., Suite 1A, Fairbanks 99701, ☎ 907/456–0527, FAX 907/456–0514). **National Park Service Alaska Regional Office** (✉ 2525 Gambell St., Anchorage 99503, ☎ 907/257–2696). **U.S. Forest Service Visitor Information Center** (✉ Centennial Hall, 101 Egan Dr., Juneau 99801, ☎ 907/586–8751). **U.S. Fish and Wildlife Service** (✉ 1011 E. Tudor Rd., Anchorage 99503, ☎ 907/786–3487, FAX 907/786–3486).

4 Southeast Alaska

Including Ketchikan, Juneau, Haines, Sitka, and Skagway

The Southeast encompasses the Inside Passage—a century ago the traditional route to the Klondike goldfields and today the centerpiece of Alaska cruises. Here are glacier-filled fjords and the justly famous Glacier Bay National Park. Juneau, the state's capital, is also in the Southeast, as are fishing villages such as Petersburg and Ketchikan, which is known for its totem-pole carving. An onion-dome cathedral accents Sitka, the onetime capital of Russian America. Each fall, up to 3,000 eagles gather outside Haines.

By Mike Miller

Updated by
Connie Saint

THE SOUTHEAST STRETCHES BELOW THE STATE like the tail of a kite. It is a world of massive glaciers, fjords, and snowcapped peaks. The largest concentration of coastal glaciers on earth can be viewed at Glacier Bay National Park and Preserve (☞ Chapter 3), one of the region's most prized attractions. Thousands of islands are blanketed with lush stands of spruce, hemlock, and cedar. Bays, coves, lakes of all sizes, and swift, icy rivers provide some of the continent's best fishing grounds—and scenery as majestic and unspoiled as any in North America. Many of Southeast Alaska's wildest and most pristine landscapes belong to the Tongass National Forest (☞ Chapter 3), which encompasses nearly 17 million acres—or 73% of the Panhandle's land.

Like anywhere else, the Southeast has its drawbacks. For one thing, it rains a lot. If you plan to spend a week or more here, you can count on showers during at least a few of those days. Die-hard Southeasterners simply throw on a light slicker and shrug off the rain. Their attitude is philosophical: without the rain, there would be no forests, no lakes, and no streams running with world-class salmon and trout, no healthy populations of brown and black bears, moose, deer, mountain goats, and wolves.

Another disadvantage—or advantage, depending on your point of view—is an almost total lack of connecting roads between the area's communities. To fill this void, Alaskans created the Marine Highway System of fast, frequent passenger and vehicle ferries, which have staterooms, observation decks, cocktail lounges, and heated, glass-enclosed solariums.

The Southeast's natural beauty and abundance of wildlife have made it one of the world's fastest-growing cruise destinations. There are about 20 big cruise ships that ply the Inside Passage during the height of the summer (☞ Chapter 2). Regular air service to the Southeast is available from the Lower 48 states and from mainland Alaska. The Southeast is closer to the Lower 48 than the rest of Alaska and is therefore the least costly to reach.

The Native peoples you'll meet in the Southeast coastal region are Tlingit, Haida, and Tsimshian. These peoples, like their coastal neighbors in British Columbia, preserve a culture rich in totemic art forms, including deeply carved poles, masks, baskets, and ceremonial objects. Many live among non-Natives in modern towns while continuing their own traditions.

A pioneer spirit dominates the towns of Southeast Alaska. Residents—some from other states, some with roots in the "old country," some who can trace their ancestors back to the Gold Rush days, and some whose ancestors came over the Bering Land Bridge from Asia tens of thousands of years ago—are an adventurous lot. The rough-and-tumble spirit of the Southeast often combines with a worldly sophistication: those who fish are also artists, loggers are often business entrepreneurs, and homemakers may be Native dance performers.

Pleasures and Pastimes

Dining

Given the region's coastal setting, it's not surprising that many of its lodges, restaurants, and cafés specialize in seafood dishes: from halibut and salmon to crab, shrimp, and clam chowder. Larger communities offer the full spectrum of dining possibilities, from fine dining

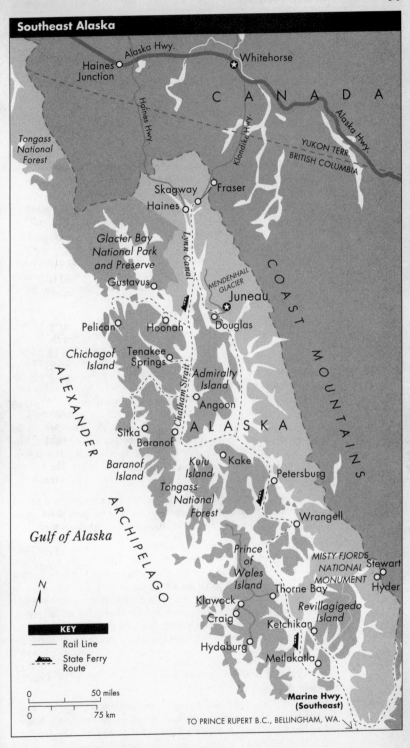

Southeast Alaska

Alaska Hwy.

Haines
Junction

Whitehorse

C A N A D A

Haines Hwy.

*Tongass
National
Forest*

Klondike Hwy.

YUKON TERR.
BRITISH COLUMBIA

Alaska Hwy.

Skagway — Fraser

Haines

Lynn Canal

*Glacier Bay
National Park
and Preserve*

MENDENHALL
GLACIER

Gustavus

Juneau

Pelican

Hoonah

Douglas

C
O
A
S
T

*Chichagof
Island*

Tenakee
Springs

Chatham Strait

*Admiralty
Island*

M
O
U
N
T
A
I
N
S

A L E X A N D E R

Angoon

Sitka
Baranof

A L A S K A

*Baranof
Island*

*Kuiu
Island*

Kake

Petersburg

A R C H I P E L A G O

*Tongass
National
Forest*

Wrangell

Gulf of Alaska

*Prince
of
Wales
Island*

*MISTY FJORDS
NATIONAL
MONUMENT*

Stewart
Hyder

N

Thorne Bay

*Revillagigedo
Island*

Klawock

Craig

Ketchikan

KEY

Hydaburg

Metlakatla

——— Rail Line

⛴ State Ferry
Route

Marine Hwy.
(Southeast)

0   50 miles

0   75 km

TO PRINCE RUPERT B.C., BELLINGHAM, WA.

to fast-food joints (of which, thankfully, there are not too many), and, as a bonus, many places offer wonderful views of the region's land- and seascapes. Reservations are generally not necessary, but you may wish to inquire in advance, particularly in the summer.

For price ranges, *see* the dining chart *in* On the Road with Fodor's.

Fishing

The Southeast is a fisherman's paradise. There are saltwater salmon charter boats, salmon fishing lodges (some near the larger communities, others remote and accessible only by floatplane), fly-in mountain-lake lodges where the fishing is for trout and char, and—bargain hunters take special note—more than 150 remote but weather-tight cabins operated by the U.S. Forest Service (☞ Visitor Information *in* Southeast Alaska A to Z, *below*) within Tongass National Forest. One of the world's great travel bargains, these public-use cabins have bunks for six to eight occupants, tables, stoves, and outdoor privies and cost only $25 per night per party. Most are fly-in units, accessible by pontoon-equipped aircraft from virtually any community in the Panhandle. You provide your own sleeping bag, food, and cooking utensils. Don't be surprised if the Forest Service recommends you carry along a 30.06- or larger-caliber rifle in the unlikely event of a bear problem.

Hiking and Backpacking

Trekking woods, mountains, and beaches is Southeast Alaska's unofficial regional sport. Many of the trails are abandoned mining and logging roads. Others are natural routes—in some sections, even game trails—meandering over ridges, through forests, and alongside streams and glaciers. A few, like the Chilkoot Trail (☞ Chapter 3) out of Skagway, rate five stars for historical significance, scenery, and hiker aids en route. The Alaska Division of Parks Southeast regional office, in Juneau (☞ Visitor Information *in* Southeast Alaska A to Z, *below*), will send you a list of state-maintained trails and parks in the Panhandle; local visitor bureaus and recreation departments can also help. For lists of operators offering hiking and backpacking trips, *see* Tour Operators *in* The Gold Guide, *and* Guided Tours *in* Chapter 3.

Lodging

Hotels, motels, lodges, and inns run the gamut in Southeast Alaska from very traditional urban hostelries—the kind you'll find almost anywhere— to charming small-town inns and rustic cabins in the boondocks.

The widest range of options is in Ketchikan and Juneau. Accommodations in any of the Panhandle communities, however, are usually not hard to come by, even in the summer, except when festivals, fishing derbies, fairs, or other special events are under way. To be on the safe side and get your first choice, you should make reservations as early as possible. With the exception of some bed-and-breakfasts, most lodgings accept major credit cards. For comprehensive listings of B&Bs, hostels, and other accommodations, contact local visitor information centers.

For price ranges, *see* the lodging charts *in* On the Road with Fodor's.

Scenic Drives

The descent (or ascent, depending on which direction you're traveling) from the high, craggy Canadian mountain country to the Southeast Alaska coast makes both the Klondike Highway into Skagway and the Haines Highway to Haines especially memorable traveling. At the top of the passes, vegetation is sparse, and pockets of snow are often present, even in summertime. The scenery is stark, with mountains silhouetted sharply against frequently blue skies. As you near the saltwater coast of the Panhandle, the forest cover becomes tall, thick, and evergreen. Both drives are worth an excursion, even if you don't intend to drive any farther than the Canadian border and return. Every city, town, and village in Southeast Alaska has one or more waterfront drives that take in bustling dock scenes and tranquil bays and beaches, and they also offer the possibility of seeing wildlife. Inquire at local information centers. Very few visitors bring their own cars to Southeast Alaska, but you can rent one.

Scuba Diving

Although the visibility is not very good in most Southeast waters, there's still a lot of scuba- and skin-diving activity throughout the region. Quarter-inch wet suits are a must. So is a buddy; stay close together. Local dive shops can steer you to the best places to dive for abalone, scallops, and crabs and advise you on the delights and dangers of underwater wrecks. Some shops also rent tanks and equipment to qualified divers.

Shopping

Totem poles, from a few inches to several feet tall, are some of the most popular handicrafts made by the Tlingit and Haida in the Southeast Panhandle. Other items include wall masks, paddles, dance rattles, baskets, and tapestries with Southeast Alaska Native designs. You'll find these items at gift shops up and down the coast. If you want to be sure of authenticity, buy items tagged with the state-approved AUTHENTIC NATIVE HANDICRAFT FROM ALASKA label. Other popular take-home items include salmon—smoked, canned, or otherwise packaged. Virtually every community has at least one canning and/or smoking operation that packs and ships local seafood.

Wildlife Viewing

From the Chilkat's gathering of bald eagles to the bears of Admiralty Island and Anan Creek, and the whales and seals of Glacier Bay, Southeast Alaska offers myriad wildlife-watching and photography opportunities. Several companies within the region conduct guided wildlife tours (☞ Chapter 3).

Exploring the Southeast

The Southeast Panhandle stretches some 500 mi from Yakutat at its northernmost to Ketchikan and Metlakatla at its southern end. At its widest the region measures only 140 mi, and in the upper Panhandle just south of Yakutat, it's a skinny 30 mi across. Most of the Panhandle consists of a sliver of mainland buffered by offshore islands.

There are more than a thousand islands up and down the Panhandle coast—most of them mountainous with lush covers of timber. Collectively they constitute the Alexander Archipelago. On the mainland to the east of the United States–Canada border lies British Columbia.

You can get to and around the area by ship or by plane, but forget traveling here by car or RV unless your destinations are Haines and Skagway; both those northern Panhandle communities are connected by road to the Alaska Highway. Elsewhere in the Southeast, the roadways that exist in these parts run at most a few dozen miles out from towns and villages, then they dead-end. (For those who wish to drive up the Alaska Highway and then visit road-isolated communities, it is possible to reserve vehicle space on Alaska's state ferries.)

Most communities are on islands rather than on the mainland. The principal exceptions are Juneau, Haines, Skagway, and the Native village of Klukwan. Island outposts include Ketchikan, Wrangell, Petersburg,

Sitka, Metlakatla, Native villages, and logging camps. Each town has its own ethnic lore, wildlife, and natural wonders.

Numbers in the text correspond to numbers in the margin and on the Ketchikan, Wrangell, Petersburg, Sitka, Juneau, Haines, and Skagway maps.

Great Itineraries

Like all of Alaska's regions, the Southeast covers a vast area (even though it represents a thin slice of the state), and most of its communities, as well as its parks, national forest lands, and other wildlands, are accessible only by boat or plane. Visitors should therefore give themselves at least a week here. For those with only a few days, it might be best to fly into one of Southeast Alaska's larger communities—like Juneau, Sitka, or Ketchikan—and then take a state ferry to other Panhandle communities. Or, fly to a remote destination. Here, as in other parts of the state, the easiest way is to go as part of a package tour; most visitors explore the Southeast on cruise ships or state ferries, which generate their own schedules. But there are plenty of adventures awaiting the ambitious independent traveler who plans ahead.

IF YOU HAVE 3 DAYS

Plan to spend them in and around Alaska's state capital, 🖼 **Juneau** ㊹–㊱. Go flightseeing or drive to the Mendenhall Glacier and visit 🖼 **Admiralty Island**'s Pack Creek (☞ Chapter 3), where brown bears can be watched as they fish for salmon (permits are required); you can overnight in one of the Forest Service cabins. Or instead of visiting Pack Creek, you might wish to overnight at the tiny village of 🖼 **Tenakee Springs.**

IF YOU HAVE 5 DAYS

Begin your trip in 🖼 **Juneau** ㊹–㊱ and spend two or three days as described above. Then go south via the state ferry to 🖼 **Sitka** ㉞–㊸, ancestral home of the Tlingit and once the capital of Russian America. Spend the next two or three days visiting White Sulphur Springs or paddling along Baranof Island's rugged coast. Or instead of going south from Juneau, another good bet is to travel north to 🖼 **Gustavus** and nearby **Glacier Bay National Park and Preserve** (☞ Chapter 3), one of America's premier parklands, where tidewater glaciers, rugged mountain scenery, and abundant marine wildlife await.

IF YOU HAVE 7 DAYS

It's possible to see a cross section of the entire region in a week via cruise ships or state ferries. Starting at 🖼 **Ketchikan** ①–⑳, known for its totem poles, the Alaska Marine Highway regularly makes stops at all of the region's larger communities: **Wrangell** ㉑–㉘, with its ancient petroglyphs; 🖼 **Petersburg** ㉙–㉝, which has a strong Norwegian influence; 🖼 **Sitka** ㉞–㊸, former capital of Russian Alaska; 🖼 **Juneau** ㊹–㊱, the state capital; **Haines** ㊹–㊳, known for its bald eagles and Native dance troupe; and 🖼 **Skagway** ㊷–㊻, a Gold Rush–era throwback; it also serves several smaller communities, like **Kake, Angoon, Tenakee,** and **Hoonah.** Give yourself time to see local sights and visit some out-of-town destinations, like **Admiralty Island, Alaska Chilkat Bald Eagle Preserve,** and **Glacier Bay National Park and Preserve** (☞ Chapter 3).

When to Tour the Southeast

The best time to visit is May through September, when the weather is mildest, daylight hours are longest, the wildlife most abundant, the fishing is best, and festivals and tourist-oriented activities are in full swing.

Ketchikan

730 mi northwest of Seattle, 850 mi southeast of Anchorage.

Ketchikan, which has more totems than anywhere in the world, is perched on a large island at the foot of Deer Mountain (3,000 ft). The site at the mouth of Ketchikan Creek was a summer fish camp of the Tlingit until white miners and fishermen came to settle the town in 1885. Gold discoveries just before the turn of the century brought more immigrants, and valuable timber and commercial fishing resources spurred new industries. By the 1930s the town bragged it was the "salmon-canning capital of the world." You will still find some of the Southeast's best salmon fishing here.

There's a lot to be seen on foot in downtown Ketchikan. The best place ❶ to begin is at the **Ketchikan Visitors Bureau** (☞ Visitor Information *in* Southeast Alaska A to Z, *below*), where you can pick up a free historic-walking-tour map. The bureau's new building is conveniently located in a municipal parking lot right next to the cruise-ship docks; a third of its space is occupied by day-tour, flightseeing, and boat-tour operators.

The U.S. Forest Service and other federal agencies provide information ❷ on Alaska's public lands at the impressive **Southeast Alaska Visitor Center,** on Main Street. The center's museum-quality exhibits focus on the resources, Native cultures, and ecosystems of Southeast Alaska; a highlight is the rain-forest exhibit. Another visitor-friendly feature is the inviting "trip-planning room," especially helpful for independent travelers; you can relax on Mission-style furniture while consulting books, maps, and videos not only on Ketchikan but on all of the towns and attractions in the Southeast. While here you can also view an award-winning multimedia show, "Mystical Southeast Alaska," in the center's theater. The show runs every 30 minutes in the summer. ☎ 907/228–6220. ☜ $4, summer. ☉ May–Sept., daily 8:30–4:30; Oct.–Apr., Tues.–Sat. 8:30–4:30.

❸ The newly finished **Spruce Mill Development** on Mill Street is modeled after 1920s-style cannery architecture. Spread over 6½ acres along the waterfront, its five buildings contain a mix of retail stores, souvenir shops, restaurants, and fish and vegetable stands.

❹ Built in 1903, **St. John's Church,** on Bawden Street, is the oldest remaining house of worship in Ketchikan, its interior formed from red cedar cut ❺ in the Native-operated sawmill in nearby Saxman. The **Seaman's Park,** next door to St. John's Church, was built in 1904 as a hospital. It later housed *Alaska Sportsman* magazine (now *Alaska*), which began pub- ❻ lication in Ketchikan in 1936. **Whale Park,** catercorner from St. John's Church, is the site of the **Knox Brother Clock,** and the **Chief Johnson Totem Pole,** raised in 1989 and a replica of the 1901 totem in the same site.

❼ At the **Tongass Historical Museum** you can browse among Native artifacts and pioneer relics of the early mining and fishing era. Among the rotating exhibits are a big and brilliantly polished lens from Tree Point Lighthouse, the bullet-riddled skull of a notorious brown bear called Old Groaner, Native ceremonial objects, and a 14-ft model of a typical Alaskan salmon-fishing seine vessel. ✉ 629 Dock St., ☎ 907/225–5600. ☜ $3. ☉ May 15–Sept., daily 8–5; Oct.–May 14, Wed.–Fri. 1–5, weekends 1–4.

At one time virtually all of Ketchikan's walkways and streets were made ❽ from wooden trestles. But now only one remains, the **Grant Street Trestle,** constructed in 1908. Get out your camera and set it for fast speed

City Park, **13**
Creek Street, **16**
Creek Street
Footbridge, **18**
Deer Mountain
Hatchery, **11**
Dolly's House, **17**
Grant Street
Trestle, **8**
Ketchikan
Visitors
Bureau, **1**
*Return of the
Eagle*, **14**
St. John's
Church, **4**
Salmon Falls, **9**
Saxman Native
Village, **20**
Seaman's Park, **5**
Southeast
Alaska Visitor
Center, **2**
Spruce Mill
Development, **3**
Thomas St., **15**
Tongass
Historical
Museum, **7**
Totem Bight
State Historical
Park, **19**
Totem Heritage
Center and
Nature Park, **12**
Westmark Cape
Fox Lodge, **10**
Whale Park, **6**

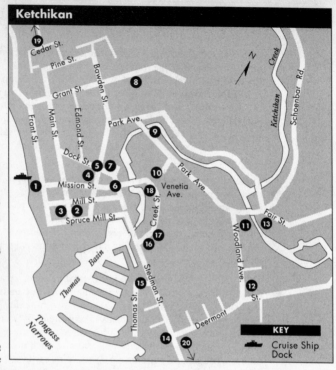

9   at the **Salmon Falls, Fish Ladder,** and **Salmon Carving,** just off Park Avenue on Married Man's Trail. When the salmon start running in midsummer, thousands literally leap the falls (or take the easier ladder route) to spawn in Ketchikan Creek's waters farther upstream. Many can also be seen in the creek feeding the falls.

10   **Westmark Cape Fox Lodge** (☞ Dining and Lodging, *below*) can be reached by walking to the top of steep Venetia Avenue. Besides a stunning view of the harbor and fine dining, the lodge offers funicular rides to and from popular Creek Street for $1.

Tens of thousands of salmon are annually dispersed into local waters

11   at **Deer Mountain Hatchery,** on Park Avenue. The hatchery, owned by the Ketchikan Indian Corporation (☞ Guided Tours, *below*), has exhibits on traditional Native American fishing and gives guided tours

12   for $5.95 per person. **Totem Heritage Center and Nature Park** is just south of the hatchery, on Deermont Street. Here you'll find an amazing collection of original totems, dating back almost two centuries, displayed for up-close viewing. ☎ 907/225–5900. ⊠ $4. ☻ May–Sept., daily 8–5; Oct.–Apr., Tues.–Fri. 1–5.

13   The Hatchery and Heritage Center lead into **City Park,** at Park and Fair
14   streets. On Stedman Street you'll see the colorful wall mural called *Return of the Eagle.* It was created by 21 Native artists on the walls of the Robertson Building on the Ketchikan campus of the University of Alaska–Southeast.

15   At **Thomas Street,** enjoy the view of Thomas Basin, a major and pictureworthy harbor. One of four harbors in Ketchikan, it is home port to a variety of pleasure and work boats.

16 **Creek Street** is the former site of Ketchikan's infamous red-light district. Today its small, quaint houses, built on stilts over the creek waters, have been restored as trendy shops. The street's most famous brothel,

17 **Dolly's House,** has been preserved as a museum (open when cruise ships are in port), complete with furnishings, beds, and a short history of the life and times of Ketchikan's best-known madam. Admission is $4.

18 **Creek Street Footbridge** offers more good salmon viewing when the fish are running.

The poles at Ketchikan's two most famous totem parks are, for the most part, 60-year-old replicas of even older totems brought in from outlying villages as part of a federal works–cultural project during the

19 1930s. **Totem Bight State Historical Park** (⊠ North Tongass Hwy., ☎ 907/247–8574) is 10 mi north of town. It has many totems and a handhewn Native tribal house and sits on a particularly scenic spit of land facing the waters of Tongass Narrows.

★ **20** **Saxman Native Village** (⊠ South Tongass Hwy., ☎ 907/225–5163) is 2 mi south of town, but don't try walking—there are no sidewalks. Saxman Village (named for a missionary who helped Native Alaskans settle here before 1900) has a tribal house believed to be the largest in the world. There's also a carver's shed nearby where totems and totemic art objects are created and a stand-up theater where a multimedia presentation tells the story of Southeast Alaska's Native peoples. You can see the **Totem Park** if you drive out on your own, but to visit the tribal house you must take a tour (☞ Guided Tours, *below*).

On the highway in either direction, you won't go far before you run out of road. The North Tongass Highway ends about 18 mi from downtown, at Settler's Cove Campground. The South Tongass Highway terminates at a power plant about 8 mi from town. Side roads soon end at campgrounds and at trailheads, viewing points, lakes, boat-launching ramps, and private property.

Dining and Lodging

$$$ ✕ **Steamers.** Anchoring the new Saw Mill Mall, this spacious restaurant has an extensive menu of fresh seafood, pasta, and meats. It also supports more beer taps than any one establishment in all of the Southeast—included in the selection is Henry Weinhart's Rootbeer—and offers more types of liquor than you ever knew existed. If you're dining with four or more, don't hesitate to order the "Ultimate Steamers Seafood Festival": the steaming mound of fresh lobster tails, steamer clams, shrimp, crabs, mussels, oysters, and potatoes is a veritable work of art. ⊠ 76 Front St., Box 9452, ☎ 907/225–1600, AE, D, DC, MC, V.

$$–$$$ ✕ **Salmon Falls Resort.** It's a half-hour drive from town, but the seafood and steaks served up in this huge, octagonal restaurant make the trip more than worthwhile. The restaurant is built of pine logs, and at the center of the dining room, supporting the roof, rises a 40-ft section of 48-inch pipe manufactured to be part of the Alaska pipeline. The dining area overlooks the waters of Clover Passage, where sunsets can be vivid red and remarkable. Seafood caught fresh from adjacent waters is especially good; try the halibut and the prawns stuffed with crabmeat. ⊠ Mile 17, N. Tongass Hwy., Box 5700, 99901, ☎ 907/225–2752 or 800/247–9059 outside Alaska. AE, MC, V.

$–$$ ✕ **Kay's Kitchen.** This simple restaurant, situated on the water 1½ mi from downtown Ketchikan, is known for its homemade soups and generous sandwiches. Other specialties include barbecued ribs and homemade desserts, including ice cream. ⊠ 2813 Tongass Ave., ☎ 907/225–5860.

$$$ ✗▣ **The Narrows Inn.** Four miles from town, the Narrows is part fishing camp, part resort conference center. The rooms are bright, with green and taupe color schemes and natural wood trim. All have balconies overlooking the Tongass Narrows. Water-based tours that begin 10 steps from your front door can be scheduled at the tour desk; order a box lunch to take along from the full service restaurant. Or, for a more urban experience, take the Narrows shuttle to town to shop or dine. Continental breakfast is included in the room rate. ⊠ *Box 8660, 99901, ☎ 907/247–2600 or 888/686–2600, FAX 907/247–2602. 44 rooms. Shuttle. AE, D, MC, V.*

$$–$$$ ✗▣ **Gilmore Hotel.** The Gilmore has a European feel, and because of such features as a 1930s-style lobby, it's on the National Register of Historic Places (though certainly the throughway from the lobby to the Baskin Robbins next door wasn't part of the original design.) There are some welcome modern touches in the rooms, but there is no elevator in this three-story building. Annabelle's Keg and Chowder House is really two restaurants. The Keg and Chowder House, with a 1920s-style decor, serves seafood, pasta, steak, and prime rib. Specialties include oysters on the half shell and steamer clams. Annabelle's Parlor is a more formal restaurant frequented by locals for its fine seafood in classic preparations. There's also an espresso bar and Annabelle's (☎ 907/225–6009), a semiformal lounge with a jukebox. ⊠ *326 Front St., 99901, ☎ 907/225–9423 or 800/275–9423, FAX 907/225–7442. 38 rooms. 2 restaurants, bar. AE, D, DC, MC, V.*

$$$$ ▣ **The Landing.** This Best Western property is named for the ferry landing site in the waters of Tongass Narrows across the street. Decor is modern, basic Best Western. A fireplace and new Mission furniture were added to the small lobby during a recent renovation, and Jeremiah's Pub, a comfortable restaurant and bar with its own cozy no-smoking lounge, opened its doors to guests in the last year. Some rooms have microwaves and kitchenettes; suites have all the comforts of home. ⊠ *3434 Tongass Ave., ☎ 907/225–5166 or 800/428–8304, FAX 907/225–6900. 76 rooms. Restaurant, café, exercise room, shuttle. AE, D, DC, MC, V.*

$$$$ ▣ **Waterfall Resort.** Remote, but boasting the ultimate in creature comforts, this upscale fishing lodge is on Prince of Wales Island near Ketchikan. At this former commercial salmon cannery you sleep in the lodge or in Cape Cod–style cottages (formerly cannery workers' cabins, but they never had it so good); eat bountiful meals of salmon, halibut steak, and all the trimmings; and fish from your own private cabin cruiser under the care of your own private fishing guide. A three-night minimum stay with all meals and floatplane fare from Ketchikan comes to around $2,700 per person. ⊠ *320 Dock St., Suite 222, Box 6440, 99901, ☎ 907/225–9461 or 800/544–5125 outside Alaska, FAX 907/225–8530. 26 cabins, 4 suites, 10 lodge rooms. Restaurant. AE, D, MC, V.*

$$$$ ▣ **Westmark Cape Fox Lodge.** One of Ketchikan's poshest properties offers fantastic views of the town and harbor from 135 ft above the village. An open ski-lodge-style lobby with roaring fire and grand piano make for a cozy, luxurious setting. Rooms are quite spacious, with Shaker-style furnishings, the traditional Tlingit tribal colors (red, black, and white), and watercolors of native Alaskan birds. All rooms provide views of either Tongass Narrows or Deer Mountain. The town's main attractions are within walking distance, but guests can take the hotel's sky tram directly to Creek Street. ⊠ *800 Venetia Way, 99901, ☎ 907/225–8001 or 800/544–0970 for reservations, FAX 907/225–8286. 72 rooms. Restaurant, lobby lounge, no-smoking rooms, room service, meeting rooms. AE, D, DC, MC, V.*

$$–$$$$ ☒ **Cedars Lodge.** Nothing in the plain, square exterior of this hotel or in its spartan lobby hints at the deluxe accommodations within. Two of the guest rooms are split-level with circular stairways; all are carpeted and have a green color scheme with natural wood trim. Many rooms have a full kitchen and whirlpool bath. Windows are large, and some give views of the busy water and air traffic in Tongass Narrows (ask for a room with a view when making reservations). Simple American fare is served at a buffet dinner and breakfast (summer only); meals can also be brought to your room from the Galley, which offers pizza and Asian food. ☒ *1471 Tongass Ave., Box 8331, 99901,* ☎ *907/225–1900,* ℻ *907/225–8604. 12 rooms. Restaurant, room service. AE, D, DC, MC, V.*

Guided Tours

Alaska Cruises (☎ 907/225–6044 or 800/228–1905 for a brochure, ℻ 907/225–8636) runs harbor cruises of the Ketchikan waterfront and leads excursions from Ketchikan to Misty Fjords National Monument. Boat transport for kayakers is also offered to and from Misty Fjords.

Cape Fox Tours (☎ 907/225–4846, ℻ 907/225–3137) conducts tours of Saxman Native Village.

Ketchikan Indian Corporation (☎ 907/225–5158 or 800/252–5158, ℻ 907/247–0429) conducts Native American heritage town tours focusing on traditional land and fishery use and Native crafts.

Outdoor Activities and Sports

CANOEING AND KAYAKING

Coastal paddling is popular here, as it is in much of the Southeast, especially in nearby Misty Fjords National Monument (☞ Chapter 3). The **Ketchikan Parks and Recreation Department** (☎ 907/225–9579) rents kayaks and canoes. **Southeast Exposure** (☎ 907/225–8829 in summer), also in Ketchikan, rents canoes and kayaks, gives kayaking classes, and guides trips.

FISHING

Sportfishing for salmon and trout is excellent in the Ketchikan area, in either saltwater or freshwater lakes and streams. Contact the **Ketchikan Visitors Bureau** (☞ Visitor Information *in* Southeast Alaska A to Z, *below*) for information on guide services and locations.

HIKING

If you're a tough hiker, the 3-mi trail from downtown to the top of **Deer Mountain** will repay your efforts with a spectacular panorama of the city below and the wilderness behind. The trail begins at the corner of Fair and Deermont streets. **Ward Cove Recreation Area,** about 6 mi north of town, offers easier hiking beside lakes and streams and beneath towering spruce and hemlock trees; they also have several designated picnic spots.

SCUBA DIVING

Alaska Diving Service (☒ 4845 N. Tongass Ave., ☎ 907/225–4667) rents tanks and equipment and guides you to the best places to dive.

Shopping

ART GALLERIES

Among the best of Southeast Alaska's galleries is the **Scanlon Gallery,** with a location in downtown Ketchikan (☒ 318 Mission St., ☎ 907/247–4730 or 800/690–4730). It handles not only major Alaska artists (Byron Birdsall, Rie Muñoz, John Fehringer, Jon Van Zyle) and local talent but also traditional and contemporary Native art, including soapstone sculptures.

Design, art, and clothing converge in the stylish **Soho Coho Contemporary Art and Craft Gallery** (⊠ 5 Creek St., ☎ 907/225–5954) where you'll find an eclectic collection of art and T-shirts, featuring the work of owner Ray Troll, best known for his fish art, as well as that of other Southeast Alaskan artists.

FOOD

For some of the Southeast's best canned or smoked salmon and halibut, try either of the two locations of **Ketchikan's Salmon Etc.** (⊠ 10 Creek St. or 322 Mission St., ☎ 907/225–6008, or 800/354–7256 outside Alaska).

Wrangell

80 mi northwest of Ketchikan.

Next up the line is Wrangell, on an island near the mouth of the fast-flowing Stikine River. A small, unassuming, timber and fishing community—though the timber mill has been closed in recent years—the town has existed under three flags. Known as Redoubt St. Dionysius when it was part of Russian America, the town was renamed Fort Stikine under the British. You can see a lot in Wrangell on foot, and a good place to start your tour is at the stalls selling local goods and souvenirs

㉑ outside the **Wrangell Visitor Center** (⊠ 107 Stikine Ave., ☎ 907/874–3901 or 800/367–9745, ℻ 907/874–3905), which is close to the docks, in the **Stikine Inn** (☞ Dining and Lodging, *below*). It's open regular hours throughout the summer. If you need information during the winter, call 907/874–2795.

㉒ **KikSadi Totem Park,** on Front Street, is a pocket park of Alaska greenery and impressive totem poles. This is the spot for a pleasant stroll.

㉓ The **Wrangell Museum** contains an historical collection that includes a bootlegger's still and historic aviation and communication memorabilia, as well as the original house totems from Chief Shakes's clan house (believed to have been carved in the late 1700s), petroglyphs, woven Native baskets from the turn of the century, and other local artifacts. It's on the lower floor of the community center, between the Presbyterian church and the high school. ⊠ *318 Church St.,* ☎ *907/874–3770.* ☜ *$2.* ☉ *May–mid-Sept., weekdays 10–5, Sat. 1–4, Sun. when the ferry or cruise ships arrive; late Sept.–Apr., Tues.–Fri. 10–4, or by appointment.*

㉔ **Chief Shakes's grave site,** on Case Avenue, is marked by two killer-whale totems. Buried here is Shakes V, who led the local Tlingit during the first half of the 19th century.

㉕ **Chief Shakes Island** is Wrangell's number-one visitor attraction. Reached by a footbridge off the harbor dock, it has some of the finest totem poles in Alaska, as well as a tribal house constructed in the 1930s as a replica of one that was home to many of the various Shakes and their peoples. ☎ *907/874–3747.* ☜ *$1.50 donation requested.* ☉ *When cruise ships are in port or by appointment.*

㉖ The **Irene Ingle Public Library** (⊠ 124 2nd St., ☎ 907/874–3535), behind the post office, has a small collection of ancient petroglyphs.

㉗ A private museum called **Our Collections,** run by Elva Bigelow, is in a large metal building on the water side of Evergreen Avenue. Literally thousands of items (clocks, animal traps, waffle irons, tools, etc.) that the Bigelows have gathered and used themselves over the past 60 years of Alaska living are on display. ☎ *907/874–3646.* ☜ *Donations accepted.* ☉ *Open for groups of cruise-ship and ferry passengers or by appointment.*

Chief Shakes's grave site, **24**

Chief Shakes Island, **25**

Irene Ingle Public Library, **26**

KikSadi Totem Park, **22**

Our Collections, **27**

Petroglyph Beach, **28**

Wrangell Museum, **23**

Wrangell Visitor Center, **21**

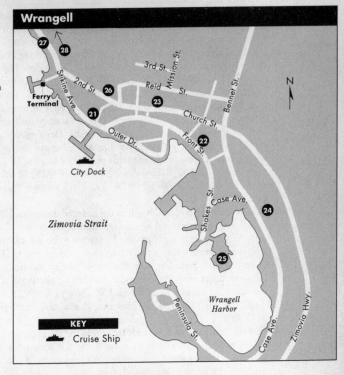

28. **Petroglyph Beach** is one of the more curious sights in Southeast Alaska. Here, scattered among other rocks, are three dozen or more large stones bearing designs and pictures chiseled by unknown, ancient artists. No one knows why the rocks were etched the way they were. Perhaps they were boundary markers or messages; possibly they were just primitive doodling. Because the petroglyphs can be damaged by physical contact, the state discourages visitors from creating a rubbing off the rocks with rice paper and crayons. Instead, you can purchase a rubber stamp duplicate of selected petroglyphs from the city museum or from a Forest Service interpreter at the cruise dock for $4.50–$6. Do not, of course, attempt to move any of the petroglyph stones.

OFF THE BEATEN PATH

ANAN WILDLIFE OBSERVATORY – About 30 mi southeast of Wrangell in the Tongass National Forest, Anan is one of Alaska's premier bear-viewing areas. Black and brown bears are the principal attractions. Each summer, from early July to mid-August, as many as 30 or 40 black bears gather at this Southeast stream to feed on pink salmon. On an average visit of about two hours, you might spot two to four bears. Forest Service interpreters are on hand to answer questions from July through September. The site is accessible only by boat or floatplane. For more information on Anan and bear-viewing regulations (among other things, dogs and food are prohibited), contact the Forest Service's Wrangell Ranger District (✉ Box 51, 99929, ☎ 907/874-2323). *See also* Guided Tours, *below.*

Dining and Lodging

$$ ✕🖭 **Roadhouse Lodge.** This waterfront lodge has a homestead atmosphere, with relics collected from all over the state; walls here are practically a museum of early Alaska. The lodge's restaurant is popular with locals and visitors alike and serves wholesome, tasty, and

ample meals. Specialties include fresh halibut, local prawns (sautéed, deep-fried, or boiled in the shell) and deep-fried Indian fry bread. The guest rooms, all of which have dark wood paneling and eclectic furnishings, were recently spruced up with new carpeting and drapes. The lodge is 4½ mi from downtown. ✉ *Mile 4.5, Zimovia Hwy, Box 1199, 99929,* ☎ *907/874–2335,* ℻ *907/874–3104. 10 rooms. Restaurant, bar, travel services, airport shuttle, car rentals. MC, V.*

$$ ✕▥ **Stikine Inn.** On the dock in the main part of town, this inn has great views of Wrangell's harbor. Rooms are simply decorated with plain, modern furnishings. The Waterfront Grill has large windows from which you'll enjoy good views of the harbor. Gourmet burgers, cross-cut waffle fries, pasta, and homemade pizzas are staples. ✉ *2 blocks from ferry terminal; 107 Stikine Ave., Box 990, 99929,* ☎ *907/874–3388 or 888/874–3388,* ℻ *907/874–3923. 33 rooms. Restaurant. AE, DC, MC, V.*

$$ ✕▥ **Thunderbird Motel.** Right in the heart of downtown Wrangell, this motel recently received some welcome updates: new beds, carpets, and paneling and a refurbished exterior. The rooms are large and bright and come with a mini-refrigerator and television. The Diamond C restaurant, popular with the locals for breakfast, serves typical Alaskan-diner fare; try the grilled halibut or prime rib if you drop in for lunch or dinner. ✉ *223 Front St., Box 110, 99929,* ☎ *907/874–3322,* ℻ *907/874–3321. 7 rooms. Restaurant, car rental. AE, D, MC, V.*

$$ ▥ **Fennimore's Bed & Breakfast.** Across the street from the ferry dock, this new B&B is tucked away at the back of Fennimore's Trading Post, a small souvenir store that reflects trading posts of old, animal pelts and all. The brightly decorated rooms, each of which has a private entrance off an outdoor deck, are completely self-sufficient, with stocked refrigerators, microwaves, and coffeemakers. Continental breakfast is included. For self-propelled touring of the local area, the owner offers guests a choice of several well-worn bikes, with "unlimited mileage." ✉ *312 Stikine Ave., Box 957, 99929,* ☎ *907/874–3012,* ℻ *907/874–3697. 3 rooms. Refrigerators, bicycles, car rental. Continental breakfast. AE, MC, V.*

$$ ▥ **Harding's Old Sourdough Lodge.** This lodge sits on the docks in a beautifully converted construction camp. The Harding family welcomes guests with home-baked sourdough breads and local seafood in the big, open dining-living room. Guest rooms have rustic paneling and modest country-style furnishings; the exterior is hand-milled cedar. A new private suite has a luxuriously large bathroom with a heated floor and a Jacuzzi. ✉ *1104 Peninsula St., Box 1062, 99929,* ☎ *907/ 874–3613 or 800/874–3613,* ℻ *907/874–3455. 16 rooms. Sauna, steam room, boating, meeting room, travel services, airport shuttle. AE, D, DC, MC, V.*

$ ▥ **Shakes Slough Cabins.** If you're a hot-springs or hot-tub enthusiast, these Forest Service cabins, accessible from both Wrangell and Petersburg, are worth checking out. Request details and reservation information from the Forest Service office in Wrangell (☎ 907/874–2323) or the regional U.S. Forest Service Information Center (✉ 101 Egan Dr., Juneau 99801, ☎ 907/586–8751). Reservations are required.

Guided Tours

Alaska Tugboat Tours (☎ 907/874–3101 or 888/488–4386) takes groups of four to six guests through the Inside Passage aboard a vintage 1967 tugboat that's been transformed into a comfortable floating resort. Enjoy fishing, wildlife viewing, beachcombing, and mountain biking. Tours range from one to 10 days and include home-cooked meals of fresh-caught fish and crabs. **Sunrise Aviation** (☎ 907/874–2319, ℻

907/874–2546) is a charter-only air carrier that offers trips to the Anan Creek Wildlife Observatory, Tracy Arm, and the LeConte Glacier (☞ *below*) and can drop you off at any number of places for a day of secluded fishing and hiking.

Outdoor Activities and Sports

FISHING

Numerous companies schedule salmon and trout fishing excursions ranging anywhere from an afternoon to a week. Contact the **Wrangell Chamber of Commerce Visitors Center** (☞ Visitor Information *in* Southeast Alaska A to Z, *below*) for information on guide services and locations.

GOLF

You can rent clubs and arrange for transportation at **Angerman's Store** (☎ 907/874–3540) in downtown Wrangell. **Muskeg Meadows Golf Course** (☎ 907/874–2381), in a wooded area just outside of town, is a 9-hole course. A driving range is scheduled to be completed by early 1999.

HIKING

Rain Walker Expeditions (☎ 907/874–2549) offers full- or half-day guided walking tours of the Tongass National Forest surrounding Wrangell, historical tours of the city itself, and hikes to pick berries and view the wildlife.

Shopping

Eagle's Wings Gallery (☎ 907/874–3330 or 888/278–4753), just off the lobby of the Stikine Inn, carries a striking selection of local crafts, including hand-carved wood bowls, furniture, jewelry, and pottery. Local marine artist Brenda Schwarts often works in her studio inside the shop.

Petersburg

35 mi northwest of Wrangell.

Getting to Petersburg is an experience, whether you take the "high road" by air or the "low road" by sea. Alaska Airlines claims the shortest jet flight in the world, from takeoff at Wrangell to landing at Petersburg. The schedule calls for 20 minutes of flying, but it's usually more like 10. At sea level only ferries and smaller cruisers can squeak through Wrangell Narrows with the aid of more than 50 buoys and range markers along the 22-mi crossing.

The inaccessibility of Petersburg is part of its off-the-beaten-path charm. Unlike in several other Southeast communities, you'll never be overwhelmed by hordes of cruise passengers.

At first sight Petersburg may make you think you're in the old country, with neat, white, Scandinavian-style homes and storefronts with steep roofs and bright-colored swirls of leaf and flower designs (called rosemaling). Row upon row of sturdy fishing vessels in the harbor invoke the spirit of Norway. No wonder. This prosperous fishing community was founded by Norwegian Peter Buschmann in 1897.

You may occasionally even hear some Norwegian spoken, especially during the Little Norway Festival held here each year on the weekend closest to May 17. If you're in town during the festival, be sure to partake in one of the fish feeds that highlight the Norwegian Independence Day celebration. You won't find better beer-batter halibut and folk dancing outside Norway.

One of the most pleasant things to do in Petersburg is to roam among the fishing vessels tied up at dockside in the town's expanding harbor.

This is one of Alaska's busiest, most prosperous fishing communities, and the variety of seacraft is enormous. You'll see small trollers, big halibut vessels, and sleek pleasure craft as well. Wander, too, around the fish-processing structures (though beware of the pungent aroma). Just watching shrimp, salmon, or halibut catches being brought ashore, you can get a real appreciation for this industry and the people who engage in it.

㉙ The **visitor center** (☎ 907/772–4636) at 1st and Fram streets is a logical spot to begin any walking (or biking) tour. From the center, wander to the **Hammer Slough reflecting pool** for a vision of houses and buildings on high stilts reflected perfectly in still, sloughy waters; it's best seen at high tide. The large, white, barnlike structure on stilts that stands just south of the pool is **Sons of Norway Hall,** headquarters of an organization devoted to keeping alive the traditions and culture of the old country.

㉚ For a longer scenic hike from the center of town, visit **Sandy Beach,** where there are picnic facilities and, frequently, good eagle viewing.

㉛ The **Clausen Memorial Museum** interprets commercial fishing and the cannery industry, the era of fish traps, the social life of Petersburg, and Tlingit culture. Don't miss the 126½-pound king salmon, the largest ever caught, as well as the Tlingit dugout canoe, two fish-trap anchors, the Cape Decision lighthouse station lens, and *Earth, Sea and Sky,* a wall piece outside. ✉ *203 Fram St., 99833,* ☎ *907/772–3598.* 🖼 *$2.* ☉ *May–mid-Sept., daily 9:30–4:30; winter schedule varies.*

㉜ The **Fall's Creek fish ladder,** at Mile 10.8 of the Mitkof Highway, is where coho and pink salmon migrate upstream in late summer and fall.

㉝ At the **Crystal Lake State Hatchery/Blind Slough Recreation Area,** at Mile 17.5 of the Mitkof Highway, more than 60,000 pounds of salmon and trout are produced each year.

OFF THE BEATEN PATH

LECONTE GLACIER – Petersburg's biggest draw lies about 25 mi east of town and is accessible only by water or air. LeConte Glacier is the continent's southernmost tidewater glacier and one of its most active, often calving off so many icebergs that the lake at its face is carpeted bank to bank with floating bergs. Ferries and cruise ships pass it at a distance. For tour information, *see* Guided Tours, *above and below.*

Dining and Lodging

$–$$ ✕ **The Homestead.** There's nothing fancy here, just basic American fare: steaks, local prawns and halibut, a salad bar, and generous breakfasts. Especially popular are the homemade pies, which include peach, blackberry, and rhubarb. ✉ *217 Main St.,* ☎ *907/772–3900. AE, MC, V.*

$ ✕ **Alaskafe.** This comfortable coffeehouse and lunch spot in downtown Petersburg, above Coastal Cold Storage, serves a variety of soups, colorful salads, and filling Italian-style panini sandwiches grilled to order. You can browse through a selection of books and magazines, or even rent their computer (by the hour), while you're waiting for your meal. ✉ *306B Nordic Dr.,* ☎ *907/772–5282. No credit cards.*

$ ✕ **Pellerito's Pizza.** This popular take-out place specializes in pizza, calzones, sub-style sandwiches (for your main course) and ice cream, cinnamon rolls, and espresso (for dessert). ✉ *1105 S. Nordic Dr., across from the ferry terminal,* ☎ *907/772–3727. MC, V.*

$$ 🏨 **Scandia House.** Exuding a Norwegian, old-country atmosphere, this hotel on Petersburg's main street, a fixture since 1910, was rebuilt in 1995 after a fire. Rosemaling designs ornament the exterior. All the squeaky-clean rooms are a showcase for traditional Western furnish-

Clausen
Memorial
Museum, **31**

Crystal Lake
State Hatchery/
Blind Slough
Recreation
Area, **33**

Fall's Creek
fish ladder, **32**

Sandy
Beach, **30**

Visitor
center, **29**

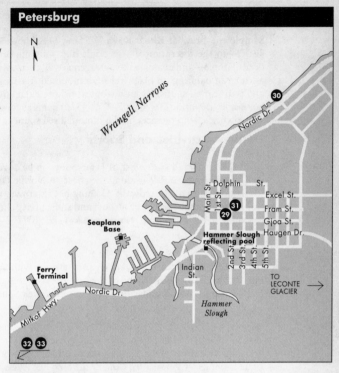

ings; some have kitchenettes and/or king-size beds and a view of the harbor. A courtesy breakfast of fresh homemade muffins and coffee warms the small but relaxing lobby in the morning. Car, boat, and bike rentals are available on the premises. ⊠ *110 Nordic Dr., Box 689, 99833,* ☎ *907/772–4281 or 800/722–5006,* FAX *907/772–4301. 33 rooms, 3 suites. Kitchenettes, minibars, beauty salon, boating, bicycles, car rental. AE, D, DC, MC, V.*

$$ 🏨 **Tides Inn.** This is the largest hotel in town, a block uphill from Petersburg's main thoroughfare. The rooms' furnishings are somewhat dated, but comfortable nonetheless; some rooms have kitchens. Rooms in the newer wing have views of the boat harbor. The coffee is always on in the small lobby, and in the morning you're welcome to complimentary juices, muffins, and pastries. Car rentals are available. ⊠ *307 N. 1st St., Box 1048, 99833,* ☎ *907/772–4288 or 800/665–8433,* FAX *907/772–4286. 48 rooms. Car rental. AE, D, DC, MC, V.*

$ 🏨 **Shakes Slough Cabins.** These Forest Service cabins are accessible from Petersburg as well as Wrangell (☞ Wrangell, *above*).

Guided Tours

Kaleidoscope Cruises (☎ 907/772–3736 or 800/868–4373) offers whale-watching and glacier ecology tours as well as sportfishing expeditions, all led by professional biologists and naturalists.

Pacific Wing, Inc. (☎ 907/772–9258) is an air-taxi operator that gets high marks from locals for its flightseeing tours over the Stikine River and LeConte Glacier.

Viking Travel (☎ 907/772–3818, FAX 907/772–3940) is a travel agency that books whale-watching, glacier, and kayaking trips with local operators.

Nightlife and the Arts

BARS AND NIGHTCLUBS

Sample the brew at **Kito's Kave** (⊠ Sing Lee Alley, ☎ 907/772–3207)—in the afternoon if you don't like your music in the high-decibel range—and examine the outrageous wall decor, which includes a Mexican painting on black velvet, a mounted Alaska king salmon, and two stuffed sailfish from a tropical fishing expedition. The **Harbor Bar**'s (⊠ Nordic Dr., ☎ 907/772–4526) name suggests its decor—ship's wheels, ship pictures, and a mounted red snapper.

Outdoor Activities and Sports

BICYCLING

Because of its small size, most of Petersburg can be covered by bicycle. A good route to ride is along the coast on Nordic Drive, past the lovely homes, to the boardwalk. Coming back to town, take the interior route and you'll pass the airport and some pretty churches before returning to the waterfront. **Northern Bikes** (☎ 907/772–3978) offers bicycle rentals.

DIVING

If you're feeling adventurous, spend an afternoon with **Southeast Diving** (☎ 907/772–2446). Some of the best Alaskan souvenirs and marine life can be found under the waters of Frederick Sound.

Shopping

Berthiel's (⊠ Nordic Dr.) sells pottery, cards, and women's fashions. A stroll down Sing Lee Alley at the south end of Nordic Drive will take you past some stores and galleries that sell local artists' work. For whalebone carvings try **Petersburg Gallery** (⊠ Sing Lee Alley, ☎ 907/772–2244). Set back off the alley in a beautiful big white house that served as a boardinghouse to fishermen and schoolteachers is **Sing Lee Alley Book Store** (☎ 907/772–4440), which has a good supply of books on Alaska, best-sellers, cards, and gifts.

Sitka

110 mi west of Petersburg.

For centuries before the 18th-century arrival of the Russians, Sitka was the ancestral home of the Tlingit nation. In canoes up to 60 ft long, they successfully fished the Alaskan Panhandle. Unfortunately for the Tlingits, Russian territorial governor Alexander Baranof coveted the Sitka site for its beauty, mild climate, and economic potential. In the island's massive timbered forests he saw raw materials for shipbuilding; its location offered trading routes as far east as Hawaii and Asia and as far south as California.

In 1799 Baranof negotiated with the local chief to build a wooden fort and trading post some 6 mi north of the present town. He called the outpost St. Michael Archangel and moved a large number of his Russian and Aleut fur hunters there from their former base on Kodiak Island.

The local peoples, Tlingits, soon took exception to the ambitions of their new neighbors. Reluctant to pledge allegiance to the czar and provide free labor, in 1802 they attacked Baranof's people and burned his buildings. Baranof, however, was away at Kodiak at the time. He returned in 1804 with a formidable force, including shipboard cannons. He attacked the Tlingits at their fort near Indian River (site of the present-day 105-acre Sitka National Historical Park) and drove them to the other side of the island.

In 1821 the Tlingits came back to Sitka to trade with the Russians, who were happy to benefit from the tribe's hunting skills. Under Baranof and succeeding managers, the Russian-American Company and the town prospered, becoming known as "the Paris of the Pacific." Besides the fur trade, the community boasted a major shipbuilding and repair facility, sawmills, and forges, and even initiated an ice industry. The Russians shipped blocks of ice from nearby Swan Lake to the booming San Francisco market. Baranof eventually shifted the capital of Russian America to Sitka from Kodiak.

The town declined after its 1867 transfer from Russia to the United States but became prosperous again during World War II, when it served as a base for the U.S. effort to drive the Japanese from the Aleutian Islands. Today its most important industries are fishing and tourism.

34 A good place to begin a tour of Sitka is the **visitors bureau**'s information booth (☎ 907/747–5940) in the **Harrigan Centennial Building,** situated near a Tlingit war canoe on Harbor Drive, behind St. Michael's Cathedral. In the Centennial Building, you'll also find a museum, an auditorium, and an art gallery.

35 To get a feel for the town, head for **Castle Hill,** where Alaska was formally handed over to the United States on October 18, 1867, and where the first 49-star U.S. flag was flown on January 3, 1959, signifying Alaska's statehood. To reach the hill and get one of Sitka's best views, make the first right off Harbor Drive just before the John O'Connell Bridge, then go into the **Baranof Castle Hill State Historic Site** entrance to the left of the Sitka Hotel. A gravel path takes you to the top of the hill, overlooking Crescent Harbor. Several Russian residences were on the hill, including Baranof's castle, which burned down in 1894.

Totem Square, below Castle Hill, has three anchors discovered in local waters and believed to be 19th-century British in origin. Look for the double-headed eagle of czarist Russia carved into the cedar of the totem pole in the park.

36 The large, four-level, red-roof structure on the northeast side of the hill with the imposing 14-ft statue in front is the **Sitka State Pioneers' Home,** the first of several state-run retirement homes and medical-care facilities for Alaska's senior citizens. The statue, symbolizing Alaska's frontier sourdough spirit, was modeled by an authentic pioneer, William "Skagway Bill" Fonda. It portrays a determined prospector with pack, pick, rifle, and supplies on his back heading for the gold country.

37 Most of Sitka's Russian dignitaries are buried in the **Russian and Lutheran cemeteries,** off Marine Street. The most distinctive grave belongs to Princess Maksutoff, wife of the last Russian governor and one of the most illustrious members of the Russian royal family to be buried on Alaskan soil.

38 One of Southeast Alaska's best-known national landmarks is **St. Michael's Cathedral,** which had its origins in a log structure erected between 1844 and 1848. In 1966 the church was destroyed in a fire that swept through the downtown business district. As the fire engulfed the building, townspeople risked their lives and rushed inside to rescue the cathedral's precious icons, religious objects, vestments, and other treasures brought to the church from Russia.

Using original measurements and blueprints, an almost exact replica of onion-domed St. Michael's was built and dedicated in 1976. Today, visitors can see what could possibly be the largest collection of Russian icons in the United States, among them the much-prized *Our Lady of Sitka* (also known as the *Sitka Madonna*) and the *Christ Pantocrator* (*Christ the Judge*) on either side of the doors of the interior altar screen. Other objects include: ornate Gospel books, chalices, cru-

108

Alaska Raptor
Rehabilitation
Center, **43**

Castle Hill, **35**

Russian and
Lutheran
cemeteries, **37**

Russian
Bishop's
House, **39**

St. Michael's
Cathedral, **38**

Sheldon
Jackson
Museum, **40**

Sitka National
Historic
Park visitor
center, **41**

Sitka State
Pioneers'
Home, **36**

Tlingit Fort
site, **42**

Visitors
bureau, **34**

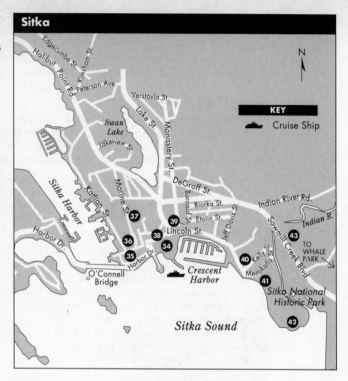

cifixes, much-used silver-gilt wedding crowns dating to 1866, and an altar cloth made by Princess Maksutoff. This is an active church and visitors are welcome to attend services. ☎ 907/747–8120. ☞ *$1 donation requested.* ☉ *May–Sept., daily 7:30–5:30; Oct.–Apr., 1:30–5:30.*

39 Facing the harbor is another registered historic landmark, the **Russian Bishop's House,** constructed by the Russian-American Company for Bishop Innocent Veniaminov in 1842. Inside the house, one of the few remaining Russian-built log structures in Alaska, are exhibits on the history of Russian America and the Room Revealed, where a portion of the house's structure is peeled away to expose Russian building techniques. ☎ 907/747–6281. ☞ *$3.* ☉ *May–Sept., daily 9–1 and 2–5; Oct.–Apr., by appointment.*

On Lincoln Street are **Sheldon Jackson College,** founded in 1878, and, **40** past it walking east, the **Sheldon Jackson Museum.** The octagonal museum, built in 1895, contains priceless Native, Aleut, and Eskimo items collected by Dr. Sheldon Jackson in the remote regions of Alaska he traveled as an educator and missionary. Carved masks, Chilkat blankets, dogsleds, kayaks—even the helmet worn by Chief Katlean during the 1804 battle against the Russians—are on display here. ☎ 907/ 747–8981. ☞ *$3.* ☉ *May 15–Sept. 15, daily 8–5; Sept. 15–May 15, Tues.–Sat. 10–4.*

Sitka National Historical Park celebrates the transfer of Alaska from Russia to the United States in 1867 and is on the site where the ex- **41** change took place. The **Sitka National Historical Park visitor center** has audiovisual programs and exhibits plus Native and Russian artifacts. In the cultural center, Native American artists and craftspeople are on hand to demonstrate silversmithing, weaving, wood carving, and basketry. ⊠ *106 Metlakatla St.,* ☎ *907/747–6281.* ☒ *Free.* ☉ *June–Sept., daily 8–5; Oct.–May, weekdays 8–5.*

㊷ A self-guided trail through the park to a beautiful grassy knoll, once the site of the **Tlingit Fort,** passes by some of the most skillfully carved totems in the state. Lost to time and the damp climate, most of the over-80-year-old totems have been replaced. Some of the replicas themselves date from the early 1930s, and all were made and raised by Native Americans and local experts in accordance with Tlingit traditions. ☎ *907/ 747–6281.* ☒ *Free.* ☉ *June–Sept., daily 8 AM–10 PM; Oct.–May, weekdays 8–5.*

㊸ At the **Alaska Raptor Rehabilitation Center** visitors have the unique experience of viewing American bald eagles and other wild Alaskan birds close-up. This nonprofit organization rescues more than 200 birds a year and houses those unable to return to the wild on a beautiful tract of land crisscrossed by hiking trails. ☎ *907/747–8662.* ☒ *$10 adults, $5 children in summer; free in winter.* ☉ *Mid-May–Sept., whenever cruise ships are in town; Oct.–mid-May, Sun. open house 2–4.*

Dining and Lodging

$$–$$$ ✕ **Channel Club.** Once you've surveyed the 35 different salads arrayed on the salad bar, you might not even make it to the steak and seafood this restaurant is known for. If you order steak, don't ask the chef for his seasoning recipe—it's a secret. The decor is nautical, with fishnet floats and whalebone carvings on the walls. A courtesy car provides door-to-door service if you're without transportation. ⊠ *Mile 3.5, 2906 Halibut Point Rd.,* ☎ *907/747–9916. AE, DC, MC, V.*

$$$$ ✕🏨 **Westmark Shee Atika.** If you stay here for a night or two, you
★ will surely come away with an increased appreciation for Southeast Alaskan Native art and culture. Artwork illustrates the history, legends, and exploits of the Tlingit people. Many rooms overlook Crescent Harbor and the islands in the waters beyond; others have mountain and forest views. The Raven Room, a pastel-color restaurant with vaulted ceilings, offers seafood, pasta, and steak. Fried halibut nuggets are a top draw. Views are of the Sitka Sound and fishing fleets amid their daily routine. ⊠ *330 Seward St., 99835,* ☎ *907/747–6241,* 🅵🅰🆇 *907/ 747–5486. 101 rooms. Restaurant, bar. AE, D, DC, MC, V.*

$$$$ 🏨 **Rockwell Lighthouse.** On an island ¾ mi from town, Burgess Bauder rents out his 1,600-square-ft, five-story lighthouse, hand-built in the 1980s with coastal woods and brass lights. The light at the top is built to Coast Guard specifications. There are accommodations for four couples. Food is not included, but there is a modern kitchen. The price includes transportation to and from the lighthouse (in summer, visitors use a small motorboat). ⊠ *Box 277, 99835,* ☎ 🅵🅰🆇 *907/747–3056. 4 rooms. Dining room, boating. No credit cards.*

$$$ 🏨 **Cascade Inn** A few miles out of town and oh-so-conveniently attached to a grocery, video, and liquor store, this new motel isn't what its modern exterior might suggest. The large rooms are decorated with contemporary furnishings and soothing colors (mauve, taupe, and wheat predominate) and all have balconies that face the water and the extinct volcano Mount Edgecumbe. A deck with a hot tub and a barbecue pit sits just above the water and is shared by all of the guests through a private entrance. ⊠ *2035 Halibut Point Rd., 99835,* ☎ *907/ 747–6804 or 800/532–0908. 10 rooms. Grocery, hot tub, bicycles, laundry service, travel services. D, MC, V.*

$ 🏨 **White Sulphur Springs Cabin.** This Tongass National Forest public-use cabin 65 mi outside Sitka has nearby hot springs. For information on this or other Forest Service cabins in the Sitka region, call 907/747–6671 or contact the U.S. Forest Service's main Tongass office (⊠ *101 Egan Dr., Juneau 99801,* ☎ *907/586–8751*).

Guided Tours

Sitka Tours (☎ 907/747–8443, ℻ 907/747–7510) meets state ferries and provides short city tours while vessels are in port, with stops at Sitka National Historical Park and the downtown shopping area. It also does a three-hour historical tour and a combined historical and raptor-center tour.

Nightlife and the Arts

BARS AND NIGHTCLUBS

Pioneer Bar (✉ 212 Katlean St., ☎ 907/747–3456), across from the harbor, offers occasional live music and pick-up pool tournaments. As far as the locals are concerned, a spot in one of the massive green-and-white vinyl booths is a destination unto itself. Tourists get a kick out of its authentic Alaskan ambience; the walls are lined with pictures of local fishing boats. **Rookies** (✉ 1617 Sawmill Creek Rd., ☎ 907/747–3285) is a sports bar with pool, air hockey, darts, and a full dinner menu. A DJ plays dance music, and their free shuttle will make sure you get home safe and sound.

DANCE

The **New Archangel Dancers of Sitka** perform authentic Russian Cossack–type dances whenever cruise ships are in port. Tickets are sold a half hour before performances; a recorded message (☎ 907/747-5516) gives their schedule a week in advance.

FESTIVALS

Southeast Alaska's major classical chamber-music festival is the annual **Sitka Summer Music Festival** (✉ Box 3333, 99835, ☎ 907/747–6774), a three-week June celebration of concerts and special events held in the Harrigan Centennial Building.

The **Sitka WhaleFest** (✉ Box 1226, 99835, ☎ 907/747–5940, ℻ 907/747–3739) is held in early November when the whales are plentiful (as many as 80) and tourists are not.

Outdoor Activities and Sports

BIRD-WATCHING AND HIKING

Sitka has unveiled two bird-watching and hiking trails just outside town. The **Starrigavan Estuary Life Interpretive Trail** provides views of spawning salmon and waterfowl, and has a platform for bird-watchers. The **Starrigavan Forest & Muskeg Interpretive Trail** has great views of the valley. Both trails are accessible to wheelchair users.

CANOEING AND KAYAKING

Alaska Travel Adventures (☎ 907/789–0052 in Juneau) does a three-hour kayaking tour in protected waters south of Sitka; instruction is provided and no experience is necessary. **Baidarka Boats** (☎ 907/747–8996) rents sea kayaks and guides trips in the Sitka area.

SCUBA DIVING

Southeast Diving & Sports (✉ 203 Lincoln St., ☎ 907/747–8279) gives diving instruction, rents tanks and equipment, provides charter services, and can advise you on the best places to dive.

Juneau

100 mi north of Sitka.

Juneau, Alaska's capital and third-largest city, is on the North American mainland but can't be reached by conventional road. The city owes its origins to two colorful sourdoughs, Joe Juneau and Dick Harris, and to a Tlingit chief named Kowee. The chief led the two men to rich reserves of gold in the outwash of the stream that now runs through the middle of town and in quartz rock formations back in the gulches and valleys. That was in 1880, and shortly after the discovery a modest stampede resulted in the formation of first a camp, then a town, then finally the Alaska district government capital in 1906.

For 60 years or so after Juneau's founding, gold was the mainstay of the economy. In its heyday the AJ (for Alaska Juneau) gold mine was the biggest low-grade ore mine in the world. It was not until World War II, when the government decided it needed Juneau's manpower for the war effort, that the AJ and other mines in the area ceased operations. After the war mining failed to start up again, and government became the city's principal employer.

Juneau is full of contrasts—it's a sophisticated and cosmopolitan frontier town. Juneau has one of the best museums in Alaska, is surrounded by beautiful wilderness, and has a glacier in its backyard.

🔴 **Marine Park,** on the dock where the cruise ships tie up, is a little gem of benches, shade trees, and shelter, and a great place to enjoy an outdoor meal purchased from Juneau's many street vendors. It also has a visitor kiosk staffed according to cruise-ship schedules.

🔴 The **Log Cabin Visitor Center** is a replica of a 19th-century structure that served first as a Presbyterian church, then as a brewery. Stop in for a walking-tour map and information on all the tours available in Juneau and the surrounding areas. ✉ *134 3rd St. at Seward St.,* ☎ *907/ 586–2201 or 888/581–2201.* ☉ *May–Sept., weekdays 8:30–5 and weekends 9–5; Oct.–Apr., weekdays 9–5.*

Buildings on South Franklin and Front streets are among the oldest and most interesting structures in the city. Many reflect the architecture of the 1920s and '30s, and some are even older. The small **Alaskan Hotel** (☞ Dining and Lodging, *below*), opened in 1913, has period trappings and is worth a visit even if you're not looking for lodging. The barroom's massive, mirrored, oak-wood back bar is accented by Tiffany lights and panels.

Also on South Franklin Street: the **Alaska Steam Laundry Building,** a 1901 structure with a windowed turret that now houses a coffeehouse, a film processor, and other stores; the **Senate Building mall,** across the street, and numerous other curio and crafts shops, snack shops, and two salmon shops. Alaska's most famous bar, the decades-old and tourist-filled **Red Dog Saloon,** is housed in frontierish quarters at 278 South Franklin Street.

★ 🔴

🔴 Constructed in 1930, the **Alaska State Capitol** has pillars of southeastern Alaska marble. The building now houses the governor's offices and other state agencies, and the state legislature meets here four months each year. ✉ *Corner of Seward and 4th Sts.,* ☎ *907/465–2479.* ☉ *Tours mid-May–mid-Sept., Sun.–Fri. 9–4:30; tours can also be arranged when legislature is in session.*

🔴 Quaint, onion-domed **St. Nicholas Russian Orthodox Church,** constructed in 1894, is the oldest Russian church building in Alaska. ✉ *326 5th St.,* ☎ *907/586–1023.* ✉ *Donation requested.* ☉ *Check Juneau visitor center for hrs.*

🔴 At the top of the hill behind the Capitol stands the **House of Wickersham,** the former residence of James Wickersham, pioneer judge and delegate to Congress. The home, constructed in 1898, contains memorabilia from the judge's travels throughout Alaska—from rare Native basketry and ivory carvings to historic photos and a Chickering grand piano that came " 'round the Horn" to Alaska while the Rus-

Alaska State
Capitol, **47**
Alaska State
Museum, **55**
Centennial
Hall, **56**
Cremation spot
of Chief
Kowee, **54**
Evergreen
Cemetery, **53**
Governor's
House, **52**
House of
Wickersham, **49**
Juneau-Douglas
City
Museum, **51**
Log Cabin
Visitor
Center, **45**
Marine
Park, **44**
Red Dog
Saloon, **46**
St. Nicholas
Russian
Orthodox
Church, **48**
State Office
Building, **50**

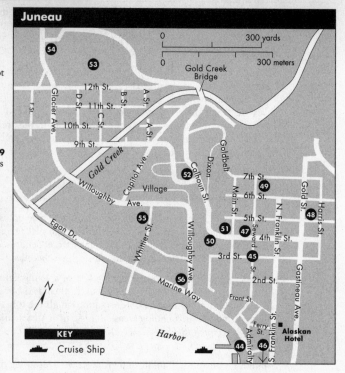

sians still ruled here. The tour includes full narration by costumed guides and tea and sourdough bread with "the judge." ⊠ *213 7th St.,* ☎ *907/ 586–9001.* ⌫ *$7.50.* ⊙ *May–Sept., Tues.–Sun. 10–3, tours on the hour; Oct.–Apr., by appointment.*

50 At the **State Office Building,** on 4th Street, you can have a picnic lunch like the state workers do and listen to organ music played in the four-story atrium on a grand old theater pipe organ, a veteran of the silent-movie era.

51 The **Juneau-Douglas City Museum** interprets local mining and Tlingit history. Among the exhibits are displays of old mining equipment, historic photos, and pioneer artifacts, including a turn-of-the-century store and kitchen. There is also a Juneau time line, exhibits on commercial fishing and steamships, historic paintings, a hands-on area for children, and a half-hour video of Juneau's history. ⊠ *114 4th St.,* ☎ *907/586–3572.* ⌫ *$2.* ⊙ *May–Sept., weekdays 9–5, weekends 10–5; Oct.–Apr., Fri.–Sat. noon–4, or by appointment.*

52 The **Governor's House,** on Calhoun Street, is a three-level colonial-style home completed in 1912. There are no tours through the house.

Many Juneau pioneers, including Joe Juneau and Dick Harris, are
53 buried in the **Evergreen Cemetery.** A meandering gravel road leads through the graveyard, and at the end of the lane you'll come to a mon-
54 ument commemorating the **cremation spot of Chief Kowee.**

55 The **Alaska State Museum** is one of Alaska's top museums. Whether your tastes run to natural-history exhibits (stuffed brown bears, a replica of a two-story-high eagle nesting tree), Native Alaskan exhibits (a 38-ft, walrus-hide umiak [whaling boat] constructed by Eskimos and a re-created interior of a Tlingit tribal house), mining exhibits, or contemporary art, the museum is almost certain to please.

⊠ *395 Whittier St.,* ☎ *907/465–2901.* ☎ *$3.* ⊙ *May 15–Sept. 15,
weekdays 9–6, weekends 9–6; Sept. 16–May 14, Tues.–Sat. 10–4.*

❺❻ Centennial Hall is the site of an excellent **information center** operated
by the U.S. Forest Service. Movies, slide shows, and information about
recreation in the surrounding Tongass National Forest and in nearby
Glacier Bay National Park and Preserve are available here. ⊠ *101 Egan
Dr.,* ☎ *907/586–8751.* ⊙ *Mid-May–mid-Sept., daily 8–5; mid-Sept.–
mid-May, weekdays 8–5.*

☪ Gold panning is fun, and sometimes children actually uncover a few
flecks of the precious metal in the bottom of their pans. You can buy
a pan at almost any Alaska hardware or sporting-goods store. Juneau
is one of the Southeast's best-known gold-panning towns; look for schedules of gold-panning excursions at visitor information centers.

If you're a beer fan, look for Alaskan Amber, Pale, Frontier, and
Smoked Porter beer, brewed and bottled in Juneau. Visitors are wel-
★ come at the **Alaskan Brewing and Bottling Company's microbrewery
plant** and can sample the product after watching the bottling operation. ⊠ *5429 Shaune Dr.,* ☎ *907/780–5866.* ☎ *Free.* ⊙ *May–Sept.,
Mon.–Sat. 11–4:30; Oct.–Apr., Thurs.–Sat. 11–4:30.*

If you want to become familiar with the salmon's life story, visit
Gastineau Salmon Hatchery, where Alaskan salmon fighting their way
up a fish ladder can be viewed through underwater windows. ⊠ *2697
Channel Dr.,* ☎ *907/463–4810.* ☎ *$2.75 adults, $1 children.* ⊙
May–Sept., weekdays 10–6, weekends noon–5.

Glacier Gardens Rainforest Adventure spreads over 30 acres of forest
with ponds, waterfalls, thousands of flowers, and unique natural tree
formations. Four miles of pathways are paved for access by golf carts,
or you can hike the natural trails to an amazing 340-degree view of
Mendenhall Glacier and downtown Juneau 7 mi away. ⊠ *7600 Glacier
Hwy.,* ☎ *907/789–5116.* ☎ *$17.50 self-guided tour, $25 full tour.* ⊙
May–Sept.

A self-guided pilgrimage to the **Shrine of St. Therese** is well worth the
23-mi journey from greater Juneau (you can take a taxi from the boat
docks or from one of the hotels). Built in the 1930s, this stone church
and its 14 Stations of the Cross are the only inhabitants of a serene
tiny island that is accessible only via a 400-ft-long pedestrian causeway.
Sunday services are held at 1 PM June through August. The "honesty-
box" gift shop sells crucifixes, books, T-shirts, and souvenirs. ⊠ *5933
Lund St.,* ☎ *907/780–6112.* ⊙ *Always open.*

Dining and Lodging

$–$$$$ ✗ **The Fiddlehead.** Juneau's favorite restaurant is actually two restau-
★ rants in one. Downstairs you can get a casual (and affordable) break-
fast, lunch, or dinner in a somewhat generic setting of light woods, gently
patterned wallpaper, stained glass, and historic photos. The food is
healthy, generously served, and eclectic. Offerings range from a light
dinner of black beans and rice to pasta Greta Garbo (locally smoked
salmon tossed with fettuccine in cream sauce). Homemade bread and
cookies from the restaurant's bakery are laudable. The Fireweed Room
upstairs has a full bar and a pricier menu: here you can sample baked
Alaskan oysters on the half-shell, grilled halibut, or seafood linguini
while rubbing elbows with the legislative elite. Smoking is not permitted.
⊠ *429 Willoughby Ave.,* ☎ *907/586–3150. AE, D, DC, MC, V.*

$$–$$$ ✗ **Hangar on the Wharf.** A new addition to the Juneau waterfront, the
Hangar is housed in the building where Alaska Airlines started busi-
ness; Wings of Alaska floatplanes still dock here. The whitewashed wood,

stainless steel accents, and vintage airplane parts and photos make for a casual dining experience. From both the bar and the restaurant you can enjoy expansive views of Gastineau Channel and Douglas Island. Live music in the bar and a wide selection of entrées, including locally caught halibut and salmon, lamb chops, and prawn fettuccine, make this a hot spot for locals and tourists alike. Upstairs are pool tables. A dance club is scheduled to be added soon. ⊠ *2 Marine Way, Merchants Wharf Mall,* ☎ *907/586–5018. AE, D, MC, V.*

$$
★ ✕ **Gold Creek Salmon Bake.** Trees, mountains, and the rushing water of Salmon Creek surround the sheltered, comfortable benches and tables at this salmon bake. Fresh-caught salmon (supplemented with ribs) is cooked over an alder fire and served with a simple but succulent sauce of brown sugar, margarine, and lemon juice. For $22 you can enjoy the salmon, along with hot baked beans, rice pilaf, salad, corn bread, and your choice of lemonade, tea, or coffee. Wine and local Alaskan Amber beer are extra. After dinner you can pan for gold in the stream (pans are available for no charge, and you can keep any gold you find) or wander up the hill to explore the remains of the Wagner Gold Mine or visit the Juneau Raptor Center and view bald eagles and falcons up close. A free bus ride from downtown hotels is included. ⊠ *1061 Salmon Lane Rd.,* ☎ *907/789–0052. AE, D, MC, V. Closed Oct.–Apr.*

$–$$ ✕ **Mike's Place.** For decades, Mike's, in the former mining community of Douglas, across the bridge from Juneau, has been serving up seafood, steak, and pasta. Its treatment of tiny Petersburg shrimp is particularly noteworthy. Rivaling the food, however, is the view from the picture windows at the rear of the restaurant. Mike's looks over the waters of Gastineau Channel to Juneau and the ruins of the AJ mine. ⊠ *1102 2nd St., Douglas,* ☎ *907/364–3271. AE, D, DC, MC, V. Closed Mon. No lunch weekends.*

$$$ ✕🏨 **Silverbow Inn.** The main building of this small inn, for years one of the town's major bakeries, was built in 1890. A funky, relaxed air surrounds the Silverbow; Johnny Love's restaurant and adjoining bagel shop are the current draw. The new owners have hopes of showing old art-house movies twice a week and live Irish music now and then. ⊠ *120 2nd St., 99801,* ☎ *907/586–4146,* 𝔽𝔸𝕏 *907/586–4242. 6 rooms. Restaurant. AE, D, DC, MC, V.*

$$–$$$ ✕🏨 **Inn at the Waterfront.** Built in 1889, this turn-of-the-century-
★ style inn mixes antiques with modern amenities. The Inn is home to the Summit, the city's most prestigious dining spot (reservations essential). This intimate, candlelit restaurant with a separate, copper-topped bar area serves mostly seafood—including prawns and halibut. For steak lovers, there is a 20–24-oz grilled Porterhouse steak. The Summit has a luxurious turn-of-the-century brothel decor and, in fact, the inn was a brothel until 1958. The rooms are eclectic but comfortable and bright. ⊠ *455 S. Franklin St., 99801,* ☎ *907/586–2050,* 𝔽𝔸𝕏 *907/ 586–2999. 21 rooms. Restaurant. AE, D, DC, MC, V.*

$$$$ 🏨 **Baranof Hotel.** For half a century the Baranof has been the city's prestige address for business travelers, legislators, lobbyists, and tourists. That designation has been challenged in recent years by the Goldbelt Hotel Juneau. The Art Deco lobby and most rooms in this nine-story hostelry have tasteful woods and a lighting style reminiscent of 1939, when the hotel first opened. The contemporary rooms feature aqua blue, pink, or maroon color schemes. Twenty rooms are equipped with either a treadmill or an exercise bike. There's an Alaska Airlines ticket counter and tour desk on site. ⊠ *127 N. Franklin St., 99801,* ☎ *907/ 586–2660 or 800/544–0970 for reservations,* 𝔽𝔸𝕏 *907/586–8315. 193 rooms. Restaurant, coffee shop, lobby lounge, beauty salon, meeting rooms, travel services. AE, D, DC, MC, V.*

$$$$ ⊞ **Goldbelt Hotel Juneau.** A high-rise by Juneau standards, the seven-story Goldbelt is across Main Street from Centennial Hall and across Egan Drive from the docks. Rooms are modern in decor; deluxe rooms have views of the Gastineau Channel. Fifteen rooms are equipped with exercise equipment—treadmills or stationary bikes. Recent renovations to the lobby and dining room have updated the hotel's ambience. ⊠ *51 W. Egan Dr., 99801,* ☎ *907/586–6900 or 800/544–0970 for reservations,* FAX *907/463–3567. 105 rooms. Restaurant, lobby lounge, meeting rooms. AE, D, DC, MC, V.*

$$$$ ⊞ **Grandma's Feather Bed.** A jewel in the rough of suburban Juneau, this hotel's friendly atmosphere makes you feel as if you're visiting someone's home. Each of the spacious rooms in the Victorian-style farmhouse is painted with cheerful, bright colors and is outfitted with Jacuzzi bathtubs and feather comforters; some have fireplaces and kitchen nooks. The complimentary breakfast is from a full menu: pancakes, omelets, French toast—all you can eat! It is hard to believe that this is a Best Western property. All hotels should be as homey and inviting as this one. ⊠ *2348 Mendenhall Loop Rd., 99801,* ☎ *907/789–5566,* FAX *907/789–2818. 14 rooms. Restaurant, airport shuttle. AE, D, DC, MC, V.*

$$$$ ⊞ **Pearson's Pond Luxury Inn and Garden Spa.** Guests at this luxurious private retreat can enjoy an amazing view of the great blue Mendenhall Glacier. Built on a small lake, the large home has a three-tiered deck with two Jacuzzis and a barbecue grill (which, in the summer, is surrounded by hundreds of flowers). The rooms are private and set up for business travelers or families. Efficiency kitchens are stocked with breakfast essentials. Activities include yoga on the deck, hiking or cross-country skiing, or relaxing in the hot tub with wine and cheese on the side. ⊠ *4541 Sawa Circle, 99801,* ☎ *907/789–3772,* FAX *907/789–6722. 3 suites. VCRs, massage, laundry service. AE, MC, V.*

$$$–$$$$ ⊞ **Country Lane Inn.** Only 4 mi from Mendenhall Glacier, this Best Western property has a somewhat sterile feel to it, although the couch and reading materials in the lobby and the baskets of multicolor flowers along the entrance walk do provide some homey accents. Rooms are decorated in country style with mauve and dusty-blue fabrics. Furnishings are kept to a minimum. Some rooms have a whirlpool bath and kitchenette. Complimentary Continental breakfast is served. ⊠ *9300 Glacier Hwy., 99801,* ☎ *907/789–5005 or 800/528–1234,* FAX *907/789–2818. 50 rooms. Kitchenettes. AE, D, DC, MC, V.*

$$$–$$$$ ⊞ **Juneau Airport TraveLodge.** The rooms and furnishings here are pretty standard. The structure, like the Mi Casa Restaurant inside, is Mexican in design and decor. The motel is the only one in the community with an indoor swimming pool and whirlpool tub—a plus if you want to unwind after a day of touring. Some rooms have mountain views. ⊠ *9200 Glacier Hwy., 99801,* ☎ *907/789–9700,* FAX *907/789–1969. 86 rooms. Restaurant, lobby lounge, in-room modem lines, indoor pool, hot tub, airport shuttle. AE, D, MC, V.*

$$$–$$$$ ⊞ **The Prospector.** A short walk west of downtown and next door to
★ the State Museum, this small but modern hotel is popular with business travelers and legislators. Here you'll find very large rooms with contemporary furnishings, bright watercolors of Alaskan nature, and views of the channel, mountains, or city. In McGuire's dining room and lounge you can enjoy outstanding prime rib. Steaks and seafood are also popular. ⊠ *375 Whittier St., 99801,* ☎ *907/586–3737 or 800/331–2711 outside Alaska, 800/478–5866 inside Alaska,* FAX *907/586–1204. 58 rooms. Restaurant, lobby lounge. AE, D, DC, MC, V.*

$$ ⊞ **Alaskan Hotel.** This historic 1913 hotel in the heart of downtown
★ Juneau is 15 mi from the ferry terminal and 9 mi from the airport (city bus service is available). Rooms are on three floors and have turn-of-

the-century antiques and iron beds. The flocked wallpaper, floral carpets, and Tiffany windows are reminiscent of the hotel's original Gold Rush−era opulence. Four hot tubs can be rented by the hour. ⊠ *167 S. Franklin St.,* ☎ *907/586−1000 or 800/327−9347,* ℻ *907/463−3775. 42 rooms, 22 with bath. Bar, hot tubs. D, DC, MC, V.*

Guided Tours

BOATING AND KAYAKING

Alaska Travel Adventures (☎ 907/789−0052) does guided float trips below the Mendenhall Glacier and sea kayaking trips in the Juneau and Sitka areas, and also leads gold-panning and sportfishing trips.

Auk Ta Shaa Discovery (☎ 907/586−8687) offers trips down the Mendenhall River accompanied by narration on aspects of natural and cultural history.

CITY TOURS

Juneau Trolley Car Company (☎ 907/789−4342) makes stops at a dozen of so of Juneau's historical and shopping attractions, providing informative narration along the way. Day passes are available.

Mount Roberts Aerial Tramway (☎ 907/463−3412 or 888-461-8726) takes visitors from the cruise terminal 2,000 ft up the side of Mt. Roberts. After the six-minute ride, passengers may take in a multimedia show on the history of the Tlingits, go for a walk on hiking trails, shop, or experience mountain-view dining.

FISHING

Angler's Choice (☎ 907/789−0052 or 800/791−2673) operates half-and full-day sportfishing charters.

Juneau Sportfishing (☎ 907/586−1887, ℻ 907/586−9769) runs charter fishing excursions for salmon and halibut, as well as whale-watching trips on its luxury yachts.

FLIGHTSEEING

Era Helicopters (☎ 907/586−2030, ℻ 907/463−3959) does one-hour flightseeing trips that include alpine country, downtown Juneau, and the Juneau Icefield, with a touchdown on a glacier. The tours include dogsled rides on a glacier, which add a real taste of the true Alaskan wilderness.

Temsco Helicopters (☎ 907/789−9501, ℻ 907/789−7989) pioneered helicopter sightseeing over Mendenhall Glacier with a touchdown and a chance to romp on the glacier.

NATIVE CULTURE

Alaska Native Tours (☎ 907/463−3231 or 800/291−0133) employs Tlingit and Haida guides, who point out historic Native village sites in the Juneau and Douglas area, explaining Native traditions along the way. Juneau is the embarkation point for two Native-oriented catamaran excursions from **Auk Nu Tours** (☎ 800/820−2628). One boat leaves downtown for sightseeing at Tracy Arm; the other operates as a ferry between Auke Bay and Gustavus before continuing to Icy Strait for wildlife watching. Both tours relate the lore of the areas visited from a Tlingit point of view.

Nightlife and the Arts

BARS AND NIGHTCLUBS

The **Alaskan Hotel Bar** (⊠ 167 S. Franklin St., ☎ 907/586−1000) is about as funky a place as you'll find in Juneau: flocked-velvet walls, antique chandeliers above the bar, and vintage Alaskan frontier brothel decor. Sit back and enjoy the live music or take turns with the locals at the open mike. It's a very popular spot.

The **Bubble Room** (⊠ 127 N. Franklin St., ☎ 907/586–2660), a comfortable lounge off the lobby in the Baranof Hotel, is quiet—and the site of more legislative lobbying than that which occurs in the nearby state capitol.

The **Red Dog Saloon** (⊠ 278 S. Franklin St., ☎ 907/463–9954) Though recently relocated, the Red Dog has been an infamous Juneau watering hole since 1890. Every conceivable surface in this two-story bar is cluttered with life preservers, business cards, and college banners; and when tourist season hits, a little atmospheric sawdust covers the floor as well. When the ships are in, the music is live, and the crowd gets livelier. One wonders if the sometimes rough-and-tumble fishing crowd even knows that the bar's namesake is actually a small shadow of a Scottie dog.

MUSIC FESTIVALS

The annual weeklong **Alaska Folk Festival** (⊠ Box 21748, 99802, ☎ 907/789–0292) is staged each April in Juneau, drawing singers, banjo masters, fiddlers, and even cloggers from all over the state, the Yukon Territory, and beyond.

During the last week of May, Juneau is the scene of **Juneau Jazz 'n Classics** (⊠ Box 22152, 99802, ☎ 907/463–3378), which celebrates music from Bach to Brubeck.

THEATER

Southeast Alaska's only professional theater company, **Perseverance Theater of Juneau** (⊠ 914 3rd St., Douglas, ☎ 907/364–2421), presents everything from Broadway plays to Shakespeare to locally written material.

Outdoor Activities and Sports

CROSS-COUNTRY SKIING

The **Parks and Recreation Department** (☎ 907/586–5226) sponsors a group ski and snowshoe outing each Wednesday morning and on Saturday when there's sufficient snow. Ski rentals are available along with suggestions for touring the trails and ridges around town from **Foggy Mountain Shop** (⊠ 134 N. Franklin St., ☎ 907/586–6780). The store also offers climbing, camping, and telemark skiing gear.

DOWNHILL SKIING

The only downhill area in the Southeast, **Eaglecrest** (⊠ 155 S. Seward St., Juneau 99801, ☎ 907/586–5284 or 907/586–5330 for recorded ski information) on Douglas Island, just 30 minutes from downtown Juneau, offers late-November to mid-April skiing and snowboarding on a well-groomed mountain with two double chairlifts, a beginner's platter pull, cross-country trails, a ski school (including downhill, Nordic, and telemark as well as snowboarding), a ski-rental shop, a cafeteria, and a tri-level day lodge. There's a vertical drop of 1,400 ft, runs up to 2 mi long, and 31 alpine trails. Enjoy the northern lights while you night-ski from January through mid-March. Because this is Southeast Alaska, knowledgeable skiers pack rain slickers along with other gear. On weekends and holidays there are bus pickups at hotels and at other stops around town.

GOLF

Juneau's par-three, nine-hole **Mendenhall Golf Course** (⊠ 2101 Industrial Blvd.; mailing address: ⊠ 9167 Parkwood Dr., 99801, ☎ 907/789–1221) is pretty modest. Still, its location beside the waters of Gastineau Channel and its full view of Mendenhall Glacier from the driving range makes it one of a kind. Club rentals are available.

HIKING
The **Parks and Recreation Department** (☎ 907/586–5226) in Juneau sponsors a group hike each Wednesday morning and on Saturday in summer. Contact the **U.S. Forest Service** for trail books & maps (☎ 907/586–8751).

TENNIS
The **Juneau Racquet Club** (✉ 2841 Riverside Dr., ☎ 907/789–2181), about 10 mi north of downtown, adjacent to Mendenhall Mall, will accommodate out-of-towners at its first-class indoor tennis and racquetball courts. Facilities include sauna, hot tub, exercise equipment, snack bar, massage tables, and sports shop. **JRC Downtown** (✉ W. Willoughby, ☎ 907/789–2181 or 907/586–5773) is a smaller club. Both charge $12.50 per day for nonmembers.

Shopping

ART GALLERIES
Knowledgeable locals frequent the **Rie Muñoz Gallery** (✉ 2101 Jordan Ave., ☎ 907/789–7411). Muñoz is one of Alaska's favorite artists, creator of a stylized, simple, and colorful design technique that is much copied but rarely equaled. Other artists' work is also on sale at the Muñoz Gallery, including wood-block prints by nationally recognized artist Dale DeArmond. Various books illustrated by Rie Muñoz and written by Alaskan children's author Jean Rogers are also available.

FOOD
Taku Smokeries (✉ 550 S. Franklin St., ☎ 800/582–5122), at the south end of town near the cruise-ship docks, processes nearly 6 million pounds of fish a year. You can view the smoking procedure through large windows and then purchase the packaged fish in the deli-style gift shop or have some shipped back home. You can also sample the local catch in the adjoining lodge-style restaurant and lounge.

OFF THE
BEATEN PATH

NATIVE VILLAGES – If you hanker to know how the Native Alaskan village peoples of Southeast Alaska live today, you can fly or take the state ferry *LeConte* to Kake, Angoon, or Hoonah. You won't find much organized touring in any of these communities, but small, clean hotel accommodations are available (advance reservations are strongly suggested), and guided fishing, natural-history, and wildlife-watching trips can be arranged by asking around. In Kake, contact the **Waterfront Lodge** (✉ Box 222, Kake 99830, ☎ 907/785–3472); in Angoon, contact **Whalers Cove Lodge** (✉ Box 101, Angoon 99820, ☎ 907/788–3123); in Hoonah, contact **Hnh Lodge** (✉ Box 320, Hoonah 99829, ☎ 907/945–3636 in summer, 360/598–6463 in winter).

Haines

80 mi northwest of Juneau.

Missionary S. Hall Young and famed naturalist John Muir picked the site for this town in 1879 as a place to bring Christianity and education to the Native peoples. They could hardly have picked a more beautiful spot—a heavily wooded peninsula with magnificent views of Portage Cove and the Coastal Mountain Range.

Unlike most other cities in Southeast Alaska, Haines can be reached by road (the 152-mi Haines Highway connects at Haines Junction with the Alaska Highway). It's also accessible by the state ferry and by scheduled plane service from Juneau. The Haines ferry terminal is 4½ mi northwest of downtown, and the airport is 4 mi west.

The town has two distinct personalities. On the northern side of the Haines Highway is the portion of Haines founded by Young and Muir. After its missionary beginnings the town served as the trailhead for the Jack Dalton Trail to the Yukon during the 1897 Gold Rush to the Klondike. The following year, when gold was discovered in nearby Porcupine (now deserted), the booming community was a supply center and jumping-off place for those goldfields as well.

South of the highway the town looks like a military post, which is what it was for nearly half a century. In 1903 the U.S. Army established a post—Ft. William Henry Seward—at Portage Cove just south of town. For 17 years (1922–39) the post (renamed Chilkoot Barracks to avoid confusion with the South Central Alaska city of Seward) was the only military base in the territory. That changed with World War II. Following the war the post closed down.

The Haines–Fort Seward community today is recognized for the enormously successful Native dance and culture center at Fort Seward, as well as for the superb fishing, camping, and outdoor recreation to be found at Chilkoot Lake, Portage Cove, Mosquito Lake, and Chilkat State Park (☞ Chapter 3) on the shores of Chilkat Inlet. The Alaska Chilkat Bald Eagle Preserve is a treasure; thousands of eagles come here annually in winter to feed on a late run of chum salmon, making it one of Alaska's premier wildlife-watching sites.

⑤⑦ You can pick up walking-tour maps of both Haines and Fort Seward at the **visitor center** (✉ 2nd Ave. near Willard St., ☎ 907/766–2234 or 800/458–3579). The easiest place to start your tour, however, is at **⑤⑧** the **Sheldon Museum and Cultural Center,** just above the boat harbor, near the foot of Main Street. The core of what's here is an Alaskan family's personal collection. Steve Sheldon began assembling Native artifacts, Russian items, and Gold Rush memorabilia, such as Jack Dalton's sawed-off shotgun, in the 1880s and started an exhibit of his finds in 1925. ✉ *11 Main St., Box 269,* ☎ *907/766–2366.* ☞ *$3.* ☉ *Mid-May–mid-Sept., daily 1–5 and most mornings and evenings; mid-Sept.–mid-May, Sun., Mon. and Wed. 1–4, Tues., Thurs., and Fri. 3–5.*

⑤⑨ Dalton City, an 1890s Gold Rush town re-created as a set for the movie *White Fang,* is less than 1 mi from downtown on the **Southeast Alaska State Fairgrounds** (☎ 907/766–2476). Attractions include carriage rides, gold panning, keepsakes from the Dalton City shops, and home-cooked meals at the Klondike Restaurant and Saloon. The state fair, held each August, is one of several official regional fall blowouts, and in its homegrown, homespun way it's a real winner. In addition to the usual collection of barnyard animals, the fair offers rides on a vintage 1920 Herschal-Spillman carousel, the finest examples of local culinary arts, and the chance to see Native dances, displays of Native totemic crafts, and some fine art and photography. ☞ *$7.*

⑥⓪ The **Haines Highway** is completely paved on the American side of the border and, except for a few remaining stretches, is almost entirely paved in Canada. At the base of the Haines Highway is **Mile 0,** the starting point of the 152-mi road to the Alaska Highway and the Canadian Yukon. Whether you plan to travel all the way or not, you should spend at least a bit of time on the scenic highway. At about Mile 6 there's a delightful picnic spot near the Chilkat River and an inflowing clear creek; at Mile 9.5 the view of Cathedral Peaks, part of the Chilkat Range, is magnificent; and from Mile 19 to Mile 21 there is good viewing of the **★ Alaska Chilkat Bald Eagle Preserve** (☞ Chapter 3). At Mile 33 is a roadside restaurant called, oddly enough, **Mile 33,** where you can refill your gas tank and coffee mug, grab a burger, and stock up on home-baked

Alaska Indian Arts, **63**

Fort William H. Seward National Historic Landmark, **62**

Halsingland Hotel, **61**

Mile 0, **60**

Sheldon Museum and Cultural Center, **58**

Southeast Alaska State Fairgrounds, **59**

Visitor center, **57**

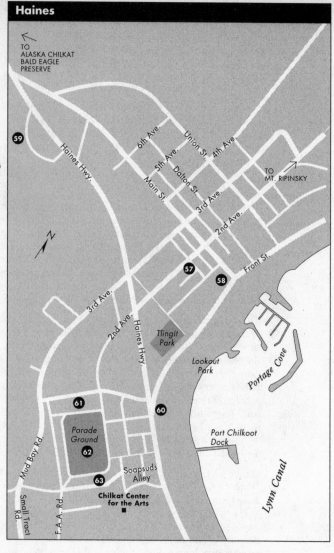

goods. The United States–Canada border lies at Mile 42. If you're traveling on to Canada, stop at Canadian customs and be sure to set your clock ahead one hour.

61 In Fort Seward, wander past the huge, stately, white-column former commanding officer's home, now a part of the **Halsingland Hotel** (☞ Dining and Lodging, *below*), on Officer's Row. Circle the flat but slop-
62 ing parade ground of the **Fort William H. Seward National Historic Landmark,** the site of the first army post built in Alaska. Here is a Native tribal house, a trapper's log cabin, and a cultural center; walking tours are regularly scheduled in summer. Contact the **Haines Visitor's Center** for more information: ⊠ *Box 530, 99827,* ☎ *800/458–3579.*

63 The former fort hospital is now a workshop for the craftspeople of **Alaska Indian Arts,** a nonprofit organization dedicated to the revival of Tlingit art. Here, between the parade ground and the Center for the Arts, you'll see Native carvers making totems and metalsmiths working in silver; you may also be able to see a performance of Native dances. ☎ *907/766–2160.* ✉ *$1 donations.* ⊙ *Weekdays 9–noon and 1–5, some evenings when cruise ships are in town.*

Dining and Lodging

$$ ✕ **Chilkat Restaurant and Bakery.** Family-style cooking is served in a homelike, no-smoking setting. Seafood, steaks, and sandwiches are cooked to order; locally grown vegetables upgrade the simple menu. Friday is all-you-can-eat Mexican night. No alcohol is served. ✉ *5th Ave. and Dalton St., Box 591,* ☎ *907/766–2920. AE, MC, V.*

$–$$ ✕ **Bamboo Room.** Pop culture meets greasy spoon in this unassuming coffee shop. The menu includes the expected sandwiches, burgers, fried chicken, and seafood, but the place really is at its best for breakfast. From the red vinyl booths diners have views of the mountains beyond. ✉ *2nd Ave. near Main St.,* ☎ *907/766–2800. AE, D, DC, MC, V.*

$$ ✕🖻 **Ft. Seward Lodge.** This lodge and restaurant has, over time, served as the fort's PX, soda fountain, bowling alley, and gymnasium. The raw wood decor and sparse interior preserves some of that heritage and somehow brings the pioneering spirit of Alaska to life. The dining room even comes with a mechanical red-velvet swing left over from wilder times. While enjoying all-you-can-eat crab dinners for around $22, or beef, chicken, or pasta from the regular menu, diners might be entertained if someone tickles the ivory (even though most of it is missing) on a vintage 1903 piano. The lodge's rooms are spacious and eclectically decorated. ✉ *Ft. Seward, 99827,* ☎ *907/766–2009 or 800/ 478–7772,* ℻ *907/766–2006. 10 rooms. Restaurant, lobby lounge, Ping-Pong, airport shuttle. DC, MC, V.*

$$ ✕🖻 **Halsingland Hotel.** The officers of old Fort Seward once lived in the big white structures that today constitute the Halsingland Hotel and a neighboring bed-and-breakfast. Many rooms have nonworking cast-iron fireplaces and original claw-foot bathtubs; most have private bath; all are carpeted and have wildlife and historic photos on the walls. The Commander's Room Restaurant and Lounge prides itself on its seafood and steaks, but burgers and fish-and-chips are also on the menu. There's a salad-and-potato bar, an extensive wine list, and a selection of Alaskan beers on tap, some from microbreweries. In summer, at the Tlingit tribal house nearby, the Halsingland prepares a nightly salmon bake called the Port Chilkoot Potlatch—$22 for all you can eat. ✉ *Fort Seward, Box 1589, 99827,* ☎ *907/766–2000, 800/542–6363 in Alaska and Lower 48, 800/478–2525 in Yukon Territory and British Columbia;* ℻ *907/766–2445. 58 rooms, 52 with bath. Restaurant, bar, travel services. AE, D, DC, MC, V.*

$$$$ 🖻 **Weeping Trout Golf and Lake Resort.** Enjoy wilderness with style at this remote resort—reachable only by boat or plane—where you can golf on a nine-hole course, fish, relax, and refresh, and *not* be bothered by telephones (the lodge does have one for emergencies). Or just enjoy a day's excursion out here and top it off with a special dinner at their popular restaurant. ✉ *Box 129, 99827,* ☎ *907/766–2827,* ℻ *907/766–2824. 4 rooms, 1 cabin sleeps 4. Travel services. AE, D, DC, MC, V.*

$$$ 🖻 **Captain's Choice Motel.** In the summer, overflowing flower boxes surround the perimeter of this contemporary yet rustic motel in downtown Haines. Rooms have cable TV, telephones, coffeemakers, and refrigerators. Almost all of the rooms have a magnificent view of Portage Cove, and the second-floor rooms open onto a deck with tables and chairs. A patio down below serves as a nightly meeting place where guests enjoy libations and conversation. ✉ *108 2nd Avenue N, Box 392, 99827,* ☎ *907/766–3111, 800/247–7153, or 800/478–2345 in Alaska. 40 rooms with bath, 3 suites. Room service, travel services, car rental. AE, D, DC, MC, V.*

Nightlife and the Arts

THE ARTS

Haines hosts a statewide drama competition called **ACTFEST** in April of odd-numbered years. The festival is held at the Chilkat Center for the Arts at Fort Seward, with entries from community theaters both large and small. For details write to Mimi Gregg, ACTFEST, Box 75, Haines 99827.

The **Chilkat Indian Dancers** perform at the **Chilkat Center for the Arts,** which was the army post's recreation hall. Some performances may be at the tribal house in the parade grounds; check posted notices for performance times. Masked performers wearing bearskins and brightly patterned dance blankets act out traditional stories. There are several performances weekly, more when cruises are in port. ⊠ *1 Theater Dr.,* ☎ *907/766–2160.* ⊡ *$10.* ☉ *May–Sept. 15.*

NIGHTLIFE

Fogcutter Bar (☎ 907/766–2555). Locals might rule the pool tables, but the jukebox is often up for grabs at this lively spot. Just don't ring the ship's bell hanging above the bar, or you'll be buying every one of your new bar friends a drink.

Harbor Bar (⊠ Front St. at the Harbor, ☎ 907/766–2444). Commercial fisherfolk gather here nightly at this old (1907) bar and restaurant. Sometimes in summer there is live music.

Outdoor Activities and Sports

CYCLING

Sockeye Cycle Company (⊠ 24 Portage St., Box 829, 99827, ☎ 907/766–2869) specializes in guided mountain tours in and around the back country of Haines; they also rent, service, and sell bikes.

FLIGHTSEEING

Wings of Alaska (⊠ 1873 Shel Simmons Dr., 99801, ☎ 907/789–0790) offers small-plane tours of Taku Glacier, Tracy Arm Glacier Fjord, and nearby Glacier Bay National Park, as well as transportation between Haines, Skagway, Juneau, and several Native fishing villages.

HIKING

One of the most rewarding hikes in the area is to the north summit of **Mt. Ripinsky,** the prominent peak that rises 3,610 ft behind the town. Be warned: it's a strenuous trek and requires a full day. The trailhead lies at the top of Young Street, along a pipeline right-of-way. For other hikes, pick up a copy of "Haines Is for Hikers" at the visitor center.

RAFTING AND KAYAKING

Alaska Cross-Country Guiding and Rafting (☎ 907/767–5522) uses three A-frame guest cabins at Mile 23 on the Haines Highway as the jumping-off point for exclusive tours and fly-in, raft-out trips down the Tsirku River, plus photo trips into the Chilkat preserve. You can also arrange for a two-day trip to DeBlondeau Glacier with an overnight stay in rustic cabins at the base of the glacier.

Chilkat Guides (☎ 907/766–2491, one of the first river-rafting tour companies in Alaska, operates out of the old telegraph office of Fort Seward, a cute little red building just across from the cruise-ship dock. Whether you have four hours or two weeks, experienced guides will accompany you on float trips through the Chilkat Bald Eagle Preserve or down the Tatshenshini or Alsek rivers.

Deishu Expeditions and Alaska Kayak Supply (⊠ 12 Portage Rd., Box 1406, 99827, ☎ 907/766–2427) rents kayaks and leads guided kayak trips. The trips—the prices of which include gear, instruction, transportation, and food—take you around the fjords, islands, and glaciers surrounding Haines. They can't guarantee it, but most day-trippers will see orca and humpback whales, sea lions, and, if the salmon are running, hungry bears at the water's edge.

Taking a river tour on pontoon boats with **Chilkoot Lake Tours** (☎ 907/766–2891) or a jet-boat ride with **River Adventures** (☎ 907/766–2050) are excellent ways to tour the glacier-carved lakes and rivers. Bring a camera, because wildlife can be abundant.

SKIING

Alaska Nature Tours and Backcountry Outfitters (✉ 2nd Ave. S, Box 491, 99827, ☎ 907/766–2876) operates a winter Nordic shuttle bus with flat-track skiing and photo tours in the Chilkat Bald Eagle Preserve and telemarking at Chilkat Pass. Ski, snowboard, and snowshoe equipment may be rented here. The company also conducts birdwatching and natural-history tours in the Chilkat preserve and leads hiking treks in summer.

Skagway

13 mi north of Haines.

Skagway is a short hop north of Haines if you take the Alaska Marine Highway ferry. If you go by road, the distance is 359 mi, as you have to take the Haines Highway up to Haines Junction, Yukon, then take the Alaska Highway 100 mi south to Whitehorse, and then drive a final 100 mi south on the Klondike Highway to Skagway. North country folk call this popular sightseeing route the Golden Horseshoe or Golden Circle tour, because it takes in a lot of Gold Rush country in addition to lake, forest, and mountain scenery.

However you get to Skagway, you'll find the town an amazingly preserved artifact from one of North America's biggest, most storied gold rushes. Most of the downtown district forms part of the Klondike Gold Rush National Historical Park, a unit of the national park system dedicated to commemorating and interpreting the frenzied stampede that extended to Dawson City in Canada's Yukon. Old false-front stores, saloons, and brothels—built to separate Gold Rush prospectors from their grubstakes going north or their gold pokes heading south—have been restored, repainted, and refurnished by the federal government and Skagway's citizens. Although it feels a little like a Disney theme park in spots, when you walk down Broadway today, the scene is not appreciably different from what the prospectors saw in the days of 1898, except the street is now paved to make your exploring easier.

Skagway had only a single cabin still standing when the Yukon Gold Rush began. At first, the argonauts, as they liked to be called, swarmed to Dyea and the Chilkoot Trail, 9 mi west of Skagway. Skagway and its White Pass Trail didn't seem as attractive until a dock was built in town. Then it mushroomed overnight into the major gateway to the Klondike, supporting a wild mixture of legitimate businesspeople, con artists (among the most cunning was Jefferson "Soapy" Smith), stampeders, and curiosity seekers.

Three months after the first boat landed in July 1897, Skagway numbered perhaps 20,000 persons and had well-laid-out streets, hotels, stores, saloons, gambling houses, and dance halls. By the spring of 1898, the superintendent of the Northwest Royal Mounted Police in neighboring Canada would label the town "little better than a hell on earth."

A lot of the "hell" ended with a shoot-out one pleasant July evening in 1898. Good guy Frank Reid (the surveyor who laid out Skagway's streets so wide and well) faced down bad guy Soapy Smith on Juneau dock downtown near the present ferry terminal. After a classic exchange of gunfire, Smith lay dead and Reid lay dying. The town built a huge monument at Reid's grave. You can see it in Gold Rush Cemetery and read the current inscription on it: "He gave his life for the honor of Skagway." For Smith, whose tombstone was continually chiseled and stolen by vandals and souvenir seekers, today's grave marker is a simple wooden plank.

When the Gold Rush played out after a few years, the town of 20,000 dwindled to 700. The White Pass & Yukon Railroad kept the town alive until 1982, when it began to run in summers only. By this time, however, tourism revenue was sufficient to compensate for any economic loss suffered as a result of the railroad's more limited schedule.

64 To begin your visit, head to the **Skagway Convention and Visitors Bureau** (⊠ 5th Ave. & Broadway, ☎ 907/983–2854) where you'll find maps and lots of friendly suggestions for seeing the town. You can't miss it—look for the row of American, Canadian, Alaskan, and Yukon flags fluttering outside.

65 **Arctic Brotherhood Hall,** on Broadway, is unlike anything else you'll see in Alaska. The Arctic Brotherhood was a fraternal organization of Alaskan and Yukon pioneers. To decorate the exterior false front of their Skagway lodge building, local members created a mosaic out of 20,000 pieces of driftwood and flotsam gathered from local beaches.

The hall now houses the **Trail of '98 Museum** (☎ 907/983–2420), where Frank Reid's will is preserved under glass, as are papers disposing of Soapy Smith's estate. Gambling paraphernalia from the old Board of Trade Saloon is on display along with Native artifacts, gold scales, a red-and-black sleigh, and a small organ. ⊠ *Broadway.* 🎫 *$2.* ☉ *Mid-May–Sept., daily 9–5; variable hrs in winter.*

★ **66** The **Klondike Gold Rush National Historical Park** (☎ 907/983–2921) is in what was once the White Pass & Yukon Route rail depot. It contains exhibits, photos, and artifacts from the White Pass and Chilkoot trails and is of special interest if you plan to take a White Pass train ride, drive the nearby Klondike Highway, or hike the Chilkoot "Trail of '98."

67 The **Golden North Hotel** (☞ Dining and Lodging, *below*) is Alaska's oldest hotel. Constructed in 1898, it has been lovingly restored to its Gold Rush–era appearance. Take a stroll through the lobby even if you're not staying there.

68 The **Klondike Highway,** which starts at the foot of State Street, often parallels the older White Pass railway route as it travels northwest to Carcross and Whitehorse in the Canadian Yukon. It merges just south of Whitehorse for a short distance with the Alaska Highway, then heads on its own again to terminate at Dawson City, on the shores of the Klondike River. From start to finish, it covers 435 mi. Along the way the road climbs steeply through forested coastal mountains with jagged, snow-covered peaks. It passes by deep, fish-filled lakes and streams in the Canadian high country, where travelers have a chance of seeing a mountain goat, moose, black bear, or grizzly.

If you're driving the Klondike Highway north from Skagway, you must stop at Canadian Customs, Mile 22. If you're traveling south to Skagway, check in at U.S. Customs, Mile 6. And remember that when it's 1 PM in Canada at the border, it's noon in Skagway.

Each year, a journey along the historic **Chilkoot Trail** (☞ Chapter 3) is the highlight of thousands of serious hikers' travels.

Arctic Brotherhood Hall and Trail of '98 Museum, **65**

Golden North Hotel, **67**

Klondike Gold Rush National Historical Park, **66**

Klondike Highway, **68**

Skagway Convention and Visitors Bureau, **64**

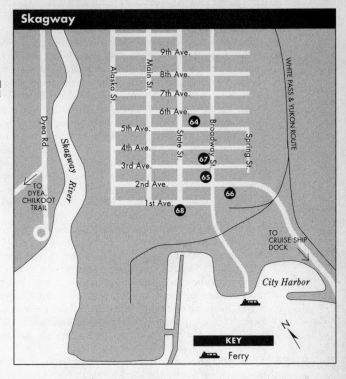

There's an easier way to travel at least partway into Gold Rush country—the **White Pass & Yukon Route** (WP & YR) narrow-gauge railroad over the "Trail of '98." The historic (started in 1898) Gold Rush railroad's diesel locomotives chug and tow vintage viewing cars up the steep inclines of the route, hugging the walls of precipitous cliff sides, and providing thousands of travelers with the view of craggy peaks, plummeting waterfalls, lakes, and forests. It's open in summertime only, and reservations are highly recommended.

Several options are available. Twice daily the WP & YR leaves Skagway for a three-hour round-trip excursion to the White Pass summit. Sights along the way include Bridal Veil Falls, Inspiration Point, and Dead Horse Gulch. The fare is $78. Through service to Whitehorse, Yukon, is offered daily as well—in the form of a train trip to Fraser, where motor-coach connections are available on to Whitehorse. The one-way fare to Whitehorse is $95. Special steam excursions, Red Caboose private railcar charters, and Chilkoot Trail hikers' service are also available. For information call 907/983–2217 or 800/343–7373.

Dining and Lodging

$$$ ✕ 🏨 **Westmark Inn.** The decor is Gold Rush style but grander and more plush than anything the stampeders ever experienced, with rich red carpeting, brass beds, and historical pictures. Make a reservation for a room in the main structure, larger and more convenient to the restaurant and lounge than those in the annex. New in 1997, the Bonanza Bar & Grill has become the local hot spot, serving up typical grill fare with an Alaskan edge and occasional live music. If it's not packed with tourists (try to avoid the 5:30 PM rush hour), the Chilkoot Dining Room offers some of Skagway's most gracious dining. ⊠ *3rd and Spring Sts.,* ☎ *907/983–2291,* 🆅🅰🆇 *907/983–6100. 209 rooms. 2 restaurants, lobby* *lounge, meeting room, travel services, car rental. AE, D, DC, MC, V. Closed Oct.–Apr.*

$$ ✕⌸ **Golden North Hotel.** No question about it, this is Alaska's most
★ historic hotel. It was built in 1898 in the heyday of the Gold Rush—
golden dome and all—and has been lovingly restored to reflect that
period. Pioneer Skagway families have contributed period furnishings
to each of the hotel's rooms, and the stories of those families are
posted on the walls of each unit. The third-floor lobby has a view of
Lynn Canal. Century-old beer recipes from the original Skagway Brewing Company have been put back to good use in a new microbrewery
inside the Golden North Restaurant. The restaurant also boats a hot
new chef; tantalizing new menu items like the pesto-stuffed rotisserie
chicken may tempt you away from the usual Alaskan specialities. ⌧
3rd Ave. and Broadway, Box 343, 99840, ☎ *907/983–2451 or 907/
983–2294,* Ⅸ *907/983–2755. 31 rooms. Restaurant, pub. AE, D, DC,
MC, V.*

$$ ✕⌸ **Skagway Inn Bed & Breakfast.** Each room in this downtown Vic-
★ torian inn is named after a different Gold Rush gal. The building, one
of Skagway's oldest, was constructed in 1897. Color schemes vary, but
rooms share a Victorian motif, with antiques and cast-iron beds; some
have mountain views. The bathrooms are shared, one to every two
rooms. The Skagway Inn Restaurant serves up a mean homemade
potpie filled with seafood, chicken, or beef every lunch hour and
freshly caught seafood every night. ⌧ *655 Broadway, Box 500, 99840,*
☎ *907/983–2289,* Ⅸ *907/983–2713. 12 rooms. Restaurant. AE, D,
MC, V.*

$$$ ⌸ **The White House.** Just about two blocks from downtown Skagway,
this recently renovated bed-and-breakfast is a welcome addition to the
roster of housing choices in Skagway. Built in 1902 by Lee Guthrie, a
gambler and owner of one of the town's most profitable Gold Rush
saloons, the white clapboard two-story house is furnished with original Skagway antiques and handmade quilts. The warm dining room
and sitting room invite conversation while serving up hearty homemade
breakfasts or, later in the day, a spot of tea and a movie on the com-
munal VCR. All rooms have private baths, cable TVs, and phones. ⌧
8th & Main Sts., Box 41, 99840, ☎ *907/983–9000,* Ⅸ *907/983–9010.
10 rooms. Laundry service, airport shuttle. AE, MC, V.*

$$ ⌸ **Wind Valley Lodge.** A long walk or a short drive from downtown,
the Wind Valley Lodge is one of Skagway's newer motels. Rooms are
modern with typical motel furniture, and there's a free shuttle to down-
town. ⌧ *22nd Ave. and State St., Box 354, 99840,* ☎ *907/983–2236,*
Ⅸ *907/983–2957. 29 rooms. AE, D, MC, V. Closed Nov.–Apr.*

Guided Tours

Skagway Street Car Co. (☎ 907/983–2908, Ⅸ 907/983–3908), in-
side a bright yellow building right across from the train station, lets
you revisit the Gold Rush days in the original 1937 White Motor
Company streetcars, complete with costumed conductors who tell the
story of the town's tumultuous history while showing you the sights.

Nightlife and the Arts

For more than 27 years, locals have performed a show called *Skag-
way in the Days of '98* at Eagles Hall. Here you'll see cancan dancers,
learn a little local history, and watch desperado Soapy Smith being sent
to his reward. If you stop in for the evening show, you can enjoy a few
warm-up rounds of mock gambling, with $1,000 worth of chips on
the house. ⌧ *Broadway and 6th Ave.,* ☎ *907/983–2545 in summer,
808/328–9132 in winter.* ⌸ *$14 adults.* ☉ *Daily 10:30 AM, 3 PM, and
7:30 PM.*

In case you want to see the world.

At American Express, we're here to make your journey a smooth one. So we have over 1,700 travel service locations in over 120 countries ready to help. What else would you expect from the world's largest travel agency?

do more ®

http://www.americanexpress.com/travel

Travel

In case you want to be welcomed there.

We're here to see that you're always welcomed at establishments everywhere. That's why millions of people carry the American Express® Card – for peace of mind, confidence, and security, around the world or just around the corner.

do more®

Cards

In case you're running low.

We're here to help with more than 118,000 Express Cash locations around the world. In order to enroll, just call American Express before you start your vacation.

do more

Express Cash

And just in case.

We're here with American Express® Travelers Cheques and Cheques *for Two.*® They're the safest way to carry money on your vacation and the surest way to get a refund, practically anywhere, anytime.

Another way we help you...

do more ®

Travelers Cheques

A longtime fixture on the Skagway scene, **Moe's Frontier Bar** (⊠ Broadway between 4th and 5th Sts., ☎ 907/983–2238) is much frequented

★ by locals. At the **Red Onion Saloon** (⊠ Broadway at 2nd St., ☎ 907/983–2222) you'll meet at least as many Skagway people as you will visitors. There's live music on Thursday night (ranging from rock to folk) and an impromptu jazz jam with cruise-ship musicians almost every afternoon. The Red Onion, whose upstairs was a Gold Rush brothel, is closed in winter.

SOUTHEAST ALASKA A TO Z

Arriving and Departing

By Bus
Year-round service between Anchorage and Skagway is available from **Alaska Direct Bus Lines** (⊠ Box 501, Anchorage 99510, ☎ 907/277–6652 or 800/770–6652).

Though it's a long ride, you can travel **Greyhound Lines of Canada** (☎ 604/662–3222) from Vancouver or Edmonton to Whitehorse and make connections there with Alaska Direct buses to Southeast Alaska.

By Car
Only Skagway and Haines, in the northern Panhandle, and tiny Hyder, just across the border from Stewart, British Columbia, are accessible by conventional highway. To reach Skagway or Haines, take the Alaska Highway to the Canadian Yukon's Whitehorse or Haines Junction, respectively, then drive the Klondike Highway or Haines Highway southwest to the Alaska Panhandle. You can reach Hyder on British Columbia's Cassiar Highway, which can be reached, in turn, from Highway 16 just north of Prince Rupert.

By Ferry
From the south, the **Alaska Marine Highway System** (⊠ Box 25535, Juneau 99802, ☎ 907/465–3941 or 800/642–0066) operates stateroom-equipped vehicle and passenger ferries from Bellingham, Washington, and from Prince Rupert, British Columbia. The vessels call at Ketchikan, Wrangell, Petersburg, Sitka, Juneau, Haines, and Skagway, and they connect with smaller vessels serving bush communities; in all, 14 Southeast towns are served by state ferries. One of the smaller ferries also operates between Hyder and Ketchikan. In the summer, staterooms on the ferries are always sold out before sailing time; reserve months in advance. For those planning to take cars on the ferry, early reservations for vehicle space are also highly recommended.

B.C. Ferries (⊠ 1112 Fort St., Victoria, British Columbia, Canada V8V 4V2, ☎ 250/386–3431) operates similar passenger and vehicle ferries from Vancouver Island, British Columbia, to Prince Rupert. From there, travelers can connect with the Alaska Marine Highway System.

By Plane
Alaska Airlines operates several flights daily from Seattle and other Pacific Coast and southwestern cities to Ketchikan, Wrangell, Petersburg, Sitka, Glacier Bay, and Juneau. The carrier connects Juneau to the northern Alaskan cities of Yakutat, Cordova, Anchorage, Fairbanks, Nome, Kotzebue, and Prudhoe Bay. In summer, **Delta Airlines** has at least one flight daily from Seattle to Juneau. **Wings of Alaska** can connect you from Juneau to several towns, including Haines and Skagway

By Train
Southeast Alaska's only railroad, the **White Pass & Yukon Railroad** (☎ 800/343–7373), operates between Skagway and Fraser, British

Columbia. The tracks follow the historic path over the White Pass summit—a mountain-climbing, cliff-hanging route of 28 mi each way. Bus connections are available at Fraser to Whitehorse, Yukon.

Getting Around

By Bus

Gray Line of Alaska (☎ 907/277–5581) offers summertime connections between Whitehorse, Anchorage, Fairbanks, Haines, and Skagway with other stops en route.

By Ferry

The **Alaska Marine Highway System** not only brings visitors into Southeast Alaska, but ferries them from town to town (☞ Arriving and Departing, *above*).

By Plane

Every large community in Southeast Alaska, and many smaller ones, have air-taxi services that fly people from town to town and, for those seeking backcountry adventures, into remote wilderness areas. Local chambers of commerce (☞ Visitor Information, *below*) can provide lists of bush-plane services.

Contacts and Resources

B&B Reservation Service

The **Alaska Bed & Breakfast Association** (✉ 1123 Timberline Ct., Juneau 99801, ☎ 907/586–2959, FAX 907/780–4673) books B&B accommodations in most Southeast communities.

Doctors and Dentists

Haines Medical Clinic (next to the Visitor Information Center, ☎ 907/766–2521). **Skagway Medical Clinic** (✉ 31011th Ave. between State St. and Broadway, ☎ 907/983–2255, 907/983–2418 for emergencies). **Wrangell General Hospital** (✉ 310 Bennett St., ☎ 907/874–7000).

Emergencies

For police or ambulance, dial **911.**

Late-Night Pharmacies

Juneau: Juneau Drug Co. (✉ 202 Front St., ☎ 907/586–1233). **Ron's Apothecary** (✉ 9101 Mendenhall Mall Rd., about 10 mi north of downtown in Mendenhall Valley, next to the Super Bear market, ☎ 907/789–0458). Ron's Apothecary's after-hours number for prescription emergencies is 907/789–9522.

Ketchikan: Downtown Drugstore (✉ 300 Front St., ☎ 907/225–3144). **Race Avenue Drugs** (✉ 2300 Tongass Ave., across from the Plaza Portwest shopping mall, ☎ 907/225–4151). After hours, call **Ketchikan General Hospital** (☎ 907/225–5171).

Petersburg: Rexall Drugs (✉ 215 N. Nordic Dr., ☎ 907/772–3265). After hours, call **Petersburg Medical Center** (☎ 907/772–4291).

Sitka: Harry Race Pharmacy (✉ 106 Lincoln St., ☎ 907/747–8006). **White's Pharmacy** (✉ 705 Halibut Point Rd., ☎ 907/747–5755).

Wrangell: Stikine Drugs (✉ 202 Front St., ☎ 907/874–3422).

Visitor Information

Hours of operation of the following visitor information centers are generally May 15–August, daily 8–5 and when cruise ships are in port; September–April, weekdays 8–5.

Southeast Alaska Tourism Council (✉ Box 20710, Juneau 99802, ☎ 907/586–4777 or 800/423–0568 for a travel planner). **Haines/Fort Seward Visitor Information Center** (✉ 2nd Ave. near Willard St., Box 530, Haines 99827, ☎ 907/766–2234 or 800/458–3579). **Juneau Convention and Visitors Bureau** (✉ 369 S. Franklin St., Suite 201, Juneau 99801, ☎ 907/586–1737). **Davis Log Cabin Visitor Center** (✉ 134 3rd St., Juneau, ☎ 907/586–2201). **Ketchikan Visitors Bureau** (✉ 131 Front St., Ketchikan 99901, ☎ 907/225–6166 or 800/770–3300). **Petersburg Visitor Information Center** (✉ 1st and Fram Sts., Box 649, Petersburg 99833, ☎ 907/772–4636). **Sitka Convention and Visitors Bureau** (✉ Lincoln St. behind St. Michael's Cathedral, Box 1226, Sitka 99835, ☎ 907/747–5940). The bureau also has a visitor information booth in the Centennial Building on Harbor Street. **Greater Sitka Chamber of Commerce** (✉ 329 Harbor Dr., Suite 209, Box 638, Sitka 99835, ☎ 907/747–8604) is not open on weekends. **Skagway Convention and Visitors Bureau** (✉ 525 5th Ave., Box 415, Skagway 99840, ☎ 907/983–2854). **Klondike Gold Rush National Historical Park** visitor center (✉ 2nd Ave. and Broadway, Box 517, Skagway 99840, ☎ 907/983–2921). **Wrangell Chamber of Commerce Visitors Center** (✉ Stikine Ave., Box 49, Wrangell 99929, ☎ 907/874–3901 or 800/367–9745) is open when cruise ships or ferries are in port and at other posted times in summer.

Alaska Department of Fish and Game (✉ Box 25526, Juneau 99802, ☎ 907/465–4112; 907/465–4180 for sportfishing seasons and regulations; 907/465–2376 for license information). **Alaska Division of Parks** (✉ 400 Willoughby Ave., Suite 400, Juneau 99801, ☎ 907/465–4563). **U.S. Forest Service** (✉ 101 Egan Dr., Juneau 99801, ☎ 907/586–8751).

5 Anchorage

Alaska's biggest city (population 240,000) is the state's only true metropolis. You'll find a varied selection of ethnic restaurants and a performing arts center—home to theater groups, an opera company, and an orchestra. The Anchorage Museum of History and Art houses an outstanding collection of historic and contemporary Alaskan art, and the Alaska Native Heritage Center celebrates the diversity of the state's original inhabitants. At nearby Lake Hood the Alaska Aviation Heritage Museum preserves rare examples of the bush planes that helped tame the wilderness.

By Robin Hill
and Howard
C. Weaver

Updated by
Don Pitcher

AMID THE WILD COUNTRYSIDE that crowds around it on all sides, Anchorage has grown into a vigorous, spirited, cosmopolitan city—by far Alaska's largest and most sophisticated. Anchorage's youth has a lot to do with its struggle for recognition. First incorporated in 1920, Anchorage's population has a median age of 30 years and an aggressive style that makes it the yuppie of Alaskan cities. Rather than earn its keep through the oil and fishing industries that fuel the state's economy, Anchorage hustles its living as the government, banking, transportation, and communications hub those businesses depend on.

The relative affluence of this white-collar city (with a sprinkling of olive drab from nearby military bases) attracts fine restaurants and pricey shops, first-rate entertainment, and world-class sporting events. Flashy modern towers stab the skyline. Traffic from the city's busy international airport, served by more than 15 international and domestic airlines, lends Anchorage a more cosmopolitan air than you might expect from a population of 240,000.

Even with such modern amenities, Anchorage has not lost touch with Alaska's frontier spirit. Dogsled races are still among the most popular events held here, and moose often roam along city bike trails.

Anchorage residents are almost all immigrants, and their having chosen to make Anchorage their home seems to give them a big stake in local events. Ferocious political battles and dedicated community activism are trademarks of the city. Although representing less than 8% of the population, Native Alaskan tribes, Eskimos, and Aleuts add, through their influence, an important cultural dimension to the city. A growing Asian population is also having an impact, with well-stocked Asian food stores and restaurants an increasingly familiar sight.

Anchorage got its start with the construction of the federally built Alaska Railroad (completed in 1917); traces of the city's railroad heritage remain today. Once the tracks were laid, the town grew because its pioneer forerunners actively sought growth by hook and—not infrequently—by crook. City officials used to delight in telling how they tricked a visiting member of Congress into dedicating a site for a not-yet-approved federal hospital.

Boom and bust periods followed major events: an influx of military bases during World War II; a massive buildup of Arctic missile-warning stations during the Cold War; and in the late 1960s, the biggest bonanza of all: the discovery of oil at Prudhoe Bay and the construction of the trans-Alaska pipeline. Not surprisingly, Anchorage positioned itself as the perfect home for the new pipeline administrators and support industries, and it attracts a large share of the state's oil-tax dollars.

These days, Anchorage residents are no longer alone in singing their city's praises. The city is welcoming international visitors from such countries as Japan and Russia, who come even in winter to savor the ski resorts, sporting events, and captivating beauty of this frontier town.

Pleasures and Pastimes

Hiking and Walking
Anchorage is a hiker's paradise, with everything from paved, in-town trails to rugged dirt paths through the Chugach Mountains. The city is laced with some 125 mi of urban trails that meander through wooded greenbelts and quiet neighborhoods. The Tony Knowles Coastal Trail

is an 11-mi ribbon of asphalt beginning downtown and stretching west to Kincaid Park. Pick up a guidebook at the Alaska Public Lands Information Center (☞ Sights to See, *below*) or at area bookstores. A note of caution: when hiking in the hills, be sure to wear sturdy shoes and to take plenty of water, rain gear, and a light jacket—the weather can change with little warning. And although bear encounters are rare, be alert and make noise when walking in thick brush.

Shopping

Anchorage offers shopping opportunities to match any taste and price range. Souvenir shops selling everything from painted gold pans to plastic totem poles can be found on virtually every downtown block. Native Alaskan handicrafts of all kinds are sold at many of the gift shops downtown. Check for the official polar-bear symbol, which means the item was made in Alaska. A hand symbol indicates an article was handcrafted locally by Native artisans. Tlingit and Haida Indian traditional arts and crafts include totem poles, button blankets, wood carvings, and silver jewelry. Athabascan Indian craftspeople are known for their beadwork, which adorns slippers, headbands, and jewelry. Eskimo handicrafts include ivory and soapstone carvings and baleen baskets. Aleut grass baskets are so fine and tightly woven that some can hold water.

EXPLORING ANCHORAGE

With the exception of downtown, Anchorage neighborhoods are widely scattered, making a city that is not particularly pedestrian-friendly. Most shops and services are clustered along busy thoroughfares, so visiting them on foot is not only unpleasant but dangerous. Downtown is the exception; it was laid out with military precision by the Army Corps of Engineers. Streets and avenues run exactly east–west and north–south, with numbers in the first direction and letters of the alphabet or Alaska place-names (Barrow, Cordova, Denali, etc.) in the other. The only aberration is the absence of a J Street—a concession, some say, to the city's early Swedish settlers, who had difficulty pronouncing the letter. It's tough to get lost in the regular grid of downtown Anchorage.

Numbers in the text correspond to numbers in the margin and on the Anchorage map.

Great Itineraries

Anchorage presents a wide variety of things to see and do, so before you put on your comfortable shoes and grab your camera, take a few minutes to figure out what you're most interested in—seeing wildlife, shopping, taking a hike in the surrounding Chugach Mountains, or soaking up some of Alaska's rich Native culture.

IF YOU HAVE 1 DAY

Take the walking tour suggested below; it'll take you by fine shops and galleries, historic sites, a museum, parks, and much more. While at the museum, take in a Native dance performance and have lunch in the atrium café. If the weather's cooperating, take a walk along the Tony Knowles Coastal Trail. If you have a car, the driving tour described below will take you by other city highlights, including the aviation museum and the new Alaska Native Heritage Center. End the day with dinner and a walk along the Delany Park Strip or do some window-shopping downtown. Several places are open late if coffee and dessert sound like the perfect nightcap.

IF YOU HAVE 3 DAYS

Follow the one-day itinerary, then head south along the Seward Highway for views of Potter Marsh and Turnagain Arm. Continue 40 mi to the community of Girdwood; there are several good restaurants, beautiful hiking trails, and interesting shops. Continue farther down the highway to Portage Glacier and the Begich-Boggs Visitor Center (☞ Chapter 6). On this drive you might see Dall sheep and beluga whales. Back in Anchorage on day three, consider visiting some of the special-interest museums or taking in a baseball game at Mulcahy Stadium (☞ Outdoor Activities and Sports, *below*). A hike along one of the city's many bike trails or in the neighboring Chugach Mountains (☞ Chugach State Park *in* Chapter 3) will give you an appreciation of the role nature plays in the lives of those who make Anchorage their home. Bears and moose roam the park, which has trails from 2 to 30 mi in length.

IF YOU HAVE 5 DAYS

Do the one-day itinerary and the drive south in the three-day itinerary then, starting on day three, spend two days on a drive north to the communities of Eagle River, Eklutna (☞ Off the Beaten Path, *below*), Palmer, and Wasilla (for the last two, *see* Chapter 6); each has a different feel. Look into a white-water raft trip, a helicopter tour, or a flightseeing trip around Mt. McKinley. On day five, if you're up to the drive, take an overnight trip to Denali National Park (☞ Chapter 3) or to the town of Seward (☞ Seward *in* Chapter 6) and a wildlife-viewing trip into Kenai Fjords National Park (☞ Chapter 3).

Downtown Anchorage

A Good Walk

Start at the **Log Cabin Visitor Information Center** ①, where friendly volunteers answer questions and racks of brochures line the walls. The marble statue in front of **Old City Hall** ②, next door, honors William Seward, the secretary of state who engineered the purchase of Alaska from Russia. Along 4th Avenue are some of Anchorage's original structures. These buildings date to 1920, when Anchorage was incorporated. Cater-corner from the Old City Hall is the **Alaska Public Lands Information Center** ③, one of four in the state that provide information on all of Alaska's public lands.

Take F Street north (downhill) to 2nd Avenue. The houses in this neighborhood are original town-site homes built by the Alaska Engineering Commission, which also built the Alaska Railroad in the early 1900s. A neighborhood marker tells of Anchorage's first mayor and the start of the Anchorage Women's Club and includes photographs from the city's early days along the banks of Ship Creek.

Walk east along 2nd Avenue, past the Eisenhower Memorial, to a set of stairs leading down to the **Alaska Railroad depot** ④, which played an important role in the city's growth. Salmon run up the creek all summer; it's easy to watch them from the **Ship Creek viewing platform** ⑤, just north of the depot. From downtown, go north on E Street, which becomes C Street, then right on Whitney Road.

Ask Anchorage residents what is the best thing about living in the city, and many will say that it's the **Tony Knowles Coastal Trail** ⑥, a recreational trail that begins west of 2nd Avenue and curls along Cook Inlet's edge. Follow 3rd Avenue westward to **Resolution Park** ⑦ with its statue of Captain Cook. From here you can admire the grand vistas over Cook Inlet to Mt. McKinley and other peaks in the Alaska Range. The **Oscar Anderson House Museum** ⑧, off the coastal trail at the north end of Elderberry Park, was Anchorage's first permanent frame house, built in 1915 by city butcher Oscar Anderson. **Elderberry Park,** just in front of the house, is a good place for kids to run off steam, watch passing trains, and look for whales off the coastline. If young travelers are getting restless, head back up the 5th Avenue hill to the **Imaginarium** ⑨, an experiential science museum with a great gift shop.

Walk down 5th Avenue past the **Egan Convention Center** (✉ 555 W. 5th Ave., ☎ 907/263–2800), whose lobby has several modern Native Alaskan sculptures and a beaded curtain that evokes the northern lights. Across the street is a park that's packed with flowers in the summer, and behind it, the **Alaska Center for the Performing Arts** ⑩.

Walk down to A Street and 7th Avenue for the entrance to the **Anchorage Museum of History and Art** ⑪, which occupies the whole block between 6th and 7th avenues. The red metal sculpture out front is a favorite hide-and-seek site for children.

TIMING

This walking tour should take three to four hours, longer if you get caught up in shopping and in the museums. There's plenty to do year-round in Anchorage, though most visitors, particularly first-timers, might be happiest in June, July, or August, when the days are longer and the temperatures warmer. Locals embrace the 18-plus hours of daylight; dog walkers, bikers, and softball players are out until it gets dark, which in late June can be nearly midnight. Spring comes late and fall early to Anchorage. These are less desirable times to visit because weather can be cool and rainy and some attractions might be closed.

Sights to See

🐾 ⑩ **Alaska Center for the Performing Arts.** This distinctive stone-and-glass building fronts on an expansive park filled with brilliant flowers all summer. Take a look inside for upcoming events, or just relax amid the blooms on a sunny afternoon. ✉ 621 W. 6th Ave., at G St., ☎ 907/ 263–2900. ☉ Daily 8–5 and for performances.

🐾 ❸ **Alaska Public Lands Information Center.** This is a great one-stop source of information on all of Alaska's public lands, including national and state parks, national forests, and wildlife refuges. Make reservations for a state ferry, watch nature videos, learn about plants and animals, or head to the theater for films highlighting different parts of the state. There's a trip-planning computer for public use, plus maps and guidebooks for sale. ✉ 605 W. 4th Ave., at F St., ☎ 907/271–2737. ☉ Summer, daily 9–5:30; winter, weekdays 10–5:30.

🐾 ❹ **Alaska Railroad depot.** Outside are totem poles and a locomotive built in 1907. A monument in front of the depot relates the history of the railroad. During February's Fur Rendezvous festival, model-train buffs set up their displays here. ✉ 411 W. 1st Ave., ☎ 907/265–2494. ☉ Daily depending on train schedules.

🐾 ⑪ **Anchorage Museum of History and Art.** A fine collection of historic and contemporary Alaskan art is exhibited here along with wonderful dioramas and displays on Alaskan history and village life. The first-floor atrium is often the site of free public events, and in summer Native dancers perform in the auditorium three times a day. There's also a café and gift shop. ✉ 121 W. 7th Ave., ☎ 907/343–4326. 🎫 $4. ☉ Summer, daily 9–6; reduced winter hrs.

🐾 ⑨ **Imaginarium.** This is an experiential science museum—a fun house for children. Here kids can stand inside a giant soap bubble, hold a starfish in the marine exhibit, or take a galaxy tour in the planetarium. ✉ 737 W. 5th Ave., ☎ 907/276–3179. 🎫 $6. ☉ Daily, hrs vary.

❶ **Log Cabin Visitor Information Center.** This log cabin, like the ones old-timers built in the Bush, has a sod roof festooned with huge hanging baskets of flowers. There's a giant jade boulder outside and a signpost depicting the mileage to some of the world's largest cities. After a stop in the cabin, walk out the back door to a more spacious visitor center filled with brochures. ⊠ *4th Ave. and F St.,* ☎ *907/274–3531.* ▣ *Free.* ⊙ *May–Sept., daily 8–6; Oct.–Apr., daily 9–4.*

❷ **Old City Hall.** The Old City Hall (⊠ 524 W. 4th Ave.), also known as Historic City Hall, was built in 1936 and now houses the **Anchorage Convention and Visitors Bureau.** It is not open for tours, but check out the marble sculpture of William Seward out front.

❽ **Oscar Anderson House Museum.** Anchorage's first permanent frame house was built in 1915 by city butcher Oscar Anderson at a time when most of Anchorage consisted of tents. Tours are available in summer; a Swedish Christmas open house is held in December. ⊠ *420 M St.,* ☎ *907/274–2336.* ▣ *$3.* ⊙ *Mid-May–mid-Sept., daily 11–4; by appointment other times of yr.*

❼ **Resolution Park.** Follow 3rd Avenue westward to tiny Resolution Park, where you'll find a cantilevered viewing platform dominated by a monument to Captain Cook. Mt. Susitna (known as the Sleeping Lady) is the prominent low mountain to the northwest. Mt. McKinley—referred to by most Alaskans by its traditional name, Denali—is often visible 125 mi away.

❺ **Ship Creek viewing platform.** Ship Creek is dammed here, with a footbridge across the dam. You'll see a waterfall, salmon running upstream, and anglers, and above it all the skyscrapers of downtown. The viewing platform is just behind the Comfort Inn (☞ Lodging, *below*), which provides fishing poles to guests. ⊠ *Whitney Rd.*

☝ ❻ **Tony Knowles Coastal Trail.** This recreational trail follows the coastline from downtown Anchorage to Kincaid Park, beyond the airport. It is used extensively by strollers, joggers, bikers, in-line skaters, and, in winter, cross-country skiers. It can be crowded on sunny summer evenings, particularly around Westchester Lagoon. The trail begins off 2nd Avenue, west of Christensen Drive, and curls along Cook Inlet for approximately 11 mi. It offers good views of Mt. Susitna (known locally as Sleeping Lady) and often of Mt. McKinley. In summer, white beluga whales roll offshore in the Cook Inlet. There is access to the trail on the waterfront at the ends of 2nd, 5th, and 9th avenues and at Westchester Lagoon.

Midtown and Beyond

If you have a car, the following sites are well worth an afternoon's drive and will give you a better feel for the city. Anchorage's official city limits extend considerably into the surrounding countryside. An old mining camp called Girdwood—now home to the Alyeska Ski Resort—is within the city's boundaries despite being 40 mi south of the city center. The municipality also stretches more than 20 mi to the north.

Although a car is necessary for most stops, a closer-in site, such as Point Woronzof, can be reached on bike; the Alaska Zoo, about 9 mi from the city center, is served by the city's People Mover bus system (☞ Getting Around *in* Anchorage A to Z, *below*).

A Good Drive

Head west on Northern Lights Boulevard to a vista point overlooking Cook Inlet. On the way you'll pass tiny **Earthquake Park,** 2 mi past Minnesota Drive, which once offered a vivid demonstration of the power of the devastating 1964 earthquake, but time has healed so well that there is virtually nothing left of the destruction. Another 1¾ mi west on Northern Lights Boulevard is **Point Woronzof,** where there are

136

Alaska Aviation
Heritage Museum, **12**

Alaska Center for the
Performing Arts, **10**

Alaska Heritage
Library and
Museum, **15**

Alaska Native Heritage
Center, **17**

Alaska Public Lands
Information Center, **3**

Alaska Railroad
depot, **4**

Alaska Zoo, **13**

Anchorage Museum of
History and Art, **11**

Elmendorf Air Force
Base Wildlife
Museum, **16**

Imaginarium, **9**

Log Cabin Visitor
Information Center, **1**

Old City Hall, **2**

Oscar Anderson
House Museum, **8**

Potter Marsh, **14**

Resolution Park, **7**

Ship Creek viewing
platform, **5**

Tony Knowles
Coastal Trail, **6**

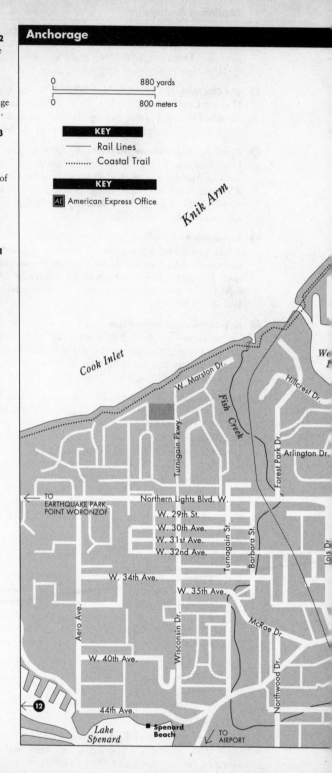

Anchorage

| 0 | | 880 yards |
| 0 | | 800 meters |

KEY
— Rail Lines
.... Coastal Trail

KEY
AE American Express Office

Knik Arm

Cook Inlet

W. Marston Dr.

Fish Creek

Hillcrest Dr.

Turnagain Pkwy.

Forest Park Dr.

Arlington Dr.

TO
EARTHQUAKE PARK,
POINT WORONZOF

Northern Lights Blvd. W.

W. 29th St.

W. 30th Ave.

W. 31st Ave.

W. 32nd Ave.

Turnagain St.

Barbara St.

Lois Dr.

W. 34th Ave.

W. 35th Ave.

Aero Ave.

Wisconsin Dr.

McRae Dr.

W. 40th Ave.

Northwood Dr.

44th Ave.

Lake
Spenand

Spenard
Beach

TO
AIRPORT

great views of Cook Inlet, Mt. Susitna, the Alaska Range, and Mt. McKinley, especially on a day when a temperature inversion (cold air is trapped on the ground by warmer air above) acts as a lens to make the mountains appear larger than life.

Turn left out of the parking lot at Point Woronzof and go back east along Northern Lights Boulevard 1½ mi to Aircraft Drive. Turn right and continue south and east along roads skirting the edge of two large lakes, Lakes Spenard and Hood. **Lake Spenard** has a beach where hardy souls may take a dip. Along **Lake Hood** you'll see geese and floatplanes take off and land—watch out for the air taxis! The **Alaska Aviation Heritage Museum** ⑫, overlooking the south end of the lake and 1½ mi from the intersection with Aircraft Drive, has more than 30 vintage aircraft.

Take the first left out of the parking lot at the Aviation Museum and, watching signs to avoid the airport traffic, head 2 mi east on International Boulevard to Minnesota Boulevard. Take Minnesota south about 9 mi (it becomes O'Malley Road and crosses Seward Highway) to the **Alaska Zoo** ⑬, which is in a wilderness setting with shaded trails. From the zoo, take a right on O'Malley and head back 2 mi to Seward Highway. Three miles south on the highway is the turnoff to **Potter Marsh** ⑭, home to the **Potter Point** game refuge, where Canada geese and other migratory birds make their home in summer.

From Potter Marsh, head north on Old Seward Highway 8 mi and turn left (west) on Northern Lights Boulevard to C Street, where you will find the **Alaska Heritage Library and Museum** ⑮. This small museum displays Native artifacts and photos. There are mounted grizzlies, polar bears, birds, moose, and more at the **Elmendorf Air Force Base Wildlife Museum** ⑯, which is 6 mi from the Alaska Heritage Library. Take Benson Boulevard (a one-way street just south of Northern Lights) back to Old Seward Highway. Go left (north), then make a right (east) on 15th Avenue, which becomes DeBarr, and a left (north) on Boniface Parkway to Elmendorf's gate. The **Alaska Native Heritage Center** ⑰ is east of here, near the intersection of Glenn Highway and Muldoon Road.

Timing

Driving the route without stopping will take about two hours. Visitors should allow from a half day to a full day, depending on the amount of time they'd like to spend at the sights.

Sights to See

☾ ⑫ **Alaska Aviation Heritage Museum.** This cramped facility presents the state's unique aviation history with more than 30 vintage aircraft, a theater, an observation deck onto Lake Hood, and special exhibits. There's an historic Fairchild American Pilgrim and a Stearman C2B, the first plane to land on Mt. McKinley back in the early 1930s. Volunteers are working to restore many of the planes and are eager to talk shop. ✉ 4721 Aircraft Dr., ☎ 907/248–5325. 🎫 $5.75. ☉ Summer, daily 9–6; reduced winter hrs.

★ ⑮ **Alaska Heritage Library and Museum.** This unassuming museum in the lobby of a large midtown bank is well organized and peaceful. Alaska Native culture is presented, and baskets, artifacts, dolls, paintings, photos, and rare books are on display. ✉ National Bank of Alaska, 301 W. Northern Lights Blvd., at C St., ☎ 907/265–2834. 🎫 Free. ☉ Weekdays noon–4.

☾ ⑰ **Alaska Native Heritage Center.** Situated on a 26-acre site facing the Chugach Mountains, this $15-million facility opens in 1999. Inside, a spacious Welcome House introduces you to Alaska's Native peoples through displays, artifacts, photographs, demonstrations, performances, and films. Also here is a café and gift shop. Visitors then head outside to circle a small lake while exploring five carefully recreated Native villages. ⊠ *Glenn Hwy and Muldoon Rd.,* ☎ *907/263–5170.* ☉ *Call for hrs.*

🖐 **13** **Alaska Zoo.** The zoo is home to Siberian tigers, musk ox, seals, brown bear, moose, and a variety of Alaskan birds. Unfortunately, the zoo's perennially most-popular animal—Annabelle the painting elephant— died in 1997. To get there from the city center, drive 9 mi south on Seward Highway to O'Malley Road; turn left (east toward the mountains) and go 2 mi. City buses also go to the zoo from downtown. ⊠ *4731 O'Malley Rd.,* ☎ *907/346–3242.* 🎟 *$6.* ☉ *Summer, daily 9–6; winter, daily 10–5.*

🖐 **16** **Elmendorf Air Force Base Wildlife Museum.** There are mounted grizzlies, polar bears, birds, moose, and more at this self-guided museum. Look for the 10½-ft brown bear, which misses the world record by only an eighth of an inch. There are also hands-on displays. ⊠ *Bldg. 4-803. Ask for directions at the Boniface Rd. gate,* ☎ *907/552–2282 for recorded information.* 🎟 *Free.* ☉ *Weekdays; call for hrs.*

🖐 **14** **Potter Marsh.** Potter Marsh, about 10 mi southof downtown on the Seward Highway, is home to the **Potter Point** game refuge. Canada geese and other migratory birds make their home here in summer; you might even spot an occasional moose or beaver. There's an elevated boardwalk for viewing. The **Potter Point Section House,** an old railroad service building, operates year-round as a state park information center. It's at the far southern end of the marsh. ☎ *907/345–5014.* ☉ *Weekdays 8–4:30.*

OFF THE
BEATEN PATH

EKLUTNA NATIVE VILLAGE – This tiny cluster of homes, a small Native community 26 mi north of Anchorage on the Glenn Highway, is the oldest continually inhabited Athabascan Indian site in the area. At the village cemetery, take note of the hand-built Siberian prayer chapel, traditional Russian Orthodox crosses, and some 80 colorful Native spirit houses. The museum at the Eklutna Historical Park (☎ 907/688–6026) is open daily in summer (mid-May to mid-Sept.) from 10 to 6 with 30-minute guided tours for $3.50. Across from the park, visitors can also tour the Mike Alex Cabin, home of the chief of the Eklutna people. There are no shops, restaurants, or overnight accommodations in Eklutna.

DINING

When it comes to eating out, many visitors to Alaska naturally think seafood. After all, fishing in Alaska is a multimillion-dollar industry employing thousands of people. For those eager to sample the fruits of those labors, dining out in Anchorage is a pleasure. Several restaurants—from formal dining rooms to casual pubs—offer such favorites as grilled Alaskan halibut and salmon, Alaskan king crab legs, scallops, oysters, and mussels. It is illegal to sell most native Alaskan foods that are hunted for subsistence purposes. You can, however, sample fiddlehead ferns and reindeer. In the last couple of years at least five microbreweries with adjoining restaurants have opened, three of them downtown, giving the area a spirited new feel. There also are a number of ethnic restaurants, especially Thai and other Asian restaurants, and a growing number of places with extensive vegetarian offerings. Downtown street vendors offer a quick lunch, and espresso bars have taken root all over town.

Most Anchorage restaurants are open daily in summer, with reduced hours in winter. Most do not require reservations, but it's always best to call ahead. For price ranges, *see* the Dining chart *in* On the Road with Fodor's.

Downtown

American

$$–$$$$ ✕ **Club Paris.** It's dark and smoky up front in the bar, where Anchorage folks have been meeting for decades. The restaurant in back serves big, tender, flavorful steaks of all kinds; halibut and fried prawns are also on the menu. There are no vegetables here except huge baked potatoes with optional cheddar-cheese sauce. If you don't have reservations, have a drink in the bar and order the hors d'oeuvres tray; this sampler of steak, cheese, and prawns could be a meal for two. ⊠ *417 W. 5th Ave.,* ☎ *907/277–6332. AE, D, DC, MC, V. No lunch Sun.*

American/Casual

$$–$$$$ ✕ **Glacier BrewHouse.** This cavernous microbrewery/restaurant is one of three relatively new microbreweries to open within a few blocks of one another. (The others are Railway Brewing Company inside the railroad depot, and Snowgoose Restaurant at W. 3rd Ave. and G St.) Popular with locals, the BrewHouse offers ales, stouts, lagers, and barley wine. Dinner selections range from thin, 10-inch pizzas to barbecued salmon, New York pepper steak, and Alaskan king crab legs. The atmosphere is loud and jovial. ⊠ *737 W. 5th Ave.,* ☎ *907/274–2739. AE, MC, V. No lunch Sun.*

$$ ✕ **Downtown Deli.** Owned by Alaska's governor, Tony Knowles, this deli serves a variety of favorites, from pastrami sandwiches to chopped chicken liver. Lunch and dinner include Alaska touches such as grilled halibut and salmon, and reindeer stew. The dark, rich chicken soup comes with either matzo balls or noodles. Breakfasts range from omelets to blintzes. Wooden booths offer privacy; if that's not your goal, sit out front at the sidewalk tables. Service is efficient and cheery. ⊠ *525 W. 4th Ave.,* ☎ *907/276–7116. Reservations not accepted. AE, D, DC, MC, V.*

Contemporary

$$$$ ✕ **Crow's Nest.** Elegant cuisine is the order of the day, along with the best view in Anchorage—every table has a window of its own. The Crow's Nest is best known for an extraordinary five-course set menu created by one of Alaska's finest chefs, R. Joseph Cooper III. The wine cellar is equally impressive. Everything is presented in an elegant atmosphere, with plenty of starched linen, brass, and teak. Local seafood is always on the menu, along with game and other meats. The Sunday brunch is especially popular. Reservations are a must, particularly if you want seats with a view of Mt. McKinley. ⊠ *On top of the Hotel Captain Cook, 5th Ave. and K St.,* ☎ *907/276–6000. Reservations essential. AE, D, DC, MC, V. No dinner Sun.*

$$$–$$$$ ✕ **Elevation 92.** Many tables have a view of the inlet, though they also face the port's industrial trappings. The ample hors d'oeuvres make great light meals—oysters in a number of permutations, sashimi, and crab-stuffed mushrooms—and there's a wide variety of wines available by the glass. The restaurant serves seafood, pasta, and steak; try the halibut Olympia, a favorite local recipe in which halibut fillets are baked in a cream-and-cheese-based sauce on a bed of onions. There's live jazz on Friday and Saturday evenings. ⊠ *1007 W. 3rd Ave.,* ☎ *907/279–1578. AE, D, DC, MC, V. No lunch weekends.*

$$$–$$$$ ✕ **Marx Brothers' Cafe.** This is one place where the food is always memorable. The little frame house on the bluff was built in 1916 and re-
★

furbished by the three "Marx Brothers"—Jack Amon, Van Hale, and Ken Brown. Chef Jack Amon's *melitzanosalata* appetizer is an Anchorage favorite—it's an eggplant spread served with Greek olives and pita bread. Or try the seafood mousse, a light pâté of smoked sturgeon, smoked salmon, and Maine lobster. The terrific made-at-your-table Caesar salad is a light meal in itself. Baked halibut with a macadamia crust served with coconut curry and mango chutney is a favorite entrée. For dessert try the warm wild-berry crisp with Alaskan birch syrup and butter pecan ice cream. The wine list is extensive. ⊠ *627 W. 3rd Ave.,* ☎ *907/278–2133. Reservations essential. AE, DC, MC, V. Closed Sun. and Sept.–May. No lunch.*

$$$–$$$$ ✕ **Sacks Café.** This cool, modern café offers light American cuisine using
★ trendy ingredients such as goat cheese, and interesting combinations of ethnic cuisines, such as Mediterranean chicken with feta cheese over pasta. Salads, which are large enough for a light meal, will leave room for the decadent chocolate gâteau. There's an extensive wine list, and Sunday brunch is available until 2:30. The owners also have a gourmet carry-out store next door, great for sandwiches, salads, baked goods, and other treats for an impromptu picnic. ⊠ *625 W. 5th Ave.,* ☎ *907/276–3546. Reservations not accepted. AE, MC, V.*

$$$–$$$$ ✕ **Simon and Seafort's Saloon and Grill.** The high ceilings and big windows here overlook Cook Inlet and light up the brass-and-wood interior. The diverse menu offers beef and pasta, but the main attraction here is seafood—fish is blackened, grilled, fried, or treated any other way you like it. Try the crab legs or grilled Alaskan salmon with toasted hazelnut butter. The brandy ice—vanilla ice cream whipped up with brandy, Kahlua, and creme de cocoa—is a good choice for dessert. The restaurant is crowded in summer, but there's usually space in the adjacent bar—a popular spot for appetizers and microbrewed beers—where you can also order from the regular menu. ⊠ *420 L St.,* ☎ *907/ 274–3502. AE, MC, V. No lunch Sun.*

$$$–$$$$ ✕ **Top of the World.** Views from this restaurant atop the Anchorage Hilton are mostly north toward Mt. McKinley. Tables away from windows are elevated, and there's an outdoor rooftop bar for sunset viewing. Etched-glass panels flank the entryway. Offerings include Alaska crab legs, lamb, and venison. Seasonal specials might include spicy duck sausage and fiddlehead ferns. Sunday brunch is served. ⊠ *Anchorage Hilton at 3rd Ave. and E. St.,* ☎ *907/265–7111. Reservations essential. AE, D, DC, MC, V. No lunch.*

Japanese

$$–$$$ ✕ **Kumagoro.** A favorite of the suit-and-tie lunch crowd, Kumagoro also has Japanese-style breakfasts, a take-out deli with such specialties as herring roe on kelp, and a sleek sushi bar (open evenings only). The best items on the dinner menu are the salmon teriyaki and the teriyaki beef dinner—a mound of steak strips grilled and brought still sizzling to your table; both are served with miso (soybean) soup and salad. The *shabu-shabu* dinner is a boiling stockpot in which you cook your own meats and vegetables. Inexpensive ramen noodle soups are also available. ⊠ *533 W. 4th Ave.,* ☎ *907/272–9905. AE, DC, MC, V.*

Thai

$$–$$$ ✕ **Thai Cuisine Too.** One of a half dozen Thai restaurants in Anchor-
★ age, Thai Cuisine Too is conveniently located right in the center of town. The atmosphere is quiet, the food is dependably good, and the menu makes for a change of pace from Alaska's ubiquitous seafood and steak houses. You'll find all the Thai standards on the menu, including fresh rolls, pad Thai, and a wonderful *tom khar gai* soup. ⊠ *328 G St.,* ☎ *907/277–8424. AE, MC, V. No lunch Sun.*

Dining
Club Paris, **26**
Crow's Nest, **14**
Double Musky, **36**
Downtown Deli, **24**
Elevation 92, **15**
Glacier BrewHouse, **18**
Gwennie's Old Alaskan
Restaurant, **28**
Jens', **5**
Kumagoro, **23**
L'Aroma Bakery &
Deli, **31**
Marx Brothers'
Café, **20**
Mexico in Alaska, **32**
Middle Way Café &
Coffeehouse, **6**
Moose's Tooth, **30**
Sacks Café, **17**
Seven Glaciers, **35**
Simon and Seafort's
Saloon and Grill, **12**
Thai Cuisine Too, **19**
Top of the World, **22**

Lodging
Alyeska Hostel, **33**
Anchorage Hilton, **21**
Anchorage Hotel, **25**
Anchorage
International Hostel, **9**
Anchorage Westmark
Hotel, **16**
Comfort Inn Ship
Creek, **27**
Copper Whale Inn, **11**
Hampton Inn, **4**
Hotel Captain
Cook, **13**
Inlet Tower Suites, **7**
Marriott Courtyard, **3**
Merrill Field Inn, **29**
Regal Alaskan Hotel, **1**
Sheraton
Anchorage, **28**
Snowshoe Inn, **8**
Voyager Hotel, **10**
Westin Alyeska Prince
Hotel, **34**

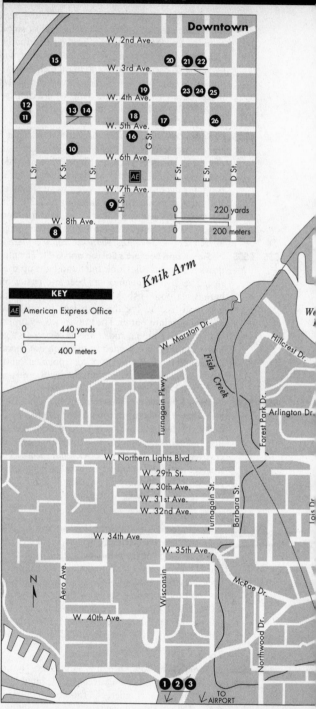

Anchorage Dining and Lodging

Downtown

W. 2nd Ave.
W. 3rd Ave.
W. 4th Ave.
W. 5th Ave.
W. 6th Ave.
W. 7th Ave.
W. 8th Ave.

L St. · K St. · I St. · H St. · G St. · F St. · E St. · D St.

AE

0   220 yards
0   200 meters

Knik Arm

KEY
AE   American Express Office
0   440 yards
0   400 meters

W. Marston Dr.
Turnagain Pkwy
Fish Creek
Hillcrest Dr.
Forest Park Dr.
Arlington Dr.

W. Northern Lights Blvd.
W. 29th St.
W. 30th Ave.
W. 31st Ave.
W. 32nd Ave.
Turnagain St.
Barbara St.

W. 34th Ave.
W. 35th Ave.
McRae Dr.

N

Aero Ave.
Wisconsin
W. 40th Ave.
Northwood Dr.

TO
AIRPORT

Greater Anchorage

American

$–$$$ ✕ **Gwennie's Old Alaskan Restaurant.** An old Anchorage favorite,
Gwennie's is filled with historic Alaskan photos, stuffed animals, and
memorabilia. Lunch and dinners are available—including an all-you-
can-eat beef barbecue for $11— but the restaurant is best known for
its old-fashioned breakfasts, available all day. Try the reindeer sausage
and eggs, the crab omelets, or the Belgian waffles. ⊠ *4333 Spenard
Rd.,* ☎ *907/243–2090. AE, D, DC, MC, V.*

Cajun/Creole

$$–$$$$ ✕ **Double Musky.** Anchorage residents say dinner here is worth the one-
★   hour drive to Girdwood. Granted, it's a little noisy and smoky (the no-
smoking section is small), and its walls are draped with tacky art and
souvenirs from trips to Mardi Gras, but this casual restaurant definitely
has its charms. For one thing, there's the setting: huge Sitka spruce are
framed in the windows. Then there's the excellent, mostly Cajun-style
menu: standard offerings like blackened salmon and chicken breasts
stuffed with Cajun sausage are outstanding. The garlic seafood pasta
is to die for and the rack of lamb and lobster kebab also are quite good.
For dessert lovers, the biggest attraction here is the Double Musky Pie.
It's got chocolate, it's got pecans, it's gooey, and it's out of this world.
Arrive by 5:30 on weekends or expect a 45-minute wait in the bar. ⊠
*Crow Creek Rd., Girdwood, south of downtown Anchorage via Se-
ward Hwy. and Alyeska Hwy.,* ☎ *907/783–2822. Reservations not
accepted. AE, MC, V. Closed Mon. and Nov. No lunch.*

Contemporary

$$$–$$$$ ✕ **Jens'.** Although this elegant dining spot is in a midtown strip mall,
★   it's comfortable and serves quite fine food. The dinner menu changes
daily; entrées often include grilled salmon and pepper steak. The lunch
menu includes Danish specialties, plus soups, salads, pastas, and veg-
etarian meals. Museum-quality art lines the walls. The wine list is ex-
tensive. ⊠ *701 W. 36th Ave.,* ☎ *907/561–5367. AE, D, DC, MC, V.
Closed Sun. and Jan. No lunch Sat., no dinner Mon.*

$$$–$$$$ ✕ **Seven Glaciers.** This elegant though relaxed restaurant is one of the
★   area's finest. An enclosed tramway (free with dinner reservation; other-
wise $18) carries you to the 2,300-ft level of Mt. Alyeska, with views
of Turnagain Arm. The dining room, from which you can see seven
glaciers, is comfortable, with most tables offering spectacular views.
Entrées include king crab with cilantro and grilled Portobello mush-
rooms, and reindeer sirloin in a shallot-whiskey sauce. Appetizers also
are out of the ordinary though pricey. The presentation is artful. ⊠
Westin Alyeska Prince Hotel (☞ Lodging, below), ☎ *907/754–2237.
Reservations essential. AE, D, DC, MC, V. Open June–Sept.; call for
hrs at other times. No lunch.*

Eclectic

$–$$ ✕ **L'Aroma Bakery & Deli.** This trendy little eatery is a popular up-
★   scale gathering place. There's deli food, such as sandwiches and stuffed
grape leaves, but the big attractions are the 9-inch California-style pizzas, featuring pesto, fresh herbs, Italian meats, seafood, and goat
cheese. Specialty breads include sourdough, raisin, and rosemary;
dozens of different pastries are also available. L'Aroma shares the
seating area with a Kaladi Brothers espresso bar and a new Sagaya grocery serving Chinese takeout. A second location, inside the Sagaya City
Market at 13th Ave. and I St., has similar fare and is closer to downtown. ⊠ *3700 Old Seward Hwy., across from the University Center
mall,* ☎ *907/562–9797. Reservations not accepted. AE, MC, V.*

Mexican

$$–$$$ ✕ **Mexico in Alaska.** Since 1972 the best Mexican food in town has been served here—subtle and ungreasy. Owner Maria Elena Ball makes everyone her friend, particularly young children. Favorite dishes include *chilaquiles* (tortilla casserole with mole sauce) and *entremesa de queso* (a platter of melted cheese, jalapeños, and onions served with home-made tortillas), and lime- marinated fried chicken. There's a buffet week-days for lunch and for dinner on Sunday. The restaurant also offers its own porter beer. ⊠ *7305 Old Seward Hwy.,* ☎ *907/349–1528. AE, D, MC, V. No lunch Sun.*

Pizza

$$–$$$ ✕ **Moose's Tooth.** This brew pub and pizzeria in midtown just off the
★ Seward Highway north of 36th Avenue has been packed since it opened in 1996. Pizzas and handcrafted beers, including more than a dozen ales, ambers, porters, and stouts, are the order of the day. In addition to the standards, pizza toppings also include artichoke hearts, Kalamata olives, sun-dried tomatoes, feta cheese, and spinach. Weekday lunches are a real bargain, starting at just $5. It's popular with the single crowd, families, and out-of-towners. ⊠ *3300 Old Seward Hwy.,* ☎ *907/258–2537. D, MC, V.*

Vegetarian

$–$$ ✕ **Middle Way Café & Coffee House.** This cramped little niche boasts a wide variety of vegetarian and nonvegetarian dishes, including dressed-up grain-and-soy burgers, hummus sandwiches, and jumbo whole-grain tortillas wrapped around combinations of fresh veggies, falafel, brown rice, and beans. There's a juice bar, fruit smoothies, espresso, and 35 choices of tea. Be sure to check out their daily specials. ⊠ *1200 W. Northern Lights Blvd.,* ☎ *907/272–6433. Reservations not accepted. No credit cards. Closed Sun.*

LODGING

There are as many lodging options in Anchorage as there are preferences. Several hotels offer top-draw amenities, with summer rates to match. There also are smaller, less expensive inns, as well as more than 100 bed-and-breakfasts; for a listing, contact the Anchorage Convention and Visitors Bureau (☞ Visitor Information *in* Anchorage A to Z, *below*). For campgrounds in and around town, contact the downtown Public Lands Information Center.

Most hotels in Anchorage are either downtown or near the airport (in the Spenard area). Girdwood, although technically within Anchorage city limits, is a ski resort 40 mi south of downtown along the Seward and Alyeska highways. In summer, reservations are a must for the major hotels; many places fill up months in advance. Winter rates are much lower than summer rates, on which these categories are based.

For price ranges, *see* the Anchorage lodging chart *in* On the Road with Fodor's.

Downtown

$$$$ ▨ **Anchorage Hilton.** The Hilton's ample lobby has big chandeliers that look like glacier ice and glass cases with menacingly posed grizzly and polar bears. Well-maintained rooms—renovated over the last few years with new furniture, carpet, drapes, and linens—have data ports and voice mail; those facing north and east have the best views. A sports bar has 18 TV screens. ⊠ *500 W. 3rd Ave., 99501,* ☎ *907/272–7411 or 800/245–2527,* FAX *907/265–7140. 591 rooms. 2 restaurants, bar, indoor pool, health club. AE, D, DC, MC, V.*

$$$$ 🏨 **Hotel Captain Cook.** The three towers of this hotel take up a full city block. The dark decor recalls Captain Cook's voyages in the South Pacific—teak paneling lines the interior walls. Most of the rooms have been recently remodeled, and all include computer ports. The best choices are the ones on the higher floors (10th and above). The most luxurious accommodations are found in the top two floors of Tower II. ✉ *5th Ave. and K St., 99501,* ☎ *907/276–6000 or 800/843–1950,* ﬁⅹ *907/278–5366. 600 rooms. 3 restaurants, room service, indoor pool, barbershop, beauty salon, hot tub, health club, racquetball, meeting rooms. AE, D, DC, MC, V.*

$$$$ 🏨 **Sheraton Anchorage.** Occupying a full city block on the east side of downtown, the 16-story Sheraton is popular with business travelers. The glass-canopied lobby has a jade-tiled staircase and acres of cream-color marble. Guest rooms all include voice mail, an iron and ironing board, hair dryer, and coffeemaker. Get a room high up on the north side to watch F-16s and other jets flying tight patterns over nearby Elmendorf Air Force Base. The Sheraton is a half mile from downtown attractions and borders a run-down part of Anchorage. ✉ *401 E. 6th Ave., 99501,* ☎ *907/276–8700 or 800/325–3535,* ﬁⅹ *907/276–7561. 375 rooms. 2 restaurants, no-smoking rooms, room service, health club, meeting rooms. AE, D, DC, MC, V.*

$$$ 🏨 **Anchorage Hotel.** The little Anchorage Hotel building has been
★ around since 1916. Experienced travelers call it the only hotel in Anchorage with charm: the original sinks and tubs have been restored, and upstairs hallways are lined with old photos of the city. The lobby, with a fireplace, has a quaint European feel. Each room includes a fully stocked minibar (the only hotel in Anchorage with this amenity), plus phone data ports, hair dryers, irons, and ironing boards. Coffee and pastries are served each morning in the lobby. ✉ *330 E St., 99501,* ☎ *907/272–4553 or 800/544–0988,* ﬁⅹ *907/277–4483. 16 rooms, 10 suites. Pub, meeting room. AE, D, DC, MC, V.*

$$$ 🏨 **Anchorage Westmark Hotel.** This 14-story downtown hotel has comfortable rooms that have been recently remodeled with dark teak furniture. Each has its own private balcony; the best vistas are from rooms on the higher floors. ✉ *720 W. 5th Ave., 99501,* ☎ *907/276–7676 or 800/544–0970,* ﬁⅹ *907/276–3615. 200 rooms. Restaurant, coffee shop, room service, meeting rooms. AE, D, DC, MC, V.*

$$$ 🏨 **Comfort Inn Ship Creek.** Popular with families, this hotel is a short walk northeast of the Alaska Railroad depot. It was built as the first phase of a plan to revitalize the area with shops, restaurants, and a microbrewery. Rooms, which can be noisy, come in a variety of configurations; some are executive suites and some have kitchens. Rooms on the north side look out on Ship Creek (a popular salmon-fishing stream) and the railroad. A limited number of bikes and fishing poles are available, and all guests receive a substantial Continental breakfast each morning. ✉ *111 Ship Creek Ave., 99501,* ☎ *907/277–6887 or 800/362–6887,* ﬁⅹ *907/274–9830. 100 rooms. Indoor pool, hot tub, business services. AE, D, DC, MC, V.*

$$$ 🏨 **Voyager Hotel.** This four-story hotel catering to both business and
★ leisure travelers offers good value. Attention to detail shows in the newly remodeled kitchens, queen-size beds, sofa beds, coffeemakers, irons and ironing boards, and high-quality linens; all rooms also have voice mail and computer and fax outlets. Smoking is not allowed anywhere in the hotel. Upstairs, west-side rooms offer views of the inlet. ✉ *501 K St., 99501,* ☎ *907/277–9501 or 800/247–9070,* ﬁⅹ *907/274–0333. 38 rooms. Restaurant, no-smoking rooms. AE, D, DC, MC, V.*

$$–$$$ 🏨 **Copper Whale Inn.** This small inn has the perfect location. It's on the edge of downtown with a view across Cook Inlet to Sleeping Lady and other mountains. Great food is available just a few steps away at

Simon and Seafort's. And the knowledgeable owner Tony Carter—a marine biologist—leads ecotours of the surrounding area. All rooms are furnished with cherry-wood beds, and most have private baths. Join other guests for a light breakfast each morning. ⊠ *440 L St., 99501,* ☎ *907/258–7999,* FAX *907/258–6213. 15 rooms. No-smoking rooms. AE, D, MC, V.*

$$ ★ 🏨 **Inlet Tower Suites.** Built in 1953, this 14-story building in a residential area several blocks south of downtown offers spacious suites for reasonable rates. Rooms have microwaves and refrigerators. Corner rooms, particularly those on the northeast side, provide expansive views. Free parking is available out front. Westchester Lagoon and bike trails are nearby. ⊠ *1200 L St., 99501,* ☎ *907/276–0110 or 800/544– 0786,* FAX *907/258–4914. 180 rooms. Restaurant, no-smoking rooms, beauty salon, sauna, exercise room, coin laundry. AE, D, DC, MC, V.*

$$ 🏨 **Merrill Field Inn.** A mile east of downtown and across from Anchorage's small-plane airfield, this well-maintained family motel has reasonable prices and spotlessly clean rooms. Each includes a microwave oven, refrigerator, and hair dryer. Kitchenettes are also available. ⊠ *420 Sitka St., 99501,* ☎ *907/276–4547 or 800/898–4547,* FAX *907/ 276–5064. 39 rooms. 2 restaurants, airport shuttle. AE, D, DC, MC, V.*

$$ 🏨 **Snowshoe Inn.** Snowshoe Inn is the opposite of downtown Anchorage's corporate motels. It's a friendly no-smoking place with comfortable rooms containing new furnishings, refrigerators, and microwaves. A Continental breakfast is served each morning in the lobby. The least-expensive rooms have a shared bath. ⊠ *826 K St., 99501,* ☎ *907/258–7669,* FAX *907/258–7463. 16 rooms. No-smoking rooms, coin laundry. AE, DC, MC, V.*

$ 🏨 **Anchorage International Hostel.** This tan cinder-block building is downtown, a block and a half from the bus depot. Guests rent linens and share kitchen, bathroom, and household chores. There's a 1 AM curfew. Accommodations are in four private rooms or in dorm-style quarters. There's a five-night limit in summer; reservations are highly recommended. ⊠ *700 H St., 99501,* ☎ *907/276–3635. 104 beds. Kitchen, coin laundry. MC, V.*

Greater Anchorage

$$$$ ★ 🏨 **Regal Alaskan Hotel.** Perched on the shore of Lake Hood—the world's busiest floatplane base—the Regal is a great place from which to watch planes come and go. And each March, the hotel becomes headquarters for the Iditarod Trail Sled Dog Race. The lobby resembles a hunting lodge with its stone fireplace and trophy heads and mounted fish on every wall. The luxuriously appointed guest rooms continue the Alaskan theme, with colorful Haida-style bedding and moose-shape cast-iron lamps. All rooms have small refrigerators, coffeemakers, hair dryers, irons, and ironing boards. Most rooms are no-smoking. The restaurant here is famous for Sunday brunch buffets ($26 with champagne or wine). ⊠ *4800 Spenard Rd., 99517,* ☎ *907/243–2300 or 800/544–0553,* FAX *907/243–8815. 248 rooms. Restaurant, room service, hot tub, exercise room, laundry service, airport shuttle. AE, D, DC, MC, V.*

$$$$ ★ 🏨 **Westin Alyeska Prince Hotel.** This large and luxurious hotel sits at the base of Mt. Alyeska Ski Resort, an hour south of Anchorage in the town of Girdwood. The hotel is surrounded by lush forests, and some rooms offer views of the Chugach Mountains. All rooms have refrigerators, safes, heated towel racks, ski-boot storage, bathrobes, and slippers; there are phones in bathrooms and bedrooms. A spectacular aerial tram transports diners to the Seven Glaciers restaurant from the

hotel. ✉ *1000 Arlberg, Box 249, Girdwood 99587,* ☎ *907/754–1111 or 800/880–3880,* FAX *907/754–2200. 307 rooms. 3 restaurants, 2 bars, room service, indoor pool, hot tub, massage, sauna, exercise room, ice-skating, cross-country skiing, downhill skiing, shops, meeting rooms. AE, D, DC, MC, V.*

$$$ 🏨 **Hampton Inn.** Midway between the airport and downtown, this is one of six new Anchorage hotels that have opened in the last two years. The Hampton has all the now-standard room features: designer furnishings, refrigerators, microwaves, coffeemakers, hair dryers, irons, ironing boards, three phones per room, data ports, and voice mail. Guests are treated to a Continental breakfast buffet, and freezer storage is available for your fresh-caught fish. ✉ *4301 Credit Union Dr., 99503,* ☎ *907/550–7000 or 800/426–7866,* FAX *907/561–7330. 101 rooms. No-smoking rooms, indoor pool, hot tub, exercise room, laundry service, meeting rooms. AE, D, DC, MC, V.*

$$$ 🏨 **Marriott Courtyard.** This new hotel near the airport is attracting business travelers. The restaurant serves breakfast and dinner, and there is limited room service in the evenings. Most rooms are designated no-smoking. Some rooms have a Jacuzzi, all have coffeemakers, hair dryers, irons, and ironing boards. Summertime guests enjoy relaxing in the grassy central courtyard. ✉ *4901 Spenard Rd., 99517,* ☎ *907/245–0322 or 800/321–2211,* FAX *907/248–1886. 154 rooms. Restaurant, room service, indoor pool, hot tub, sauna, exercise room, laundry service, meeting rooms, airport shuttle. AE, D, DC, MC, V.*

$ 🏨 **Alyeska Hostel.** Located 35 mi south of Anchorage in the resort town of Girdwood, this small, rustic cabin is the perfect place for budget travelers who don't mind taking a sauna instead of a shower. The adventurous also won't mind the wood heat and gas lights. Guests have a midnight curfew and are assigned a small housekeeping chore. It's also best if you bring your own bedding. There's a four-night maximum stay. ✉ *Alpina St., Girdwood 99510 (mailing address: Box 10-4099, Anchorage 99510);* ☎ *907/783–2099. 12 beds. Kitchen, sauna. No credit cards.*

NIGHTLIFE AND THE ARTS

The Arts

Visitors and those new to Anchorage are often surprised by the variety—and high quality—of cultural activities in this town of 240,000 people. In addition to top-name touring groups and performers, routinely there are opportunities to attend local productions, including provocative theater, winning student performances at the university, thought-provoking poetry readings, literary brunches, or Native Alaskan dance or storytelling performances. Tickets for many cultural events can be purchased at any Carr's grocery store. Carr's Tix (☎ 907/263–2901 or 907/263–2787) offers recorded information on cultural events of the week and the option to buy tickets by phone.

The **Alaska Center for the Performing Arts** (✉ 621 W. 6th Ave., ☎ 907/263–2787 or 907/263–2900) has three theaters and occupies the block between 5th and 6th avenues at G Street in the heart of downtown. The lobby box office, open Monday to Saturday 10–6, sells tickets to a variety of productions and is a good all-around source of cultural information.

Opera and Classical Music

The **Anchorage Opera** produces two or three operas during its November-to-March season. The **Anchorage Symphony Orchestra** performs classical concerts October through April. The box office of the Alaska Center for the Performing Arts (☞ *above*) sells tickets for both.

Theater

The **Alaska Center for the Performing Arts** (☞ *above*) is the major venue.

Cyrano's Off-Center Playhouse (✉ 4th Ave. and D St., ☎ 907/274–2599) mounts innovative productions in an intimate theater that is connected to a café, an art movie house, and a bookstore that bear its name.

Out North Theatre Co. (✉ 1325 Primrose St., just west of Bragaw off DeBarr Rd., ☎ 907/279–8200), whose productions are thought-provoking and, at times, controversial, often earns critical acclaim from local reviewers.

Student productions from the **University of Alaska Anchorage Theater** (✉ 3211 Providence Dr., ☎ 907/786–4721) are timely and well done. The theater is intimate, with seating on three sides.

Nightlife

Anchorage does not shut down when it gets dark. Bars here—and throughout Alaska—open early (in the morning) and close as late as 3 AM on weekends. The *Anchorage Daily News* entertainment section, published on Friday, has an exhaustive listing of entertainment options, ranging from concerts and theater to movie listings and a roundup of nightspots featuring live music. The Alaska Center for the Performing Arts has three theaters and hosts local performing groups as well as traveling production companies that in the last few years have brought *Cats, Les Miserables,* and *Phantom of the Opera* to the Anchorage stage.

Bars and Nightclubs

Chilkoot Charlie's (✉ 2435 Spenard Rd., ☎ 907/272–1010). A rambling timber building with sawdust floors, three stages, very loud music seven nights a week, and rowdy customers, this place is where younger Alaskans go to get crazy. Not for the faint of heart.

Club Paris (✉ 417 W. 5th Ave., ☎ 907/277–6332). Lots of old-timers favor this dark, smoky bar. Once the classiest place in downtown Anchorage, with its Paris mural and French street lamps hanging behind the bar, it has lost the glamour but not the faithful. There's mostly swing on the jukebox. (☞ Dining, *above*.)

Fletcher's (✉ 5th Ave. and K St., ☎ 907/276–6000). The Captain Cook Hotel's bar has lead glass and dark wood, and a genteel atmosphere. Good food is served, including fresh pasta and gourmet pizzas.

Simon and Seafort's Saloon and Grill (✉ 420 L St., ☎ 907/274–3502). An "in" place for the dressy thirtysomething crowd, the bar at Simon's has fantastic views of Cook Inlet, a special Scotch menu, and an extensive selection of imported beers. There are deliciously decadent desserts, too. (☞ Dining, *above*.)

Comedy

Fly by Night Club. Mr. Whitekeys is the proprietor of this self-proclaimed "sleazy Spenard nightclub." Every summer he produces a revue called the "Whale Fat Follies" (with tacky Alaska jokes), accomplished singing, and the boogie-woogie piano of Mr. Whitekeys himself. Three other equally wacky shows are presented at other times of the year. To really appreciate all the inside jokes, it helps to attend with a local. Shows start at 8; it's a good idea to reserve a week in advance. The club is smoke-free Tuesday, Wednesday, and Thursday nights. ✉ *3300 Spenard Rd.,* ☎ *907/279–7726. Closed Sun. and Mon. and Jan.–Mar.*

Live Music

Most of the larger hotels have live bands playing in at least one of their bars. See Friday editions of the *Anchorage Daily News* for complete listings of live music. On most Fridays during the summer, open-air concerts are performed at noon on the stage in front of the **Old City Hall** (⊠ 4th Ave. between E and F Sts.). Performers can also be heard at the **Saturday Market** (⊠ 3rd Ave. and E St.) in summer.

A-K Korral Saloon (⊠ 2421 E. Tudor Rd., ☎ 907/562–6552). If it's country you want, it's country you'll get at this big east-side favorite. Tony Lamas and Wranglers are the uniform of choice. Free country-western dance lessons are offered Tuesday through Thursday nights.

Blues Central/Chef's Inn (⊠ 825 W. Northern Lights Blvd., ☎ 907/272–1341). This modest and smoky eatery is a blues mecca that features hot live bands on weekend nights.

Humpy's Great Alaskan Alehouse (⊠ 610 W. 6th Ave., ☎ 907/276–2337). Rock, blues, and folk, along with dozens of microbrews and tasty pub grub are offered at Humpy's. It's popular, noisy, smoky, and always packed with a thirtysomething crowd of locals and travelers.

The Wave (⊠ 3103 Spenard Rd., ☎ 907/561–9283). A favorite haunt of Anchorage's party-hardy crowd, this big box of a place is usually packed with both gay and straight patrons who dance practically non-stop to the DJ tunes.

OUTDOOR ACTIVITIES AND SPORTS

Participant Sports

Bicycling, Jogging, and Walking

Anchorage has more than 125 mi of bicycle trails, and many streets have marked bike lanes. Although busy during the day, downtown streets are uncrowded and safe for cyclists in the evening. The **Tony Knowles Coastal Trail** (☞ Exploring Anchorage, *above*) and other bike trails in Anchorage are used by runners, cyclists, rollerbladers, and walkers. The trail from Westchester Lagoon at the end of 15th Avenue runs 2 mi to Earthquake Park and an additional 7 mi to Kincaid Park.

Bike rentals are available from **Adventure Cafe** (⊠ 414 K St., ☎ 907/276–8282 or 800/288–3134), and **Downtown Bicycle Rental** (☎ 907/279–5293).

Canoeing and Kayaking

Local lakes and lagoons, such as Westchester Lagoon, Goose Lake, and Jewel Lake, offer good boating. **Rental kayaks and canoes** are available from **Adventure Cafe** (⊠ 414 K St., ☎ 907/276–8282 or 800/288–3134) and from **Recreational Equipment Inc.** (⊠ 1200 W. Northern Lights Blvd., ☎ 907/272–4565).

Fishing

Nearly 30 local lakes are stocked with trout. You must have a valid Alaska sportfishing license. Jewel Lake in south Anchorage and Mirror and Fire lakes near Eagle River all hold fish. Coho salmon return to Ship Creek (downtown) in August, while king salmon are caught between late May and early July. Campbell Creek and Bird Creek just south of town are also popular spots. Fishing licenses may be purchased at any Carr's grocery store. Call the **Alaska Department of Fish and Game** (☎ 907/267–2218) for information.

Golf

Russian Jack Springs (☎ 907/333–8338) is run by the city and generally is open May–September. It has nine holes, synthetic greens, and clubs for rent. **Tanglewood Lakes Golf Club** (☎ 907/345–4600) is a relatively new, nine-hole course in South Anchorage. **Anchorage Golf Course** (☎ 907/522–3363) on O'Malley Road has 18 holes with greens. Golf carts and clubs are available for rent.

Ice-Skating

Ben Boeke indoor ice arena (✉ 334 E. 16th Ave., ☎ 907/274–5715) offers open skating. The **University of Alaska** also has an indoor ice rink (✉ 3211 Providence Dr., ☎ 907/786–1231) open to the public weekdays noon–1:45 PM and on weekends; call for hours.

Racquet Sports

The park strip at 9th Avenue and C Street has several **tennis courts.** The **Alaska Club** (✉ 5201 E. Tudor Rd., ☎ 907/337–9550) has a pool, weight room, indoor track, and golf cage, as well as tennis, racquetball, and squash courts. Visitors may buy a day pass for $15 but must be accompanied by a member.

Rafting

Both **Midnight Sun River Runners** (✉ Box 211561, Anchorage 99521, ☎ 907/338–7238 or 800/825–7238, FAX 907/333–6170), and **NOVA** (✉ Box 1129, Chickaloon 99674, ☎ 907/745–5753 or 800/746–5753, FAX 907/745–5754) offer white-water and float trips in the Anchorage area. Check with the Log Cabin Information Center or the Anchorage Yellow Pages for additional listings.

Skiing

Alyeska Ski Resort (☎ 907/754–1111, 907/754–7669 recorded information, or 800/880–3880), at Girdwood, 40 mi south of the city, is a full-service resort with a day lodge, hotel, restaurants, six chairlifts, a tram, a vertical drop of 2,500 ft, and runs for all abilities. The tram is open during the summer, providing access to a mountaintop restaurant and hiking trails. **Alyeska Accommodations** (☎ 907/783–2000, FAX 907/783–2425) can set you up in a privately owned cabin or condo. Closer to town are two smaller ski areas: **Alpenglow at Arctic Valley** (☎ 907/428–1208, 907/249–9292 recorded information) and **Hilltop Ski Area** (☎ 907/346–1446).

Cross-country skiing is extremely popular; locals ski trails in town at Kincaid Park or Hillside, and farther away at Girdwood Valley, Turnagain Pass, and Chugach State Park.

Rental skis are available from Recreational Equipment Inc. (✉ 1200 W. Northern Lights Blvd., ☎ 907/272–4565) and **Alaska Mountaineering and Hiking** (✉ 2633 Spenard, ☎ 907/272–1811).

Spectator Sports

Baseball

Anchorage is home to the **Anchorage Bucs** and the **Glacier Pilots,** teams composed of college players here for the summer. Games are played at **Mulcahy Stadium** next to the Sullivan Arena (✉ 1600 Gambell St., ☎ 907/279–2596).

Basketball

The University of Alaska Anchorage hosts the **Great Alaska Shootout** in Anchorage over Thanksgiving weekend. Games are at Sullivan Arena (☞ Baseball, *above*).

Dogsled Races

World Championship races are run in mid-February, with three consecutive 25-mi heats through downtown Anchorage, out into the foothills, and back. People line the route with cups of coffee in hand to cheer on their favorite mushers. The three-day races are part of the annual **Fur Rendezvous,** one of the largest winter festivals in the United States; the festival office (⊠ 327 Eagle St., 99501, ☎ 907/277–8615) has a guide to events.

In March, mushers and their dogs compete in the 1,049-mi **Iditarod Trail Sled Dog Race** (Iditarod Trail Headquarters, ☎ 907/376–5155) The race commemorates the delivery of serum to Nome by dog mushers during the diphtheria epidemic of 1925. The serum run was the inspiration for the animated family film *Balto.* Dog teams leave downtown Anchorage and wind through the Alaska range, across the Interior, out to the Bering seacoast, and on to Nome. Depending on weather and trail conditions, winners can complete the race in nine days.

Hockey

The **University of Alaska Anchorage** has a Division I NCAA hockey team that draws several thousand loyal fans to home games at the Sullivan Arena. The West Coast Hockey League's **Anchorage Aces** (☎ 907/258–2237) also play the arena.

SHOPPING

Art

Artique (⊠ 314 G St., ☎ 907/277–1663) sells paintings, prints, and jewelry by Alaskan artists. **Decker/Morris Gallery** (⊠ 621 W. 6th Ave., south side of Alaska Center for the Performing Arts, ☎ 907/272–1489) carries works by better-known Alaskan artists—both Native and non-Native—and features contemporary originals and prints, jewelry, and sculpture. Monthly solo exhibits also are featured.

Books

Barnes & Noble Booksellers (⊠ 200 E. Northern Lights Blvd., at A St., ☎ 907/279–7323) features an enormous variety of books and magazines, plus a café serving Starbucks coffees.

Borders Books & Music (⊠ 1100 E. Dimond Blvd., west of Seward Hwy., ☎ 907/344–4099) has an extensive inventory and a small café.

Cook Inlet Book Company (⊠ 415 W. 5th Ave., ☎ 907/258–4544) has a wide collection of books on Alaska and an extensive newspaper and magazine section.

Metro Music & Book Store (⊠ 530 E. Benson Blvd., ☎ 907/279–8622) is great for browsing and carries a well-thought-out inventory of fiction and nonfiction. The collection of CDs and tapes here is easily the best in Anchorage.

Fur

Fur buyers can find merchants on 4th Avenue between A and C streets and on 5th and 6th avenues downtown. Not all furs sold in Alaska come from Alaska; ask the furrier to explain the origin of the item. At the Fur Rendezvous in February, raw furs can be bought at auction.

Gift Ideas

Anchorage's **Saturday Market** is open in the parking lot at 3rd Avenue and E Street all summer long; browse here for Alaskan-made crafts, fresh produce, and food. **Alaska Native Arts and Crafts** (⊠ 333 W. 4th Ave., ☎ 907/274–2932) sells items from all Native groups and carries work by the best-known Native carvers, silversmiths, beadworkers, skin sewers, printmakers, and basket weavers, as well as unknown, but highly skilled, artists. The best buys on Native Alaskan artists' work can be found at the **Alaska Native Medical Center** gift shop (⊠ 4315 Diplomacy Dr., at Tudor Rd. and Bragaw, ☎ 907/563–2662), which is open weekdays 10–2 and from 11–2 on the first Saturday of the month. **Oomingmak** (⊠ 6th Ave. and H St., ☎ 907/272–9225), the musk-ox producers' cooperative, sells items made of qiviut, the warm undercoat of the musk ox. Scarves, shawls, and tunics are knitted in traditional patterns. Frozen seafood and smoked fish packed for shipping are available from **10th and M Seafoods** (⊠ 1020 M St., ☎ 907/272–3474; ⊠ 301 Muldoon Rd., ☎ 907/337–8831) or **New Sagaya City Market** (⊠ 900 W. 13th Ave., ☎ 907/274–6173). You can carry your purchases on your flight back or ship them. Give them a day's lead time to pack your order.

Jewelry

The **Kobuk Valley Jade Co.** (⊠ Olympic Circle, Girdwood, ☎ 907/783–2764), at the base of Mt. Alyeska, sells a wide variety of hand-polished jade pieces as well as Native masks, baskets, and jewelry.

ANCHORAGE A TO Z

Arriving and Departing

By Boat

Cruise ships sailing the Gulf of Alaska and the Alaska Marine ferries call in Seward, several hours by train south of Anchorage. The South Central route of the **Alaska Marine Highway** (⊠ Box 25535, Juneau 99802-5535, ☎ 907/465–3941 or 800/642–0066, FAX 907/277–4829) connects Kodiak, Port Lions, Homer, Seldovia, Seward, Valdez, Cordova, and Whittier.

By Car

There is only one road into Anchorage from the north and only one road out to the south. The Glenn Highway enters Anchorage from the north and becomes 5th Avenue near Merrill Field; this route will lead you directly into downtown. Gambell Street leads out of town to the south, turning into Seward Highway at about 20th Avenue.

By Plane

Anchorage International Airport is 6 mi from downtown Anchorage on International Airport Road. It is served by Alaska, America West, Continental, Delta, Northwest, Reno Air, and United airlines, along with a number of international carriers (☞ Air Travel *in* the Gold Guide). Several carriers, including ERA, PenAir, Reeve Aleutian Airways, SouthCentral Air, and Yute Air, connect Anchorage with smaller Alaskan communities. Air-taxi operators and helicopters serve the area from **Lake Hood,** which is adjacent to and part of Anchorage International Airport. There are also air taxis and air-charter operations at **Merrill Field,** 2 mi east of downtown on 5th Avenue.

BETWEEN THE AIRPORT AND CITY CENTER

Taxis line up at the lower level of the airport terminal outside the baggage-claim area. Alaska Cab, Checker Cab, Yellow Cab, and Taxi Cab (☞ By Taxi *in* Getting Around, *below*) all operate here; you'll get whichever cab is next in line. All charge about $12, excluding tip, for the ride to downtown hotels.

By Train

The **Alaska Railroad** (☞ Train Travel *in* the Gold Guide) runs between Anchorage and Fairbanks via Denali National Park and Preserve daily, mid-May to September, and also south between Anchorage and Seward during the same period.

Getting Around

By Bus

The municipal **People Mover** bus system (☎ 907/343–6543) covers the whole Anchorage bowl. The central bus depot is at 6th Avenue and G Street. Schedules and information are available there. The one-way fare is $1 for rides outside the downtown area; rides within downtown are free.

By Recreational Vehicle

Many visitors to Alaska bring their RV or rent one on arrival. Parking downtown on weekdays is challenging for an RV. The big parking lot on 3rd Avenue between C and E streets is a good place to park and walk. Parking usually is not a problem in other parts of town, and most of the big discount stores allow free parking in their lots.

By Taxi

Prices for taxis start at $2 for pickup and an additional $1.50 for each mile. Most people in Anchorage telephone for a cab; it is not common to hail one. Allow 20 minutes for arrival of the cab during morning and evening rush hours. **Alaska Cab** (☎ 907/563–5353). **Checker Cab** (☎ 907/276–1234). **Taxi Cab** (☎ 907/278–8000). **Yellow Cab** (☎ 907/272–2422).

Contacts and Resources

B&B Reservation Services

For reservations at B&Bs in the Anchorage area, contact the following reservation services: **Alaska Adventures & Accommodations** (✉ 200 W. 34th Ave., No. 342, Anchorage 99503, ☎ 907/344–4676 or 888/655–4723, FAX 907/349–4676); **Alaska Available B&B Reservation Service** (✉ 3800 Delwood Pl., Anchorage 99504, ☎ 907/337–3414, FAX 800/474–2262); **Alaska Private Lodgings/Stay With A Friend** (✉ 704 W. 2nd Ave., Anchorage 99501, ☎ 907/258–1717, FAX 907/258–6613);or **Alaska Sourdough Bed & Breakfast Association** (✉ 889 Cardigan Circle, Anchorage 99503, ☎ 907/563–6244).

Bird-Watching

The local chapter of the **Audubon Society** (☎ 907/278–3007) offers referrals to local birders who will advise you on the best bird-watching spots. Birding classes and field trips also are offered. There's a bird hot line (☎ 907/338–2473) for the latest sightings in town.

Doctors and Dentists

Alaska Regional Hospital (✉ 2801 DeBarr Rd., ☎ 907/276–1131). **Providence Hospital** (✉ 3200 Providence Dr., ☎ 907/562–2211). **U.S. Air Force Hospital** on Elmendorf AFB (☎ 907/552–5555). Both civilian hospitals also operate a physician-referral service (☎ 907/562–3737 at Providence, 907/264–1722 at Alaska Regional).

First Care (✉ 3710 Woodland Dr., ☎ 907/248–1122; ✉ 1301 Huffman Rd., ☎ 907/345–1199) offers minor emergency care on a walk-in basis. It's open daily 7 AM–11 PM.

Emergencies

Dial **911** for police and ambulance. **Poison Control Center,** 907/261–3193.

Guided Tours

FLIGHTSEEING

Any air-taxi company (check the Anchorage Yellow Pages) can arrange for a flightseeing trip over Anchorage and environs. The fee will be determined by the length of time you are airborne and the size of the plane. Tours of about an hour and a half generally cost around $150 to $200 per person. Three-hour flights over Mt. McKinley, including a landing on a remote backcountry lake, run about $200 per person. **Rust's Flying Service** (☎ 907/243–1595) also offers ski-plane flights over McKinley that include a landing on Ruth Glacier—a spectacular alpine amphitheater high on the mountain.

ERA Helicopters (☎ 907/248–4422 or 800/843–1947, FAX 907/266–8349) offers a 50-minute trip over Anchorage and the Chugach Mountains. The trip is available year-round and costs $179 per person. A second, longer tour costs $279 per person.

Aviation buffs, take note. **Alaska World Tours** (☎ 907/272–2255, FAX 907/272–2256) offers a "Nostalgia Air Cruise" to Mt. McKinley or Knik Glacier on a DC-3, an aircraft that had its heyday in the 1940s. Flight attendants dress in '40s-style uniforms, and in-flight reading material and music are also from that era. Flights are conducted by ERA Aviation.

ORIENTATION TOURS

The **Anchorage City Trolley** (✉ 630 W. 4th Ave., Anchorage 99501, ☎ 907/257–5603) offers hour-long tours of downtown Anchorage for $10. **Alaska Sightseeing/Cruise West** (✉ 513 W. 4th Ave., Anchorage 99501, ☎ 907/276–1305 or 800/426–7702, FAX 907/272–5617) and **Gray Line of Alaska** (✉ 745 W. 4th Ave., #200, Anchorage 99501, ☎ 907/277–5581 or 800/544–2206) provide longer **bus tours** of the city and environs.

WILDLIFE VIEWING

Kenai Coastal Tours (✉ 319 F St., ☎ 907/276–6249 or 800/468–8068, FAX 907/276–1064) offers day packages to Kenai Fjords National Park (☞ Chapter 3) April–October. Allow three hours if first driving to Seward from Anchorage.

Late-Night Pharmacy

Carr's grocery-store pharmacy (✉ 1650 W. Northern Lights Blvd., at Minnesota Dr., ☎ 907/276–3921) is open 24 hours.

Visitor Information

The **Anchorage Convention and Visitors Bureau** (ACVB, ✉ 524 W. 4th Ave., 99501-2212, ☎ 907/276–4118, FAX 907/278–5559) will send information to visitors planning a trip to Anchorage. It operates the **Log Cabin Visitor Information Center** (✉ 4th Ave. and F St., ☎ 907/274–3531), where volunteers answer questions and distribute literature daily from 8 to 6 May–September and from 9 to 4 October–April.

There is also an **information center** (☎ 907/266–2437) run by the Anchorage Convention and Visitors Bureau at the **airport** in the main terminal building on the lower level among the baggage-claim areas. It's open daily 9–4. For a telephone recording of **daily events,** call 907/276–3200.

In summer the **Alaska Public Lands Information Center** (✉ 4th Ave. and F St., ☎ 907/271–2737) offers daily video presentations about Alaska, as well as trip-planning services, displays, maps, and guidebooks.

6 South Central Alaska

Including Prince William Sound, Homer, and the Kenai Peninsula

Beyond Anchorage, South Central is an outdoor playground for fishing, hiking, wildlife watching, and rafting. The truly adventurous can ski in Valdez. Kodiak, just offshore in the Gulf of Alaska, is the second-largest island in the United States. Known as the Emerald Island for its green-carpeted mountains, this is the home of the famous Kodiak brown bear, which can weigh up to 1,200 pounds and is the biggest terrestrial carnivore on earth.

By Robin
Mackey Hill
and Kent
Sturgis

Updated
by Tom Reale

ANCHORAGE MAY DOMINATE THE REGION IN SIZE, recognition, and political clout, but don't let that mislead you into thinking Anchorage *is* South Central Alaska. The city is actually an anomaly—a modern, urban environment amid historic ports, wilderness outposts, and fishing towns.

South Central starts with the port towns on the Gulf of Alaska—Cordova, Valdez, Whittier, Seward, Seldovia, Kodiak, Homer, Kenai—with their harbors, ferries, glaciers, and ocean life. Then come the mountains, curled like an arm embracing the region. Talkeetna, at the western limits of South Central, is where mountaineers gather to launch their assaults on towering Mt. McKinley. On the eastern border, the defunct copper mine outside McCarthy lies at the foot of the Wrangell Mountains. South Central is also Alaska's farm country. In the Matanuska-Susitna Valley, under an ever-present summertime sun, 75-pound cabbages are a common occurrence.

Portage Glacier is an accessible ice field near Anchorage. Kenai Fjords National Park and the Kenai National Wildlife Refuge (☞ Chapter 3) provide outstanding opportunities for viewing wildlife—from whales, seals, and otters to moose.

Unlike the towns and cities of Interior Alaska, where the common theme of Gold Rush history links most of the communities, South Central towns and cities have very different personalities. Kodiak, for example, is a busy commercial fishing port, while Homer is a funky tourist town and artist colony on beautiful Kachemak Bay.

Pleasures and Pastimes

Boating
Opportunities for boating on lakes, rivers, and the ocean are abundant in South Central. Boaters should exercise caution, however, because local waters are icy cold and can be deadly. Even a life jacket will not save you if hypothermia sets in. Ask locals about conditions before setting out on any but the smallest, most placid lakes.

In addition to Prince William Sound and Kachemak Bay, canoe and kayak parties are attracted to the Tangle Lakes region of South Central. Access is off the Denali Highway, 20 mi west of Paxson. This mountainous country on the southern flank of the Alaska Range forms the headwaters of the Delta River. Possibilities for paddling here range from a few lazy hours near the road to an extended trip requiring overnight camping and portages. Contact the Bureau of Land Management (☞ Visitor Information *in* South Central Alaska A to Z, *below*) for camping information.

Dining
There are a variety of good restaurants in South Central, many of them—not surprisingly—featuring local seafood, such as halibut, salmon, clams, mussels, crab, scallops, and oysters. Roadside burger joints often serve surprisingly good fare. Espresso bars have taken root throughout the region, making it easy to grab a good cup of coffee for the road. Another trend that has worked its way north is the brew pub. Anchorage has several excellent examples downtown, and others can be found in Eagle River and Juneau, with more surely to come as the trend grows.

Because many restaurants vary their hours by season, it's always a good idea to call ahead. Many close for the winter or are open only for dinner on selected evenings. For price ranges, *see* the dining chart *in* On the Road with Fodor's.

Fishing

South Central has Alaska's most accessible fishing. Thousands of tourists flock to the Kenai River and its tributaries for trophy king salmon, which can reach nearly 100 pounds. Saltwater fishing yields huge halibut, cod, and shellfish. Boat rentals and guide services are available all along the South Central coastline; drift boats are a popular means of access to the fishing holes.

A prime fishing ground is on the west side of the Kenai Peninsula, where the rivers and streams empty into Cook Inlet and along Kachemak Bay. Because this area is readily accessible to the large population in and around Anchorage, the popular spots can be lined with people fishing shoulder to shoulder. Campgrounds can be crowded to overflowing at the height of the salmon runs. Still, at their peaks, these salmon runs are so strong that chances are good for a catch.

Soldotna is the headquarters for those fishing for salmon on the western Kenai Peninsula. Salmon are also taken in Homer, but Homer is best known as the place for landing whopper halibut and for digging razor clams. Halibut of 100 pounds or more are taken here frequently; sometimes a fishing party will land one that weighs well over 300 pounds.

Clam digging is subject to bag limits and seasons just as other sport-fishing is, and it is a skill best learned by observation. There's more to successful clamming than just digging a shovel into the sand. However, Alaskans are known for being friendly—ask a local about conditions.

Lodging

As with other parts of the state, accommodations across South Central vary from rustic to Alaskan elegance; don't be shy about asking proprietors for detailed descriptions of their facilities. Most communities offer a variety of lodging options ranging from standard motels to quaint B&Bs. Reservation agencies and local tourist information centers can provide suggestions. Places fill up quickly between Memorial Day and Labor Day, so it's best to make reservations early. If you are here in winter, remember that some properties close for the season while others remain open subject to weather conditions.

Summer rates are quoted; rates between seasons may vary widely in some places. For price ranges, *see* the lodging chart *in* On the Road with Fodor's.

Exploring South Central

South Central is a vast area stretching south from Anchorage down the Kenai Peninsula to the coastal communities of Homer and Seldovia, north through the Matanuska-Susitna Valley to Talkeetna and Wrangell–St. Elias National Park and Preserve, and east to the communities on Prince William Sound. The region is ideal for exploring by boat, train, car, or RV. All but a couple of the coastal communities are on the road system. For the most part, roads have two lanes and are paved. Traffic, especially on the Kenai Peninsula, can be bumper to bumper on summer weekends, so give yourself plenty of time; better yet, try to travel midweek. Long summer days give you plenty of daylight for exploring.

Numbers in the text correspond to numbers in the margin and on the South Central Alaska map.

BONUS MILES MAKE
GREAT SOUVENIRS.

Earn Miles With Your MCI Card.

Take the MCI Card along on this trip and start earning miles for the next one. You'll earn frequent flyer miles on all your calls and save with the low rates you've come to expect from MCI. Before you know it, you'll be on your way to some other international destination.

Sign up for MCI by calling 1-800-FLY-FREE

Is this a great time, or what? :-)

Earn Frequent Flyer Miles.

HAWAIIAN AIRLINES.

MIDWEST EXPRESS AIRLINES

NORTHWEST AIRLINES WORLDPERKS®

Rapid Rewards™ SOUTHWEST AIRLINES®

MILEAGE PLUS. United Airlines

US AIRWAYS DIVIDEND MILES

You've read the book. Now book the trip.

© 1998 Preview Travel Inc. CST #2022036-40

For all the best deals on flights, hotels, rental cars, and vacation packages, book them online at www.previewtravel.com. Then click on our Destination Guides featuring content from Fodor's and more. You'll find hotels, restaurants, attractions, and things to do around the globe. There are even interactive maps, videos, and weather forecasts. You'll have everything you need to make your vacation exactly what you want it to be. All it takes is a trip online.

Travel on Your Terms™
www.previewtravel.com
aol keyword: previewtravel

preview travel SM

Great Itineraries

As noted above, South Central Alaska can be broken down into three general subregions—communities south of Anchorage along the Kenai Peninsula, communities north of Anchorage in the Matanuska-Susitna (Mat-Su) Valley and beyond, and the waters and towns of Prince William Sound.

IF YOU HAVE 3 DAYS

Spend them on the Kenai Peninsula. Head south out of **Anchorage** (☞ Chapter 5) along the Seward Highway and Turnagain Arm and stop in the ski town of **Girdwood** (☞ Chapter 5) for a light lunch and a stroll before continuing south to **Portage Glacier** ① and the Begich-Boggs Visitor Center. Take a day hike out of **Hope** ④ or a boat trip into **Kenai Fjords National Park** (☞ Chapter 3) out of Seward. After spending the night in 🏨 **Seward** ⑤, work your way down to 🏨 **Homer** ⑦. There's plenty to see and do along **Kachemak Bay,** including a dinner cruise over to **Halibut Cove** or trying your luck at landing a killer halibut. On your way back up to Anchorage, stop for a bite to eat in **Soldotna** ⑥ and make any other stops you missed during the trip down.

IF YOU HAVE 5 DAYS

Follow the three-day itinerary above, return to 🏨 **Anchorage,** and head north out of town the next day along the Glenn Highway. Wander the back roads between **Palmer** ⑩ and **Wasilla** ⑪, continuing up to Hatcher Pass and the **Independence Mine.** Visit a couple of area attractions, such as the **Musk Ox Farm** or the **Iditarod Headquarters** before working your way up to 🏨 **Talkeetna** ⑫ for the night. On your way back to Anchorage, stop along the roadside for a short hike or picnic.

IF YOU HAVE 7 DAYS

Follow the five-day itinerary before cutting over to 🏨 **Valdez** ②, which you should use as a base. Take a day trip past **Columbia Glacier,** see the sites in town, or take a hike in the surrounding Chugach Mountains. Consider flying across the sound to **Cordova** ③ or into McCarthy and the nearby **Kennicott Mine,** in **Wrangell–St. Elias National Park and Preserve** (☞ Chapter 3). If hiking is your passion, you can spend the entire seven days on a guided backcountry trip through the park. Or if exploring Prince William Sound is more to your liking, arrange for a kayak trip out of Valdez or Cordova.

When to Tour South Central

The region is most alive between Memorial Day and Labor Day, which is also when it is the most crowded. Summer means fishing, hiking, boating, and all the other things for which the region is most noted. Fall comes early to South Central but can be a gorgeous time to travel. Trees are painted gold and orange, and mountaintops are dusted with snow. For those interested in winter sports, the region has it all. A pristine quietness blankets the region, making it a peaceful time to visit. Be aware, however, that dining and lodging options may be limited in winter, as many businesses close during the off-season.

PRINCE WILLIAM SOUND

The sound covers some 15,000 square mi, making it 15 times the size of San Francisco Bay. It receives an average of 150 inches of rain a year and is home to more than 150 glaciers, 20 of them reaching tidewater. Along its shoreline are quiet bays, trickling waterfalls, and hidden coves perfect for camping. In addition to brown bears, gray wolves, and marten, the sound is home to a variety of birds and to all manner of marine life, including salmon, halibut, humpback and killer whales,

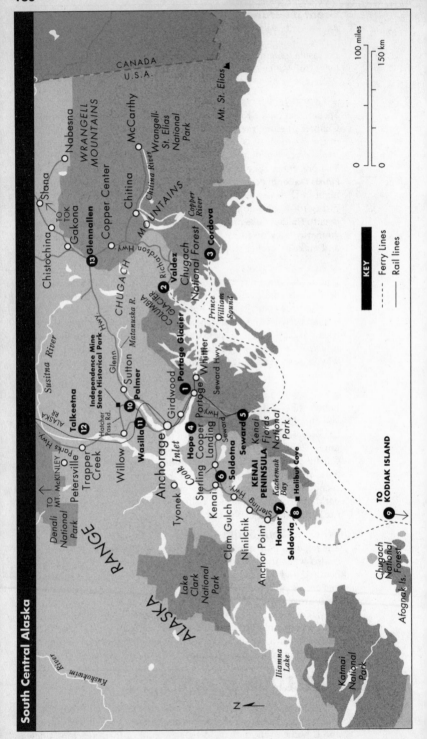

South Central Alaska

sea otters, sea lions, and porpoises. Bald eagles often soar overhead or perch in tall trees.

The sound was heavily damaged by the *Exxon Valdez* oil spill in 1989. The oil has sunk into the beaches below the surface. What lasting effect this lurking oil, which is sometimes uncovered after storms and high tides, will have on the area is still being studied and remains the topic of much debate.

Portage Glacier

★ ☾ ❶ *54 mi southeast of Anchorage via the Seward Hwy.*

Portage Glacier is one of Alaska's most frequently visited tourist destinations. A 6-mi side road off the Seward Highway leads to the **Begich-Boggs Visitor Center** (☎ 907/783–2326), on the shore of Portage Lake. Unfortunately, the glacier is receding rapidly, so the view across the lake is not as good as it used to be.

The mountains surrounding Portage Glacier are covered with smaller glaciers. A short hike to **Byron Glacier** overlook, about 1 mi west, is popular. In summer, naturalists lead free weekly treks in search of microscopic ice worms. There are several popular hiking trails accessible from the Seward Highway, including the Old Johnson Trail and the path up Bird Ridge. Both offer spectacular views of **Turnagain Arm**, where explorer Captain Cook searched for the Northwest Passage. Local lore has it that the arm is so named because Cook entered it repeatedly, only to be turned back by the huge tides, forcing him to turn around again. The tide is so powerful it sometimes rushes up the arm as a tidal bore—a wall of water that goes up an inlet. Keep an eye out for black bears in all the Portage side valleys in the summer (☞ Bears *in* the Gold Guide).

☾ **Big Game Alaska** is a 45-acre drive-through animal park just before the Portage Glacier turnoff. Moose, bison, elk, caribou, Sitka black-tailed deer, musk ox, and a bald eagle, many of them orphaned in the wild, now live in the park. There are also snack and gift shops. ⊠ *Mile 79, Seward Hwy.,* ☎ *907/783–2025,* FAX *907/783–2370.* 🎫 *$5.* ☉ *Summer, daily 9 AM–7:30 PM; winter, daily 9–5.*

Little remains of the community of **Portage,** thanks to the 1964 earthquake. A tumbledown building or two still stand along the highway; there's also a café at the turnoff to Portage Glacier. Portage is mainly the pickup point for those going to Whittier (☞ En Route, *below*) by train. Tickets may be purchased at the Alaska Railroad depot in Anchorage or at the ticket booth at the Portage pullout. (The loading area is 47 mi from Anchorage and 1½ mi before the turnoff to the glacier.) Trains run several times daily in summer, and less frequently in winter. Passage may be purchased for RVs, boats, and bikes.

Guided Tours

Gray Line of Alaska (☎ 907/277–5581 or 800/478–6388) offers summer boat tours (from mid-May to mid-September) along the face of Portage Glacier aboard the 200-passenger *Ptarmigan*. The one-hour cruise costs $25.

Shopping

On your way to Portage, look for **Indian Valley Meats** (⊠ Huot Circle, 23 mi south of Anchorage on the Seward Hwy., ☎ 907/653–7511), where workers sell the smoked salmon and musk ox, reindeer, and buffalo sausage they make on the premises. They'll also smoke, can, and package your fish and arrange for shipping anywhere in the world.

En Route   Access to the small community of **Whittier** is generally by railroad (30 minutes from Portage) or state ferry, though you could fly; the area is not yet connected to the state's highway system, but work is underway to complete a road link by the spring of 2000. Through no fault of its own, this former army supply port has become little more than a launching site for those traveling by boat into Prince William Sound. State ferries traveling from Cordova and Valdez dock here and cruiseship passengers often disembark in town for the bus ride to Anchorage. You will probably find little reason to linger here—there are other towns more picturesque and entertaining, but on a clear day the sound and surrounding snowcapped mountains make for fabulous views. There are two inns and a handful of restaurants and small shops.

Valdez

❷   *6 hours from Portage by water; 304 mi east of Anchorage via the Glenn Hwy. and the Richardson Hwy.*

Of the three major Prince William Sound communities—Valdez, Whittier, and Cordova—only Valdez (pronounced val-*deez*), which lies at the southern end of the Richardson Highway, can be reached by road. This community, with its year-round ice-free port, originally was the entry point for people and goods going to the Interior during the Gold Rush. Today that flow has been reversed, with Valdez harbor being the southern terminus of the trans-Alaska pipeline, which carries crude oil from Prudhoe Bay and surrounding oil fields nearly 800 mi to the north. This region, with its dependence on commercial fishing, is still feeling the aftereffects of 1989's massive oil spill.

Much of Valdez looks new because the business area was relocated and rebuilt after its destruction by the 1964 Good Friday Earthquake.

Many Alaskan communities have summer **fishing derbies,** but Valdez may hold the record for the number of such contests, stretching from late May into September for halibut and various runs of salmon. If you go fishing, by all means enter the appropriate derby. Every summer the newspapers run sob stories about tourists who landed possible prizewinners but couldn't share in the glory because they hadn't forked over the five bucks to officially enter the contest. The Valdez Silver Salmon Derby is held the entire month of August. Fishing charters abound in this area of Prince William Sound, and for a good reason: these fertile waters provide some of the best saltwater sportfishing in all of Alaska.

☝   A pleasant attraction on a rainy day, if you ever tire of gazing at the 5,000-ft mountain peaks surrounding Valdez, is the **Valdez Museum.** It depicts the lives, livelihoods, and events significant to Valdez and surrounding regions. Exhibits include a restored 1880s Gleason & Baily hand-pumped fire engine, a 19th-century saloon, a saltwater aquarium, and a model of the pipeline terminus. ✉ *217 Egan Dr.,* ☎ *907/ 835–2764.* ⌑ *$3.* ⊙ *June–Aug., daily 9–6; Sept.–May, Tues.–Sat. noon–5.*

★   A visit to **Columbia Glacier,** which flows from the surrounding Chugach Mountains, certainly should be on the agenda. Its deep aquamarine face is 5 mi across, and it calves new icebergs with resounding cannonades. This glacier is one of the largest and most readily accessible of Alaska's coastal glaciers. The state ferry travels past the face of the glacier, and scheduled tours of the glaciers and the rest of the sound are available by boat and aircraft from Valdez and Whittier.

Dining and Lodging

$–$$ ✕ **Mike's Palace.** This busy restaurant with typical Italian-diner decor is popular with locals. The menu includes veal, terrific pizza, beer-battered halibut, steaks, and Greek specialties, including gyros. ✉ *On the harbor, 201 N. Harbor Dr.,* ☎ *907/835–2365. MC, V.*

$ ✕ **Gold Rush Cafe.** This café serves fresh homemade pastries and espresso in the mornings, along with breakfast sandwiches and burritos. The main event here, though, is lunch, with pasta, homemade soups and gourmet sandwiches, vegetarian entrées and, in summer, local seafood. Soups range from salmon chowder in summer to curry vegetable. There is no smoking in the café. ✉ *310 Egan Dr.,* ☎ *907/835–5455. No credit cards. Closed Sun. No dinner.*

$$$$ ✕🏨 **Westmark Valdez Hotel.** This is another efficient hotel in the Westmark chain, next to the small-boat harbor. Rooms come in various configurations; ask for one overlooking the harbor. The Captain's Table restaurant ($$–$$$) overlooks the water and offers everything from shrimp and chips to pasta, fried chicken, and steak. ✉ *100 Fidalgo Dr., 99686,* ☎ *907/835–4391 or 800/544–0970,* 𝔽𝔸𝕏 *907/835–2308. 97 rooms. Restaurant, bar, barbershop. AE, D, DC, MC, V.*

Guided Tours

Numerous charter operators, including **Alaskan Wilderness Sailing & Kayaking** (✉ Box 1313, Valdez 99686, ☎ 907/835–5175, 𝔽𝔸𝕏 907/835–3765), offer tours of this portion of Prince William Sound aboard a 40-ft sailboat. They also conduct naturalist-led sea kayaking tours and rent kayaks and equipment. **Columbia Glacier Wildlife Cruises/Lu-lu Belle** (☎ 907/835–5141 or 800/411–0090, 𝔽𝔸𝕏 907/835–5899 in summer or ☎ 𝔽𝔸𝕏 206/842–9123 off-season) specializes in small-group wildlife viewing and cruise tours to Columbia Glacier. **One Call Does It All** (☎ 907/835–4988, 𝔽𝔸𝕏 907/835–5865) can arrange lodging, car rental, fishing, flightseeing, kayaking, and glacier-viewing cruises. **Stan Stephens Cruises** (☎ 907/835–4731 or 800/992–1297, 𝔽𝔸𝕏 907/835–3765) is based in Valdez and offers various Prince William Sound options: glacier cruises, island cookouts, overnight trips, and wilderness camps.

Alpine Aviation Adventures (☎ 907/835–4304 or 800/478–4304 in Alaska, 𝔽𝔸𝕏 907/835–2523) has aerial tours of Columbia Glacier, Prince William Sound, and the Wrangell Mountains. Unlike many such flightseeing services, they do not provide hunting drop-offs.

Gray Line of Alaska (☎ 907/277–5581 or 800/478–6388) conducts tours of the pipeline terminal May–September, departing from the Westmark Valdez Hotel (☞ Dining and Lodging *in* Valdez, *above*).

Ketchum Air Service (☎ 907/835–3789 or 800/433–9114) offers flightseeing tours of Columbia Glacier, Shoup Glacier, or the Thompson Pass area, site of the Extreme Skiing and Snowboarding championships.

Keystone Raft & Kayak Adventures (☎ 907/835–2606 or 800/328–8460, 𝔽𝔸𝕏 907/835–4638) provides all gear for guided raft and kayak tours on rivers rated up to Class V.

Cordova

❸ *6 hours from Valdez by water; 150 mi east of Anchorage by air.*

Perched on Orca Inlet in eastern Prince William Sound, Cordova began life early this century as the port city for the Copper River–Northwestern Railway, which was built to serve the Kennicott copper mines 191 mi away in the Wrangell Mountains. With the mines and the railroad shut down since 1938, Cordova's economy now depends heavily on fishing. Attempts to develop a road along the abandoned railroad line connecting to the state highway system were dashed by the 1964 earthquake, so Cordova remains isolated. Access to the community is limited to airplane or ferry. A small town with the spectacular backdrop of snowy Mt. Eccles, Cordova is the gateway to the Copper River delta—one of the great birding areas of North America.

The **Cordova Historical Museum** is strong on Native artifacts as well as on pioneer, mining, and fishing history. There's also an 1840s hand-crafted lighthouse lens and an 800-pound stuffed leatherback turtle. They also offer afternoon video programs and an interesting brochure that outlines a self-guided walking tour of the town's historical build-ings. The gift shop sells baskets, masks, pottery, children's books, and a nice selection of local postcards. ⊠ *622 1st St.,* ☏ *907/424–6665.* ☞ *$1.* ⊙ *Mid-May–mid-Sept., Mon.–Sat. 10–6, Sun. 2–4..*

Drive out of town along the Copper River Highway and visit the **Million Dollar Bridge,** a good vantage point for glacier viewing, at Mile 48. The glacier in question is **Childs Glacier,** which doesn't have a vis-itor center. There is, however, a covered viewing area that enables you to watch the face of the glacier, and you can read the informational plaques while you wait for a huge chunk of ice to topple into the river. The waves produced by falling ice frequently wash migrating salmon onto the riverbank, and the local brown bears have been known to pa-trol the river's edge looking for an easy meal, so keep your eyes wide open.

Dining and Lodging

$$–$$$ ✕ **Ambrosia.** Pastas, hamburgers, and steaks are available here, but it's the pizzas, basic and hearty, that have earned this place its repu-tation among locals. ⊠ *410 1st St.,* ☏ *907/424–7175. MC, V.*

$$–$$$ ✕ **Powder House Bar & Restaurant.** On clear summer evenings cus-tomers relax on the deck overlooking Eyak Lake and enjoy homemade soups, sandwiches, sushi, and seasonal seafood; dinner is whatever the cook's in the mood to fix. The staff will cook your seafood catch. On Friday and Saturday, shrimp and steak are added to the menu, and there's live music on occasion. ⊠ *Mile 2.1, Copper River Hwy.,* ☏ *907/424–3529. AE, MC, V.*

$ ✕ **Killer Whale Cafe.** Have a breakfast of espresso and baked goods
★ or an omelet, and for lunch choose from a deli menu of soups, salads, and sandwiches, followed by a fresh, homemade dessert. In a popular bookstore, the café has a back balcony that overlooks the harbor; those in the front balcony have a view of the town's main street. ⊠ *507 1st St.,* ☏ *907/424–7733. No credit cards. Closed Sun. No dinner.*

$$–$$$$ ✕🏠 **Reluctant Fisherman Inn.** This waterfront restaurant with its Alaskan decor is a good place to watch the commercial-fishing fleet and sample local halibut or salmon. The inn caters to tourists, sport-fishermen, and businesspeople. Many of the comfortable, nautical-theme rooms overlook the harbor. Don't miss the collection of Native art and artifacts in the restaurant and lounge. The restaurant serves local seafood, including a king salmon chili, as well as pastas and espresso. ⊠ *407 Railroad Ave.,* ☏ *907/424–3272 or 800/770–3272,* 🆇 *907/424–7465. 41 rooms. Restaurant, bar, coin laundry, travel services, car rental. AE, D, DC, MC, V.*

$$ 🏠 **Northern Nights Inn B&B.** Commanding a dramatic view of Orca Inlet just a couple of blocks above downtown Cordova, this bed-and-breakfast has rooms furnished with turn-of-the-century period an-tiques. If owner Becky Chapek doesn't have room for you, she'll serve as a valuable source of information on other B&Bs in town. She also operates van tours around town and to the Million Dollar Bridge, and she can transport you to and from the airport as well. ⊠ *500 3rd St., Box 1564, 99574,* ☏ *907/424–5356. 4 rooms. AE, MC, V.*

Guided Tours

Cordova Air Service (☎ 907/424–3289 or 800/424–7608 in Alaska, ℻ 907/424–3495) offers aerial tours of Prince William Sound on planes with wheels, skis, or floats. **Cordova Alaskan Adventures and Outfitters** (☎ 907/424–5757 or 800/881–7948, ℻ 702/677–2648) can arrange fishing, canoeing, whale-watching, hiking, and mountain-biking trips, or extended stays in a fishing camp or aboard their fully equipped floating cabin. **Ketchum Air Service** (☎ 907/243–5525 or 800/433–9114, ℻ 907/243–8311) features a 1 ¼-hour floatplane flight-seeing tour of Sheridan Glacier and the Copper River Delta, with views of the Sound and Wrangell–St. Elias National Park and Preserve, for $155. **Prince William Sound Adventures** (☎ 907/424–3350) offers flightseeing as well as sportfishing and other air charters.

Outdoor Activities and Sports

BIRD-WATCHING

Spring migration to the **Copper River delta** (☞ Wrangell–St. Elias National Park and Preserve *in* Chapter 3) provides some of the finest avian spectacles in the world. Species including the Western sandpiper, American dipper, orange-crowned warbler, and short-billed dowitcher number 14 million. Trumpeter swans and dusky Canada geese also can be seen. The **Copper River Delta Shorebird Festival** (☎ 907/424–7212), held the first week of May, includes five days of workshops and guided field trips.

Shopping

Orca Book & Sound Co. is much more than a bookstore. In addition to things written, there's music, art supplies, children's toys, and locally produced art for sale. The walls often double as a gallery for local works or traveling exhibits. In the back is the Killer Whale Cafe. ⊠ 507 1st St., ☎ 907/424–5305. ☉ Mon.–Sat. 7–5. No credit cards.

KENAI PENINSULA

The Kenai Peninsula, thrusting into the Gulf of Alaska south of Anchorage, is South Central's playground, offering salmon and halibut fishing, spectacular scenery, and wildlife viewing. Commercial fishing is important to the area's economy, and the city of Kenai, on the peninsula's northwest coast, is the base for the Cook Inlet offshore oil fields.

The area is dotted with roadside campgrounds and trailheads for backwoods hiking. Along the way, you can explore three major federal holdings on the peninsula—the western end of the sprawling Chugach National Forest, Kenai National Wildlife Refuge, and Kenai Fjords National Park (☞ Chapter 3).

Hope

❹ *39 mi from Portage via the Seward and Hope Hwys.; 87 mi from Anchorage.*

The little gold-mining community of Hope is 87 mi south of Anchorage by road, but just across Turnagain Arm. To visit, however, you must drive all the way around, as there is no ferry service. Hope was founded by miners in 1896 but now consists mainly of retirement homes for former Anchorage residents. The old log cabins and weathered frame buildings in the town center are popular with photographers. Gold panning, fishing, and hiking are also popular here. Contact the U.S. Forest Service (☞ Visitor Information *in* South Central Alaska A to Z, *below*) for information on campgrounds, cabin rentals, and hikes in this area.

Dining and Lodging

$ ✕ **Discovery Café.** This four-table, storefront café serves sandwiches, burgers, salads, milk shakes, and homemade pies, as well as beer and wine. ⊠ *Downtown Hope,* ☎ *907/782–3274. No credit cards.*

$$ ✕🏨 **Bear Creek Lodge.** There are six cabins here, four of them around a pond and two down by the creek. Each is carpeted and has both a woodstove and an electric heater. The cabins vary in size, with the largest sleeping up to six. A central bathhouse offers hot showers and toilets. The lodge café serves lunch and dinner daily in summer; only dinner is served in the winter. Try the stir fry, pork chops, or pasta with meat sauce, or, if you want something lighter, homemade bread and soup. Beer and wine are available. ⊠ *Mile 15.7 Hope Hwy. (mailing address: Box 90, Hope 99605),* ☎ *907/782–3141. 6 cabins without bath. Café. MC, V.*

Seward

❺ *74 mi south of Hope; 127 mi south of Anchorage via the Seward Hwy.*

One of the peninsula's major communities is the city of Seward, at the head of Resurrection Bay. It lies at the south end of the Seward Highway, which connects with Anchorage, and is the southern terminus of the Alaska Railroad. Seward also is the launching point for excursions into Kenai Fjords National Park (☞ Chapter 3), home to calving glaciers, sea lions, whales, and otters.

Seward was founded in 1903 when survey crews arrived at this ice-free port to begin planning for a railroad to the Interior. Since then the town has come to rely heavily on tourism and commercial fishing, and its harbor is important for loading coal bound for Asia.

Seward, like Valdez, was badly damaged by the 1964 earthquake. A movie about the quake is shown daily (except Sunday and holidays) at 2 PM in the **Seward Community Library,** and it illustrates the upheaval caused by the disaster. Paintings by prominent Alaskan artists and Russian icons are on exhibit, and there's an annual photo show in summer. ⊠ *5th Ave. and Adams St.,* ☎ *907/224–3646.* 🎟 *$3.* ☉ *Weekdays noon–8, Sat. noon–6.*

The **Resurrection Bay Historical Society** operates a museum displaying photographs of the quake's damage, as well as model rooms and artifacts from the early pioneers. ⊠ *336 3rd Ave., at Jefferson St.,* ☎ *907/224–3902.* 🎟 *$2.* ☉ *Early May–Sept., daily 9–5; winter, weekends noon–4*

The first mile of the historic original **Iditarod Trail** runs along the beach and makes for a nice, easy stroll, as does the city's printed walking tour. For a different view of the town, drive out **Nash Road,** around Resurrection Bay, and see Seward as it appears nestled at the base of the surrounding mountains.

★ ☺ The **Alaska SeaLife Center,** which opened in May 1998, is a world-class research and visitor facility complete with massive cold-water tanks and outdoor viewing decks. Featuring displays on Alaska's abundant marine life, including seals and sea lions, as well as films, hands-on activities, a gift shop, and a snack bar, the center was built with reparations money from the Exxon *Valdez* oil spill. The center functions as a center for cold-water research on fish, seabirds, and marine mammals; provides educational experiences for the general public and school groups; and serves as a rehabilitation center for injured marine wildlife. ⊠ *Railway Ave., at the foot of 4th Ave., Mile 0 of the Seward Hwy.,* ☎ *907/224–3080,* 🖷 *907/224–5391.* 🎟 *$12.50.* ☉ *Early May–Sept., daily 9–9:30; winter, Wed.–Sun. 10–5.*

★ ☾ A short walk from the parking lot along a paved path will bring you face to face with **Exit Glacier,** just outside Seward. Look for the turnoff as you enter town or ask locals for directions.

Dining and Lodging

$$–$$$$ ✕ **Harbor Dinner Club & Lounge.** Local seafood is the best choice in this comfy, family-run restaurant; try a halibut burger and fries for lunch, prime rib or lobster for dinner. There's also dancing in the lounge. ✉ *220 5th Ave.,* ☎ *907/224–3012. AE, D, DC, MC, V.*

$$–$$$$ ✕ **Ray's Waterfront.** True to its name, this popular dining spot has views of the bay and small-boat harbor. Sea otters and sea lions have occasionally been known to swim right past the large picture windows. Not surprisingly, seafood is the specialty here; the seafood chowder is excellent. ✉ *Small-boat harbor,* ☎ *907/224–5606. AE, D, DC, MC, V. Closed Nov.–Mar.*

$$$$ ★ 🏨 **Great Alaska Fish Camp.** You don't need to be a fisherman to appreciate the hospitality of the Great Alaska Fish Camp, midway between Seward and Homer. Daily activities are individually scheduled. Mornings begin with coffee delivered to your room; afternoons culminate in a complimentary happy hour. Activities include a range of natural history and soft adventure options. And if you do fish, this is definitely the place to be: the guides are top-notch, and five world records have been set from the camp's riverbanks. Rates, which start at $300 a day per person, include lodging, meals, and most activities. There are guest rooms in the main lodge or in riverside cabins. There's also a separate, remote, bear-viewing camp. ✉ *Mile 82, Sterling Hwy. (mailing address: HC 1 Box 218, Sterling 99672; in winter: Box 2670, Poulsbo, WA 98370),* ☎ *907/262–4515 or 800/544–2261,* 🆑 *907/ 262–8797;* ☎ *360/697–6454,* 🆑 *360/697–7850 in winter. 18 rooms. Hiking, boating, fishing. MC, V. Closed Oct.–mid-May.*

$$$$ ★ 🏨 **Kenai Princess Lodge.** Elegantly rustic might best describe this sprawling complex approximately 45 mi from Seward on a bluff overlooking the famed Kenai River. Paths lead from the main lodge to charming log cabins, each containing four spacious units. Buildings higher on the bluff house eight units. Rooms have a king or two queen-size beds, TV, comfortable sitting areas, and porches. There's also a nature trail. The lodge, popular with Anchorage residents and groups, is about two hours southwest of Anchorage and an hour north of Seward. Staff can arrange for fishing, flightseeing, horseback riding, and river rafting. The Eagle's Crest Restaurant serves local seafood and caribou. ✉ *Mile 47.7, Sterling Hwy., Box 676, Cooper Landing 99572,* ☎ *907/ 595–1425 or 800/426–0500,* 🆑 *907/595–1424 or 206/443–1979. 70 rooms. Restaurant, bar, 3 outdoor hot tubs, exercise room, camping, shops. AE, DC, MC, V.*

$$$$ 🏨 **Seward Windsong Lodge.** Opened in 1997 as part of a statewide chain of lodges, the Seward Windsong rests in a forested setting near the banks of the Resurrection River. Rooms have either mountain or river views and are done in warm plaids, with pine furniture, Alaskan prints on the wall, coffeemakers, and TVs. The lodge, which plans to expand to 72 rooms for the 1999 season, is just down the road from Exit Glacier. A full-service restaurant is on the premises. ✉ *Mile 0.6 Exit, Glacier Rd., about 2 mi north of Seward (mailing address: Box 221011, Anchorage 99522),* ☎ *907/245–0200 or 800/208–0200;* 🆑 *907/245–0400. 48 rooms. Restaurant. AE, D, MC, V.*

$$$–$$$$ 🏨 **Best Western Hotel Seward.** This downtown hotel is decorated in Gold Rush style. Rooms are rather fancy—each has a VCR, king- or queen-size bed, and a phone in the bathroom as well as the bedroom—and some have bay views. The hotel runs a shuttle to the harbor and is close to the ferry, restaurants, and the SeaLife Center. They also have

a very deluxe cabin for rent, perched on a cliff overlooking the small-boat harbor, the cruise-ship docks, and Resurrection Bay. Furnished with two queen-size brass beds, an outdoor hot tub, a small kitchen, and all the comforts of home—and then some—it rents for $300 a night. ⊠ *221 5th Ave. (mailing address: Box 670, 99664),* ☎ *907/224–2378 or 800/528–1234,* FAX *907/224–3112. 38 rooms. Refrigerators, in-room VCRs. AE, D, DC, MC, V.*

$$$–$$$$ 🏨 **Breeze Inn** This big, new, modern hotel is very convenient to the small-boat harbor. The rooms are bright, airy, and well furnished. Alaskan wildlife photos adorn the walls, and custom-made wooden furnishings accent the decor. The annex building is all no-smoking, and the preferred rooms overlook the harbor. ⊠ *Box 2147, 99664,* ☎ *907/ 224–5237 or 888/224–5237,* FAX *907/224–7024. 86 rooms. Restaurant, lobby lounge, refrigerators. AE, MC, V.*

$$$ 🏨 **Trail Lake Lodge.** A companion to the Seward Windsong, the Trail Lake Lodge is in the sedate little town of Moose Pass, 30 mi north of Seward. Sitting on the shore of Trail Lake, this reasonably priced lodge offers neat, clean accommodations and lakeside dining on a deck. Rooms have private baths, satellite TV, and a variety of bed configurations. ⊠ *Mile 29.4 Seward Hwy. (mailing address: Box 221011, Anchorage 99522),* ☎ *907/245–0200 or 800/208–0200;* FAX *907/ 245–0400. 21 rooms. Restaurant. AE, D, MC, V.*

$$ 🏨 **Alaska's Treehouse B&B.** There are spectacular views of the Chugach
★   Mountains from the solarium and from the hot tub on the tiered deck, and the hand-built wood-fired sauna is perfect for relaxing in after a hike or ski along nearby trails. Breakfast, included in the room rate, includes sourdough pancakes with homemade wild-berry sauces. A two-bedroom suite sleeps five comfortably, while another room has a queen-size bed and shared bath. ⊠ *½ mi off Seward Hwy. at Mile 7 (mailing address: Box 861, 99664),* ☎ *907/224–3867. 1 suite, 1 room. Hot tub, sauna. MC, V.*

$$ 🏨 **Teddy's Inn the Woods** Set back from the road in a forest of spruce
★   trees in parklike surroundings, this bed-and-breakfast offers room for up to six in a newly refurbished outbuilding. The furnishings are impeccable, and two decks afford the opportunity for lounging in the sun. Two cubbyhole bunks are especially kid-friendly, and the breakfast of fresh homemade pastries just might be complemented with freshly smoked salmon. ⊠ *Mile 23, Seward Hwy. in Moose Pass (mailing address: HCR 64, Box 515, 99664),* ☎ *907/288–3126. 1 room. MC, V.*

Guided Tours

Alaska Wildland Adventures (☎ 907/783–2928 or 800/334–8730), in Cooper Landing, operates a tidy, pleasant compound on the Kenai River, at Mile 50.1 of the Sterling Highway, and offers a wide selection of outdoor adventures. Two-hour scenic float trips are offered three times daily in summer. Drift boats and raft trips are available, as are multiday fishing trips (through September) and five- to 14-day natural history safaris. Lodge accommodations are available for extended stays on Skilak Lake on the Kenai peninsula or at the Denali Backcountry Lodge. Prices for trips range from $42 for the short raft trip up to $4,000 for the two-week trip.

Fish House (⊠ Small-boat harbor, ☎ 907/224–3674 or 800/257–7760) is Seward's oldest booking agency for deep-sea fishing.

If you're in Seward, a boat trip through the nearby **Kenai Fjords National Park** is an absolute must. You'll get close-up looks at marine birds and mammals (including bird and sea-lion rookeries), watch icebergs drop into the sea from tidewater glaciers, and gain an appreciation of the subarctic marine environment. Several companies offer tours of the park. **Kenai Coastal Tours** (☎ 907/277–2131 or 800/770–9119) leads day trips into Kenai Fjords National Park. They also offer combination train/cruise/motor-coach trips from Anchorage: you take the train down to Seward along Turnagain Arm and then through the scenic Kenai Mountains, embark on a boat trip, and then return to town via motor coach. **Mariah Tours** (☎ 907/224–8623 or 800/270–1238, FAX 907/224–8625) operates smaller boats through the park and into the Chiswell Islands with a maximum of 16 passengers per boat. Closed mid-September–May 1. **Kenai Fjords Tours** (☎ 907/224–8068 in Seward, 907/276–6249 or 800/478–8068, FAX 907/276–1064) is the oldest and largest company offering tours through the park. They have a large fleet of boats and offer a variety of packages that combine cruises of varying lengths, various transportation options to and from Anchorage, tours of the SeaLife Center, and meal stops or overnight stays at their lodge on Fox Island in Resurrection Bay.

Outdoor Activities and Sports

RUNNING

The footrace best known among Alaskans is Seward's annual **Mt. Marathon** (☎ 907/224–8051), run on the 4th of July since 1915. It doesn't take the winners very long—44 minutes or so—but the route is straight up the mountain (3,022 ft) and back down to the center of town. The field is very limited, past participants have priority, and early registration is required. For more info, contact the Seward Chamber of Commerce at Box 749, Seward, 99664.

Shopping

Bardarson Studio (✉ Across from the small-boat harbor, ☎ 907/224–5448), selling everything from fine art—watercolors to sculpture—to beaded earrings, is a browser's dream. There's a kiddie cave for children and a video-viewing area for nonshoppers.

The **Resurrect Art Coffee House Gallery** (✉ 320 3rd Ave., ☎ 907/224–7161) occupies a former church. The gallery sells original works by local artists, and there are espresso drinks, Italian sodas, and light snacks in the café. There's often live entertainment on summer evenings, and outdoor garden seating when the weather cooperates.

Soldotna

❻ *116 mi from Seward, 148 mi from Anchorage via the Seward and Sterling Hwys.*

Soldotna, with its strategic location, takes its name from a nearby stream; it's a corruption of the Russian word for "soldier," although some say the name came from an Indian word meaning "stream fork." Today, this city of 3,900 residents is the commercial and sportfishing hub of the Kenai Peninsula. Along with its sister city of Kenai, it is home to Cook Inlet oil-field workers and their families. Soldotna's commercial center stretches along the Sterling Highway, making this a popular stopping point for those traveling up and down the peninsula.

This portion of the peninsula is level and forested, with numerous lakes and streams dotting and crisscrossing the area. Trumpeter swans return here in the spring and sightings of moose and caribou are common.

In addition to fishing, there's also clam digging at **Clam Gulch,** 24 mi south of Soldotna on the Sterling Highway. This is a favorite of local children, who love any excuse to dig in the muddy, sloppy goo. Ask locals on the beach how to find the giant razor clams (recognized by their dimples in the sand). The clam digging is best when tides are minus 4 or 5 ft. A sportfishing license, available at all grocery stores, is required.

Dining and Lodging

$$–$$$ ✕ **Through the Seasons.** On part of a large tract that was once a
  ★   homestead, this restaurant emphasizes locally harvested foods, including salmon, halibut, and wild berries. There's homemade pasta and New York steak, and lighter meals can be made of soup, salad, and homemade bread. ✉ *Sterling Hwy. at the Kenai turnoff,* ☎ *907/262–5006. MC, V.* ⊘ *Call for winter hrs. No lunch Sun.*

$$$ 🏨 **Kenai River Lodge.** The highway crosses the Kenai River near this sprawling motel. Clean, modern rooms, all of which overlook the river, have coffeemakers, TVs, and nondescript decor—but there's spectacular fishing right outside the back door. One more-expensive room has a kitchen. A $100 deposit (payable by check or money order, nonrefundable after May 1) is required per room, per reservation. ✉ *393 West Riverside Dr., 99669,* ☎ *907/262–4292,* 🅵🅰🆇 *907/262–7332. 25 rooms. Refrigerators, fishing. MC, V.*

Outdoor Activities and Sports

FISHING

Anglers from around the world come for the salmon-choked streams and rivers, most notably the **Kenai River** and its companion, the **Russian River.** Deep-sea fishing out of **Deep Creek** also is popular; the local campground and RV lot is packed on summer weekends.

Area phone books list some 300 **fishing charters** and guides, all of whom stay busy during the hectic summer fishing season. For more information, contact the local chamber of commerce or visitor information center (☞ Visitor Information *in* South Central Alaska A to Z, *below*).

Homer

★ ❼   *77 mi south of Soldotna via the Sterling Hwy.; 226 mi south of Anchorage via the Seward and Sterling Hwys.*

At the southern end of the Sterling Highway lies the city of Homer, on the head of a narrow spit that juts into beautiful Kachemak Bay. This community was founded just before the turn of the century as a gold-prospecting camp and later was used as a coal-mining headquarters. Today the town of Homer is a funky fishing port with picturesque buildings and good seafood. The town at the end of the road also is home to a talented and diverse artistic community, including author and radio personality Tom Bodett. The galleries on and around Pioneer Avenue are good places to find works by the town's residents. Halibut fishing is especially good in this area, and numerous charters are available. In addition to highway and air access, Homer also has regular ferry service to Seldovia.

★ ☾   The **Pratt Museum** has a saltwater aquarium, an exhibit on the 1989 Prince William Sound oil spill, a wildflower garden, a gift shop, and pioneer, Russian, and Alaska Native displays. There's also a refurbished homestead cabin, outdoor summer exhibits along the trail out back, and museum-sponsored historic tours of the harbor. ✉ *Bartlett St., just off Pioneer Ave.,* ☎ *907/235–8635.* 💲 *$4, $10 for harbor tour.* ⊘ *Summer, daily 10–6; winter, Tues.–Sun. noon–5. Closed Jan.*

Kachemak Bay abounds in wildlife. Tour operators take visitors past bird rookeries in the bay or across the bay to gravel beaches for clam digging. Most fishing charters will include an opportunity to view whales, seals, porpoises, and birds close up. A walk along the docks on Homer Spit at the end of the day is a pleasant chance to watch commercial fishing boats and charter boats unload their catch. The bay supports a large population of puffins and eagles.

Directly across from the end of the Homer Spit is **Halibut Cove,** a small community of people who make their living on the bay or by selling handicrafts. It's a good place to while away the afternoon or evening, meandering along the boardwalk and visiting galleries. The cove itself is lovely, especially during salmon runs, when fish leap and splash in the clear water. There are also several lodges on this side of the bay, on pristine coves away from summer crowds. The *Danny J* ferries people across from Homer Spit, with a stop at the rookery at Gull Island and two–three hours to walk around Halibut Cove, for $36. **Central Charters** (☞ Guided Tours, *below*) handles all booking.

Dining and Lodging

$$$–$$$$ ✕ **Homestead Restaurant.** This former log roadhouse 8 mi from town
★ is a favorite of locals who appreciate artfully presented fine food. The Homestead specializes in steak, prime rib, and seasonal seafood. Local fish and shellfish are prepared with garlic, citrus fruits, macadamia nuts, or spicy ethnic sauces. Outside are views of the bay, mountains, and hanging glaciers; the view inside includes contemporary museum-quality art. ⊠ *Mile 8.2, East End Rd.,* ☎ *907/235–8723. AE, MC, V. Closed Jan. and Feb.*

$$–$$$$ ✕ **Saltry in Halibut Cove.** Local seafood is served as sushi or is pre-
★ pared exotically here with curries and pastas, and a wide selection of imported beers is available. The deck overlooks the boat dock and the cove. Dinner seatings are at 6 and 7:30; diners spend the time before or after their seating exploring Halibut Cove. Reservations are essential for the ferry (at a reduced $21 round-trip, with dinner extra), which leaves Homer Spit at 5 PM. ⊠ *Halibut Cove, contact Central Charters (☞ Guided Tours, below). Reservations essential. AE, D, MC, V. Closed early Sept.–late May.*

$$$–$$$$ ✕🖬 **Land's End.** This sprawling gray-and-white complex at the very
★ end of the spit has wide-open views of the bay. The recently renovated rooms, half of which face the bay (and are much preferred over the rooms facing the parking lot), have telephones and TVs, but otherwise vary widely: the decor in some is nautical, in others floral; some are perfect for a couple, some big enough for a family—one 425-square-ft room has a loft. As might be expected, the restaurant ($$–$$$$), a popular place with locals, specializes in local seafood, including halibut, scallops, oysters and clams; burgers and steak are also available. ⊠ *4786 Homer Spit Rd., 99603,* ☎ *907/235–0400 or 800/478–0400 in Alaska,* FAX *907/235–0420. 61 rooms. Restaurant, bar, spa, exercise room. AE, D, DC, MC, V.*

$$–$$$$ 🖬 **Driftwood Inn.** Rooms in this cozy inn are bright and come in var-
★ ious configurations. Downstairs there's a comfortable sitting room with fireplace, TV, books, and videos. There's also a small eating area with serve-yourself coffee, tea, pastries, and cold cereal. A microwave, refrigerator, barbecue, and fish cooker and cleaning area are available for guest use. Ask for a room in the back, overlooking Bishop's Beach and the bay. The inn is perfect for families traveling with children, and the staff is friendly. ⊠ *135 West Bunnell Ave., 99603,* ☎ *907/235– 8019 or 800/478–8019,* FAX *907/235–8019. 12 rooms with bath, 9 rooms share 2 baths. Dining room, camping, coin laundry. AE, D, DC, MC, V.*

Guided Tours

Central Charters (⊠ 4241 Homer Spit Rd., 99603, ☎ 907/235–7847 or 800/478–7847) can arrange fishing, sailing, and ferry trips to Halibut Cove, around Kachemak Bay, and across to Seldovia. They can also set up daylong guided sea kayaking trips in the bay, complete with lunch and boat drop-off. **Homer Ocean Charters** (☎ 907/235–6212) offers fishing, hunting, and sightseeing trips.

Nightlife

★ Dance to lively bands at **Alice's** (☎ 907/235–7650). The spit's **Salty Dawg Saloon** (☎ 907/235–9990) is a tumbledown lighthouse, sure to be playing host to a carousing fisherman or two when you visit. The **Waterfront Bar** (☎ 907/235–9949) is in town across from the Driftwood Inn and is a favorite of fishermen.

Shopping

Alaska Wild Berry Products (⊠ 528 Pioneer Ave., ☎ 907/235–8858) sells jams, jellies, sauces, syrups, chocolate-covered candies, and juices made from wild berries handpicked on the Kenai Peninsula. Although once produced here, most items are now made at the company's Anchorage location. The gift shop at the **Pratt Museum** (☞ *above*) has an excellent inventory of natural history books, locally crafted or inspired jewelry, note cards, and gifts for children. **Ptarmigan Arts** (⊠ 471 Pioneer Ave., ☎ 907/235–5345) sells pottery, watercolors, leather work, beaded jewelry, handwoven clothing, and wildflower kaleidoscopes.

The **Bunnell Street Gallery** (⊠ Corner of Main and Bunnell Sts., ☎ 907/235–2662) exhibits innovative contemporary art produced primarily in Alaska. The gallery, which occupies the first floor of a historic trading post, hosts workshops, lectures, musical performances, and other community events. Sharing the same front porch, **Two Sisters Bakery** (☎ 907/235–2280), open daily 7–6, is a great place for coffee, muffins, soup, or pizza.

Seldovia

❽ *16 mi south of Homer, by air or water.*

Seldovia, isolated across the bay from Homer, retains the charm of an earlier Alaska. The town's Russian bloodline shows in its onion-dome church and its name, meaning "herring bay." Those who fish use plenty of herring for bait, catching record-size salmon, halibut, and king or Dungeness crab. You'll find excellent fishing whether you drop your line into the deep waters of Kachemak Bay or cast into the surf for silver salmon on the shore of Outside Beach, near town. Stroll through town and along the slough, where frame homes rest on pilings.

Dining and Lodging

$ ✕ **The Buzz.** This coffee shop sells espresso, monster baked goods, breakfast burritos, quiche, and homemade granola. For lunch, try soup with homemade bread, pasta, or chili. They also rent mountain bikes here. ⊠ *Main St., near the grocery,* ☎ *907/234–7479. MC, V.* ☻ *6–6. Closed Oct.–Feb.*

$$ 🏨 **Seldovia Boardwalk Hotel.** This hotel with a fabulous view of the harbor has immaculate modern rooms, of which half face the water. There's a large, sunlit parlor downstairs with a woodstove and coffee service. Many guests visit this no-smoking hotel as part of a tour from Homer that includes a narrated wildlife cruise and a 30-minute flight-seeing trip back to Homer. The proprietors can also arrange charter fishing or sea kayaking trips. ⊠ *Box 72, 99663,* ☎ *907/234–7816 or 800/238–7862 in summer, 907/345–5510 off-season. 14 rooms. Bicycles, no-smoking rooms. MC, V. Closed Oct.–Apr.*

$–$$ 🏨 **Across the Bay Tent & Breakfast Adventure Co.** This place is a real
★ find! A step up the comfort ladder from camping, this beachfront compound is reachable via water taxi from Homer. Guests stay in sturdy canvas-floor tents with twin beds. Prices vary depending on whether guests do their own cooking. There's a propane stove and grill for cooking, as well as pots, pans, and picnic tables. Host-prepared meals are

hearty and served family style. There's great beach walking and clamming; escorted kayak trips and mountain bikes are available for an extra charge. ⊠ *Mile 8, Jakalof Bay Rd., 8 mi from Seldovia (mailing address: Box 81, Seldovia 99663, in summer;* ⊠ *Box 112054, Anchorage 99511, in winter),* ☎ *907/235–3633 in summer, 907/345–2571 in winter. 5 tents. Sauna, boating, bicycles. MC, V. Closed late Sept.– early May.*

KODIAK ISLAND

⑨ *248 air mi from Anchorage by air.*

Alaska's largest island is accessible only by air from Anchorage and by ferry from Homer and Seward. Russian explorers discovered the island in 1763, and Kodiak served as Alaska's first capital until 1804, when the government was moved to Sitka. Situated as it is in the northwestern Gulf of Alaska, Kodiak has been subjected to several natural disasters. In 1912 a volcanic eruption on the nearby Alaska Peninsula covered the town site in knee-deep drifts of ash and pumice. A tidal wave resulting from the 1964 earthquake destroyed the island's large fishing fleet and smashed Kodiak's low-lying downtown area.

Today, commercial fishing is king in Kodiak. Despite its small population—about 15,000 people scattered among the several islands in the Kodiak group—the city is among the busiest fishing ports in the United States. The harbor is also an important supply point for small communities on the Aleutian Islands and the Alaska Peninsula.

Floatplane and boat charters are available from Kodiak to numerous remote attractions not served by roads. Chief among these areas is the 1.6-million-acre **Kodiak National Wildlife Refuge** (☞ Chapter 3), lying partly on Kodiak Island and partly on Afognak Island to the north, where spotting the enormous Kodiak brown bears is the main goal of a trip.

Kodiak figured in America's North Pacific defense in World War II and was the site of an important naval station, now occupied by the coast guard fleet that patrols the surrounding fishing grounds. Part of the old military installation has been incorporated into **Abercrombie State Park and Campground** (contact the Kodiak Island Convention and Visitors Bureau, ☞ Visitor Information *in* South Central Alaska A to Z, *below*), 3½ mi north of Kodiak on Rezanof Drive. Self-guided tours take you by cement bunkers and gun emplacements.

The **Baranov Museum** portrays the area's Russian origins. On the National Register of Historic Places, the building was built in 1808 by Alexander Baranov to warehouse precious sea-otter pelts; W. J. Erskine made it his home in 1911. On display today are samovars, Russian Easter eggs, native baskets, and other relics from the early native Koniags and the later Russian settlers. ⊠ *101 Marine Way,* ☎ *907/ 486–5920,* 𝖥𝖠𝖷 *907/486–3166.* 🖼 *$2.* ☼ *Summer, daily 11–6; winter, Mon.–Wed. and Fri. 11–3, Sat. noon–3.*

The ornate **Holy Resurrection Russian Orthodox Church** is a visual feast, both inside and out. Three different churches have stood on this site since 1796; the present structure was built in 1945 and is on the National Register of Historic Places. ☎ *907/486–3854 (parish priest).* ☼ *Summer, daily 1–3; winter, by appointment.*

★ ℭ The **Alutiiq Museum & Archaeological Repository** is home to one of the largest collections of Eskimo materials in the world and contains archaeological and ethnographic items dating back 8,000 years. Only a fraction of the museum's more than 100,000 artifacts are on display. Among the exhibits are harpoons, masks, dolls, stone tools, seal-gut parkas, grass baskets, and pottery fragments. The gift shop sells fine Alaskan gifts, including beadwork, jewelry, ivory carvings, baskets, and skin goods such as gloves and hats. ⊠ *215 Mission Rd., Suite 101,* ☎ *907/486–7004.* ⊠ *$2 donation requested.* ⊙ *Summer, Mon.–Sat. 10–4, Sun. noon–4; winter, Tues.–Fri. 10–4, Sat. noon–4.*

Dining and Lodging

$$–$$$ ✕ **Road's End.** You know a place is good if locals are willing to drive 42 mi each way to eat—30 of those miles along a gravel road. Such is the case at this lunch and dinner place out the Chiniak Road from Kodiak. There are steaks, hamburgers, homemade pies, and a seafood platter that includes halibut, shrimp, and scallops. What better reason to get out and explore a bit? ⊠ *Mile 42 Chiniak Rd.,* ☎ *907/486–2885. No credit cards. Closed Mon. Oct.–Apr.*

$ ✕ **Beryl's.** Kodiak's only sweet shop serves espresso, ice cream, and baked goods as well as breakfast and lunch (hamburgers, sandwiches, and salads). ⊠ *202 Center Ave.,* ☎ *907/486–3323. MC, V. No dinner.*

$$$$ ✕▤ **Kodiak Buskin River Inn.** This modern lodge is near the airport,
★ about 4½ mi from downtown. Rooms are large and well kept (some have voice mail and data ports), and service is friendly. Guests can fish for salmon in the river out back. Like many Alaskan restaurants, the Eagle's Nest ($$–$$$$) features local seafood, including king crab, scallops, and a chilled seafood sampler. There also are Cajun prawns, tempura vegetables, pasta, and a variety of steaks. The atmosphere is semiformal, with candlelike lamps on each table. ⊠ *1395 Airport Way, 99615,* ☎ *907/487–2700 or 800/544–2202,* ℻ *907/487–4447. 51 rooms. Restaurant, bar, fishing, airport shuttle. AE, D, DC, MC, V.*

$$$$ ▤ **Kodiak Inn.** Rooms here have soothing floral decor; some overlook the harbor. The Chartroom Restaurant has harbor views and serves local seafood and standard American fare, including steak and pasta. ⊠ *236 Rezanof St. W, 99615,* ☎ *907/486–5712 or 888/563–4254,* ℻ *907/486–3430. 81 rooms. Restaurant, bar, refrigerators, microwaves, hot tub. AE, D, DC, MC, V.*

Guided Tours

Dig Afognak (⊠ Box 1277, 99615, ☎ 907/486–6014 or 800/770–6014, ℻ 907/486–2514) gives archaeologist wanna-bes a chance to work alongside professionals during a seven-day dig and a chance to learn about the island's natural history. Guests stay in sturdy weather ports with solid floors and skylights and eat together in a common enclosure. There's also a Native-style sauna for bathing.

Kodiak Island Charters (☎ ℻ 907/486–5380 or 800/575–5380,) operates boat tours for fishing, hunting, and sightseeing. **Kodiak Nautical Discoveries** (☎ 907/486–4269) has saltwater fishing and sightseeing tours. **Wavetamer** (☎ ℻ 907/486–2604) leads guided sea-kayaking tours.

MATANUSKA-SUSITNA VALLEY

Giant homegrown vegetables and the headquarters of the best-known dogsled race in the world are among the most prominent attractions of the Mat-Su Valley.

The valley, lying an hour north of Anchorage by road, draws its name from its two largest rivers, the Matanuska and the Susitna, and is bisected by the Parks and the Glenn highways. Major cities are Wasilla on the Parks Highway and Palmer on the Glenn Highway. To the east, the Glenn Highway connects to the Richardson Highway by way of several high mountain passes sandwiched between the Chugach Mountains to the south and the Talkeetnas to the north. At Mile 103 of the Glenn Highway, the massive **Matanuska Glacier** comes almost to the road.

Palmer

⑩ *40 mi north of Anchorage via the Glenn Hwy.*

In 1935 the federal government relocated about 200 farm families from the Depression-ridden Midwest to the Mat-Su Valley, and some elements of these early farms remain around Palmer. The valley has developed into the state's major agricultural region. Good growing conditions result in some outsize vegetables—such as 100-pound cabbages. You'll find these and other attractions at the **Alaska State Fair,** which runs 11 days, ending on Labor Day (1999 dates are Aug. 27– Sept. 6). ⊠ *Alaska State Fairgrounds, Mile 40.2, Glenn Hwy., 2075 Glenn Hwy., Palmer 99645,* ☎ *907/745–4827 or 800/850–3247,* FAX *907/746–2699.* 🎫 *$6 weekdays, $8 weekends.*

On a sunny day the town of Palmer looks like a Swiss calendar photo, with its old barns and log houses silhouetted against craggy Pioneer Peak. On nearby farms (on the Bodenburg Loop off the old Palmer Highway) you can pay to pick your own raspberries and other fruits and vegetables. Visit **Pyrah's Pioneer Peak Farm** (⊠ Mile 2.8 Bodenburg Loop, ☎ 907/745–4511) to see what's growin'. They cultivate 35 kinds of fruits and vegetables and begin harvesting at the end of June, with the peak picking time occurring around mid-July.

The **Musk-Ox Farm** is the world's only domestic musk-ox farm and has 30-minute guided tours from May to September. In addition to the 40-some animals roaming outside, there are indoor displays and a gift shop. ⊠ *Mile 50.1, Glenn Hwy.,* ☎ *907/745–4151.* 🎫 *$7.* ☉ *May– Sept., daily 10–6; by appointment rest of yr.*

The valley abounds with good fishing, especially for salmon and trout, and numerous charter services are available, by both air and boat, to carry visitors into remote areas. Gold mining was an early mainstay of the valley's economy; visitors today may tour the long-dormant **Independence Mine** on the Hatcher Pass Road, a loop that in summer connects to the Parks Highway just north of Willow to the Glenn Highway near Palmer. (The gravel roads leading to the gold mine are rough and full of potholes, even under the best of conditions, so be careful.) In the 1940s as many as 200 workers were employed by the mine. Today it is a 271-acre state park that is a popular cross-country ski area in winter. Only the wooden buildings remain, one of them a red-roof mine manager's headquarters now serving as a visitor center. ⊠ *Independence Mine State Historical Park, 19 mi from Glenn Hwy. on Hatcher Pass Rd.,* ☎ *907/745–3975.* 🎫 *$5 per vehicle; tours $3.* ☉ *Visitor center Memorial Day–Labor Day, daily 11–7, grounds year-round.*

Dining and Lodging

$$–$$$ ✕🏨 **Hatcher Pass Lodge.** This lodge has spectacular views and can serve as base camp for hiking, berry picking, and—in fall and winter—skiing. Most rooms and cabins have queen-size beds. The cabins have chemical toilets and water coolers; guests shower in the lodge. The restaurant serves a Continental menu ($$–$$$), including fondues, halibut, and gourmet pizzas; there are domestic and imported beers, cappuccino, and hot buttered rum. ⊠ *Box 763, 99645,* ☎ *907/745–5897,* FAX *907/745–1200. 3 rooms, 9 cabins. Restaurant, sauna. AE, D, MC, V.*

$$ ✕🏨 **Colony Inn.** All guest rooms in this lovingly restored historic building are tastefully decorated with antiques and quilts. The build-

ing was used as a women's dormitory during the farm colonization of the 1930s. The small café serves light breakfasts, lunches, and Friday night dinners. The homemade pies are blue-ribbon winners at the Alaska State Fair. Inn reservations and check-in are handled at the neighboring Valley Hotel (☞ *below*). There is no smoking anywhere in the inn. ✉ *325 E. Elmwood,* ☎ *907/745–3330,* 𝖥𝖠𝖷 *907/746–3330. 12 rooms. Restaurant, no-smoking rooms. AE, MC, V.*

$$ 🏨 **Valley Hotel.** This three-story frame hotel is popular with budget travelers. Most rooms have recently been repainted and have new quilts and carpets. Built in 1948, the building also houses a 24-hour no-smoking coffee shop, a beauty salon, a lounge, and a massage therapist. ✉ *606 S. Alaska St., 99645,* ☎ *907/745–3330,* 𝖥𝖠𝖷 *907/746– 3330. 30 rooms. Bar, coffee shop, beauty salon. AE, MC, V.*

Wasilla

❶ *42 mi north of Anchorage via the Parks Hwy.; 10 mi from Palmer via the Trunk Rd. and the Parks Hwy.*

Wasilla is one of the valley's original pioneer communities and over time has served as a supply center for farmers, gold miners, and mushers. Today, fast-food restaurants and strip malls line the Parks Highway. Rolling hills and more scenic vistas can be found by wandering the area's back roads.

The **Museum of Alaska Transportation and Industry,** on a 15-acre site, exhibits some of the machines that helped develop Alaska, from dogsleds to jet aircraft, and everything in between. The Don Sheldon Building houses aviation artifacts as well as antique autos and photographic displays. A Gold Rush exhibit also is on display. ✉ *Turn-off at Mile 47, Parks Hwy. and follow the signs.* ☎ *907/376–1211,* 𝖥𝖠𝖷 *907/376–3082.* 🎫 *$5.* ⊙ *May–Sept., daily 10–6; Oct.–Apr., Tues.– Sat. 9–5.*

Wasilla is the headquarters and official starting point for the Iditarod Trail Sled Dog Race, run each March from here to Nome, more than 1,000 mi to the northwest. (A ceremonial start is held on Anchorage's 4th Avenue the previous day.) The **Iditarod Trail Headquarters** is open year-round with its displays of dogsleds, mushers' clothing, and trail gear as well as video highlights of past races. The gift shop sells Iditarod items. ✉ *Mile 2.2, Knik Rd.,* ☎ *907/376–5155.* 🎫 *Free.* ⊙ *Summer, daily 8–7; winter, weekdays 8–5.*

Dining and Lodging

There are several lovely rural B&Bs among the farms and woods of this area. Contact the **Wasilla Chamber of Commerce** (☞ Visitor Information *in* South Central Alaska A to Z, *below*).

$$–$$$ ✕ **Evangelo's Trattoria.** The food is good and the servings ample at this spacious local favorite on the Parks Highway at the north end of town. Try the garlic-sautéed shrimp in a white-wine butter sauce or a mammoth calzone. The pizzas are loaded with goodies and there's also a respectable salad bar. The atmosphere is spiffed-up casual. ✉ *Frontier Mall, Mile 42.5, Parks Hwy.,* ☎ *907/376–1212. AE, MC, V.*

$$$–$$$$ 🏨 **Best Western Lake Lucille Inn.** This attractive, well-maintained re-
★   sort sits right on Lake Lucille (at Mile 43.5 on the Parks Highway) and provides easy access to several recreational activities, including boating in summer and ice-skating and snowmobiling in winter. The inn's rooms are bright and cheery. Half of them have private balconies overlooking the lake, and there's an outdoor deck with spectacular views of the mountains and water. ✉ *1300 W. Lake Lucille Dr., 99654,* ☎

907/373–1776 or 800/528–1234, FAX *907/376–6199. 50 rooms, 4 suites. Restaurant, lobby lounge, sauna, health club, boating. AE, D, DC, MC, V.*

$$ ☒ **Yukon Don's B&B.** Each of the spacious, immaculate, log-partitioned
★ rooms in this converted barn is decorated according to a theme. The Denali Room has posters of the mountain, snowshoes, crampons, and other climbing gear; there's a dogsled and other race paraphernalia in the Iditarod Room. A rooftop room offers a spectacular, 360-degree panorama of the mountains and river valleys. A bear coat that guests are welcome to try on and mounted grizzlies and sheep are in the large sitting room. Host Yukon Don can arrange dogsled rides and other adventure packages. ☒ *2221 Yukon Circle (mailing address: 1830 E. Parks Hwy., Suite 386, 99654),* ☎ *907/376–7472,* FAX *907/376–6515. 3 suites, 4 rooms with shared bath. Sauna, exercise room. MC, V.*

Guided Tours

Tri-River Charters (☒ Box 312, Talkeetna 99676, ☎ 907/733–2400) operates fishing trips out of Talkeetna and can provide all the necessary tackle and gear if necessary. They start fishing the first week of May and run clear through September. You can book a guided or drop-off trip, half- or full-day, and pursue the wily rainbow, grayling, and all five species of Pacific salmon. They also offer scenic cruises on the rivers.

Talkeetna

⑫ *56 mi north from Wasilla via the Parks Hwy. and Talkeetna Spur Rd.; 112 mi from Anchorage.*

Talkeetna lies at the end of a spur road near Mile 99 of the Parks Highway. Mountaineers congregate here to begin their assaults on Mt. McKinley in **Denali National Park** (☞ Chapter 3). The Denali mountain rangers have their climbing headquarters here, as do most glacier pilots who fly climbing parties to the mountain. The community maintains a museum of the history of Mt. McKinley climbs, as well as a carved pole at the town cemetery, honoring deceased mountaineers.

Dining and Lodging

$$$ ✕☒ **Swiss-Alaska Inn.** Family-run since 1976, this rustic-style property is popular with those who come to fish in the Talkeetna, Susitna, and Chulitna rivers. Rooms are bright and homey and have a floral decor. Two rooms are accessible for people who use wheelchairs. Menu selections at the restaurant ($$) include halibut, salmon, buffalo burgers, and the owner's secret-recipe Swiss-style French toast. (Mention Fodor's and the owner will give you a 10% discount.) ☒ *East Talkeetna, by the boat launch (mailing address: Box 565, 99676),* ☎ *907/733–2424,* FAX *907/733–2425. 20 rooms. Restaurant, no-smoking rooms. AE, D, MC, V.*

$$ ✕☒ **Talkeetna Roadhouse.** This log roadhouse has a common sitting area and plain rooms in a variety of sizes, including two bunk rooms with four beds each. Homemade bread, bagels, scones, and cinnamon rolls are the order of the day at the restaurant ($–$$), along with sizable breakfasts, soup-and-salad combos, and sandwiches, desserts, and pies, all made from scratch and using local berries and produce whenever possible. It's a popular place with locals and with climbers who use Talkeetna's air taxis to reach nearby Mt. McKinley. ☒ *Main St. (mailing address: Box 604, 99676),* ☎ *907/733–1351,* FAX *907/733–1353. 8 rooms and a cabin share 4 baths. Restaurant. D, MC, V. Restaurant closed mid-Sept.–mid-May; hotel operates as a bed-and-breakfast in winter.*

$$–$$$ 🖭 **Talkeetna Motel.** This all-purpose roadside A-frame downtown has a cocktail lounge with dancing and a full-service restaurant. Rooms, which have wood paneling and brightly patterned bedspreads, are well maintained. Each has a private bath and satellite TV. ⊠ *Box 115, 99676,* ☎ *907/733–2323. 23 rooms. Restaurant, bar. MC, V.*

Guided Tours

Doug Geeting Aviation (☎ 907/733–2366 or 800/770–2366, ℻ 907/733–1000) offers glacier landings and air transportation for fly-in fishing and skiing and climbing trips. There's also a Pitts S2-B aerobatic plane for loop-de-loops if you're feeling especially adventurous. **K2 Aviation** (☎ 907/733–2291 or 800/764–2291, ℻ 907/733–1221) lands you on a glacier and also offers overnight trips to Denali National Park. Floatplanes provide access to area lakes for fly-in activities. **Talkeetna Air Taxi** (☎ 907/733–2218 or 800/533–2219, ℻ 907/733–1434) offers a breathtaking exploration flight close to the massive Mt. McKinley, as well as fly-in hiking and fishing service.

Mahay's Riverboat Service (☎ 907/733–2223 or 800/736–2210) offers guided jet-boat tours, scenic cruises, and fishing on the Susitna and Talkeetna rivers. Their newest boat is the 51-passenger *Talkeetna Queen,* an enclosed and climate-controlled boat that can safely navigate the rivers in any weather. **Talkeetna Riverboat Service** (☎ 907/733–2281) offers guided or drop-off fishing trips and river cabins.

Glennallen

⑬   *187 mi from Anchorage on the Glenn Hwy.*

This community of 900 residents is the gateway to Wrangell–St. Elias National Park and Preserve (☞ Chapter 3); it's 124 mi from Glennallen to McCarthy, the last 58 on unpaved gravel. This town is also the service center for the Copper River basin and is a fly-in base for several wilderness outfitters.

Dining and Lodging

$$ ✕ **Caribou Cafe Family Restaurant.** This friendly place serves such typical roadside fare as burgers, hot sandwiches, meat loaf, pancakes, and charbroiled steak. Bakery items, such as sweet rolls and pies, are baked fresh daily. ⊠ *Downtown Glennallen, Mile 187, Glenn Hwy.,* ☎ *907/822–3656. AE, D, MC, V.*

$$$ 🖭 **Caribou Hotel.** This modern hotel is clean and comfortable, with rooms done in mauve and sea green. Unless you're on a strict budget, be sure to ask for a room in the main building and not in the trailer-like annex out front—rooms there are spartan and share a bath at the end of the hall. Several rooms in the main building have hot tubs; there are three suites with kitchens. The owners operate two other nearby properties. One is a B&B that has two rooms with bath and two rooms that share a bath. The other property has three two-bedroom apartments and a one-bedroom apartment. ⊠ *Box 329, 99588,* ☎ *907/822–3302 or 800/478–3302,* ℻ *907/822–3711. 83 rooms, 63 with bath; 3 suites. AE, D, DC, MC, V.*

SOUTH CENTRAL ALASKA A TO Z

Arriving and Departing

Most visitors to South Central Alaska arrive through Anchorage (☞ Anchorage A to Z *in* Chapter 5).

Getting Around

The Alaska Range to the north mirrors the gentle curve of the Gulf of Alaska in the south, creating natural borders for the South Central region. Compared with the Interior and Bush regions, South Central is somewhat more compact, and the distances you will have to travel between destinations aren't as vast.

Anchorage is the central hub, connected by rail and road to Seward and (at least for the time being) by rail only to Whittier. Valdez can be reached by a rather indirect but interesting road route (the Glenn Highway to the Richardson Highway) out of Anchorage. The Seward and Sterling highways connect to most of the places you'll want to see on the Kenai Peninsula, including the small towns of Hope, Soldotna, and Homer.

South Central's other "highway," the ferry-driven Marine Highway, connects with Kodiak, Whittier, Seward, Valdez, Dutch Harbor, and Cordova via the gulf.

Heading north of Anchorage, the Glenn and Parks highways are your only options, with the Parks Highway skirting Denali National Park as it heads on to Fairbanks.

Air taxis are also a viable means of transportation around South Central.

By Bus

There's year-round service between Fairbanks and Anchorage by way of Denali National Park and also down to Homer, at the very tip of the Kenai Peninsula. **Alaska Direct Bus Line** (☎ 907/277–6652 or 800/770–6652, ℻ 907/338–1951) offers service between Anchorage and Fairbanks and also to White Horse and Skagway. **The Park Connection** (☎ 800/208–0200, 907/224–7116 for Seward same-day bookings, or 907/683–1240 for Denali same-day bookings) provides regularly scheduled shuttle service between Seward, Anchorage, and Denali National Park mid-May to mid-September. **Seward Bus Line** (☎ 907/563–0800 or 907/224–3608, ℻ 907/224–7237). serves Anchorage, Portage, and Seward. A subsidiary offers service between Anchorage and Homer.

By Car

Driving may be the best way to see Alaska, but keep in mind that all but a few miles of the road system consist of two-lane highways, not all of which are paved. For hot-line reports on highways during snow season, call the **State Department of Transportation in Anchorage** (☎ 907/243–7675).

Two highway routes offer a choice for travel by car **between Fairbanks and Anchorage.** Heading north from Anchorage, the Parks Highway (turn left off Glenn Highway near Palmer) passes through Wasilla and up the Susitna River drainage area and through a low pass in the Alaska Range, then down into the Tanana Valley and Fairbanks. This route passes the entrance to Denali National Park and roughly parallels the Alaska Railroad.

A longer route (436 mi) follows the Glenn Highway to the Richardson Highway, then heads north to Fairbanks through the Copper River valley. This route makes possible a side trip to Valdez, and it offers the most direct connection to the Alaska Highway, joining it at Tok.

Anchorage can be used as a base for **side trips** over the Seward and Sterling highways to the Kenai Peninsula and its smorgasbord of outdoor recreation. And watch the side roads for short trips to such places as Portage Glacier, off the Seward Highway, and Hope, an isolated community across Cook Inlet.

By Ferry

Ferries are a great way to explore the South Central coast, with its glaciers, mountains, fjords, and sea mammals. The ferries between Valdez and Whittier run by way of Columbia Glacier in summer, where it is not unusual to witness giant fragments of ice calving from the face of the glacier into Prince William Sound.

The **Alaska Marine Highway** (✉ Box 25535, Juneau 99802, ☎ 907/465–3941 or 800/642–0066, FAX 907/277–4829), the state-run ferry operator, offers scheduled service to Valdez, Cordova, Whittier, Seward, Homer, and Seldovia on the mainland, to Kodiak and Port Lions on Kodiak Island, and to the port of Dutch Harbor in the Aleutian Islands. The same agency runs the ferries that operate in Southeast Alaska, but the two systems do not connect. The system operates on two schedules; summer (May–September) sailings are considerably more frequent than fall and winter service. Check your schedules carefully: ferries do not stop at all ports every day. Reservations are required on all routes; they should be made as far in advance as possible, particularly in summer.

By Plane

Anchorage is the air hub of the South Central region, served by major national and international airlines and well stocked with smaller carriers and local air-taxi operators.

ERA Aviation flies to Homer, Kenai, Valdez, Cordova, and Kodiak. Reservations are handled by Alaska Airlines (☎ 907/243–3300).

By Train

The **Alaska Railroad Corporation** (✉ Box 107500, Anchorage 99510, ☎ 907/265–2494 or 800/544–0552, FAX 907/265–2323) operates the Alaska Railroad, which is said to be the last railroad in North America that still makes flag stops to accommodate the homesteaders, hikers, fishing parties, and other travelers who get on and off in remote places. The 470-mi main line runs up Alaska's rail belt between Seward and Fairbanks via Anchorage. A branch south of Anchorage connects to Whittier on Prince William Sound. There's daily service in summer, and weekly service between Anchorage and Fairbanks in the winter. Service to Seward from Anchorage runs mid-May to September 1 only. Adults are allowed two pieces of luggage, to a maximum of 50 pounds. There's a $20 charge for bicycles; camping equipment is allowed on a space-available basis.

For information on the luxury-class **Ultradome service** between Anchorage and Fairbanks, contact **Princess Tours** (☎ 206/728–4202 or 800/835–8907) about its *Midnight Sun Express* or **Westours/Gray Line of Alaska** (☎ 907/277–5581 or 800/544–2206) about its *McKinley Explorer.*

Contacts and Resources

B&B Reservation Services

Contact **Alaska Private Lodgings/Stay With A Friend** (✉ 704 W. 2nd Ave., Anchorage 99501, ☎ 907/258–1717, FAX 907/258–6613) for bed-and-breakfast bookings throughout the state. For information on B&Bs on the Kenai Peninsula, contact **Accommodations on the Kenai** (✉ Box 2956-MP, Soldotna 99669, ☎ 907/262–2139).

Emergencies

Dial 911 for local police or ambulance emergency assistance in Anchorage and other larger communities.

The **Alaska State Troopers** maintain detachments throughout the region, although funding cuts have made staffing sparse and calls frequently are routed to detachments several miles away: Anchorage (☎ 907/269–5722), Glennallen (☎ 907/822–3263), Homer (☎ 907/ 235–8239), Kodiak (☎ 907/486–4121), Palmer (☎ 907/745–2131), Seward (☎ 907/224–3346), Soldotna (☎ 907/262–4052), Valdez (☎ 907/835–4359).

Hiking

Information on locations and difficulty of trails is available at the Alaska Public Lands Information Center at 4th and F streets in Anchorage (☞ *below*). Another good resource is *55 Ways to the Wilderness in Southcentral Alaska,* published by the Mountaineers and available at most local bookstores.

Hospitals and Clinics

Anchorage: Alaska Regional Hospital (☎ 907/276–1131); **Providence Alaska Medical Center** (☎ 907/562–2211); **U.S. Air Force Hospital** (☎ 907/552–5555). **Cordova: Cordova Medical Center** (☎ 907/424–8000). **Glennallen: Crossroads Medical Center** (☎ 907/822–3203). **Homer: South Peninsula Hospital** (☎ 907/235–8101). **Kodiak: Kodiak Island Hospital** (☎ 907/486–3281). **Palmer: Valley Hospital** (☎ 907/746–8600). **Seldovia: Seldovia Medical Clinic** (☎ 907/234–7825). **Seward: Providence Seward Medical Center** (☎ 907/224–5205). **Soldotna: Central Peninsula General Hospital** (☎ 907/262–4404). **Valdez: Community Hospital** (☎ 907/835–2249).

Visitor Information

Alaska Public Lands Information Center (✉ 605 W. 4th Ave., Anchorage 99501, ☎ 907/271–2737) handles reservations for Chugach National Forest recreational cabins and provides a wealth of information on the area and its activities. It's a good first stop when doing trip planning.

Bureau of Land Management (✉ Box 147, Glennallen 99588, ☎ 907/ 822–3217). **Cordova Chamber of Commerce** (✉ Box 99, Cordova 99574, ☎ 907/424–7260). **Homer Chamber of Commerce** (✉ 135 Sterling Hwy., Box 541, Homer 99603, ☎ 907/235–5300). **Kenai Peninsula Visitor Information Center** (✉ 44790 Sterling Hwy., Soldotna 99669, ☎ 907/262–1337). **Kodiak Island Convention and Visitors Bureau** (✉ 100 Marine Way, Kodiak 99615, ☎ 907/486–4782). **Palmer Chamber of Commerce** (✉ Box 45, Palmer 99645, ☎ 907/745– 2880). **Seward Visitors Bureau** (✉ Mile 2, Seward Hwy., Box 749, Seward 99664, ☎ 907/224–8051). **U.S. Fish and Wildlife Service** (✉ Alaska Regional Office, 1011 E. Tudor Rd., Anchorage 99503, ☎ 907/786– 3487). **U.S. Forest Service** (✉ 3301 C St., Room 300, Anchorage 99503, ☎ 907/271–2500) disseminates information about the Chugach National Forest. **Valdez Convention and Visitors Bureau** (✉ 200 Chenega St., Box 1603, Valdez 99686, ☎ 907/835–2984). **Wasilla Chamber of Commerce** (✉ 1830 E. Parks Hwy., A-116, Wasilla 99654, ☎ 907/376–1299).

7 The Interior

Including Fairbanks, the Dalton Highway, and the Yukon

Bounded by the Brooks Range to the north and the Alaska Range to the south, the Interior is home to Mt. McKinley, the highest peak in North America, and to Denali National Park. Fairbanks, founded in 1901 by a merchant and a prospector who struck it rich in their respective endeavors, is Alaska's second-largest city. It is the gateway to the Far North—the Arctic and the Bering Coast—and to Canada's Yukon Territory, whose Gold Rush history is preserved in towns such as Dawson City and Whitehorse.

By Kent Sturgis

Updated by
Tom Reale

THE IMAGE OF TURN-OF-THE-CENTURY ALASKA, with its heady gold rushes set to the jangling accompaniment of honky-tonk saloons, has its roots in the Interior. Gold fever struck in Circle and Eagle in the 1890s, spread into Canada's Yukon Territory in the big Klondike Gold Rush of 1898, then came back to Alaska's Interior when Fairbanks hit pay dirt in the 1900s. The broad, swift Yukon River was the rush's main highway. Flowing almost 2,300 mi from Canada to the Bering Sea, just below the Arctic Circle, it carried prospectors across the border in search of instant fortune.

Although Fairbanks has grown up into a small city, many towns and communities in the Interior seem little changed. Soaking in the water of the Chena Hot Springs Resort, you can almost hear the whispers of the gold seekers exaggerating their finds and claims, ever alert for the newest strike.

Early missionaries set up schools in the Bush, and the nomadic Alaskan Native peoples were herded to these regional centers for schooling and "salvation." Interior Alaska is still flecked with Indian villages. Fort Yukon, on the Arctic Circle, is the largest Athabascan village in the state.

Alaska's most recent gold rush—the pipeline carrying black gold from the oil fields in Prudhoe Bay south to the port of Valdez—snakes its way through the heart of the Interior. The pipeline itself is something of an enigma: it's a symbol of commercial interests against the environment yet also a monumental construction that hugs the land as a giant necklace. The Richardson Highway, which got its start as a gold stampeders' trail, parallels the trans-Alaska pipeline on its route south of Fairbanks.

Gold itself is glittering anew in the Interior. Fairbanks, the site of the largest gold production in Alaska in pre–World War II days, now is the location for the recently opened Fort Knox Gold Mine, which is expected to double Alaska's gold production. The start-up of the mine is occurring a century after the discovery of gold in the Klondike in 1896 and the massive stampede of prospectors to Dawson City in 1898.

Pleasures and Pastimes

Dining
Why fight it? Salmon and freshwater fish are plentiful and among the better values on most menus; unless you're a confirmed fish hater, try the local specialty. There will, of course, be other dishes available. Among those at Fairbanks-area restaurants are caribou stew, reindeer in cranberry sauce, and buffalo burgers.

Restaurants in outlying areas, which are mostly small family-run establishments, vary their hours with the season. Call ahead to be sure they're open. Outside Fairbanks, reservations are rarely necessary.

For price ranges, *see* the dining chart *in* On the Road with Fodor's.

Hiking
Several developed trails in the area offer hikers everything from an afternoon outing to an expedition of several days. Water is often scarce along the trails, so make sure you pack enough. Those adventuresome souls interested in following their own paths off the developed trails will find lots of space to go exploring. However, be well informed before you start. Although still beautiful and mostly wild, Alaska has many

dangers for the unsuspecting, and private property needs to be respected here as it is elsewhere. A necessary stop for hikers is at the Alaska Public Lands Information Center in Fairbanks (☞ Visitor Information *in* Interior A to Z, *below*). The staff there is helpful, knowledgeable, and in many cases can tell you about areas from personal experience.

Hot Springs Retreats

Forty below zero isn't a temperature that brings thoughts of going for a swim, but that's what visitors have done for many years at the three hot-springs resorts in the Interior. The discovery by early miners of natural hot springs in the frozen wilderness just north of Fairbanks sent them scrambling to build communities around this heaven-sent phenomenon. The areas around the hot springs also make excellent bases for fishing, hiking, snowshoeing, or cross-country skiing. Each of the resorts is accessible by road and air from Fairbanks.

Lodging

The Interior has a surprising range of lodging, from wilderness lodges to hot-springs spas and up-to-date modern hotels. However, be aware that as a rule the farther away from civilization centers you get, the more basic the lodging gets. For example, most lodging along the Dalton Highway is made from service trailers formerly used to house pipeline workers. It is clean and fairly comfortable but expensive and not fancy.

For price ranges, *see* the lodging chart *in* On the Road with Fodor's.

Mushing

Alaska is to dog mushing what Kentucky is to horse racing, and the Interior is arguably the prime mushing spot in Alaska. A host of dog-mushing races are held here, including everything from short sprint races with small teams to the Yukon Quest International, the second-longest sled-dog race in the world next to the Iditarod. But mushing isn't a sport solely for racers. Many people live in the Interior just so they can spend their free time in winter mushing their dogs. Skijoring—being pulled on skis by dogs—is also popular here. A web of trails surrounds many communities. Find out more information at the Alaska Public Lands Information Center (☞ Visitor Information *in* Interior A to Z, *below*).

Exploring the Interior

Interior Alaska is neatly sandwiched between two monumental mountain ranges—the Brooks Range to the north and the Alaska Range to the south. Important cities and towns are spread along two major transportation routes. The Yukon River flows east–west in the northern half of the region.

Interior Alaskans often define their area by the road system. Only a few highways cut through this great land, and only one connects Alaska to the rest of the world. The Alaska Highway, still often referred to as the Alcan, enters Alaska by way of Yukon Territory, Canada.

On the eastern edge of the state lies Fortymile Country and just across the border, the Yukon Territory. The histories of both are steeped in gold rushes, and both are home to rugged individuals who are willing to battle the elements for a place to live. These areas are still mostly wild, rugged lands with pockets of civilization. In Alaska the Taylor Highway cuts through Fortymile Country, connecting Eagle, a Gold Rush town, to the Alaska Highway. A cutoff connects the Taylor to the Top of the World Highway, which runs through Dawson City, a town that's a celebration of mining history. Both highways are gravel.

The Alaska Highway officially ends in Delta Junction, where the Richardson Highway leads travelers to Fairbanks. Many people follow this route, which started as a dirt trail years and years ago. The highways run through fairly flat land by Alaska standards, though they do get close to some mountains. Woods are abundant along this stretch of road, and a sharp eye might be able to pick out some wild animals.

The Parks Highway connects Fairbanks to Anchorage and passes right by Denali National Park (☞ Chapter 3). This is a beautiful drive, and the park is, of course, stunning.

North of Fairbanks are three highways, one of which stretches into the Arctic. All three wind through rugged, wooded country. The Steese Highway heads northeast and dead-ends in Circle at the Yukon River. Along the way the highway leads travelers into alpine country. A cutoff before Circle heads to Circle Hot Springs. The Elliott Highway takes you northwest to the beginning of the Dalton Highway and then to a dead end at Manley Hot Springs on the Tanana River. The final main highway in the Interior is the Dalton, which goes to the north coast of Alaska. The highway cuts through the Brooks Range, an impressive collection of rocky arctic peaks, and spills out onto the tundra of the North Slope.

The Denali Highway, oddly enough, isn't in Denali National Park. It connects the towns of Paxson and Cantwell, running for 135 mi through tundra and spruce forests. Most of the road is unpaved, and services are few and far between, so it's not a trip to be taken too lightly. Before attempting to drive end to end on the Denali, make sure you've got a full tank of gas, and at least one real spare tire, not one of those cheesy space-saver models. On a clear day, the views north to the Alaska range are stunning, and it's well worth the three to five hours it takes to make the drive. You can use the Denali to add some variety to the Anchorage to Fairbanks trip.

Numbers in the text correspond to numbers in the margin and on the Interior and the Yukon, Fairbanks, and Dawson City maps.

Great Itineraries

Alaska is immense, but the limited number of roads helps narrow down what you can see and do, and a few places are must-sees. Even a short trip can give you a taste for Alaska's raw beauty, varied terrain, rugged individualism, and gold-mining history.

IF YOU HAVE 3 DAYS

Spend a day in 🖬 **Fairbanks** ①–⑪, taking in the trans-Alaska pipeline, the University of Alaska Museum, and the Riverboat Discovery tour. Try to end your day at Alaskaland so that you can have dinner at the Alaska Salmon Bake. The next day head to 🖬 **Denali National Park** (☞ Chapter 3) and do some hiking or take a white-water rafting trip down the nearby Nenana River. Spend the night in the park area, but be sure to call ahead for room or campsite reservations, and for seats on the bus—the park area is very popular in the summer. The next morning get up early to take a shuttle bus to Eielson Visitor Center at the park entrance, and start the third day exploring the national park. Head back to Fairbanks that evening and catch dinner and a show at the **Ester Gold Camp** (☞ Nightlife and the Arts *in* Fairbanks, *below*).

IF YOU HAVE 5 DAYS

Follow the three-day itinerary, then spend the next day in Fairbanks, taking the tour of **El Dorado Gold Mine** (☞ Outdoor Activities and Sports *in* Fairbanks, *below*), where you can pan for gold, and visiting the **Fairbanks Ice Museum** ② if you missed it earlier. That afternoon head out

Interior and the Yukon

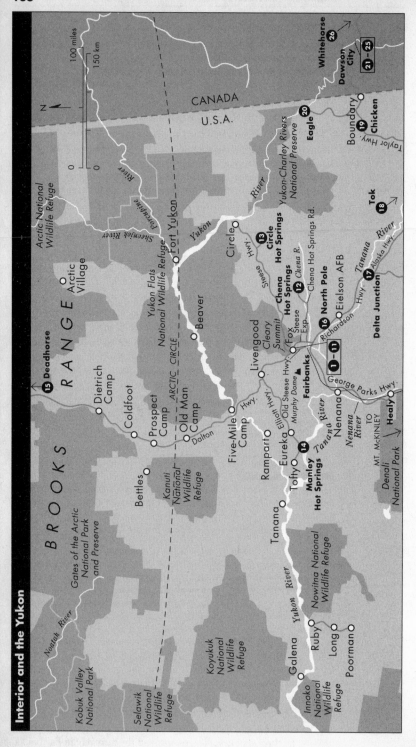

to the scenic Chena Hot Springs Road for some delicious homemade pie at Tack's General Store and a relaxing soak at Chena Hot Springs Resort in ⌘ **Chena Hot Springs** ⑫. Spend the night at the resort or head back to town and consider stopping for dinner at Two Rivers Lodge.

IF YOU HAVE 10 DAYS

Follow the five-day itinerary, then head east to the Fortymile and Klondike Gold Rush areas, visiting some of the unique attractions along the Richardson and Alaska highways, such as the Santa Claus House in **North Pole** ⑯, the Knotty Shop just south of North Pole, and Rika's Roadhouse in **Delta Junction** ⑰. Spend the night in ⌘ **Tok** ⑱. The next day take the gravel Taylor Highway up to ⌘ **Eagle** ⑳ and the Yukon River. Take the walking tour of Eagle in the morning, then drive to ⌘ **Dawson City** ㉑–㉕, spending a day or two there. From Dawson you can go back to Fairbanks the way you came, or you can continue on to **Whitehorse** ㉖, on the Alaska Highway. If a long drive doesn't suit you, hop a flight to Dawson, spend a couple of days there, and then return for more Fairbanks attractions.

When to Tour the Interior

The Interior is characterized by bitter cold in winter with temperatures as low as minus 80 degrees. But summers are among the warmest in Alaska, with a few days each month from May to August that have temperatures in the high 80s or 90s. From the first week of May to the middle of August, it's bright enough at midnight to read a newspaper outdoors. Sunny days or partly cloudy ones, sometimes punctuated with afternoon cloudbursts, are the norm.

Tourism is big business in Alaska, but many of the attractions shut down after tourist season, which generally runs from Memorial Day to Labor Day. Consider coming early or late in the season to avoid the rush. Higher elevations and northern areas could have snow early in the season. It's been known to snow in Fairbanks in May. Late season brings fall colors, ripening berries, and active wildlife, but it also brings more chance of rain. Also, the fall season is short and is over quicker at higher elevations and farther north. In any case, you would be prudent to make reservations early. Things can be especially tight at peak season, including shuttle-bus passes into Denali National Park.

People who love winter sports or are interested in unique experiences should come to Interior Alaska in the winter. March is generally the best winter month. The dark days of deep winter are over, lots of snow blankets the ground, and if the temperature does drop far below zero at night, the sun generally warms it up so it's fairly comfortable during the day. In March you can go skiing or snowmobiling and catch sled-dog races, winter carnivals, and ice carving in Fairbanks. It is also one of the best times to catch spectacular displays of the northern lights.

FAIRBANKS AND CHENA HOT SPRINGS

Fairbanks

120 mi north of Denali National Park, 100 mi northwest of Delta Junction, 600 mi northwest of Whitehorse, 489 mi south of Prudhoe Bay, 5,300 mi northwest of Miami.

Its nickname, the Golden Heart, reflects Fairbanks's economic history as well as its geographical location. Surrounded by wilderness, it lies between the rugged Alaska and Brooks mountain ranges and serves as the hub of the Interior. Here the Parks and Richardson highways end and several bush commuter air services base their operations. But Fairbanks got its start as a gold-mining town in 1901, and that is what is celebrated by its residents. Many of the old homes and commercial buildings trace their history to the early days of the city, especially in the older downtown area, with its narrow, winding streets following the contours of the Chena River.

❶ The **Fairbanks Convention and Visitors Bureau** (☞ Visitor Information *in* Interior A to Z, *below*), on the river at the Cushman Street Bridge, provides a map for a self-guided 1½-hour walking tour through the historic downtown area. The bureau also has maps for a two-hour do-it-yourself driving tour. Points of interest on the tours include **Golden Heart Park,** home of the *Unknown First Family* statue; the **Clay Street Cemetery,** with its marked and unmarked graves of early pioneers; the **Empress Theater,** the first cement structure in Interior Alaska; the stately **Falcon Joslin Home,** the oldest frame house in Fairbanks still at its original location; **The Line,** home of the red-light district until the mid-1950s; **Odd Fellows Hall,** a bathhouse for gold miners until the pipes froze in the winter of 1910–11; and the historic **Immaculate Conception Church,** which was raised off its foundation in 1911 and rolled across the frozen Chena River on logs pulled by horses.

❷ The **Fairbanks Ice Museum** gives visitors a taste of the ice carvings that help decorate Fairbanks in winter, especially the Ice Art competition held in March. The prime attraction of the museum is the Ice Showcase, a large glass-walled display kept at 20°F. The chilly environment allows ice sculptors to demonstrate their skills and sculptures throughout the summer. The museum is in the historic Lacey Street Theater, on the corner of 2nd Avenue and Lacey Street. ⊠ *500 2nd Ave.,* ☎ *907/451–8222,* ℻ *907/456–1951.* ☜ *$6.* ☉ *Late May–mid-Oct., daily 10–9.*

❸ The new **Fairbanks Exploration Industrial Complex** shows visitors just how much work went into building equipment like the gold dredges, steam shovels, and other apparatus so necessary for moving vast amounts of soil so the miners could reach pay dirt. The complex, which is on the National Registry of Historic Sites, is the latest mining-related attraction restored by Big John Reeves, whose previous efforts had been directed at *Gold Dredge Number 8* (☞ *below*). The machine shop still manufactures gold pans of copper, brass, and steel. Along with tours of the complex, you'll receive a small gold pan and can watch a video that shows the history of the place and its importance to gold mining in the Interior. ⊠ *612 Illinois St.,* ☎ *907/452–6058.* ☜ *$10.* ☉ *May 15–Sept. 15, daily 9–6.*

Imagine a giant gold dredge literally making its own waterway as it chews through the gold pay dirt, crawling along at a snail's pace and processing tons of rock and gravel. Built by Bethlehem Shipbuilders in 1928, the dredge was operated by the Fairbanks Exploration Company until its retirement in 1959. The five-deck ship is more than 250 ft long and took millions of dollars' worth of gold out of the Goldstream and Engineer creeks north of Fairbanks. **Gold Dredge Number 8** has been ❹ declared a National Historic District by the National Park Service, one of the few privately owned districts in the nation. This unique mining vessel came to rest at Mile 9, Old Steese Highway, where she was lovingly restored by Big John Reeves and his wife, Ramona, who have collected many other mining artifacts and brought them to the grounds. The price of admission entitles visitors to the necessary tools, some gold-panning instructions, and a chance to find "colors" at the sluice or to independently seek gold in old tailings from the mining days. A sit-down, family-style miner's pot-roast stew is served from 11 AM to 3 PM for $8. Recently purchased by Holland America, the dredge is a

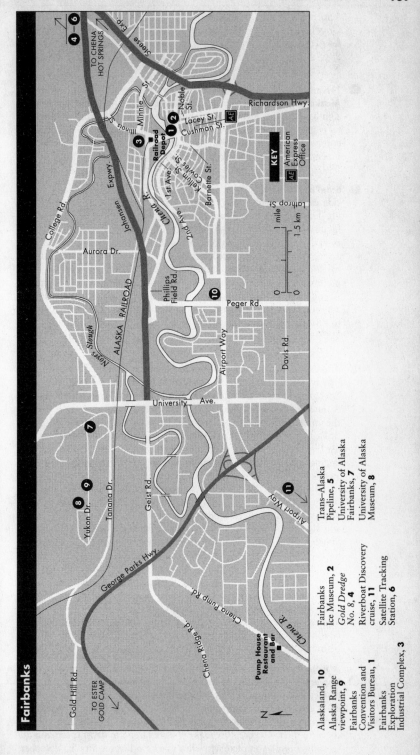

Fairbanks

KEY
AE American Express Office

Railroad Depot

TO CHENA HOT SPRINGS

Richardson Hwy.

Steese Expy.

Noble St.
Minnie St.
Illinois St.
Lacey St.
Cushman St.
Kellum St.
Cowles St.
1st Ave.
2nd Ave.
Barnette St.
Lathrop St.

College Rd.
Johansen Expwy.
Aurora Dr.
Chena R.
ALASKA RAILROAD
Noyes Slough
Phillips Field Rd.
Peger Rd.
Airport Way
Davis Rd.
University Ave.
Geist Rd.
Tanana Dr.
Yukon Dr.
George Parks Hwy.
Chena Pump Rd.
Chena Ridge Rd.
Gold Hill Rd.
Chena R.

TO ESTER GOLD CAMP

Pump House Restaurant and Bar

N

0   1 mile
0   1.5 km

Alaskaland, **10**
Alaska Range
viewpoint, **9**
Fairbanks
Convention and
Visitors Bureau, **1**
Fairbanks
Exploration
Industrial Complex, **3**

Fairbanks
Ice Museum, **2**
*Gold Dredge
No. 8*, **4**
Riverboat Discovery
cruise, **11**
Satellite Tracking
Station, **6**

Trans-Alaska
Pipeline, **5**
University of Alaska
Fairbanks, **7**
University of Alaska
Museum, **8**

featured stop on all of the Fairbanks city tours offered by the firm's Gray Line of Alaska. The four-hour tour price of $57 includes the entry fee to the dredge and the miner's stew. ⊠ *Gold Dredge Number 8, Mile 9, Old Steese Hwy.,* ☎ *907/456–7741 or 907/452–3646.* ⊠ *$19.50.* ☉ *May–Sept., daily 9–6.*

❺ Just north of Fairbanks visitors can see and touch the famous **trans-Alaska pipeline.** The parking lot, just off the Steese Highway, has a sign loaded with information about the pipeline. A small visitor center is staffed by informative guides and has a small gift shop with pipeline company memorabilia. Although the center is closed in winter, the pipeline is accessible year-round. ⊠ *Mile 7.5, Steese Hwy.,* ☎ *907/456–9391,* ⅎ⅄ *907/456–9392.* ⊠ *Free.* ☉ *Mid-May–Sept., daily 8–5.*

❻ **Satellite Tracking Station.** Weather and technology buffs can get an inside view of the National Oceanic Atmospheric Administration Satellite Tracking Station, on the Steese Highway north of Fairbanks. The facility has huge satellite dishes (including two that are 85 ft in diameter) that receive information from satellites orbiting hundreds of miles above the Earth. Equipment at the station turns that electronic information into video images of the Earth's surface. The front hall features pictures of the Gulf Stream flowing along the Atlantic Coast up to the Arctic Ocean. Tour guides only work during the summer, but special arrangements can be made. Postcards of the station are provided free to visitors. ⊠ *Mile 13.5, Steese Hwy., 1300 Eisele Rd.,* ☎ *907/451–1200,* ⅎ⅄ *907/451–1209.* ⊠ *Free.* ☉ *June–Aug., weekdays 8–4:30, Sat. 9–3.*

❼ The **University of Alaska Fairbanks** has an international reputation for its Arctic research, including a study of the aurora borealis, or northern lights. Tours of the following campus facilities are offered: the **Large Animal Research Station** (⊠ Yankovitch Rd., off Ballaine Rd. behind the university), which houses caribou, musk ox, and reindeer; the **Arctic Region Supercomputing Center** (Butrovitch Bldg.), where researchers use high-performance supercomputers to solve problems in science and engineering for the high latitudes and the Arctic; the **Geophysical Institute** (⊠ West Ridge, about 1 mi from the center of campus), a center of atmospheric and earthquake research; the **Poker Flat Research Range** (⊠ Steese Hwy., 33 mi northeast of Fairbanks), where the university launches rockets studying the aurora borealis; and the **Georgeson Botanical Garden of the Agricultural and Forestry Experiment Station Farm** (⊠ West end of the campus), where researchers study Interior Alaska's unique, short, but intense, midnight-sun growing season. A 2-mi, two-hour guided walking tour of the campus is also offered (if you prefer, guide yourself by picking up a campus map at the Office of University Relations). ⊠ *University of Alaska, Office of University Relations, 202 Eielson Building,* ☎ *907/474–7581.* ☉ *Tour schedule varies; call for details or inquire at the Fairbanks Convention and Visitor Center (☞ Visitor Information in Interior A to Z, below).*

★ ❽ A stuffed grizzly bear—8 ft, 9 inches tall—guards the entrance to the **University of Alaska Museum,** a history and natural sciences collection divided into five Alaska regions: Southeast, Interior, South Central, Southwest, and the Western Arctic Coast. A featured artifact is Blue Babe, a mummified steppe bison that lived 38,000 years ago during the Pleistocene epoch. The creature was preserved in permafrost (permanently frozen ground), complete with claw marks indicating attack by a saber-toothed tiger. The bison's remains were found by gold miners in 1979. For every "don't touch" exhibit, the museum features a "please touch" item, including the molars of a mammoth and a mastodon, a gray whale skull, and a 5,495-pound copper nugget. The museum has two summer shows, one on the northern lights and one on the events of the World Eskimo Indian Olympics. ⌧ *907 Yukon Dr., West Ridge, University of Alaska campus,* ☎ *907/474–7505,* FAX *907/474–5469.* ☞ *$5.* ☉ *June–Aug., daily 9–7; May and Sept., daily 9–5; Oct.–May, weekdays 9–5, weekends noon–5.*

The Interior offers many mountain vistas in the Alaska Range to the south. The most accessible viewpoint in Fairbanks is on the West Ridge of the University of Alaska Fairbanks campus on Yukon Drive. (Look for the parking area just east of the University of Alaska Museum.) At the **Alaska Range viewpoint,** the entire north side of the range is visible. Many of the Alaska Range panoramas seen in magazines and travel brochures are photographed from this point. It also is a favorite spot for time-lapse photography of the midwinter sun just peeking over the southern horizon on a low arc. Nearly always distinguishable on a clear day are three major peaks, called the Three Sisters because they appear quite similar to one another. They are, from your left: **Mt. Hayes,** 13,832 ft; **Mt. Hess,** 11,940 ft; and **Mt. Deborah,** 12,339 ft. Much farther to the right, toward the southwest, lies **Mt. McKinley,** the highest peak in North America. On some seemingly clear days it's not visible at all. At other times the base is easy to see but the peak is cloud-covered. Often when Mt. McKinley is entirely visible, **Mt. Foraker,** the second-highest peak in the Alaska Range, also can be seen. It appears as a small pyramid just to the right of the base of Mt. McKinley. It seems small because it is 75 mi farther away than Mt. McKinley.

★ ☾ ⑩ **Alaskaland,** a 44-acre park set along the Chena River near downtown Fairbanks, has several museums, a theater, an art gallery, a civic center, a native village, a large children's playground, a miniature golf course, an antique merry-go-round, restaurants, and a Gold Rush town consisting of historic buildings saved from urban renewal. The complex has log-cabin gift shops and **Mining Valley,** an outdoor museum of mining artifacts situated around an indoor-outdoor salmon-bake restaurant (☞ Dining and Lodging, *below*). Then there is the restored *Denali,* a plush railcar in which President Warren Harding traveled when he came north in 1923 to hammer the golden spike on the Alaska Railroad. Also restored is the 227-ft stern-wheeler *Nenana,* the second-largest wooden vessel in existence. A national historic landmark, the *Nenana* was built by the railroad in 1933 to serve the rivers of Interior Alaska. Inside is a diorama of the course the riverboat took on the Yukon and Tanana rivers around the turn of the century. The **Crooked Creek and Whiskey Island Railroad,** a small-gauge train, circles the park. No-frills RV camping is available for $9 a night in the west end of the large parking lot on Airport Way. ⌧ *Alaskaland Park, Airport Way and Peger Rd.,* ☎ *907/459–1087,* FAX *907/459–1199.* ☞ *Free.* ☉ *Daily 11–9.*

★ ☾ ⑪ The excitement and color of the city's riverboat history and the Interior's cultural heritage are relived each summer aboard the popular **Riverboat Discovery cruise,** a four-hour narrated trip by stern-wheeler along the Chena and Tanana rivers to a rustic Native village setting on the Tanana. The cruise offers a glimpse of the lifestyle of the dog mushers, subsistence fishermen, traders, and Native Alaskans who populate the Yukon River drainage. Sights along the way include operating fish wheels, a bush airfield, floatplanes, a smokehouse and cache, log cabins, and Iditarod champion Susan Butcher's dog kennels. Captain Jim Binkley, his wife, Mary, and their children have operated the Discovery cruises for nearly 50 years. Their family, with its four generations of river pilots, has run great rivers of the north for more than 100 years. ⌧ *Alaska Riverways, Dale Rd. Landing, near Fairbanks*

International Airport, ☎ *907/479–6673.* 🖃 *$39.95.* ☉ *Mid-May–mid-Sept., cruises daily, 8:45* AM *and 2* PM.

Dining and Lodging

$$–$$$$ ✕ **Ivory Jack's.** Jack "Ivory" O'Brien used to deal in Alaskan ivory
★ and whalebone out of this small restaurant tucked into the gold-rich hills of the Goldstream Valley on the outskirts of Fairbanks. Now it's a favorite spot in which to eat delectable steaks and seafood—or to try its specialty of reindeer in cranberry sauce, which is available as an appetizer or an entrée. ⊠ *2581 Goldstream Rd.,* ☎ *907/455–6665 or 907/455–6666. AE, DC, MC, V. Closed Mon. No lunch.*

$$–$$$$ ✕ **Pike's Landing.** Enjoy lunch on a huge outside deck (it seats 420) overlooking the Chena River, or dine inside in the elegant dining room of an extended log cabin. The meals are expensive, up to $55 for steak and crab legs, but excellent. For a less expensive dinner, something in the $10 range, relax in the sports bar and catch a view of the river. Lunch, dinner, and Sunday brunch are served. ⊠ *4438 Airport Way,* ☎ *907/479–7113. AE, D, DC, MC, V.*

$–$$$ ✕ **Don Pilos Mexican Restaurant.** Delicious homemade Mexican food served in abundant proportions makes this arguably the best Mexican restaurant in the Alaskan Interior. House specials include crab enchiladas and *barbacoa* (steam-cooked beef cheeks served on flour or corn tortillas). ⊠ *206 Eagle St.,* ☎ *907/457–7456. MC, V.*

$$ ✕ **Alaska Salmon Bake.** This indoor-outdoor restaurant in Alaskaland's Mining Valley (☞ *above*) serves mouthwatering salmon cooked over an open fire with a special lemon and brown sugar sauce. Also available at the all-you-can-eat dinner buffet are halibut, barbecued beef ribs, and 19-ounce porterhouse steaks, an all-you-can-eat salad bar, and homemade blueberry cake. ⊠ *Airport Way and Peger Rd.,* ☎ *907/452–7274 or 800/354–7274.* ☉ *Open for dinner mid-May–mid-Sept., 5–9* PM. *Lunch is served mid-June–mid-Aug., noon–2.*

$$ ✕ **Gambardella's Pasta Bella.** Known simply as Gambardella's, this family-run Italian restaurant is a favorite among locals and is centrally located at the edge of downtown. The place is small but cozy, with covered outside seating in the summer. Delicious offerings include salads, pasta, pizza, and submarine sandwiches on homemade bread. Its specialty, however, is lasagna, which the *Seattle Times* recently described as "the lasagna of all lasagnas." On special order you can get its clam pizza. There are several vegetarian entrées. ⊠ *706 2nd Ave.,* ☎ *907/456–3417,* 🖷 *907/456–3425. AE, MC, V. No lunch Sun.*

$$ ✕ **Pump House Restaurant.** This mining pump-station turned restau-
★ rant built alongside the Chena River serves American and specifically Alaskan seafood dishes. You can't go wrong with its house specialties of seafood chowder and Alaskan caribou stew. Just stepping into the restaurant is a treat. The furnishings and floor are rich, polished wood. A huge Alaskan brown bear in a glass case is on sentry next to the hostess station. Bill and Vivian Bubbel, who in the late 1980s made the restaurant a Fairbanks favorite, purchased the Pump House in January 1996 and brought in a new chef to keep the restaurant a top choice of Interior residents and visitors. A spacious deck offers riverside dining. ⊠ *Mile 1.3, Chena Pump Rd.,* ☎ *907/479–8452. AE, MC, V. No lunch Oct.–Mar.*

$–$$ ✕ **Raven's Nest.** On the menu are grilled steak, halibut, and salmon—and there's a bird's-eye view of downtown Fairbanks from the top of the 12-story Northern Lights Hotel as well. ⊠ *427 1st Ave.,* ☎ *907/452–1484. AE, DC, MC, V.*

$$$$ 🏨 **Comfort Inn–Chena River.** Situated on a wooded bank of the Chena River directly across the water from Alaskaland, this Comfort Inn opened in May 1996. It boasts a full-length, glass-enclosed indoor pool with

a spa. The rooms have televisions equipped with free cable programming, including HBO, and some rooms have small refrigerators, and microwaves; 60% are smoke-free. The room rate includes free local telephone calls and a Continental breakfast. ⊠ *1908 Chena Landings Loop, 99701,* ☎ *907/479–8080 or 800/201–9199,* FAX *907/479–8063. 74 rooms. No-smoking rooms, refrigerators, airport shuttle. AE, D, DC, MC, V.*

$$$$ ⊞ **Fairbanks Princess Hotel.** The newest luxury hotel in Fairbanks, the
★ Princess has a beautiful setting on the banks of the Chena River just off the road to Fairbanks International Airport. The mauve and green decor is highlighted by wooden floors and polished birch trim. Its Edgewater Restaurant features a popular Sunday brunch. Diners in suits and evening gowns or duct tape–patched Carhartts work clothes are equally welcome. The expansive wooden deck, which is encircled by manicured lawns and faces a lovely section of the Chena River, attracts a crowd in summer. It's a favorite spot for an enjoyable lunch or for spending a lazy evening watching water-skiers and the occasional floatplane landing. ⊠ *4477 Pikes Landing Rd., 99709,* ☎ *907/455–4477 or 800/426–0500,* FAX *907/455–4476. 200 rooms. 2 restaurants, bar, steam room, health club, meeting rooms, airport shuttle. AE, DC, MC, V.*

$$$$ ⊞ **Northern Lights Hotel.** This completely remodeled hotel is within a quick walk of the downtown Visitor Information Center. Some of the rooms offer views of the Chena River and the hills beyond. ⊠ *427 1st Ave., 99701,* ☎ *907/452–4456, 800/235–6546 or 888/563–0055,* FAX *907/456–2696. 134 rooms. Restaurant, bar, airport shuttle. AE, D, DC, MC, V.*

$$$$ ⊞ **Regency Fairbanks Hotel.** In a large building near downtown, this hotel has a lobby with Victorian-style decor and large, modern rooms. The bathrooms have deep bathtubs, tasteful wall hangings, and bricklike tile. Some rooms include kitchenettes with a full-size refrigerator, range, and microwave. Third-floor rooms have whirlpool baths. ⊠ *95 10th Ave., 99701,* ☎ *907/452–3200, 800/348–1349 from outside Alaska, 800/478–1320 in Alaska,* FAX *907/452–6505. 130 rooms, 9 suites. Restaurant, bar, kitchenettes, coin laundry, laundry service, airport shuttle. AE, DC, MC, V.*

$$$$ ⊞ **Sophie Station Hotel.** This spacious hotel near the airport is one of
★ the best in Fairbanks, thanks to its quiet location, helpful staff, and pleasant pastel decor. All rooms are suites with kitchens that feature a full-size range and refrigerator. The furniture is comfortable, with rich velvetlike upholstery. Its restaurant, Zach's, offers breakfast, lunch, and dinner, with specialties like buffalo burgers or all-you-can-eat crab for $25.95. ⊠ *1717 University Ave., 99709,* ☎ *907/479–3650 or 800/528–4916,* FAX *907/479–7951. 147 suites. Restaurant, bar, kitchenettes, airport shuttle. AE, D, DC, MC, V.*

$$$$ ⊞ **The Villages.** Though close to downtown, this new establishment is tucked away in a wooded area. Studios and one-, two-, and three-bedroom suites are available. The full kitchens have dining tables that seat four, and the sitting rooms feature living room–size sofas, comfortable easy chairs and 25-inch stereo monitors. The dark burgundy carpeting adds warmth to some of the rooms, which seem bright because of the off-white wallpaper. All the suites come with 19-inch portable television sets equipped with VCRs and full cable programming, including free HBO and Showtime channels. ⊠ *205 Palace Circle, 99701,* ☎ *907/456–7612 or 800/770–7612,* FAX *907/456–8358. 30 rooms. Kitchenettes, laundry service. AE, D, DC, MC, V.*

$$$$ ⊞ **Westmark Fairbanks.** This full-service hotel, close to downtown, is built around a courtyard on a quiet street. All rooms have a rose-and-burgundy motif and a writing desk; some have a StairMaster or stationary bike. The hotel underwent a $4.5-million renovation in 1998,

adding a new conference center, a new entrance and lobby, and several new rooms. Each room now has a voice mail system, and there's a new bar and grill, the Bear 'n Seal. ⊠ *813 Noble St., 99701,* ☎ *907/456–7722 or 800/544–0970,* FAX *907/451–7478. 237 rooms. 2 restaurants, bar, laundry service, airport shuttle. AE, D, DC, MC, V.*

$$ 🏠 **Alaskan Iris B&B.** Just a 20-minute drive from downtown Fairbanks, the Alaskan Iris is a beautifully kept home set in the wooded wilderness of the Alaskan Interior. The grounds include a garden and greenhouse surrounded by trees, and the cozy guest rooms are decorated with elegant Alaskan country furnishings. A full, multicourse breakfast is included in the price of the room. ⊠ *751 Nordale Rd., 99711,* ☎ *907/488–2308 or 800/464–7262. 3 rooms with shared bath. Laundry room. AE, MC, V.*

$$ 🏠 **Cranberry Ridge B&B.** From the hills north of Fairbanks off Farmers Loop Road, guests at this small B&B can enjoy magnificent views of the Alaska Range, sometimes even catching a glimpse of Mt. McKinley. The two rooms available to visitors share a bath and a large sitting and family area and can be taken together as a suite. A separate downstairs entrance for the guest rooms affords privacy. Each morning visitors can expect fresh baked pastries (possibly peach cobbler, a specialty of the house) in addition to a large fruit tray and coffee. The proprietors, Mike and Floss Caskey, a fifth-generation Alaskan family, drew the plans and built the home themselves. Caskey offers flightseeing tours in his Cessna 185; he can take up to three passengers for a charter rate of $250 an hour. ⊠ *705 Cranberry Ridge Dr., 99712,* ☎ *907/457–4424. 2 rooms with shared bath. AE, D, DC, MC, V.*

$ 🏠 **Birch Grove Inn.** This bed-and-breakfast located in a stand of tall birch trees above Farmers Loop Road has an extra-large room with its own private deck overlooking the wooded hills north of Fairbanks, and two smaller rooms with garden views. The rooms have shared baths. Breakfasts are full-size; the inn's specialty is sourdough blueberry pancakes served with reindeer sausage. The inn is close to the Farmers Loop bike and cross-country ski trail that leads to the University of Alaska Fairbanks campus, 2 mi away. Gold-panning equipment and fishing poles can be borrowed. ⊠ *691 DePauw Dr., 99708,* ☎ *907/479–5781 or 800/478–5781 in Alaska. 3 rooms with shared bath. D, MC, V.*

Guided Tours

CanoeAlaska (⊠ Mile 1, Chena Small Tracts Rd., Box 81750, 99708, ☎ 907/479–5183, FAX 907/479-5383) has been offering guided canoe trips on several Interior Alaska rivers for 20 years. Trips begin in mid-May and continue through Labor Day. They range from two to seven days on rivers that vary in difficulty and remoteness. CanoeAlaska also offers weekend instructional clinics for the inexperienced.

Northern Alaska Tour Company–Arctic Circle Adventure (⊠ Box 82991, Fairbanks 99708, ☎ 907/474–8600, FAX 907/474–4767) offers half- and full-day bus trips to the Arctic Circle and Yukon River, and two- and three-day fly-drive tours to Prudhoe Bay and Barrow. The company caters to the independent traveler. Those who cross the Arctic Circle with the firm receive an Arctic Circle Adventure Certificate.

Wynfromere Farms Trail Rides (☎ 907/457–7902) will put you on horseback and take you to see the pipeline.

Nightlife and the Arts

Fairbanks supports a year-round arts program that would be the envy of many larger communities. Summer visitors to Fairbanks will find that the lack of a true "night"—thanks to the midnight sun—doesn't seem to hinder nightlife at all. Check the Kaleidoscope section in the

Thursday *Fairbanks Daily News–Miner* for current nightspots, plays, concerts, and art shows.

ARTS FESTIVAL

The **Fairbanks Summer Arts Festival** has grown from a small jazz festival for adults to a major University of Alaska Fairbanks–affiliated annual event attracting students worldwide. Spread over two weeks in late July and early August, the festival offers music, dance, theater, opera, ice-skating, and visual-arts instruction. Dozens of noted guest artists attend to perform and to present workshops. ⊠ *Box 80845, Fairbanks 99708,* ☎ *907/474–8869,* FAX *907/479–4329.*

CABARET THEATER

For an evening of varied and high-quality entertainment head to **Ester Gold Camp,** a former gold-mining town about 6 mi south of Fairbanks reached via the Parks Highway. Its 11 historical structures date to the early 1900s and include the rustic **Malemute Saloon,** which is open daily from 2 PM to midnight. The camp, which is on the National Register of Historic Places, comes alive at night with a show in the saloon featuring Gold Rush–era songs and stories and Robert Service poetry, a beautiful northern lights photography show in the **Firehouse Theatre,** and a dinner buffet offering crab, halibut, and reindeer stew in yet another building. Plan your evening to catch dinner and all the shows. The camp has a hotel with semiprivate bathrooms, RV parking, a gift shop, and complimentary evening bus service to and from Fairbanks. ⊠ *3175 College Rd., No. 1, Ester 99709-3703,* ☎ *907/479–2500 or 800/676–6925,* FAX *907/474–1780.* ▣ *Saloon show $12, photography show $6.* ☼ *Late May–early Sept.*

The **Palace Theatre and Saloon** at Alaskaland (☎ 907/456–5960 or 800/354–7274) is one of the livelier summer spots. The Palace's *Golden Heart Revue,* a musical-comedy show about the founding and building of Fairbanks, begins at 8:15 nightly. A later performance, *Into the Bush,* which pokes fun at the Alaskan lifestyle, is offered at 10 PM from mid-May to mid-September. ▣ *$12.*

SALOONS

A favorite watering hole among miners, truckers, university students, homesteaders, ex-hippies, and the younger set is the **Howling Dog Saloon** (⊠ 2160 Old Steese Hwy., ☎ 907/457–8780), in Fox, 11 mi north of Fairbanks. Be ready for a big crowd and loud, authentic rock and roll. All-night volleyball games out back are part of the ambience of the Dog, which also serves up pizza. But don't head to the Dog in the winter, as it hibernates after Halloween. However, the **Blue Loon Saloon** (☎ 907/457–5666), at Mile 353.5, Parks Highway, between Ester and Fairbanks, offers year-round rock and roll and folk music and sells a variety of microbrews to complement its pizza and snacks. The Blue Loon also has two volleyball courts, a campfire area outside, and RV parking. The **Senator's Saloon** at the **Pump House Restaurant** (☎ 907/479–8452) is the place for easy-listening music alongside the Chena River on a warm summer evening.

SQUARE DANCING

There are square-dancing clubs in Fairbanks, North Pole, Delta Junction, and Tok. The groups are affiliated with the **Alaskaland Dance Center** (☎ 907/452–5699), which holds frequent dances where visitors are welcome. Call for current dance schedules.

Outdoor Activities and Sports

BASEBALL

Scores of baseball players, including Tom Seaver, have passed through Fairbanks on their way to the major leagues. The Interior city is home to the **Alaska Goldpanners** (☎ 907/451–0095), a member of the Alaska League, a string of semiprofessional baseball organizations throughout the state. Players are recruited from college teams nationwide, and the summer season (late June–early August) generates top-caliber competition. Home games are played at **Growden Field,** along Lower 2nd Avenue at Wilbur Street, not far from Alaskaland. This baseball park is the home of the traditional **Midnight Sun Baseball Game,** in which the Goldpanners play baseball at midnight of the summer solstice without benefit of artificial lights. This is thrilling (and possibly chilly—bring a thermos of something hot) to watch on a clear, sunny evening when the daylight never ends.

BICYCLING

Bicyclists in Fairbanks have paved paths from the University of Alaska campus around Farmers Loop to the Steese Highway. Another path follows Geist and Chena Pump roads into downtown Fairbanks. A shorter, less strenuous route is via the bike path between downtown and Alaskaland along the south side of the Chena River. Maps showing all the bike paths are available at the **Fairbanks Convention and Visitors Bureau** (☞ Visitor Information *in* Interior A to Z, *below*). Mountain bikers can test their skills during the summer on the ski trails of the University of Alaska Fairbanks and the Birch Hill Recreation Area, or on many of the trails and dirt roads around Fairbanks. The **Alaska Public Lands Information Center** (☞ Visitor Information *in* Interior A to Z, *below*) is a good resource for mountain biking.

BOATING

For relaxing boating in or near Fairbanks, use Chena River access points at Nordale Road east of the city, at the Cushman and Wendell Street bridges near downtown, at Alaskaland park above the Peger River Bridge, at the state campground, and at the University Avenue Bridge.

The Tanana is riverboat country. On this river and others in the Yukon River drainage, Alaskans use long, wide flat-bottom boats powered by one or two large outboard engines. The boats include a lift to raise the engine a few inches, allowing passage through the shallows, and some of the engines are equipped with a jet unit instead of a propeller to allow more bottom clearance. Arrangements for riverboat charters can be made in almost any river community. Ask at the Fairbanks Convention and Visitors Bureau (☞ Visitor Information *in* Interior A to Z, *below*).

CURLING

Hundreds of Fairbanksans participate each year in curling, an odd game in which people with brooms play a giant version of shuffleboard on ice. This ancient Scottish game was brought to Alaska and the Yukon during the Klondike Gold Rush. Visitors are welcome at the **Fairbanks Curling Club** (⊠ 1962 2nd Ave., 99701, ☎ 907/452–2875), which hosts an annual international bonspiel (match) on the first weekend of April.

FISHING

Although a few fish can be caught right in town from the Chena River, avid fishermen can find outstanding angling by hopping a plane or riverboat. Popular fishing trips include air charters to **Lake Minchumina** (an hour's flight from Fairbanks), known for good pike fishing and a rare view of the north sides of Mt. McKinley and Mt. Foraker.

Another popular charter trip by riverboat or floatplane will take you pike fishing in the **Minto Flats,** west of Fairbanks off the Tanana River, where the mouth of the Chatanika River spreads through miles of marsh and sloughs.

Salmon run up the **Tanana River,** too, most of the summer, but they're not usually caught on hook-and-line gear. Residents take them from the Tanana with gill nets and fish wheels, using special commercial and subsistence permits. For more information on fishing, *see* Pleasures and Pastimes *in* Chapter 1. For a list of operators offering fishing trips, *see* Tour Operators *in* the Gold Guide, *and* Guided Tours *in* Chapter 3. Also check the Outdoors section in the Friday *Fairbanks Daily News–Miner* newspaper for weekly updates on fishing in the Interior.

GOLD PANNING

There are several places where you can pan for gold without fear of jumping a claim. **Alaska Prospectors** (⊠ 504 College Rd., ☎ 907/452–7398) is the oldest mining and prospecting supply store in the Alaskan Interior. In addition to a collection of rocks and minerals, they sell gold pans, and books and videos on mining. They can offer lots of valuable advice for the neophyte gold bug, so don't be put off by the store's outward appearance—once you get inside, you'll find enough interesting material to keep you occupied for hours. **El Dorado Gold Mine** (⊠ Mile 1.3, Elliott Hwy., ☎ 907/479–7613) offers tours of a seasonal mining operation, which include a ride on a narrow-gauge railroad. Also try the **Chatanika Gold Camp** (⊠ Mile 27.9, Steese Hwy., ☎ 907/389–2414), formerly the Old F. E. Gold Camp. **Gold Dredge Number 8** (⊠ 1755 Old Steese Hwy. N., ☎ 907/457–6058, FAX 907/457–8888) is another option.

GOLF

Golfers have three choices: **Chena Bend** (☎ 907/353–6223), an army course open to civilians, is an 18-hole spread on nearby Ft. Wainwright. This beautiful little course was recently renovated to the tune of $3.5 million. The nine-hole course at the **Fairbanks Golf and Country Club** (☎ 907/479–6555) straddles Farmers Loop just north of the university. The nine-hole course at the **North Star Golf Club** (☎ 907/457–4653, FAX 907/457–3945) is off the Old Steese Highway just past Chena Hot Springs Road.

HIKING

On the edge of Fairbanks is the 1,800-acre **Creamer's Field Migratory Waterfowl Refuge** (⊠ 1300 College Rd., 99701, ☎ 907/459–7307 or 907/459-7301), which has three nature trails; the longest is 2 mi, and one is accessible for people who use wheelchairs. The barns and buildings are still standing and the farmhouse is now a nature/visitor center. It is a great place to view historic buildings, waterfowl, cranes, songbirds, and moose, and to learn about the history of Fairbanks. Creamer's Dairy, from 1910 to 1966 the farthest-north dairy in North America and now on the National Register of Historic Places, is also here.

HOCKEY

During the winter, the **Gold Kings** professional hockey team (☎ 907/456–7825) hosts teams from other states and one from Russia. At the nearby University of Alaska Fairbanks, the **Nanooks** (☎ 907/474–6868) play NCAA Division I hockey.

MUSHING

Dog mushing is one of the top winter draws. From November to March, there is a constant string of sled-dog races throughout the region, culminating in the **North American Open Sled-Dog Championship,** which attracts international competition to Fairbanks. Throughout Alaska, sprint races, freight hauling, and long-distance endurance runs are held in late February and March, that popular Alaska season when the winter's snow remains but there's more daylight in which to enjoy it. Men and women often compete in the same classes in the major races. For children, there are various racing classes based on age, starting with the one-dog category for the youngest. In Fairbanks many of the sprint races are organized by the **Alaska Dog Mushers Association** (☎ 907/457–6874), one of the oldest organizations of its kind in the Arctic, at its **Jeff Studdert Sled Dog Racegrounds** at Mile 4, Farmers Loop. The **Yukon Quest International** is an endurance race covering more than 1,000 mi between Fairbanks and Whitehorse, Yukon Territory, via Dawson and the Yukon River. It's held in February; you can get more details from the visitor centers in either city or by calling the Yukon Quest office (☎ 907/452–7954) in Fairbanks.

At **Tivi Haus** (✉ Mile 2, Kallenberg Rd., off Cripple Creek Rd. at Mile 349, Parks Hwy.; call first for directions, ☎ 907/474–8702, ℻ 907/479–7601), learn about the official state sport from a family of dog mushers who offer dinner and then a ride with the dogs. In summer (mid-June–Labor Day) ride on the dog-powered Arfmobile. In winter (Dec.–Mar.), take a dogsled ride and possibly see the northern lights. Overnight lodging and cross-country skiing are also available.

RIVERBOAT RACING

Another summer highlight is riverboat racing sanctioned by the **Fairbanks Outboard Association.** These specially built 22-ft racing boats are powered by 60-horsepower engines and reach speeds of 70 mi per hour. Weekend races throughout the summer and fall begin and end either at the Pump House Restaurant, on Chena Pump Road, or at Pike's Landing, just off Airport Way near Fairbanks International Airport. The season's big event in late June is the **Yukon 800 Marathon,** a two-day, 800-mi race between Fairbanks and Galena by way of the Chena, Tanana, and Yukon rivers. The **Roland Lord Memorial Race,** from Fairbanks to Nenana and back, is held in early August.

RUNNING

Two of Fairbanks' most popular runs are the **Midnight Sun Run** each June on the weekend nearest the summer solstice and the September **Equinox Marathon,** a tough run up and down the large Ester Dome, northwest of the city. Check with local sporting goods stores for race schedules.

SKIING

The Interior has some of the best weather and terrain in the nation for **cross-country skiing,** especially during the late fall and early spring. Among the developed trails in the Fairbanks area, the ones at the **Birch Hill Recreation Area,** on the city's north side, and the **University of Alaska Fairbanks** are lighted to extend their use into the winter nights. Cross-country ski racing is a staple at several courses on winter weekends. The season stretches from October to late March or early April. Other developed trails can be found at **Chena Hot Springs Resort, White Mountain National Recreation Area,** the **Chena Lakes Recreation Area,** and the **Two Rivers Recreation Area.** For more information check with the **Alaska Public Lands Information Center** (☞ Visitor Information *in* Interior A to Z, *below*).

For **downhill skiing,** Mt. Aurora/Skiland (☎ 907/456–7669), with a chairlift and 1,100-ft vertical drop, on the Steese Highway about 20 mi from Fairbanks at Cleary Summit, is open weekends in the winter. **Moose Mountain** (☎ 907/479–8362), off Murphy Dome Road, has beginner, intermediate, and a few advanced slopes; open November–April, Thursday–Sunday. **Birch Hill** (☎ 907/353–7053), in Ft. Wainwright, open November–April, Thursday–Sunday, has a chairlift and beginner and intermediate runs.

Shopping

CRAFTS

The **Arctic Travelers Gift Shop** (⊠ 201 Cushman St., ☎ 907/456–7080) has a terrific selection of Athabascan beadwork. **Beads and Things** (⊠ 537 2nd Ave., ☎ 907/456–2323) sells native handicrafts from around the state. The **Great Alaskan Bowl Company** (⊠ 4630 Old Airport Rd., ☎ 907/474–9663) sells bowls machine-carved out of Alaskan trees.

FUR

The **Fur Factory** (⊠ 121 Dunkel St., ☎ 907/452–6240) sells 250 different items, such as mukluks, hats, and coats made from a variety of wild animal furs, including fox, mink, beaver, wolf, and sheep. **Gerald Victor Furs** (⊠ 100 Barnette St., ☎ 907/456–3877) has a large selection of fur garments, including headbands, earmuffs, hats, coats, and items that reverse to fabric or leather.

JEWELRY

In her small eponymous shop **Judie Gumm Designs** (⊠ 3600 Main St., Ester, ☎ 907/479–4568), Ms. Gumm fashions stunning silver and gold designs drawn from Alaska's favorite plants and wildlife. She has silver and gold caribou, Dall sheep, and bears, as well as earrings, bracelets, and pins that mimic the lines of high bush and low bush cranberries, blueberries, and wild roses. For precious stones, she frequently uses Alaskan garnet or jade. Ester is 5 mi west of Fairbanks off the George Parks Highway.

OUTERWEAR AND OUTDOOR GEAR

All Weather Sports (⊠ 4001 Geist Rd., No. 12, ☎ 907/474–8184) Simon Rakower, the owner of this Far North bike shop, invented the double-wide mountain bike rim—the Snow-Cat—so that competitors in IditaSport, a mountain bike, snowshoe, and ski version of the Iditarod Trail Sled Dog Race, would be able to pedal their bikes on snow-packed trails. His shop offers a full line of extra-wide rim wheels, studded bicycle tires, and other items hard to find anywhere else.

Apocalypse Design (⊠ 101 College Rd., ☎ 907/451–7555) makes its own, highly specialized, cold-weather clothing for dog mushers and winter bicyclists. Travelers from colder sections of the Lower 48 will appreciate the double-layer fleece mittens, among other items. Of course, the dog booties, used by mushers to protect their dogs' feet from ice-crusted snow, can make great protectors for bracelets or other jewelry.

Chena Hot Springs

⑫ *62 mi northeast of Fairbanks via Steese Hwy. and Chena Hot Springs Rd.*

The 57-mi, paved, Chena Hot Springs Road, which starts 5 mi outside Fairbanks, leads to Chena Hot Springs, a popular playground of many Fairbanks residents. Several attractions lie along the road, including Tack's General Store and Greenhouse Cafe, Chena River State Recreation Area, and Chena Hot Springs Resort (☞ *below*).

Dining and Lodging

$$–$$$$ ✕ **Two Rivers Lodge.** This popular restaurant serves up fine beef and Alaskan seafood dishes and often has crab specials. Many Fairbanksans make the 40-mi round-trip for the delicious dinners. The building has a rustic log decor, and some of the tables are made from carved tree burls. ⊠ *Mile 16, Chena Hot Springs Rd.,* ☎ *907/488–6815,* FAX *907/488–9761. MC, D, V. No lunch.*

$ ✕ **Tack's General Store and Greenhouse Cafe.** Tack's, an almost essential pit stop, serves up homemade pies that draw locals back again and again. Many people plan a hard day of play in the nearby Chena River State Recreation Area, with a stop at Tack's on the way back. The café is open for breakfast, lunch, and dinner from 8 to 8. The main building is an old-fashioned general store, and in summer the owners operate a greenhouse next door. ⊠ *Mile 23.5, Chena Hot Springs Rd.,* ☎ *907/488–3242,* ℻ *907/488–9010. MC, V.*

$$–$$$$ 🏨 ⛷ **Chena Hot Springs Resort.** This resort at the end of Chena Hot Springs Road is popular among Fairbanksans for day outings, especially in winter. Summer activities include fishing, horseback riding, gold panning, camping, flightseeing, and mountain biking. In winter you can go cross-country skiing, snowmobiling, dogsledding, sleigh riding, and Snow-Cat touring. All year round you can soak in the hot springs–warmed hot tubs or swimming pool. A new feature is the Aurora Nest, a large, glassed-in room for viewing the northern lights. The dining room serves three meals a day. There are sports-equipment rentals, camping sites, RV hookups, and heated cabins without running water. ⊠ *Box 73440, Fairbanks 99707,* ☎ *907/452–7867 or 800/ 478–4681 in AK,* ℻ *907/456–3122. Restaurant, coin laundry. AE, D, DC, MC, V.*

Outdoor Activities and Sports

BOATING
CanoeAlaska (☞ Guided Tours *in* Fairbanks, *above*) offers classes on river canoeing, which include time on the upper Chena River, and two-day guided trips down the Chena. Additionally, it offers "playboating" trips to the white water of the Nenana River.

The **Chena River State Recreation Area,** along Chena Hot Springs Road from Mile 26 to Mile 51, contains numerous well-marked river-access points. The lower sections of the river area are placid, but the area above the third bridge, at Mile 44.1, can be hazardous for inexperienced boaters. For more detailed information check with the **Alaska Public Lands Information Center** (☞ Visitor Information *in* Interior A to Z, *below*).

HIKING
The **Chena River State Recreation Area,** which straddles Chena Hot Springs Road from Mile 26 to Mile 51, has a few hiking trails. A popular daylong trip is the **Granite Tors Trail,** a 15-mi loop that offers a view of the upper Chena Valley. Carry plenty of drinking water on this trip, because there are few reliable water sources. A popular shorter hike is the 3½-mi **Angel Rocks Trail,** near the eastern boundary of the area. This area is managed by the **Alaska Division of Parks** (☎ 907/ 451–2695), which also maintains five area public-use cabins, although only one is reachable by car.

NORTH OF FAIRBANKS

The three roads north of Fairbanks head straight out of civilization. They all dead-end at water—two at rivers and one on the Arctic Ocean. This is the direction in which to head if you want to see untamed Alaska and meet some rugged, independent people.

Steese Highway

From Fairbanks: 128 mi to Central, 136 mi to Circle Hot Springs, 162 mi to Circle.

The Steese Highway follows the Chatanika River and several other creeks along the southern part of the White Mountains. It eventually climbs into weatherworn alpine mountains, peaking at Eagle Summit (3,624 ft), about 100 mi from Fairbanks, and drops back down into forested creek beds en route to Central. At Central you can drive the 30-plus mi on a winding gravel road to Circle, a small town on the Yukon River, or you can take the 8-mi road south to **Circle Hot Springs,** a popular destination. The highway is paved to Mile 44 and is usually in good shape. However, in winter, Eagle Summit is sometimes closed due to drifting snow.

Lodging and Camping

$$–$$$$ ⊞ ⚠ **Circle Hot Springs.** A three- to four-hour drive from Fairbanks, Circle Hot Springs has an original hotel dating from 1930, a hostel on the fourth floor, cabins, and a small campground (with room for six motor homes). The hot springs feed an Olympic-size outdoor pool, and snowmobiling, cross-country skiing, and hiking trails are in the area; dogsled rides are available in the winter. This resort is at the end of an 8-mi spur road that begins at Central on the Steese Highway. A small airstrip nearby allows the resort to be reached by small plane from Fairbanks. ⊠ *Mile 8.3, Circle Hot Springs Rd., Box 69, Central 99730,* ☎ *907/520–5113,* ⚐ *907/520–5116. 29 rooms; 11 cabins in summer, 7 in winter. Restaurant, bar, pool, massage, exercise room. MC, V.*

$$ ⊞ ⚠ **Chatanika Gold Camp.** Formerly known as the Old F. E. Gold Camp, this lodge was the bunkhouse for the miners working the dredges for the F. E. Gold Co. in the early 1900s. The 48-acre site is on the National Register of Historic Places. The dining room features the world's largest coal cookstove still in operation. The rooms in the 40-bed hotel share bathrooms. Additionally, there are two four-room log cabins, each with two shared bathrooms. The area is popular with local winter-sports enthusiasts, summertime hikers, and international travelers who come to see the aurora. ⊠ *Mile 27.5, Steese Hwy., 5555 Steese Hwy., Fairbank, 99712,* ☎ *907/389–2414. 26 rooms with shared bath. Restaurant, meeting room. No credit cards.*

$$ ⊞ ⚠ **Chatanika Lodge.** This log lodge is a gathering spot for rocket scientists from the nearby Poker Flat Research Range and for mushers (guests can take dogsled rides), snowmobilers, and recreational gold panners. The eclecticism of clientele is matched by that of the furnishings: the decor includes diamond willow lamps and a variety of wild animal trophy heads and skins, including bear, lynx, and wolf. The rooms generally have a double bed and a single bed, a sink and a television set. The bathrooms and showers are down the hall. ⊠ *Mile 28.6, Steese Hwy. (mailing address: 5760 Old Steese Hwy. N, Fairbanks 99712),* ☎ *907/389–2164,* ⚐ *907/389–2166. 10 rooms with shared bath. Restaurant, bar, snowmobiling. MC, V.*

Outdoor Activities and Sports

BOATING

The **Chatanika River,** popular with canoeists and kayakers, has a wilderness feel to it yet is fairly close to Fairbanks. The most northerly access point is at Cripple Creek campground, near Mile 60 of the Steese Highway. Other commonly used access points are at Long Creek (Mile 45, Steese Highway), at the state campground where the Chatanika River crosses the Steese Highway at Mile 39, and at the state's Whitefish Campground, where the river crosses the Elliott Highway at Mile 11. Below this point, the stream flows into the Minto Flats, and access is more difficult.

Water in the Chatanika River may or may not be clear, depending on mining activities along its upper tributaries. In times of very low water, the upper Chatanika River will be shallow and difficult to navigate. Avoid the river in times of high water, especially after heavy rains, because of the danger of sweepers, floating debris, and hidden gravel bars.

Farther north, in the **Steese National Conservation Area,** you can take a four- to five-day float trip on the **Birch Creek** (☞ Wild and Scenic Rivers *in* Chapter 3).

CROSS-COUNTRY SKIING, SNOWMOBILING, AND SNOWSHOEING

Once past Mile 20 of the Steese Highway, even though it's within an hour of downtown Fairbanks, travelers enter a countryside that seems to have changed little in 100 years. Mountains loom in the distance, and in winter, a solid snowpack of 4–5 ft makes the area excellent for riding snowmobiles, snowshoeing, and backcountry skiing. Recent Arctic Cat snowmobiles can be rented at **Snow-RV** (✉ 5760 Old Steese Hwy., off Steese Hwy. at Mile 28.5, at Chatanika Lodge (mailing address: 740 Leuthold Dr. E, Fairbanks, 99712); ☎ 907/389–7669, FAX 907/389–5665) Rentals are available by the hour or for several days; guided rides are required for those from out of state.

HIKING

The Bureau of Land Management (BLM) maintains the **Pinnell Mountain National Recreation Trail,** connecting Twelve-Mile Summit and Eagle Summit on the Steese Highway. This trail, 27 mi long, passes through alpine meadows and along mountain ridges, all above the tree line. It has two emergency shelters. No dependable water supply is available in the immediate vicinity. Most hikers spend three days making the trip. The **Alaska Public Lands Information Center** (☞ Visitor Information *in* Interior A to Z, *below*) has information on the trail.

The **Circle-Fairbanks Historic Trail** stretches 58 mi from the vicinity of Cleary Summit to Twelve-Mile Summit. This route, which is not for novices, follows the old summer trail used by gold miners; in winter they generally used the frozen Chatanika River to make this journey. The trail has been roughly marked and cleared, but there are no facilities and water is scarce along much of it. Most of the trail is on state land, but it does cross valid mining claims, which must be respected. Although there are rock cairns and mileposts along it, there is no well-defined tread the whole way, so it's easy to become disoriented. The State Department of Natural Resources strongly recommends that backpackers on this trail equip themselves with the following USGS topographical maps: Livengood (A-1) and Circle (A-6), (A-5), and (B-4). The **Alaska Public Lands Information Center** (☞ Visitor Information *in* Interior A to Z, *below*) has detailed information about the trail.

Elliott Highway

From Fairbanks: 28 mi to Wickersham Dome, 73 mi to Dalton Hwy. junction, 152 mi to Manley.

The Elliott Highway, which starts in Fox, takes travelers to the Tanana ⑭ River and a small community called **Manley Hot Springs,** a colorful, close-knit "end-of-the-road" place. This town originally was a trading center for placer miners who worked the nearby creeks. Residents maintain a small public campground. Northern pike are caught in the nearby slough, and a dirt road leads to the Tanana River with its summer runs of salmon. The Manley Hot Springs Resort recently closed, but the hot springs is only a short walk from the campground. The highway is paved for 28 mi outside Fairbanks.

Lodging and Camping

$$ 🏠 ⛺ **Manley Roadhouse.** Built in 1906 in the midst of the Gold Rush into the Interior, this roadhouse is among the oldest in Alaska. Today it caters to a diverse crowd of vacationers, miners, and road maintenance crews. The restaurant serves breakfast, lunch, and dinner. Rather than the food or the accommodations (including rooms in the original roadhouse and several cabins), it is its bar that the roadhouse boasts about. They say it is the best stocked in Alaska, with 250 brands of liquor and 20 varieties of beer. Activities in the area include summer fishing charters, ice fishing, snowmobiling, and dog mushing. ✉ *Mile 152, Elliott Hwy. (mailing address: Box 1), Manley Hot Springs 99756,* ☎ *907/672–3161. 14 rooms, 6 with bath; 3 cabins. Restaurant, bar. D, MC, V.*

Outdoor Activities and Sports

HIKING

The BLM maintains the 22-mi **Summit Trail** from the Elliott Highway, near Wickersham Dome, north into the **White Mountain National Recreation Area** (☞ Chapter 3).

Dalton Highway

From Fairbanks: 140 mi to the Yukon River, 199 mi to the Arctic Circle, 259 mi to Coldfoot, 329 mi to Atigun Pass, 499 mi to Deadhorse. Take the Steese Hwy. to Mile 11, then the Elliot Hwy. to Mile 73.

The Dalton Highway is a road of "onlys." It's the only road that goes to the Beaufort Sea, it's the only Alaskan road to cross the Arctic Circle, and it has the state's only bridge across the Yukon River. The 415-mi gravel road runs northwest of Fairbanks to the North Slope oil fields at Prudhoe Bay. It was built in 1974–75 to open a truck route necessary to build the facilities at Prudhoe and the northern half of the trans-Alaska pipeline. For a few months a ferry was used to carry loads across the Yukon River, until the present bridge was completed late in 1975.

The road is named for James Dalton, a pioneer Alaskan engineer who recognized early the potential of oil on the North Slope. If you are planning to drive the Dalton Highway, remember these tips: slow down and move to the side of the road for trucks; leave your headlights on at all times; yield on one-lane bridges; pull to the side of the road when stopping for pictures or the view; carry at least one spare tire; consider bringing extra gas and purchasing a citizen's band radio if you do not already have one. Remember there are no services between Coldfoot and Prudhoe Bay, a distance of nearly 250 mi.

The Dalton Highway has two **visitor centers** open in the summer. One is just north of the Yukon River bridge and has no phone. The other is in Coldfoot (☎ 907/678–5209). The centers are operated by the Fish and Wildlife Service, the National Park Service, and the BLM. A picnic area and a large, colorful sign mark the spot where the road crosses the Arctic Circle.

The **Wiseman Trading Co.,** a museum and general store 12 mi north of Coldfoot, is run by Coldfoot Services–Slate Creek Inn (☞ Lodging, *below*).

Today the road is still used to carry oil-field supplies and is now open **⑮** all the way to **Deadhorse,** just shy of the Arctic coast. This town exists mainly to service the oil fields of Prudhoe Bay. It's not scenic, but it does have important facilities for travelers, including fuel, vehicle maintenance, a general store, an airport, a post office, hotels, and restaurants. Oil-field tours and shuttles to the Arctic Ocean leave daily from the three hotels in town (☞ *below*). For tour reservations call **Tour Arc-**

tic (☎ 907/659–2368, ☎ 907/659–2840 in winter) or the **Prudhoe Bay Hotel** (☞ *below*).

Guided Tours

Westours (☎ 907/456–7741 or 800/478–6388) runs tour buses on the Dalton from Fairbanks all the way to Prudhoe Bay, with a variety of services, including an overnight at Coldfoot, a tour of the oil field, and air service from Prudhoe back to Fairbanks or Anchorage. Tours operate from June 1 to the end of August. **Princess Tours** (☎ 907/479–9640 or 800/835–8907) leads similar bus/air tours on the Dalton Highway up to Prudhoe Bay. Van tours are available from **Northern Alaska Tour Company** (☎ 907/474–8600) and **Trans Arctic Circle Treks** (☎ 907/479–5451) also leads van tours.

Arctic Adventures Touring and Outfitting Company (☎ 907/678–5201), out of Coldfoot, also offers tours of the area, including one to Prudhoe Bay.

Yukon River Tours (✉ 214 2nd Ave., Fairbanks 99701-4811, ☎ 907/452–7162, FAX 907/452–5063) takes people from the Yukon River bridge on the Dalton Highway on a tour of the Yukon River. You travel in a 45-ft, enclosed riverboat with big windows so you can see everything. The tours last about 90 minutes and run all week, three times a day, from June 1 to September 1. There are opportunities to sight black bears, waterfowl, and numerous other animals. Also, by mid-August, the leaves start turning, and the area provides an early taste of autumn. An overnight option is available. The company also offers custom tours into the Yukon Flats National Wildlife Refuge.

Lodging and Camping

There are five camping areas plus many scenic turnouts along the road. Only one of the camping areas (Marion Creek, at Mile 180) is developed. Most of the rest are gravel pads, sometimes with outhouses. Call the Alaska Public Lands Information Center (☞ Visitor Information *in* Interior A to Z, *below*) for more information.

$$$$ 🏨 ⛰ **Coldfoot Services–Slate Creek Inn.** Fuel, tire repairs, and towing are available here. Basic and clean rooms are built from surplus pipeline-worker housing. The 24-hour restaurant serves generous portions of food cooked to satisfy truckers. The complex has a 20-space RV hookup and post office. ✉ *Mile 175, Dalton Hwy., Box 9041, Coldfoot 99701,* ☎ *907/678–5201,* FAX *907/678–5202. 81 rooms, 52 with bath. Restaurant, bar, shops, coin laundry. D, MC, V.*

$$$$ 🏨 **Prudhoe Bay Hotel.** This hotel is in the community of Deadhorse, although the post office serving the area is named Prudhoe Bay. Like much of the town, the hotel was built mainly to house pipeline workers, and as a result the guest rooms are spartan but comfortable. There is a TV room with a big-screen TV. The restaurant (all meals are included in the room rate) serves good basic American fare in an all-you-can-eat buffet—and fresh gourmet pizza. ✉ *Airport Rd., across from the airport (mailing address: Pouch 340004, Prudhoe Bay 99734),* ☎ *907/659–2449,* FAX *907/659–2752. 180 rooms, 15 with bath. Restaurant, exercise room. AE, MC, V.*

$$$–$$$$ 🏨 **Arctic Caribou Inn.** This hotel, made of trailer-type units similar to those of the Prudhoe Bay Hotel, opened in 1988. Rooms are very basic. The restaurant serves a predictable American menu in an all-you-can-eat buffet. ✉ *Airport Rd. (mailing address: Box 340111, Deadhorse 99734),* ☎ *907/659–2368,* FAX *907/659–2432. 45 rooms. Restaurant, coin laundry. AE, MC, V. Closed Labor Day–Memorial Day.*

$$$ 🏨 **Yukon Ventures Alaska.** On the Yukon River, this property has a motel, a tire repair shop, and gasoline, diesel fuel, and propane. The motel is basic and clean, built from surplus pipeline-worker housing. None of the rooms have private baths, but there are two (one for men, one for women); both have showers and are centrally located. The restaurant offers large portions of trucker fare. ⊠ *Mile 56, Dalton Hwy., Box 60947, Fairbanks 99706,* ☎ *907/655–9001. 18 rooms with shared bath. Restaurant. MC, V.*

Outdoor Activities and Sports

FISHING

Although this is not a prime fishing area, there are fish, mostly grayling, in the streams along the Dalton. You'll do better if you are willing to hike more than ¼ mi from the road, where fishing pressure is the heaviest. Lakes along the road have grayling, and some have lake trout and arctic char. The Alaska Department of Fish and Game (☞ Visitor Information *in* Interior A to Z, *below*) puts out a pamphlet titled "Sport Fishing Along the Dalton Highway," which is also available at the Alaska Public Lands Information Center (☞ Visitor Information *in* Interior A to Z, *below*).

HIKING

No trails have been officially established along the road, but hikers willing to pick their own route can explore much of the area. The road passes near the **Yukon Flats National Wildlife Refuge,** the **Kanuti National Wildlife Refuge,** the **Arctic National Wildlife Refuge,** and just east of **Gates of the Arctic National Park and Preserve** (☞ Chapter 3). Check with the **Alaska Public Lands Information Center** (☞ Visitor Information *in* Interior A to Z, *below*). Chances of seeing wildlife are fairly good; this is grizzly bear and caribou habitat.

SOUTH OF FAIRBANKS

Healy

109 mi south of Fairbanks, 248 mi north of Anchorage, and 11 mi north of the entrance to Denali National Park.

Coal mining fuels the economy of Healy, which is home to the **Usibelli Coal Mine,** the largest mine of its kind in the state and Alaska's only commercially viable coal mining operation. Each summer overflow crowds from Denali National Park stream into this small community of 500 people on the George Parks Highway, north of the entrance, to park. However, more and more frequently, Fairbanks-area residents and visitors from the Lower 48 and other countries are seeking out the all-year lodging and the magnificent views that Healy offers. Healy is close to the **Stampede Trail,** which offers those interested in snowmobiling, mushing, cross-country skiing, and mountain biking a way to enter the northern expanse of Denali National Park. This wide, well-traveled path begins where Stampede Road ends and leads to the former Gold Rush boomtown of Kantishna, 90 mi inside the park. Take the George Parks Highway 2 mi north of Healy to Mile 251.1, where Stampede Road intersects the highway. Eight miles west on Stampede Road is a parking lot and the start of the Stampede Trail.

Dining and Lodging

$$–$$$ ✕ **Totem Inn.** For standard American fare at reasonable prices, this all-★ year restaurant draws a crowd from travelers along the George Parks Highway and visitors to Healy and Denali National Park. The kitchen is open 7 AM–11 PM, seven days a week. ⊠ *Mile 248.7, George Parks Hwy.,* ☎ *907/683–2420. D, MC, V.*

$$$ ⌂ **Dome Home.** This all-year bed-and-breakfast is housed in a huge, 7,200-square-ft, modified geodesic dome. Each guest room has a pri-

vate bath, a television set, VCR, and a phone; one has a sauna. Guests
are welcome in the 24-by-30-ft TV and fireplace room and there are
Alaska-related books and videos to read and watch. The fireplace accommodates 5-ft-long logs and the high ceiling is enhanced by tall windows that provide excellent views of nearby mountains. A full breakfast
comes with the room rate. ⊠ *137 Healy Spur Rd., Box 262, 99743,*
☎ *907/683–1239,* ⒻⒶⓍ *907/683–2322. 6 rooms. Breakfast room, in-
room VCRs. AE, D, MC, V.*

$$$ 🔟 **Motel Nord Haven.** This new motel, with wood trim throughout,
features one or two queen-size beds, a telephone, television, and pri-
vate bath in all rooms. Its location on 5 wooded acres means the motel
is protected from the road. As a result it offers a secluded feeling other
lodgings along the George Parks Highway lack. An expansion com-
pleted in June 1997 added eight new rooms, including one specifically
designed for travelers with disabilities. Rooms with two queen beds
can accommodate up to five people at no additional charge. ⊠ *Mile
249.5, George Parks Hwy., Box 458, Healy 99743,* ☎ *907/683–
4500,* ⒻⒶⓍ *907/683–4503. 24 rooms. AE, MC, V.*

$$ 🔟 **Stampede Lodge.** New owners have toned down the appearance of
the former Healy Hotel, which had been a bright blue. Now it's gray
with dark blue trim. All the rooms have private baths and phones. Breakfast, lunch, and dinner are available at the lodge's restaurant, the
Bushmaster Grill. ⊠ *Mile 248.8, George Parks Hwy., Box 380, Healy
99701,* ☎ *907/683–2242,* ⒻⒶⓍ *907/683–2243. 29 rooms. Restaurant.
AE, D, MC, V.*

RICHARDSON HIGHWAY

The Richardson Highway stretches 364 mi, from Fairbanks to the all-
year, ice-free port of Valdez. The Richardson takes travelers the final
98 mi from the official end of the Alaska Highway in Delta Junction
to Fairbanks, but it is not a mere connecting route. The first road built
in Alaska, the Richardson offers fantastic mountain views while also
providing opportunities for excellent river and lake fishing. Named after Gen. Wilds P. Richardson, first president of the Alaska Road Commission, the highway evolved from a pack train trail and dogsled route
that mail carriers and gold seekers followed in the early 1900s to a two-
lane, asphalt highway in 1957. It's a four-lane, divided highway from
Fairbanks to North Pole, home of the Santa Claus House gift shop,
with its towering Santa silhouette, and the North Pole Coffee Roast-
ing Company, which provides many Fairbanks-area restaurants with
fresh-roasted coffee. The Richardson also links Fairbanks with Delta's
farm country and the winter and summer recreation areas near Summit Lake in the Alaska Range. At Paxson, the Richardson takes travelers to the Denali Highway, a gravel road leading west through the
Alaska Range to campgrounds and fishing in the Tangle Lakes area
and, later, to Denali National Park. Fifty-six miles south of the Denali
Highway, the Richardson borders Wrangell–St. Elias National Park,
the largest U.S. national park. The Richardson provides more spectacular
scenery as it crosses the Chugach Mountains before entering Valdez.

North Pole

🔟 *15 mi southeast of Fairbanks, 85 mi northwest of Delta Junction.*

Christmas lives in North Pole all year long. Many of the street names
maintain the theme, including Santa Claus Lane and St. Nicholas
Drive. The prime attraction here is the ☾ **Santa Claus House** (☞
Shopping, *below*), a must-see if you have young children. Also popular with locals is the Chena Lakes Recreation Area.

Off the Richardson Highway just south of North Pole, **Chena Lakes Recreation Area** offers hiking, swimming, boating, camping, picnicking, dog mushing, and cross-country skiing. Created by the Army Corps of Engineers as part of the Chena River Flood-Control Project, it is now operated by the local government, the **Fairbanks North Star** Borough (Parks and Recreation Dept., ☎ 907/488–1655).

Outdoor Activities and Sports

FISHING

Rainbow trout are not native to the Interior, but they are stocked in some lakes. **Birch Lake** (✉ Mile 303.5), **Harding Lake** (✉ Mile 321.4, Richardson Hwy.), and **Quartz Lake** (✉ Mile 277.8), easily accessible from the Richardson Highway between Fairbanks and Delta Junction, are popular trout-fishing spots. All have campgrounds and boat launching areas.

The **Salcha River,** 40 mi below Fairbanks on the Richardson Highway, is a popular spot for catching migrating salmon in the fall.

Shopping

The **Knotty Shop** (✉ Mile 332, Richardson Hwy., 32 mi south of Fairbanks, ☎ 907/488–3014) has a large selection of Alaskan handicrafts, as well as a mounted wildlife display and a yard full of spruce burl sculptures, including a 6-ft mosquito. They also serve soft drinks and ice cream over a counter carved from spruce burl.

The **Santa Claus House Gift Shop** (✉ Mile 349, Richardson Hwy., 14 mi south of Fairbanks, ☎ 907/488–2200) is hard to miss. Look for the giant Santa statue and the Christmas mural on the side of the building. The store has a variety of toys, gifts, and Alaskan handicrafts. Santa is often on duty to talk to children. Two reindeer are kept in a pen outside the store. The store closes in January and February.

Delta Junction

⑰ *100 mi southeast of Fairbanks, 106 mi northwest of Tok, 266 mi north of Valdez.*

As the hub of the state Delta Agricultural Project, Delta Junction usually has the manner of a small farming town. Although the project has had many difficulties, grain and dairy farms still define the area. In summer Delta becomes a bustling rest stop for road-weary tourists traveling the Alaska and Richardson highways. Delta is also known for its access to good fishing and its proximity to the Delta Bison Range. However, don't expect to see the elusive bison, as they roam free and generally avoid people.

Dining and Lodging

$–$$ ✕ **Pizza Bella.** This popular restaurant serves up delicious pizzas and other Italian and American entrées. The decor is a slice of Italy. ✉ *Mile 265, Richardson Hwy.,* ☎ *907/895–4841 or 907/895–4524. AE, D, MC, V.*

$ ✕ **Rika's Roadhouse.** This historic landmark near Big Delta State Historical Park serves delectable baked goods and homemade soups and sandwiches. It's open 9–5 and has a gift shop. ✉ *Mile 275, Richardson Hwy.,* ☎ *907/895–4201,* ☒ *907/895–4787. AE, D, MC, V. No dinner.*

$$ ▣ **Alaska 7 Motel.** Cheap and clean accommodations right off the highway are what you get here—small refrigerators in each room, and color televisions, too. Some units have kitchenettes, and some have phones. ✉ *Mile 270.3, Richardson Hwy., Box 1115, 99737,* ☎ *907/895–4848. 16 rooms. Kitchenettes, refrigerators. AE, D, DC, MC, V.*

$$ ⊞ **Black Spruce Lodge.** This comfortable, rustic lodge with 10 cabins is a 10-minute pontoon-boat shuttle ride from the parking area at a nearby campground. Nearby Quartz Lake is rife with rainbow trout, arctic char, and landlocked silver salmon. Bring on the fish! ⊠ *10 mi northwest of Delta Junction (mailing address: Box 265, 99737),* ☎ *907/ 895–4668. 10 cabins. Bar, boating, fishing. MC, V. Closed Oct.– Nov. and Apr.*

$$ ⊞ **Kelly's Country Inn Motel.** Delta residents most often put visitors up at this downtown motel. Units are modern; some have kitchenettes. ⊠ *Mile 266.5, Richardson Hwy., Box 849, 99737,* ☎ *907/895–4667,* FAX *907/895–4481. 21 rooms. AE, MC, V.*

$$ ⊞ **Tangle Lakes Lodge.** This rustic lodge 22 mi from Paxson consists of a main lodge building housing the restaurant ($$–$$$) and bar, and 10 log cabins set on the shores of the lake. (One of the cabins is large enough to sleep 10–12 and rents for $150 a night). The cabins are heated by wood or oil stoves, and the lights are propane. The main building has running water, showers, and two bathrooms. Here you're surrounded by rolling tundra, home to moose, caribou, grizzly bears, and wolves, and the fishing for grayling, salmon, rainbow, and lake trout is exceptional. The proprietors also lead birders tours and can arrange guided fishing trips. ⊠ *Mile 22, Denali Hwy., Box 670386, Chigiak 99567,* ☎ *907/688–9173,* FAX *907/688–9175. 10 rooms. Restaurant, bar. MC, V.*

FORTYMILE COUNTRY

A trip through the Fortymile Country up the Taylor Highway will take you back in time nearly a century—when gold was the lure that drew hardy travelers to Interior Alaska. It's still one of the few places to see active mining without leaving the road system.

The 160-mi Taylor Highway runs north from the Alaska Highway at Tetlin Junction, 12½ mi south of Delta Junction. It's a narrow rough-gravel road that winds along mountain ridges and through valleys of the Fortymile River. The road passes the tiny community of Chicken and ends in Eagle at the Yukon River. This is one of only three places in Alaska where the river can be reached by road. A cutoff just south of Eagle connects to the Canadian Top of the World Highway leading to Dawson City in the Yukon Territory. This is the route many Alaskans take to Dawson City. The highway is not plowed in winter, so it is snowed shut from fall to spring. Watch for road reconstruction.

Tok

18 *12 mi from Tetlin Junction, where the Taylor Hwy. starts, 78 mi from Chicken, 173 mi from Eagle, 175 mi from Dawson City.*

If you can't travel into the Fortymile Country itself, you can catch the flavor of the region at the **Tok Main Street Visitors Center** (☞ Visitor Information *in* Interior A to Z, *below*). At the junction of the Glenn Highway (which leads to Anchorage) and the Alaska Highway (which leads to Fairbanks), Tok is a main supply center for the loggers, miners, and hunting guides who live and work along the surrounding streams or in the millions of acres of spruce forest nearby. Each summer Tok, with a resident population of less than 1,500, becomes temporary home to thousands of travelers, including those traveling up the Alaska highway from the Lower 48.

Dining and Lodging

$$–$$$$ ✕ **Fast Eddy's Restaurant.** It's much better than the name would indicate: the chef makes his own noodles for chicken noodle soup, and

the hoagies and pizza are a welcome relief from the roadhouse hamburgers served by most Alaska Highway restaurants. It's open 6 AM–midnight (but no soup after 5 PM). ⊠ *Mile 1313.3, Alaska Hwy.,* ☎ *907/883–4411. AE, MC, V.*

$$$–$$$$ 🏨 **Westmark Tok.** This hotel, part of a chain, is reliable, comfortable, and well appointed. ⊠ *Junction of Alaska and Glenn Hwys.,* ☎ *907/ 883–5174 or 800/544–0970,* FAX *907/883–5178. 72 rooms. Restaurant, bar, shops. AE, D, DC, MC, V. Closed Oct.–May.*

Shopping

The **Burnt Paw** (⊠ Intersection of Alaska and Glenn Hwys., ☎ 907/ 883–4121, FAX 907/883–5680) sells jade and ivory, Alaskan ceramics, crafts, paintings, smoked salmon—even sled-dog puppies.

In Northway, south of Tok, **Naabia Niign** (⊠ Mile 1264, Alaska Hwy., ☎ 907/778–2298, FAX 907/778–2366) is a Native-owned crafts gallery with fine Athabascan beadwork and baskets.

Chicken

⑲ *78 mi from Tok, 95 mi from Eagle, 109 mi from Dawson City.*

Chicken was once in the heart of major gold-mining operations, and the remains of many of these works are visible along the highway. Here you'll find a country store, bar, liquor store, café, and gas station. Be careful not to trespass on private property. Miners rarely have a sense of humor about trespassing.

Outdoor Activities and Sports

CANOEING

Canoeing on the **Fortymile River** (☞ Wild and Scenic Rivers *in* Chapter 3) is popular among Alaskans.

Eagle

⑳ *95 mi from Chicken, 173 mi from Tok, 144 mi from Dawson City.*

Eagle was once a seat of government and commerce for the Interior. An army post (Ft. Egbert) was operated here until 1911, and territorial judge James Wickersham had his headquarters in Eagle until Fairbanks began to grow from the gold strike there. The population peaked at 1,700 in 1898. Today it is fewer than 200.

Eagle Historical Society (☎ 907/547–2325) offers a two-hour walking tour, beginning at the courthouse at 9 each morning from mid-May to mid-September, visiting five museum buildings, and telling tales of the famous people who have passed through this historic Yukon River border town. For a small extra fee, the society will lead tours at other times of the day and year by appointment. For the next five years over the 4th of July holidays, Eagle will be celebrating various centennial milestones in town history, inviting relatives of noteworthy figures from the Gold Rush days.

Eagle is a popular jumping-off point for the **Yukon–Charley Rivers National Preserve** (☞ Chapter 3).

YUKON TERRITORY

Gold! That's what called Canada's Yukon Territory to the world's attention with the Klondike Gold Rush of 1897–98. And, although Yukon gold mining today is mainly in the hands of a few large companies that go almost unnoticed by the visitor, the territory's history is alive and thriving.

Though the international border divides Alaska from Yukon Territory, the Yukon River tends to unify the region. Early prospectors, miners, traders, and camp followers moved readily up and down the river with little regard to national boundaries. An earlier Alaska strike preceded the Klondike find by years, yet Circle was all but abandoned in the stampede to the creeks around Dawson City. Later gold discoveries in the Alaskan Fortymile Country, Nome, and Fairbanks reversed that flow across the border into Alaska.

Dawson City

337 mi from Whitehorse, 109 mi from Chicken, 144 mi from Eagle, 175 mi from Tok.

Dawson City today forms the heart of the Yukon's Gold Rush remembrances. In the hundred years since the first swell of the Gold Rush, many of the original buildings are gone, victims of fire, flood, and weathering. But enough of them have been preserved and restored to give more than a glimpse of the city's onetime grandeur. In a period of three years up to the turn of the century, Dawson was transformed into the largest, most refined city north of San Francisco and west of Winnipeg. It had grand new buildings and boasted running water, telephones, and electricity. The city's population, only about 1,500 now, numbered almost 30,000 in 1899.

Regular air service to Dawson is available from Fairbanks. You also may drive the Taylor Highway route, leaving the Alaska Highway at Tetlin Junction and winding through the Fortymile Country past the little communities of Chicken and Jack Wade Camp into Canada. The border is open 8 AM to 8 PM in summer. The Canadian section of the Taylor Highway is called Top of the World Highway. Broad views of range after range of tundra-covered mountains stretch in every direction. Travelers heading north on the Alaska Highway can turn north at Whitehorse to Dawson City, then rejoin the Alaska Highway by taking the Taylor south. This adds about 100 mi to the trip.

Today you can recapture some of the city's former magnificence at the
㉑ reconstructed **Palace Grand Revue** (✉ King St. between 2nd and 3rd Aves., ☎ 867/993–6217). Every summer night except Tuesdays, there are performances of the Gaslight Follies. Another major attraction is
㉒ **Diamond Tooth Gertie's Gambling Hall** (✉ Arctic Brotherhood Hall, Queen St., ☎ 867/993–5575), adults 19 and over only, which features live entertainment and three different cancan shows three times a night, seven days a week. It is the only authentic, legal gambling establishment operating in all of the North. Yes, there really was a Diamond Tooth Gertie—Gertie Lovejoy, a prominent dance-hall queen who had a diamond between her two front teeth.

㉓ The **Dawson City Museum** has Gold Rush exhibits, and numerous relics are next door, including trains from the Klondike Road Railroad that operated along the gold creeks. ✉ *Territorial Administration Bldg., 5th Ave.,* ☎ *867/993–5291.* 🎫 *$4.* ☉ *Mid-May–Labor Day, daily 10–6.*

Scholars still argue the precise details of the tenure of writers Robert Service and Jack London in Dawson City, but there's no question that between Service's poems and London's short stories, the two did more
㉔ than anyone else to popularize and romanticize the Yukon. **Robert Service's cabin** (☎ 867/993–5566) on 8th Avenue has been restored, and
㉕ twice daily his poetry is read. **Jack London's cabin** (☎ 867/993–6317) has been moved to 8th Avenue in town from Henderson Creek, and presentations of his work take place there daily.

Dawson City Museum, **23**

Diamond Tooth Gertie's Gambling Hall, **22**

Jack London's cabin, **25**

Palace Grand Revue, **21**

Robert Service's cabin, **24**

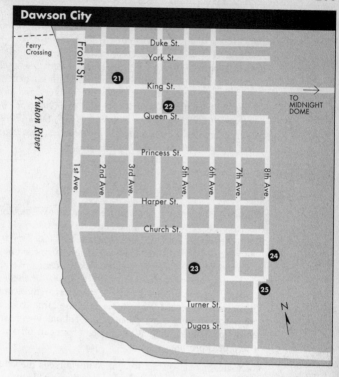

Dawson City

Tours visit the old "diggings." A highlight is a visit to **Bonanza Creek and Dredge Number 4,** a wooden-hulled gold dredge about 10 minutes outside town.

Dining and Lodging

$–$$ ✕ **Marina's.** This restaurant serves a full menu, including fresh pizzas, salads, lasagna, and a light, crisp, fried-calamari appetizer. It is a popular spot with college students working in local tourist attractions for the summer. ⊠ *5th Ave. across from the Westmark,* ☎ *867/993–6800. AE, DC, MC, V.*

$$ ✕🏨 **Downtown Hotel.** The early 1900s decor of this hotel is accented with a large collection of artwork, especially mushing scenes, from area artists. The rooms are refined and have a Klondike Gold Rush motif. The Jack London Grill is a best bet: go for the Canadian and American regional specialties, especially the Yukon River king salmon. The menu also includes a calorie-counter dinner selection. The restaurant, which serves three meals a day, has an outside deck for summer dining. ⊠ *2nd Ave. and Queen St., Box 780, Y0B 1G0,* ☎ *867/993–5346, 800/764–4653 in AK, or 800/661–0514 in Yukon Territory and northern British Columbia;* FAX *867/993–5076. 60 rooms. Restaurant, bar, hot tub, coin laundry, meeting room, airport shuttle. AE, D, DC, MC, V.*

$$$–$$$$ 🏨 **Westmark Dawson City.** This two-story hotel is built around a central courtyard. The Gold Rush–era decor in the lobby includes flocked wallpaper and lace curtains. Rooms are decorated in soft blues and greens. ⊠ *5th Ave. and Harper St., Box 420, Y0B 1G0,* ☎ *867/993–5542 or 800/544–0970,* FAX *867/993–5623. 132 rooms. Dining room, bar. AE, D, DC, MC, V. Closed Sept. 10–May 14.*

$$$ 🏨 **Eldorado Hotel.** The lobby of this popular hotel has Gold Rush–era decor. Rooms, some with kitchenettes, are modern. ⊠ *3rd Ave. and*

*Princess St., Box 338, Y0B 1G0, ☎ 867/993–5451, FAX 867/993–5256.
52 rooms. Dining room, bar, laundry service, airport shuttle. AE, D,
DC, MC, V.*

$$$ 🖼 **Triple "J" Hotel.** This clean, quiet compound of little log cabins is
next to Diamond Tooth Gertie's. There is a central hotel, a detached
motel-like addition, and little log cabins with kitchenettes are avail-
able. All rooms have TVs and small coffeemakers, and most of the cab-
ins have kitchenettes as well. ⌧ *5th Ave. and Queen St., Box 359, Y0B
1G0, ☎ 867/993–5323 or 800/764–3555, FAX 867/993–5030. 27
rooms, 20 cabins. Restaurant, bar, kitchenettes, coin laundry, meeting
room, airport shuttle. AE, DC, MC, V.*

Whitehorse

㉖ *337 mi from Dawson City, 396 mi from Tok.*

Whitehorse began as an encampment near the White Horse Rapids of
the Yukon River. It was a logical layover point for gold rushers in the
late 1890s—most coming north along the Chilkoot Trail from Alaska—
who headed north toward Dawson to seek their fortune. Today's city
of more than 22,000 residents is the Yukon's center of commerce, com-
munication, and transportation and is the seat of the territorial gov-
ernment. It is not, however, a city of any great architectural distinction.
Visitors should regard Whitehorse as a base camp from which to ven-
ture out to explore other parts of the Yukon. There are, however, a
few points of interest in Whitehorse, which can fill a well-spent day
or two of exploring.

The logical place to start touring Whitehorse is the **Whitehorse Visi-
tor Reception Centre,** which is housed in the new block-long, pine-sided
headquarters for Yukon Tourism. Anything to do with the Yukon can
be found in the reception center, including hundreds of brochures on
outfitters, bed-and-breakfast operations, hotels, and restaurants. ⌧ *100
Hanson St., ☎ 867/667–3084, FAX 867/667–3546. ☉ May–Sept.,
daily, 8–8; Oct.–Apr., weekdays 9–noon, 1–4:30.*

Near the Whitehorse Visitor Reception Centre is the **Yukon Territo-
rial Government Building.** It is worth a quick visit to see the **Yukon
Permanent Art Collection,** a display of works by Yukon artists depict-
ing northern people and their culture. In addition to the collection on
the premises, there's a brochure available that leads you on an art walk
through the neighborhood, giving the locations of galleries and art shops.
⌧ *2nd Ave. and Hanson St., ☎ 867/667–5811. ▣ Free. ☉ Weekdays
8:30–5.*

The **MacBride Museum** is your best general introduction to the spirit
and heritage of the Yukon. Over 5,000 square ft of exhibits display
artifacts, natural history specimens, historic photographs, maps, dia-
grams, and heritage buildings from prehistory to the present. ⌧ *1st
Ave. and Wood St., ☎ 867/667–2709, FAX 867/633–6607. ▣ $4. ☉
Mid-May–Labor Day, daily 10–6; winter, Thurs.–Sat. noon–4.*

The **Waterfront Walkway** along the Yukon River will take you past a
few stops of interest. Your walk starts on the path along the river just
east of the MacBride Museum entrance on 1st Avenue. Traveling up-
stream (south) you'll go by the old White Pass & Yukon Route Build-
ing, on Main Street.

The former Yukon Visitors Reception Centre on the Alaska Highway
at the Whitehorse Airport is the home of the new **Yukon Beringia In-
terpretive Centre,** which presents the story of the Yukon during the ice
age. Beringia is the name given to the large subcontinental landmass

of eastern Siberia and Interior Alaska and the Yukon, which were linked by the Bering Land Bridge during the ice age. ⊠ ☎ 867/667–3516. 🖾 $6. ☉ May–Sept., daily 8–9.

★ The **S.S. *Klondike,*** a national historic site, is in Rotary Park. The 35-ft stern-wheeler was built in 1929, sank in 1936, and was rebuilt in 1937. In the days when the Yukon River was the transportation link between Whitehorse and Dawson, the *Klondike* was the largest boat plying the river. Today it is dry-docked and has been restored to its 1930s glory. ⊠ *S. Access Rd. and 2nd Ave.,* ☎ 867/667–4511. 🖾 $3. ☉ *May–Sept., daily 9–6:30.*

If you're in Whitehorse during late summer, it's possible to see the chinook (king) salmon that hold one of nature's great endurance records: longest fish migration in the world. The **Whitehorse Rapids Dam and Fish Ladder** has interpretive exhibits, display tanks of freshwater fish, and a platform for viewing the fish ladder. The best time to visit is August, when between 150 and 2,100 salmon (average count is 800) use the ladder to bypass the dam. ⊠ *End of Nisutlin Dr.,* ☎ 867/633–5965. 🖾 *Free.* ☉ *June–Labor Day, daily; hrs vary, so call ahead.*

Miles Canyon, a 10-minute drive south of Whitehorse, is both picturesque and historic. Although the dam below it now makes the canyon seem relatively tame, it was this perilous stretch of the Yukon River that determined the location of Whitehorse as the starting point for river travel north. In 1897 Jack London won the admiration—and the cash—of fellow Stampeders headed north to the Klondike gold fields because of his steady hand as pilot of hand-hewn wooden boats here. You can hike on trails along the canyon or take a two-hour cruise aboard the *M.V. Schwatka* and experience the canyon from the waters of Lake Schwatka, which obliterated the Whitehorse Rapids in 1959. ⊠ *Miles Canyon Rd., 2 mi south of Whitehorse (mailing address: Box 4001, Whitehorse, Yukon Territory Y1A 3S9),* ☎ 867/668–4716, FAX 867/633–5574. 🖾 $18. ☉ *Cruises early–mid-June and mid-Aug.–early Sept., daily at 2; mid-June–mid-Aug., daily at 2 and 7.*

At **Takhini Hot Springs,** off the Klondike Highway, there's swimming in the spring-warmed water (suits and towels are available for rent), horseback riding, camping, areas for picnicking, and a coffee shop. ⊠ *Km 9.6 on Takhini Hot Springs Rd., 17 mi north of Whitehorse,* ☎ 867/633–2706. 🖾 *$4; campsites $12 with power, $10 without.* ☉ *Summer, daily 7 AM–10 PM; winter, Thurs.–Sun. 10–10.*

The **Yukon Wildlife Preserve** offers a fail-safe way of photographing rarely spotted animals in a natural setting. Animals roaming freely here include elk, caribou, mountain goats, musk oxen, bison, mule deer, and Dall and Stone sheep. Two-hour tours can be arranged through Gray Line. ⊠ *Gray Line Yukon, 208G Steele St.,* ☎ 867/668–3225. 🖾 $12. ☉ *Tour mid-May–mid-Sept., daily.*

Dining and Lodging

$–$$$ ✕ **Antonio's Vineyard.** Though this restaurant is now operating under
★ a new name (it was formerly known as Angelo's), the menu remains the same. It has the best views of any restaurant in town. Classic Greek and Italian cuisine is complemented by such local delicacies as king salmon, Alaskan halibut, and king crab, and game dishes such as musk ox, caribou, and venison. The calamari is especially wonderful. Now open for lunch, there's a pasta and salad bar, soups, and Greek specialties. ⊠ *202 Strickland St.,* ☎ 867/668–6266. *Reservations essential.* MC, V.

$–$$$ ✕🖭 **Westmark Hotel.** Centrally located, this full-service hotel has some rooms with either a StairMaster or a stationary bike. A nightly

Klondike vaudeville show is performed in summer. Its restaurant, which is open for all three meals, serves very good pork chops, filet mignon, salmon, and calorie-counter selections. ⊠ *2nd Ave. and Wood St., Box 4250, Y1A 3T3, ☎ 867/668–4700 or 800/544–0970, ℻ 867/668–2789. 176 rooms, 5 suites. Restaurant, bar, barbershop, travel services. AE, MC, V.*

$$–$$$ 🏨 **High Country Inn.** Rooms are clean, well maintained, and nicely decorated in pastels; deluxe suites have kitchenettes. Renovations have enlarged some of the smaller rooms, which reduced the number of rooms by more than 10%. Public areas are cozy, and the location is close to the S.S. *Klondike* and the public swimming pool. ⊠ *4051 4th Ave., Y1A 1H1, ☎ 867/667–4471 or 800/554–4471, ℻ 867/667–6457. 95 rooms. Restaurant, bar, kitchenettes, coin laundry. AE, DC, MC, V.*

Outdoor Activities and Sports

HIKING

The **Kluane National Park and Reserve** (☞ Wrangell–St. Elias National Park and Preserve *in* Chapter 3), west of Whitehorse, has millions of acres for hiking.

MUSHING

Whitehorse and Fairbanks organize the **Yukon Quest International Sled-Dog Race** (☎ 867/668–4711) in February; the race's starting line alternates yearly between the two cities. This is one of the longest and toughest races in the North.

INTERIOR A TO Z

Arriving and Departing

By Bus

Several tour companies and bus lines offer bus service between Anchorage and Fairbanks (☞ By Bus *in* Getting Around, *below*). Fairbanks has a city bus system. For information about schedules ask at the **Fairbanks Convention and Visitors Bureau** (☞ Visitor Information, *below*).

By Car

Only one road connects Alaska to the Outside—the Alaska Highway. The highway starts in Dawson Creek, British Columbia, in Canada. It is paved but long, almost 1,500 mi to Fairbanks, Alaska. Lots of people make this trek in the summer, so there are ample restaurants and motels along the way. Winter driving takes more planning, as many businesses shut down for the season. An alternative route through part of Canada is the Cassiar Highway, which leaves the Yellowhead Highway several miles northwest of Prince Rupert and connects to the Alaska Highway just outside Watson Lake. The Cassiar is a more scenic drive but may have long sections of gravel road. Summer road construction somewhere along the Alaska Highway is a given.

People flying into Anchorage and renting a car can reach the Interior on the Parks Highway or the Glenn and Richardson Highways. All are paved, in good condition, and offer spectacular views. The Parks Highway route is shorter by a few miles and passes by Denali National Park, but traffic is busier.

For road reports call the **State Department of Transportation** in Fairbanks (☎ 907/456–7623) or Canada's Yukon Territory (☎ 867/667–8215).

By Plane

Alaska Airlines and **Delta Airlines** fly the Anchorage-Fairbanks route. Both have connecting routes to the Lower 48 states.

If you fly from Fairbanks to Anchorage, sit on the right side of the plane for a dazzling view of Mt. McKinley (if the weather cooperates).

By Train

Between late May and early September, daily passenger service is offered between Anchorage and Fairbanks by way of Talkeetna and Denali National Park. Passengers may ride in one of the window-dome cars with luxury seating and gourmet dining, operated by **Princess Tours** (☎ 800/835–8907) and **Holland America/Westours** (☎ 907/456–7741 or 800/478–6388), or they can choose more conventional and considerably less expensive seating in reconditioned coach cars with access to dining, lounge, and dome cars, operated by the **Alaska Railroad** (☎ 907/456–4155 or 800/544–0552). Because of the scenery, there is no such thing as a poor seat on the Alaska Railroad. Beyond your window, a panorama will unfold: scenes of alpine meadows and snowcapped peaks, and the muddy rivers and taiga forests of the Interior.

Getting Around

By Bus

The most common run is between Fairbanks and Anchorage by way of Denali National Park. However, you can take side trips by bus or van to such places as Circle Hot Springs, on the Steese Highway north of Fairbanks, and into the Yukon Territory. For more information about bus service throughout the Interior, contact **Fireweed Express** (☎ 888/505–8267), which provides some winter service and operates a regular summer schedule with 15-passenger vans along the George Parks Highway. **Gray Line of Alaska** (☎ 907/456–7741 or 800/887–7741 in AK; 800/544–2206 outside AK) has summer service and winter charters. **Princess Tours Alaska and Canada** (☎ 800/426–0442) has seasonal service. **Alaska Direct Bus Lines** (☎ 907/277–6652 or 800/770–6652) has year-round service. **The Park Connection** (☎ 800/208–0200, 907/224–7116 for Seward same-day bookings, or 907/683–1240 for Denali same-day bookings) provides regularly scheduled shuttle service between Seward, Anchorage, and Denali National Park mid-May to mid-September. **Denali Overland Transportation** (☎ 907/733–2384, FAX 907/733–2385) serves Anchorage, Talkeetna, and Denali National Park with charter bus and van service.

By Car

In the Interior your choices of side trips by road from Fairbanks include the **Steese Highway** to historic Circle on the Yukon, with its legacy of gold mining; the **Dalton Highway**, across the Yukon and along the trans-Alaska pipeline; and the **Taylor Highway** (closed in winter), connecting the Alaska Highway near Tok with the historic towns of Eagle on the Alaska side of the border and Dawson City, Yukon Territory, in Canada. These are mainly well-maintained gravel roads. However, summer rain can make them slick and dangerous. Hot-line reports on highways, especially during the snow season, can be important (☞ Arriving and Departing, *above*).

By Plane

Air North (☎ 800/764–0407) has the only direct, scheduled air service between Alaska and Canada, flying regular runs from Fairbanks and Juneau to the Yukon Territory towns of Dawson City and Whitehorse.

In much of the Bush, federally subsidized mail runs make regular air schedules possible. From Fairbanks, you can easily catch a ride on the mail run to small, predominantly Indian villages along the Yukon River or to Eskimo settlements on the Arctic coast.

Airlines with bush service from Fairbanks include **Frontier Flying Service** (☎ 907/474–0014), **Larry's Flying Service** (☎ 907/474–9169), **Tanana Air Service** (☎ 907/474–0301), and **Wright Air Service** (☎ 907/474–0502). For commuter flights out of Anchorage, try **ERA Aviation** (☎ 907/243–6633 or 800/866–8394), **Peninsula Airways** (☎ 907/243–2323), **SouthCentral Air** (☎ 907/283–3926 or 800/478–2550), or **Yute Air** (☎ 907/243–7000 or 888/359–9883).

Contacts and Resources

Car Rentals

Avis Rent A Car (☎ 907/474–0900 or 800/478–2847 in Alaska, 800/331–1212 worldwide). **Budget Car and Truck Rental** (☎ 907/474–0855 or 800/248–0150 in Alaska). **Hertz Rent A Car** (☎ 907/452–4444, 907/456–4004, or 800/654–3131). **Payless Car Rental** (☎ 907/474–0177).

Doctors and Dentists

Dawson City (Yukon Territory): Dawson City Nursing Station (☎ 867/993–4444). **Fairbanks: Bassett Army Hospital** (☎ 907/353–5172 or 800/478–5172); **Fairbanks Memorial Hospital** (☎ 907/452–8181); **Medical Dental Arts Building** (☎ 907/452–1866 or 907/452–7007). **Tok: Public Health Clinic** (☎ 907/883–4101). **Whitehorse (Yukon Territory): General Hospital** (☎ 867/668–9444).

Emergencies

Dial **911** for local police or emergency assistance in Fairbanks and other larger communities.

Alaska State Troopers: Delta Junction (☎ 907/895–4344), Fairbanks (☎ 907/451–5100), Nenana (☎ 907/832–5554), Tok (☎ 907/883–5111).

Royal Canadian Mounted Police: Dawson Creek (☎ 250/782–5211), Whitehorse (☎ 867/667–5555).

Travel Agencies

Eagle Travel (✉ 529 6th Ave., Fairbanks 99701, ☎ 907/451–9767). **Sweetwater Travel** (✉ 119 N. Cushman St., Suite 103, Fairbanks 99701, ☎ 907/451–8100). **USTravel** (✉ 609 2nd Ave., Fairbanks 99701, ☎ 907/452–8992 or 800/622–6449, FAX 907/452–5765). **Vista Travel** (✉ 1211 Cushman St., Fairbanks 99701, ☎ 907/456–7888, FAX 907/456–8420).

Visitor Information

Contact the **Alaska Public Lands Information Center** for information on parks, reserves, and other state and federal lands; northern plants and animals; and recreational opportunities in Alaska. ✉ *250 Cushman St., Suite 1A, Fairbanks 99701,* ☎ *907/456–0527 or 907/456–0532 TTY,* FAX *907/456–0514.* ☉ *Memorial Day–Labor Day, daily 9–6; rest of year, Tues.–Sat. 10–6.*

Alaska Department of Fish and Game (✉ 1300 College Rd., Fairbanks 99701, ☎ 907/459–7207). **Delta Chamber of Commerce** (✉ Mile 1422, Alaska Hwy., 99737, ☎ 907/895–5068). **Fairbanks Convention and Visitors Bureau** (✉ 550 1st Ave., 99701, ☎ 907/456–5774 or 800/327–5774, FAX 907/452–4190). **Klondike Visitors Association** (✉ Front and King Sts., Box 389F, Dawson City Y0B 1G0, ☎ 867/993–5575). **Nenana Visitor Center** (✉ A and 4th Sts., 99760, ☎ 907/832–9953). **Tok Main Street Visitors Center** (✉ Mile 1314, Alaska Hwy., 99780, ☎ 907/883–5775). **Whitehorse Visitor Reception Centre** (✉ 100 Hanson St., Box 2703, Whitehorse Y1A 2C6, ☎ 867/667–3084).

8 The Bush

Including Nome, Barrow, Prudhoe Bay, and the Aleutian Islands

The Bush, more a spirit than a place, is the last frontier of the Last Frontier. In the Southwest are coastal lands and waters rich in wildlife. Farther north, from Nome to Barrow, much of the ground is permanently frozen, and for months at a time the sun never sets— or never rises. In the Arctic are the Eskimo, the Prudhoe Bay oil fields, and Barrow, America's northernmost community.

By Stanton H.
Patty

Updated by
Bill Sherwonit

ALASKANS CALL IT THE BUSH—those wild and lonely bands of territory beyond cities, towns, highways, and railroad corridors, stretching from the Alaska Peninsula and Aleutian Islands in the south through the Yukon-Kuskokwim Delta and into the northern High Arctic. It is a land where caribou roam and the sun really does shine at midnight. It is a land that knows the soft footsteps of the Eskimos and the Aleuts, the scratchings of those who search for oil and gold, and the ghosts of almost-forgotten battlefields of World War II.

It is a vast, misunderstood wonderland—bleak yet beautiful, harsh yet bountiful. A look across the Arctic tundra in summer yields the miracle of bright wildflowers growing from a sponge of permafrost ice water. In the long, dark Arctic winter, a painter's-blue kind of twilight rises from the ice and snowscapes at midday. Spring and fall are fleeting moments when the tundra awakens from its winter slumber or turns briefly brilliant with autumn colors.

The Arctic is separated by the Brooks Range from the rest of the state, and the Brooks Range itself is so grand that it contains several mountain systems. Each has its own particular character, ranging from pale, softly rounded limestone mountains in the east and west to the towering granite spires and faces of the Arrigetch Peaks in the heart of the range.

North of the Brooks Range, a great apron of land tilts gently until it slides under the Beaufort Sea and the Arctic Ocean. The vast sweep of this frozen tundra brightens each summer with yellow Arctic poppies and dozens of other wildflower species that seem to stretch into infinite distances. Permafrost has worked over this land for centuries and fragmented it into giant polygons that make a fascinating pattern when viewed from the sky. North-flowing Arctic rivers form into lacy patterns, freezing to the bottom in the winter and not entirely melting in the summer. Thousands of lakes and ponds glimmer in the slanting summer sunlight (the sun never gets directly overhead), and hundreds of thousands of birds nest here. Pingos—frost upheavals like small frozen volcanoes—make landmarks for foot travelers.

Great herds of caribou—hundreds of thousands of them—move in slow waves across the tundra, feeding and fattening for the next winter and attempting to stay clear of wolves and grizzlies. And out on the Arctic Ocean's Beaufort Sea, polar bears, stained a light gold from the oil of seals they have killed, pose like monarchs on ice floes, swinging their heads as if warning humans to keep their distance.

The rivers that drain the Brooks Range have names like Kongakut, Kobuk, and Sheenjek. These speak of the Native peoples who have lived here through countless thousands of years. The great Noatak River defies the Arctic's northerly drainage pattern and runs east–west, making a right-angle turn before emptying into Kotzebue Sound.

The Northwest has its surprises: here stretch the inland deserts (the 25-square-mi Great Kobuk Sand Dunes, the Little Kobuk Sand Dunes, and the Hunt River Sand Dunes), with Saharan characteristics including temperatures that can rise above 100 shimmering degrees. The sands of these dunes are actually formed from glacial river deposits moved by wind and rain. The dunes are accessible by foot from the Kobuk River. Also in the Northwest, the tundra community meets and mingles with the boreal forest, and lichen-carpeted meadows are spiked with spruce and stands of graceful birch.

During the Ice Age, sections of the Northwest lay open to the Bering Land Bridge that linked North America to Russia. Early settlers found their way to this continent across this bridge of land, then probably about 900 mi wide and now lying under the Bering Sea. Traces of their travel thousands of years ago abound in such places as Onion Portage on the Kobuk River. This particular archaeological site is considered among the most important in the Arctic. The colorful Eskimo town of Kotzebue (*kots*-eh-bew) is the jumping-off point to much of this area; it is the largest Native village in the state. Eskimo ceremonial dances are demonstrated at Kotzebue's Living Museum of the Arctic, as is the Eskimo blanket toss, a sport dating to ancient times, when Eskimo hunters were bounced high in the air so they could see across ice ridges in their search for seals and other wildlife.

Another coastal community, this one first settled by prospectors, is the former Gold Rush boomtown of Nome, where you can still pan for gold. In the spring, the going gets wild when Nome hosts a zany golf tournament with "greens" painted on the ice of the Bering seacoast. Nome also serves as the end of the 1,049-mi Iditarod Trail Sled Dog Race, which begins in Anchorage the first Saturday in March.

The Northwest is also where you will find the Bering Land Bridge National Monument and the Cape Krusenstern National Monument (☞ Chapter 3).

Within Southwest Alaska is the Yukon-Kuskokwim Delta, wetlands that are highly productive. Sloughs, ponds, marshes, mud, streams, and puddles in these flat regions near sea level can slow water travel to a standstill. Birds thrive here, and the waters teeming with life offshore testify to the importance of these unique places. Farther south, Bristol Bay is the site of the largest salmon runs in the world. And on the upper Alaska Peninsula, the brown bears of Katmai rule a vast national park, sharing salmon and trout streams with wary sportfishermen and always receiving the right-of-way.

Also in the Southwest are the lower Alaska Peninsula and the Aleutian Islands. Here Alaska reaches well into the Pacific Ocean at its closest point to Japan. This chain beckoned Russian explorers to Alaska in the 18th century. Along the islands, weathered onion-domed Russian Orthodox churches in Aleut villages brace against the fierce Pacific winds. The debris of war—rusted Quonset huts, weed-covered bunkers, and shell casings—still litter the foggy Aleutians, where American and Japanese forces fought bitter campaigns during World War II. There are few blue days in these treeless, windswept islands, yet there are occasional summer sightings of wild orchids.

Dutch Harbor, in the Aleutians, a former U.S. Navy base pounded by Japanese bombs in 1942, is one of America's busiest commercial-fishing ports. Deep-sea trawlers and factory ships venture from here into the stormy north Pacific Ocean and the Bering Sea for harvests of bottom fish, crab, and other catches. One of the most profitable and abundant species these days is Alaska pollock, which is turned into a paste called *surimi*, re-formed, flavored, and sold as the imitation crab we buy for seafood salads. Unalaska, an ancient Aleut village, is Dutch Harbor's across-the-bay neighbor and home to one of the oldest Russian Orthodox churches in Alaska.

North of the Aleutian chain in the Bering Sea, the remote volcanic islands called the Pribilofs support immense populations of birds and sea mammals as well as two small Aleut communities, St. George and St. Paul. Near St. Paul, the world's largest herds of northern fur seals haul out onto wave-lashed breeding rookeries, while far above, on sheer cliffs, puffins, cormorants, and other seabirds put on a show that delights birders equipped with binoculars and zoom lenses.

The Bush also is where America's largest oil field, Prudhoe Bay, was discovered in 1968. At its peak, more than 2 million barrels a day of North Slope crude from Prudhoe and neighboring lesser basins flowed southward via the 800-mi pipeline to the port of Valdez, on Prince William Sound in South Central Alaska, to help fuel the Lower 48 states. Now the flow has diminished to about 1.4 million barrels per day.

As roads in the Bush are few, airplanes—from jetliners to small bush planes—are the lifelines. Visitors throughout Alaska hear about the legendary pilots of the Far North—Noel and Sig Wien, Bob Reeve, Ben Eielson, Harold Gillam, Joe Crosson, Jack Jefford, and the others—who won their wings in the early years. They are Alaska's counterparts to the cowboy heroes of the Wild West. The Bush is where America's favorite humorist, Will Rogers, died in a crash with famed aviator Wiley Post in 1935. It happened just a few miles from Barrow, America's northernmost community. Today's pilots in Alaska, well equipped with dependable instruments and aircraft, make bush flying seem almost routine. Regional bush centers, such as Nome, Kotzebue, Barrow, and Bethel, though with smaller populations than most Lower 48 small towns, can count on daily jet service. The jets carry more than passengers; they also bring freight—from fresh vegetables to disposable diapers—that makes life livable in rural Alaska.

Bush Alaskans have a deep affection for their often-raw land, which is difficult to explain to strangers. They talk of living "close to nature," a cliché, perhaps, until one realizes that these Alaskans reside in the Bush all year long, adapting to brutal winter weather and isolation. They talk of a love for freewheeling frontier life, yet there is hardly a bush family that hasn't been touched by tragedy, from drownings to airplane crashes. They have accepted the Bush for what it is: dramatic and unforgiving. They have swapped big-city cultural amenities and supermarkets for wide-open spaces and distance from bureaucracy.

Visitors, still in city clothes, hop aboard jets in Anchorage and Fairbanks and head into the Bush like pampered explorers. Tour companies are waiting at the end of the line in the Arctic and near-Arctic with warm parkas that travelers can borrow for their stay. Even in summer, the weather can be chilly here.

Visitors should be aware that many of the bush communities have voted to be dry areas in order to fight alcohol-abuse problems affecting Alaska's Native people. Enforcement is strict, and bootlegging is a felony. Nome, of course, remains wet, with numerous lively saloons.

Pleasures and Pastimes

Dining

Visitors to the Bush should anticipate few dining choices. Expect prices to be higher, reflecting the remote locale and the need for supplies to be barged or flown in over long distances. Meals are hearty, often with too much deep-fat cooking for cholesterol- and calorie-conscious travelers. Mexican and Chinese foods are popular transplants. Local specialties, such as reindeer stew and Arctic sheefish, are served in some restaurants. The reindeer are herded by the Eskimo-owned NANA Regional Corporation, and their mild, lean meat is reminiscent of veal.

Virtually all restaurants in the Bush are small family-run establishments whose hours vary widely from one season to the next. Your best bet is to call ahead. Addresses are listed below whenever possible. In some towns, residents literally do not refer to their main street as anything other than "in town." Don't worry. These places are small and friendly enough to make getting lost impossible. For price ranges, *see* the dining chart *in* On the Road with Fodor's.

Fishing

Alaska's bush regions offer some of the state's premier sportfishing opportunities. Southwest Alaska is especially well known around the world for its remarkable salmon migrations and healthy populations of native rainbow trout. The easiest way to find the fish is to arrange for a guided trip—many sportfishing guides combine fishing and river-floating adventures—or visit a lodge. The Alaska Department of Fish and Game, National Park Service, and U.S. Fish and Wildlife Service can provide lists of guides and outfitters who operate in the region's parks and refuges (☞ Contacts and Resources *in* the Bush A to Z, *below*).

Lodging

In the Bush, accommodations are few and, as with dining, prices may seem high. Keep in mind that these towns are small outposts of civilization. And take note that limited lodging space is often reserved by tour groups. Add to that a visitor season lasting only about 110 days, from mid-May through mid-September, and the necessity of reservations becomes apparent.

Accommodations in outlying areas are plain but comfortable. Water supplies are often limited in the Arctic—your shower water may drain into your toilet tank. Ask about bed-and-breakfasts; their numbers are slowly growing. It's also sometimes possible to arrange to stay with a local family through bush airlines serving outlying villages. If you decide to head out to a wilderness lodge, be prepared to pay top dollar: the cost of transporting guests, not to mention supplies, to these remote locations often adds up to a daily rate of more than $200 per person, including meals. Remote lodges that also offer guided sportfishing commonly charge their clients $2,000–$4,000 per week. For price ranges, *see* the lodging chart *in* On the Road with Fodor's.

Native Culture

More and more, Native communities throughout Alaska are reconnecting with and celebrating their cultural traditions. Nowhere is this movement stronger than in the Bush. At the same time, many rural communities are recognizing the value of tourism to local economies, and a growing number of cultural tours and activities are being offered in rural villages—from drumming and dancing to potlucks, traditional Native games, and arts-and-crafts exhibits.

Shopping

Alaska's Arctic is known for Eskimo arts, ranging from wildlife figures carved from walrus ivory to bracelets and other jewelry fashioned from ivory, gold, Alaska jade, and other local materials. The Marine Mammals Act permits the purchase of walrus-ivory goods from Native Alaskans. Nome, Kotzebue, and Barrow all have reputable gift shops. Prices range from about $10 for tiny earrings to hundreds of dollars for ceremonial masks and other major pieces.

Wildlife Viewing

From the brown bears of Katmai National Park to the seals and seabirds of the Pribilofs and the caribou herds of the Arctic, the Bush in spring and summer is a place of great activity. The Alaska Peninsula has Alaska's—and the world's—largest gathering of brown bears, which congregate at clear-water streams to feed on the huge runs of salmon that return each summer. Millions of sea- and shorebirds breed in the Aleutian and Pribilof islands annually, and all sorts of marine mammals—sea lions, seals, sea otters, porpoises, and whales—inhabit coastal waters. And two of the continent's largest caribou herds, the Western Arctic and Porcupine, roam across the Arctic's mountains, valleys, and coastal plains. By far the easiest way for most travelers to see wildlife is to participate in guided tours, though independent travelers can also expect to see abundant animals if they do their homework before visiting Alaska and plan trips well in advance (☞ Chapter 3).

Exploring the Bush

Philosophically speaking, the Bush is where you find it. Technically, it's a place in Alaska that can't be reached by road. For the purposes of this chapter, we have contained our discussion to the major destinations of the Bush—remote communities that are beyond the scope of previous chapters yet still draw significant numbers of tourists.

Beginning in the southwestern part of the state, our tour of the Bush begins on the Alaska Peninsula, which juts out between the Pacific Ocean and the Bering Sea. The Aleutian Islands start where the peninsula ends, and sweep off toward Japan.

The Pribilof Islands lie north of the Aleutians, 200 mi off Alaska's coast. Head farther north and you encounter the undeveloped wilderness of Nunivak Island. Due east, back on the mainland, is Bethel, an important bush outpost on the Yukon-Kuskokwim Delta. As you continue north along the Bering seacoast, the next major stop is Nome, a predominantly white community with a Gold Rush heritage, just below the Arctic Circle. Kotzebue, just above the circle, is a coastal Eskimo town surrounded by sea and tundra. Barrow, another Eskimo community, sits at the very top of the state, the northernmost town in the United States. Follow the Arctic coastline eastward, and you reach Deadhorse, on Prudhoe Bay, the custodian to the region's important oil and gas reserves.

Numbers in the text correspond to numbers in the margin and on the Bush and Alaska Peninsula, Aleutians, and Pribilofs maps.

Great Itineraries

Because of its immense size—the Bush encompasses a third of the state—and the expense of transportation, it's best to give yourself a week or more when exploring Alaska's rural regions. But even with a week or two, you're likely to see no more than a small slice of Alaska's wildest and most remote parts. The easiest way to go, of course, is through a package tour. For those with shorter amounts of time, many companies offer one-, two-, or three-day tours to Arctic communities.

IF YOU HAVE 3 DAYS

Visit Katmai National Park's ⊞ **Brooks Falls and Camp** (☞ Chapter 3), where brown bears can be seen fishing for salmon, and take the bus tour to the **Valley of Ten Thousand Smokes,** formed in 1912 by a giant volcanic eruption. Or visit ⊞ **Dutch Harbor** ② and **Unalaska** in the **Aleutian Islands,** where guided fishing and wildlife-watching trips can be arranged. If you're visiting in winter, consider ⊞ **Bethel** ①, which hosts one of the state's premier dogsled races, the Kuskokwim 300, each January and the Camai Dance Festival in late March (☞ Festivals and Seasonal Events *in* Chapter 1).

IF YOU HAVE 5 DAYS

On guided wildlife tours, visit ⊞ **St. Paul Island** ③ or ⊞ **St. George Island,** two of the **Pribilof Islands** in the Bering Sea. Or if fishing is your thing, stay at one of the region's many lodges; there are several in and around **Katmai National Park** (☞ Chapter 3). Another popular way

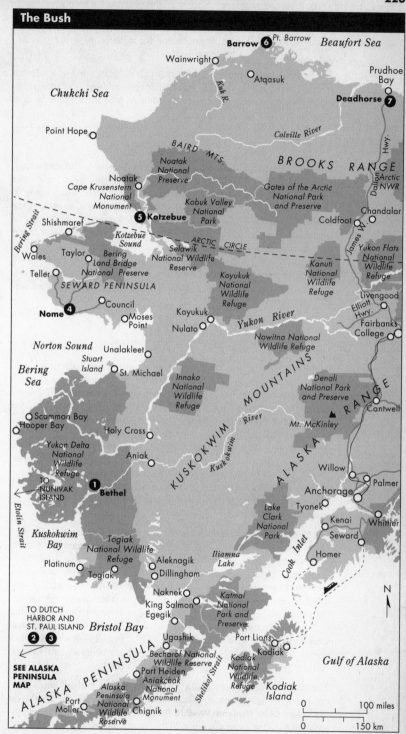

Beaufort Sea

Chukchi Sea

Barrow 6 Pt. Barrow
Wainwright

Atqasuk

Prudhoe Bay

Deadhorse 7

Point Hope

Kuk R.

Colville River

BAIRD MTS.

BROOKS RANGE

Noatak National Preserve

Gates of the Arctic National Park and Preserve

Dalton Hwy.

Arctic NWR

Noatak
Cape Krusenstern National Monument

Kobuk Valley National Park

Chandalar

Coldfoot

Shishmaref

5 **Kotzebue**

Kotzebue Sound

ARCTIC CIRCLE

Selawik National Wildlife Reserve

James W.

Yukon Flats National Wildlife Refuge

Bering Strait

Wales

Taylor

Bering Land Bridge National Preserve

Koyukuk National Wildlife Refuge

Kanuti National Wildlife Refuge

Teller

SEWARD PENINSULA

Livengood

Elliott Hwy.

Nome 4

Council

Koyukuk

Yukon River

Fairbanks

RANGE

College

Moses Point

Nulato

Nowitna National Wildlife Refuge

Norton Sound

Unalakleet

Bering Sea

Stuart Island

St. Michael

Innoko National Wildlife Refuge

KUSKOKWIM MOUNTAINS

Denali National Park and Preserve

Cantwell

Scammon Bay
Hooper Bay

Holy Cross

Yukon Delta National Wildlife Refuge

Aniak

Kuskokwim River

Mt. McKinley

ALASKA

Willow

Palmer

TO NUNIVAK ISLAND

1 **Bethel**

Anchorage

Tyonek

Kenai

Whittier

Etolin Strait

Kuskokwim Bay

Togiak National Wildlife Refuge

Lake Clark National Park

Seward

Platinum

Aleknagik

Iliamna Lake

Cook Inlet

Homer

Togiak

Dillingham

Naknek

Katmai National Park and Preserve

TO DUTCH HARBOR AND ST. PAUL ISLAND

King Salmon

Egegik

Port Lions

2 3

Ugashik

Kodiak

Gulf of Alaska

Bristol Bay

SEE ALASKA PENINSULA MAP

Becharof National Wildlife Reserve

Port Heiden

Aniakchak National Monument

Shelikof Strait

Kodiak National Wildlife Refuge

Kodiak Island

ALASKA PENINSULA

Port Moller

Alaska Peninsula National Wildlife Reserve

Chignik

N

0   100 miles

0   150 km

to see the region is on a guided river-floating trip on one of Southwest or Arctic Alaska's many pristine waterways, where you're likely to see lots of birds and perhaps bears fishing for salmon.

When to Tour the Bush

The best time to visit is from June through August, when the weather is mildest (though you should still anticipate cool, wet, and sometimes stormy weather), daylight hours are longest, and the wildlife is most abundant.

SOUTHWEST

The Southwest region encompasses some of Alaska's most remote, inaccessible, and rugged land- and seascapes. Ranging from the Alaska Peninsula down through the Aleutian Chain, it also includes many islands within the Bering Sea, among them the Pribilofs, as well as the Bristol Bay watershed and the Yukon-Kuskokwim Delta. A place of enormous biologic richness, it is seasonal home to many of North America's largest breeding populations of seabirds and waterfowl and also supports the world's densest population of brown bears and the world's greatest salmon runs. Here, too, are dozens of rural communities, most of them small, remote Native villages whose residents continue to lead subsistence lifestyles.

Bethel

❶ *400 mi west of Anchorage.*

Huddled on a sweeping curve of the Kuskokwim River, Bethel is a rough-hewn frontier town with 4,500 or so residents. One of rural Alaska's most important trading centers, it is a hub for more than 50 Native villages in a region roughly the size of the state of Oregon. The surrounding tundra is woven with pastel hues in summer, and the fishing for salmon, Arctic grayling, and Dolly Varden trout just a few miles outside town is excellent. Though visitor accommodations are limited, Bethel does have radio and television stations, a theater, a hotel, two banks, a credit union, a newspaper, a child-care center, a college, and the largest Alaska Native Health Service field hospital in the state, which is contracted to the tribally owned Yukon-Kuskokwim Health Corporation.

The **Yugtarvik Regional Museum** (⊠ Convention Center, ☎ 907/543–1819) holds Eskimo artifacts and is the place to buy contemporary crafts of western Alaska and the Yukon-Kuskokwim Delta area. It is a nonprofit marketplace for all the villages of the Kuskokwim area and is operated by volunteers, so its hours are usually Tuesday–Saturday, noon–5. Items for sale include water-grass baskets, wooden spirit masks, ivory-handle knives, grass and reindeer-beard dance fans, yo-yos, dolls, and seal-gut raincoats. Admission to the museum is free. The nearby **Moravian Bookstore** (⊠ 301 Third Ave., ☎ 907/543–2474) stocks a variety of arts and crafts as well as books about religion and Eskimo culture. It is open Monday–Saturday 11–5:30.

The Yukon-Kuskokwim Delta surrounds Bethel and abounds with moose, wolves, beavers, muskrats, fish, and birds. To the northwest the **Yukon Delta National Wildlife Refuge** (☎ 907/543–3151) encompasses one of the largest waterfowl breeding grounds in the world. Despite modern encroachment, Yupik Eskimos in the delta continue their centuries-old subsistence lifestyle. Refuge staff can provide tips on fishing, wildlife viewing, and boating opportunities, as well as guides and outfitters who operate in the refuge. For more information on the

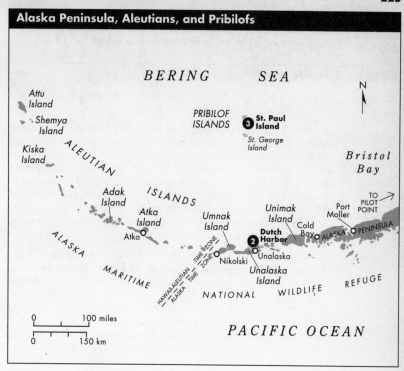

refuge contact Alaska Public Lands Information Center (☞ *Visitor Information in* the Bush A to Z, *below*).

Dining and Lodging

$$–$$$ ✕ **Alice's Kitchen.** This downtown restaurant specializes in Chinese food, with daily lunch and dinner specials. ⊠ *473 Ridgecrest St., Box 1915, Bethel 99559,* ☎ *907/543–2272. No credit cards.*

$$$–$$$$ 🏠 **Bentley's Porter House B&B.** This inn sits on Front Street, along the banks of the Kuskokwim River in downtown Bethel, and prides itself on Alaska-style hospitality. In addition to the simply furnished bedrooms there are sitting rooms with TVs, VCRs, and reading material. The price includes a full breakfast. ⊠ *624 Front St., Box 529, Bethel 99559,* ☎ *907/543–3552,* ⅀ *907/543–3561. 23 rooms with shared bath. AE, D, DC, MC, V.*

$$–$$$ 🏠 **Pacifica Guest House.** This inn offers a quiet stay and insightful tips from the Bush-savvy owners. Suites are furnished in Queen Anne style; standard rooms have typical hotel furnishings. The restaurant, Diane's Café, is just next door in a solarium setting. It offers gourmet meals, by bush or any standards. You can sample Alaska salmon or halibut, steaks or roasts, or go with the vegetarian and heart-healthy meals. ⊠ *1220 Hoffman Hwy., Box 1208, Bethel 99559,* ☎ *907/543–4305,* ⅀ *907/543–3403 or 907/543–5461. 24 rooms, 10 with bath; 11 suites. Restaurant, sauna, exercise room, meeting room, travel services, airport shuttle. AE, D, DC, MC, V.*

OFF THE
BEATEN PATH

NUNIVAK ISLAND – Due west of Bethel, and separated from the Yukon-Kuskokwim Delta by Etolin Strait, Nunivak Island is an important wildlife refuge. Home of the **Nunivak National Wildlife Refuge,** this site is noted for its large herd of reindeer, a transplanted herd of musk ox, and the Eskimo settlement of **Mekoryuk.** For information on the island, contact the **U.S. Fish and Wildlife Service** (☎ 907/543–3151) in Bethel. Visitors, lured by fine ivory carvings, masks, and items knit from *qiviut* (musk ox) wool, should check with **ERA Aviation** (☎ 800/866–8394) about accommodations, which are limited and far from deluxe.

Aleutian Islands

The Aleutians begin 540 mi southwest of Anchorage and stretch more than 1,000 mi.

Separating the North Pacific Ocean from the Bering Sea, the Aleutian Islands (also called the Chain) stretch from the Alaska Peninsula in a southwesterly arc toward Japan. The distance from the point nearest the Alaska mainland, Unimak Island, to the most distant island, Attu, is more than 1,000 mi. This volcanic, treeless archipelago consists of about 20 large islands and several hundred smaller ones. The Aleutian Islands and surrounding coastal waters make up one of the most biologically rich areas in Alaska, with abundant seabird, marine mammal, and fish populations.

Before the Russians came, the islands were dotted with Aleut villages. Today's communities include **Nikolski,** on Umnak Island; **Unalaska,** on Unalaska Island; **Atka,** on Atka Island; and **Cold Bay,** at the peninsula's tip. The hardy Aleuts work at commercial fishing or in canneries and as expert guides for those who hunt and fish. With the exception of U.S. military bases, the settlements are quite small, and accommodations are scarce. Visitors are not allowed to visit Adak or Shemya, another military base, without special permission. The military is shutting down its Adak operation and there's been talk of using the base's infrastructure to start a new town.

❷ Dutch Harbor, on Unalaska Island, is by far the most populous and popular destination in the Aleutian Islands and in recent years has served as its tourism center. The Japanese bombed Dutch Harbor during World War II, and visitors can still see concrete bunkers, gun batteries, and a partially sunken ship left over from the war. In addition to military history, you'll find a hotel and restaurants that rival those on Alaska's mainland, and a variety of guided adventure tours.

Dining and Lodging

$–$$ ✕ **Stormy's Restaurant.** A variety of American and ethnic foods are served at this family-style restaurant, including Chinese and Japanese (there's even a sushi bar). Dishes include pizza, fried chicken, and seafoods. Less than 1 mi across the bridge from downtown Dutch Harbor, this is Unalaska's oldest eatery. ⊠ *2nd Ave. and Broadway, Unalaska village,* ☎ *907/581–1565. MC, V.*

$$$$ ✕🏨 **Grand Aleutian Hotel.** This hotel won an architectural award for
★   its chalet-inspired design, which includes a stone fireplace in its three-story atrium lobby. Guest rooms have views of Margaret Bay or Unalaska Bay. In-room amenities include hair dryer, clock radio, and cable TV; some suites have a whirlpool tub. The Chart Room Restaurant and Lounge offers fine dining, specializing in Pacific Rim cuisine featuring locally caught seafood. Guided activities include hiking, mountain biking, bird-watching, and halibut and salmon fishing. ⊠ *498 Salmon Way, Box 921169, Dutch Harbor 99692-1169,* ☎ *907/ 581–3844 or 800/891–1194,* ℻ *907/581–7150. 112 rooms, 6 suites. 2 restaurants, 2 bars, meeting rooms, travel services, airport shuttle. AE, D, DC, MC, V.*

$$$ ✕🏨 **Unisea Inn.** Rooms at this hotel right on the water are simple yet comfortable and have cable TV and telephones. Try to book a room with a view of the small-boat harbor. Mexican fare, burgers, and sand-

wiches are served in the Unisea Inn Sports Bar and Grill. Sit back and watch satellite broadcasts of spectator sports or try your hand at darts, pool, or video games. Live bands play Top-40 or country music six nights a week. ⊠ *185 Gilman Rd., Box 921169, Dutch Harbor 99692,* ☏ *907/581–1325 or 800/891–1194 for reservations,* ℻ *907/581–1633. 42 rooms. Restaurant, sports bar, beauty salon, airport shuttle. AE, D, DC, MC, V.*

Pribilof Islands

200 mi north of the Aleutians, 800 mi southwest of Anchorage.

The Pribilof Islands are misty, fogbound breeding grounds of seabirds and northern fur seals. Five islets make up the Pribilof group—a tiny, green, treeless oasis, with rippling belts of lush grass contrasting with red volcanic soil. In early summer seals come home from far Pacific waters to mate, and the larger islands, St. Paul and St. George, are overwhelmed with scenes of frenzied activity. Their sounds can roll out several miles to sea.

The islands are a 1,600-mi round-trip from Anchorage, over the massive snowy peaks of the Alaska Peninsula and past the rocky islands of the Aleutian chain. This was the supply route for U.S. forces during World War II, when Japan invaded Attu and Kiska islands toward the tip of the chain. During the Bering Sea leg, there may be a playful pod of whales below.

Wildlife watching is what brings nearly all visitors to the Pribilof Islands. Together, St. Paul and St. George islands are seasonal homes to nearly 1 million fur seals (about 80% of them on St. Paul) and 200 species of birds. Some birds migrate here from as far away as Argentina, while others are year-round residents. Of special interest to birders are the rare Asian vagrants sometimes blown here by strong western winds. Most spectacular of all is the islands' seabird population: each summer more than 2 million seabirds gather at traditional Pribilof nesting grounds; about 90% of them breed on St. George. The Pribilofs are also home to foxes, and sea lions and whales are occasionally spotted off their shores.

For most travelers, it is much easier and more cost-efficient to participate in packaged tours that arrange air travel from Anchorage, lodging, ground transportation on the islands, and guided activities. Anyone planning to come here on their own should be aware that visitor accommodations in the Pribilofs are very limited.

❸ At **St. Paul Island,** nature lovers can watch members of the largest northern fur seal herd in the world and more than 180 varieties of birds. In town, you can visit with local residents; about 500 descendants of Aleut-Russians live here now, in the shadow of the old Russian Orthodox church and the vestiges of Aleut culture. **St. George Island** is home to nearly to 2 million nesting seabirds, but it is much less frequently visited because no organized tours go there and accommodations are limited.

Dining and Lodging

\$\$ ✕ **Trident Sea Foods.** This cafeteria-style eatery—the island's only restaurant—serves fish processors as well as visitors to St. Paul Island. Plan your day carefully because meals are served according to a strict schedule: breakfast, 7–8 AM; lunch noon–1; and dinner 5–6 PM. ⊠ *Downtown St. Paul, 2 blocks from the King Eider Hotel,* ☏ *907/546–2377. No credit cards.*

$$$$ ⊡ **King Eider Hotel.** Filled in summer by tour groups, this hotel has rooms that are simply furnished. The original part of the hotel dates to the late 1800s; it's been expanded four times since. There are TV and reading rooms and a gift shop. If you are traveling on your own, make reservations months in advance. ⊠ *523 Tolstoi St., Box 88, St. Paul 99660,* ☎ *907/546–2477,* FAX *907/546–5026. 25 rooms with shared bath. Travel services. AE, MC, V.*

$$$$ ⊡ **St. George Tanaq Hotel.** A national historic landmark, St. George Island's only hotel is a small, spare building with 10 simply furnished rooms and shared baths. There is a shared kitchen and dining area, with stove, refrigerator, and cooking utensils—important on an island with no restaurant. ⊠ *Downtown, Box 939, St. George 99591,* ☎ *907/ 272–9886 or 907/859–2255,* FAX *907/859–2230. 10 rooms with shared bath. MC, V.*

Guided Tours

Contact **Reeve Aleutian Airways** (⊠ 4700 W. International Airport Rd., Anchorage 99502, ☎ 800/544–2248) for St. Paul Island tour information.

NORTHWEST AND THE ARCTIC

This is a largely roadless region of long, dark, sunless winters and short, bright summers, when the sun remains in the sky around the clock for nearly three months. It's the land of Eskimos and huge caribou herds and polar bears, a place where people still lead subsistence lifestyles and where traditional Native culture is making a strong comeback. It's also a place of gold rushes and America's largest oil field.

Nome

❹ *540 mi northwest of Anchorage on the Seward Peninsula.*

It has been 100 years since a great stampede for gold put a speck of wilderness called Nome on the Alaska map, but gold mining and noisy saloons are still mainstays in this frontier community on the icy Bering Sea. Mainly a collection of ramshackle houses and low-slung commercial buildings, Nome looks like a vintage gold-mining camp or the neglected set of a western movie—rawboned, rugged, and somewhat shabby. What the town lacks in appearance is made up for with a cheerful hospitality and colorful history.

Only 165 mi from the coast of Siberia, Nome is considerably closer to Russia than either Anchorage or Fairbanks. And though there's a local road system, to get to Nome you must either fly or mush a team of sled dogs.

Nome's golden years began in 1898, when three prospectors—known as the "Lucky Swedes"—struck rich deposits on Anvil Creek, about 4 mi from what became Nome. The news spread quickly. When the Bering Sea ice parted the next spring, ships from Puget Sound, down by Seattle, arrived in Nome with eager stampeders. An estimated 15,000 people landed in Nome between June and October of 1900. Among the gold-rush luminaries were Wyatt Earp, the old gunfighter from the O.K. Corral, who mined the gold of Nome by opening a posh saloon; Tex Rickard, the boxing promoter, who operated another Nome saloon; and Rex Beach, the novelist.

Nome is also proud to be the hometown of General James H. Doolittle, the Tokyo raider of World War II. When Doolittle's bombers hit Japan in a daring raid in 1942, the headline in the *Nome Nugget* proudly announced: "NOME TOWN BOY MAKES GOOD!"

A network of 250 mi or so of **gravel roads** around the town leads to creeks and rivers for gold panning or fishing for trout, salmon, and Arctic grayling. You can also see reindeer, bears, foxes, and moose in the wild on the back roads that used to connect early mining camps and hamlets. Independent travelers with hardy vehicles should go exploring. You can rent a Jeep, pickup truck, or van in Nome for $65–$110 a day (**Alaska Cab Garage,** ☎ 907/443–2939; or **Stampede Car Rentals,** ☎ 907/443–5598). Because the sun stays up late in the summer months, drive to the top of **Anvil Mountain,** near Nome, for a panoramic view of the old gold town and the Bering Sea. Be sure to carry mosquito repellent.

For exploring downtown, make the **Nome Convention and Visitor's Bureau** (⊠ Front St., Box 240, Nome 99762, ☎ 907/443–5535, FAX 907/443–5832) your first stop. You can pick up an historic-walking-tour map, a city map, and information on local activities from flight-seeing to bird-watching. There are also slide shows and a video presentation (call for screening times).

Dining, Lodging, and Camping

$$–$$$$ ✕ **Fort Davis Roadhouse.** The Roadhouse, which specializes in prime rib and seafood, is where locals go for a night out. Friday and Saturday are buffet nights. Some visitors fall for the Bering Ball, a infamously potent cocktail that most locals seem to avoid. Taxis serve the area. ⊠ *Nome–Council Rd., 1½ mi east of town,* ☎ 907/443–2660. MC, V. Closed Sun., Mon. No lunch.

$$ ✕ **Nacho's Mexican Restaurant.** The authentic Mexican food at this café-style restaurant is popular with the locals, so you may have to wait. Chinese food also is served. ⊠ *Front St., downtown,* ☎ 907/443–5503. MC, V.

$–$$ ✕ **Fat Freddie's.** This popular eatery overlooking the Bering Sea serves
★ buffalo and musk ox burgers, steak, and seafood in season. Guests at the Nome Nugget Inn (☞ *below*) can enter directly from the hotel. ⊠ *50 Front St.,* ☎ 907/443–5899. AE, MC, V.

$–$$ ✕ **Polar Cub.** Standard American diner food, from omelets to steak, fills the menu here. Locals like to linger over coffee, making it a good place to eavesdrop on area issues or just gaze out at the Bering Sea. With its sea views, good prices, and friendly service, the Cub is a great place for early-morning breakfast. ⊠ *Next to the seawall, off Front St., downtown,* ☎ 907/443–5191. AE, MC, V.

$$$$ ⌂ **Camp Bendeleben.** This lodge is in Council, an early 1900s gold-mining camp, about 75 mi northeast of Nome. Visitors can fish for arctic char, grayling, and four species of salmon; other outdoor diversions include bird-watching and photography. Packages include all meals and transportation between the lodge and Nome. Prices vary considerably, depending on whether guests stay at the lodge or remote tent camps and whether or not they choose to be guided when fishing. There is a three-night minimum. *In summer:* ⊠ *Council, Box 1045, Nome 99762; in winter:* ⊠ *654 Highlander Circle, Anchorage 99518;* ☎ *907/443–2880 summer, 907/349–9589 winter;* FAX *907/443–2880. 3 rooms. Dining room, fishing. No credit cards. Closed Oct.–mid-June.*

$$$ ⌂ **Nome Nugget Inn.** The architecture and decor of the Nugget Inn combine every cliché of the Victorian gold-rush era. Authentic it's not, but fun it is. Outside, a signpost marks the mileage to various points, serious and silly, around the globe. Inside, frontier memorabilia abounds in the lobby and lounge. Rooms are simple, modern, and clean but not nearly as atmospheric. Arctic tour groups stay here. ⊠ *Box 430, Front St., Nome 99762,* ☎ 907/443–2323, FAX 907/443–5966. 47 rooms. Restaurant, bar. AE, DC, MC, V.

$$ 🏠 **June's B&B.** A genuine gold miner's daughter regales visitors with
★ tall tales of Nome's past in this remodeled home downtown. Rooms
have handmade quilts and stenciled walls. Breakfast is Swedish pan-
cakes or sourdough pancakes made from dough that was started 100
years ago. (It made the legendary trip over the Chilkoot Trail during
the Klondike Gold Rush of 1897–98.) The small garage in the front
yard is where June's dad used to keep his train. Make sure you ask her
about it. ⊠ *231 E. Fourth St., Box 489, Nome 99762,* ☎ *907/443–
5984 in summer, 800/494–6994 in winter. 3 rooms share 2 baths. V.
Closed Oct.–Apr.*

$ 🏕 **Bureau of Land Management Campground.** BLM manages a free
campground at Mile 40 of the Nome-Taylor Highway. The camp-
ground has six tent sites, toilet facilities, and nearby fishing. The max-
imum length of stay is 14 days. The campground has a pit toilet and
fire rings for cooking, but the only water is in nearby Salmon Lake and
Pilgrim River; it must be boiled or otherwise treated. ⊠ *Bureau of Land
Management, Nome Field Office, Box 925, Nome 99762,* ☎ *907/443–
2177 in Nome or 800/437–7021 in Fairbanks. Reservations not ac-
cepted. No credit cards. Closed Oct.–Apr.*

Outdoor Activities and Sports

The famed 1,049-mi **Iditarod Trail Sled Dog Race**—the Olympics of sled-
dog racing—reaches its climax in Nome in mid-March. Racers start
in Anchorage for a trip of 10 days to two weeks. The arrival of the
mushers heralds a winter carnival. For dates, starting times, and other
information, contact the **Iditarod Trail Committee** (⊠ Box 870800,
Wasilla 99687, ☎ 907/376–5155).

Shopping

Nome is one of the best places to buy **ivory**, because many of the Es-
kimo carvers from outlying villages come to Nome first to offer their
wares to dealers. The **Arctic Trading Post** (⊠ Bering and Front Sts., ☎
907/443–2686) has an extensive stock of authentic Eskimo ivory carv-
ings and other Alaskan artwork and books. Also try the **Board of Trade
Ivory Shop** (☎ 907/443–2611), **Maruskiya's** (☎ 907/443–2955), and
the other shops on **Front Street** downtown. **Chukotka–Alaska** (⊠ W.
1st St., ☎ 907/443–4128) has both Alaskan and **Russian artwork** and
handicrafts.

Kotzebue

❺ *170 mi northwest of Nome.*

It happens all the time. An Alaska Airlines jetliner bound for Kotze-
bue nears the Arctic Circle. "Please fasten your seat belts," the pilot
cautions. "We usually get a bump when we cross the circle." Moments
later, the plane takes a roller-coaster dip that has passengers shrieking
and laughing.

Kotzebue, Alaska's largest Eskimo community, is home to around
3,500 residents. It lies 26 mi above the Arctic Circle, on Alaska's
northwestern coast. "We have four seasons—June, July, August, and
winter," a tour guide jests. But don't worry about the sometimes-chilly
weather—the local sightseeing company has snug, bright loaner parkas
for visitors on package tours.

Strung out in clusters of weather-bleached little houses and a few pub-
lic buildings on the gravelly shore of Kotzebue Sound, Kotzebue pro-
vides visitors with a glimpse of the way Alaska's Eskimos live today.
It was an ancient Eskimo trading center; now it is an example of the
new spirit nudging Alaska's Natives into the state's mainstream cul-
ture without leaving their traditions behind.

The NANA (Northwest Alaska Native Association) Regional Corporation, one of the 13 Native corporations formed when Congress settled the Alaskan Natives' aboriginal land claims in 1971, has its headquarters in Kotzebue. It was NANA (☎ 907/442–3301 or 800/478–3301) that built the $1 million **Living Museum of the Arctic** (☎ 907/442–3747 or 907/442–3301) in 1977 and turned it into one of Alaska's top-rated museums: visitors sit on bleachers facing a stage where stories are told; after the storytelling, there is a cultural slide show relating the wisdom of the elders, followed by traditional Eskimo singing and dancing and a blanket toss in which audience members are invited to participate. It may look like a game, but it was serious business in the early days, when Eskimo hunters were launched high in the air from blankets of walrus or seal hide to scan the seas for game. You may even be urged to take a turn on the bouncing blanket. The gift shop stocks a good selection of Native crafts as well as T-shirts, sweatshirts, and postcards. The museum's hours are 9–7 daily from mid-May through mid-September; at other times of the year you can call to make special arrangements to have it opened for you. Admission to the museum is free, but the cost is $20 to attend cultural programs. Tours can be arranged through NANA's Tour Arctic program (☞ *below.*)

NANA also has a **Tour Arctic** program (☎ 907/442–3301), in which visitors may participate in a guided Kotzebue Tour or a Native Village Excursion. Prices vary, depending on the nature of the tour.

Visitors hiking the wildflower-carpeted tundra around Kotzebue enter a living museum dedicated to **permafrost,** the permanently frozen ground that lies just a few inches below the spongy tundra. Even Kotzebue's 6,000-ft airport runway is built on permafrost—with a 6-inch insulating layer between the frozen ground and the airfield surface to ensure that landings are smooth, not slippery.

Kotzebue serves as a gateway for three exceptional national **wilderness areas:** Noatak National Preserve, Kobuk Valley National Park, and Cape Krusenstern National Monument (☞ Chapter 3). North and east of Kotzebue is the **Brooks Range,** one of Alaska's great mountain ranges. Stretching across the state, much of the range is protected by Gates of the Arctic National Park and Preserve and the Arctic National Wildlife Refuge (☞ Chapter 3).

Dining and Lodging

$$ ✕ **Arctic Dragon.** In the center of town, this family-style restaurant is known for its traditional Chinese fare as well as its American-style meals. ⊠ *Bison St., downtown,* ☎ *907/442–3770. AE, MC, V.*

$–$$ ✕ **Kotzebue Pizza House.** Although this restaurant serves pizza and Chinese food, locals especially tout the burgers here, which are among the best in the state. ⊠ *2nd Ave. and Bison St., downtown,* ☎ *907/442–3432. No credit cards.*

$$$ 🏨 **Nullagvik Hotel.** This downtown hotel overlooking Kotzebue Sound is built on pilings driven into the ground because the heat of the building would melt the underlying permafrost and cause the hotel to sink. The modern rooms, decorated with images of Eskimo life, have sitting areas and cable TV; suites have couches in the sitting areas. There are public sitting areas on each floor with picture-window views of the bay. Insist on a ground-floor room; there's no elevator to the second or third floors, and rooms there can get unbearably hot. The hotel's coffee shop–restaurant serves standard American fare in addition to a few local specialties, such as reindeer and fresh Arctic fish. Meals are sometimes served buffet style when big tour groups are in the hotel. ⊠ *301 Shore Ave., Box 336, Kotzebue 99752,* ☎ *907/442–3331, FAX 907/442–3340. 75 rooms, 4 suites. Restaurant, travel services. AE, DC, MC, V.*

Barrow

6 *330 mi north of Kotzebue.*

The northernmost community in the United States, Barrow sits just 1,300 mi from the North Pole on the Beaufort Sea. For 82 days, from May to August, the sun stays above the horizon; it is the best place in Alaska to catch the legendary midnight sun. An umiak (Eskimo skin boat), a fish-drying rack, and drifting Arctic pack ice, often close to shore, complete the scene. Barrow's 4,000 residents, many of them Natives (only Kotzebue has a larger Eskimo population), live in a modern village but maintain traditional Eskimo activities such as whale hunting. The Barrow airport is the site of the **Will Rogers and Wiley Post Monument,** commemorating the 1935 crash of the American humorist and the pilot 15 mi south of town.

Visitors arriving in Barrow usually come on a one- or two-day tour from Alaska Airlines (☞ *Guided Tours in* the Bush A to Z, *below*). Packages include a bus tour of the town's dusty roads and major sights. A highlight is **Mound 44,** where the frozen body of a 500-year-old Eskimo was discovered. Scientists have been studying her remains to learn more about pre-outside-contact Eskimo life and culture. You'll also pass by an **early warning radar installation,** which once watched for incoming Soviet missiles. The air force has since mothballed its big dishes, but Barrow duty must have given special meaning to the term "Cold War." Without a doubt, the best part about visiting the top of the world is walking along the sandy beach and seeing the pack ice, stretching across the horizon even in the middle of summer.

Dining and Lodging

$$–$$$$ ✕ **Pepe's North of the Border.** The warmth of Pepe's will make you forget that you're in the middle of the Arctic tundra. Murals depicting Mexican village scenes highlight the Mission-style decor, and an extensive selection of Mexican dishes makes this restaurant a favorite of locals and visitors alike. Dinner at Pepe's is surprisingly refined for being on the very fringe of civilization. ⊠ *Next to the Top of the World Hotel,* ☎ *907/852–8200. DC, MC, V.*

$–$$$ ✕ **Ken's Restaurant.** Basic burgers and Chinese food are the staples at this restaurant, with good daily specials and the best prices in town. ⊠ *Above the airport terminal building,* ☎ *907/852–8888. No credit cards.*

$$$$ 🏨 **Barrow Airport Inn.** As the name says, this modern and well-appointed property is conveniently near the airport. Standard rooms come with cable TV and telephones; nine rooms have full kitchenettes and the others have a microwave and refrigerator. Complimentary morning coffee is served in the lobby. ⊠ *1815 Momegana St., Box 933, Barrow 99723,* ☎ *907/852–2525,* 𝖥𝖠𝖷 *907/852–2316. 14 rooms. Travel services. AE, D, MC, V.*

$$$$ 🏨 **Top of the World Hotel.** Frontier touches at this popular hotel on
  ★   the shore of the Arctic Ocean include one complete stuffed polar bear and the mounted head of another. All rooms have cable TV and telephone. Guests can mingle in the lobby at the coffee bar or in front of the community television. Several rooms are brand new and others have been remodeled. Ask for a room with an ocean view. ⊠ *1200 Agviq St., Box 189, Barrow 99723,* ☎ *907/852–3900 or 800/882–8478; 800/478–8520 in AK;* 𝖥𝖠𝖷 *907/852–6752. 50 rooms. Coffee shop. AE, D, DC, MC, V.*

Shopping

The AC Value Center or, as it's known locally, **Stuaqpak** (the "Big Store," ⊠ Agviq St., near Borough Bldg., ☎ 907/852–6711) is the largest store in town for both groceries and Eskimo products, including furs, parkas, mukluks, and ceremonial masks. Be sure to visit the lobby of the **North Slope Borough Building** (✉ 1274 Agviq St., ☎ 907/852–2611), which has a fine display case of Eskimo arts and crafts from all the villages along the North Slope. For sale are such items as baleen baskets and artwork, sealskin bags, and ivory carvings. This is a nonprofit operation, so the money goes directly to the artisans. Credit cards (MC, V) are accepted for certain items only.

Prudhoe Bay

250 mi southeast of Barrow.

❼ Most towns have museums that chronicle local history and achievements. **Deadhorse** is the town anchoring life along Prudhoe Bay, but it could serve also as a museum dedicated to humankind's hunt for energy and our ability to adapt to harsh conditions.

The costly, much-publicized Arctic oil and gas project is complex and varied. One-day tours explore the tundra terrain from oil pipes to sandpipers. Along with spotting caribou, wildflowers, and an unusual stand of willow trees at the edge of the Arctic Ocean, the field tour surveys oil wells, stations, and oil-company residential complexes—small cities themselves. Your guide will discuss the multimillion-dollar research programs aimed at preserving the region's ecology and point out special tundra vehicles known as Rollagons, whose great weight is distributed so that they scarcely make a dent as they pass over delicate terrain.

In the past, individual travelers rarely turned up in Deadhorse and Prudhoe Bay. But now that the Dalton Highway has been opened as far north as Deadhorse, adventurous independent travelers are finding their way north. Still, most people traveling to Deadhorse either work here or come on a tour with one of Alaska's airlines or motor-coach operators (☞ Guided Tours *in* the Bush A to Z, *below*). And even those who travel here on their own must join a guided tour (arranged through the Arctic Caribou Inn, ☞ *below*) if they wish to cross the oil fields to get to the Arctic Ocean. Visitors traveling on their own should also be aware that there are no restaurants here, though meals can sometimes be arranged through the hotel.

Lodging

$$$ 🏨 **Arctic Caribou Inn.** This one-story hotel, owned by the NANA Corporation, was created with trailers left over from the building of the trans-Alaska pipeline. The simply furnished wood-paneled rooms have twin beds and private bathrooms. There is a buffet-style restaurant with limited hours and a TV lounge. ✉ *Deadhorse, near airport, Pouch 340111, Prudhoe Bay 99734,* ☎ *907/659–2368 or 907/659–2840,* FAX *907/659–2289. 140 rooms with bath. Restaurant, exercise room, recreation room. D, DC, MC, V.*

THE BUSH A TO Z

Arriving and Departing

By Boat

The Alaska state ferry *Tustumena* (Alaska Marine Highway System, ✉ Box 25535, Juneau 99802-5535, ☎ 907/465–3941 or 800/642–0066, FAX 907/277–4829) makes monthly trips May through September to Dutch Harbor/Unalaska, Kodiak, the Aleutian Islands, and several other bush communities in Southwestern Alaska.

By Bus

The only bus service in the Bush is up the Dalton Highway to Prudhoe Bay (☞ Guided Tours, *below*).

By Car

The **James W. Dalton Highway**—formerly the construction road for the trans-Alaska pipeline—is Alaska's only highway to the High Arctic. Popularly known as the Haul Road, this 414-mi, all-gravel road begins about 73 mi north of Fairbanks, connecting with the Steese and Elliott highways to points south. Private vehicles may travel the entire length of the highway to Deadhorse. However, access to oil company facilities and the shore of the Arctic Ocean is limited to commercial operators.

Vehicle services are limited along the highway. There are plans to add new facilities, but currently fuel, repairs, food, and lodging are available at only three places: the Yukon River crossing (Mile 56), Coldfoot (Mile 175), and Deadhorse (Mile 414). Motorists are cautioned not to expect assistance from truckers shuttling between Prudhoe Bay and Fairbanks. For Dalton Highway information, contact the Fairbanks office of the **Alaska Public Lands Information Center** (⊠ 250 Cushman St., Suite 1A, Fairbanks 99701, ☎ 907/456–0527).

The Arctic and near-Arctic communities of Nome, Kotzebue, and Barrow do not have highway connections to the rest of Alaska, nor do Bethel, the Aleutian Chain, or the Pribilofs.

By Plane

Alaska Airlines (☎ 800/426–0333) is among the major carriers serving Alaska from Seattle, and it flies within Alaska to most major communities. **Reeve Aleutian Airways** (☎ 907/243–4700 or 800/544–2248) has scheduled service to points in Southwest Alaska, including the Alaska Peninsula, the Aleutian Islands, and the Pribilof Islands.

Many Anchorage and Fairbanks air taxis serve the Bush in addition to Bush-based carriers such as **Bering Air Inc.** (⊠ Box 1650, Nome 99762, ☎ 907/443–5464 or 800/478–5422 in AK; 907/443–5620 Russian desk; FAX 907/443–5919), which also offers local flightseeing tours, and weather and politics permitting, flights to Provideniya, on the Siberian coast across the Bering Strait. **Cape Smythe Air Service** (⊠ Box 549, Barrow 99723, ☎ 907/852–8333 or 800/478–8333 in AK; FAX 907/852–2509) serves the communities of the North Slope plus Kotzebue. **Frontier Flying Service** (⊠ 3820 University Ave., Fairbanks 99709, ☎ 907/474–0014, FAX 907/474–0774) serves the Interior and the Bering and Arctic coasts. **Peninsula Airways** (⊠ 6100 Boeing Ave., Anchorage 99502, ☎ 907/243–2323 or 800/448–4226, FAX 907/243–6848) serves the communities on the Alaskan Peninsula, the Aleutians and Pribilofs, Kodiak, and parts of the Interior and Northwest. **Wright Air Service** (⊠ Box 60142, Fairbanks 99706, ☎ 907/474–0502 or 800/478–0502 in AK; FAX 907/474–0375) flies to all of the Alaskan Bush as well as the Interior.

Contacts and Resources

Doctors and Dentists

A statewide air-ambulance service operates through **Columbia Alaska Regional Lifeflight** (☎ 800/478–9111) in Anchorage. The **Maniilaq Health Center** (☎ 907/442–3321) is in Kotzebue. **Norton Sound Regional Hospital** (☎ 907/443–3311) is the major hospital in the Nome area. The Arctic Slope Native Association operates **Samuel Simmonds Memorial Hospital** (☎ 907/852–4611) in Barrow.

Emergencies

Contact the **police** at: Barrow (☎ 907/852–6111), Kotzebue (☎ 907/442–3351), Nome (☎ 907/443–5262). For services outside the city limits, contact the **state troopers:** Barrow (☎ 907/852–3783), Kotzebue (☎ 907/442–3222 or 800/789–3222), Nome (☎ 907/443–5525).

Guided Tours

Package tours are the most common way of traveling the Bush, where making your flight connections and having a room to sleep in at the end of the line are no small feats. Independent travel, particularly for campers and hikers, can be highly rewarding, but it takes careful planning. During peak season—late May through Labor Day—planes, state ferries, hotels, and sportfishing lodges are likely to be crowded with travelers on organized tours. Booking well ahead is recommended; many Alaska travelers make their reservations a year in advance.

The type of tour you choose will determine how you get there. On air tours—which include travel to most bush communities—you will fly to and from your destination. On motor-coach tours to Deadhorse and Prudhoe Bay, you will travel at least one way by coach. Each type of tour has its own advantages: air travel is faster and gives you the unique perspective of the Arctic from the air; motor-coach tours travel at a more leisurely pace and give you a ground-level view of sweeping tundra vistas. But the visitor has no choice but to fly to most bush locales.

Most tours to the Arctic are short—one, two, or three days. These often can be combined with visits to other regions of the state. Packages may include stays at wilderness lodges (☞ Lodging *in* Pleasures and Pastimes, *above*).

The Bush is home to many Native Alaskan groups, many of which are active in tourism. Often, local Native corporations act as your hosts—running the tours, hotels, and attractions. **Nome Tour and Marketing** (book through Alaska Airlines Vacations; ☞ *below*), in Nome provides ground transportation, accommodations, and other services for visitors. The **NANA Development Corporation** (☎ 800/478–3301, or book through Princess Tours or Gray Line of Alaska; ☞ *below*) provides ground transportation and accommodations in Kotzebue as well as at Prudhoe Bay, in conjunction with motor-coach tours. If you visit Barrow and stay at the Top of the World Hotel, **Tundra Tours** (book through Alaska Airlines Vacations; ☞ *below*), another Native operation, will be your host. On **Gambell Island** (book through Alaska Village Tours; ☞ *below*), local residents also run all the ground operations.

BY BUS

In the summer tourist season, tour operators run trips up the **Dalton Highway** out of Fairbanks and Anchorage. Travelers go one way by air, the other by motor coach. The route crosses the rugged Brooks Range, the Arctic Circle, and the Yukon River. It also brushes the edges of the Gates of the Arctic National Park and the Arctic National Wildlife Refuge (☞ Chapter 3). **Gray Line of Alaska** (✉ 1980 S. Cushman, Fairbanks 99701, ☎ 907/452–3646 or 800/887–7741 in AK) operates package tours that travel the Dalton Highway to Deadhorse. **Princess Tours** (✉ 2815 2nd Ave., Suite 400, Seattle, WA 98121, ☎ 206/728–4202, 907/479–9660, or 800/835–8907 for reservations) also runs tours along the Dalton Highway.

The **Northern Alaska Tour Company** (✉ Box 82991, Fairbanks 99708, ☎ 907/474–8600, FAX 907/474–4767) runs ecotours to the Arctic Circle and Prudhoe Bay that emphasize natural and cultural history, wildlife, and geology. Groups are limited to 25 people on Arctic day tours and to 10 on Prudhoe Bay overnight trips. Some tours are completely ground-based; others include a mix of ground and air travel.

BY PLANE

Alaska Airlines Vacations (⊠ Box 68900, SEARV, Seattle, WA 98168, ☎ 800/468–2248) packages air tours to Barrow, Nome, and Kotzebue; local arrangements are taken care of by Native ground operators. These trips are especially good for travelers who would otherwise move about independently. **Alaska Village Tours** (⊠ 1577 C St., Suite 304, Anchorage 99501, ☎ 907/276–7568 or 800/478–2332 in AK; FAX 907/263–9971) arranges day trips from Nome or Anchorage to Gambell Island in the Bering Sea; the company can also put you in touch with local guides to more remote Native villages. **Reeve Aleutian Airways** (⊠ 4700 W. International Airport Rd., Anchorage 99502, ☎ 907/243–4700 or 800/544–2248, FAX 907/249–2276) sells packages to the Pribilof Islands.

Visitor Information

Contact the following for general information: **Alaska State Division of Tourism** (⊠ Box 110801, Juneau 99811-0801, ☎ 907/465–2010 or 800/762–5275 to receive a vacation planner, FAX 907/465–2287). **Alaska Native Tourism Council** (⊠ 1577 C St., Suite 304, Anchorage 99501, ☎ 907/274–5400, FAX 907/263–9971). **Southwest Alaska Municipal Conference** (⊠ 3300 Arctic Blvd., Suite 203, Anchorage 99503, ☎ 907/562–7380, FAX 907/562–0438). **Bethel Chamber of Commerce** (⊠ Box 329, Bethel 99559, ☎ 907/543–2911, FAX 907/543–2255). **Nome Convention & Visitors Bureau** (⊠ Box 240, Nome 99762, ☎ 907/443–5535, FAX 907/443–5832). **Unalaska-Dutch Harbor Convention and Visitors Bureau** (⊠ Box 545, Unalaska 99685, ☎ 907/581–2612, FAX 907/581–2613).

For information about camping, hiking, and fishing, contact the following. **Alaska Public Lands Information Center** (⊠ 605 W. 4th Ave., Suite 105, Anchorage 99501, ☎ 907/271–2737). **Alaska Department of Fish and Game** (⊠ Box 25526, Juneau 99802-5526, ☎ 907/465–4180 for sportfishing seasons and regulations or 907/465–2376 for licenses). **U.S. Fish and Wildlife Service** (⊠ 1011 E. Tudor Rd., Anchorage 99503, ☎ 907/786–3487, FAX 907/786–3486). **National Park Service** (⊠ 2525 Gambell St., Anchorage 99503, ☎ 907/257–2690).

9 Vancouver and Victoria

Cosmopolitan Vancouver, Canada's answer to San Francisco, enjoys a spectacular setting. Tall fir trees stand practically downtown, rock spires tower close by, the ocean laps at your doorstep, and people from every corner of the earth create a vibrant atmosphere. On Vancouver Island just west of Vancouver, the capital of British Columbia, Victoria, is as British a city as you'll find outside England, but you'll still see many signs of the distinctive heritage of the Pacific Northwest.

VANCOUVER AND VICTORIA AREN'T IN ALASKA, but so many Alaska cruises originate or make a stop here, we thought a short chapter on these British Columbia cities would be appreciated. We've concentrated on a neighborhood or two in each city, trying not to wear you out running all around either city in a short time—and possibly covering too much ground to enjoy any of it. We haven't included three- and five-day itineraries in this chapter as in the others because it has been written with time constraints in mind. If you have more time, you'll want to range further afield.

By Melissa
Rivers

Updated by
Sue Kernaghan

Pleasures and Pastimes

Dining

Cosmopolitan Vancouver (and, to a lesser extent, Victoria) offer the visitor a diverse gastronomic experience. A new wave of Asian immigration and tourism has brought a proliferation of upscale Asian restaurants. Cutting-edge restaurants currently perfecting and defining Pacific Northwest fare—including such homegrown regional favorites as salmon and oysters, accompanied by British Columbia and Washington State wines—have become some of the city's leading attractions.

For price ranges, *see* the dining chart *in* On the Road with Fodor's.

Lodging

The hotel industry has become a major business for Vancouver, which hosts large numbers of conventioneers, Asian businesspeople, and others who are used to an above-average level of service. Although by some standards pricey, properties here are highly competitive, and you can expect the service to reflect this. In Victoria as in Vancouver, there are a wide range of accommodations, from luxury hotels and chains to bed-and-breakfast inns.

For price ranges, *see* the lodging chart *in* On the Road with Fodor's.

VANCOUVER

Vancouver is a young city, even by North American standards. Just over 100 years old, it was not yet a town in 1871, when British Columbia became part of the Canadian confederation. Still, Vancouver's history, such as it is, remains visible to the naked eye: eras are stacked east to west along the waterfront like some century-old archaeological dig— from cobblestoned, late-Victorian Gastown to shiny postmodern glass cathedrals of commerce.

Exploring Vancouver

Vancouver may be small when compared with New York or San Francisco, but it still takes time to explore. There is much to see and do here, but when time is limited (as it usually is for cruise-ship passengers), the most popular options are a walking tour of Gastown and Chinatown and a driving or biking tour of Stanley Park, one of two 1,000-acre wilderness parks within the city limits. These sights of interest are concentrated in the hemmed-in peninsula of Downtown Vancouver. The heart of Vancouver—which includes the downtown area, Stanley Park, and the West End high-rise residential neighborhood—sits on this peninsula bordered by English Bay and the Pacific Ocean to the west; by False Creek, the inlet home to Granville Island, to the south; and by Burrard Inlet, the working port of the city, to the north, past which loom the North Shore mountains. Gastown and Chinatown were declared historic districts in the late 1970s and have been revitalized. Gastown is now chock-a-block with boutiques, cafés, loft apartments, and souvenir shops and Chinatown is an expanding, vital neighborhood fueled by investment from Vancouver's most notable newcomers—immigrants from Hong Kong.

Numbers in the text correspond to numbers in the margin and on the Gastown and Chinatown and Stanley Park maps.

A Good Walk—Gastown and Chinatown

Pick up Water Street at Richards Street and head east into Gastown, named for saloon keeper "Gassy" Jack Deighton. At the corner of Water and Cambie streets, you can see and hear the world's first **steam-powered clock** ① (it chimes on the quarter hour). About two blocks east, you'll pass **Gaoler's Mews** ②, which are tucked behind 12 Water Street. Two buildings of historical and architectural note are the **Byrnes Block** ③ on the corner of Water and Carrall streets and the **Hotel Europe** (1908–09) at Powell and Alexander streets, Vancouver's first reinforced concrete structure. A statue of Gassy Jack stands on the west side of Maple Tree Square, at the intersection of Water, Powell, Alexander, and Carrall streets, where he built his first saloon.

From Maple Tree Square, it's only three blocks south on Carrall Street to Pender Street, where Chinatown begins. However, this route passes through a rough part of town, so it's far safer to backtrack two blocks on Water Street through Gastown to Cambie Street, then head south to Pender and east to Carrall. The corner of Carrall and Pender streets, now the western boundary of Chinatown, is one of the neighborhood's most historic and photogenic spots. It's here that you'll find the **Sam Kee Building** ④, the **Chinese/Freemasons Building** ⑤ (circa 1913), and, directly across Carrall Street, the **Chinese Times Building** ⑥ (circa 1902). Across Pender is the first living classical Chinese garden built outside China, **Dr. Sun Yat-Sen Garden** ⑦, tucked behind the Chinese Cultural Center, which houses exhibition space, classrooms, and the occasional mah-jongg tournament. The south side of Pender Street here is a good spot from which to view the buildings in Chinatown. You'll see important details that adorn the upper stories. The style of architecture in Vancouver's Chinatown, unique among Canadian cities, is patterned on that of Canton. Finish up by poking around in the open-front markets and import shops that line several blocks of Pender running east.

TIMING

The walk itself will take about an hour depending on your pace; allow extra time for shopping and the guided tour of the garden in Chinatown. Daylight hours are best for seeing the sights, although shops and restaurants are open into the night in both areas. There are few traffic signals for safe crossings in Gastown, so avoid commuter rush hours.

A Good Biking or Driving Tour—Stanley Park

A morning or afternoon in Stanley Park gives you a capsule tour of Vancouver that includes beaches, the ocean, the harbor, Douglas fir and cedar forests, and a good look at the North Shore mountains.

One of the most popular ways to see the park is to walk, rollerblade, or cycle along Vancouver's famous seawall, a 9 km (5½) mi seaside pathway around the park's circumference. At press time, work was under way to extend the seawall to the cruise-ship terminal at Canada Place, so you should be able to start your ride from there. Alternatively, rent a bike on Denman Street near the park entrance and start your ride at

Byrnes Block, **3**

Chinese/
Freemasons
Building, **5**

Chinese Times
Building, **6**

Dr. Sun Yat-Sen
Garden, **7**

Gaoler's
Mews, **2**

Sam Kee
Building, **4**

Steam-powered
clock, **1**

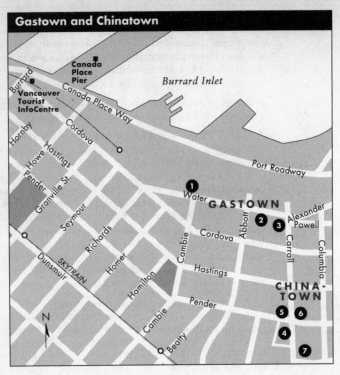

the foot of Alberni Street beside Lost Lagoon. Go through the underpass, veer right, and follow the cycle path markings to the seawall. Cyclists must ride in a counterclockwise direction, wear a helmet, and stay on their side of the path.

It's also possible to see the park by car, entering at the foot of Georgia Street and driving counterclockwise around the one-way Stanley Park Drive. An even better option is to take the **Stanley Park Shuttle,** a new service expected to provide free and frequent transportation between the park entrance and all the major sights from mid-May to mid-September.

Whether you're driving, cycling, or blading, the first sight you'll pass on your right is the Tudor-style **Vancouver Rowing Club,** a private athletic club established in 1903. Watch for the information booth on the left, and the turnoff to the renowned **Vancouver Aquarium** ⑧ and to the **Miniature Railway and Children's Farmyard** ⑨. Continuing along the main road or the seawall, the next thing you'll pass is the **Royal Vancouver Yacht Club.** About ½ km (⅓ mi) along is the causeway to **Deadman's Island,** a former burial ground for the local Salish people and now a small naval training base that is not open to the public. The **totem poles** ⑩, which are a bit farther down the road and slightly inland on your left, make a popular photo stop. Just ahead at the water's edge is the **Nine O'Clock Gun** ⑪. To the north is Brockton Point and its small but functional lighthouse and foghorn.

At km 3 (mi 2) is **Lumberman's Arch,** a huge log archway dedicated to workers in Vancouver's first industry. The **Children's Water Park** across the road is also popular throughout the summer. About 2 km (1¼ mi) farther is the Lions Gate Bridge—the halfway point of the seawall. Just past the bridge is **Prospect Point** ⑫. From the seawall you

Stanley Park

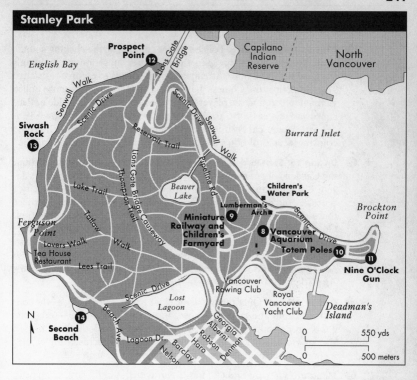

can see where cormorants nest; the drive climbs high to a viewing point, snack bar, and restaurant at the top of Prospect Point. Continuing around the seawall or the drive, you'll come to the English Bay side and the beginning of sandy beaches. The imposing rock just offshore is **Siwash Rock** ⑬, the focus of a Native legend.

The road and the seawall pass the large heated pool at **Second Beach** ⑭ and emerge from the park into a high-rise residential neighborhood, the West End. There are plenty of places to stop for coffee, ice cream, or a drink along Denman, Davie, or Robson streets.

TIMING

You'll find parking lots near most of the sights in the park; if you're driving, take the time to stop and get a better look or take pictures. With that advice in mind, expect a driving tour to take about an hour. Your biking time will depend on your speed, but with stops to see the sights, expect it to take several hours. Add at least two hours to thoroughly tour the aquarium, and you've filled a half- to full-day tour.

Sights to See

③ **Byrnes Block.** This building was constructed on the site of Gassy Jack's second saloon after the 1886 Great Fire. The date is just visible at the top of the building above the door where it says "Herman Block," which was its name for a short time. ✉ *2 Water St.*

⑤ **Chinese/Freemasons Building.** Two completely different facades distinguish a fascinating structure on the northwest corner of Pender and Carrall streets: the side facing Pender presents a fine example of Cantonese-imported recessed balconies; the Carrall Street side displays the standard Victorian style common throughout the British Empire. It was in this building that Dr. Sun Yat-Sen hid for months from the agents of the Manchu dynasty while he raised funds for its overthrow, which he accomplished in 1911. ⊠ *3 W. Pender St.*

❻ Chinese Times Building. Police officers could hear the clicking sounds of clandestine mah-jongg games played after sunset on the building's hidden mezzanine floor. Attempts by vice squads to enforce restrictive policies against the Chinese gamblers proved fruitless, because police were unable to find the players. The building on the north side of Pender Street just east of Carrall dates to 1902. Meandering down Pender Street, you can still hear mah-jongg games going on behind the colorful facades of other buildings in Chinatown. ⊠ *1 E. Pender St.*

★ **❼ Dr. Sun Yat-Sen Garden.** Built in the 1980s by 52 artisans from Suzhou, the Garden City of the People's Republic, this garden incorporates design elements and traditional materials from several of that city's centuries-old private gardens. As you walk along the paths, remember that no power tools, screws, or nails were used in the construction. Guided tours, included in the price of admission, are offered throughout the day; telephone for times. The free public park next door is also in the style of a traditional Chinese garden. ⊠ *578 Carrall St.,* ☎ *604/ 689–7133.* ☞ *C$5.25.* ☉ *June 15–Sept. 15, daily 10–7:30; Sept. 16– Apr. 30, daily 10–4:30; May 1–June 14, daily 10–6.*

❷ Gaoler's Mews. Once the site of the city's first civic buildings—the constable's cabin and customs house, and a two-cell log jail—today the cobblestone courtyard and the mews leading off it look like a hidden slice of Victorian England. The mews are home to architectural offices, a courtyard café, and an Irish pub. ⊠ *Behind 12 Water St.*

☙ **❾ Miniature Railway and Children's Farmyard.** A child-size steam train takes kids and adults on a ride through the woods of Stanley Park. Just next door is a farmyard full of tame, pettable critters, including goats, rabbits, and guinea pigs. ⊠ *Off Pipeline Rd., in Stanley Park,* ☎ *604/ 257–8530.* ☞ *C$2.25 for each site.* ☉ *Apr.–Sept., daily 11–4; Oct. 1–Dec. 4 and Jan. 4–Apr 1, weekends 11–4:00; Dec. 5–Dec. 12, daily 5–9; Dec. 13–Jan 4, daily 2–9.*

⓫ Nine O'Clock Gun. This cannonlike apparatus by the water was originally used to alert fishermen to a curfew ending weekend fishing; now it signals 9 o'clock every night.

⓬ Prospect Point. Here cormorants build their seaweed nests along the cliff's ledges. The large black diving birds are distinguished by their long necks and beaks; when not nesting, they often perch atop floating logs or boulders. Another remarkable bird found along the park's shore is the beautiful great blue heron, which reaches up to 4 ft tall and has a wing span of 6 ft. Herons prey on passing fish in the waters here; the oldest heron rookery in British Columbia is in the trees near the aquarium.

❹ Sam Kee Building. *Ripley's Believe It or Not!* recognizes this structure as the narrowest office building in the world. In 1913, when the city confiscated most of Chang Toy's land to widen Pender Street, in protest he built on what he had left—just 6 ft. These days the building houses an insurance agency whose employees make do with the 4-ft 10-inch wide interior. ⊠ *8 W. Pender St.*

☙ **⓮ Second Beach.** In summer the main draw is the 50-meter pool with water slides and lifeguards. The shallow end fills up on hot days, but the lap-swimming section is usually deserted. Nearby you'll also find a sandy beach, a playground, and covered picnic sites. ⊠ *Stanley Park.* ☞ *Free.* ☉ *June–Labor Day, daily 9:30–8.*

⑬ **Siwash Rock.** Legend tells of a Native American who, about to become a father, bathed persistently to wash his sins away so that his son could be born pure. For his devotion he was blessed by the gods and immortalized in the shape of Siwash Rock, just offshore. Two small rocks, said to be his wife and child, are up on the cliff just above the site.

❶ **Steam-powered clock.** The world's first steam-powered clock, built by Ray Saunders of Landmark Clocks, is driven by an underground steam system. On the quarter hour a whistle blows, on the hour a huge cloud of steam spews from the clock. ⊠ *123 Cambie St.,* ☎ *604/669–3525.*

❿ **Totem poles.** Totem poles were not made in the Vancouver area; these, carved of cedar by the Kwakiutl and Haida peoples late in the last century, were brought to the park from the north coast of British Columbia. The combination of carved animals, fish, birds, and mythological creatures represent clan history.

★ ☾ ❽ **Vancouver Aquarium.** The humid Amazon rain-forest gallery has piranhas, giant cockroaches, alligators, tropical birds, and jungle vegetation. Other displays show the underwater life of coastal British Columbia, the Canadian arctic, and other areas of the world. Huge tanks (populated with orca and beluga whales and playful sea otters) have large windows for underwater viewing. ⊠ *Stanley Park,* ☎ *604/ 682–1118.* ⌑ *July–Labor Day, C$12; Labor Day–June, C$10.* ☉ *July–Labor Day, daily 9:30–7; Labor Day–June, daily 10–5:30.*

Dining

$$$–$$$$ ✕ **Diva at the Met.** This multitiered restaurant at the Metropolitan Hotel opened in 1996 and quickly scooped up a fistful of awards. The presentation of the innovative contemporary cuisine is as appealing as the Art Deco decor. The menu changes seasonally; recent winning creations from the open kitchen have included smoked Alaskan black cod and porcini-crusted veal loin steak. The after-theater crowd heads here for late-evening snacks and desserts: prawn tempura, vegetable chips, fresh sorbets, and Stilton cheesecake are available until midnight. The creative weekend brunches are also popular. ⊠ *645 Howe St.,* ☎ *604/ 602–7788. AE, DC, MC, V.*

$$$–$$$$ ✕ **Teahouse Restaurant.** This former officers' mess in Stanley Park is perfectly poised for watching sunsets over the water. Try for a seat in the glassed-in wing that resembles a conservatory or, in the summer, on the patio. The West Coast Continental menu includes cream of carrot soup, lamb with herb crust, and perfectly grilled fish. ⊠ *7501 Stanley Park Dr., at Ferguson Point, Stanley Park,* ☎ *604/669–3281. Reservations essential. AE, MC, V.*

$$–$$$$ ✕ **Imperial Chinese Seafood.** This elegant Cantonese restaurant in the Art Deco Marine Building, two blocks west of the Canada Place cruiseship terminal, has two-story floor-to-ceiling windows with stupendous views of Stanley Park and the North Shore mountains across Burrard Inlet. Any dish featuring lobster, crab, or shrimp from the live tanks is recommended, as is the dim sum served every day from 11 to 2:30. Portions tend to be small and pricey (especially the abalone, shark's fin, and bird's nest delicacies) but never fail to please. ⊠ *355 Burrard St.,* ☎ *604/688–8191. Reservations essential. AE, DC, MC, V.*

$$–$$$$ ✕ **Raintree at the Landing.** In a beautifully renovated heritage building in busy Gastown, this cool, spacious restaurant has waterfront views, a local menu, and a wine list with Pacific Northwest vintages. The kitchen, focusing on healthy cuisine using local ingredients, teeters between willfully eccentric and exceedingly simple; it bakes its own bread and makes luxurious soups. Main courses, which change daily, may include salmon with toasted hazelnut sorrel-butter sauce and pan-seared halibut in ginger-butter sauce. ✉ *375 Water St.,* ☎ *604/688–5570. Reservations essential. AE, DC, MC, V.*

$$–$$$ ✕ **Liliget Feast House.** Unique in Vancouver, this longhouse near English Bay serves genuine Pacific Northwest First Nations' cuisine in a soothing setting, enhanced by traditional Native music (piped in) and Northwest Coast art on the walls. The restaurant affords a rare opportunity to try dishes like traditional panfried bannock bread, sweet potato with hazelnuts, alder-grilled salmon, toasted seaweed with rice, steamed fern shoots, barbecued venison, a dessert made of soapberries, and the Northwest coast staple—oolichan (candlefish) grease. ✉ *1724 Davie St.,* ☎ *604/681–7044. Reservations essential. AE, DC, MC, V. No lunch.*

$$ ✕ **Delilah's.** Cherubs dance on the ceiling, candles flicker on the tables, and martini glasses clink in toasts at this popular West End restaurant. Under the direction of chef Peg Montgomery, the West Coast Continental cuisine is delicious, innovative, and beautifully presented. The menu, which changes seasonally, lets you choose two- or five-course prix-fixe dinners. Try the pancetta, pine nut, Asiago, and mozzarella fritters with sun-dried tomato aioli and the grilled swordfish with blueberry-lemon compote if they're available. Patrons have been known to line up before the restaurant even opens for dinner. ✉ *1789 Comox St.,* ☎ *604/687–3424. Reservations not accepted, except for parties of 6 or more. AE, DC, MC, V. No lunch.*

$ ✕ **La Luna Café.** This unpretentious bi-level deli in the heart of Gastown serves fragrant coffees and teas and fresh soup-and-salad lunches, but it's the luscious sourdough cinnamon rolls that steal the show. Have one heated and slathered with butter if you plan to eat in at one of the small tables, or get the staff to bag a roll to go. These rolls are not to be missed! ✉ *117 Water St.,* ☎ *604/687–5862. No credit cards.*

Lodging

$$$$ 🏨 **Pan Pacific Hotel.** Sprawling Canada Place, Vancouver's main cruise-ship terminal and convention center, houses the luxurious Pan Pacific Hotel. The three-story atrium lobby has a dramatic totem pole and waterfall, and the lounge, the Five Sails restaurant (a glorious spot for that special occasion dinner), and the café all have huge expanses of glass with views of the harbor and mountains. Guest rooms were newly decorated in 1998. Nearly 80% of the rooms have a water view, though corner rooms overlooking the harbor are favorites. The fitness facilities are among the best in the city. ✉ *300–999 Canada Pl., V6C 3B5,* ☎ *604/662–8111, 800/663–1515 in Canada, or 800/937–1515 in the U.S.;* ℻ *604/685–8690. 467 rooms, 39 suites. 2 restaurants, café, coffee shop, lobby lounge, in-room modem lines, in-room safes, minibars, no-smoking floors, in-room VCRs, pool, barbershop, beauty salon, outdoor hot tub, spa, aerobics, health club, indoor track, paddle tennis, racquetball, squash, shops, baby-sitting, laundry service and dry cleaning, concierge, business services, convention center, meeting rooms, travel services, parking (fee). AE, DC, MC, V.*

$$$$ 🏨 **Sutton Place.** The staff here makes guest service a priority and, despite its size, this hotel achieves and maintains a significant level of intimacy and exclusivity. With its sumptuous carpets, enormous displays of flowers, and elegant European furniture, the feel is more like that of an exclusive guest house than of a large hotel. The rooms are furnished with rich, dark woods reminiscent of 19th-century France. The Fleuri Restaurant concentrates on Continental cuisine and serves one of the best Sunday brunches in town. Top shopping options are within walking distance. ✉ *845 Burrard St., V6Z 2K6,* ☎ *604/682–5511 or 800/961–7555,* ℻ *604/682–5513. 350 rooms, 47 suites. Restaurant,* bar, kitchenettes, minibars, no-smoking floors, room service, indoor pool, beauty salon, spa, health club, bicycles, laundry service and dry cleaning, concierge, business services, meeting rooms, travel services, parking (fee). AE, D, DC, MC, V.

$$$-$$$$ ▥ **Waterfront Centre Hotel.** Dramatically elegant, this 23-story glass hotel opened in 1991 across from Canada Place, which can be reached from the hotel by an underground walkway. The lobby and 70% of the guest rooms face Burrard Inlet; the rest of the rooms give onto a fragrant, terraced herb garden. The large corner rooms have the best views. The rooms are attractively furnished with contemporary paintings; armoires conceal the TV. A string quartet entertains in the lobby restaurant, Herons, during Sunday brunch. ✉ 900 Canada Pl. Way, V6C 3L5, ☎ 604/691–1991 or 800/441–1414, ℻ 604/691–1999. 460 rooms, 29 suites. Restaurant, lobby lounge, some in-room modems, pool, steam room, health club, shops, meeting rooms, concierge. AE, D, DC, MC, V.

$$$ ▥ **O Canada House.** This beautifully restored 1897 Victorian within walking distance from downtown is the house in which the first version of O Canada, the national anthem, was written in 1909. Winner of Vancouver's top Heritage Restoration award, this B&B oozes with period charm. Each of the spacious bedrooms is appointed with late-Victorian antiques; modern comforts, such as in-room TVs, VCRs, phones, bathrobes, and even teddy bears, help make things especially homey. The enormous top-floor room has two double beds and a private sitting area. Guests also enjoy the use of a guest pantry and a front parlor with a fireplace. Breakfast, served in the dining room or on the wraparound porch, is lavish. O Canada is popular, so book well ahead if you plan to visit in the summer. ✉ 1114 Barclay St., V6E 1H1, ☎ 604/688–0555, ℻ 604/488–0556. 5 rooms. Free parking. MC, V.

Nightlife and the Arts

Summer arts festivals provide some of the best opportunities to enjoy the performing arts in Vancouver, though year-round you'll find everything from opera, symphonic music, and touring musicals to off-off Broadway shows and live jazz, blues, and rock concerts. Leading festivals include the **Vancouver International Jazz Festival** (☎ 604/682–0706) which brings international performers to 37 venues around town every June, **Bard on the Beach** (☎ 604/739–0559), a summer series of Shakespeare's plays performed under a huge tent on the beach at Vanier Park, and **The Fringe** (☎ 604/257–0350), Vancouver's live theatrical arts festival, held in September. For information on events, pick up a free copy of the Georgia Straight (available at cafés and bookstores around town), or look in the entertainment section of the Vancouver Sun (Thursday's paper has listings in the "What's On" column). A **jazz and blues hot line** (☎ 604/682–0706) gives you current information on concerts and clubs. Call the **Arts Hotline** (☎ 604/684–2787) for the latest lineups in a wide range of entertainment. For tickets, book through **Ticketmaster** (☎ 604/280–3311).

Microbreweries

At **Steam Works** (✉ 375 Water St., ☎ 604/689–2739) on the edge of bustling Gastown, they use an age-old steam brewing process and large copper kettles (visible through glass walls in the dining room downstairs) to whip up six to nine brews. The **Yaletown Brewing Company** (✉ 1111 Mainland St., ☎ 604/681–2739) is based in a huge renovated warehouse with a glassed-in brewery turning out eight tasty microbrews; it also has a darts and billiards pub and a restaurant with an open-grill kitchen.

VICTORIA

71 km (44 mi) south of Vancouver; about 2½ hours by direct ferry from Seattle.

Anglophile Victoria is the oldest city on Canada's west coast and the first European settlement on Vancouver Island, but the founding date (1843) doesn't qualify as particularly old by eastern Canadian standards. Today Victoria is a compact seaside town laced with tea shops and gardens. Though it's quite touristy during the high summer season, it's also at its prettiest, with flowers hanging from turn-of-the-century lampposts and strollers enjoying the beauty of Victoria's natural harbor.

Exploring Victoria

Great views, lush gardens, and fine museums are the highlights of a visit to Victoria's walkable downtown. There are also many places to shop and stop for a cup of tea along the way. From the point of view of a visitor on a short stop in Victoria, a trip to popular Butchart Gardens is "off the beaten path" (☞ *below*), but it's worthwhile, if you've got the time.

Numbers in the text correspond to numbers in the margin and on the Downtown Victoria map.

A Good Walk and Tour

For some wonderful views, begin your tour of Victoria on the waterfront at the **Tourism Victoria** (☞ Visitor Information *in* Vancouver and Victoria A to Z, *below*). Just across the way is the **Empress Hotel** ⑮, a majestic railway hotel that originally opened in 1908. Across Belleville Street is the **Parliament Buildings** ⑯ complex, typical of the style of much of the city's architecture. Follow Belleville Street one block east to reach the **Royal British Columbia Museum** ⑰, where you can explore thousands of years of history. Just behind the museum and bordering Douglas Street is Thunderbird Park, where totem poles and a ceremonial longhouse stand in one corner of the garden of **Helmcken House** ⑱, the oldest house in British Columbia. A few blocks south on Douglas Street will take you to beautiful seaside **Beacon Hill Park.** From the park, go north on Douglas Street and stop off at the glass-roof **Crystal Garden** ⑲, where you can see 75 varieties of birds, hundreds of flowers, and monkeys.

From Crystal Garden, continue north on Douglas Street to View Street, then west to the original site of Fort Victoria and the Hudson's Bay Company trading post, **Bastion Square,** with its gas lamps, restaurants, cobblestone streets, and small shops. While you're here, you can stop in at the **Maritime Museum of British Columbia** ⑳ and learn about an important part of the province's history. West of Government Street, between Pandora Avenue and Johnson Street, is **Market Square** ㉑, one of the most picturesque shopping districts in the city. Just around the corner from Market Square is Fisgard Street, the heart of **Chinatown** ㉒. A 15-minute walk or a short drive east on Fort Street will take you to Joan Crescent and lavish **Craigdarroch Castle** ㉓ and the nearby **Art Gallery of Greater Victoria.**

TIMING

Many of the sights are within easy walking distance of one another and could be covered in half a day, but there's so much to see at the Royal British Columbia Museum and the other museums that you should plan on a full day. This would allow time for some shopping and a visit to Craigdarroch Castle, too.

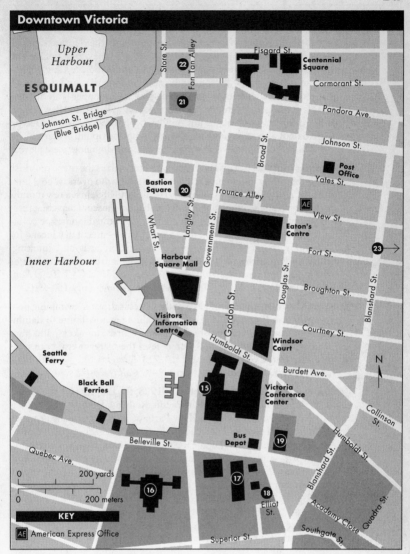

Downtown Victoria

Upper Harbour

ESQUIMALT

Johnson St. Bridge (Blue Bridge)

Inner Harbour

Store St.

Fan Tan Alley

Fisgard St.

Centennial Square

Cormorant St.

Pandora Ave.

Johnson St.

Broad St.

Post Office

Yates St.

Bastion Square

Trounce Alley

View St.

Langley St.

Government St.

Eaton's Centre

Fort St.

Harbour Square Mall

Wharf St.

Douglas St.

Broughton St.

Visitors Information Centre

Gordon St.

Courtney St.

Humboldt St.

Windsor Court

Burdett Ave.

Blanshard St.

Seattle Ferry

Victoria Conference Center

Black Ball Ferries

Collinson St.

Humboldt St.

Belleville St.

Bus Depot

N

Quebec Ave.

0   200 yards

0   200 meters

Elliot St.

Blanshard St.

Academy Close

Quadra St.

KEY

Superior St.

Southgate St.

AE American Express Office

15 16 17 18 19 20 21 22 23

Chinatown, **22**

Craigdarroch Castle, **23**

Crystal Garden, **19**

Empress Hotel, **15**

Helmcken House, **18**

Maritime Museum of British Columbia, **20**

Market Square, **21**

Parliament Buildings, **16**

Royal British Columbia Museum, **17**

Sights to See

㉒ Chinatown. The Chinese were responsible for building much of the Canadian Pacific Railway in the 19th century, and their influences still mark the region. If you enter Chinatown (one of the oldest in Canada) from Government Street, you'll walk under the elaborate **Gate of Harmonious Interest,** made from Taiwanese ceramic tiles and decorative panels. Along the street, merchants display fragile paper lanterns, embroidered silks, imported fruits, and vegetables. **Fan Tan Alley,** just off Fisgard Street, holds claim not only to being the narrowest street in Canada but also to having been the gambling and opium center of Chinatown, where games of mah-jongg, fan-tan, and dominoes were played.

㉓ Craigdarroch Castle. This lavish mansion was built as the home of British Columbia's first millionaire, Robert Dunsmuir, who oversaw coal mining for the Hudson's Bay Company. He died in 1889, just a few months before the castle's completion. Converted into a museum depicting turn-of-the-century life, the castle has elaborately framed landscape paintings, stained-glass windows, carved woodwork—precut in Chicago for Dunsmuir and sent by rail—and rooms for billiards and smoking. There's a wonderful view of downtown Victoria from the fourth-floor tower. ⊠ *1050 Joan Crescent,* ☎ *250/592–5323.* ☞ *C$7.50.* ☉ *Mid-June–early Sept., daily 9–7; mid-Sept.–mid-June, daily 10–4:30.*

⑲ Crystal Garden. Opened in 1925 as the largest saltwater swimming pool in the British Empire, this glass-roof building is now home to flamingos, macaws, 75 varieties of other tropical birds, monkeys, and hundreds of blooming flowers. At street level there are several boutiques and the Water Club restaurant. ⊠ *713 Douglas St.,* ☎ *250/381–1213.* ☞ *C$7.* ☉ *May–Aug., daily 8–8. Call for off-season hrs.*

⑮ Empress Hotel. Originally opened in 1908, the Empress is a symbol of both the city and the Canadian Pacific Railway. Designed by Francis Rattenbury, who also designed the Parliament Buildings, the property is another of the great châteaus built by Canadian Pacific, still the owners. The ingredients that made the 483-room hotel a tourist attraction in the past—old-world architecture and ornate decor, a commanding view of the Inner Harbour—are still here. The hotel staff runs tours daily in summer, and the archives, an historical photo display, are open to the public anytime. Nonguests can also stop by the Empress for a traditional afternoon tea (reservations are essential but hats and gloves are no longer required), meet for a curry under the tiger skin in the Bengal Room, or enjoy the superb regional cuisine in the Empress Room restaurant. ⊠ *721 Government St.,* ☎ *250/384–8111.* ☞ *Free; historical tours are C$6.*

⑱ Helmcken House. The oldest house in British Columbia was built in 1852 by pioneer doctor and statesman John Sebastian Helmcken. It is a treasure trove of history, from the early Victorian furnishings to an intriguing collection of 19th-century medical tools. Audio tours last 20 minutes. **Thunderbird Park,** with totem poles and a ceremonial longhouse constructed by Kwakiutl Chief Mungo Martin, occupies one corner of the garden. Next door, and also open to the public, is **St. Ann's Schoolhouse,** one of British Columbia's oldest schools. ⊠ *Helmcken House, 10 Elliot St.,* ☎ *250/361–0021.* ☞ *C$4.* ☉ *May–Sept., daily 10–5; call for winter hrs.*

⑳ Maritime Museum of British Columbia. In Victoria's original courthouse, dugout canoes, model ships, Royal Navy charts, photographs, uniforms, and ship's bells chronicle Victoria's seafaring history. A seldom-used 100-year-old cage lift, believed to be the oldest in North America, ascends to the third floor. ⊠ *28 Bastion Sq.,* ☎ *250/385–4222.* ☞ *C$5.* ☉ *Daily 9:30–4:30.*

㉑ Market Square. During Victoria's late-19th century heyday, this two-level square, originally the courtyard of an old inn, provided everything a sailor, miner, or up-country lumberjack could want. Now, beautifully restored to its original architectural, if not commercial, character, it's a traffic-free, café- and boutique-lined hangout—now, as then, a great spot for people-watching. ⊠ *West of Government St., between Pandora Ave. and Johnson St.*

★ **⑯ Parliament Buildings.** The massive stone structures, completed in 1897, dominate the Inner Harbour and are flanked by statues of two men: Sir James Douglas, who chose the site where Victoria was built, and Sir Matthew Baille Begbie, the man in charge of law and order during the Gold Rush. Atop the central dome is a gilded statue of Captain George Vancouver, the first European to sail around Vancouver Island. A statue of Queen Victoria stands in front of the complex; more than 3,000 lights outline the buildings at night. Another of Francis Rattenbury's creations, the complex is a good example of the rigid symmetry and European elegance that characterize much of the city's architecture. From the public gallery, when the legislature is in session, you can watch British Columbian democracy at work; tradition has the opposing parties sitting two sword lengths apart. The free half-hour tours are very informative. ⊠ *501 Belleville St.,* ☎ *250/387–3046.* ✆ *Free.* ☉ *June–Aug., daily 9–5; up to 23 tours a day. Sept.–late May, weekdays 8:30–5; tours at 4 PM daily. Closed holidays.*

★ ♨ **⑰ Royal British Columbia Museum.** Easily the best attraction in Victoria, this museum is as much a research and educational center as a diversion for tourists, and its exhibits, gripping with their sound, scent, and visual effects, are all informed by historical context. The definitive First People's exhibit includes a genuine Kwakwaka'wakw longhouse (the builders retain rights to its ceremonial use) and provides insights into the daily life, art, and mythology of both coastal and interior peoples, before and after the arrival of Europeans. The Modern History Gallery recreates most of a frontier town, complete with cobblestone streets, silent movies, and rumbling train sounds. The Natural History Gallery realistically re-creates the sights, sounds, and smells of many B.C. natural habitats, and the Open Ocean exhibit mimics, all too realistically, a submarine journey. A new on-site IMAX theatre shows National Geographic films on a six-story-high screen. ⊠ *675 Belleville St.,* ☎ *250/387–3701 or 800/661–5411.* ✆ *June–Sept., C$7; Oct.–May, C$5.35; theater, C$9.* ☉ *Daily 9–5. Theater, 9–8 in winter, 9–9 in summer.*

OFF THE BEATEN PATH
BUTCHART GARDENS – This impressive 50-acre garden, 21 km (13 mi) north of downtown Victoria, on the way to the Swartz Bay ferry terminal, grows more than 700 varieties of flowers in its sunken, Italian, Japanese, and rose gardens. In summer, many of the exhibits are illuminated at night, and fireworks light the sky over the gardens every Saturday night. Also on the premises are a conservatory, seed and gift shop, teahouse, and restaurants. ⊠ *800 Benvenuto Ave., Brentwood Bay,* ☎ *250/652–5256 or 250/652–4422.* ✆ *C$15.50; discounted rates in winter.* ☉ *June 15–Sept. 15, 9 AM–10:30 PM, rest of the year, 9 AM–dusk.*

Dining

$$–$$$$ ✗ **Il Terrazzo.** A charming redbrick terrace edged by potted greenery, ★ lit by flickering candles, and warmed by fireplaces and overhead heaters make Il Terrazzo, tucked away off Waddington Alley and not visible from the street, the locals' choice for romantic alfresco dining in Victoria. Baked garlic served with warm Cambozola cheese and focaccia;

scallops dipped in roasted pistachios and garnished with arugula, Belgian endive, and mango salsa; grilled lamb chops on angel-hair pasta with tomatoes, garlic, mint, and black pepper; and other hearty Northern Italian dishes come piping hot from the restaurant's authentic wood oven. Anything from the daily fresh sheet is worth a try here. ⊠ *555 Johnson St., off Waddington Alley (call for directions),* ☎ *250/361-0028. Reservations essential. AE, MC, V. No lunch Sun.*

$$–$$$ ✕ **Herald Street Caffe.** This jazz and art-filled bistro in Victoria's ware-
★   house district is an established favorite among Victorians and visitors alike. The menu changes seasonally but always features fresh, local cuisine, daily fish grills, and great pastas, many prepared with intriguing Asian accents. If they're offering it, try the calamari in tomato-dill ratatouille with crumbled feta; bouillabaisse in fennel chardonnay broth; or the roasted chicken breast in a cashew crust. Ask one of the knowledgeable staff members to help you choose from the many wines available by the glass. ⊠ *546 Herald St.,* ☎ *250/381-1441. Reservations essential. AE, DC, MC, V. No lunch Mon. and Tues.*

$$–$$$ ✕ **Pagliacci's.** Quiches, veal, and chicken in marsala sauce are among the standout dishes served at this fine trattoria where the pastas are all made in-house. Pagliacci's is popular and lively. Diners are surrounded by orange walls covered with photos of Hollywood movie stars, with upbeat opera and jazz for background music. Save room for the cheesecake. ⊠ *1011 Broad St.,* ☎ *250/386-1662. Reservations not accepted. AE, MC, V.*

$$–$$$ ✕ **Pescatore's Fish House.** Conveniently situated across from the Inner Harbour, upbeat Pescatore's specializes in fresh seafood. Its oyster bar features East and West Coast varieties, hot or on the half shell, and its fish tanks are stocked with live crabs and lobsters. The lunch specials, usually fresh fish, are a good value and popular with the downtown business crowd. Come evening, there's live dinner music on the grand piano. ⊠ *614 Humboldt St.,* ☎ *250/385-4512. AE, DC, MC, V. No lunch Sun.*

$–$$$ ✕ **Siam Thai.** The Thai chefs at Siam work wonders with both hot and mild Thai dishes. The *phad Thai goong* (fried rice noodles with prawns, tofu, peanuts, bean sprouts, and green onions), *panang* (choice of meat in curry and coconut milk), *bami goreng* (a noodle-based dish with shreds of shrimp, pork, vegetables, and an Indonesian blend of spices), and *satay* (grilled, marinated cubes of meat served with a spicy peanut sauce) are particularly good options. The restaurant is spacious and conveniently near the Inner Harbour. The well-stocked bar has a variety of beers suited to the spices used here. ⊠ *512 Fort St.,* ☎ *250/383-9911. Reservations essential. AE, MC, V. No lunch Sun.*

$ ✕ **Barb's Place.** This funky, blue-painted takeout shack is on Fisherman's Wharf, on the south side of Victoria Harbour west of the Inner Harbour, just off Marine Drive, where fishing boats come in. It has become an institution in Victoria, and the locals consider the authentic fish (halibut) and chips to be the best. You can catch a ferry to Fisherman's Wharf from the Inner Harbour, pick up an order, and take another ferry to Songhees Point for a picnic. ⊠ *310 Lawrence St.,* ☎ *250/384-6515. No credit cards. Closed Nov.–Mar.*

Lodging

$$$$ 🏨 **Clarion Hotel Grand Pacific.** One of Victoria's finest modern hotels has mahogany furniture and an elegant ambience. Overlooking the harbor and adjacent to the legislative buildings, the hotel accommodates business travelers and vacationers looking for comfort, convenience, and great scenery. All rooms have balconies and most have views of either the harbor or the Olympic Mountains. The elaborate health club

is one of the best in the city. ⊠ *450 Quebec St., V8V 1W5,* ☎ *250/ 386–0450 or 800/663–7550,* FAX *250/386–8779. 130 rooms, 15 suites. Dining room, bar, in-room safes, in-room modem lines, no-smoking rooms, indoor pool, sauna, health club, racquetball, squash, laundry service and dry cleaning, business services, meeting rooms, free parking. AE, D, DC, MC, V.*

$$$$ 🏨 **The Empress.** As far as movie stars and minor nobles are concerned,
★ the Empress is the only place to stay in Victoria. Opened in 1908, this Canadian Pacific Château has aged gracefully; its sympathetically restored Edwardian decor, modern amenities, and service standards (including bellhops and page boys) all date back to a more gracious age. A concierge floor, called Entrée Gold, offers boutique-hotel intimacy within the larger hotel. ⊠ *721 Government St., V8W 1W5,* ☎ *250/ 384–8111 or 800/441–1414,* FAX *250/381–4334. 474 rooms, 36 suites. 2 restaurants, no-smoking rooms, indoor pool, hot tub, sauna, exercise room, shops, laundry service and dry cleaning, concierge floor, business services, convention center, parking (fee). AE, D, DC, MC, V.*

$$$–$$$$ 🏨 **Abigail's Hotel.** A Tudor-style country inn with gardens and crys-
★ tal chandeliers, Abigail's is not only lovely but also convenient—it's within walking distance of the shops and restaurants of downtown. The guest rooms are prettily detailed in soothing pastel colors. Down comforters, together with Jacuzzis and fireplaces in some, add to the pampering atmosphere. The elegant informality in this no-smoking hotel is especially noticeable in the guest library and sitting room, where hors d'oeuvres are served each evening. Breakfast, included in the room rate, is served in the downstairs dining room. ⊠ *906 McClure St., V8V 3E7,* ☎ *250/388–5363 or 800/561–6565,* FAX *250/388–7787. 16 rooms, 6 suites. Breakfast room, no-smoking rooms, library, concierge, free parking. MC, V.*

$$$ 🏨 **Admiral Motel.** On Victoria Harbour along the tourist strip, this small, modern motel is in the center of things, although it is relatively quiet in the evening. If you're looking for basic, clean lodging, the Admiral is just that. The amiable owners take good care of the rooms, and small pets are permitted. Kids under 12 stay free in their parents' room. ⊠ *257 Belleville St., V8V 1X1,* ☎ FAX *250/388–6267. 22 rooms, 10 suites. Kitchenettes, no-smoking rooms, coin laundry, free parking. AE, D, MC, V.*

$$$ 🏨 **Swans.** When English-born shepherd Michael Williams bought supplies for his kennel at the Buckerfield Company Feed Store during the 1950s, he never dreamed he would one day own the building and turn it into a waterfront hotel. Extensive renovations have given the 1913 brick warehouse a new look: there's a brewery, bistro, and pub on the first floor and a jazz bar in the cellar. Large, apartment-like suites, all with kitchens and decorated with Pacific Northwest art, fill the upper floors. Swans is a good choice for families. ⊠ *506 Pandora Ave., V8W 1N6,* ☎ *250/361–3310 or 800/668–7926,* FAX *250/361–3491. 29 suites. Restaurant, pub, kitchenettes, no-smoking rooms, nightclub, coin laundry, laundry service, business services, meeting rooms, parking (fee). AE, DC, MC, V.*

Nightlife and the Arts

Cultural institutions include the **Victoria Symphony** (☎ 250/386– 6121) and the **Pacific Opera Victoria** (☎ 250/386–6121). Several venues in town present live theater. The **TerriVic Jazz Party** (☎ 250/ 953–2011) showcases internationally acclaimed musicians every April. The **Victoria Jazz Society** (☎ 250/388–4423) organizes an annual JazzFest International in late June; it has featured such jazz, blues, and world-beat artists as Dizzy Gillespie, Frank Morgan, and Ellis Marsalis.

VANCOUVER AND VICTORIA A TO Z

Arriving and Departing

By Car

From the south, I–5 from Seattle becomes **Highway 99** at the U.S.–Canada border. Vancouver is a three-hour drive (226 km, or 140 mi) from Seattle. It's best to avoid border crossings during peak times such as holidays and weekends. Highway 1, the **Trans-Canada Highway,** enters Vancouver from the east. To avoid traffic, arrive after rush hour (8:30 AM).

By Ferry

B.C. Ferries (☎ 250/386–3431; 888/223–3779 in British Columbia only) operates daily service between Vancouver and Victoria. The Vancouver terminal is in Tsawwassen, 38 km (24 mi) southwest of downtown. In Victoria, ferries arrive at and depart from the Swartz Bay Terminal at the end of Highway 17, 32 km (20 mi) north of downtown Victoria.

Clipper Navigation (☎ 250/382-8100 in Victoria; 206/448-5000 in Seattle; or 800/888–2535 elsewhere) operates year-round passenger-only service between Victoria and Seattle on the **Victoria Clipper,** and summer-only vehicle and passenger service on the **Princess Marguerite III.**

Washington State Ferries (☎ 250/381–1551; 206/464–6400 in the U.S.; 800/843–3779 in WA only) cross daily, year-round, between Sidney, just north of Victoria, and Anacortes, Washington. **Black Ball Transport** (☎ 250/386–2202; 360/457–4491 in the U.S.) operates between Victoria and Port Angeles, Washington.

By Plane

Vancouver International Airport is on an island about 14 km (9 mi) south of downtown. An airport improvement fee is assessed on all flight departures: C$5 for flights within British Columbia, C$10 for flights within Canada, and C$15 for international flights. American Airlines, Air Canada, Canadian Airlines, Continental Airlines, Delta, Horizon Air, and United fly into the airport.

Victoria International Airport is served by Air B.C., Canadian Airlines, and Horizon Air. **West Coast Air** (☎ 604/688–9115 or 800/347–2222) and **Harbour Air** (☎ 604/688–1277 or 800/665–0212) both offer 35-minute harbor-to-harbor service (downtown Vancouver to downtown Victoria) several times a day. **Kenmore Air** (☎ 425/486–1257 or 800/543–9595) offers direct daily floatplane service from Seattle to Victoria's Inner Harbour.

Helijet Airways (☎ 800/665–4354, 604/273–1414, or 250/382–6222) has helicopter service from downtown Vancouver and downtown Seattle to downtown Victoria. The heliport is near Vancouver's Pan Pacific Hotel (☞ Lodging *in* Vancouver, *above*).

BETWEEN THE AIRPORT AND DOWNTOWN

The drive from the airport to downtown Vancouver takes 20–45 minutes, depending on the time of day. Airport hotels offer free shuttle service to and from the airport. The **Vancouver Airporter Service** (☎ 604/946–8866) provides service to major downtown hotels from 5 AM until midnight for C$10 one-way, C$18 round-trip. Taxi fare to downtown is about C$22. Area cab companies are **Yellow** (☎ 604/681–1111) and **Black Top** (☎ 604/681–2181). Limousine service from **Airlimo** (☎ 604/273–1331) costs about C$30 one-way.

In Victoria, taxis are available from **Empress Taxi** (☎ 250/381–2222) and **Victoria Taxi** (☎ 250/383–7111). The fare to downtown is about C$38.

By Train

In Vancouver, the **Pacific Central Station** (✉ Main St. and Terminal Ave., near the Main St. SkyTrain station), is the hub for rail and bus service. From here, **VIA Rail** (☎ 800/561–8630) provides transcontinental service through Jasper to Toronto three times a week, and **Amtrak** (☎ 800/872–7245) has one round-trip per day between Seattle and Vancouver. Passenger trains leave the **B.C. Rail** station (✉ 1311 W. 1st. St., ☎ 604/631–3500 or 800/663–8238) in North Vancouver for Whistler and the interior of British Columbia. In Victoria, the **VIA Rail** station on Pandora Street (☎ 800/561–8630) provides service between Victoria and Nanaimo.

Getting Around

By Bus

Vancouver's **B. C. Transit** system (☎ 604/521–0400), comprising buses, the SeaBus, and the SkyTrain, can get you just about anywhere you need to go. Exact change ($1.50 in Vancouver, $2.25 to the suburbs) or a FareSaver ticket (available from newsagents) is required. For route details, pick up the free visitor's transit guide, called *Discover Vancouver on Transit,* at the Tourist InfoCentre (☞ Visitor Information, *below*).

B. C. Transit (☎ 250/382–6161) also runs a fairly extensive service in Victoria and the surrounding areas. An all-day pass costs C$5.50.

By Car

Because no freeways cross Vancouver, rush-hour traffic still tends to be horrendous. The worst bottlenecks outside the city center are the North Shore bridges, the George Massey Tunnel on Highway 99 south of Vancouver, and Highway 1 through Coquitlam and Surrey. Parking downtown is both expensive and tricky to find.

By Ferry

In Vancouver, the **SeaBus** is a 400-passenger commuter ferry that crosses Burrard Inlet from the foot of Lonsdale (North Vancouver) to downtown. The ride takes 13 minutes and costs the same as the transit bus (and it's much faster). With a transfer, connection can be made with any B.C. Transit bus or SkyTrain. **Aquabus Ferries** (☎ 604/689–5858) and **False Creek Ferries** (☎ 604/684–7781) connect several stations on False Creek including Science World, Granville Island, Stamp's Landing, and the Hornby Street dock.

In Victoria, **Victoria Harbour Ferries** (☎ 250/480–0971) operate between March and October, making eight stops around the Inner Harbour, including the Empress Hotel and Fisherman's Wharf.

Contacts and Resources

B&B Reservation Agencies

Supernatural B.C. (☎ 800/663–6000) can book accommodations anywhere in the province. **Best Canadian Bed and Breakfast Network** (✉ 1064 Balfour Ave., Vancouver V6H 1X1, ☎ 604/738–7207, FAX 604/732–4998), **Town & Country Bed and Breakfast Reservations Service** (✉ 2803 W. 4th Ave., Box 74543, Vancouver V6K 1K2, ☎ 604/731–5942), and **Garden City B&B Reservation Service** (✉ 660 Jones Terr., Victoria V8Z 2L7, ☎ 250/479–1986, FAX 250/479–9999) all specialize in B&B's.

Doctors and Dentists

Medicentre(☎ 604/683–8138) and its counterpart **Dentacentre** (✉ 1055 Dunsmuir St., lower level, Vancouver, ☎ 604/669–6700) are drop-in clinics open weekdays. **St. Paul's Hospital** (✉ 1081 Burrard St., Vancouver, ☎ 604/682–2344) has an emergency ward. **Victoria General Hospital** (✉ 35 Helmcken Rd., Victoria, ☎ 250/727–4212).

Emergencies

Call **911** for police, fire department, and ambulance.

Guided Tours

Gray Line (☎ 604/879–3363 in Vancouver; 250/388–5248 in Victoria), the largest tour operator, offers orientation tours of both cities.

The **Vancouver Trolley Company** (☎ 604/451–5581) runs turn of the century–style trolleys through Vancouver on a two-hour narrated tour of Stanley Park, Gastown, English Bay, Granville Island, and Chinatown, among other sights. From April to October a day pass (C$20) allows you to complete one full circuit, getting off and on as often as you like.

Tally-Ho Horsedrawn Tours (☎ 250/383–5067) offers a get-acquainted session with downtown Victoria that includes Beacon Hill Park. **Victoria Carriage Tours** (☎ 250/383–2207) has horse-drawn tours of the city. From April through September it's possible to tour downtown Victoria by pedicab; contact **Kabuki Kabs** (☎ 250/385–4243).

Late-Night Pharmacy

Vancouver: Shopper's Drug Mart (✉ 1125 Davie St., ☎ 604/669–2424) has 24-hour service daily. **Victoria: London Drugs** (✉ 911 Yates, ☎ 250/381–1113) is open until 10 PM.

Visitor Information

Vancouver Tourist InfoCentre (✉ 200 Burrard St., ☎ 604/683–2000, FAX 604/682–6839) provides maps and information about the city and is open daily 8–6 from late May through August, and Monday–Saturday 9–5 for the remainder of the year. There's also a visitor information booth open during the summer at the corner of Georgia and Granville streets, downtown.

For Victoria, contact **Tourism Victoria** (✉ 812 Wharf St., V8W 1T3, ☎ 250/953–2033, FAX 250/382–6539), which maintains an visitor center on Wharf Street that is open daily.

Supernatural B.C. (☎ 800/663–6000) is available year-round to assist with tourist information and reservations.

10 Portraits of Alaska

Native Alaskans

Alaska: A Geological Story

NATIVE ALASKANS

THE HISTORY of Alaska's native peoples—Eskimos, Indians, and Aleuts—is not unlike that of aboriginal people throughout Central and North America. After they had held domain over their land for thousands of years, their elaborate societies were besieged by a rapid onslaught of white settlers. Unable to stem the tide, they were forced into retreat.

The first European to visit Alaska—in 1728—was Vitus Bering, a Dane serving in the Russian navy. Bering died on his journey home, but survivors returned to Russia with a rich booty of sea-otter furs, sparking a stampede that would crush the traditional lifestyles of Alaska's native peoples. The way was open for eager Russian fur traders who plundered Aleut territory along the Aleutian Islands.

Records indicate that the native population of the Aleutian chain dropped from perhaps 20,000 to about 2,500 in the first 50 years of Russian rule. Diseases took a heavy toll, but the more ruthless among the Russian frontiersmen were also responsible—killing Aleut leaders to discourage uprisings. Stories of brutality are common. One trader, Feodor Solovief, reportedly tied together 12 Aleuts and fired a musket ball through them to see how far it would penetrate. It stopped in the body of the ninth man.

In 1867, when the United States purchased Alaska, the natives were classified in the Treaty of Cession as "uncivilized tribes." To early tourists, they were little more than "those charming folk you take pictures of in their quaint villages."

Early missionaries and government teachers in Southeast Alaska ordered Indian totem poles destroyed, mistakenly believing them to be pagan symbols. Important works of art were lost. The totems of the Tlingit and Haida Indians were—and still are—simply the decorative record of outstanding events in the life of a family or clan.

The plight of the natives improved little as Alaska grew more prosperous by exploiting its great natural resources. A painful split between traditional and modern living developed—public health experts call it "a syndrome of grief." Under increasing pressure from this clash of cultures, alcoholism grew to epidemic levels, and the suicide rate of Alaskan natives climbed to twice that of Indians living on reservations in the continental United States. Still, by the 1960s, native groups were making major strides toward claiming overdue political clout. In 1966, native leaders from across the state gathered and organized the present Alaska Foundation of Natives. It was a fragile coalition of differing cultures, but the meeting was a significant move. With 16% of the state's population, a unified native voice was suddenly a political force to be reckoned with.

At the same time, Eskimo leaders founded the *Tundra Times* and selected Howard Rock, a quiet, articulate man from Point Hope village, as its editor. Rock, whose background was in art rather than journalism, quickly prodded natives to press their aboriginal land claims.

"The natives are reticent by nature, and time was passing them by," the Eskimo editor said. "At first, it was kind of discouraging. Nothing happened. And then, one by one, the native leaders started speaking up."

The *Tundra Times* helped file the first suit for native land claims. More lawsuits followed, and soon the whole state was tied up in litigation. Oil companies, hungry to build a pipeline from the newly discovered giant oil field at Prudhoe Bay to Valdez, on Alaska's southern coast, soon realized they could not get federal construction permits until the native land claims were settled.

In 1971, the natives won a spectacular settlement in Congress: 40 million acres of land and almost $1 billion in cash. The settlement has not been a cure-all for the many problems of Alaska's natives. Poverty is still widespread, as little of the land-claims money (allocated mostly to 13 regional, for-profit native corporations by Congress) has trickled down to the village level. But the settlement has given many a sense of dignity and purpose. Several villages in the Arctic have voted themselves "dry" (prohibiting alcohol) to combat drinking problems. A new cadre of bright native leaders is taking charge to help its people.

Today, the fundamental issue is whether the natives will be allowed by the larger Alaskan society to pursue their own future, says Byron Mallott, former chief operating officer of Sealaska Corp., the regional native corporation for Southeast Alaska.

"In one way, Alaska is truly the last frontier," Mallott says. "Will the final chapter of the total and unremitting decimation of our nation's Native American people be written in Alaska—or will, with the benefit of the lesson of history, Alaska be the place where native peoples finally are able to become a part of the overall society with their pride, strength, and ethnicity intact?" There are, he adds, few guideposts to suggest the answer.

Most of Alaska's natives still reside in widely scattered communities spread across the half-million square miles of Alaska. Unlike the Indians of the Lower 48 states, the Alaskan natives have never been restricted to reservations. Many villages remain isolated, the preference of traditional villagers; others have plunged into modern life with mixed results.

Recently, Alaska's native peoples have become more enterprising in the tourist business. No longer content to let out-of-state tour operators have all the business, they are now starting to take charge of tours in their communities.

The various native peoples tend to group in well-defined regions. Here is a brief look at the different native cultures and their locations.

Eskimos. Most of Alaska's more than 40,000 Eskimos are found in scattered settlements along the Bering Sea and Arctic Ocean coasts, the deltas of the lower Yukon and Kuskokwim rivers in Western Alaska, and on remote islands in the Bering Sea such as St. Lawrence, Nunivak, and Little Diomede. The principal Arctic and sub-Arctic Eskimo communities include Barrow, Kotzebue, Nome, Gambell, Savoonga, Point Hope, Wainwright, and Shishmaref.

The Eskimos are divided into two linguistic groups: the Inupiat of the Far North and the Yup'ik, who reside mostly along the coastal regions of the west. The Yup'ik share the same dialect as the Eskimos of Siberia. Both groups are famed for their hunting and fishing skills. They are also noted craftspeople, carving animals and creating jewelry from native materials.

Indians. Alaska has four major Indian cultures: Tlingit, Haida, Athabascan, and Tsimshian.

Once among North America's most powerful tribes, the **Tlingits** (pronounced "Klink-its") are found mostly throughout coastal Southeast Alaska. They number about 13,000 and are found in cities such as Juneau, Ketchikan, and Sitka, and in villages from Hoonah, near Juneau, to Klukwan, near Haines.

The Tlingits developed a highly sophisticated culture and fought hard against Russian incursions. Social status among early Tlingits depended on elaborate feasts called potlatches. Heads of families and clans vied in giving away vast quantities of valuable goods, their generosity so extravagant at times that the hosts fell into a form of ancient bankruptcy. There are still potlatches for important occasions, such as funerals, but they are greatly scaled down from earlier times.

Haidas are also found mainly in Southeast Alaska, as well as in British Columbia. They number only about 1,000 in Alaska. Their principal community is Hydaburg on Prince of Wales Island, near Ketchikan. The Queen Charlotte Islands of British Columbia are another Haida center.

Historically, the Haidas were far-ranging voyagers and traders. Some historians credit the artistic Haidas with originating totem carving among Alaska's natives.

Most of Alaska's 7,000 or so **Athabascan** Indians are found in the villages of Alaska's vast Interior, including Ft. Yukon, Stevens Village, Beaver, Chalkyitsik, and Minto, near Fairbanks. Other Athabascans are scattered from the Kenai Peninsula–Cook Inlet area, near Anchorage, to the Copper River area near Cordova.

Linguistically, the Athabascans are related to the Navajos and Apaches of the American Southwest. They were driven out of Canada by Cree tribes more than 700 years ago.

The ancestral home of the **Tsimshian** (pronounced "Simp-shee-ann") Indians was British Columbia, but Tsimshian historians say their forebears roamed through much of Southeastern Alaska fishing, hunting, and trading long before the arrival of the white man. The 1,000 or so Tsimshians of Alaska settled in 1887 on Annette Island, near Ketchikan, when a dissident Church of England lay missionary, William Duncan, led them out of British Columbia to escape religious persecution. The town of Metlakatla on Annette Island is their principal community. Their artwork includes a variety of wood carvings, from totems to ceremonial masks.

Aleuts. With their villages on the Aleutian Islands, curving between Siberia and Alaska like broken beads, the Aleuts (pronounced "Al-ee-oots") were first in the path of early explorers and ruthless fur traders.

There are about 7,000 Aleuts in Alaska today, their principal communities being Dutch Harbor/Unalaska, Akutan, Nikolski, and Atka in the Aleutians, and St. Paul and St. George in the Pribilof Islands. Grass basketry, classed by museums as some of the best in the world, is the principal art of the Aleuts. Finely woven baskets from Attu, at the tip of the Aleutian chain—where villages were destroyed in American-Japanese combat during World War II and never rebuilt—are difficult-to-obtain treasures.

—Stanton H. Patty

ALASKA: A GEOLOGICAL STORY

MOST PEOPLE KNOW about Alaska's oil and gold. But did you know that the state has a desert? That camels once roamed here? That there's a fault line nearly twice as long as the San Andreas Fault? That the largest earthquake ever to hit North America struck Alaska in 1964 and affected the entire planet? That the state has 80 potentially active volcanoes and approximately 100,000 glaciers?

All these physical wonders are geological in origin and are in addition to a North Slope oil supply that accounts for 25% of U.S. production and more than 10% of U.S. consumption; and caches of gold that fueled more than 20 rushes.

Nearly all visitors will have at least one encounter with a glacier (with 29,000 square miles of them, they're hard to miss). Courtesy of the Pleistocene Ice Ages, high latitude location, and abundant moisture from the North Pacific, Alaska is home to approximately 100,000 of these large sheets of ice. The vast majority are in the southern and southeastern parts of the state as these are the areas with the most moisture. How much moisture? Portions of the Chugach Mountains can gather 600 inches of snow each year, an amount that is comparable, in rain, to the annual precipitation in Seattle. In north-central Alaska, the Brooks Range contains a glacial field of approximately 280 square miles. Although small by Alaskan standards, it is larger than all the glacial fields in the rest of the United States combined, which comprise approximately 230 square miles.

There are alpine or valley glaciers, those that form high in mountain valleys and travel to lower elevations. Alaska is home to several of the great alpine glaciers in the world, found in the high country of the Alaska Range, the Talkeetna, Wrangell, Chugach, St. Elias, and Coast Mountains. Some, such as the Bering Glacier, come tantalizingly close to the water. At over 100 miles in length, and with an area of more than 2,250 square miles, the Bering is the longest and largest Alaskan glacier, its seclusion guarded by Cape St. Elias and

the stormy waters of the Gulf of Alaska. Also impressive are the Hubbard, its imposing terminus dominating the head of isolated Yakutat Bay; and the Columbia, foreboding and threatening, calving icebergs that tack-in-line like Nelson's fleet across the mouth of Valdez Arm.

The Malaspina Glacier is an unusual piedmont glacier. Formed by the coalescence of several glaciers, this 850 square-mile mass is lobate, or fan-shaped, and occupies a benchland on the northwest side of Yakutat Bay. So much of the Alaska Range, Wrangell, Chugach, St. Elias, and Coast Mountains are covered by glacial ice that it is often more appropriate to talk about ice fields than individual glaciers.

Then there are the great tidewater glaciers of Prince William Sound and southeastern Alaska. Alpine glaciers that come right to the water's edge, they creak, moan, thunder, and calve-off great bergs and little bergeys. The world's longest is the previously mentioned Hubbard Glacier, which, because it stretches over 70 miles from its head in Canada to its terminus in Yakutat Bay, is both an alpine and a tidewater glacier. Sixteen tidewater glaciers can be found in Glacier Bay National Park; 20 in Prince William Sound. Some are advancing, some retreating. Hubbard has not only advanced in recent years, it has surged. In 1986, a surge by Hubbard blocked the Russell Fjord at the upper end of Yakutat Bay, turning it into Russell Lake. Later that year, the portion of the glacier acting as a dam in front of Russell Lake gave way, violently releasing the backed-up water to an elevation of 83 feet above sea level. Pretty impressive when you stop to think that the Russell Fjord is normally at sea level. Surging glaciers can move downhill hundreds of feet per day. The Hubbard's greatest surge was in September 1899 when it advanced a half mile into the bay in just five minutes, courtesy of an earthquake.

Glaciologists are interested in knowing more about how glaciers, especially tidewater glaciers, advance and retreat. The Columbia Glacier, both an alpine and a tidewater glacier like the Hubbard, in

Prince William Sound is approximately 40 miles long, covers more than 400 square miles, and flows to sea level from 10,000–12,000-foot peaks in the Chugach Range. Its width at the terminus can be as much as 4 miles; its ice thickness can reach 900 feet (on average 300 feet above the water and 600 feet below). It is also only 8 miles from the shipping lanes traveled by oil tankers leaving the Alaska pipeline terminal at Valdez. Columbia has been receding since the early 1980s, sending berg after berg into Prince William Sound and into the shipping lanes to Valdez; and now that it's receding, it has the potential to calve even more bergs. Although a shallow sill, or shoal of underwater glacial deposits keeps icebergs more than 100 feet thick from entering Prince William Sound, some big bergs still make it to the shipping lanes. Columbia's calving took its toll just after midnight on March 29, 1989 when Captain Hazlewood of the Exxon *Valdez* steered too far east while trying to avoid bergs in Valdez Arm and ran aground on Bligh Reef.

YOU CAN SEE many glaciers from the Alaska Marine Highway. The tidewater glaciers of Glacier Bay and the Malaspina and Hubbard glaciers in Yakutat Bay are best seen by boat or ship. Sailing into Valdez Arm you may see more of the Columbia Glacier than you want—it's often coming to see you in the form of scores of bergs and bergeys—often forcing you east toward Bligh Reef. Once safely ashore in Valdez it's time to look at valley glaciers. You can access either the Valdez or Worthington Glacier by road. If in the Matanuska Valley, go see the Matanuska Glacier. If on the Kenai Peninsula, try either the Exit or Portage glaciers. If visiting Juneau, the Mendenhall Glacier is on the outskirts of town.

More than 80 volcanoes in Alaska are potentially active. Novarupta, Pavlof, Augustine, Redoubt, and Spurr are Alaskan volcanoes that are part of the "Ring of Fire," the volcanic rim of the Pacific. From Mt. Wrangell at 144 degrees west longitude in southeast Alaska to Cape Wrangell at 173 degrees east longitude at the tip of the Aleutian archipelago, southern Alaska exists, to paraphrase historian Will Durant, by volcanic decree . . . subject to change.

Anchorage (and the greater Cook Inlet area) is a great place to watch volcanoes erupt. Augustine, Redoubt, and Spurr volcanoes have put on shows up and down the Cook Inlet in recent years; the Mt. Spurr eruption of August 1992 temporarily stopped air travel in and out of Anchorage. The most violent Alaskan eruption? The two-and-a-half day eruption of Novarupta in 1912 in what is now Katmai National Park. The two-and-a-half cubic miles of ash deposited there has left an Alaskan legacy: the surreal Valley of Ten Thousand Smokes.

The length of a fault system and whether or not the fault is straight over great distances are of interest to geologists. Fault length is related to earthquake magnitude. Generally speaking, the longer a fault, the greater the potential magnitude. Impressed by the 600-mile length of California's San Andreas? The onshore portion of the Denali Fault System is more than 1,000 miles long. Numerous long faults around the world move horizontally. This produces some interesting results if the fault trace is not straight. A fault system such as the Denali has a large component of horizontal movement (called strike-slip motion): Crustal blocks on either side move past each other, rather than up or down. If a strike-slip fault bends, one of two situations results: a gap or hole in the crust (usually filled by volcanic outbreaks and/or sediments sloughing into the hole), or a compression of the bend, resulting in vertical uplift (mountains). Which condition occurs is a function of fault motion, whether into or out of the bend. South of Fairbanks, the Denali Fault System changes trend, from northwest–southeast to northeast–southwest. The sense of horizontal motion is into the bend, resulting in vertical uplift. What mountain just happens to be in the vicinity? Mt. McKinley, at 20,320 feet, the tallest mountain in North America. Moreover, its relief (difference in elevation between the base and top of the mountain), at 18,000 feet, is unsurpassed. Mt. Everest is more than 29,000 feet, but "only" 11,000 feet above the Tibetan Plateau that forms its base.

With such big faults, it's no wonder geologists look at Alaska as big earthquake country. Seward, Valdez, Whittier, and Anchorage are just some of the more prominent names associated with the Good Friday Earthquake of 1964. Upgraded in

1977 to magnitude 9.2, the Good Friday quake is the largest on record for North America. Fifteen to 30 seconds is not unusual for ground motion in a big, destructive earthquake; Alaskans shook for three to four minutes during the Good Friday quake. The epicenter was about 6 miles east of College Fjord in Prince William Sound, some 70 miles east of Anchorage. Vertical deformation (uplift or downdropping of the land) affected an area of 100,000 square miles. By the time shaking had stopped, the area of Latouche Island had moved 60 feet to the southeast and portions of the Montague Island area were uplifted by as much as 30 feet. The area of Portage was downdropped by approximately 10 feet. The largest tsunami (often misnamed as a tidal wave) that hit Hilo, Hawaii checked in at 12.5 feet; the largest at Crescent City, California was 13 feet; and in Chenega, Alaska, native residents were never sure what rose from the sea to smite them . . . just that it was 90 feet tall. The entire planet was affected: The area in which the quake was felt by people is estimated at 500,000 square miles—South Africa checked in to report that groundwater was sloshing around in wells.

Geologists generally describe tsunamis with respect to displacement on a fault underwater. They use the more general term seismic sea wave when other things, such as submarine landslides, cause enormous waves. The 90-foot seismic sea wave that hit Chenega was topped by the 220-foot wave reported from the Valdez Arm area. But a few years earlier in southeastern Alaska, on the evening of July 9, 1958, an earthquake in the Yakutat area dumped an enormous landslide into the head of Lituya Bay. The result was a seiche, or splash wave, which traveled 1,740 feet up the opposite mountainside.

IMPRESSED YET? In the last century the average recurrence interval for Alaskan earthquakes in excess of 8.0 on the Richter Scale is 10 years. The recurrence interval for earthquakes over 7.0 is just over a year. Never mind California—Alaska in the most seismically active state in the Union. Volcanic hazard? Well, Pavlof has averaged an eruption every six years over the last 240.

Earthquakes, volcanoes—it's not called the "Ring of Fire" for nuthin'. The North American and Pacific tectonic plates are battling all the way from California to Japan. The two battle awfully hard in Alaska.

And now about that desert. The North Slope of Alaska is 80,000 square miles of frozen, windswept desert where Inupiat Eskimos live. It's a desert from the climatological perspective that the North Slope receives less than 10 inches of precipitation each year. If you go around the west end of the Brooks Range you can even find sand dunes—Great Kobuk, Little Kobuk, and Hunt River sand dune fields. Temperatures during the short, cool summers are usually between 30°F and 40°F. Temperatures during the winter can average −20°F. In winter, the Arctic Ocean moderates temperatures on the North Slope . . . but there is nothing to moderate the wind.

The first people to "come into the country" came across the Bering Land Bridge from Asia, between 10,000 and 40,000 years ago. The Bering Land Bridge was a product of the Pleistocene Epoch—"The Great Ice Age"—that lowered sea level enough for the bridge to form. Inupiat life, Alaskan life, changed dramatically with the discovery of oil. At the start of the Mesozoic Era (beginning about 245 million years before the present), sandstones and conglomerates deposited in a warm, shallow sea marked the beginning of Prudhoe Bay. That abundant organic matter is now abundant oil under the North Slope. As Alaska approaches the millennium, the state still runs on oil—approximately three-fourths of the general revenue is provided by it. Also during the Mesozoic Era, oil-bearing shales were deposited in the Cook Inlet, home of Alaska's first oil boom; copper and silver deposits were formed in what is now the Copper River country; Cretaceous swamps in south-central Alaska became the Matanuska coalfield; and gold was emplaced around present-day Fairbanks and near Nome on the Seward Peninsula.

The oldest rocks in Alaska are of Precambrian age (the "Time before Life") and are in southwestern Alaska. They have been dated at 2 billion years of age, nearly half the age of the earth. Rocks 1 billion years old have been identified in the area of the Brooks Range south to the Yukon River. Interestingly, the 1 billion year old rocks are native; the 2 billion year old rocks are expatriates. In fact, southern and southeastern Alaska are composed of a mosaic or quilt of microplates, all much smaller than continent size. Some terranes (blocks or fragments of the earth's crust that may vary in age, geologic character, or site of origin) arrived in Alaska from as far south as the equator.

Certain Alaskan rocks tell a tale of warm climates and seas. Evidence? Hike the Holitna River basin in southwest Alaska and look for the many types of trilobites present (those now-extinct three-lobed marine arthropods that scavenged the bottoms of warm, shallow, Cambrian seas—parents, if you don't know what they look like, ask your children). The central interior of Alaska evidently was never covered by ice, but was instead a cool steppe land roamed by mammoths, bison, horses, saber-toothed cats, and camels. Yes, camels.

Alaska's stunning expanse incorporates fire and ice, wind and rain, volcano, glacier, windswept tundra, towering rain forest, and mist-shrouded island. Its geologic story covers a great deal of time and distance and has produced (and is producing) some of the most exquisite land anywhere. In the north, the rocks tell a story of relative stability—geological homebodies born and raised. In the south, the patchwork terranes tell a tale of far-traveled expatriates coming into the country. Geological processes that have produced, and are still producing, both homebodies and expatriates create a land in constant flux. But the majesty of the land . . . that is the unchanging legacy of Alaska.

—Dr. Charles Lane

INDEX

A

Abercrombie State Park and Campsite, *173*
ACTFEST (festival), *122*
Addresses and numbers. ☞ Contacts and resources
Admiralty Island National Monument, *11, 52, 94*
Air taxis, *86*
Air travel. ☞ Plane travel
Alaska Aviation Heritage Museum, *138*
Alaska Center for the Performing Arts, *134*
Alaska Chilkat Bald Eagle Preserve, *12, 52, 94, 119*
Alaska Folk Festival, *117*
Alaska Goldpanners, *196*
Alaska Heritage Library and Museum, *138*
Alaska Indian Arts, *120–121*
Alaska Marine Highway, *52*
Alaska Native Heritage Center, *138–139*
Alaska Public Lands Information Center, *133, 134*
Alaska Railroad, *12, 133, 134, 153–154*
Alaska Range Viewpoint, *191*
Alaska Raptor Rehabilitation Center, *109*
Alaska SeaLife Center, *10, 166*
Alaska State Capitol, *111*
Alaska State Fair, *175*
Alaska State Museum, *112–113*
Alaska Steam Laundry Building, *111*
Alaska Zoo, *138, 139*
Alaskaland (theme park), *191*
Alaskan Brewing and Bottling Company's microbrewery plant, *113*
Alaskan Hotel, *111*
Albert Loop Trail, *67*
Aleutian Islands, *222, 226–227*
Alutiiq Museum & Archaeological Repository, *173–174*
Anan Wildlife Observatory, *101*
Anchorage, *5, 11, 131–155, 159*
bird-watching, 53, 154
children, attractions for, 134, 135, 138–139
climate, xxxiv
contacts and resources, 154–155
emergencies, 154
guided tours, 155
hotels, 10, 145–148
itineraries, 132–133
nightlife and the arts, 148–150
outdoor activities and sports, 131–132, 150–152
restaurants, 139–141, 144–145
shopping, 132, 152–153
shore excursions, 37
sightseeing, 132–135, 138–139
transportation, 153–154
visitor information, 133, 134–135, 155
Anchorage Audubon Society, *53*
Anchorage Museum of History and Art, *134*
Anderson, Oscar, *133, 135*
Angoon, *94, 118*
Aniakchak National Monument and Preserve, *80*
Anvil Mountain, *229*
Apartment and villa rentals, *xxii–xxiii*
Aquariums, *10, 166, 240, 243*
Arctic Brotherhood Hall, *124*
Arctic National Wildlife Refuge, *80–81*
Arctic Region Supercomputing Center, *190*
Art galleries, *99–100, 118, 120–121, 152, 169, 172, 212, 246*
Art Gallery of Greater Victoria, *246*
Arts
Anchorage, 148–149
Interior, 194–195
Southeast Alaska, 106, 110, 116–117, 122, 126–127
Vancouver, British Columbia, 245
Victoria, British Columbia, 251
Atka, *226*
Australian travelers, tips for, *xviii, xxvi*

B

Backpacking, *46–47, 48, 49, 92*
Baranof Castle Hill State Historic Site, *107*
Baranov Museum, *173*
Bard on the Beach (festival), *245*
Barrow, *xxxiv, 12, 232–233*
Bars. ☞ Nightlife
Bartlett Cove, *61*
Baseball, *151, 195–196*
Basketball, *151*
Bastion Square (Victoria, British Columbia), *246*
Beacon Hill Park, *246*

Bears, *xii–xiii, 13, 52–53, 85, 101*
Beaver Creek, *79*
Bed-and-breakfasts, *xxiii, 128, 154, 180, 253.* ☞ Also Hotels and motels
Begich-Boggs Visitor Center, *66, 161*
Bering Land Bridge National Preserve, *81*
Bethel, *222, 224–226*
Bicycling, *xiii, xxix, 6, 106, 122, 150, 196, 239–243*
Big Game Alaska, *161*
Birch Creek, *79*
Birch Lake, *202, 207*
Bird-watching, *xxix, 53, 109, 110, 119, 154, 165, 170, 224–225*
Boat travel
Anchorage, 153
the Bush, 233
Boating, *xxix, 6–7, 157, 196, 200, 201–202.* ☞ Also Riverboats
Bonanza Creek and Dredge Number 4, *211*
Brew pubs and breweries, *13, 113, 245*
British Columbia, *238–254*
Brooks Falls and Camp, *82, 222*
Brooks Range, *231*
Brooks River, *83*
Bus travel, *xiii–xiv*
Anchorage, 154
British Columbia, 253
the Bush, 234
Interior, 214, 215
South Central Alaska, 179
Southeast Alaska, 127, 128
the Bush, 5–6, 218–236
camping, 84, 86, 230
car rentals, 229
contacts and resources, 234–236
emergencies, 235
fishing, 221
guided tours, 83, 88, 228, 231, 235–236
hotels, 82, 84, 85, 86, 221, 225, 226–227, 228, 229–230, 231, 232, 233
itineraries, 222, 224
Northwest and the Arctic, 228–233
outdoor activities and sports, 82, 221, 230
parks, wilderness areas, and wildlife refuges, 80–86, 231
restaurants, 220–221, 225, 226–227, 229, 230, 232
shopping, 221, 230, 232–233
sightseeing, 222, 224–226, 227, 228–229, 230–231, 232, 233

Southwest, *224–228*
timing the visit, *224*
transportation, *233–234*
visitor information, *225–226,
229, 236*
wildlife viewing, *221–222,
224–226*
Butchart Gardens, *249*
Byrnes Block (Vancouver,
British Columbia), *239, 241*
Byron Glacier, *161*

C

Cameras and computers, *xiv*
Camping, *xxiii, xxix, 47, 48,
58–59, 65, 67, 68, 69, 70,
72, 77–78, 79, 84, 86, 173,
200, 201, 203, 204, 230*
Canadian travelers, tips for,
xviii
Canoeing, *xxix, 6, 99, 110,
150, 209*
**Cape Krusenstern National
Monument,** *81*
Caribou, *53, 80–81*
Car rentals, *xiv–xv, 216, 229*
Car travel, *xv–xvii*
Anchorage, *153*
British Columbia, *252, 253*
the Bush, *234*
Interior, *214, 215*
parks, wildlife refuges, and
wilderness adventures, *86*
South Central Alaska, *179–
180*
Southeast Alaska, *127*
Castle Hill, *107*
Cemeteries, *107, 112, 188*
Centennial Hall, *113*
Chatanika River, *201–202*
Chena Hot Springs Resort,
187, 199–200
**Chena Lakes Recreation
Area,** *207*
Chicken, *209*
Chief Johnson Totem Pole, *95*
**Chief Kowee, cremation spot
of,** *112*
Chief Shakes Island, *100*
Chief Shakes's grave site,
100
Children, attractions for
Anchorage, *134, 135, 138–
139*
Interior, *190, 191–192, 206*
South Central Alaska, *161,
162, 166, 167, 169, 170,
173–174, 175, 176*
Southeast Alaska, *97, 112,
113*
Vancouver, British Columbia,
242, 243
Victoria, British Columbia,
249
Children, traveling with,
xvii–xviii
Children's Water Park, *240*
Childs Glacier, *164*

Chilkat Center for the Arts,
122
Chilkat Indian Dancers, *122*
Chilkat State Park, *58–59*
Chilkoot Trail, *59, 124*
Chinatown (Vancouver, British
Columbia), *239*
Chinatown (Victoria, British
Columbia), *246, 248*
**Chinese/Freemasons
Building,** *239, 241–242*
Chinese Times Building, *239,
242*
Chugach National Forest, *66–
67*
Chugach State Park, *67*
Churches, *95, 107–108, 111,
113, 173, 188*
**Circle-Fairbanks Historic
Trail,** *202*
Circle Hot Springs, *201*
City Park, *96*
Clam digging, *169*
Clam Gulch, *169*
Clausen Memorial Museum,
104
Clay Street Cemetery, *188*
Climate, *xxxiv*
Cold Bay, *226*
Columbia Glacier, *159, 162*
Comedy, *149*
Consumer protection, *xviii*
Contacts and resources
Anchorage, *154–155*
British Columbia, *253–354*
the Bush, *234–236*
Interior, *216*
parks, wildlife refuges, and
wilderness adventures, *87–
88*
South Central Alaska, *180–
181*
Southeast Alaska, *128–129*
Cordova, *159, 163–165*
Cordova Historical Museum,
164
Crafts, native, *xxvii, 9, 199,
224, 230, 232–233*
Craigdarroch Castle, *246,
248*
**Creamer's Field Migratory
Waterfowl Refuge,** *53*
Creek Street Footbridge, *97*
**Crooked Creek and Whiskey
Island Railroad,** *191*
Cruises, *10–11, 12–13, 18–41*
booking, *22–27*
coastal cruisers, *19, 32–35*
choosing, *18–22*
costs, *21*
cruise experience, *19–20*
cruise fleet, *27, 29–37*
deals and discounts, *25–26*
expedition ships, *19, 32*
itineraries, *20–21*
ocean liners, *19, 27, 29–32*
payment, *26–27*
riverboat, *191–192*
ships, types of, *19*

shore excursions, *37–31*
small ships, *32–35*
special-interest cruises, *35–37*
timing your cruise, *21*
tours, *20–21*
whale-watching, *57–58*
Crystal Garden, *246, 248*
**Crystal Lake State
Hatchery/Blind Slough
Recreation Area,** *104*
Curling, *196*
Curry-Kesugi Ridge, *68*
Customs and duties, *xviii–xix*

D

Dalton Highway, *203–205*
Dance, *110, 122, 195*
Dancing, Cossack, *110*
Dancing, Indian, *122*
Dawson City, Yukon Territory,
187, 210–212
Dawson City Museum, *210*
Deadhorse, *203–204, 233*
Deadman's Island, *240*
Deer Mountain Hatchery, *96*
Delta Junction, *187, 207–208*
**Denali National Park and
Preserve,** *11–12, 52, 53,
74, 76–78, 177, 185*
Denali State Park, *67–68*
**Diamond Tooth Gertie's
Gambling Hall,** *210*
Dillingham, *86*
Dining. ☞ Restaurants
Disabilities and accessibility,
xix–xx
Discounts and deals, *xx–xxi*
Dr. Sun Yat-Sen Garden, *239,
242*
Dogsled races, *152, 197–198,
214, 230*
Dogsledding, *xxx, 54.* ☞
Also Mushing
Dolly's House, *97*
Dutch Harbor, *222, 226*

E

Eagle, *187, 209*
Eagle Historical Society, *209*
Eagle preserves, *12, 52, 94,
119*
Eagle River Nature Center, *67*
**Early warning radar
installation,** *232*
Earthquake Park, *135*
Ecotourism, *xxi, 48*
Egan Convention Center, *134*
Eklutna Native Village, *139*
El Dorado Gold Mine, *185*
Elderberry Park, *133*
Elliott Highway, *202–203*
**Elmendorf Air Force Base
Wildlife Museum,** *138, 139*
Emergencies
Anchorage, *154*
British Columbia, *254*
the Bush, *235*
Interior, *216*

South Central Alaska, 180–181

Southeast Alaska, 128

Empress Hotel, *246, 248*

Empress Theater, *188*

Equinox Marathon, *198*

Ester Gold Camp, *185*

Evergreen Cemetery, *112*

Exit Glacier, *12, 167*

F

Fairbanks, *185, 187–188, 190–199*

bird-watching, 53

climate, xxxiv

Fairbanks Convention and Visitors Bureau, *188*

Fairbanks Exploration Industrial Complex, *188*

Fairbanks Ice Museum, *185, 188*

Fairbanks Summer Arts Festival, *195*

Falcon Joslin Home, *188*

Falls Creek fish ladder, *104*

Fan Tan Alley (Victoria, British Columbia), *248*

Ferries, *xxx, 87, 127, 128, 180, 233, 252, 253*

Festivals and seasonal events, *15–16, 110, 117, 122, 151, 152, 162, 175, 195, 196, 197–198, 214, 230, 245, 251*

Fish hatcheries, *96, 104, 113*

Fishing, *xxv, xxxi, 7–8, 46, 92, 99, 103, 116, 150, 158, 162, 170, 196–197, 205, 207, 221*

derbies, 162

Flattop Mountain, *67*

Flightseeing, *8, 116, 122, 155*

Food, *8, 13*

Forests, *49.* ☞ *Also* National parks and forests; Parks, wildlife refuges, and wilderness adventures

Fort William H. Seward National Historic Landmark, *120*

Fortymile Country, *208–209*

Fortymile River, *79, 209*

Fringe (festival), *245*

Fur Rendezvous (festival), *152*

G

Gaoler's Mews (Vancouver, British Columbia), *239, 242*

Gardens, *8, 113, 190, 239, 242, 246, 248, 249*

Gastineau Salmon Hatchery, *113*

Gastown (Vancouver, British Columbia), *239*

Gate of Harmonious Interest, *248*

Gates of the Arctic National Park and Preserve, *81–82*

Gay and lesbian travelers, tips for, *xxi*

Geophysical Institute, *190*

Georgeson Botanical Garden of the Agricultural and Forestry Experiment Station Farm, *190*

Girdwood, *159*

Glacier Bay National Park and Preserve, *12, 52, 59, 61–64, 94*

Glacier Gardens Rainforest Adventure, *113*

Glaciers, *12, 52, 59, 66, 94, 104, 113, 159, 161–162, 164, 167, 175*

Glennallen, *178*

Gold Dredge No. 8, 188, 190

Gold panning, *113, 188, 190, 197*

Golden Heart Park, *188*

Golden North Hotel, *124*

Golf, *103, 116, 151, 197*

Governor's House, *112*

Grant Street Trestle, *95*

Great Alaska Shootout, *151*

Great Kobuk Sand Dunes, *84*

Gustavus, *12, 61–62*

H

Haines, *94, 118–123*

bird-watching, 53

shore excursions, 37–38

Haines Highway, *119*

Haines Visitor's Center, *120*

Halibut Cove, *12, 159, 171*

Halsingland Hotel, *120*

Hammer Slough reflecting pool, *104*

Harding Icefield, *70*

Harding Lake, *207*

Health concerns, *xxi–xxii*

Healy, *205–206*

Helmcken House, *246, 248*

Hiking, *xxx, 46–47, 48, 49, 79, 92, 99, 103, 110, 118, 122, 131–132, 181, 183–184, 197, 200, 202, 203, 205, 214*

Hockey, *152, 197*

Holidays, *xxii*

Holy Resurrection Russian Orthodox Church, *173*

Home exchanges, *xxiii*

Homer, *159, 170–172*

Hoonah, *94, 118*

Hope, *159, 165–166*

Horsepacking, *55*

Hostels, *xxiii–xxiv*

Hotel Europe, *239*

Hotels and motels, *xxiv, 14.* ☞ *Also* Apartments and villa rentals; Bed-and-breakfasts; Home exchanges; Hostels; Lighthouse accommodations; Wilderness lodges

Anchorage, 10, 145–148

the Bush, 82, 84, 85, 86, 221, 225, 226–227, 228, 229–230, 231, 232, 233

Interior, 76–77, 78, 184, 192–194, 200, 201, 203, 204–206, 207–208, 209, 211–212, 213–214

South Central Alaska, 66, 68–70, 71, 72, 158, 163, 164, 166, 167–168, 170, 171, 172–173, 174, 175–178

Southeast Alaska, 62–63, 65, 92, 98–99, 101–102, 104–105, 109, 114–116, 121, 125–126

Vancouver, British Columbia, 238, 244–245

Victoria, British Columbia, 238, 250–251

Hot springs retreats, *184, 187, 199–200, 201, 202, 213*

House of Wickersham, *111–112*

I

Ice hockey, *152, 197*

Ice-skating, *151*

Iditarod Trail, *166*

Iditarod Trail Headquarters, *159, 176*

Iditarod Trail Sled Dog Race, *152, 230*

Imaginarium (museum), *134*

Immaculate Conception Church, *188*

Imuruk lava flow, *81*

Independence Mine, *159, 175*

Insurance, *xxi*

rental cars, xv

Interior, *5, 183–216*

camping, 77–78, 79, 200, 201, 203, 204

car rentals, 216

children, attractions for, 190, 191–192, 206

contacts and resources, 216

emergencies, 216

Fairbanks and Chena Hot Springs, 185, 187–188, 190–200

Fortymile Country, 208–209

guided tours, 78, 87, 194, 203–204

hiking, 183–184, 197, 200, 202, 203, 205, 214

hot spring retreats, 184, 187, 199–200, 201, 202, 213

hotels, 76–77, 78, 184, 192–194, 200, 201, 203, 204–206, 207–208, 209, 211–212, 213–214

itineraries, 185, 187

mushing, 184, 197–198, 214

nightlife and the arts, 194–195

North of Fairbanks, 200–205

outdoor activities and sports, *78, 79, 183–184, 195–198, 200, 201–202, 203, 205, 207, 209, 214*

parks, wilderness areas, and wildlife refuges, 72–74, 76–80

restaurants, 76, 183, 192, 199–200, 205, 207, 208–209, 211, 213–214

Richardson Highway, 206–208

shopping, 199, 207, 209

sightseeing, 184–185, 187–188, 190–192, 200–201, 202, 203–204, 205, 206–207, 208, 209–211, 212–213

South of Fairbanks, 205–206

timing the visit, 187

transportation, 214–216

visitor information, 188, 203, 208, 212, 216

wild and scenic rivers, 79

Yukon Territory, 209–214

Internet sites, *9–10*

Itineraries, *11–12*

Irene Ingle Public Library, *100*

J

Jogging, *150*

John Hopkins Glacier, *59*

Juneau, *11, 94, 110–118*

bird-watching, 53

guided tours, 10

shore excursions, 38

Juneau-Douglas City Museum, *112*

Juneau Jazz'n Classics (festival), *117*

K

Kachemak Bay, *159, 170*

Kake, *94, 118*

Katmai National Park and Preserve, *12, 52–53, 82–84, 222*

Kayaking, *xxix, 6, 56–57, 63–64, 99, 110, 116, 122–123, 150*

Kenai Fjords National Park, *12–13, 52, 69–70, 159, 168–169*

Kenai National Wildlife Refuge, *70*

Kenai Peninsula, *12, 165–173*

Kennicott Mine, *13, 71, 159*

Ketchikan, *12, 94, 95–100*

guided tours, 10

shore excursions, 39

Ketchikan Visitors Bureau, *95*

Kiana, *85*

KikSadi Totem Park, *100*

Klondike Gold Rush National Historical Park, *59, 124*

Klondike Highway, *124*

Kluane National Park and Reserve, *214*

Knox Brothers Clock, *95*

Kobuk, *85*

Kobuk River, *84*

Kobuk Valley National Park, *84–85*

Kodiak Island, *173–174*

Kodiak National Wildlife Refuge, *53, 85*

Kotzebue, *12, 230–231*

L

Lake Clark National Park and Preserve, *70–71*

Lake Hood, *138*

Lake Minchumina, *196*

Lake Spenard, *138*

Large Animal Research Station, *190*

Learning tours, *xxx*

LeConte Glacier, *104*

Libraries, *100, 138, 166*

Lighthouse accommodations, *10*

The Line (former red-light district; Fairbanks), *188*

Little Rodak Trail, *67*

Living Museum of the Arctic, *231*

Lodging. ☞ Apartment and villa rentals; Bed-and-breakfasts; Camping; Home exchanges; Hostels; Hotels and motels; Lighthouse accommodations; Wilderness lodges

Log Cabin, *59*

Log Cabin Visitor Information Centers, *111, 133, 134–135*

London, Jack, *210*

Luggage, *xxv–xxvi*

Lumberman's Arch, *240*

Lutheran Cemetery, *107*

M

MacBride Museum, *212*

Manley Hot Springs, *202*

Marathons, *169, 198*

Marine animals, *53*

Marine Park, *111*

Maritime Museum of British Columbia, *246, 248*

Market Square (Victoria, British Columbia), *246, 249*

Matanuska Glacier, *175*

Matanuska-Susitna Valley, *174–178*

McCarthy, *13, 71*

McNeil River State Game Sanctuary, *13, 52*

Mekoryuk, *225*

Mendenhall Wetlands State Game Refuge, *53*

Midnight Sun Baseball Game, *196*

Midnight Sun Run, *198*

Mile 33, *119–120*

Mile 0, *119*

Miles Canyon, *213*

Million Dollar Bridge, *164*

Miniature Railway and Children's Farmyard, *240, 242*

Mining Valley (museum), *191*

Minto Flats, *196*

Misty Fjords National Monument, *12, 64*

Money, *xxiv–xxv*

Moravian Bookstore, *224*

Mound 44, *232*

Mt. Deborah, *191*

Mt. Fairweather, *61*

Mt. Foraker, *191*

Mt. Hayes, *191*

Mt. Hess, *191*

Mt. Iliamna, *70*

Mt. Katmai, *83*

Mt. Marathon, *169*

Mt. McKinley, *11, 13, 191*

Mt. Redoubt, *70*

Mt. Ripinsky, *122*

Museum of Alaska Transportation and Industry, *176*

Museum of the Aleutians, *10*

Museums, *10*

Anchorage, 133, 134, 135, 138, 139

the Bush, 224, 231

Interior, 185, 188, 190–191, 209, 210, 212–213

South Central Alaska, 162, 164, 166, 170, 173–174, 176

Southeast Alaska, 95, 97, 100, 104, 108, 112–113, 119, 120–121, 124

Victoria, British Columbia, 246, 248, 249

Mushing, *184, 197–198, 214.* ☞ Also Dogsledding

Music festivals, *110, 117, 245, 251*

Musk Ox Farm, *159, 175*

N

Nabesna Road, *71–72*

Naknek Lake, *83*

Nash Road, *166*

National monuments, *11, 12, 52, 64, 80, 81, 94.* ☞ Also National parks and forests; Parks, wildlife refuges, and wilderness adventures

National parks and forests, *xxv, 8–9.* ☞ Also Parks, wildlife refuges, and wilderness adventures

Native crafts, *xxvii, 9, 199, 224, 230, 232–233*

Native tours, *xxx, 10, 116, 221, 231*

Native villages, *97, 118, 139, 226, 230–231*

Natural history tours, *xxxi*

New Zealanders, tips for, *xviii–xix, xxvi*

Nightlife, *14.* ☞ Also specific place

Nikolski, 226
Nine O'Clock Gun, 240, 242
Noatak National Preserve, 85
Nome, 228–230.
Nome Convention and Visitor's Bureau, 229
North of Fairbanks, 200–205
North Pole, 187, 206–207
Novarupta mountain, 83
Nunivak Island, 225–226
Nunivak National Wildlife Refuge, 225

O

Odd Fellows Hall, 188
Old City Hall (Anchorage), 133, 135
Opera, 148–149, 251
Oscar Anderson House Museum, 133, 135
Our Collections (museum), 100
Outdoor activities and sports, xxvi, 6–8, 9
Anchorage, 131–132, 150–152
the Bush, 82, 221, 230
Interior, 78, 79, 183–184, 195–198, 200, 201–202, 203, 205, 207, 209, 214
parks, wildlife refuges, and wilderness adventures, 53–58, 63–64, 78, 79, 82
South Central Alaska, 157, 158, 165, 169, 170, 181
Southeast Alaska, 63–64, 92, 93, 99, 103, 106, 110, 117–118, 122–123

P

Pack Creek, 52, 64
Packing for the trip, xxv–xxvi
Palace Grand Revue, 210
Palmer, 159, 175–176
Parks, wildlife refuges, and wilderness adventures, xxxi, 43–88. ☞ Also National parks and forests
the Bush, 80–86, 231
contacts and resources, 87–88
dining, lodging, and camping, 46, 47–48, 58–59, 62–63, 65, 66–67, 68–70, 71, 72, 76–79, 82, 83, 85, 86
ecotourism, xxi, 48
equipment, 48–49
exploring, 58–59, 61–74, 76–86
fishing, 46
guided tours, 59, 63, 64–65, 69, 78, 83, 87–88
hiking and backpacking, 46–47, 48, 49, 79
Interior, 72–74, 76–80
outdoor activities and sports, 53–58, 63–64, 78, 79, 82
planning, 47–53
safety, 50

South Central Alaska, 65–72
Southeast Alaska, 58–59, 61–65
terrain, 49–50
transportation, 86–87
visitor information, 88
wildlife viewing, 47, 50–53
Parliament Buildings, 246, 249
Passports, xxvi
Permafrost museum, 231
Peters Hills, 68
Petersburg, 12, 94, 103–106
Petroglyph Beach, 101
Photographers, tips for, xiv
Photography tours, xxxi
Pinnell Mountain National Recreation Trail, 202
Plane travel, x–xii
airports, xii
Anchorage, 153
British Columbia, 252–253
the Bush, 234
with children, xvii
Interior, 214–216
luggage restrictions, xxv
South Central Alaska, 180
Southeast Alaska, 127, 128
Point Woronzof, 135, 138
Poker Flat Research Range, 190
Porcupine Caribou Herd, 80–81
Portage, 161
Portage Glacier, 66, 159, 161–162
Potter Marsh, 138, 139
Pratt Museum, 170
Pribilof Islands, 53, 222, 227–228
Prince William Sound, 159, 161–165
Prospect Point, 240–241, 242
Prudhoe Bay, 233
Pyrah's Pioneer Peak Farm, 175

Q

Quartz Lake, 207

R

Racquet sports, 151
Rafting, xxix, 6–7, 122–123, 151
Red Dog Saloon, 111
Resolution Park, 133, 135
Restaurants, 8, 13–14
Anchorage, 139–141, 144–145
the Bush, 220–221, 225, 226–227, 229, 230, 232
Interior, 76, 183, 192, 199–200, 205, 207, 208–209, 211, 213–214
South Central Alaska, 157–158, 162–163, 164, 166, 167, 170, 171, 172, 174, 175–176, 177, 178

Southeast Alaska, 62, 90, 92, 97–98, 101–102, 104, 109, 113–114, 121, 125–126
Vancouver, British Columbia, 238, 243–244
Victoria, British Columbia, 238, 249–250
Resurrection Bay, 12–13
Resurrection Bay Historical Society, 166
Richardson Highway, 206–208
Riverboat Discovery cruise, 191–192
Riverboat racing, 198
Riverboats, 191–192
Rivers, 79
crossing, 49
Round Island, 53
Royal British Columbia Museum, 246, 249
Royal Vancouver Yacht Club, 240
Running, 169, 198
Russian Bishop's House, 108
Russian cemetery, 107
RV, traveling by, xxxi, 154

S

S.S. *Klondike*, 213
Safety, 50
St. George Island, 222, 227
St. John's Church, 95
St. Michael's Cathedral, 107–108
St. Nicholas Russian Orthodox Church, 111
St. Paul Island, 222, 227
Salcha River, 207
Salmon Falls, Fish Ladder, and Salmon Carving, 96
Sam Kee Building, 239, 242
Sandy Beach, 104
Santa Claus House, 206
Satellite Tracking Station, 190
Saxman Native Village, 97
Scenic drives, 92–93
Scuba diving, 93, 99, 106, 110
Seaman's Park, 95
Second Beach, 241, 242
Seldovia, 172–173
Senate Building mall, 111
Senior citizens, tips for, xxvi–xxvii
Service, Robert, 210
Seward, 11, 12, 159, 166–169
shore excursions, 39–40
Seward Community Library, 166
Sheldon Jackson Museum, 108
Sheldon Museum and Cultural Center, 119
Ship Creekviewing platform, 133, 135

Shopping, *xxvii,* 9. ☞ See also specific place
Shrine of St. Therese, *113*
Shuyak Island State Park, *85–86*
Sightseeing tours, *xxvii*
Sitka, *12, 94, 106–110*
shore excursions, 40
Sitka National Historical Park, *13, 108–109*
Sitka State Pioneers' Home, *107*
Sitka Summer Music Festival, *110*
Sitka WhaleFest, *110*
Siwash Rock, *241, 243*
Skagway, *12, 94, 123–127*
shore excursions, 40–41
Skagway Convention and Visitors Bureau, *124*
Skiing, *9, 117, 123, 151, 198, 202*
Skilak Lake, *70*
Snowmobiling, *202*
Snowshoeing, *202*
Soldotna, *159, 169–170*
Sons of Norway Hall, *104*
South of Fairbanks, *205–206*
South Central Alaska, *5, 157–181*
boating, 157
camping, 67, 68, 69, 70, 72, 173
children, attractions for, 161, 162, 166, 167, 169, 170, 173–174, 175, 176
contacts and resources, 180–181
emergencies, 180–181
fishing, 158, 162, 170
guided tours, 69, 72, 87, 161, 163, 165, 168–169, 171, 174, 177, 178
hiking, 181
hotels, 66, 68–70, 71, 72, 158, 163, 164, 166, 167–168, 170, 171, 172–173, 174, 175–178
itineraries, 159
Kenai Peninsula, 12, 165–173
Kodiak Island, 173–174
Matanuska-Susitna Valley, 174–178
nightlife, 172
outdoor activities and sports, 157, 158, 165, 169, 170, 181
parks, wilderness areas, and wildlife refuges, 65–72
Prince William Sound, 159, 161–165
restaurants, 157–158, 162–163, 164, 166, 167, 170, 171, 172, 174, 175–176, 177, 178
shopping, 161, 165, 169, 172
sightseeing, 158–159, 161, 162, 163–164, 165, 166–167, 169, 170, 172, 173–175, 176, 177, 178

timing the visit, 159
transportation, 178–180
visitor information, 161, 181
Southeast Alaska, *5, 90–129*
backpacking, 92
camping, 58–59, 65
children, attractions for, 97, 112, 113
contacts and resources, 128–129
emergencies, 128
fishing, 92, 99, 103, 116
guided tours, 59, 63, 64–65, 87, 99, 102–103, 105, 110, 116, 126
Haines, 37–38, 53, 94, 118–123
hiking, 92, 99, 103, 110, 118, 122
hotels, 62–63, 65, 92, 98–99, 101–102, 104–105, 109, 114–116, 121, 125–126
itineraries, 94
Juneau, 10, 11, 38, 53, 94, 110–118
Ketchikan, 10, 12, 39, 94, 95–100
nightlife and the arts, 106, 110, 116–117, 122, 126–127
outdoor activities and sports, 63–64, 92, 93, 99, 103, 106, 110, 117–118, 122–123
parks, wilderness areas, and wildlife refuges, 58–59, 61–65
Petersburg, 12, 94, 103–106
restaurants, 62, 90, 92, 97–98, 101–102, 104, 109, 113–114, 121, 125–126
scenic drives, 92–93
scuba diving, 93, 99, 106, 110
shopping, 93, 99–100, 103, 106, 118
sightseeing, 93–97, 100–101, 103–104, 106–109, 110–113, 118–121, 123–125
Sitka, 12, 40, 94, 106–110
Skagway, 12, 40–41, 94, 123–127
timing the visit, 94
transportation, 127–128
visitor information, 95, 100, 104, 107, 108–109, 111, 119, 120, 128, 128–129
wildlife viewing, 93, 101, 109
Wrangell, 41, 94, 100–103
Southeast Alaska State Fairgrounds, *119*
Southeast Alaska Visitor Center, *95*
Sports. ☞ Outdoor activities and sports; specific sports
Spruce Mill Development, *95*
Square dancing, *195*
Stampede Trail, *205*
Stanley Park (Vancouver, British Columbia), *239–243*

Stanley Park Shuttle, *240*
State Office Building, *112*
Steam-powered clock, *239, 243*
Steese Highway, *200–202*
Steese Mountain National Conservation Area, *78–79*
Student travel, *xxvii*
Summit Trail, *79, 203*

T
Takhini Hot Springs, *213*
Talkeetna, *159, 177–178*
Tanana River, *197*
Taxis, *153, 154*
Telephones, *xxvii*
Tenakee Springs, *94*
Tennis, *118*
Terrain, *49–50*
TerriVic Jazz Party (festival), *251*
Theater
Anchorage, 149
Interior, 195, 210
Southeast Alaska, 117, 122
Vancouver, 245
Thomas Street, *96*
Timing your visit, *xxxiii–xxxiv*
Tlingit Fort, *109*
Tok, *187, 208–209*
Tongass Historical Museum, *95*
Tongass National Forest, *64–65*
Tony Knowles Coastal Trail, *133, 135*
Totem Bight State Historical Park, *97*
Totem Heritage Center and Nature Park, *96*
Totem poles, *95, 96, 97, 100, 107, 240, 243*
Totem Square, *107*
Tours, *xxvii–xxxi*
Anchorage, 155
bird-watching, xxix
boat, 116
British Columbia, 254
the Bush, 83, 88, 228, 235–236
camping, xxix
canoeing, kayaking, and rafting, xxix, 56–57, 63–64, 116
cruise, 20–21
dogsledding, xxx, 54–55
ferry, xxx
fishing, xxxi, 116
flightseeing, 8, 116, 122, 155
hiking, xxx
horsepacking, 55
Interior, 78, 87, 194, 203–204
learning, xxx
native, xxx, 10, 116, 221, 231
natural history, xxxi
photography, xxxi
RV, xxxi
sightseeing, xxvii

South Central Alaska, 69, 72, 87, 161, 163, 165, 168–169, 171, 174, 177, 178

Southeast Alaska, 59, 63, 64–65, 87, 99, 102–103, 105, 110, 116, 126

whale-watching cruises, 57–58

wilderness high adventures, xxxi

Trail of '98, 13

Trail of '98 Museum, 124

Train travel, xxxi–xxxii

Anchorage, 153–154

British Columbia, 253

Interior, 215

parks, wildlife refuges, and wilderness adventures, 87

South Central Alaska, 180

Southeast Alaska, 128–129

Trans-Alaska pipeline, 190

Transportation, 10

Anchorage, 153–154

British Columbia, 252–253

the Bush, 233–234

Interior, 214–216

parks, wildlife refuges, and wilderness adventures, 86–87

South Central Alaska, 178–180

Southeast Alaska, 127–128

Travel agencies, xxxii

Travel gear, xxxii

Tundra, 50

Turnagain Arm, 161

Tustumena Lake, 70

U

U.K. travelers, tips for, xix, xxii, xxvi, xxxiii

Umnak Island, 226

Unalaska, 222, 226

University of Alaska Fairbanks, 190

University of Alaska Museum, 190–191

V

Valdez, 159, 162–163

shore excursions, 41

Valdez Museum, 162

Valley of Ten Thousand Smokes, 83, 222

Valley Overlook, 83

Vancouver, British Columbia, 238–254

children, attractions for, 242, 243

Chinatown, 239

contacts and resources, 253–254

emergencies, 254

Gastown, 239

guided tours, 254

hotels, 238, 244–245

nightlife and the arts, 245

restaurants, 238, 243–244

sightseeing, 238–243

Stanley Park, 239–243

transportation, 252–253

visitor information, 254

Vancouver Aquarium, 240, 243

Vancouver International Jazz Festival, 245

Vancouver Rowing Club, 240

Vegetables, giant, 8

Victoria, British Columbia, 238, 246–254

children, attractions for, 249

contacts and resources, 253–254

emergencies, 254

guided tours, 254

hotels, 238, 250–251

nightlife and the arts, 251

restaurants, 238, 249–250

sightseeing, 246, 248–249

transportation, 252–253

visitor information, 246, 254

Victoria Jazz Society, 251

Visas, xxvi

Visitor information, xxxii–xxxiii

Anchorage, 133, 134–135, 155

British Columbia, 246, 254

the Bush, 225–226, 229, 236

Interior, 188, 203, 208, 212, 216

parks, wildlife refuges, and wilderness adventures, 88

South Central Alaska, 161, 181

Southeast Alaska, 95, 100, 104, 107, 108–109, 111, 119, 120, 124, 128–129

W

Walking, 131–132, 150

Walrus Islands State Game Sanctuary, 86

Wasilla, 159, 176–177

Waterfront Walkway, 212

Weather, xxxiii–xxxiv

Westmark Cape Fox Lodge, 96

Whale festival, 110

Whale Park (Ketchikan), 95

Whale-watching cruises, 57–58

Whitehorse, Yukon Territory, 187, 212–214

Whitehorse Rapids Dam and Fish Ladder, 213

Whitehorse Visitor Reception Centre, 212

White Mountain National Recreation Area, 78–79, 203

White Pass & Yukon Route, 125

Whittier, 11, 162

Wilderness adventures, xxxi. ☞ Also Parks, wildlife refuges, and wilderness adventures

Wilderness lodges, xxiv. ☞ Also Hotels and motels

Wildlife refuges. ☞ Parks, wildlife refuges, and wilderness adventures

Wildlife viewing, 47, 50–53, 80–81, 85, 86, 93, 101, 109, 133, 135, 155, 161, 170, 213, 221–222, 224–226

Will Rogers and Wiley Post Monument, 232

Wiseman Trading Co., 203

Wood-Tikchik State Park, 86

Wrangell, 94, 100–103

shore excursions, 41

Wrangell Museum, 100

Wrangell–Saint Elias National Park and Preserve, 12, 71–72, 159

Wrangell Visitor Center, 100

Y

Yugtarvik Regional Museum, 224

Yukon Beringia Interpretive Centre, 212–213

Yukon-Charley Rivers National Preserve, 79–80, 209

Yukon Delta National Wildlife Refuge, 224–225

Yukon Permanent Art Collection, 212

Yukon Territory, 209–214

Yukon Wildlife Preserve, 213

Z

Zoo, 138, 139

WHEREVER YOU TRAVEL, *H*ELP IS NEVER FAR AWAY.

From planning your trip to

providing travel assistance along

the way, American Express®

Travel Service Offices are

always there to help

you do more.